UNDERSTANDING MOTIVATION AND EMOTION

Second Edition

Johnmarshall Reeve
University of Wisconsin-Milwaukee

Harcourt Brace College Publishers

Fort Worth Philadelphia San Diego New York Orlando Austin San Antonio
Toronto Montreal London Sydney Tokyo

Publisher	Christopher P. Klein
Acquisitions Editor	Earl McPeek
Production Manager	Melinda Esco
Art Director	Vicki Whistler

Cover Image © Cutler/SIS

Harcourt Brace College Publishers may provide complimentary instructional aids and supplements or supplement packages to those adopters qualified under our adoption policy. Please contact your sales representative for more information. If as an adopter or potential user you receive supplements you do not need, please return them to your sales representative or send them to: Attn: Returns Department, Troy Warehouse, 465 South Lincoln Drive, Troy, MO 63379.

Address for Editorial Correspondence:
Harcourt Brace College Publishers
301 Commerce Street, Suite 3700
Fort Worth, TX 76102

Address for Orders:
Harcourt Brace & Company
6277 Sea Harbor Drive
Orlando, FL 32887-6777
1-800-782-4479

Library of Congress Catalog Card Number: 96-78387

Printed in the United States of America

ISBN 0-15-502654-2

6 7 8 9 0 1 2 3 4 5   067   9 8 7 6 5 4 3 2 1

Dedication

To Richard Troelstrup, who introduced me to psychology.
To Edwin Guthrie, who interested me in psychology.
To Steven Cole, who mentored me so I could participate in this wonderful profession.

PREFACE

I write to introduce you to what I think is some of the most exciting and useful information in psychology and life. Motivation is about human strivings, wants, desires, and aspirations. Its study concerns all those conditions that exist within the person and in the environment and culture that explain why we want what we want and why we do what we do. By the end of the book, I hope you will feel comfortable with motivation study at two levels. First, theoretically, an understanding of motivation and emotion involves a journey to answer questions such as, "Why did she do that?" and "From where does the sense of 'want to' come?" Second, practically, an understanding of motivation and emotion involves a journey to develop the art of motivating both the self and other people. I also harbor a third objective that I have kept in mind in writing each page of the book. I hope to pass on to you some of my fascination with motivation study as I try to help you discover for yourself motivation's appeal, excitement, and usefulness.

I assumed some background knowledge on the part of the reader, such as an introductory course in psychology. The intended audience is undergraduates enrolled in courses in a department of psychology. I also write for students in other disciplines, such as education and business, as the book concentrates fully on human, rather than nonhuman, motivation. The book includes some experiments in which rats, dogs, and monkeys served as research participants, but the information gleaned from these studies is always framed within an analysis of human motivation.

Recommended Readings

My experience in working with students teaches me that many desire tips and suggestions to guide their future self-determined study. For these students, each chapter ends with a list of 10 recommended readings. I chose each entry on the reading list based on four criteria: (1) its methodology and data analysis are reader-friendly; (2) its topic is both interesting and central to the chapter; (3) its length is short, so the student will have time to read several articles rather than just one or two; and (4) it showcases a journal that is central to motivation study. These readings provide a firsthand exposure to original articles in motivation.

For more specialized study, I want to point out another feature of the book designed to promote further self-determined study. The book is rich in theories, findings, and experiments, and in presenting each of these, I have tried to enter into a dialogue with the reader in which I supply a supportive reference for each statement and conclusion offered. The reference (e.g., Ben & Jerry, 1996) strives to accomplish two purposes: (1) give credibility to the statement or conclusion offered by citing supportive evidence and (2) give the reader a lead for further reading and investigation. In addition, I recommend spending a day or two in the library flipping through the articles in motivation's primary journals, such as *Motivation and Emotion* and *Cognition and Emotion*. Motivation articles appear in a wide range of journals, and several of these concentrate on motivation's relevance to a particular area of application. For special areas of study, I recommend the following: for education, *Journal of Educational Psychology* and *Review of Educational Research*; for sports, *Journal of Sport and Exercise Psychology*; for therapy, *Journal of Humanistic Psychology* and *Cognitive Therapy and Research*; for work, *Journal of Applied Psychology*; and for major theoretical articles, *Psychological Review* and *Psychological Bulletin*. And, the reader will find an article related to either motivation and emotion in each issue of the *Journal of Personality and Social Psychology*.

I also offer the chapter-ending readings for a second purpose. I offer the readings to professors as a way of linking the flow of ideas in the book to the flow of ideas in the classroom between professor and student and between student and student. I suggest that the recommended readings might stimulate class discussions, give substance to oral presentations, and form the basis of student papers.

Plan of the Book

The book argues that four constructs define the subject matter of motivation study: needs, cognitions, emotions, and external events. Chapter 1 introduces these four motivational constructs and also presents 10 themes that effectively organize motivation study's wide range of assumptions, findings, hypotheses, and theories. Chapter 2 summarizes motivation study in historical perspective. Following this introduction, the subject matter of motivation is presented in four parts.

Part 1 covers human needs. Chapter 3 introduces physiological needs by discussing thirst, hunger, and sex. Chapter 4 adds the organismic psychological needs to the discussion by introducing self-determination, competence, and relatedness. Chapter 5 introduces the motivational significance of external events by pointing out how external events generate extrinsic motivation and how external events affect organismic psychological needs via intrinsic motivation. Chapter 6 completes part 1 by discussing the acquired needs, including situationally induced quasi-needs and the social needs of achievement, affiliation, intimacy, and power.

Part 2 covers cognition. Chapter 7 introduces the motivational aspects of cognitive discrepancies by focusing on plans, goals, and dissonance. Chapter 8 discusses the four expectancy-based phenomena of self-efficacy, expectancy-times-value theory, learned helplessness, and reactance theory. Chapter 9 links attributions to a wide range of motivational phenomena. Chapter 10 focuses on the three motivational aspects of the self—self-concept, identity, and agency.

Part 3 covers the emotions. Chapter 11 addresses the nature of emotion via four fundamental questions—what causes an emotion, how many emotions are there, what is the relationship between emotion and motivation, and what is the difference between emotion and mood? Chapter 12 highlights the biological aspects of emotion. Chapter 13 highlights emotion's cognitive aspects, including the social/cultural constructivistic perspective.

Part 4 adds a layer of complexity to motivation study by outlining the motivational significance of individual differences. Chapter 14 discusses five personality characteristics—extraversion, sensation seeking, affect intensity, causality orientations, and desire for control. Chapter 15 focuses on growth motivation by presenting the humanistic perspective on motivation study. Chapter 16 focuses on unconscious motivation by presenting the psychoanalytic perspective on motivation study.

Chapter 17 concludes the discussion by making explicit a couple of points. It offers a concise statement of what I see to be the central subject matter of contemporary motivation study, its central themes, and a perspective on the art and science of motivating others. It is no accident that the chapter ends with a discussion called *Motivating Others*, because I hope the book speaks to the reader in ways that are not only theoretical and academic but also practical and useful.

Acknowledgments

Many voices speak within the pages of the book. To acknowledge these voices, my first expression of gratitude goes to all those colleagues who, formally and informally, knowingly and unknowingly, shared their ideas in conversation: Roy Baumeister, Daniel Berlyne, Virginia Blankenship, Jerry Burger, Steven Cole, Mihaly Csikszentmihalyi, Richard deCharms, Ed Deci, Paula Gottlieb, Wendy Grolnick, Carroll Izard, Alice Isen, Randy Larsen, David McClelland, Henry Newell, Angela O'Donnell, Brad Olson, Tom Rocklin, Carl Rogers, Lynn Smith-Lovin, Richard Solomon, Silvan Tomkins, Wayne Ludvingson, Dawn Robinson, Richard Ryan, Robert Vallerand, and Dan Wegner. I consider these people my colleagues, mentors, and kindred spirits in the struggle to understand human strivings. My second expression of gratitude goes to those who explicitly donated their time and energy to reviewing the early drafts of the book, including Sandor B. Brent, Robert Emmons, Wayne Harrison, John Hinson, Wesley J. Kasprow, John Kounios, Michael McCall, James J. Ryan, Peter Senkowski, Michael Sylvester, and A. Bond Woodruff.

I also want to thank all the students I have had the pleasure to know over the years. It was back at Ithaca College that I first became convinced that my students wanted and needed such a book. In a very real sense, I wrote the first edition for them. The students who dominate my attention and perspective now are those with me at the University of Wisconsin-Milwaukee. For readers who are familiar with the first edition, the second edition takes on a tone that is decidedly more practical and applied in its emphasis. That applied orientation comes directly from my interactions and relationships with my students here in Milwaukee.

Ithaca is doubly important to me because it was in this beautiful town in upstate New York that I met Deborah Van Patten, of Harcourt Brace. Deborah was at least as responsible for getting the book off the ground as I was. I express my deep gratitude to you, Deborah. My colleagues at University Graphics, Inc. worked the manuscript into shape for me, so I want to express my gratitude to each member of the production team in York, PA, especially Barbara Merritt and Sandra Gormley. The professionals at Harcourt Brace have been wonderful. Everyone at Harcourt Brace has been both a valuable resource and a source of pleasure. I am especially grateful for the advice, assistance, and direction given to me by Product Manager, Susan Kindel, Acquisitions Editor, Earl McPeek, and Psychology Editor, John Haley.

CONTENTS IN BRIEF

CONTENTS

Chapter 4
ORGANISMIC PSYCHOLOGICAL NEEDS   74

Chapter 5
EXTERNAL EVENTS: EXTRINSIC AND INTRINSIC MOTIVATIONS   102

Chapter 6
ACQUIRED PSYCHOLOGICAL NEEDS   127

PART 2
Cognition   155

Chapter 7
DISCREPANCIES   157

Chapter 9
ATTRIBUTIONS   213

Chapter 10
THE SELF   237

PART 3
Emotions   257

Chapter 11
THE NATURE OF EMOTION   259

Chapter 12
BIOLOGICAL ASPECTS OF EMOTION   286

Chapter 13
COGNITIVE ASPECTS OF EMOTION   315

PART 4
Individual Differences   339

Chapter 14
PERSONALITY CHARACTERISTICS   341

Chapter 15
GROWTH MOTIVATION   375

Chapter 16
UNCONSCIOUS MOTIVATION   399

Chapter 17
CONCLUSION   424

Chapter 1

INTRODUCTION TO THE STUDY OF MOTIVATION

Perennial Questions in the Study of Motivation
Subject Matter in the Study of Motivation
    Motives
    External Events
Expressions of Motivation
    Overt Behavior
    Physiology
    Self-Report
Themes in the Study of Motivation
    Motivation Includes Both Approach and Avoidance Tendencies
    Motivation Varies Not Only in Its Intensity but Also in Its Type
    Motivation Can Be Self-Regulated or Environmentally Regulated
    Motivation Is More Than Personal Willpower
    Motivation Is a Dynamic Process
    Motive Strengths Vary Over Time and Influence the Stream of Behavior
    Motives Have Been Arranged Hierarchically
    We Are Not Always Consciously Aware of the Motivational Basis of our Behavior
    Motivational Principles Can be Applied
    There is Nothing So Practical As a Good Theory

Human striving, desire, want, need, aspiration, longing, hope, wish, fear, pressure, anxiety—such phenomena lie at the heart of understanding motivation and emotion. Many students tell me that these phenomena poses a special attraction, and I trace that appeal to three roots.

First, few topics spark and entertain the imagination so well. Motivation's spark comes from its promise to inform us about who we are, why we want what we want, and how we can use motivation to improve our lives. Motivation study also helps us understand other people, why they want what they want, and how we can use motivation to improve their lives too. Second, motivation has an air of mystery about it, because our desire and sense of purpose is sometimes strong and resilient but other times it wanes or disappears altogether. This mystery about motivation and the intuition that it is somehow very important combine to attract our interest enough to find out what motivation theories have to say about topics such as sex and the psychological need to belong, strivings for achievement and self-actualization, fear and anger, altruism and aggression, self-efficacy and doubt, mastery and helplessness, sensation seeking and sensation avoiding, unconscious desires and inhibitions, and even human nature itself. Third, understanding motivation is an extremely practical undertaking. It can be quite useful to know where motivation comes from, how and why it changes, and which conditions work to increase or decrease motivation. Such understandings apply very nicely to situations such as trying to do our best in school, motivate employees, coach athletes, counsel clients, raise our children, or change our own ways of thinking, feeling, and behaving. Motivation study therefore promises to equip us with both the theoretical understanding and the practical know-how we need to accomplish whatever it is we think is important.

To introduce motivation study, consider exercise. Think about it for a moment—why would anyone *want* to exercise? Why would anyone want to run laps around a track, jump up and down during an aerobics class, or swim laps back and forth in a pool? Why run when you know your lungs will collapse for want of air; why jump and stretch when you know your muscles will rip and tear; why take an hour or two out of the day when your schedule will not allow it; or why exercise when life offers so many other things to do? Of course, there are plenty of good reasons to exercise. Children exercise spontaneously—they run and jump and chase and they do so simply for the sheer fun of it (i.e., intrinsic motivation, chapter 4). Most of us, however, exercise in response to more utilitarian motives, such as a desire to lose weight or to please a coach (i.e., extrinsic motivation, chapter 5). Goal setting (chapter 7) can motivate exercise, as some people care very much whether they can run a mile in 6:00 or less. Other people sometimes inspire us to exercise, such as an athlete we want to be like or a model who is slim and trim (possible selves, chapter 10). And exercise offers us a challenge, a standard of excellence to pursue, such as a biker who tries for 25 miles (achievement strivings, chapter 6). Some of the motivation to exercise grows out of a sense of accomplishment and satisfaction from a job well done (competence, chapter 4). A few people tell me that running and marathoning gives them an emotional kick, a runner's high (opponent process theory, chapter 12). Sometimes beautiful weather can pick up our mood and invigorate us so that we exercise spontaneously, without even knowing why we skip along or walk briskly (positive affect; chapter 11). Others exercise to relieve stress and gain a sense of personal control over the events in their lives (personal control beliefs, chapter 8). And exercise is often a social event, a time simply to enjoy hanging out with friends (relatedness, chapter 4) or an arena to test our abilities against those of others (social comparison, chapter 10). For those people who find exercise to be important, motivation study speaks theoretically to the question of why people want to exercise and it speaks practically to the effort to increase people's desire to exercise.

PERENNIAL QUESTIONS IN THE STUDY OF MOTIVATION

The fundamental questions in motivation study are these: "What causes behavior?" and "Why do they want to do that?" To answer these questions, it helps to ask more specific questions: "How does behavior start?" "Where does want come from?" "Once begun, what sustains behavior over time?" "Why is behavior directed toward some ends yet away from others?" "Why does behavior change its direction or its intensity?" "How does behavior stop?" It is not enough to ask what causes a person to train, or what causes a child to read. We must also ask why athletes begin to practice in the first place. What energizes their effort hour after hour, day after day? Why do they practice that sport rather than another? Why are they practicing now, rather than, say, hanging out with their friends? When they do practice, why do they quit, either during the day or during their lifetimes? We can ask these same questions for children reading a book: Why begin? What maintains their reading past the first page, and past the first chapter? Why did they pick those particular books rather than the others sitting on the bookshelf? Why will they stop? Will they continue to read for years?

These questions introduce the first essential problem in motivation study, namely to make sense of behavior's instigation, persistence, change, goal directedness, and termination. This is either one grand question (What causes behavior?) or five interrelated questions, but the first essential problem to solve is to understand how motivation participates in and influences the stream of behavior. For a more personal example, let me ask you to consider your own immediate behavior of reading this book. Why did you open this book? Will you continue reading to the end of the chapter, or to the end of the book? At what point in your reading will you stop? What factors will determine when to stop? When you stop, what will you do next? Why?

A second perennial question in motivation study asks why behavior varies in its intensity. Often, behavior expresses a special distinctiveness, such as unusually high or low effort, persistence, intensity, promptness, or liveliness. Some days an employee works rapidly and diligently; other days the work is lethargic. One day a student shows strong enthusiasm, strives for excellence, and shows determined goal-directed striving; yet, the next day the same student is listless, does only the minimal amount of work, and avoids being challenged academically. The problem is to explain why the same person shows strong and persistent motivation at one time yet weak and unenthusiastic motivation at another time. Why does the worker perform so well on Monday but not on Tuesday? Why do children say they are not hungry in the morning yet complain of urgent hunger in the afternoon? Why does the driver get so angry and upset when stuck in traffic at one time but remain calm and undisturbed at another? Behavior's intensity varies from time to time and from day to day, so the second problem to solve in a motivational analysis is to identify the forces that determine behavior's intensity—from one moment to the next, from one day to the next, and from one decade to the next.

The third perennial problem in a motivational analysis of behavior asks, "Why do people differ in what motivates them?" We all share the same basic motivations (hunger, need for affiliation, anger, and so on), but many motives are relatively strong for one person yet relatively weak for another. Why is one person a sensation seeker who continually seeks out strong sources of stimulation such as motorcycling or bungee jumping whereas another person is a sensation avoider who finds such strong stimulation more an irritant than a source of excitement? In a contest, who do some people strive diligently to win whereas others care little about winning and strive more to make friends? Some people seem so easy to anger whereas others seem rarely upset. For those motives in which there exist wide individual differences, motivation study investigates how such differences arise and what implications they hold. So, this third problem recognizes that individuals differ in what motivates them and that under identical conditions some people show strong motivation while others do not.

In summary, the starting point in a motivational analysis of behavior is to answer questions such as "What causes behavior?" and "Why do they want to do that?" To answer such questions, people who study motivation wrestle with three perennial problems:

1. How does motivation affect behavior's initiation, persistence, change, goal-directedness, and termination?
2. Why does behavior vary in its intensity from one moment to the next?
3. What are the motivational differences among individuals, how do such differences arise, and what are the implications of individual differences in motivation?

SUBJECT MATTER IN THE STUDY OF MOTIVATION

To explain why people do what they do, we need a theory of motivation. The usefulness of our motivation theory is that it allows us to explain what gives a person's behavior its energy and its direction. It is some motive that energizes the athlete, directs the student's behavior toward particular goals, makes employees enthusiastic and focuses their attention, and gives purpose to everyday life. *Motivation study deals with the processes that give behavior its energy and direction.* Energy implies that behavior is relatively strong, intense, and persistent. Direction implies that behavior is aimed toward achieving a particular purpose or goal. So, the subject matter in the study of motivation centers on all those processes that energize and direct behavior.

The processes that energize and direct behavior emanate both from forces within the individual and from external forces in the environment. Figure 1.1 organizes motivational processes in terms of internal individual motives and external environmental events. Motives are internal events—needs, cognitions, and emotions—that energize the individual's approach and avoidance goal-directed tendencies. External events are environmental incentives that attract or repel the individual to engage or not in certain behavior.

Motives

Motive is a general term that identifies the common ground shared by needs, cognitions, and emotions (each is an internal process that energizes and directs behavior). The difference between a motive on the one hand and a need, cognition, or emotion on the other hand is simply the level of analysis (general versus specific; Fig. 1.1).

Needs are physiological or psychological states that energize and direct action —or pain avoiding in either a deficiency-remedying or a growth-promoting way. Hunger (from food deprivation) and thirst (from water deprivation) exemplify two physiological deficiency-remedying needs. Competence (desire for environmental mastery) and strivings to actualize the self exemplify two psychological growth-promoting needs. Needs generate strivings, wants, and desires either to remove some psychological or physiological deficiency or to promote psychological growth and development. Part 2 discusses specific types of physiological and psychological needs: physiological needs

FIGURE 1–1
Hierarchical Categorization of the Four Sources of Motivation

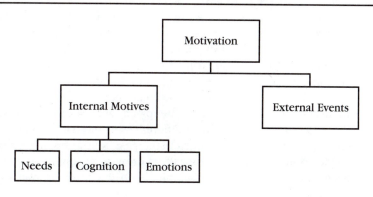

(chapter 3), organismic psychological needs (chapter 4), and acquired psychological needs (chapter 6).

Cognitions refer to mental events such as beliefs, expectations, and self-concept. Cognitive sources of motivation revolve around the person's relatively enduring ways of thinking. For instance, as students, athletes, or salespersons engage a task, they have in mind some plan or goal and they hold beliefs about their ability, expectations for success and failure, ways of explaining success and failure (i.e., attributional style), and understanding of who they are and what their place in society is (i.e., self-concept, identity), and so forth. Part 3 discusses specific cognitive sources of motivation: discrepancies (chapter 7), expectancies (chapter 8), attributions (chapter 9), and the self (chapter 10).

Emotions are complex phenomena that organize and orchestrate four aspects of experience that allow us to react adaptively to the important events in our lives—how we feel, how our body changes to meet situational demands, what we want or strive to accomplish, and how we express our inner experience to others. During fear, for instance, we feel terror, our heart races, we desire to escape, and the corners of our lips are drawn backward in such a way that others can recognize and respond to our fear. Part 4 discusses different aspects of the emotions: the nature of emotion (chapter 11), biological aspects of emotion (chapter 12), and cognitive aspects of emotion (chapter 13).

External Events

External events are environmental incentives that cause energy and direction in the person. For instance, money motivates approach behavior, a hostile audience motivates defensive avoidance, and the promise of having one's name in the newspaper motivates trying hard in sports. The incentive signals the likelihood that a behavior will or will not produce rewarding or punishing consequences. Those incentives that signal positive consequences cause forthcoming approach behaviors, while those incentives that signal negative consequences cause forthcoming avoidance and escape behaviors. Chapter 5 discusses how incentives (and rewards and punishers) add to a motivational analysis of behavior.

From a broader perspective, external events also include environmental contexts, social situations, climates (e.g., those that emerge in the classroom and workplace), and sociological forces such as culture. Discussion of these environmental agents of motivation are dispersed throughout each chapter of the book.

The chapters in Part 5 add a final layer of complexity by overviewing the role of personality and individual differences in motivation. A study of individual differences allows us to address the third essential problem in motivation study, namely, "What are the motivational differences among people, how do such differences arise, and what are the implications of individual differences in motives?" Chapter 14 focuses on several specific personality characteristics (e.g., extraversion), chapter 15 adds the humanistic approach and its emphasis on growth strivings, and chapter 16 adds the psychoanalytic approach and its emphasis on unconscious wants and desires.

EXPRESSIONS OF MOTIVATION

Thus far, we have introduced the perennial problems that define motivation study and the basic vocabulary of the field—motivation, motives, needs, cognitions, emotions, and incentives. One more introductory task remains, namely, specifying how motivation is expressed. In other words, when someone is motivated, how do you know? Or, as you watch two people behave, how do you know that one person is more motivated than the other? The primary way to infer motivation is by observing its manifestations. To infer hunger, for instance, we watch to see whether Joe eats more quickly than usual, chews vigorously, talks about eating during conversation, and forgoes social manners for the opportunity to eat.

A second means to infer motivation in others is to pay close attention to antecedents known to give rise to motivational states. After 72 hours of food deprivation, a person will be hungry; after feeling threatened, a person will feel fear; after winning a competition, a person will feel competent; and so on. Food deprivation leads to hunger, a threat appraisal leads to fear, and objective messages of effectance lead to feelings of competence. Because the antecedents to many motivational states are known, we are not always left in the precarious position of having to infer motivation from behavior.

But the antecedents to motivated action are not always known. Sometimes, motivation must be inferred from its behavioral expressions. Three categories of activity express motivation: overt behavior, physiology, and self-report.

Overt Behavior

Six aspects of overt behavior express both the presence and intensity of motivation (from Atkinson & Birch, 1970, 1978; Bolles, 1975): latency, persistence, choice, intensity, probability of response, and facial expressions and bodily gestures.

LATENCY. Latency is the time a person delays a response on an initial exposure to a stimulus event. For example, if a child cries immediately after separation from the mother, such a quick reaction allows us to infer high separation anxiety relative to another child who cries moments or hours after such a separation. Or, if a child wastes no time picking a toy up from the ground to play with it, such a quick reaction to the toy allows us to infer high task interest. In these examples, latency is the number of seconds or minutes between separation from the mother (the stimulus event) and the crying, or the number of seconds between seeing the toy and picking it up. As a rule of thumb, as response latency decreases, the presence and intensity of motivation increases.

PERSISTENCE. Persistence is the time between the initiation of a response until its cessation. In the previous two examples, persistence is the number of seconds or minutes the child continues to cry once begun or the number of minutes the child continues to play with the toy once begun. Response persistence is proportional to the intensity of the motive for that activity (and inversely proportional to the motive intensity to engage in an alternative activity). The person who continues a goal-directed course of action for an extended period expresses the more intense motive than does the person who quickly quits.

CHOICE. Choice, or preference for one stimulus object over another, presents the individual with two or more options in which he or she selects one course of action over another. At any given time, we typically face a large number of options from which to choose. For instance, you can read this book, go to the refrigerator for a drink, pick up the phone to call a friend, take a nap, hit the remote control to watch television, and so on. Preference of one course of action over another expresses an underlying motive. In designing an experiment on altruism, for instance, a researcher might give the participant the choice between either helping or not helping, and the participants who choose to help express the greater altruism.

INTENSITY. Intensity is the amplitude of the individual's response to a stimulus event. In a study of males' reactions to photographs of attractive women, researchers assessed the diameter of each male's pupils while looking at each of 10 different photographs (Hess, 1975). The researchers inferred the intensity of the males' attraction via the size of their pupils. Similarly, the more intensely a person pulls back the zygomatic muscles of the cheek and mouth (the smile muscles), the stronger his or her felt joy (Pope & Smith, 1994). As a rule of thumb, the greater the intensity of the behavior, the greater the strength of the motive.

PROBABILITY OF RESPONSE. Probability of response refers to the number of occasions a goal-directed response occurs per number of opportunities the response might have occurred. If two people are put into a situation 10 times, the person who performs the response 8 times expresses the more intense motive than does the person who performs the response 3 times. Thus, other things being equal, the person who telephones his friends 8 nights out of 10 expresses the stronger need for affiliation than does the person who telephones his friends only 3 nights out of 10 (e.g., Lansing & Heyns, 1959).

FACIAL EXPRESSIONS AND BODILY GESTURES. Facial expressions and bodily gestures communicate, in part, the emotional aspects of behavior. A smile communicates an underlying joy or friendship; furrowed eyebrows communicate an underlying anger or determination to overcome an obstacle. Similarly, posture, weight shifts, and the movements of the legs, arms, and hands (e.g., a clenched fist) communicate emotions and desires. Consider, for example, the next time you find yourself engaged in a rather boring face-to-face conversation. When you wish to terminate the conversation, you will consciously or unconsciously signal your desire to depart by (1) shifting your weight from an equal to an unequal distribution, (2) crossing your legs (while standing), and (3) moving away from the other person (Lockard et al., 1978). Shifting your weight, crossing your legs, and increasing the distance between yourself and your conversant all express a desire to escape the interaction.

OVERVIEW. These six aspects of behavior provide the observer with data to infer the presence and intensity of another person's motivation. When behavior shows a short latency, long persistence, high probability of occurrence, is intense, offers facial or gestural expressiveness, or when the individual pursues a specific goal-object in lieu of another, such is the evidence to infer the presence of a relatively intense motive. When behavior shows a long latency, short persistence, low probability of occurrence, is not intense, offers minimal facial and gestural expressiveness, or the individual pursues an alternative goal-object, such is the evidence to infer an absence of a motive, or at least a relatively weak motive.

Physiology

As human beings prepare to engage in various activities, the nervous and endocrine systems manufacture and release various chemical substances (e.g., neurotransmitters, hormones) that provide the biological underpinnings of motivation and emotion (Andreassi, 1986; Coles, Ponchin, & Porges, 1986). In the course of a public speech, for example, speakers experience acute emotional stress (to various degrees), and that emotionality manifests itself physiologically through a major rise in plasma catecholamines (e.g., adrenaline) (Bolm-Avdorff et al., 1989). The rise in catecholamines serves as the biological underpinning of the felt stress. To measure various neural and hormonal changes, researchers use blood tests, saliva tests, urine analyses, and a host of psychophysiological measures involving complex electrical equipment (electromyograph, galvanic skin response, and so on). Using these measures, motivation researchers monitor an individual's heart rate, blood pressure, respiratory rate, pupil diameter, skin conductance, contents of blood plasma, and other indices of physiological functioning to infer the presence and intensity of motivational and emotional states.

PSYCHOPHYSIOLOGY. Psychophysiology is an amalgamation of psychology and physiology. The goals of psychophysiological experiments are (1) to observe how the body prepares its biological systems to perform psychologically and behaviorally and (2) to use that knowledge to understand the physiology of motivation and emotion. The five bodily arousal systems that express aspects of motivation and emotion are cardiovascular, plasma, ocular (eye), electrodermal, and skeletal muscle activity.

Cardiovascular activity (cardia, heart; vascular, blood vessels) increases with the pursuit of difficult and challenging tasks as well as attractive incentives (Fowles, 1983). For instance, intensity of cardiac activity is proportional to intensity of a monetary incentive (Fowles, Fisher, & Tranel, 1982; Tranel, Fisher, & Fowles, 1982) and therefore expresses want or desire. On the other hand, cardiac activity decreases when the individual needs to pay close attention to some aspect of the environment (Lacey et al., 1963; Reeve, 1993) and therefore expresses attention or interest.

Plasma activity involves the contents of the blood stream, particularly the cate-cholamines of epinephrine and norepinephrine (which regulate the fight-or-flight re-action). Epinephrine coincides with feelings of tension and anxiety, whereas nor-epinephrine coincides with aggressive strivings (e.g., Dimsdale & Moss, 1980). *Ocular activity* involves eye behavior—pupil size, eye blinks, and eye movements. Pupil size correlates rather well with the extent of mental activity required to com-plete a task (Beatty, 1982, 1986; Kahneman, 1973; Stern, Walrath, & Goldstein, 1984). Eye blinks (the involuntary ones) express changing cognitive states, allocation of at-tention, and transition points in the information processing flow (Stern *et al.*, 1984). Lateral eye movements increase in frequency when the person engages in reflective thought (Woods, Beecher, & Ris, 1978), as during an interview (Meskin & Singer, 1974; Woods & Steigman, 1978). *Electrodermal activity* refers to the electrical changes on the surface of the skin, as during sweating. Novel, emotional, threaten-ing, and attention-getting stimuli all evoke electrodermal activity (Raskin, 1973) and therefore express threat or aversion. *Skeletal activity* involves the musculature, and emotion researchers routinely record skeletal muscular activity during facial ex-pressions (Cacioppo et al., 1986; Fridlund & Izard, 1983; Larsen, Kasimatis, & Frey, 1992; Sackeim, Gur, & Saucy, 1978; Schwartz, 1986; Schwartz, Brown, & Ahern, 1980). People react to emotional stimuli with significant facial muscular activity, such as pulling back the zygomatic cheek muscle when happy or pressing the lips firmly together when angry (Ekman & Friesen, 1975).

Self-Report

A third way to collect data regarding the presence and intensity of motivation is sim-ply to ask. Typically people can introspect and self-report their level of motivation, as in an interview or on a questionnaire. An interviewer might assess anxiety, for in-stance, by asking how anxious the interviewee feels in particular settings or by ask-ing the interviewee to report anxiety-related symptoms such as an upset stomach, sweaty palms, or self-derogating thoughts. These same questions could also be asked on a pencil-and-paper or computer questionnaire. For instance, a questionnaire might ask, "When interacting with strangers, how anxious do you feel?" and include a 1 to 4 response scale in which 1 indicates not at all, 2 indicates a little, 3 indicates some, and 4 indicates highly anxious.

Questionnaires have several advantages that recommend them. Questionnaires are easy to administer, can be administered to many people simultaneously, and can ask specific information (Carlsmith, Ellsworth, & Aronson, 1976). There are, how-ever, at least four reasons that self-report ratings might not reflect a person's true motivation (Mitchell & Jolley, 1988). First, people might intentionally distort their self-reports to produce socially desirable, rather than actual, ratings. Recognizing this, questionnaire developers go to great lengths to validate their measures (e.g., people who score a high sensation seekers on the Sensation-Seeking Scale do indeed seek thrills and adventures in life via speeding in a car, sexual promiscuity, risk taking, and so on; Zuckerman, 1994). Second, people may not know their own motives

(Nisbett & Wilson, 1977). It is a difficult task, even when being fully honest, to report precisely what one's sex drive, achievement striving, or level of fear is at any moment. Third, self-report ratings frequently ask for a retrospective account (e.g., "How nervous do you feel when talking to strangers?") and therefore depend on memory for accuracy. Fourth, self-report questionnaires are not applicable to animals, infants, or verbally handicapped individuals (Plutchik, 1980).

So, while questionnaires have advantages that recommend them, questionnaires also have pitfalls that raise a red flag of caution as to their usefulness. Many researchers in motivation lament the lack of correspondence between what people say they do and what they actually do (for reviews, see Quattrone, 1985; Wicker, 1969). The task of measuring motivation gets a bit more difficult still because self-report measures do not correspond particularly well with physiological measures either (e.g., Hodgson & Rachman, 1974; Rachman & Hodgson, 1974). Hence, what people say their motives are sometimes are not what people's behavioral and physiological expressions suggest their motives are. What conclusion, for instance, can we draw on those occasions when a person verbally reports low anger but shows a quick latency to aggress and rapid heart rate acceleration? Because of such discrepancies, and because self-report measures are plagued by problems such as social desirability, conscious awareness, accuracy of recollection, and limited application, motivation researchers typically rely on only a conservative use of self-report measures. In contrast, motivation researchers trust and rely heavily on behavioral and physiological measures, and therefore use self-report measures mostly to confirm the validity of their behavioral and physiological measures.

THEMES IN THE STUDY OF MOTIVATION

Motivation study includes a wide range of assumptions, findings, hypotheses, and theories. But motivation study also has a number of unifying themes that integrate these assumptions, findings, hypotheses, and theories into a coherent field of study. Here are 10 themes that run throughout this text:

- Motivation includes both approach and avoidance tendencies.
- Motivation varies not only in its intensity but also in its type.
- Motivation can be self-regulated or environmentally regulated.
- Motivation is more than personal willpower.
- Motivation is a dynamic process.
- Motive strengths vary over time and influence the stream of behavior.
- Motives have been arranged hierarchically.
- We are not always consciously aware of the motivational basis of our behavior.
- Motivational principles can be applied.
- There is nothing so practical as a good theory.

Motivation Includes Both Approach and Avoidance Tendencies

Generally speaking, people presuppose that to be motivated is better than to be un-motivated. Indeed, the two most frequent questions I am asked as a professor of motivation are, "How can I motivate myself to do better (or more)?" and "How can I motivate another person to do better (or more)?" In other words, I am frequently asked how one might get more motivation than one presently has, either for one-self or for others. What I hear in these conversations is that motivation is a state that people long to achieve for themselves and for others.

The problem is that several motivational systems are aversive in nature. Pain, hunger, distress, fear, anxiety, dissonance, and deadlines are frequent and potent sources of motivation. In fact, the early motivation theorists (whom we will meet in chapter 2) conceptualized human beings as continually struggling to ward off nox-ious states of affairs. In Freudian theory, for example, the individual is perpetually warding off instinctual energies of sex and aggression, and the escape from anxiety explained motivated activity. In Hullian theory, motivation occurs with biological deprivation states (e.g., deprivation of food, deprivation of water). In cognitive dis-sonance theory (Festinger, 1957), inconsistent beliefs (i.e., "I believe X, but not-X also seems to be true") create an affectively aversive state that pokes a psychologi-cal needle in the side until the person adjusts either the way of thinking or behav-ing. In all these theories, the human body harbors a multitude of response poten-tials that lie in wait until ignited to activity by some aversive motivation (i.e., hunger, thirst, dissonance). And, "the greater the irritation, the greater the change" (in mo-tivation, emotion, and behavior) (Kimble, 1990, p. 36). So, when others ask me how they can motivate themselves or how they can motivate others more, I do not think they have in mind an answer like instinctual urges, biological deprivations, or in-consistent belief systems.

As motivation research matures, more and more positive motivations occupy re-searchers' interests. Contemporary research recognizes that people are curious, in-trinsically motivated, sensation-seeking animals with goals and plans striving to mas-ter challenges, develop warm interpersonal relationships, and move themselves towards attractive environmental incentives, psychological development, and growth. At the same time, however, it is equally true that people are stressed, frus-trated, pressured, depressed, afraid, and in pain; they encounter aversive situations from which they wish to flee. The first theme therefore offers the reader a caution of perspective: whereas some motives create approach tendencies and positive af-fect, many motives create avoidance tendencies and negative affect.

Motivation Varies Not Only in Its Intensity but Also in Its Type

In many people's mind, motivation is a unitary concept. In other words, the only feature of motivation that varies is its amount, or its intensity, and the only concern about motivation is how much. In contrast, several motivation theorists suggest that types of motivations exist and can be distinguished (Ames, 1987; Ames & Archer, 1988; Atkinson, 1964; Condry & Stokker, 1992; Deci, 1992a). For instance, Deci (1992a) distinguished between intrinsic motivation and extrinsic motivation. Ames and Archer (1988) distinguished between motivation to learn and motivation to perform. Atkinson (1964) distinguished between the tendency to approach success and the tendency to avoid failure.

It is important and helpful to pay attention to motivation's intensity, but the second theme in motivation study is that it is also fruitful to think about types of motivation. Watch as an athlete practices, a student studies, an employee works, and a doctor cares for a patient and you will see variations in the intensity of motivation. An equally important question, however, asks why the athlete practices, the student studies, the employee works, and the doctor provides care. Some types of motivation are more productive and psychologically healthy than others. For instance, students who learn out of an intrinsic motivation (via interest, challenge, curiosity) do so with more creativity and positive emotionality than do students who learn out of an extrinsic motivation (via grades, stickers, deadlines) (Deci & Ryan, 1987). Emotions too show that type of motivation matters at least as much as intensity. For instance, a person who is intensely angry would be expected to behave quite differently from a person who was intensely afraid. So, a complete motivational analysis of behavior answers both questions of how much and what type.

Motivation Can Be Self-Regulated or Environmentally Regulated

Recall that behavior can be motivated by intrinsic motives (e.g., needs, emotions) or by extrinsic incentives (e.g., money, rules). Environmentally regulated behavior is caused by incentives and extrinsic motivators in general. For an automobile assembly line worker, for example, some extrinsic motivators might be money, praise, and a positive evaluation from the boss. Each of these extrinsic motivators represents a socially arranged consequence of putting together an automobile. Thus, aspects of the environment—external agents—provide the motivation to assemble the automobile. Self-regulated behavior is caused by internal motives that originate from needs, beliefs, and emotions. For the automobile worker, a need for competence, beliefs of high ability, and emotions such as interest and enjoyment explain why the worker puts together the automobile. Thus, aspects of the self—internal agents— provide the motivation to assemble the automobile.

The distinction between self-regulated motivation and environmentally regulated motivation has implications for not only our own motivation but for any attempt to motivate others (Deci & Ryan, 1985a; Katzell & Thompson, 1990; Ryan, Connell, & Grolnick, 1992). If you want to motivate yourself to study more, to exercise more, or to be more productive at work, how would you do it? Likewise, if you wanted to motivate someone else to study more, exercise more, or be more productive at work, how would you do that? The distinction between intrinsic and extrinsic motivators emphasizes that you have at least two options, motivation via self-regulation and motivation via environmental regulation. Chapter 5 focuses specifically on the efficacy of these two options.

Motivation Is More Than Personal Willpower

Motivation constitutes more than personal willpower to try harder or to increase commitment to a sought-after goal. Trying to marshal effort to study more, to begin an exercise routine, or to overcome a smoking habit are central motivational problems, but the belief that these problems can be overcome by increased willpower is simplistic. For instance, increased effort and commitment do not go very far in the attempt to quit smoking (Cohen et al., 1989), and effort follows from, rather than causes, academic achievement (MacIver, Stipek, & Daniel, 1991). To increase effort in the name of increasing motivation is to put the proverbial cart before the horse, so to speak. Effort is an expression, rather than a cause, of motivation. By analogy, consider when you are in a sour mood and somebody walks up to you and says, "Smile, let's see that happy face!" Smiling will not necessarily create happiness any more than effort will create motivation.

If personal willpower and inspirational speeches are relatively unreliable sources of motivation, then what are the more reliable sources of motivation? Motivation arises from four sources—needs, cognitions, emotions, and incentives. So in the effort to quit smoking, for instance, I recommend looking to physiological needs (how nicotine is addictive and disturbs homeostasis), psychological needs (affiliative need to be accepted by peers who also smoke), cognitive beliefs (does smoking cause cancer?) and expectations (if I smoke a pack a day, will I lose weight?), emotions (e.g., anxiety, pleasure, coping with stress), and personality factors (e.g., sensation seeking). Thus, in offering this fourth theme, I ask the reader to consider the merits of putting the will somewhere on the back shelf of the ways to explain motivation and make room for four new ways of explaining motivated action—needs, cognitions, emotions, and incentives.

Another way of framing this theme in motivation is to ask, "How do people change?" Or, "How do people accomplish the goals they seek?" Imagine being in an experiment with the following presentation:

> We all have things in our lives that we would like to change. For example, people would like to quit smoking, or would like to suddenly quit their jobs and start new careers, or would like to leave abusive relationships. Please try to recall if there is any aspect of your life that you would like to suddenly and dramatically change. If so, please describe the reasons that you believe have prevented you from achieving this change. Provide as much detail as possible. (Heatherton & Nichols, 1994, p. 667).

Change is a complex process that involves motivational, emotional, interpersonal, situational, and cognitive aspects, and change is sometimes successful and other times unsuccessful. In the failure narratives, participants in this study wrote about their attempts to change in terms of personal willpower. In the success narratives, themes such as escape from strong negative affect, change in interpersonal relationships or environments (i.e., moving), and incorporating a new identity emerged (Heatherton & Nichols, 1994).

Motivation Is a Dynamic Process

Motivation is a dynamic process rather than a discrete event or static condition. By calling motivation dynamic, one affirms that motivational states are perpetually rising and falling. Many (but not all) motives conform to a recurring process of (1) anticipation, (2) activation, (3) action and feedback, and (4) outcome (e.g., Folkman & Lazarus, 1985). During the anticipation stage, the individual has some expectation of the emergence of the motive into consciousness and recognizes the situation as an opportunity for motive satisfaction. Some aspect of the situation arouses the motive, and the motive, once aroused, provides purpose or direction for the forthcoming behavior. During the action and feedback stage, the individual performs goal-directed acts, and these coping efforts produce environmental feedback such as success or failure or acceptance or rejection. During the outcome stage, the environment provides consequences that lead to motive satiation or frustration. If the motive is satiated, it typically loses some of its salience in consciousness and another motive takes its place; if the motive is not satiated (i.e., is frustrated), the previous behavioral action typically persists, perhaps in a modified form.

Different emotions characterize different stages of the dynamic rise and decline of a motive (Folkman & Lazarus, 1985). Anticipation typically involves emotions such as hope or fear; activation typically involves emotions such as interest and enthusiasm; action typically involves delight or dejection; and outcome typically involves triumph or anguish. This pattern of changing emotions indicates that motives follow a dynamic process of increase and decline that occurs over time (Buck, 1988).

Motive Strengths Vary Over Time and Influence the Stream of Behavior

We always experience more than one motive. At any time, we harbor a multitude of motives; one motive is strongest while others are relatively subordinate. The strongest motive typically has the greatest influence on our behavior, but each subordinate motive can become dominant and therefore influence the ongoing stream of behavior.

As an illustration, consider a typical study session in which a student sits at a desk with book in hand. Our scholar's goal is to read the book, a relatively strong motive on this occasion because of an important examination the next morning. The student reads for an hour, but during this time various subordinate motives begin to increase in strength, motives such as hunger and affiliation. Perhaps the smell of popcorn from a neighbor's room makes its way to the desk or perhaps the sight of a close friend passing by increases the relative strength and salience of his hunger and affiliation motives. Plus, the hour of reading might increase fatigue or satisfy curiosity and therefore undermine the intensity of the goal to read further. If the affil-

iative motive increases in strength to a dominant level, our scholar's stream of behavior will shift its direction from studying to affiliating.

Figure 1.2 illustrates a stream of behavior in which a person performs a set of
three behaviors, X, Y, and Z (e.g., studying, eating, and affiliating; after Atkinson,
Bongort, & Price, 1977). The figure plots the changes in the strength of each of these
three motives that produce the observed stream of behavior. At time 1, motive X
(to study) is the dominant motive while motives Y and Z are relatively subordinate.
At time 2, motive Y (to eat) has increased in strength above motive X while motive
Z remains subordinate. At time 3, motive Z (to affiliate) gains relative dominance and
exerts its influence on the stream of behavior. Overall, Figure 1.2 illustrates that (a)
motive strengths change over time and (b) people forever harbor a multitude of motives of various intensities, any of which might participate in the stream of behavior, given the appropriate circumstances.

Motives Have Been Arranged Hierarchically

Human beings possess a multitude of motives, but it is difficult to say just how many.
Do people have a basic few motives, say five or six or do people have hundreds of
motives (e.g., see Kleinginna & Kleinginna, 1981)? It is hard to say how many motives we have, because, as Maslow (1987) once put it, "If we wished, we could have
such a list (of motives) containing anywhere from one to one million, depending en-
tirely on the specificity of analysis." His solution to the number issue was to propose a need hierarchy that clustered all motives into five broad categories: physiological needs, safety needs, belongingness needs, esteem needs, and self-actualization

FIGURE 1–2
Stream of Behavior and Changes in Strength of Motives That Produce It

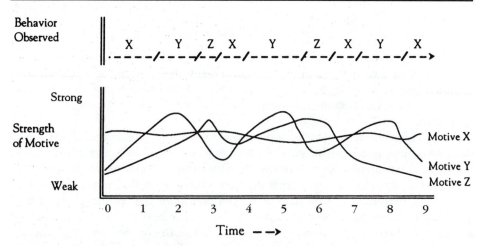

SOURCE: Adapted from Birch, D., Atkinson, J.W., & Bongort, K. (1974). Cognitive control of action. In
B. Weiner's (Ed). *Cognitive view of human maturation* (pp. 71-84). New York: Academic Press.

needs (arranged in a hierarchy in which physiological needs were most basic whereas self-actualization was most unique; Maslow, 1943). Such a hierarchy answers the number of individual motives question by changing the question to the number of general categories. Its advantage is that most of us will disagree on whether we have 5, 12, or 20 physiological needs, but most of us will agree that we have a general survival-based category of needs. Buck (1985) provides a more contemporary hierarchical arrangement that features five major motivational/emotional systems: instincts, primary drives, acquired drives, primary affects (i.e., emotions), and effectance (or competence).

The guiding principle contemporary motivation researchers use to arrange motivation systems is the neuroanatomical structure of the brain (e.g., Derryberry & Tucker, 1991). The human brain has an onionlike structure, such that the core of the brain (i.e., brainstem) regulates basic physiological motives. The next onion layer is the limbic system, which regulates biological motives (e.g., hunger) and the arousal aspects of the basic emotions (e.g., anger). The next neuroanatomical layer up is the paralimbic cortex, which includes neural projections connecting the limbic system to the neocortical brain centers and thus adds cognitive input to needs like hunger and emotions like anger. The outside layer is the neocortex, which brings complex cognitive processes and structures (e.g., self-concept) into behavior. While one does not need to be an expert neurophysiologist to arrange human motives into a sensible hierarchy, the brain's onionlike structure does make the task more substantive than it might otherwise be. The benefit of any such hierarchical arrangement is that it provides a framework that organizes the otherwise overwhelming number of motives into general categories that illustrate the commonalities between individual motivations.

We Are Not Always Consciously Aware of the Motivational Basis of Our Behavior

Motives can be obvious or not so obvious, conscious or unconscious, simple to explain or downright mysterious. This principle simply cautions the reader that the motives for behavior might not be immediately obvious, either to an observer or to the actor. For example, in one study participants were positioned into either a slumped or an erect posture while they worked on an experimental task (Riskind & Gotay, 1982). The task was unsolvable, because the researchers wanted to know what effect posture would have on each performer's persistence. Erect participants persisted significantly longer than did slumped participants, although the two groups did *not* report any difference in their emotion. In a similar study, participants solved a problem and reported how much pride they felt after the experimenter manipulated their posture as either erect or slumped. Erect achievers reported significantly more pride than did slumped achievers (Stepper & Strack, 1993). Thus, posture affected persistence and pride, but it did so in a way that the performer remained fully unaware.

Consider four experimental findings. People who feel good after receiving an unexpected gift are more likely to help a stranger in need than are people in neutral moods (Isen, 1987). People are more friendly and sociable on a sunny day than they are on a cloudy day (Kraut & Johnston, 1979). People commit more acts of violence and aggression in summer months than in nonsummer months (Anderson, 1989). And people commit acts without knowing why after receiving a suggestion to do so during a hypnosis session by a therapist (Hilgard & Hilgard, 1983). In each of these examples, it would not be immediately obvious to the person why he or she committed the social or antisocial act. Few people, for instance, would say they helped a stranger because they felt good, and few say they commit murder because of the hot temperature. Still, these are conditions that cause motivations. The brief lesson behind these empirical examples is that the motives that regulate human behavior are not always immediately obvious.

Consider an example in which heat leads to aggression in ways that we are not consciously aware of (from Anderson, Deuser, & DeNeve, 1995). Heat increases hostile affect, hostile cognition, and physiological arousal, so how might heat contribute to aggression? Imagine driving home in dense traffic on a hot summer afternoon in a car with a broken air conditioner. The temperature biases your affect, schemas, and arousal such that you feel miserable and your thoughts are not necessarily sugar and spice. Suddenly, a car that has been riding your rear bumper for the last mile zooms carelessly around you and almost causes an accident. A typical reaction is anger and a blasting of the horn. In working through the example, the authors ask what difference a working air conditioner would have made to your affect, cognition, arousal, and reaction to the other driver. With your affect, cognition, and arousal not biased by the heat, you would more than likely have dismissed the other driver's actions as irresponsible and left it at that. Such aggression and impulse control frequently affect us in ways that remain outside our conscious awareness.

One final question—why do major league baseball pitchers intentionally hit batters on the opposing team? Not many people attribute such motivated aggression to the high temperature, but the relationship between temperature and this act of aggression is linear; the higher the temperature is, the more likely it is that the pitchers will become aggressive in pitching to batters (Reifman, Larrick, & Fein, 1991).

Motivational Principles Can Be Applied

Throughout this book, the reader will find frequent illustrations as to how motivation principles can be applied. Four areas of application are stressed: (1) education, (2) therapy, (3) work, and (4) sports. Enhancing academic achievement and the desire for lifelong learning, improving mental and emotional well-being, improving worker productivity and satisfaction, and improving athletic participation and performance are all attractive aspirations that can create a better, happier society. Motivation study provides insights in how to attain the objectives we and others seek (McClelland, 1978).

Let me forewarn the reader that the tricky part of motivating the self and others is that there are at least two markedly different approaches to do so (Ryan, Connell, & Grolnick, 1992). One approach assumes that motivation is something people lack and it therefore needs to be produced from the outside. A teacher, employer, coach, or the like uses incentives and rewards as means to create enthusiasm about working toward a particular goal. An alternative approach is to support students', clients', workers', and athletes' motivation from within. This more humanistic approach assumes that motivation is something inherent in us all and the means of facilitating motivation is to nurture the inner motivational resources people already possess (e.g., competence, curiosity, interest).

I suggest you begin to observe and perhaps even classify the strategies and techniques people use when they try to motivate others (e.g., teacher and student, coach and athlete). As you watch one person try to motivate another or as you participate in these interactions yourself (e.g., at work, in school), monitor how active versus passive the person being motivated seems, how he or she reacts emotionally, and ask whose well-being is being served—the motivator's or the subject's? If you do so, you will observe that not all attempts to motivate the self and others are successful and there really is an art to motivating the self and others.

There Is Nothing So Practical As a Good Theory

Consider how you might answer a motivational question, such as, "What causes Joe to study so hard and so long?" To generate an answer, you might first begin with a commonsense analysis. Alternatively, you might recall a similar instance from your personal experience and generalize that solution to this particular situation. A third strategy might be to seek out a person you consider to be an expert on studying and ask his or her opinion. These are all fine and informative resources to fall back on to answer motivational questions, but I want to offer the benefits of yet another resource—a good theory.

A theory is a set of variables (e.g., ability beliefs, goals, effort) and the relationships that are assumed to exist among those variables (e.g., strong ability beliefs encourage people to set difficult goals, and difficult goals once set encourage high effort expenditures). Theories provide a conceptual framework to interpret behavioral observations and function as intellectual bridges that link motivational questions with answers and solutions. With a motivation theory in mind, the researcher approaches a question or problem along the lines of, "Well, according to goal-setting theory, . . ." or "According to the attributional theory of achievement motivation, . . ." As you read through the pages of each chapter, I invite you to become familiar with the motivation theories and to consider their usefulness in answering the motivational questions you care about most.

Table 1.1 introduces 30 or so motivation theories that are outlined in the chapters to come. I list the theories here for two reasons. First, I want simply to introduce the idea that the heart and soul of a motivational analysis of behavior is its theories. Instead of existing as abstract, dry, and idealistic playthings of scientists, I want to offer the idea that for the student, teacher, therapist, parent, coach, and manager, a good theory is the most practical, useable tool for solving the problems we face. To paraphrase Kurt Lewin (chapter 7), there is nothing so practical as a good theory. Second, I list the theories here as a check that you can refer back to throughout your reading to monitor your growing familiarity and comprehensive under-

TABLE 1–1

Some Theories in the Study of Motivation and Emotion (with a Supportive Reference)

MOTIVATION THEORY	SUPPORTIVE REFERENCE CITATION
Achievement motivation	Atkinson (1964)
Affect control	Smith-Lovin (1991)
Appraisal of emotion	Lazarus (1991a)
Arousal	Berlyne (1967)
Attribution	Weiner (1986)
Cognitive dissonance	Festinger (1957)
Cognitive evaluation	Deci & Ryan (1985a)
Control	Klein (1991)
Control process of emotion	Carver & Scheier (1990)
Differential emotions	Izard (1991)
Drive	Bolles (1975)
Dual process of curiosity	Spielberger & Starr (1994)
Dynamics of action	Atkinson & Birch (1978)
Effectance motivation	Harter (1981)
Ego development	Loevinger (1976)
Expectancy × value	Vroom (1964)
Facial feedback hypothesis	Laird (1974)
Flow	Csikszentmihalyi & Rathunde (1993)
Goal setting	Locke & Latham (1990)
Intrinsic motivation	Deci & Ryan (1985a)
Learned helplessness	Abramson, Seligman, & Teasdale (1978)
Opponent process	Solomon (1980)
Personal control	Peterson, Maier, & Seligman (1993)
Positive affect	Isen (1987)
Psychodynamics	Freud (1917)
Reactance	Wortman & Brehm (1975)
Self-actualization	Rogers (1959)
Self-determination	Rigby, Deci, Patrick, & Ryan (1992)
Self-efficacy	Bandura (1993)
Self-schemas	Markus & Nurius (1986)
Sensation seeking	Zuckerman (1994)
Social cognitive	Bandura (1986)
Stress and coping	Lazarus (1991a)

standing of contemporary motivation study. To the extent that you feel comfortable with the range of theories listed in Table 1.1, then you can be confident that you are developing a sophisticated and complete understanding of motivation and emotion. When you know motivation theories, you know motivation.

SUMMARY

The journey to understand motivation and emotion begins by asking, "What causes behavior?" and "Why did that person do that?" Such questions prompt more questions, ones that constitute the core problems to be solved in a motivational analysis of behavior: What starts behavior? From where does a sense of want come? How is behavior sustained over time? Why is behavior directed toward some ends but away from others? Once initiated, how does behavior stop? What are the forces that determine behavior's intensity? Why does a person behave one way in a particular situation at one time yet behaves in a different way at another time? What are the motivational differences among individuals and how do such differences arise?

Motivation study involves the processes that give behavior its energy and direction. The four processes that motivate behavior and therefore define the subject matter of motivation study are needs, cognitions, emotions, and incentives. Needs are physiological or psychological states of the person that energize and direct action to restore deficits or promote growth. Cognitions are mental events, such as beliefs, expectations, attributions, and self-concept, that represent rather enduring ways of thinking. Emotions are complex phenomena that organize and orchestrate the following four aspects of experience into a coherent response to some environmental condition—how we feel, how our body reacts, our sense of purpose, and how we express our experience to others. External events are environmental incentives that energize and direct behavior toward those events that signal positive consequences and away from those events that signal aversive consequences. When considered broadly, external events also include environmental contexts, situations, and climates, as well as sociological forces such as culture.

Motivation expresses itself in both its presence and its intensity through three types of expression—overt behavior, physiological activity, and self-report ratings. Six aspects of overt behavior express the presence and intensity of motivation, including latency of response, persistence, choice, intensity, probability of response, and facial and gestural expressiveness. Psychophysiological states such as the activities of the central nervous and hormonal systems further provide data necessary to infer the biological underpinnings of motivation. Self-report ratings, as from an interview or a questionnaire, also measure motivational states. All three of these expressions of motivation can be helpful in inferring motivation, but researchers rely rather heavily on behavioral and physiological indicators and only lightly on self-report indicators.

Ten themes run through motivation study. These themes are as follows: (1) motivation includes both approach and avoidance tendencies; (2) motivation varies not only in intensity but also in type; (3) motivation can be self-regulated or environmentally regulated; (4) motivation is more than personal willpower; (5) motivation is a dynamic process; (6) motive strengths vary over time and influence the stream of behavior; (7) motives have been viewed as hierarchically arranged; (8) we are not always consciously aware of the motivational basis of our behavior; (9) motivational principles can be applied; and (10) there is nothing so practical as a good theory.

Chapter 2

Motivation in Historical Perspective

Imagine it is 100 years ago. Two travelers are walking the dirt path to town and pass by a laboring farmer. One asks the other, "Why is that farmer working so hard?" Our nineteenth-century traveler's answer to this *What causes behavior?* question would be very different from the answers you will read in this book. A hundred or so years ago, the explanation overheard might be, "Work or starve; live or die; it's that simple." Perhaps the explanation would be more psychological: "He's a man; he has an instinct to work; it's his nature." Or perhaps it would be more ecclesiastical: "To earn his heavenly reward; to avoid a hellish punishment." Hedonism, instincts, and ecclesiastical aspirations were in vogue; no nineteenth-century thinker would have explained the farmer's effort in terms of achievement strivings, resilient self-efficacy beliefs, goal setting, a possible farmer self, growth strivings for self-actualization, identity maintenance, autonomous ego development, the pleasure of optimal challenge, sunny weather–induced positive affect, or unconscious sublimation of repressed sexual desires. I am sure the traveler would not invoke such motivational analyses because none of these existed 100 years ago. So, where did these ideas come from? From where did the notions of achievement motivation, possible selves, autonomous ego development, and so on, come? Its an interesting story, and here we go.

PHILOSOPHICAL ORIGINS OF MOTIVATIONAL CONCEPTS

We can trace the origins of motivation as a concept back to at least the ancient Greeks—Socrates, Plato, and Aristotle. Plato (Socrates' student) proposed that motivation flowed from a hierarchically arranged soul that featured appetitive (bodily demands and desires such as hunger and thirst), competitive (other-referenced standards such as shame and honor), and calculating (decision-making capacities such as reason and choosing among options). Plato's portrayal of how these aspects of the mind interacted with one another anticipated Sigmund Freud's psychodynamics (introduced later in this chapter and discussed fully in chapter 16). In *The Republic* Plato wrote, "In all of us, even in good men, there is a lawless wild beast nature." At times, but most notably during sleep, "reasoning" and "shame" take a back seat and the beast within "goes forth to satisfy his desires; and there is no conceivable folly or crime . . . (he) may not be ready to commit" (Book IX, pp. 280–281). Roughly speaking, Plato's reason corresponds to Freud's ego, Plato's shame to Freud's superego, and Plato's wild beast to Freud's id (Erdelyi, 1985). Thus, Plato offered two principles: (1) different aspects of the psyche motivate different realms of behavior, and (2) these different aspects sometimes act in opposition to one another to produce one goal-directed action rather than another (i.e., psychodynamics).

Aristotle continued to endorse Plato's hierarchically arranged soul, though he used slightly different terminology. Aristotle's hierarchically arranged soul featured nutritive, sensitive, and rational components. Both the nutritive and sensitive components were body related and motivational in nature. The nutritive component provided the motivation necessary for bodily growth and regulation. The sensitive component provided motivation from sensory experience in the form of pleasure and pain. These components provided irrational, impulsive motivational forces. The rational component of the soul, in contrast, contained all the intellectual aspects of the soul; it was idea related, intellectual in nature, and featured the will. The will provided rational, intentional motivational forces. This distinction between rational and irrational motivational agents completed Plato's conception of the mind; the rational component housed "reason" and "shame" while the irrational component housed "the beast within." By postulating the hierarchical mind, the ancient Greeks presented the first theoretical explanation for motivated behavior—the desires of the body, the pleasures and pains of the senses, and the calculating reason of the will. Together, these three aspects provided an early answer to the question, what causes behavior?

Hundreds of years later, the Greek's tripartite soul/mind was reduced to two parts—the passions of the body and the reason of the mind. The impetus for this reinterpretation rested mostly in the era's intellectual commitment to motivational forces that emphasized dichotomies, such as passion versus reason, good versus evil, and animal nature versus human soul. Thomas Aquinas, for example, suggested that the body provided irrational, pleasure-based motivational impulses, whereas the mind provided rational, will-based motivations.

In the modern (post-Renaissance) era, Descartes promoted a distinction between the passive and active aspects of motivation. The body was a motivationally passive agent, whereas the will was a motivationally active agent. The body was a physical entity that possessed nutritive needs and responded to the environment in mechanistic ways through its senses, reflexes, and physiology. The hand touched a hot flame, and the body's senses and reflexes mechanically and automatically energized and directed protective behavior. If you wanted to understand bodily motives, then a passive, physiological, mechanistic analysis of behavior was needed. The mind, however, was a spiritual, immaterial, and thinking entity that possessed a purposive will. The will moved the hand in an active, intellectual, purposive way. If you wanted to understand purposive motives (how purpose moved the hand), then an analysis of the will was needed.

THE FIRST GRAND THEORY: WILL

For Descartes, the will was the ultimate motivational force. The will initiated and directed action, choosing both whether to act and what to do when acting. Passions, pleasures, and pains certainly arose from the body, but instead of motivating behavior directly, these passions merely excited the will. Passion, pleasure, and pain could excite the will, but the direct cause of motivation was always the will. By assigning exclusive powers of motivation to the human will, Descartes provided philosophy with its first grand theory of motivation. I use the term *grand theory* here and throughout the chapter to connote a theory that is all encompassing and seeks to explain the full range of motivated action—why we eat, drink, work, play, compete, read, fall in love, and so on.

The philosopher's hope was this: If he or she could understand the essence of the will, then an understanding of motivation and an understanding of why people do what they do would inevitably unfold. For this reason, a great deal of philosophical energy was invested in the study of the will. After two centuries of philosophical analysis and debate, the conclusion reached was rather disappointing. The will turned out to be an ill-understood property of the mind that arose, somehow, out of a congeries of sensations, ideas, and reflections upon itself. In other words, somewhere in the cauldron of innate capacities, experience, and introspection, a will emerged. Further, once emerged, the will somehow became endowed with its intentions and purposes. It also turned out that some people showed more will power than did others. To make a long story short, philosophers found the will to be as difficult to explain as was the motivation it supposedly generated.

By adopting the will as the agent of motivation, philosophers painted themselves into the proverbial corner by using two unexplainable phenomena—motivation and will. Philosophers were actually worse off using the concept of will than not using it because now they had to explain not only motivation but also the will. For this reason, those involved with the new science of psychology (which emerged in the 1870s; Schultz, 1987) searched for a less ambiguous motivational principle. They found one, but not within the field of philosophy. Psychology's substitute motivational principle emerged from the field of physiology.

THE SECOND GRAND THEORY: INSTINCT

Charles Darwin's biological determinism provided biology with its most important idea (evolution), but it did more. Darwin's ideas turn the mood of scientific thinking away from mentalistic motivational concepts (i.e., will) toward more mechanistic ones (i.e., biological systems). Animal behavior seemed to be largely unlearned, automated, and mechanistic (Darwin, 1859, 1872). With or without experience, the shepherd's dog hunted hares, birds built nests, and hens brooded. To explain unlearned, automated behavior, Darwin proposed the instinct.

Instinct could explain what the philosopher's will could not, namely, where the motivational force came from in the first place. Instincts arose from the individual's genetic endowment, that is, from a physical substance. Instincts motivated behavior through an inherited set of complex reflexes. Instincts were in the genes, and instincts expressed themselves through bodily reflexes. Given the presence of the appropriate stimulus, the dog hunted, the bird built a nest, and the hen brooded, all because each had a genetically endowed, biologically aroused impulse to do so.

The first psychologist to popularize an instinct theory of motivation was William James (1890). Borrowing heavily from the intellectual climate of Darwin and other contemporary theorists, James endowed human beings with a generous number of physical (e.g., sucking, locomotion) and mental instincts. Here are James' 17 mental instincts:

James' instincts

- Imitation
- Emulation/rivalry
- Anger/pugnacity
- Sympathy
- Hunting
- Acquisitiveness/appropriation
- Cleanliness
- Modesty/shame
- Constructiveness
- Play
- Curiosity
- Sociability/shyness
- Secretiveness
- Jealousy
- Love
- Parental love
- Fear

Instincts were predispositions to behave in a specific, goal-directed way. All that was needed to translate an instinct into behavior was the presence of an appropriate stimulus. Cats chase mice, run from dogs, avoid fires—simply because they biologically must. For the cat, the mouse brings out the instinct to chase, the dog brings out the instinct to flee, and the fire's flames bring out the instinct to protect. Thus, the sight of a mouse (or dog or fire) activates a complex set of inherited reflexes in the cat's nervous system that generates impulses to specific actions. The sight of the mouse sets in motion the cat's reflexes to stalk it, spring upon it, tear at it, and devour it. To initiate such motivated action, the animal needed only its instincts; it needed no education as to which goals to pursue or which behaviors to perform. Birds fly, even if raised in total isolation from other birds, and therefore never learning from other birds how to fly.

After James popularized instinct as motivator, psychology's affection for its second grand theory of motivation grew rapidly. The next generation's most outspoken instinct proponent was McDougall (1908). Here are McDougall's 12 major human instincts (the list grew to 17 by 1930):

McDougall's instincts

- To desire food
- To reject certain substances or things
- To explore new places or things
- To escape from dangers
- To fight when challenged
- To have sexual desire
- To care for the young (mothering)
- To seek company (gregariousness)

- To seek to dominate (self-assertion)
- To accept inferior status (submission)
- To make things
- To collect things

McDougall regarded instincts as irrational and compelling sources of behavior, motivational forces that oriented a person toward some particular goal. For McDougall, it was the instinct that "determines its possessor to perceive, and to pay attention to, objects of a certain class . . . and to act in regard to it in a particular manner, or, at least, to experience an impulse to action" (McDougall, 1908, p. 30). Thus, instincts were the motivational mechanisms that explained the goal-directed quality so readily apparent in human behavior. In many respects, McDougall's instinct doctrine paralleled that of James'. Perhaps the greatest difference between the two was McDougall's rather extreme assertion that without instincts human beings would initiate no action. Without these prime movers, human beings would be inert lumps, bodies without impulses to action, bodies without motives and with about as much behavior as a tree or a rock. In other words, human motivation owes its origin fully to a collection of genetically endowed instincts.

Decline of Instinct Theory

Bernard (1924) wrote a book that began to close the door on instinct theory. He compared the lists of instincts authored by James, McDougall, and others, and found that collectively these authors endowed human beings with 6000 different instincts. The instinct doctrine was hopelessly out of control. A few years earlier, Dunlap (1919) had voiced essentially the same complaint. The plight of compiling lists of instincts became, "If he goes with his fellows, it is the 'herd instinct' which activates him; if he walks alone, it is the 'antisocial instinct'; if he twiddles his thumbs, it is the 'thumb-twiddling instinct'; if he does not twiddle his thumbs, it is the 'thumb-not-twiddling instinct.' Thus, everything is explained with the facility of magic— word magic" (Holt, 1931, p. 428). The problem here is the tendency to confuse naming with explaining. As McClelland (1987) put it, "It is like saying that because a plant grows it wants to grow, or because the apple falls it wants to fall" (p. 33). Confusing naming with explaining adds nothing to our understanding of motivation and emotion.

Concurrent with these critiques, an equally devastating criticism of the instinct concept emerged. The logic underlying instinct theory was exposed as circular (Kuo, 1921; Tolman, 1923). Consider the explanation of how the instinct to fight motivates people to aggression. The only evidence that people possess a fighting instinct is the aggressive behavior the instinct supposedly explains. For the theorist, this is the worse kind of circularity: the cause (instinct) explains its effect (the behavior) and the effect in turn is used to justify its cause (i.e., the instinct explains the fighting and the fighting justifies the instinct). Instead of inferring motivation from behavior, the theorist needed some independent way of measuring (and therefore verifying the existence of) the instinct. One way is to rear two very similar animals (i.e., animals endowed with similar instincts) in a way that gives them different life experiences. Then, wait until they mature into adulthood and check to see if their behaviors are essentially the same. If instincts direct behavior, then two genetically matched animals should behave in essentially the same way despite the differences in their life circumstances and experiences.

Consider the mothering instinct in the rat (Birch, 1956). During pregnancy, female rats engage in frequent licking of their own genitalia, and during birth, the female rats smear their vaginal tissues on their pups. Resisting the temptation to embrace a mothering instinct, Birch hypothesized that the licking (i.e., the mothering behavior) was regulated not by an instinct but, rather, by her familiar odor. To test his hypothesis, he placed cuffs on some females' forepaws to prevent self-licking and their means to transfer vaginal tissues (and its familiar odor) to their pups. The rats had normal pregnancies, but after giving birth these mothers paid little attention to their pups. When the mothers did attend to their odorless pups, they ate them. Surely the mothers did not have an instinct to eat their pups!

Investigations such as those on the mothering instinct and the handedness instinct (see Watson, 1924, p. 86) led to the decline of the instinct as the grand theory of motivation. Originally, the instinct concept arose to fill a gap of what motivation is and from where it came (Beach, 1955). Psychology's affair with instinct theory began with wholehearted acceptance, but ended with sweeping denial. Just as psychology previously abandoned the will, psychology abandoned the instinct. Once again, psychology searched for an alternate motivational concept.

Contemporary Instinct Theory

Psychology no longer uses the instinct to explain human motivation and behavior. Nonetheless, the proposition that nonhuman animals show consistent, unlearned, stereotypical patterns of behavior is an undeniable observation. Bees build hexagonal cells, the male stickleback fish attacks red coloration, and birds build nests, fly, and lay their eggs. Contemporary psychologists (but especially ethologists) concede that such stereotypical acts can be attributed to instincts in animals. As James wrote over a century ago, "that instincts . . . exist on an enormous scale in the animal kingdom needs no proof" (1890, p. 383). Rather than use the term *instinct*, ethologists (Eibl-Eibesfeldt, 1989; Lorenz, 1965; Moltz, 1965) now speak of inherited neuronal structures that are unmodified by the environment during development. These inherited neuronal structures give rise not to general behavior but to particular bits of situationally specific behavior referred to as *fixed action patterns*. Changing instinct's focus from the cause of complex behavior to the cause of bits of behavior (fixed action patterns) proved to be a comfortable theoretical compromise. While theoretically expedient, such a compromise clearly shows the decline of a grand theory. Explaining bits of behavior or bits of motivation is just not the same as explaining all of behavior and all of motivation.

THE THIRD GRAND THEORY: DRIVE

The motivational concept that arose to replace instinct was drive (introduced by Woodworth, 1918). The two most widely embraced drive theories came from Sigmund Freud (1915) and Clark Hull (1943).

Freud's Drive Theory

Working from a clinical perspective, Freud suggested that human beings are born with ever-present biological urges (or instinctual *drives*, after Bolles, 1975). Freud did not mean the instinct of the instinct theorist. Freud's concept of *Trieb*, which regrettably was translated as instinct, has more in common with psychologists' concept of drive than it does with ethologists' concept of instinct. Freud, a physiologist by training, believed the nervous system has an inherited tendency to maintain a constant low level of energy. Though the nervous system strives to maintain low energy, these biological urges—drives—forge a continuous production of energy that opposes nervous system stability. Any buildup in energy therefore feels psychologically uncomfortable. If the energy buildup rises unchecked, it could become health threatening. To alleviate aversive, health-threatening levels of energy, the individual behaved. Behavior was the means to eliminate or reduce excessive internal stimulation. One way to understand Freud's view of psychic energy (i.e., libido) is through the analogy of a hydraulic system in which psychic energy (like water) continues to rise and rise. As the bodily drives continue their steady buildup of energy, the urge to discharge the energy becomes increasingly urgent and expedient (i.e., the water would overflow). As the drives persist, the need for their release builds to a threshold intensity and generates an impulse to action. The impulse to act—a motivational urge born out of physiological activators—motivates behavior.

Despite its creativity, Freud's drive theory was plagued by serious criticisms. The following were among the most serious: (1) Freud overestimated the contribution of biological forces to human motivation; (2) Freud's ideas arose from case studies of disturbed individuals rather than from experimental research with more representative samples; and (3) many of Freud's ideas are not scientifically (i.e., experimentally) testable. This third criticism is perhaps most devastating, because without scientific confirmation, constructs and ideas must be embraced only with skepticism, as creative analogies rather than as scientific facts. On a more positive note, however, contemporary researchers are becoming increasingly apt at putting Freud's ideas to empirical test (as discussed in chapter 16). None of these three criticisms apply, however, to the second major drive theory—Hull's.

Hull's Drive Theory

For Hull (1943, 1952), drive was a pooled energy source comprised all current physiological (bodily) disturbances. In other words, particular needs for food, water, sex, sleep, and so forth summed to constitute a total physiological need. For Hull, as for Freud, motivation (i.e., drive) had a purely physiological basis.

The outstanding feature of Hull's drive theory was that motivation could be predicted from antecedent conditions in the environment before it occurred, unlike motivation arising from either the will or the instinct. If an animal was deprived of food, water, sex, or sleep, drive would inevitably increase in accordance with the duration of that deprivation. Drive was an increasing monotonic function of total physiological need. Once it arose, drive activated behavior (Bolles, 1975). A hungry animal was an energized, active animal. Although drive energized behavior, it did not contribute to the direction of behavior. Habit, not drive, directed behavior. Habits came from learning, and learning occurred as a consequence of reinforcement. Hull believed that if a response was quickly followed by a reduction in drive, learning occurred and habit was reinforced. Any response that decreased drive (e.g., eating, drinking, mating) produced reinforcement, and the animal learned what response produced drive reduction in that particular situation. Any response that did not produce drive reduction (e.g., grooming, sneezing, climbing) produced no reinforcement and consequently no learning and no habit formation.

Hull (1943) developed the following formula to show how habit and drive (i.e., learning and motivation) combine to produce behavior:

$$sEr = sHr \times D$$

In Hull's formula, sEr is the strength of behavior (excitatory potential) in the presence of a particular stimulus, sHr is habit strength, or probability of a particular drive-reducing response given a particular stimulus, and D is drive.[1] The observable aspects of behavior are denoted by sEr; sHr and D referred to behavior's underlying, unobservable causes. The multiplication sign is important in that behavior occurred only when habit and drive were at nonzero levels. In other words, without drive (D = 0) or habit (H = 0), there is no excitatory potential (E = 0).

Later, Hull (1952) extended his behavior system beyond H × D to include a third cause of behavior, incentive motivation, abbreviated as K.[2] In addition to D, the incentive value of a goal object (its quality, its quantity or both) also energized the animal. After all, people work harder for $50 than they do for $1, and a grilled steak is more attractive than is wet spinach. Because he recognized that motivation could arise from either internal (D) or external (K) sources, Hull (1952) proposed the following formula:

$$sEr = sHr \times D \times K$$

Both D and K were motivational terms. The principle difference between the two was that D was rooted in physiological disturbances, whereas K was rooted in qualitative and quantitative aspects of the environment.

---

[1]The subscripts s and r stand for stimulus and response to communicate that H refers to a particular response tendency in the presence of a particular stimulus while E refers to the potential energy of that response in the presence of that stimulus.

[2]Incidentally, if you happen to wonder why incentive motivation was abbreviated as *K* instead of *I* (as I certainly did when I was a student), *K* stood for Kenneth Spence (Weiner, 1972). Spence convinced Hull of the necessity of incorporating incentive motivation into his behavior system; besides, *I* was used for another variable, inhibition, which is not discussed here.

Hull's behavior theory gained *enormous* popularity. In its zenith, Hull's drive theory was as popular as any theory in the history of psychology. This is a strong statement, but consider that approximately half of all the articles published in the leading psychology journals in the early 1950s (e.g., *Psychological Review, Journal of Experimental Psychology*) included a reference to Hull's 1943 book. In that same decade (1950–1960) the American Psychological Association (APA) invited its members to list the most important figures in the history of psychology. Table 2.1 reports the top 10 psychologists in psychology's first 50 years; notice that the two drive theorists, Freud and Hull, appear at the top of the list.

Decline of Drive Theory

The fundamental assumptions of drive theory (including both Freudian and Hullian approaches) were that (1) drive emerged from physiological needs, (2) drive reduction was reinforcing and produced learning, and (3) drive energized behavior. Throughout the 1950s, however, empirical tests of these theoretical foundations revealed reasons for concern. First, research found that a motive could exist with or without any corresponding biological need. For instance, anorexics do not eat (and do not want to eat) despite a strong biological need to do so (Klien, 1954). Thus, motivation must emerge from sources other than just the physiological activators. Second, research found that learning often occurred without drive reduction. Hungry rats, for instance, learn even when reinforced only by a nonnutritive saccharin reward (Sheffield & Roby, 1950). Still other research documented that learning could occur with drive induction (i.e., with drive *increase*; Harlow, 1953). Thus, drive induction could produce learning, and learning could occur in ways unrelated to drive reduction. Third, research recognized the importance of external (nonphysiological) sources of motivation. For example, a person who is not necessarily thirsty can feel a rather strong motive to drink upon tasting (or seeing or smelling) a favorite beverage. While Hull included incentive motivation (K), the important point here for drive theory is that motives arose from more than just internal, physiological sources.

TABLE 2–1

Mid-Century Rankings of the 10 Most Important Historical Figures in Psychology

1. Sigmund Freud
2. Clark Hull
3. Wilhelm Wundt
4. Ivan Pavlov
5. John Watson
6. Edward Thorndike
7. William James
8. Max Wertheimer
9. Edward Tolman
10. Kurt Lewin

Motives also arose from external, environmental sources, motives that frequently overwhelmed physiologically based motives (e.g., we sometimes eat the pleasant-tasting, visually appealing desert even when we are as full as a pumpkin). To explain motivational phenomena like eating, drinking, and having sex, it became increasingly clear that attention had to be focused not only on internal physiological sources of motivation (i.e., D) but on external environmental sources as well (i.e., K).

Hull's drive theory was not "wrong." The research conducted within its framework was sound research and should not be discarded. After all, each of its three major assumptions is correct, to a degree. Some motivation does emerge from physiological needs, drive reduction generally does reinforce learning, and drive generally does energize behavior. Rather than being wrong, drive theory simply proved to be unnecessarily limited in its scope of application. It just had too many exceptions and loopholes to permit it to serve as *the* theoretical explanation for all motivated behavior.

INCENTIVE AS A MOTIVATIONAL PRINCIPLE. In explaining goal-directed strivings such as eating, drinking, and having sex, motivational psychologists of the 1950s began to emphasize external environmental motivators. By the 1960s, the concept of incentive had replaced drive as motivation's central explanatory concept. An incentive is an external event, object, condition, or stimulus in the environment that induces a state of arousal that energizes behavior (Cofer, 1972). Hence, motivation study focused on how incentives such as speaking to an audience (event), receiving a paycheck (object), facing a time deadline (condition), or reacting to another person in the room (environmental stimulus) moved the person to action. The incentive theories that emerged fundamentally sought to explain why people approached positive incentives and avoided negative ones. How the person came to characterize any particular incentive as either positive or negative was largely a function of learning. Through experience, people acquired associations between the environmental events around them and the gratifying versus painful consequences those events produced. Through learning, people formed associations (or expectancies) that some environmental objects were gratifying and thus deserved approach responses whereas other objects were pain-inflicting and thus deserved avoidance responses. The fundamental advancement incentive theories had to offer over their predecessors was that they could speak more successfully to the moment-to-moment goal-directed quality of human behavior that was not so well explained by the less flexible constructs of instinct and drive (Cofer, 1972).

RISE OF THE MINITHEORIES

The 1960s and 1970s were transitional decades in the historical study of motivation. In the 1950s, the prevalent motivation theories were well-known historically entrenched grand theories. The prominent midcentury motivational theories centered on drive (Hull, 1952; Bolles, 1975), optimal level of arousal (Hebb, 1955; Berlyne,

1967), pleasure centers in the brain (Olds, 1956, 1969; Olds & Milner, 1954), universal human needs (Murray, 1938), conditioned motives (Miller, 1948), self-actualization (Rogers, 1959), and psychoanalysis (Freud, 1915; Rapaport, 1960). As motivation study progressed, it became clear that if progress was to be made, the field was going to have to step outside of the boundaries of its grand theories. In the 1960s and 1970s psychologists began to embrace *minitheories* of motivation (Dember, 1965).

Unlike grand theories that attempt to explain the full range of motivation, minitheories limit their domain of explanation to more limited behavioral phenomenon. Minitheories seek to understand or investigate particular behavioral phenomena (e.g., doing well versus poorly in school), the motivational significance of a particular set of circumstances (e.g., failure feedback, the presence of an audience), a particular question (e.g., what is the relationship between cognition and emotion?), or the motivational problems or tendencies of a particular group of people (e.g., extraverts, children, workers). A minitheory explains some, but not all, of a motivational analysis of behavior. Thus, achievement motivation theory (a minitheory) arose out of the attempt to explain why some people give up in the face of failure whereas others work even harder than before; the cognitive dissonance minitheory arose out of the attempt to explain why people strive for consistency in their attitudes and behaviors; and research on sensation seekers versus sensation avoiders arose to explain why some people seek out and find pleasure in arousing activities such as riding motorcycles and engaging in promiscuous sexual activity. For a sampling of some of the minitheories that emerged in the late 1960s–1970s era, I provide an abbreviated list of the minitheories (with its seminal reference) that arose to replace the fading grand theories:

- Achievement motivation theory (Atkinson, 1964)
- Attributional theory of achievement motivation (Weiner, 1972)
- Cognitive dissonance theory (Festinger, 1957)
- Effectance motivation (White, 1959; Harter, 1978a)
- Expectancy times value theory (Vroom, 1964)
- Intrinsic motivation (Deci, 1975)
- Goal-setting theory (Locke, 1968)
- Learned helplessness theory (Seligman, 1975)
- Reactance theory (Brehm, 1966)
- Self-efficacy theory (Bandura, 1977)
- Self-schemas (Markus, 1977)

Three historical trends explain why motivation study left behind its grand theories in favor of minitheories. First, motivation study reevaluated the wisdom of its commitment to the idea that human beings are inherently passive. The next section discusses this trend. Second, motivation, like all of psychology, turned markedly cognitive in its emphasis. This second trend became known as the *cognitive revolution*. And third, motivation researchers became increasingly interested in applied, socially relevant questions and problems. In addition to these three historical trends, the first journal devoted exclusively to the topic of motivation emerged in 1977, *Motivation and Emotion*. Throughout its two decades, *Motivation and Emotion* has focused almost all of its attention on empirical exploration of the minitheories in motivation. Parenthetically, a second journal, *Cognition and Emotion*, debuted in 1987 to focus on empirical study of the interrelationships between mental processes and emotional experience.

The Active Nature of the Person

The purpose of the drive theory was to explain how an inactive animal became active (Weiner, 1990). The midcentury assumption was that animals (and, hence, human beings) are naturally inactive, are inert, and the role of motivation was to arouse the passive to become the active. Indeed, the term *motive* derives from the Latin word meaning *to move*; so drives, like all other early motivational constructs, were offered to explain the instigating motors of behavior. The psychologist of the second half of the century saw things differently, emphasizing that the person was always getting to and doing something, "The human organism is inherently active, and there is perhaps no place where this is more evident than in little children. They pick things up, shake them, smell them, taste them, throw them across the room, and keep asking, 'What's this?' They are unendingly curious" (Deci & Ryan, 1985a, p. 11). In their mid-1960s review of motivation theories, Cofer and Appley (1964) divided the motivation theories of the day into those that assumed a passive, energy-conserving organism and those that assumed an active, growth-seeking organism. Throughout the 1970s, motivation theories increasingly adopted the notion of the active organism. When compared to their historical predecessors, contemporary motivational ideas take a decidedly different tone (e.g., Appley, 1991; Benjamin & Jones, 1978; Rapaport, 1960; White, 1960), having less and less to do with deficit motivations (e.g., tension reduction, homeostasis, equilibrium) and more and more to do with growth motivations (e.g., creativity, competence, possible selves, self-actualization).

The Cognitive Revolution

The psychological *Zeitgeist* of the 1970s turned decidedly cognitive (Gardner, 1985). The so-called cognitive revolution argued for the importance of internal processes such as expectancies, beliefs, and meaning representations to provide insight to explain behavior's direction. Along with the rest of psychology, motivation too assimilated the cognitive revolution (D'Amato, 1974; Dember, 1974). Throughout the book (especially chapters 7 through 10) we will see the fruits of the cognitive revolution in understanding how mental events such as plans (Miller, Galanter, & Pribram, 1960), expectations and beliefs (Bandura, 1977), attributions (Weiner, 1972), and self-concept (Markus, 1977) explain behavior's direction toward some goals and away from others.

The cognitive revolution had another, more subtle, effect on thinking about motivation. An emphasis on cognitive constructs and a deemphasis on structural constructs (e.g., environmental stimuli and rewards) changed psychology's image of human nature to become "*human* rather than mechanical" (McKeachie, 1976, p. 831). Mechanical portrayals of human motives gave way to dynamic portrayals (e.g., Carver & Scheier, 1981, 1990; Marcus & Wurf, 1987), and this ideological shift was captured nicely in the title of one of the popular motivation texts of the day, *Theories of Motivation: From Mechanism to Cognition* (Weiner, 1972). The motivation studies of the 1960s to 1970s show a marked decline in experiments manipulating the deprivation states of rats and a marked increase in experiments manipulating success or failure feedback given to human performance (Weiner, 1990). The experimental design is not much different, but the focus on human instead of nonhuman animals is unmistakable.

The changing view of motivation study complemented another emerging movement—humanism. Humanistic psychologists critiqued the popular motivation theories of the day as decidedly ahuman. Humanists resist the machine metaphor that portrays motivation in a deterministic fashion in response to unyielding biological forces, developmental fates such as childhood experiences, or controls in the environment or in the structures of society (Bugental, 1967; Wertheimer, 1978). The ideas about motivation from theorists like Maslow and Rogers (chapter 15) were a manifestation of psychology's new understanding of human beings as inherently active, cognitively flexible, and growth motivated (Berlyne, 1975; Maslow, 1987).

Applied, Socially Relevant Research

A third important change occurred as researchers turned their attention to questions that were relevant to solving the motivational problems people faced in their lives (McClelland, 1978)—at work (Locke & Latham, 1984), in school (Weiner, 1979), in coping with life's stress (Lazarus, 1966), and so on. As researchers turned from nonhuman animals to humans, they discovered a wealth of naturally occurring instances of motivation, particularly in domains such as achievement and affiliation and in settings such as work and school. Hence, motivation researchers began to focus increasingly on socially relevant, applied questions and problems. Overall, the field became less interested in studying, say, hunger as a motive and more interested in studying the motivations underlying eating, dieting, obesity, and bulimia (Rodin, 1981).

Final Thoughts on Motivation's Attempt at a Grand Theory

The decline of the grand theories and portrayal of humans as passive and mechanical—along with the rise of cognitive psychology, humanistic psychology, and a commitment to address applied concerns—endowed motivation study with a dramatically different face, emphasis, and vision.

Kuhn (1962) described the history of most sciences as a cyclical pattern in which progress occurs both continuously and discontinuously. With continuous progress, new data add to and supplant old data, and new ideas add to and supplant outworn ideas. Through ongoing modification, the scientific discipline grows and gradually matures. With discontinuous progress, radical ideas appear and rival, rather than add to, old ideas. If the radical ideas gain acceptance, researchers' ways of thinking change, sometimes drastically. In Kuhn's terminology, the continuous growth of a discipline represents a "normal stage," whereas discontinuous growth represents a "crisis stage." In the normal stage, contributors share a common theoretical and methodological framework. This shared framework (a paradigm) allows each contributor to understand the science's subject matter in much the same way and subsequently guides emerging theories and research. As the discipline increases its knowledge base and makes new discoveries, the inadequacies of the prevalent modes of thinking eventually become apparent. These newly found inadequacies give rise to a general discomfort that soon runs throughout the field. With ever-increasing discomfort, the discipline enters a crisis stage, and its contributors become increasingly willing to work outside the established paradigm. As a result, fresh insights and new discoveries arise, and these insights and discoveries breed a new way of thinking. Armed with their new way of thinking, researchers then settle into a new and improved paradigm and the scientific process returns to "normal."

Motivation as a field has participated in the rise and fall of (at least) three major focuses of thinking: will, instinct, and drive. In its philosophical era, motivation's main focus was the will. In its eventual discontent with the will, the field looked to Darwin's biological determinism for a new and improved theoretical concept, which was instinct. Instinct gained wide acceptance, but its empirical test left researchers entertaining considerable doubt. With the abandonment of instinct, motivation embraced the drive concept as yet another improved focus. Drive theory, like will and instinct, eventually, and perhaps inevitably, proved to be unnecessarily limited. The field's theoretical fallout with drive theory initiated its third historical crisis stage. Contemporary motivation remains theoretically discontent and in want of the fresh ideas and new discoveries that can help the field to progress its fourth normal stage.

MOTIVATION'S FOURTH GRAND THEORY? In the field's quest for a sense of unity (i.e., a normal stage of scientific progress), motivation came close to adopting a fourth grand theory—equilibrium or discrepancy (Appley, 1991; Carver & Scheier, 1981; Hunt, 1965; Stagner, 1977). Equilibrium as a motivational concept works as follows. People seek equilibrium, and motivational states arise as discrepancies emerge from upsetting environmental events. Detecting a discrepancy from equilibrium (in domains such as hunger, competence, self-concept, and so on) gives rise to arousal-based energetic behavior. Arousal explains behavior's energy, and discrepancy-reduction coping responses explain behavior's direction. Restoration of equilibrium dissipates the motivational state.

Without a doubt, the last quarter-century has produced many fresh insights, new discoveries, and new ways of thinking about motivation. What is clear, however, is that a few grand concepts (i.e., drive, arousal, rewards, equilibrium, discrepancy) simply cannot carry the whole burden of explaining motivation. Equilibrium and discrepancy as a grand theory had one critical difference with the earlier grand theories of will, instinct, and drive—namely, that few argued that discrepancy/equilibrium was *the* universal motivational principle. Rather than being wrong, the issue is whether discrepancy and equilibrium "stretches far enough to cover the full range of motivational phenomena" (Appley, 1991, p. 12). It does not, but discrepancy remains a prominent theme in contemporary motivation study. After all, the seventh chapter in this book is titled Discrepancies. But dozens of other themes and motivational principles deserve at least an equal standing with discrepancy and equilibrium. The contemporary landscape of motivation study is therefore one characterized by diversity of theories (a crisis stage) rather than by consensus of theories (a normal stage).

The Current Minitheories Era

The transition from grand theories to minitheories produced consequences that were both good and bad. On the bad side, motivation was dethroned as perhaps psychology's most important discipline to a sort of second-class field of study. The dethronement of motivation was so severe that, to some degree, the field disappeared for a decade and a half. If that statement sounds too strong, I invite you to try a demonstration. Ask the psychology professors in almost any department in the world (including your own) what their special field of study is. I suspect that you will find a good number of cognitive, physiological, developmental, personality, social, clinical, and counselling specialists; I suspect that you will also find some who categorize their speciality as learning, industrial/organizational, school, educational, forensic, or health. I would be surprised, however, if you were to find many motivation specialists. There will be some, but not too many. So, the down side was rather severe.

But motivation study did not disappear. The questions that define motivation, discussed in chapter 1, endured. Instead of disappearing, motivation specialists dispersed themselves into virtually all areas of psychology. What emerged were theories of social motivation (Pittman & Heller, 1988), of physiological motivation (Stellar & Stellar, 1985), of cognitive motivation (Sorrentino & Higgins, 1986), of developmental motivation (Kagan, 1972), and so on. Further, motivation theories specific to a particular domain of application emerged, theories to explain the motivation of dieting and binging (Polivy & Herman, 1985), the motivation to work (Locke & Latham, 1984, 1990; Vroom, 1964), sports motivation (Roberts, 1992; Straub & Williams, 1984), motivation in the schools (Weiner, 1979), and so on. By 1980, motivation psychologists were in literally every area of psychology investigating the motivational underpinnings of cognition, of social interaction, of health, of personality, of education, and so on. Although motivation did not exist as its own coherent field of study, its problems proved to be significant for and relevant to practically every aspect of psychology. The end result of motivation branching out and forming alliances with other fields of psychology resulted in motivation's dispersion into a loose network of researchers who shared a common concern and commitment to motivationally-relevant questions and problems.

CONTEMPORARY MOTIVATION STUDY. There are two ways to conceptualize contemporary study motivation. Figure 1.1 (from chapter 1) represents the first way by arguing that four constructs define the subject matter of motivation—needs, cognitions, emotions, and external events. All motivation researchers emphasize the contribution of one or more of these constructs to explain behavior's energy and direction. In the study of needs, for instance, some theorists argue that "the study of human motivation is the study of human needs and the dynamic processes related to these needs" (Deci, 1980, p. 31). Emotion-minded motivational theorists argue that "emotions are the primary motivation system" (Tomkins, 1970, p. 101). A cognitive study of motivation assumes "people's . . . beliefs determine their level of motivation" (Bandura, 1989, p. 1176). Others focus on the motivational properties of external events and favor a careful analysis of how environmental stimuli and social incentives energize and direct behavior (Baldwin & Baldwin, 1986, Skinner, 1953). The organization of chapters in this book reflects this first conceptualization of motivation study.

A second way to conceptualize contemporary motivation study focuses on the relationships among motivation researchers and researchers in other disciplines. Figure 2.1 relates the basic questions in motivation to psychology's basic aspects. The figure has two purposes. First, it illustrates the loose boundaries that currently exist between motivation and related fields. Second, it illustrates explicitly how motivation links itself with the reader's other courses in the study of psychology. That is, courses in social psychology, personality, and educational psychology will have some content that is decidedly motivational. Because of this overlap, it is sometimes difficult to say where cognition study ends and where the study of motivation begins (Sorrentino & Higgins, 1986) or where the study of perception ends and where the study of motivation begins (Bindra, 1979). Weak boundaries between motivation

FIGURE 2–1
Relationship of Motivation and Emotion to Basic Aspects of Psychology

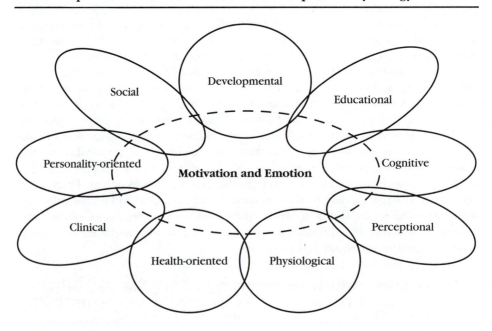

and other fields of study generally suggest an identity crisis within motivation study, but this identity crisis need not have negative consequences. In fact, the absence of sharp boundaries between motivation and other fields facilitates the exchange of ideas and theoretical constructs and it fosters exposure to different perspectives and methodologies (Feshbach, 1984). Motivation's overlap with other fields has also led to alliances outside of psychology (e.g., sociology; Turner, 1987). As a consequence, contemporary motivation study has a special richness and interest.

THE RETURN OF MOTIVATION STUDY. Starting in 1952, the University of Nebraska invited the most prominent motivation theorists of the day to gather annually for a symposium on motivational topics. In its inaugural year, contributors included Harry Harlow, Judson Brown, and Hobart Mowrer (rather famous names in motivation study). The next year John Atkinson and Leon Festinger presented papers, and Abraham Maslow, David McClelland, James Olds, and Jullian Rotter presented papers in the third year (again, all famous names in motivation study, as will be evident in the chapters to come). The symposium quickly became a success and served a leadership role in defining the field. The symposium continued uninterrupted for twenty-five years, until a fundamental change occurred in 1978 (Benjamin & Jones, 1978). In 1979 the symposium discontinued its motivational theme and, instead, considered topics that changed from one year to the next, none of which had much if anything to do with motivation. The 1979 symposium focused on *beliefs, attitudes, and values*, and later symposiums focused on annual topics such as *socioemotional development, psychology and gender, alcohol and addictive behaviors*, and *psychology and aging*. Recall, these years correspond to motivation's dethronement as perhaps psychology's most important field to a sort of second-class field of study. Basically, the Nebraska Symposium, like psychology in general, lost interest in the study of motivation (for reasons described earlier). Motivation study lost its focus and identity.

In recognition of motivation's revival and its contemporary accomplishments, the organizers of the 1990 Nebraska Symposium once again invited prominent motivation researchers to gather for a symposium devoted exclusively to the concept of motivation (Dienstbier, 1991). During that conference, the organizers asked the participants—Mortimer Appley, Albert Bandura, Edward L. Deci, Douglas Derryberry, Carole Dweck, Don Tucker, Richard Ryan, and Bernard Weiner—if they thought motivation was once again strong enough and mature enough as a field to support a return to motivation topics exclusively. Unanimously and enthusiastically, the contributors agreed that motivation was once again a rich enough field of study to justify an annual gathering in Nebraska. The organizers agreed and, in doing so, gave motivation study a vote of confidence and a sense of public identity. Every year since, the symposium has continued its focus on motivation.

In the 1970s, motivation study was on the brink of extinction, "flat on its back" as one pair of researchers put it (Sorrentino & Higgins, 1986, p. 8). It survived by allying itself with other fields of study, and the 1990 Nebraska Symposium symbolically heralds its return as an integrated, coherent field of study. As it enters the millennium, motivation study once again has its critical mass of interested and prominent participants. Table 1.1 (in chapter 1) provides the reader with theories and theorists in contemporary subject matter in motivation study. In the 15 chapters that remain, the reader can expect to encounter a growing field at its best.

SUMMARY

A historical view of motivation study allows the reader to consider how the concept of motivation came to prominence, how it changed and developed, how motivational ideas have been challenged and replaced, and finally, how it reemerged and brought together various disciplines within psychology (Bolles, 1975). Motivation study has philosophical origins. From the ancient Greeks through the European Renaissance, the principal motivational construct was the will. Unfortunately, the will as a construct turned out to be a dead end that actually explained very little about motivation and raised more questions than it was able to answer. The burden of explaining motivation passed from philosophy to psychology in the late 1800s. To explain motivation, psychology chose the mechanistic, genetically endowed concept of the instinct. Despite two decades of popularity, the instinct also proved to be a dead end as the basis of motivation theory. Its logic was shown to be hopelessly circular and its usefulness proved to be only in the naming, not the explaining, of motivated action. Motivation's third and final grand theory was based on drive. Like will and instinct, drive appeared to be full of promise and enjoyed wide acceptance as a useful motivational construct, especially as manifest in the drive theories of Freud and Hull. In the end, drive theory too proved itself to be a dead end, and with the rejection of drive theory came the disillusionment with grand theories in general.

Eventually, it became clear that if substantial progress was to be made in understanding motivation, the field had to be willing to step outside of the boundaries of its grand theories and embrace the less ambitious but more promising minitheories. While motivation researchers were stepping gently out of their past, they got a strong shove to hurry it up from three historical trends. First, motivation study rejected its commitment to a passive view of human nature and adopted a more active portrayal of human beings. Second, motivation turned decidedly cognitive and humanistic in its subject matter. Third, the field focused its attention on applied socially relevant problems. The outcome of all this stepping and shoving was part disaster and part good fortune. As to disaster, motivation lost its comfortable status as psychology's flagship discipline and fell to a second-class field of study. In reaction, motivation study became dispersed into virtually all areas of psychology (e.g., social, personality, developmental, physiological, clinical) and forged alliances with other fields to share ideas, constructs, methodologies, and perspectives. This turned out to be motivation's good fortune, because the field successfully developed a host of enlightening minitheories that might otherwise have been overlooked. Contemporary motivation study is now characterized by a host of minitheories that are so theoretically and practically enriching that they collectively restored motivation study to a first-class field.

The theme that runs throughout the chapter is that motivation study has undergone a constant maturational process. In retrospect, motivation study has featured a forward-moving developmental trajectory in which it has progressed from relatively simplistic conceptualizations to an ever-increasing collection of new discoveries and fresh insights. As the turn of the millennium approaches, it seems clear that the era of the grand theories has passed. Motivation study simply knows too much to reduce its way of thinking to a few general (grand) theoretical principles. What history teaches us is that human motivation is an extremely complex phenomenon that exists at overlapping levels of concreteness, including motivators that arise from genetic, physiological, psychological, social-interpersonal, and sociological-cultural sources. No single theory is therefore going to be general enough to encompass all the faces of human motivation. What has arisen to replace a once unified field dominated by a grand theory is an eclectic group of researchers who embrace three commonalities: (1) core questions (e.g., What causes energetic and directed behavior?); core constructs (i.e., needs, cognitions, emotions, and external events), and (3) a shared history.

RECOMMENDED READINGS

Appley, M. H. (1991). Motivation, equilibration, and stress. In R. A. Dienstbier (Ed.), *Nebraska symposium on motivation* (Vol. 38, pp. 1–67). Lincoln: University of Nebraska Press.

Benjamin, Jr., L. T., & Jones, M. R. (1978). From motivational theory to social cognitive development: Twenty-five years of the Nebraska Symposium. *Nebraska symposium on motivation* (Vol. 26, pp. ix–xix). Lincoln: University of Nebraska Press.

Bolles, R. C. (1975). Historical origins of motivational concepts. In *A theory of motivation* 2e, (Chpt. 2, pp. 21–50). New York: Harper & Row.

Cofer, C. N., & Appley, M. H. (1964). Motivation in historical perspective. In *Motivation: Theory and research* (Chpt 2, pp. 19–55). New York: Wiley.

Dember, W. N. (1965). The new look in motivation. *American Scientist, 53,* 409–427.

Dember, W. N. (1974). Motivation and the cognitive revolution. *American Psychologist, 29,* 161–168.

Hull, C. L. (1943). Primary motivation and reaction potential. In *Principles of behavior* (Chpt 14, pp. 238–253). New York: Appleton-Century-Crofts.

Koch, S. (1951). The current status of motivational psychology. *Psychological Review, 58,* 147–154.

Kuo, Z. Y. (1921). Giving up instincts in psychology. *Journal of Philosophy, 17,* 645–664.

Weiner, B. (1990). History of motivational research in education. *Journal of Educational Psychology, 82,* 616–622.

PART ONE

Needs

Chapter 3

PHYSIOLOGICAL NEEDS

Need
  Definition of Need
  Relationship of Needs to Cognition, Emotion, and Behavior
Fundamentals of Regulation
  Physiological Need
  Drive
  Homeostasis
  Multiple Inputs/Multiple Outputs
  Negative Feedback
  Intraorganismic Mechanisms
  Extraorganismic Mechanisms
Thirst
  Physiological Regulation
  Environmental Influences
Hunger
  Physiological Regulation
  Environmental Influences
Sex
  Physiological Regulation
  Environmental Influences

Suppose a researcher invites you to participate in an experiment. She promises that you will be paid a handsome amount of money; all you have to do is try to gain 10% of your present body weight. It sounds easy and profitable enough; you accept. At first, all goes well and you gain four pounds in week 1 and two more in week 2. By week 3, however, your appetite wanes and at times seems to disappear altogether. You find it increasingly difficult to gain another pound, let alone the nine still needed to achieve your 10% increase. By the end of the fourth week, in fact, you have to eat an abundance of high caloric foods just to maintain the six pounds previously gained. You realize that increasing your body weight is going to be more difficult than you first suspected.

After six weeks of struggle, the experiment seems pointless and you decide to drop out. Increasing your body weight by 10% is simply too much to ask. The experimenter understands and decides to turn the tables. She asks you to participate in a different experiment; this time, you will try to lose 10% of your body weight. You reason that you might be better at losing weight than you are at gaining it, so, again, you accept. You begin a strict diet, but the food deprivation is even more miserable than was the food excess. It takes two months of continual effort, but, in the end, you lose the weight. But to do so you have to continually restrain yourself and suppress or ignore your bodily cues to eat. Despite the accomplishment, you feel perpetually grouchy. Following the experiment, a month of more typical eating passes and you eventually regain your preexperimental body weight. Interestingly, the return to your normal weight coincides with the alleviation of your misery and crankiness.

After the experiments are over, two things have changed. On the one hand, you have a lot more money; but on the other hand, you think about hunger, eating, and weight control a little differently. Your experience shows that the body has a predispositional, somewhat automated guide to how much it should weigh. As we shall see throughout the chapter, the body does indeed feature many self-regulatory guides, and when these self-regulatory guides are upset, ignored, or outright rejected, motivational states arise. Such motivational states (e.g., hunger, misery) will continue until the individual acts to correct the upset regulatory guides. Thus, the thesis of the present chapter is that needs, behavior, and biologically based guides act in concert with one another to achieve physiological regulation.

NEED

Need describes a condition of the individual that produces energy and behavioral direction. That condition can be rooted in biological forces, human nature, or ways of thinking (beliefs and values) that are acquired through experience. Hence, human beings possess physiological, organismic, and acquired needs. Examples of biological needs include thirst, hunger, and sex. Examples of organismic needs include self-determination, competence, and relatedness. Examples of acquired needs include achievement, affiliation, and power.

Figure 3.1 diagrams the relationship among the basic categories of needs.

FIGURE 3–1
Relationships among Categories of Needs

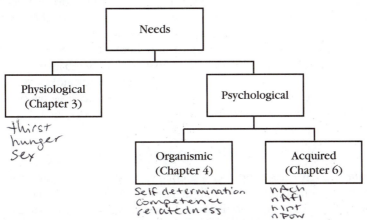

Physiological needs revolve around regulating biological systems such as neural brain circuits, hormones, and bodily organs. Physiological needs, when unmet for an extended period, signal life-threatening emergencies and therefore dominate consciousness. When gratified, physiological needs lose their salience in consciousness, and we mostly forget about them. Psychological needs revolve around the processes of the central nervous system. Psychological needs do not conform to a cyclical time course as do the physiological needs. Rather, they are always present in consciousness to some extent, though specific environmental conditions make some psychological needs more salient than others (e.g., when you are hanging out with friends, your needs for affiliation and relatedness are relatively more salient than are achievement needs). The distinction between organismic and acquired psychological needs is that organismic needs are innate and exist as an inherent part of development and human nature; acquired psychological needs are gained through experience, as through socialization or learned ways of coping and adjusting. Thus, all people inherit pretty much the same constellation of organismic psychological needs, but each of us accrues a unique constellation of acquired psychological needs, at least to the extent to which our life histories and experiences vary.

Important distinctions exist among the categories of needs beyond those highlighted in Figure 3.1. All needs generate energy. Yet, needs differ from one another in their directional effects on feelings, desires, and behaviors (Murray, 1937). A hunger need is different from a thirst need, not in the amount of energy it generates but in directing that energy to seeking out either food or water as the need-satisfying goal object. Similarly, a competence need is different from a relatedness need not in the amount of motivation aroused but in the ensuing desire to seek out either optimal challenges or intimate relationships.

A second distinction among needs is that some cause deficiency motivation whereas others cause growth motivation (Maslow, 1987). With deficiency needs, people exist in a state of deprivation and want to interact with their surroundings to satisfy the deficit (i.e., return toward homeostasis). In his characterization of affiliation as a deficiency need, for instance, Maslow wrote that "it is a hole which has to be filled, an emptiness into which love is poured" (Maslow, 1987, p. 134). With growth needs the person initiates behavior in the pursuit of a forward-moving developmental trajectory. Rather than trying to satisfy a deficit and reestablish equilibrium, growth motivation energizes differentiation and integration processes in which the individual strives to become more complex than he or she presently is (differentiation) and also strives to bring that increased complexity to a coherent whole (integration) (Deci & Ryan, 1991). The emotions that accompany deficiency and growth needs also differ; deficiency needs are expressed in feelings of anxiety, frustration, and relief whereas feelings of interest and enjoyment accompany growth needs.

Definition of Need

The definition given earlier for need—a condition of the individual that produces energy and behavioral direction—could be applied to other (nonneed) motivational states. For instance, emotions too describe a condition of an individual that produces energy and behavioral direction. Some ways of thinking (cognitions) also produce energy and direction. We can distinguish needs from emotions and cognitions by offering the following comprehensive definition of need—*a deficiency-satisfying or growth-promoting condition of the individual that produces energy and behavioral direction*.

Relationship of Needs to Cognition, Emotion, and Behavior

Need is the cornerstone construct in motivation study (e.g., Deci, 1992a). Of course, cognition, emotion, and external events are important constructs as well, but needs are particularly important because of their effects on these other motivational processes. That is, needs affect cognitions, emotions, and behaviors. Needs affect our cognitions, such that a person with a strong need for affiliation thinks disproportionately about friends, relationships, conversations, world harmony, and interpersonal interactions (McAdams & Losoff, 1984). Needs affect our emotions, such that opportunities to satisfy needs bring emotions such as enjoyment and pride (Weiner, 1986). Needs affect our behaviors, such that when needs arise we narrow our ways of behaving to specific need-directed courses of action (McAdams, Jackson, & Kirshnit, 1984). It is also true, however, that cognitions, emotions, and behaviors, in turn, affect our needs. But the point I would like to make here is that needs not only energize and direct behavior but also affect the full range of motivational processes.

Consider two examples of how a need affects how we think, feel, and behave (Biner, Angle, Park, Mellinger, & Barber, 1995). In one study, college students performed a task either after skipping both breakfast and lunch or after eating both breakfast and lunch. If they succeeded, they earned a McDonald's Big Mac sandwich. Before performing the task, participants estimated their skill at the task and their chance of winning the food prize. The food-deprived students overestimated both their chances of winning and their task-related skill, compared with the food-satiated students. Hence, need (hunger, via food-deprivation) affected cognitions (confidence of winning and estimate of skill). In a second study, the same researchers found that low-income individuals (having financial need) believed they possessed greater skill at winning lottery games than did high-income individuals, and they played the lottery games more. Hence, need affected not only ways of thinking but also ways of behaving. The authors did not assess need's effect on emotions, but it seems likely that need would further affect emotions like hope (of winning) and pride (my skill caused the win).

These illustrations speak to how needs affect small episodes of our thoughts, emotions, and behaviors. But needs also affect our enduring ways of thinking, including the appraisals of our abilities, the values we embrace, and the construction of our self-concept. Needs further affect our most enduring ways of feeling, such as whether or not we find our jobs interesting or whether we are happy or depressed. As to behaviors, needs affect our lifestyles, the habits we keep, and fundamental courses of action we pursue such as a career choice or the extent to which we devote energy to developing and maintaining a network of friends.

FUNDAMENTALS OF REGULATION

A half century ago, Hull (1943) described a biologically based theory of motivation referred to as *drive theory* (recall the discussion in chapter 2). According to drive theory, physiological deprivations and deficits (e.g., lack of water, food, sleep) give rise to bodily needs. If the need continues unsatisfied, the biological deprivation becomes potent enough to occupy consciousness and generate psychological drive. *Drive* is a theoretical term used to depict the psychological discomfort (felt tension and restlessness) stemming from a persistent biological deficit. For Hull, drive was a motivational condition that energized the animal to find a behavioral means to gratify its bodily deficit. The behavioral end of gratifying a need was referred to as *drive reduction*.

Figure 3.2 illustrates the physiological need and psychological drive process. After drinking a glass of water or having breakfast, the individual experiences a satiated (i.e., full) biological condition (1) in which neither thirst nor hunger is of motivational consequence. As time goes by, the individual evaporates water and expends calories. With the loss of water and nutrients, physiological imbalance develops (2). If the physiological imbalance persists, continued deprivation produces a physiological need (3) as the individual biologically requires increased water or calories to maintain optimal functioning. The physiological need intensifies enough to produce felt tension and restlessness, which is the psychological drive (4). Once motivated by drive, the person engages in a goal-directed pattern of behavior (5). When the thirsty person finds and drinks water or the hungry person locates and eats food, consummatory behavior occurs (6). The water and food intake satisfies the physiological need. Need satiety removes the physiological basis of thirst or hunger from consciousness, causing drive reduction (7). Following drive reduction, the individual returns to a satiated (i.e., unmotivated) state (1).

FIGURE 3–2
Schematic Model of Need → Drive → Behavior Sequence

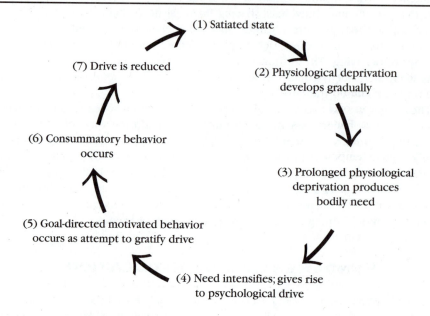

Figure 3.2 graphs the fundamental, cyclical pattern of physiological need and psychological drive. Such biological regulation features seven core processes: need, drive, homeostasis, multiple inputs/multiple outputs, negative feedback, intraorganismic mechanisms, and extraorganismic mechanisms.

Physiological Need

Physiological need describes a deficiency-satisfying biological condition of a person that produces energy and behavioral direction. Physiological needs occur with tissue and bloodstream deficits, as from water loss, nutrient deprivation, or physical injury. If neglected such that the person does not engage in goal-directed, need-satisfying consummatory behavior, bodily pathology follows. Hence, physiological needs, when unmet and intense in consciousness, represent life-threatening emergencies. Restoration of the water or food levels or recovery from the physical injury removes the physiological need (and thus the biological emergency).

Drive

Drive is a psychological, not a biological, term. Drive is the psychological manifestation of a biological deprivation, and it has motivational properties. Drive produces energy. Although we are not consciously aware of how much glucose circulates through our bloodstream or to what extent our fat cells are extended (physiological conditions), we are aware that we are hungry (a drive exists). When aroused, drive readies the individual to perform a particular set of goal-directed behaviors. Thus, the hungry individual seeks food and performs food-getting behaviors to a greater extent than does the nonhungry individual.

Homeostasis

Homeostasis is the bodily tendency to maintain a steady, constant state. Homeostasis and its regulation over time represents the body's ability to maintain a stable internal environment. For instance, the bloodstream maintains a constant water content, constant salt level, constant sugar level, constant calcium level, constant oxygen level, constant temperature, constant acidity, as well as constant levels of proteins and fats (Cannon, 1932, Dempsey, 1951). Because people suffer deprivation conditions and because people face changing environments, the body is continually displaced from homeostasis. As conditions of deprivation upset homeostasis, so do conditions of excess. Thus, in response to homeostatic tendencies, people learn that meals should be small and they develop aversions to consuming large meals (Woods, 1991).

The role of physiological need–motivated behavior is to restore homeostasis or to prevent homeostatic upset before it occurs. Homeostasis for the body's temperature, for instance, is 98.6°F. If body temperature drops below 98.6°, the body can shiver and break down fats to generate a compensatory amount of heat. People also put on coats, wear gloves, and stay inside a warm house to prevent body temperature from falling below 98.6°. If body temperature rises above 98.6°, the body can perspire or find its way to an air conditioner to generate a compensatory amount of cooling. People buy air conditioners, drink fluids, and stay inside a cool house to prevent body temperature from rising above 98.6°. Thus, the body has both a tendency to maintain a steady state and the behavioral means to do so.

Multiple Inputs/Multiple Outputs

Drive has various means of activation. One can feel thirsty, for example, after sweating, eating salty foods, giving blood at the Red Cross center, electrical stimulation of a particular brain structure, or simply at a particular time of the day. In much the same way, drive has multiple outlets, or behavioral responses, that satisfy it. When cold, the person can put on a jacket, turn up the furnace, engage in exercise, or shiver. Each of these behaviors achieves the same end, a raised body temperature. The basic idea is that drive (or motives in general) can arise from a number of different sources (inputs) and can be expressed in a number of different ways (outputs). The convergence of multiple inputs with multiple outputs, shown in Figure 3.3, is actually what makes drive such an appealing motivational construct. In theoretical terms, drive is an *intervening variable*, one that clarifies the relationships among several otherwise diverse input and output variables. The intervening variable of pain, for example, greatly helps to explain the motivational processes that occur immediately after a hammer strikes the hand (antecedent 1), a hand touches

FIGURE 3–3
Drive as Intervening Variable

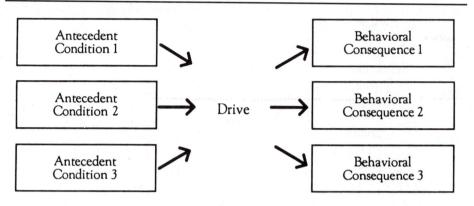

a hot stove (antecedent 2), or a bare foot scrapes across a nail (antecedent 3) to the time that the person shakes his or her hand frantically (consequence 1), pours cold water over the hand (consequence 2), or hops around on one foot while holding the injured other (consequence 3). Drive therefore intervenes between states of deprivation (input stimuli) and restorative actions (output responses), being caused by an input and causing the output.

Consider the theoretical advantage of using drive as an intervening variable to connect multiple inputs with multiple outputs. Imagine that the three inputs in Figure 3.3 were hours of food deprivation, percentage of decrease in recent body weight, and appeal of cooked food aroma and that the three outputs were calories consumed, latency to begin eating, and probability of eating versus skipping lunch. Without drive as an intervening variable, we need to keep track of all the effects each input has on each output (e.g., how hours of deprivation affects amount eaten, latency to eat, and probability of lunching, and so on for all the inputs). This would be a difficult task even for those among us with excellent memories and extensive experience with such matters. Hunger, our intervening variable, allows us a theoretical common ground in which the focus is on how each input affects hunger and how hunger affects each output.

The present chapter applies this multiple input/multiple output framework to the three physiological needs of thirst, hunger, and sex. But the model depicted in Figure 3.3 also applied to other motives as well, and we will see its relevance in practically every chapter to come. For instance, consider the need for achievement (chapter 5). The need for achievement inputs could be optimal challenge, rapid feedback, and personal responsibility for outcomes; its outputs could be persistence in the face of failure, choice of moderately difficult undertakings, and entrepreneurship. As in Figure 3.3., three environmental events are related to three behavioral courses of action through the single motivational and explanatory construct of need for achievement.

Negative Feedback

Negative feedback refers to drive's physiological stop system (Mook, 1988). People eat until they are no longer hungry, and people sleep until they are no longer tired. Drive initiates motivated behavior; feedback stops it. Without feedback, without a way of inhibiting motivated behavior once the underlying need is satiated, human beings would be like the fabled sorcerer's apprentice (from Dukas' tone poem and popularized by Walt Disney's Phantasia; to borrow an example from Cofer & Appley, 1964). As the story goes, the apprentice, by imitating the sorcerer, learned how to command a broom to bring a bucket of water. Sure enough, the broom obeyed and brought the apprentice a bucket of water. After a couple of buckets, the apprentice had enough water but the broom continued to bring bucket after bucket after bucket. Most regrettably, the apprentice forgot to learn how to command the broom to quit bringing water. Were the body unable to inhibit a drive, bodily disaster would result. If people were unable to shut off hunger, they might literally eat themselves to death.

The household furnace provides an analogy for how feedback operates in concert with homeostasis. The temperature setting on the thermostat determines the optimal (i.e., homeostatic) room temperature and a mechanical feedback system controls the furnace output. If room temperature is the same as the thermostat setting, the furnace output remains constant. If room temperature falls below the thermostat setting, the furnace output increases and heat pours into the room. The furnace continues to heat until room temperature rises to the thermostat setting. When the temperature in the room exceeds the thermostat setting, furnace output decreases due to *negative feedback*, which corrects for an excess. In the body, negative feedback systems actually signal satiety well before the physiological need is fully replenished (Adolph, 1980). At first people eat and drink rapidly, but the rate of eating and drinking decreases quickly over the course of a meal (Spitzer & Rodin, 1981). As people digest food and water, the body displays an amazing aptitude to estimate how much of the food or water, when transformed and transplanted, is needed to gratify the underlying physiological need. During drinking, for example, the body continuously monitors the volume of fluid ingested on each swallow and uses that information to predict how much water will eventually make its way into the bloodstream and bodily cells. Understanding precisely how the body signals satiety is the heart of the study of negative feedback systems.

Intraorganismic Mechanisms

Intraorganismic regulatory mechanisms include all the biological systems that act in concert to activate, maintain, and terminate the physiological need that regulates drive. Brain centers, the endocrine system, and bodily organs constitute the three main categories of intraorganismic regulating mechanisms. Intraorganismic mechanisms for hunger regulation, for example, include hypothalamic brain structures, glucose and insulin hormones (endocrine system), and the stomach and liver (bodily organs). Together, the hypothalamus, glucose, insulin, stomach, and liver (as well as other intraorganismic mechanisms) create the bodily conditions of need (i.e., deprivation) and satiety (i.e., gratification) that activate, maintain, and terminate hunger. For each need the intraorganismic mechanisms are different, as will be described in the pages that follow.

Extraorganismic Mechanisms

Extraorganismic mechanisms include all the nonbiological mechanisms that energize and direct behavior toward or away from need-satisfying behaviors such as eating, drinking, and copulating. Cognitive, environmental, social, and cultural influences constitute the four main categories of extraorganismic regulating mechanisms. Extraorganismic influences on eating, for example, include beliefs about calories and weight control (cognitive influences), the smell of food and the time of day (environmental influences), the presence of others and peer pressure to eat or not (social influences), and sex roles and endorsement of an ideal body shape (cultural influences). Together, beliefs, expectations, smells, the daily schedule, the presence of others, pressures to eat and to diet, internalization of sex roles, and a sought-after body image create the environmental conditions that combine with physiological intraorganismic mechanisms to energize and direct behaviors related to eating and refraining from eating. For each need, the extraorganismic mechanisms are different, as will be discussed in the pages that follow. As we will see, extraorganismic regulatory processes can play as important a role as intraorganismic regulatory processes.

Many biological needs exist and create motivational states, but this chapter focuses only on three—thirst, hunger, and sex. Thirst, hunger, and sex represent perhaps the most pervasive motivation systems, and the physiological needs that underlie them range from mostly physiological and regulated by intraorganismic mechanisms (i.e., thirst) through equally physiological and environmental and regulated equally by intraorganismic and extraorganismic mechanisms (i.e., hunger) to mostly environmental and regulated by extraorganismic mechanisms (i.e., sex). That is, thirst is the most prototypical physiological need. Hunger is about 50/50 physiological and environmental. Sex is largely environmental or social.

THIRST

The body continually loses water through perspiration, exhalation, urination, and even through bleeding, vomiting, and sneezing (multiple need inputs). Loss of water, to below an optimal homeostatic level, gives rise to the physiological need underlying thirst. Thirst, therefore, is a motivational state manifest in consciousness to ready the body to perform behaviors necessary to replenish its water deficit.

Physiological Regulation

The water inside the human body lies in intracellular and extracellular fluids. The intracellular fluid consists of all the water inside the cells (approximately 40% of body weight). The extracellular fluid (approximately 20% of body weight) consists of all the water outside the cells; it is divided between the blood plasma and the interstitial fluid. Water is water no matter where it is in the body, but the differentiation is important because thirst arises from two distinct sources. Because thirst arises from both intracellular and extracellular deficits, physiologists endorse the *double-depletion* model of thirst activation (Epstein, 1973). When the intracellular fluid needs replenishment, *osmotic thirst* arises; that is, cellular dehydration causes osmotic thirst. When the extracellular fluid needs replenishment, *volemic thirst* arises; that is, hypovolemia (reduction of plasma volume) causes volemic thirst.

THIRST ACTIVATION. Osmotic and volemic thirsts represent separate means of physiological regulation. Consider the standard water deprivation study in which laboratory animals are deprived of water, but not food, for about 24 hours (e.g., Rolls, Wood, & Rolls, 1980). Following the 24 hours of water deprivation, the researchers selectively replace either the intracellular or the extracellular water (using special infusion techniques). After confirming that the water replacement occurred, the researchers compare the animals' drinking behavior to that of animals that were water deprived without selective replenishment. The procedure yields three conditions: (1) 24-hour water deprivation but intracellular fluid replenished; (2) 24-hour water deprivation but extracellular fluid replenished; and (3) 24-hour water deprivation with no fluid replenishment. The amount of water drunk by animals in the third group (no fluid replenished) was used as a standard of normal thirst and drinking. Replenishment of the intracellular fluid reduced drinking behavior by 85% whereas replenishment of the extracellular fluid reduced it by only 5%. When given a chance to drink, animals extracellular replenishment drank as much as the fully deprived animals whereas animals with intracellular fluid drank as if they were nearly full. These results tell us that osmotic thirst is primary whereas volemic thirst is of secondary importance.

THIRST SATIETY. People do not drink forever. Something alerts the body to quit drinking (i.e., a negative feedback mechanism). During drinking, water passes from the mouth and esophagus to the stomach and intestines and is then absorbed into the bloodstream, hence into the extracellular fluid. Water passes from the extracellular to the intracellular fluid via cellular osmosis. The negative feedback mechanism must therefore lie in one (or more) of these body sites—mouth, stomach, intestines, bloodstream, cells.

To locate thirst's negative feedback mechanism(s), physiologists devised a number of experiments. In one, animals drank water but the experimenters arranged for the water to pass through the mouth but not reach the stomach (or intestines, bloodstream, or cells; Blass & Hall, 1976). The animals, on average, drank four times their normal amount of water, but they did eventually stop drinking. Thus, water passing through the mouth does provide one means of thirst inhibition, albeit a weak one. The mouth's negative feedback signal is the number of swallows during drinking (Mook & Wagner, 1989). After many swallows (but not necessarily after one drinks a large volume of water), drinking stops.

Subsequent studies arranged for animals to drink so that water passed from the mouth to the stomach but not into the intestines, bloodstream, or cells (Hall, 1973). These animals drank twice as much as normal. Thus, the stomach, like the mouth, also has a thirst inhibitory mechanism, albeit another weak one.

Other studies allowed animals to drink with water passing through the mouth to the stomach and into the intestines and extracellular fluids (Mook & Kozub, 1968). The solution the rats drank, however, was a salt solution. Drinking the salt solution allowed much water into the extracellular fluid but little into the intracellular fluid. (Salty water does not diffuse into intracellular areas, following the principles of osmosis.) These animals drank more than normal. Therefore, the cells themselves must house a negative feedback mechanism for thirst. Evidently, water consumption does not alleviate thirst and stop drinking unless it enters and hydrates bodily cells (Mook, 1996).

Deductive logic from each of these three studies implies that three separate types of negative feedback mechanisms exist—in the mouth, stomach, and cells. Such findings on thirst's physiological stop systems have important practical implications because the body wants not only to replenish its water deficits but also to prevent water intoxication—drinking too much water and causing cellular disfunction serious enough to threaten death. The body needs to regulate its water intake carefully, and it uses multiple feedback signals and mechanisms to do so.

HYPOTHALAMUS AND LIVER. The mouth, stomach, and cells coordinate thirst activation and satiety, but so do the liver, hypothalamus, and specific hormones. The brain (through the hypothalamus) monitors intracellular shrinkage (due to low water levels) and releases a hormone into the blood plasma that sends a message to the liver to conserve its water reserves (by producing concentrated, rather than diluted, urine). While the hypothalamus is managing the involuntary behavior of the liver, it also creates the psychological state of thirst in consciousness that directs the body's voluntary behavior into water-replenishing courses of action. It is the hypothalamus that creates the psychological experience of thirst.

Environmental Influences

Perception of water availability, adherence to drinking schedules, and taste are three extraorganismic mechanisms of drinking behavior. Drinking behavior depends on the amount of water available for consumption in the animal's environment (Toates, 1979). Animals with water-plentiful environments drink less than do animals with water-restricted environments. Animals also acquire and closely adhere to drinking schedules, irrespective of physiological need (Toates, 1979). The most important environmental influence, or extraorganismic mechanism, for drinking behavior, however, is taste (Pfaffmann, 1961, 1982).

Pure water is tasteless; it therefore offers no incentive value beyond water replenishment. When water is given a taste, however, drinking behavior changes in accordance with the incentive value of the fluid. Figure 3.4 graphs the incentive value of four tastes: sweet, sour, salty, and bitter at various stimulus intensities. Using tasteless water as a baseline (0% pleasantness), any taste is at least slightly pleasant

FIGURE 3–4
Relative Pleasantness of Four Taste Solutions

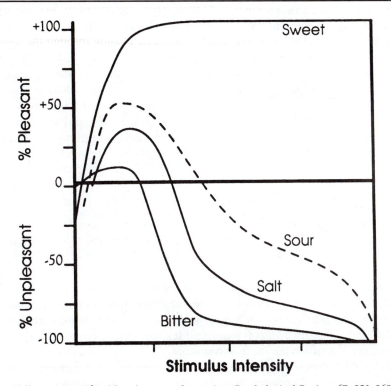

SOURCE: Pfaffmann, C. (1960). The pleasures of sensation. *Psychological Review*, 67, 253–268.

at very low stimulus intensities. At more substantial intensities, sucrose-flavored (sweet) water is markedly more pleasant than is tasteless water. Tartartic acid (sour), salt, and quinine (bitter) -flavored water are all markedly more unpleasant than taste-less water. When factors such as a sweet taste offer a high incentive value for drink-ing, human beings drink excessively and sometimes dangerously, biologically speak-ing (Rolls, Wood, & Rolls, 1980). Additional complications emerge with water-based drinks that contain alcohol or caffeine. Alcohol and caffeine generate addictions, and they therefore introduce a number of additional physiological processes. Further, a number of social and cultural influences surround the drinking of alcoholic and caf-feinated beverages that make drinking behavior more complex than thirst-regulated water consumption. Overall, however, we can offer this conclusion: Drinking oc-curs for two reasons, not just one: (1) water replenishment and (2) subjective sen-sations of pleasure.[1]

---

[1]The relationship between taste and drinking behavior is made more complicated by the fact that water deprivation affects the perception of the taste of water. Water becomes increasingly more hedonically positive (more rewarding) with increased deprivation, and water becomes increasingly more hedonically aversive with water satiation (Beck, 1979).

HUNGER

The physiological regulation of hunger is relatively more complex than that of thirst. Water loss instigates thirst and water replenishment satiates it. Hunger, then, might simply involve the cyclical loss and replenishment of food. Hunger, however, is both short-term and long-term regulated. Hunger regulation, as we shall see, is an interaction between short-term processes operating under homeostatic regulation (e.g., caloric intake) and long-term processes operating under metabolic regulation (e.g., metabolism and fat cells). To further complicate the picture, hunger and eating behavior are affected substantially by cognitive, environmental, and social influences, so much in fact that an understanding of hunger and eating requires both physiological and environmental models (Weingarten, 1985).

Physiological Regulation

Hunger arises from both brain and peripheral (nonbrain) bodily cues. The major brain hunger cue is the lateral hypothalamus (LH). Electrical simulation of the LH produces extensive eating behavior, even if an animal has just eaten a full meal moments before (Delgado & Anand, 1953). A separate hypothalamic nucleus, the ventromedial hypothalamus (VMH), inhibits hunger (Miller, 1960). Rats with a lesioned ventromedial hypothalamus tend to eat about twice as much food as normal and consequently typically double their body weight (Stevenson, 1969). The absence of the ventromedial hypothalamus (via surgical lesioning) translates into an absence of one of hunger's negative feedback systems.

Hunger also arises from peripheral bodily cues, such as the mouth (Cabanac & Duclaux, 1970), stomach distentions (Deutsch, Young, & Kalogeris, 1978), and body temperature (Brobeck, 1960). The two principal peripheral body cues that activate hunger, however, are the body's levels of glucose and fat. The idea that glucose levels regulate hunger is referred to as the *glucostatic hypothesis*; the idea that body fats regulate hunger is referred to as the *lipostatic hypothesis*.

GLUCOSTATIC HYPOTHESIS. Cells require glucose for energy production, and when the cell's capacity for energy production drops, a physiological need for glucose arises that, in turn, gives rise to the psychological experience of hunger (Mayer, 1952, 1953). In one study, animals received an intravenous injection of glucose and researchers plotted the extent of subsequent neural firing in the lateral and ventromedial hypothalamic nuclei (Anand, Chhina, & Singh, 1962). Activity in the LH (the hunger center) decreased, whereas activity in the VMH (the satiety center) increased. Hence, high glucose levels activate the VMH with a negative feedback signal whereas low glucose levels activate the LH with a hunger signal. It is the liver that constantly detects the level of glucose in the body and communicates that information to the hypothalamus (Russek, 1971). When the glucose level is at or above an optimal level, the liver sends an inhibitory signal to the lateral hypothalamus, thereby minimizing hunger (Schmitt, 1973). Thus, the glucostatic hypothesis proposes the following sequence of events for the short-term regulation of hunger and satiety: a drop in plasma glucose leads to liver detection of glucose deprivation, which leads to stimulation of the lateral hypothalamus, which leads to activation of hunger, which causes consummatory behavior, which increases plasma glucose and allows the liver to detect and signal glucose satiety to the VMH.

The glucostatic hypothesis is appealing as an approach to the study of hunger regulation, but it does have one major drawback. Diabetics sometimes experience both a high glucose level and hunger. Mayer recognized the contradiction that diabetes posed for his glucostatic hypothesis and altered his conceptualization by proposing that the important determinant of hunger was glucose level in the cells rather than in the bloodstream. This modification explains why diabetics can be hungry even with a great deal of glucose circulating in the bloodstream. Insulin, the hormone that diabetics lack, is the critical determinant of whether glucose is able to pass from the bloodstream into and through the membranes of body cells. Insulin affects cell membrane permeability, and when insulin increases the cells' permeability, glucose flows freely from the bloodstream into the cells.

LIPOSTATIC HYPOTHESIS. Like glucose, free fatty acids also produce bodily energy. According to the *lipostatic* (lipo, fatty; static, in equilibrium) hypothesis, when the body's store of fat drops below its homeostatic balance, feeding behavior becomes more probable (Hoebel & Teitelbaum, 1966). Eating is therefore a means to maintain or increase stored fat (i.e., adipose tissue). The body monitors its fat cells quite precisely (Faust, Johnson, & Hirsch, 1977a, 1977b). Unfortunately, however, no study has yet found the alleged receptor that monitors the level of body fat. For this reason, the lipostatic hypothesis remains largely theoretical as researchers study possible bodily means of monitoring fat levels (see Keesey & Powley, 1975; Wirtshafter & Davis, 1977; Woods, Decke, & Vaselli, 1974). What is known is that the liver is the organ involved in the producing and breaking down of fat. When the liver relies on plasma glucose for energy, it sends an inhibitory signal to the VMH, as discussed previously. When plasma glucose is low, however, the liver falls back on free fatty acids for energy and simultaneously sends an excitatory signal to the LH to stimulate hunger and eating behavior for glucose (Friedman & Stricker, 1976). The picture that emerges is that the liver monitors glucose levels and manufactures free fatty acids and uses both for energy. Which is used—glucose or free fatty acids—depends first on glucose availability and second on depletion versus excess of stored body fat.

A spin-off version of the lipostatic hypothesis is *set-point* theory (Keesey, 1980; Keesey, Boyle, Kemnitz, & Mitchell, 1976; Keesey & Powley, 1975; Powley & Keesey, 1970). Set-point theory suggests that each individual has a biologically determined body weight or fat thermostat, set either at birth or shortly thereafter. The body weight, or fat content, is determined in large part by the number of fat cells a person has. One person might be born with few fat cells whereas another might be born with many. The more fat cells, the greater the body weight, generally speaking. In set-point theory, hunger activation and satiety depend on the size of one's fat cells, which vary with time. When fat cells are relatively small, hunger follows. Thus, the person with many fat cells who shrinks the size of those many fats cells (e.g., through dieting) feels a hunger that persists until feeding behavior allows the fat cells to return to their natural (set-point) size. Evidence for set-point theory comes from research such as that with obese individuals who participate in extensive treatment programs. While in treatment programs they do indeed lose pounds by the dozens, but after treatment ends they routinely see their body weights gradually rise and rise until they return back to their original starting points (Brownell, 1982).

STOMACH'S ROLE IN HUNGER. Stomach distension further participates in hunger regulation (McHugh & Moran, 1985). If an animal's stomach is artificially stretched (e.g., by the implantation of a water-filled balloon), neural activity in the VMH increases (Sharma, Anand, Due, & Singh, 1961). Under normal conditions, the stomach empties itself at a calorie-constant rate (about 2.1 kcal/min for humans). For this reason, the energy content of food put into the stomach affects how fast it empties and how soon hunger returns. Thus, a person who eats 8 ounces of low-calorie food feels hungry sooner than a person who eats 8 ounces of high-calorie food, despite the fact that they ate the same food volume. Stomach distension—its extent but most particularly its duration—therefore provides regulatory information relevant to forthcoming meal sizes and time intervals from one meal to the next (McHugh & Moran, 1985).

After a meal, when the stomach is full and distended, people report feeling no hunger, as you might expect. As the stomach and intestine digest the food and begin to empty, people continue to report feeling no hunger. By the time the stomach empties 60% of its contents, people report a hint of some hunger. As the stomach continues to empty (at a calorie-constant rate), however, individual reports of hunger continue to increase accordingly. By the time the stomach empties 90% of its food stuff, people report maximal hunger, despite the fact that food is still in the stomach (Sepple & Read, 1989).[2]

Environmental Influences

The sight, smell, appearance, and taste of food, the time of day, and stress are all antecedents to eating behavior. Feeding behavior increases significantly, for instance, when an individual confronts a variety of foods, a variety of nutrients, a variety of tastes, and particular shapes of food (Rolls, 1979; Rolls, Rowe, & Rolls, 1982). The mere availability of food variety encourages more eating than does a monotonous diet (Sclafani & Springer, 1976). Even when the individual has only one type of food

---

[2]Deutsch and Gonzalez (1980) further find that the stomach signals not only food volume information but food content information as well. Deutsch and Gonzalez removed specific nutrients from an animal's food and found that the animal responded by eating foods that had those particular nutrients and refusing foods without those nutrients. Thus, the stomach monitors food content and food volume, and both food content and food volume regulate hunger and its satiety.

(e.g., ice cream), variety in the number of flavors available increases food intake (Beatty, 1982).

Eating is also a social occasion. Human beings eat more in the presence of others (who are also eating) than when alone (Berry, Beatty, & Klesges, 1985). One demonstration of the social facilitation of eating behavior involved asking college students to participate in an ice cream tasting experiment. Half the students ate alone whereas the other half ate in a group of three. Ice cream eaters also had either no choice or three flavors from which to choose (a variety manipulation). Table 3.1 shows the number of grams of ice cream eaten by males and females (1) when alone versus with others and (2) when offered one versus three flavors. Everyone (males and females) ate more in the presence of others and when offered variety.

Like the mere presence of others, situational pressure to eat or not serves as an environmental influence on eating behavior. Binge eating, for instance, is an acquired behavioral pattern under substantial social control (Crandall, 1988). Binge eating seems to occur in small groups, such as athletic teams (Crago et al., 1985) and cheerleading squads (Squire, 1983), largely because small groups develop and enforce norms about what is appropriate behavior. Deviation from these norms typically results in some form of interpersonal rejection and a reduction in popularity. If eating is an important behavior for the group, then group acceptance might become a more potent regulator of eating than one's physiology.

RESTRAINT-RELEASE SITUATIONS. Much in the same way that group acceptance pressures can override physiological regulation, dieting too can override physiological guides. By dieting, the dieter attempts to bring eating behavior under cognitive, rather than physiological, control (e.g., "I will eat this much at this time" rather than "I will eat when I feel hungry"). More often than not, dieting causes binge eating because the dieter becomes increasingly susceptible to eating disinhibition (or *restraint release*), especially under conditions of anxiety, stress, alcohol, depression, or exposure to high-calorie foods (Greeno & Wing, 1994; Polivy & Herman, 1983, 1985). One study, for example, found that dieters generally eat less ice cream than

TABLE 3-1

Ice Cream Intake (in Grams) for Students Alone versus in Group and with One versus Three Flavors

	SOCIAL SETTING			
	ALONE		3-PERSON GROUP	
	NUMBER OF FLAVORS		NUMBER OF FLAVORS	
	1	3	1	3
Males	113.8	211.1	245.6	215.6
Females	76.9	137.7	128.5	170.8

SOURCE: Berry, S.L. Beatty, W.W. & Klesges, R.C. (1985). Sensory and social influences on ice cream consumption by males and females in a laboratory setting. *Appetite, 6,* 41-45.

do nondieters, as you would expect, *except* when dieters and nondieters first drink a 15-ounce milk shake. After the dieters drink the high-calorie food, they go on to binge (Herman, Polivy, & Esses, 1987), a phenomenon known as restraint release and a pattern of binging described as *counterregulation* (Polivy & Herman, 1985).

Counterregulation describes the paradoxical pattern displayed by dieters who eat very little when just nibbling (as during a social occasion or party) but who eat very much after consuming a large, high-calorie preload (Herman & Mack, 1975; Polivy, 1976; Ruderman & Wilson, 1979; Spencer & Fremouw, 1979; Woody et al., 1981). Consuming high-calorie food is only one of many conditions that unleash dieters' binge eating. Depression also triggers restraint release among dieters; depressed dieters typically gain weight whereas depressed nondieters typically lose weight (Polivy & Herman, 1976a). The same pattern holds for anxiety; as anxious or distressed dieters eat more than do anxious or distressed nondieters (Baucom & Aiken, 1981). Others find that ego threats in general—fear from physical harm, failure at an easy task, and making a speech before an evaluative audience—lead restrained eaters to eat more than unrestrained eaters (Heatherton, Herman, & Polivy, 1991). Again, the same pattern emerges for alcohol; dieters eat voraciously following alcohol consumption whereas nondieters eat less (Polivy & Herman, 1976b). The conclusion therefore is that several disinhibitors can release dieters from their self-imposed restraint and lead to binge eating (Polivy & Herman, 1985). Taken as a whole, the research on social facilitation, social pressure, and the restraint release of dieters documents that eating behavior can and often does move away from physiological regulation and toward some type of nonphysiological regulation, such as social or cognitive regulation.

COGNITIVELY REGULATED EATING STYLE. As illustrated by the glucostatic and lipostatic hypotheses and by set-point theory, the body defends its weight. Sometimes, however, people come to the conclusion that their physiologically managed body weight does not measure up well to their personal or cultural aspirations. Rather like a civil war, people decide that it is time for the mind, or their will, to take over and regulate body weight. The revolt occurs when cognitive controls supplant physiologically regulated controls. Successful dieting (in terms of weight loss goals) requires that the dieter substitute cognitive controls for physiological ones. The problem, however, is that cognitive controls feature no negative feedback system and dieters are therefore vulnerable to binge eating when situational events interfere with cognitive inhibitions (e.g., the presence of others, depression, anxiety, alcohol, intake of high-calorie preloads).[3]

---

[3]Restraint eating is problematic not only because it relies on cognitive rather than physiological cues for hunger and satiety but also because it drops the individual below set-point weight status (Lowe, 1993). The binge eating of restrained eaters can therefore be explained in part by cognitive restraint and its absence of negative feedback mechanisms and in part by the influence of low weight status. Self-imposed restraint is therefore a double whammy against homeostatic eating behavior.

OBESITY. Obesity is a surplus of body fat in individuals who are 20% over their ideal body weight for their height (Jeffrey & Knauss, 1981). It is a complex, multifactorial phenomenon (Rodin, 1982) that features causes and influences that are both genetic (Foch & McClearn, 1980; Price, 1987; Stunkard, 1988) and environmental (Grilo & Pogue-Geile, 1991; Jeffrey & Knauss, 1981). To explore the hypothesis that the cause of obesity is undue attention to environmental cues to eating, early research tested the idea that obese individuals are overresponsive to external cues and underresponsive to inner cues to signal hunger and satiety (Schachter, 1968, 1971a, 1971b; Schachter, Goldman, & Gordon, 1968; Schachter & Gross, 1968; Schachter & Rodin, 1974). Despite a collection of impressive early research that supported the hypothesis, subsequent research concluded that overweight persons are *not* more responsive to external cues than persons of average weight (Lowe & Fisher, 1983; Ruderman, 1983). Overweight persons are relatively more responsive to external cues, but so are those of average weight. In the last decade, research identified specific environmental influences that lead people to become at risk for obesity, though most of these factors are only tangentially related to motivation: child-rearing practices (Birch, Zimmerman, & Hind, 1980); child-feeding practices (Klesges et al., 1983); socioeconomic status (Sobal & Stunkard, 1989); fat content in one's diet (Sclafani, 1980); lack of exercise (Stern & Lowney, 1986); and stress (Greeno & Wing, 1994).

Obesity is not a direct function of amount of food consumed. Obesity is a function of genetic forces such as hypothalamic signals, metabolic rate, number of fat cells, and liver disorders. Obesity is also a function of environmental forces such as socioeconomic status, child-feeding practices, stress, exercise, and fat content in the diet. Obesity is not a function of how much food a person consumes; two people with different metabolisms or set-point levels can ingest the same amounts of food yet gain different amounts of weight. And, food intake and hunger are regulated by genetic factors largely outside of the individual's control (or willpower), factors such as number of fat cells, and rate of metabolism. Once food is consumed, some bodies are genetically predisposed to hoard their fat resources more than do other bodies, and all bodies come equipped with sophisticated mechanisms to resist losing weight.

SEX

In lower animals, sexual motivation and behavior occur only during the female's ovulation period (Parkes & Bruce, 1961). During ovulation, the female secretes a pheromone and its scent stimulates sexual advances from the male. For the male, injections of testosterone, a gonad hormone, can further increase his sexual behavior. Hence, in the lower animals, sex conforms nicely to the cyclical physiological need and psychological drive process shown in Figure 3.2.

The farther one goes up the evolutionary scale, the less physiological forces govern sexual motives and behaviors. In human sexual motivation and behavior, physiological forces actually play a relatively minor role, augmenting rather than governing sexual motivation. For humans, environmental forces—cognitive, social, cultural, and evolutionary influences—play the dominant role. Some cognitive forces, for instance, include beliefs of romantic love, expectations of romance, and sexual scripts (discussed later); some social forces include judgments of physical attractiveness, social exchange, and the social feelings of loneliness and love; some cultural forces include religious and moral attitudes towards sex, cultural attitudes toward women, and gender role identification; some evolutionary forces include fertility assessment, commitment seeking and avoidance, and parental certainty and investment. That being said, physiological influences do affect sexual motivation and behavior.

Physiological Regulation

The sex hormones are the androgens and estrogens. Though present in both sexes, androgens predominate in males and estrogens predominate in females. Androgens are a set of sex hormones, the most important of which is testosterone. Estrogens are also a set of hormones, the most important of which is estradiol. Surgical or pharmacological removal of androgens and estrogens suppresses sexual motives for both males and females (Money et al., 1976), but the sex hormones are not necessary for human sexual motivation. Hormones mostly promote the individual's responsiveness to external stimuli (e.g., a potential partner), but nonhormonal factors (e.g., sight, smell, touch) also promote responsiveness to external stimuli. Although androgens and estrogens affect sexual motives, it is the hypothalamus, through its regulation of the endocrine (or hormonal) system, that controls the release of androgens and estrogens into the bloodstream. The hypothalamus stimulates the (anterior) pituitary, and the pituitary releases two executive hormones that regulate sexual motives: FSH (follicle-stimulating hormone), which activates sperm production in males and estrogen release in females; and LH (luteinizing hormone), which stimulates testosterone production in males and ovulation in females.

Sexual arousal is a second physiological contributor to sexual motivation. Human males and females follow a culturally universal four-phase sexual response cycle (Masters & Johnson, 1966). During the first phase, *excitation*, muscle tension and blood flow around the sexual organs increase toward an upper limit. The second phase of the sexual response cycle, *plateau*, occurs when excitation is at its upper limit. The third phase, *orgasm*, starts with rapid breathing and a series of rhythmic contractions of the pelvic muscles and ends with an experience of pleasure, a feeling that emanates mostly from release of muscle tension and blood swell but also partly from psychological intimacy and relatedness. The fourth and final phase is *resolution*. In males, resolution is short-lived and quickly returns the male to the preexcitatory phase. In females, resolution can continue longer. If sexual stimulation continues, resolution is delayed because females can continue with multiple orgasm phases (phase 3). If sexual stimulation ceases, resolution returns the female, like the male, to the preexcitatory phase.

Environmental Influences

VISUAL CUES TO SEXUAL MOTIVATION: FACIALMETRICS. The physical attractiveness of another person strongly affects our sexual motivation toward him or her.

Western cultures generally rate a slim body build for women as attractive (Singh, 1993a, 1993b). Standards of physical attractiveness, however, vary from one culture to the next, because they are to some extent learned and thus acquired through experience and through cultural knowledge and socialization (Mahoney, 1983). I say somewhat learned because some universal characteristics are viewed as physically attractive in almost all cultures, including health (e.g., clear skin; Symons, 1992) and youthfulness (Cunningham, 1986), physical characteristics that have adaptive significance in terms of being associated with greater reproductive value (e.g., Singh, 1993a). Although men (and women) rate slim females as attractive, women's perception of male attractiveness generally has little consensus as to what body shapes or body parts are attractive (Beck, Ward-Hull, & McLear, 1976; Horvath, 1979, 1981; Lavrakas, 1975). The main significant predictor of women's rating of attractiveness in men's bodies is waist-to-hip ratio (WHR, a measure that ranges typically from 0.7 to 1.0; it is calculated via the narrowest circumference of the waist divided by the widest circumference of the hips/buttocks). Women rate moderately slim WHRs in males as most attractive, presumably because it reflects a positive health status (Singh, 1995).

Although the standards for physically attractive bodies vary from culture to culture, cultures show an impressive convergence in what facial characteristics they judge as attractive and unattractive. The study of people's judgments of the attractiveness of facial characteristics is called *facialmetrics* (Cunningham, 1986; Cunningham, Barbee, & Pike, 1990; Cunningham, Roberts, Barbee, Druen, & Wu, 1995). Consider the face shown in Figure 3.5 and its facialmetric parameters. On what dimensions do faces vary from each other and which of those dimensions determine which faces are attractive and which are not? Faces vary in a host of structural characteristics, and Figure 3.5 illustrates 24 of these (e.g., eye size, mouth width, cheekbone prominence). Three categories mainly explain which faces are judged attractive: neonatal features, sexual maturity features, and expressive features. Neonatal features correspond to those associated with the newborn infant, such as large eyes and a small nose, and are associated with attractive nonverbal messages of youth, openness, and agreeableness (Berry & McArthur, 1985, 1986). Sexual maturity features correspond to those associated with postpubescent status, such as prominent cheekbones and, for males, thick facial and eyebrow hair, and are associated with attractive nonverbal messages of strength, status, and competency (Keating, Mazur, & Segall, 1981). Expressive features such as a wide smile (or mouth) and higher-set eyebrows are means to express positive emotions such as happiness and social approachability and thus positive motivational dispositions to potential mates (McGinley, McGinley, & Nicholas, 1978).

Facialmetrics research proceeds by showing dozens of different faces of men and women (via overhead slides) to a group of opposite-sexed heterosexual (or same-sex homosexual; Donovan, Hill, & Jankowiak, 1989) raters. The raters judge each face on a variety of dimensions (e.g., how attractive? how desirous as a sexual partner?), and the experimenters painstakingly measure each face on all the facial metric dimensions listed in Figure 3.5. With these data in hand, the researchers investigate the emerging correlations between attractiveness ratings and facial characteristics. Facialmetrics do indeed predict physical attractiveness ratings, and

FIGURE 3–5
Male and Female Facialmetric Parameters

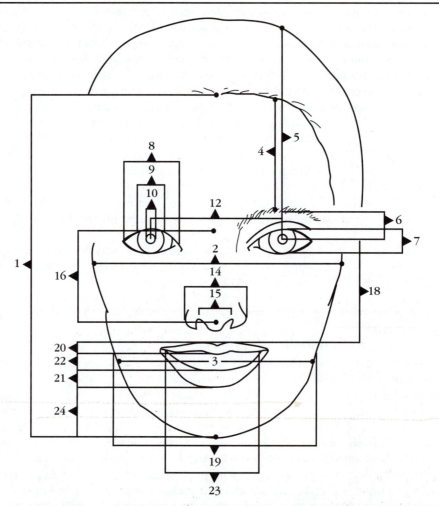

1, Length of face, distance from hairline to base of chin; *2,* Width of face at cheekbones, distance between outer edges of cheekbones at most prominent point; *3,* Width of face at mouth, distance between outer edges of cheeks at the level of the middle of the smile; *4,* Height of forehead, distance from eyebrow to hairline—length of face: *5,* Height of upper head, measured from pupil center to top of head estimated without hair—length of face; *6,* Height of eyebrows, measured from pupil center to lower edge of eyebrow—ratio to length of face; *7,* Height of eyes, distance from upper to lower edge of visible eye within eyelids at pupil center—length of face; *8,* Width of eyes, inner corner to outer corner of eye—width of face at cheekbones; *9,* Width of iris, measured diameter—width of face at cheekbones; *10,* Width of pupil, measured diameter—width of face at cheekbones; *11,* Standardized width of pupil, calculated as a ratio of the width of the pupil to the width of the iris—width of face at cheekbones (not shown). *12,* Separation of eyes, distance between pupil centers—width of face at cheekbones: *13,* Cheekbone width, an assessment of relative cheekbone prominence calculated as difference between the width of the face at the cheekbones and the width of the face at the mouth—length of the face (not shown). *14,* Nostril width, width of nose at outer edges of nostrils at widest point—width of face at mouth; *15,* Nose tip width, width of protrusion at tip of nose, usually associated with crease from nostril—width of face at mouth; *16,* Length of nose, measured from forehead bridge at level of upper edge of visible eye to nose tip—length of face; *17,* Nose area, calculated as the product of the length of nose and width of nose at they do so for the faces of women (Cunningham, 1986), for the faces of men (Cunningham, Barbee, & Pike, 1990), across different cultures (Cunningham et al., 1995), and across different age groups (Symons, 1992). For women's faces, the facialmetrics associated with physical attractiveness include mostly neonatal features (large eyes, small nose, small chin), but also sexual maturity (cheekbone prominence and thinness) and expressive characteristics (eyebrow height and smile height and width). For men's faces, the facialmetrics associated with physical attractiveness include mostly sexual maturity features (thick eyebrows and prominent chin length) but also expressive features (smile height and width).

SEXUAL SCRIPTS. The complexity of adult human sexuality requires inclusion of social, cultural, and developmental perspectives. For instance, the individual's history of socialization and enculturation leads to the creation of a cognitive *sexual script* (Gagnon, 1974, 1977; Simon & Gagnon, 1986). A sexual script is essentially one's mental representation of how sexual episodes are to be enacted. A sexual script, not unlike a movie script, includes specific actors, motives and feelings of those actors, and a set of appropriate verbal and nonverbal behaviors that should take place to conclude sexual behavior successfully (Gagnon, 1974). In its essence, the sexual script is the individual's story line of what a typical sexual encouter involves.

The initial basis of a sexual script is the culture-bound gender script one learns early in life. Children learn what boys do, what girls do, and how boys and girls behave together. Stereotypical gender-appropriate behavior is the crude beginning of a soon-to-be-complex sexual script. Though the preadolescent schoolchild does not yet have a sexual script, he or she does have a vast knowledge of gender-appropriate behaviors. With adolescence, masturbatory fantasies (in males, mostly) combine with gender roles and lay the foundation for a rudimentary sexual script. In masturbatory fantasies, the male coordinates physical activity with an ongoing sexual script that features actors, moral or not-so-moral motives and feelings, and also nonsexual activities (e.g., walking on the beach). Panel *A* of Figure 3.6 shows the coordination of an emerging sexual script with self-stimulatory physical activity (i.e., Masters and Johnson's four-phase sexual response cycle). The young male learns to coordinate his sexual script to coincide with each of the four stages of excitement, plateau, orgasm, and resolution. A more sophisticated male sexual script eventually features images and behav-

---

the tip—length of the face (not shown). *18,* Midface length, distance from pupil center to upper edge of upper lip, calculated by subtracting from the length of face the height of forehead, height of eyebrows, width of upper lip, height of smile, width of lower lip, and length of chin—length of face: *19,* Width of cheeks, calculated as an assessment of facial roundness based on the measured width of face at mouth—length of face; *20,* Thickness of upper lip, measured vertically at center—length of face; *21,* Thickness of lower lip, measured vertically at center—length of face; *22,* Height of smile, vertical distance between lips at center of smile—length of face; *23,* Width of smile, distance between mouth inner corners—width of face at mouth; *24,* Length of chin, distance from lower edge of lower lip to base of chin—length of face.

SOURCE: Cunningham, M.R. (1986). Measuring the physical in physical attractiveness: Quasi-experiments on the sociobiology of female facial beauty. *Journal of Personality and Social Psychology,* 50, 925–935. Copyright © (1986) by the American Psychological Association. Reprinted by permission.

FIGURE 3–6

Sexual Arousal Cycle in Early Adolescent Masturbation and Coitus of Early Adult Male and Female

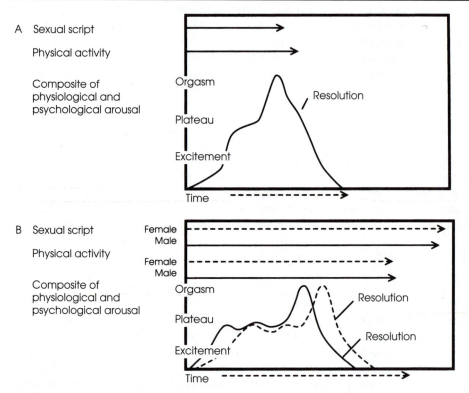

SOURCE: Adapted from Gagnon, H. (1974). Scripts and the coordination of sexual conduct. In J. K. Cole & R. Diensteiber (Eds.), *Nebraska symposium on motivation* (Vol. 21, pp. 27-59). Lincoln: University of Nebraska.

iors coinciding with excitement increase, images and behaviors coinciding with plateau, images and behaviors coinciding with orgasm, and images and behaviors coinciding with resolution. The function of the rudimentary sexual script is the coordination of imagined interpersonal behavior with the physiological desires that elicit and sustain sexual arousal.

For females the coordination of sexual script and physical activity is more awkward, because fewer females masturbate in early adolescence. Further, for females the content of emerging sexual scripts contains little material that is sexual (from the male point of view). The sexual content of the female is more likely to include events such as falling in love (rather than participating in sex). Nonetheless, such events do contain romantic and anticipatory excitement (phase 1) and therefore allow the female a first means to coordinate imagined interpersonal behavior with sexual activity. Later in adolescence, females' sexual scripts conform more closely to the four-stage sexual response cycle.

With dating, both the male and female sexual scripts begin a process of transition from an autonomous, fantasy-based script to an interpersonal, interdependent, teamlike script. In petting, the young couple explores nonsexual behaviors that they have learned as appropriate from the culture. Each physically touches the dressed other. The behavior is exciting, but it does not produce orgasm. The excitement without orgasm leads the male to adjust his rudimentary sexual script to include an excitement phase that does not end with orgasm. The excitement without orgasm leads the female to adjust her script to include the experience of arousal via a sequence of activities instigated by the male. With repeated petting, both sexes master experiences of sexual excitement and gain the practice that will form the foundation for the general complexities of the coital situation (Gagnon, 1974). Later, there is practice in mutual disrobing, learning the social skills to secure privacy, focusing attention on the other, and so forth. At this stage, sexual performance is awkward, anxiety ridden, and frequently unsuccessful. Continued practice improves the couple's ability to coordinate their sexual scripts with each other's four phases of the sexual response cycle. Finally, workable sequences of behavior become conventionalized, and the couple's sexual scripts begin to have a normal order and character to them. As couples find an interpersonal script that allows each to realize sexual pleasure, there is a tendency to fix or pararitualize that workable script (Simon & Gagnon, 1986). Such an achievement of coordinated sexual scripts is an additive, adaptive, and reeducative process for both sexes. This is the learned order of sexual conduct shown in panel *B* of Figure 3.6.

SEXUAL SCHEMAS. People differ in their cognitive representations of their sexual selves (Anderson & Cyranowski, 1994). Sexual self-schemas are cognitive generalizations about the sexual self that are derived from past experience and manifest themselves in day-to-day thought and behavior. Sexual schemas include both positive approach aspects as well as negative avoidance aspects. On the positive side, people's cognitive representation of their sexual self includes an inclination to experience passionate romantic emotions and a behavioral openness to sexual participation; on the negative side, people's cognitive representation of their sexual self includes a degree of embarrassment or conservativism that is frequently a deterrent to sexual romantic emotions and actions. Sexual schemas affect the sexual experience itself such that positive elements of sexual schemas promote sexual desire and the phases of the sexual response cycle—excitement, plateau, orgasm, and resolution; the negative elements of sexual schemas inhibit sexual desire and the phases of the sexual response cycle (Anderson & Cyranowski, 1994).

SEXUAL ORIENTATION. A key component of postpubescent sexual scripts is the establishment of one's sexual orientation, or one's preference for sexual partners of the same or other sex. Sexual orientation actually exists on a continuum, and about a third of all adolescents have participated in at least one homosexual act (with more boys than girls having done so; Money, 1988). The sexual orientation continuum extends from exclusively heterosexual through a bisexual orientation and continues to an exclusively homosexual orientation. Most adolescents rather routinely commit to a heterosexual orientation, but about 4% do not. Though still far from conclusive, research suggests that sexual orientation is not a choice; it is something that happens to the adolescent rather than something that is more deliberate and results from soul-searching (Money, 1988). Part of the explanation for why some people develop a homosexual rather than heterosexual orientation is genetic (see the twin studies by Bailey & Pillard, 1991; Bailey et al., 1993), and part of the explanation is environmental. Unfortunately, this literature is characterized more by rejected hypotheses than by confirmed ones. The idea that homosexuality emanates from a domineering mother and weak father has pretty much been refuted (Bell, Weinberg, & Hammersmith, 1981) as has the idea that homosexuality emanates from an older same-sex seducer (Money, 1988). Actually, this is a frustrating literature, because it is littered with so many rejected hypothesis and pseudo-explanations, especially those related to psychodynamic or behavioral points of view. The most promising leads exist in the domain of genetics and prenatal hormonal environment (Berenbaum & Snyder, 1995; Paul, 1993).

IS SEX PHYSIOLOGICALLY BASED? By admitting that sexual motives are regulated mostly by environment, one must ask whether sex is physiologically based or not. More and more, it appears that sexual arousal depends little on hormonal activity and much on the sensory awareness of a sexual partner (Holt, 1989) and social forces that range from peer promiscuity to sociological institutions like churches (Rogers & Rowe, 1993). That is, the sight, smell, and touch of a sexual partner and the beliefs and actions of other people seem to be the strongest input stimuli to sexual motivation and behavior. The most potent internal stimuli to sexual arousal, in fact, are not the sex hormones but images, fantasies, and scripts, all of which are cognitive events with social and developmental histories that are acquired through interactions with the environment. That is not to say that the physiological underpinnings of sex are not important, just that they are relatively less potent compared to thirst and hunger.

IS SEX EVOLUTIONARY? Sexual motivation and behavior have an obvious evolutionary function and basis. In an evolutionary analysis, men and women are hypothesized to have evolved distinct psychological mechanisms that underlie their sexual motivations and mating strategies (Buss & Schmitt, 1993). It is difficult to say with confidence whether men's and women's mating strategies and preferences are conscious or unconscious, but it is clear that the two sexes use distinct sexual/ mating strategies. Compared to women, men have more short-term sexual motivations, impose less stringent standards, are less exclusionary, value cues of sexual accessibility such as youth and attractiveness, become jealous for different reasons, and value chastity in mates; compared to men, women value signs of a man's resources (spends money, gives gifts, lives an extravagant lifestyle), social status and ambition, and promising career potential (Buss & Schmitt, 1993).

Table 3.2 summarizes the essential differences between the sexes in mate selection preferences (from Sprecher, Sullivan, & Hatfield, 1994). The table confirms that, essentially, men find youth and physical attractiveness important in selecting women partners, whereas women find earning potential important in selecting men

TABLE 3–2

Gender Differences in Mate Preferences

VARIABLES	MEN	WOMEN	F RATIO
Physical Appearance			
Not good-looking	3.41	4.42	172.39**
Age			
Older by five years	4.15	5.29	182.48**
Younger by five years	4.54	2.80	394.17**
Earning Potential			
Not likely to hold a steady job	2.73	1.62	213.25**
Earns less	4.60	3.76	88.44**
Earns more	5.19	5.93	98.89**
More education	5.22	5.82	73.69**
Less education	4.67	4.08	39.00**
Other Variables			
Married before	3.35	3.44	2.03
Has children	2.84	3.11	9.56*
Different religion	4.24	4.31	0.76
Different race	3.08	2.84	12.97**

$^*p < .05$, $^{**}p < .01$.

SOURCE: Sprecher, S., Sullivan, Q., & Hatfield, E. (1994). Mate selection preferences: Gender differences examined in a national sample. *Journal of Personality and Social Psychology*, 66, 1074–1080. Copyright © (1994) by the American Psychological Association. Adapted with permission.

partners. These data come from asking thousands of unmarried black and white men and women the question, "How willing would you be to marry someone who...," and then asking each participant to respond on a scale ranging from 1 (not at all willing) to 7 (very willing). The table shows the mean scores for men and women for each item organized into the categories of physical attractiveness, age, earning potential, and other variables. The F ratio is a statistical term that communicates the magnitude of the mean difference. Any F ratio followed by an asterisk or two denotes a significant mean difference between men and women on that mate selection preference.

Although these conclusions are blatantly and undeniably sexist, they nonetheless represent the expressed preferences of men and women. Such preferences might not be consistent with cultural aspirations, but they are consistent with evolutionary aspirations. They are consistent with heterosexual aspirations anyway, but some differences emerge when examining the mating preference of homosexuals (Bailey et al., 1994). Like heterosexual males, homosexual males rate interest in visual sexual stimuli and rate the physical attractiveness of their partners as very important, but unlike heterosexual males they do not show a strong preference for younger partners and are not so prone to sexual jealousy. Mate preferences of course apply to include literally 100 possible mates, so understanding the act of choosing a single mate who will be a life companion still requires an analysis of romantic infatuation and pair bonding (Lykken & Tellegen, 1993). Thus, sexual activity is based in evolutionary motives, just as it, also, is based in nonevolutionary influences—hormones, facialmetrics, cognitive scripts, social contagion, religious beliefs, and so on.

SUMMARY

The three physiological needs of thirst, hunger, and sex can be organized into a continuum according to the relative degree of physiological versus environmental regulation. At the biological end of the continuum is thirst, and at the environmental end of the continuum is sex, with hunger somewhere in between the two. This continuum is useful because other physiological needs not discussed in this chapter could be understood via their placement on the continuum. For instance, toward the physiological end we could put temperature regulation; pain would be somewhere in the middle but more toward the physiological side; and aggression would be best placed nearest the environmental end of the continuum.

The anchor point of the chapter was Hull's biologically based drive theory (Fig. 3.2). According to drive theory, physiological deprivations and deficits give rise to bodily need states, which in turn give rise to a psychological drive. More completely, drive theory proposes the following sequence of events: Physiological deprivation leads to the emergence of biological need, expressed as a felt psychological drive, which causes motivated consummatory behavior resulting in drive reduction, time goes by and physiological deprivations recur, and so on. The chapter outlined the physiological regulatory processes of thirst, hunger, and sex and, in doing so, introduced seven fundamental regulatory processes common to each physiological motive: physiological need, drive, homeostasis, multiple inputs and outputs, negative feedback, intraorganismic variables, and extraorganismic variables.

Thirst activation and satiety is rather straightforward. Water depletion inside the cells (intracellular thirst) and water depletion outside the cells (extracellular thirst) activate thirst. Of the two, intracellular dehydration is the more critical thirst activator. Water restoration satiates thirst. Once initiated, drinking behavior continues until inhibited by separate negative feedback mechanisms in the mouth, stomach, and cells. These negative feedback systems prevent water intoxication, which can be as dangerous a threat to homeostasis and physical well-being as water deprivation. Drinking behavior is further regulated by extraorganismic variables, such as water availability and taste, which give water added incentive value.

Hunger and feeding behavior involve a complex regulatory system of both short-term (glucostatic hypothesis) and long-term (lipostatic hypothesis, including set-point theory) regulation. According to the glucostatic hypothesis, glucose deficiency stimulates the lateral hypothalamus to activate hunger and glucose excess stimulates the ventromedial hypothalamus to inhibit it. According to the lipostatic hypothesis, smaller cells initiate hunger whereas normal or larger fat cells inhibit it. Some important environmental eating cues include the sight, smell, and taste of food, time of day, stress, presence of others, and situational pressures such as conforming to a group norm. Environmental factors are such substantial contributors to eating behavior that they sometimes overwhelm and supplant physiological factors. Dieting, for instance, is the prototypical manifestation of the person's attempt to supplant involuntary physiological controls over eating with voluntary cognitive controls. Such a cognitively regulated eating style has implications associated with binging, restraint release, and obesity.

The physiological basis of human sexual behavior involves the sex hormones (androgens and estrogens) and the four-stage sexual response cycle of excitement, plateau, orgasm, and resolution. But human sexual behavior is governed mostly by cognitive, social, and cultural forces. The physical characteristics of a potential sexual partner are among the most important determinants of how much sexual motivation we experience toward that person. Attractive bodily characteristics are mostly culturally determined, but many facial characteristics are considered attractive across different cultures and ages. Sexual scripts add a distinct cognitive influence to sexual motivation. From their childhood learning of sex and gender roles and adolescent experiences with masturbation, young males and females develop rudimentary sexual scripts to bridge the gap between self-stimulatory sexual activity and interpersonal sexual behavior. The research on the determinants of sexual orientation is inconclusive, but it points tentatively toward the importance of genetics and prenatal development and away from environmental influences. Sexual motivation is also regulated, in part, by evolutionary influences such that men and women inherit distinct psychological mechanisms that regulate their sexual motivation and mating strategies.

RECOMMENDED READINGS

Anderson, B. L., & Cyranowski, J. M. (1994). Women's sexual self-schema. *Journal of Personality and Social Psychology, 67*, 1079-1100.

Berry, S. L., Beatty, W. W., & Klesges, R. C. (1985). Sensory and social influences on ice cream consumption by males and females in a laboratory setting. *Appetite, 6*, 41-45.

Blass, E. M., & Hall, W. G. (1976). Drinking termination: Interactions among hydrational, orogastic, and behavioral control in rats. *Psychological Review, 83*, 356-374.

Cunningham, M. R. (1986). Measuring the physical in physical attractiveness: Quasi-experiments on the sociobiology of female facial beauty. *Journal of Personality and Social Psychology, 50*, 925-935.

Crandall, C. S. (1988). Social cognition of binge eating. *Journal of Personality and Social Psychology, 55*, 588-598.

Gagnon, H. (1974). Scripts and the coordination of sexual conduct. In J. K. Cole & R. Dienstbier (Eds.), *Nebraska symposium on motivation* (Vol. 21, pp. 27-59). Lincoln: University of Nebraska Press.

Keesey, R. E., & Powley, T. L. (1975). Hypothalamic regulation of body weight. *American Scientist, 63*, 558-565.

Polivy, J., & Herman, C. P. (1985). Dieting and binging. *American Psychologist, 40*, 193-201.

Sepple, C. P., & Read, N. W. (1989). Gastrointestinal correlates of the development of hunger in man. *Appetite, 13*, 183-191.

Toates, F. M. (1979). Homeostasis and drinking. *Behavior and Brain Sciences, 2*, 95-102.

Chapter 4

ORGANISMIC PSYCHOLOGICAL NEEDS

Imagine visiting a lake, at a campground or state park, for instance. As you lie on the shore soaking up the sun's rays, you notice a young girl playfully skipping stones across the water. Before each toss, she studiously inspects piles of stones to find the flattest one. With stone in hand, she puts all her effort into the toss. Each time a rock skips according to plan, she smiles and her enthusiasm grows. Each dud brings a frown, but also increased determination. Despite the family fish fry, her rock skipping continues. At first, she tries to make each stone skip once off the surface. After a half-hour of practice, she uses three or four finely tuned techniques—short skips with many hops, a long skip with a single hop, and so forth. And, she pretends to throw some stones like a baseball and others, the big and heavy ones, like hand grenades, because these splashes look like explosions in her imagination.

The child is at play. For her, an urban child, the lake is a relatively novel setting. It allows her to use her imagination in a way that is different from every day. As she plays, she feels excited and entertained. Each rock and each toss provides her with a different, surprising result. She seems challenged. She feels competent as she exercises and then develops her imagination and rock-tossing competencies, and, more generally, her object-tossing skills. From the perspective of the next two chapters, such behavior is more than frivolous play—it is integral to healthy development. The lake setting provides the child with yet another opportunity in life to exercise and to develop skills, to feel competent and self-determining, and to learn to enjoy an activity solely for the experience and the positive emotion it provides.

PSYCHOLOGICAL NEEDS

Human beings are inherently active. As children, we push and pull things; we shake, throw, carry, explore, and ask questions about the objects that surround us. As adults, we continue to explore and to play. We play games, solve mysteries, undertake challenges, pursue hobbies, build and organize, and do any number of activities for little apparent reason other than the interest and enjoyment they provide. I say "apparent" because there is reason in our motivation; namely, playing games, solving mysteries, and undertaking optimal challenges provides an arena to involve and satisfy the full range of our psychological needs. When an activity involves our needs, we feel interest; when an activity satisfies our needs, we feel enjoyment. So, although we apparently engage in activities out of interest and enjoyment (i.e., "I play tennis because it's fun."), this chapter argues that the underlying cause of engaging our environment to exercise and challenge our skills is psychological need involvement (one origin of interest) and psychological need satisfaction (one origin of enjoyment).

Psychological needs are important additions to our analysis of motivated behavior. As discussed in the last chapter, physiological needs for water, sugar, fat, and so on emanate from biological deficits and function to alert the person (via psychological drive) to the existence of biological emergencies. The changing conditions of biological systems automatically produce the arousal (i.e., involvement) and satiation (i.e., satisfaction) of physiological needs. The motivation to instigate physiological need-gratifying behavior is essentially reactive, in the sense of becoming aware of and then eliminating a deficit bodily condition. Psychological needs are of a qualitatively different nature. Psychological needs provide proactive energy. Psychological needs motivate environmental exploration and challenge seeking.

Need Structure

Types of needs exist, and these types can be organized within a *need structure* (recall Fig. 3.1; see also Deci, 1980). Physiological needs are inherent within the workings of biological systems (chapter 3). Organismic psychological needs are inherent within the strivings of human nature and healthy development (this chapter). Acquired psychological needs are derived from experience, learning, and our socialization histories (chapter 6). Organismic psychological needs include self-determination, competence, and relatedness, and these needs are innate in all of us. Acquired psychological needs include achievement, affiliation, intimacy, and power (among others); these needs arise from our unique personal experiences and thus vary considerably from one person to the next.

Organismic Approach to Motivation

Organismic theories get their name from the term *organism*, an entity that is alive and in active exchange with its environment (Blasi, 1976). The survival of any organism depends on its environment, and all organisms are equipped to engage in and to initiate environmental exchanges (unlike machines, for instance, that are exposed to and react to the environment). Environments change and hence organisms need flexibility to adjust and accommodate to those changes. To adapt, organisms must learn to substitute a new response for a previously successful but now outdated one (because the environment changed). Hence, organisms change, grow, and develop in part due to their own maturation but also in accordance with the demands, changes, and affordances of their surroundings. Hence, organisms have motives to engage the environment (organismic psychological needs), and organisms acquire new motives as they struggle to adapt successfully to their surroundings (acquired psychological needs).

The opposite of an organismic approach is a mechanistic one. In mechanistic theories, the environment acts on the person. The person, in turn, reacts in a predictable, largely passive manner. For instance, in the case of physiological thirst, environments produce heat and the person responds in a rather predictable and passive way—by sweating. Sweating leads to water loss; when the biological systems detect water loss, thirst arises rather automatically (or mechanistically). Chapter 3 discussed thirst and hunger as mechanistically regulated motives. Later chapters will discuss other mechanistic motives (e.g., reinforcements, chapter 5; TOTE unit, chapter 7). In each of these approaches, the relationship between the person and the environment is largely one-way such that the environment acts on the person and the person reacts.

Organismic theories reject the one-way portrayal and instead emphasize the person-environment dialectic (Deci & Ryan, 1991). In a dialectic, the environment acts on the person and the person acts on the environment. Organismic theories of motivation emphasize both the person's (i.e., organism's) intrinsic motivation to seek out and effect changes in the environment as well as the environment's capacity to generate in the person an extrinsic motivation to adjust and accommodate to the demands in the environment (Deci & Ryan, 1985a). The outcome of the person-environment dialectic is an ever-changing synthesis in which the person's needs are fulfilled by the environment and the environment produces in the person new forms of motivation. As an illustration, consider the athlete's motivation in competition. A relatedness need might lead one person to participate in team sports, whereas a competence need might motivate another to seek out interpersonal competitions. The competitive setting's emphasis on winning, however, produces in the athlete an artificial need to win, or perhaps a need to gain status or public recognition (Deci & Olson, 1987; Vallerand, Gauvin, & Halliwell, 1986). After some history of interpersonal competition, the athlete's motivation to compete emanates partly from inherent strivings for belonging and mastery and partly from a socially acquired desire to win.

The following two assumptions define an organismic approach to motivation:

1. Human beings are inherently active.
2. The principles of differentiation and integration guide the development of internal structures.

The organismic approach to motivation begins with the assumption that the organism is inherently active. The motivational source of that inherent activity is a set of organismic psychological needs that collectively generate in the person an *intrinsic motivation* (Deci & Ryan, 1985a). Intrinsic motivation explains why people actively and continually initiate voluntary interactions with their environment—because they want to involve and satisfy their organismic psychological needs of self-determination, competence, and relatedness. Such self-initiated engagement with the environment in the service of psychological needs explains the first assumption of the organismic approach to motivation.

Differentiation and integration describe the two complementary developmental processes that underlie the organism's tendency toward a more elaborate organization. Differentiation involves elaboration, a developmental tendency toward ever-increasing complexity. Integration involves organization and refinement, a tendency toward coherence, wholeness, or unity (Deci & Ryan, 1991). Differentiation occurs because people are inherently active. Inherently active people explore, seek out challenges, encounter new situations, strive to expand their capabilities, and discover new interests within themselves. As a result, people grow (i.e., differentiate themselves) in complexity. Integration occurs because people seek to synthesize their expanding complexity into a higher level of organization. As people grow in complexity, they need to organize their expanding interests and capacities with other aspects of the self (e.g., "I am a traditional male who is currently learning about cooking, so how can I make sense of who I am? How can I integrate these new interests and skills into my old self?"). Such tendencies toward organized complexity explain the second assumption of the organismic approach to motivation.

ORGANISMIC PSYCHOLOGICAL NEEDS. Consider the motivational dynamics that underlie people's desires to exercise and develop their competencies. Consider why people experiment with, practice, and seek to improve skills such as walking, talking, reading, swimming, driving, drawing, riding a bicycle, hitting a baseball, solving crossword puzzles, making friends, telling jokes, and hundreds of other such competencies. In part, these competencies emerge maturationally, but they also emerge in part through motivated learning (Gibson, 1988; White, 1959). Much of what motivates such learning is the organismic psychological need (Deci & Ryan, 1985a; White, 1959). Young children best illustrate how organismic psychological needs motivate skill exercise and development. The desire to interact effectively with their surroundings (i.e., the competence need) motivates the exercise, practice, and development of skills such as crawling, walking, and talking. Endlessly, young children motor about from one place to another just to do so. Further, they desire to carry out their skill-testing experiments on the world on their own terms (i.e., showing the self-determination need).

The three organismic psychological needs of self-determination, competence, and relatedness collectively provide individuals with a natural motivation to learn, grow, and develop in a way that is healthy and allows them to progressively transform the self (through differentiation and integration) from simple and immature to complex and mature. In brief, the need for self-determination speaks to people's agency strivings to initiate behaviors and environmental transactions that emanate from within the self. The need for competence speaks to people's effectance strivings to produce intentional changes in their environmental surroundings. The need for relatedness speaks to people's strivings to relate the self authentically to others in a caring and emotionally meaningful way. Three assumptions follow: (1) these organismic needs are inherent in healthy development and human nature, (2) people are naturally desirous of being self-determining, competent, and interpersonally related to others, and (3) when environments allow people to be self-determining, competent, and interpersonally related, motivation is strong, affect is positive, and development is growth oriented.

SELF-DETERMINATION

We all desire choice when deciding when to act and what to do. That is, we want to exercise choice in the initiation and regulation of our behavior rather than having someone else tell us what to do, when to do it, how to do it, and when to stop doing it. We want to have our choices, rather than environmental rewards and pressures, determine our actions. As initiators of our own behavior, we want to select what goals we will pursue and how we will go about achieving those aspirations that are important to us. We prefer to choose behaviors based on our interests, preferences, wants, and desires. In other words, we have a need for self-determination.

Behavior is self-determined when our interests, preferences, and beliefs guide the decision whether or not to engage in a particular activity. We are not self-determining (i.e., our behaviors are other-determined) when some outside force pressures us to think, feel, or behave in particular ways (Deci, 1980). Formally, self-determination is the need to experience choice in the initiation and regulation of behavior, and it reflects the desire to have one's choices rather than environmental rewards and pressures determine one's actions (Deci & Ryan, 1985a).

The fundamental concept of self-determination is *perceived locus of causality* (Heider, 1958). Perceived locus of causality (PLOC) refers to an individual's understanding of the cause of his or her motivated actions. PLOC exists on a continuum that ranges from internal to external. An internal PLOC is synonymous with self-determination whereas an external PLOC is synonymous with other-determination (or environment-determination, since external events such as rewards and deadlines can cause our behavior much as other people can). When individuals believe that personal interests, thoughts, and desires motivate their behavior, the PLOC is internal; when individuals believe that environmental incentives and pressures motivate their behavior, the PLOC is external.

Some theorists use the terms *origins* and *pawns* to communicate the distinction between a person whose behavior is free and self-determined and emanates from an internal PLOC versus a person whose behavior is forced and other-determined and emanates from an external PLOC (deCharms, 1976, 1984; Ryan & Grolnick, 1986). Because people have a need for self-determination, they strive to be the causal agents of their behavior, to be origins, to be the primary locus of causality for their behavior. Origins *origin*ate their own intentional behavior. The pawn metaphor refers to chess. You can think of the game that powerful other people play as they push their subordinates around like game pieces, or *like pawns*—employers ordering employees to do something, military sergeants commanding privates, teachers telling students what to do, and so on. In contrast to origins who are active and take personal responsibility for their goals and actions, pawns are relatively passive, reactive, and show little personal responsibility for their goals and courses of action (Ryan & Grolnick, 1986). When treated as a pawn, play becomes work, leisure becomes obligation, and the intrinsic motivational orientation becomes the extrinsic motivational orientation. Exercising, reading a book, or talking on the telephone out of personal choice have a phenomenological tone of play, leisure, and fun, whereas being told to exercise, read a book, or talk on the telephone because of a job requirement or a parental demand has a tone of work, obligation, and stress. In each case, the activity is the same—exercising, reading, talking—but the experience of an origin is characterized by self-determination and an intrinsic motivational orientation whereas the experience of a pawn is characterized by other-determination and an extrinsic motivational orientation.

Involving and Satisfying the Need for Self-Determination

Specific environmental elements and social contexts in general vary in how much versus how little they support a person's need for self-determination. Environmental elements include, for instance, rewards (Lepper, Greene, & Nisbett, 1973), prizes (Harackiewicz, 1979), money (Deci, 1971), deadlines or time limits (Amabile, DeJong, & Lepper, 1976), surveillance (Pittman et al., 1980), threats of punishment (Deci &

Cascio, 1972), external evaluations (Benware & Deci, 1984), limits or rules (Koestner et al., 1984), competition (Reeve & Deci, 1996), and opportunities for choice (Zuckerman et al., 1978). Social contexts include, for instance, households (Deci et al., 1993), classrooms (Deci, Schwartz, Scheinman, & Ryan, 1981), gymnasiums or fields (Gould, Hodge, Peterson, & Giannini, 1989), and work settings (Deci, Connell, & Ryan, 1989). These environmental elements and social contexts vary along a continuum of how controlling versus autonomy supportive they are. Controlling elements and contexts promote an external PLOC by pressuring a person to think, feel, or behave in a particular way. They do little to involve or satisfy the need for self-determination; rather, they frustrate self-determined strivings. Autonomy-supportive elements promote an internal PLOC by encouraging a person to initiate intentional behaviors and pursue personally valued goals. Autonomy-supportive elements and contexts optimally involve and satisfy the need for self-determination.

Autonomy-Supportive Environments

A synonym for self-determination is autonomy. So, an autonomy-supportive environment is one that involves, nurtures, and satisfies the need for self-determination.

Autonomy-supportive environments encourage people to make their own choices, set their own goals, choose their own ways of achieving personal goals, solve problems in their own way, and basically pursue their own agendas. Autonomy-supportive environments are *not* laissez-faire, hands-off, permissive social contexts. Rather, autonomy-supportive environments strongly attempt to identify and support the interests, needs, and strivings of others. Table 4.1 summarizes the four essential ingredients that work together to create an autonomy-supportive environment (adapted from Deci, Connell, & Ryan, 1989; Deci et al., 1994; Koestner et al., 1984).

AUTONOMY-SUPPORTIVE ENVIRONMENTS EMPHASIZE THE INDIVIDUAL'S POINT OF VIEW. At the heart of an autonomy-supportive environment is a striving of one person to understand, acknowledge, appreciate, and respond to another person's perspective or point of view. To do so, teachers, employers, coaches, therapists, parents, and others need to put the proverbial shoe on the other foot to best identify the interests, needs, preferences, beliefs, and feelings of their students, employees, athletes, clients, and children, respectively. One way an employer can begin to understand how employees' experience their jobs is to spend time doing that

TABLE 4–1

Four Elements of an Autonomy-Supportive Environment

Autonomy-Supportive Environments
1. Emphasize the individual's point of view.
2. Encourage choice and initiative.
3. Communicate rationale for social control—that is, for any behavioral rules, limits, or constraints placed on the individual's plans and behaviors.
4. Use a communication style rich in noncontrolling, positive feedback.

job, or at least carefully observe as others work. The employer-manager would soon understand what it feels like to answer the phone, listen to customer complaints, type memos, write reports, be frustrated by a lack of resources, participate in committee discussions, worry about child care, relate to difficult co-workers, and so on. After taking the role of the employee, the manager would then be better able to identify the needs and feelings of the employees. The employer could then make decisions that reflected not only the employer's perspective but also the employee's perspective. When employers identify workers' concerns in an emotionally meaningful way and when they foster a responsive working environment, they enable employees' work to take place in an air of trust, interest, and self-determined motivational strivings rather than in an air of suspicion, pressure, and conflict (Csikszentmihalyi & LeFevre, 1989; Deci, Connell, & Ryan, 1989).

AUTONOMY-SUPPORTIVE ENVIRONMENTS ENCOURAGE CHOICE AND INITIATIVE. As individuals identify the interests, needs, desires, and feelings of another, they are better positioned to create for that person meaningful opportunities for choice, initiative, and self-reliance (McCombs & Pope, 1994). In a work setting, greater opportunities for choice occur when employees are given a variety of projects to pursue, appropriate and flexible challenges, flexibility in their schedules, options of whom to work with, and options of which tasks to perform and in what order to do them. Greater opportunities for initiative revolve around employees making decisions, setting priorities, diagnosing problems, and implementing their own ways of solving problems and overcoming the obstacles that arise. Greater opportunities for self-reliance occur as employees receive more time for (directed) independent work and greater personal responsibility for their own performance, production, and outcomes. This provision for choice, initiative, and self-reliance applies equally well to employers as it does to teachers, coaches, therapists, parents, and others (e.g., Deci & Ryan, 1987).

AUTONOMY-SUPPORTIVE ENVIRONMENTS COMMUNICATE THE RATIONALE FOR RULES, LIMITS, OR CONSTRAINTS. Rules, limits, and constraints are a necessary and important part of the structure for any social context. The important point is not whether rules, constraints, and limits are necessary in the home, classroom, workplace, and gymnasium (because they are), but rather in how these elements of structure are used. There are two major ways of promoting internalization and self-regulation in others, one that relies on control and essentially bypasses people's need for self-determination and the other that relies on information and speaks directly to people's need for self-determination (Ryan, Connell, & Grolnick, 1992). When informational (as opposed to controlling), the person imposing the rules, limits, and constraints on another communicates the rationale for behavioral limits (e.g., "be on time," "don't smoke") by explaining the importance and necessity of the constraints and by clearly and unambiguously spelling out what the good reason behind the "no talking," "be on time," and "do not smoke in here" constraints are (Deci & Ryan, 1985a; Koestner et al., 1984). Explaining the good reasons for behavioral limits—

why they are important, why they are necessary—constitutes the essence of informational limit setting. The logic in communicating the information-rich rationale for social control is that the person being constrained or limited is more likely to internalize and voluntarily accept the structure's rules, constraints, and limits.

AUTONOMY-SUPPORTIVE ENVIRONMENTS USE A COMMUNICATION STYLE RICH IN NONCONTROLLING, POSITIVE FEEDBACK. At times, self-determining people perform poorly or behave inappropriately. Autonomy-supportive environments treat poor performance and behavioral problems as problems to be solved rather than as targets for criticism (Deci, Connell, & Ryan, 1989). A noncontrolling communication style begins with resisting coercive, pressuring language, such as saying that the other person should, must, ought to, or has to do such and such (e.g., "Johnny, you should try harder," "Johnny, you must finish the project before four o'clock"). Instead, a noncontrolling, autonomy-supportive communication style takes the other person's point of view and asks why the performance is poor or why the behavior is maladaptive. More often than not, the individual has some insight as to why performance is poor or behavior is maladaptive (e.g., insufficient resources, lack of training, the task seems pointless or irrelevant). A noncontrolling social context functions to provide the individual with the resources, training, and rationale as to why the task is important. When so supported or informed, individuals can then diagnose the cause of poor performance or misbehavior and then initiate their own solutions to the problems they face. A noncontrolling coach, for instance, would ask, "Johnny, I've noticed that your scoring average has declined lately; do you have any idea why this might be?" As to positive feedback, an autonomy-supportive communication style resists critically negative feedback (e.g., "Your workmanship is sloppy") and instead makes a special effort to identify points of improvement and progress (e.g., "I noticed real progress in the liveliness of your writing style"; "I've noticed that your running times improved steadily in January but not in February."). Noncontrolling communications invite poor performers to initiate their own solutions; positive feedback informs poor performers of points of progress and achievement.

AUTONOMY-SUPPORTIVE AND CONTROLLING ENVIRONMENTS IN MOMENT-TO-MOMENT INTERACTION. The four characteristics in Table 4.1 describe the general goals autonomy-supportive people embrace as they try to motivate others. In addition to these general goals, autonomy-supportive individuals exhibit characteristic moment-to-moment behaviors. Consider, for instance, the specific behaviors exhibited by autonomy-supportive tutors (as compared to controlling tutors) during a twenty-minute teaching-learning session (Deci et al., 1982). Using a two-group experimental design, the researchers told one group of tutors that their role was to help the learner learn. The researchers told the second group that it was their job and responsibility to make sure their learners performed up to high standards on a forthcoming test. The first group therefore tutored in a way that was supportive of the learner's autonomy; the second group tutored in a controlling way (as they pressured the learners toward particular outcomes). The researchers videotaped each tutoring session and then compared the teaching styles of autonomy-supportive teachers with that of their controlling counterparts. The controlling teachers talked more, were more critical, gave more praise, gave more directives and commands, invoked deadlines, and allowed their learner's less choice and autonomy. In contrast, the autonomy-supportive teachers gave learner's more choice, allowed them leeway to experiment, provided more time to work independently, came across as less demanding and controlling, promoted conceptual rather than factual understanding, and were rated as generally more likeable.

Positive Outcomes from Autonomy-Supportive Environments

Autonomy-supportive teachers, tutors, employers, coaches, therapists, and parents relate to students, tutees, workers, athletes, clients, and children in ways that are different from their controlling counterparts. These different styles are important because of their implications for people's self-determination and because autonomy-supportive social contexts, compared to controlling ones, produce a number of positive outcomes related to learning, development, emotionality, and performance (Deci & Ryan, 1987). People learning, working, and performing in autonomy-supportive, as opposed to controlling, environments show the following:

- Higher achievement
- Greater perceived competence
- Enhanced sense of self-worth and self-esteem
- Greater creativity
- Enhanced conceptual learning
- Preference for optimal challenge
- Positive emotional tone
- Trusting interpersonal relationships
- Maintenance of behavioral change

HIGHER ACHIEVEMENT AND GREATER PERCEIVED COMPETENCE. In school settings, students show higher academic achievement when teachers support their autonomous learning and behaving, and the positive effect of autonomy support holds true whether achievement is defined by standardized test scores (Boggiano et al., 1991; Deci, Schwartz, Scheinman, & Ryan 1981; Flink et al., 1992) or by classroom grades (deCharms, 1976). Autonomy support also increases students' perceived academic competence (Deci, Schwartz, Sheinman, & Ryan, 1981; Ryan & Grolnick, 1986). The logic of how self-determination bolsters perceived academic competence is that when teachers ask students to take personal responsibility for their own learning and for solving their own academic problems, students rely more and more on their own inner motivational resources and less and less on outer resources (such as the teacher, deadlines, or tests). Teacher support for students' self-reliance affirms and strengthens students' sense of competence (Deci, Nezlek, & Sheinman, 1981; Williams et al., 1994).

HIGHER SENSE OF SELF-WORTH AND SELF-ESTEEM. Self-worth is a particularly important developmental outcome because it serves as an index for a child's overall adjustment and well-being (Harter, 1982). The more self-determined children perceive themselves to be, the higher self-worth they report (Harter, 1981, 1982; Ryan & Grolnick, 1986). Further, in school, students of autonomy-supportive teachers report higher self-esteem than do students of controlling teachers (Deci, Schwartz, Sheinman & Ryan 1981). The link between self-determination and self-worth occurs because gains in self-worth occur as children (1) feel personally responsible for their own actions and accomplishments and (2) perceive that significant others support and respect their autonomous functioning.

ENHANCED CREATIVITY, CONCEPTUAL UNDERSTANDING, AND PREFERENCE FOR CHALLENGE. Being controlled by others diminishes creativity. Specifically, creativity decreases when people expect their work to be evaluated (Amabile, 1979), during surveillance by others (Amabile, 1983), when people are pressured (Koestner et al., 1984), when they try to impress others (Amabile, 1985), and when extrinsic rewards are at stake for expert performance (Amabile, Hennessey & Grossman, 1986). In contrast, creativity thrives when people are self-determining, that is, when they are motivated by the interest, enjoyment, satisfaction, and challenge of the work itself (Amabile & Hennessey, 1992). As to enhanced conceptual thinking, learners in autonomy-supportive environments, compared to learners in controlling ones, show greater flexibility in their way of thinking (McGraw & McCullers, 1979) and a more active mode of information processing (Grolnick & Ryan, 1987) and learn in a way that is conceptual rather than rote (Benware & Deci, 1984; Boggiano et al., 1994; Boggiano et al., 1993; Flink, Boggiano, & Barrett, 1990; Grolnick & Ryan, 1987). As to preference for challenge, when people are controlled by environmental pressures (i.e., grades, scholarships, pleasing others), they routinely prefer easy versions of a task (Harter, 1974, 1978b; Pittman, Emery, & Boggiano, 1982; Shapira, 1976). The rationale behind avoiding challenge is that by doing so a person is best positioned to gain the reward at stake (i.e., make an A, keep the scholarship, make one's parents proud). In contrast, self-determined individuals routinely choose the optimally challenging version of a task, because their reason to engage in the task in the first place is not for external gain but to strive for mastery, improvement, and the development of personal skills (Shapira, 1976) and because they derive maximum pleasure from mastery of optimal challenges (Harter, 1978b).

POSITIVE EMOTIONAL TONE AND INTERPERSONAL TRUST. When people find themselves in autonomy-supportive environments, their moment-to-moment emotional tone centers around the positive emotions of interest and enjoyment (Csikszentmihalyi, 1985; Csikszentmihalyi & Rathunde, 1993; Ryan & Connell, 1989), because opportunities to involve a psychological need (i.e., self-determination) generate interest whereas experiences of need satisfaction generate enjoyment (Reeve, 1993). In contrast, controlling environments engender a negative emotional tone because others force them to think or behave in a way with which they are not necessarily comfortable (Ryan, 1982; Ryan & Connell, 1989). Controlling environments generally lead people to feel more alienated, tense, pressured, anxious, distressed, and even angrier than they otherwise would (Patrick, Skinner, & Connell, 1993). As to trust, employees at a major corporation who had bosses interested in creating an autonomy-supportive working climate reported greater trust and more positive interpersonal relationships at work than did workers with controlling bosses and in less supportive working climates (Deci, Connell, & Ryan, 1989).

MAINTENANCE OF BEHAVIORAL CHANGE. The principle objective in a controlling environment is to pressure people to behave in a particular way. So, if there is virtue to controlling environments, it should show up in attempts to produce behavioral change in others. After all, environments such as the military and prison seem successful in pressuring people's behavior toward particular goals. Controlling social contexts can and often do promote behavioral change. When controlled by threats of punishment, reward programs, token economies, and other such salient controls and incentives, people change their behaviors such that they go to school more, lose weight, exercise more, and so on (Baldwin & Baldwin, 1986). But when these controls and reward programs are removed, people typically revert back to their former ways of behaving—absenteeism, weight gain, and lackadaisical lifestyles. That is, behavior change frequently persists only as long as the contingent controls and rewards persist. When behavior change is self-determined, however, it is significantly more likely to be maintained over time and more likely to be transferred to new situations, because the self-determined reasons for the behavior change continue in a way that external incentives and controls do not (Deci & Ryan, 1985a; Vallerand & Bissonnette, 1992; Williams et al., 1996).

COMPETENCE

We all want to be competent. We desire to interact effectively with our surroundings—in school, at work, in relationships, and during recreation and sports. We want to develop skills, and we want to expand our capacities. We feel an energy to improve ourselves beyond our current abilities. And mastery experiences provide us with some of our most positive and satisfying emotional experiences. In other words, we have a need for competence.

Competence is a psychological need that provides an inherent source of motivation to seek out and master optimal challenges. Defined formally, competence is the need to be effective in interactions with the environment and reflects the desire to exercise one's capacities and skills and, in doing so, seek out and master optimal challenges (Deci & Ryan, 1985a).

Competence as Effectance Motivation

Infants engage their environment with only the most basic of skills, such as sucking and grasping. Throughout early infancy, additional motor competencies emerge, including shaking, reaching, carrying, and tossing (Gibson, 1988). In late infancy, infants gain competencies related to language and to locomotion. By early childhood, children engage their environment with social skills and with abilities such as dressing, reading, and skipping rope. The same timely emergence of new skills continues throughout the school years and throughout adolescence and adulthood. To engage one's environment effectively, countless physical, social, and academic skills must emerge and undergo refinement. To be effective, skills must emerge and be exercised, stretched, improved, and refined. It is the need for competence that motivates people's desire and voluntary willingness to seek out situations that allow them the opportunity to exercise, stretch, improve, and refine personal skills and capacities.

When people exercise their skills, they affect the environment. A responsive environment communicates the extent to which personal skills can or cannot alter the environment in a desired way. For example, exercising computer skills can produce an impressive document or a lot of beeps and error messages. An entertainer can tell a joke and hear the audience's laughter or cold silence. A gardener can plant and care for flowers and later see them either grow or die. A pet owner can instruct a dog to sit and watch as the dog either complies or stares off into space. The perception that a person can manipulate and affect the environment in ways that are consistent with personal intentions is the insight that cultivates a sense of competence.

Over time and across innumerable skill areas, an accumulated history of competent experiences builds in individuals a personal belief that, yes, they possess the skills and competencies necessary to interact successfully (i.e., competently) with their environment. This accumulated sense of whether they can (or cannot) interact effectively in the world constitutes *effectance motivation* (Harter, 1978a; White, 1959). The greater one's effectance motivation, the greater one's desire to seek out and approach situations that challenge existing skills. Figure 4.1 illustrates White's (1959) classic description of how effectance motivation energizes and directs (intrinsically motivated) behavior. Effectance motivation creates the desire to exercise skills and capacities in the first place. When skills are used, the ensuing behaviors

FIGURE 4–1
Model of Effectance Motivation

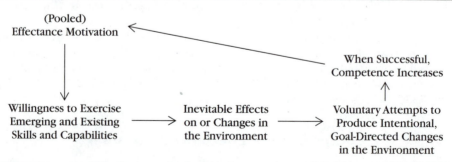

SOURCE: Reeve, J. (1996). *Motivating others: Nurturing inner motivational resources.* Copyright © 1996 by Allyn and Bacon. Reprinted by permission.

produce changes in the environment, some of which are intentional and strategic and others of which are incidental and superfluous. Cooking a meal, for instance, produces food and feedback about personal culinary skills, but cooking also incidentally and accidentally raises the temperature in the room and invites people in other rooms to wander toward the kitchen. As people act on their environment, they learn the extent to which their skills influence their environment. Knowing whether and how their actions influence their environment, people then attempt to effect purposive, intentional, goal-directed adjustments in their surroundings. Some of these intended adjustments are successful, and when skills successfully effect intentional change ("I meant to do that!"), the need for competence is satisfied and effectance motivation increases. Each experience in the self-perception of competence increases the individual's pooled reservoir of effectance motivation. Finally, the greater one's pooled effectance motivation, the greater is one's desire to seek out and master optimal challenges.

Competence as a Need

A portrayal of competence as a psychological need extends the concept of competence beyond that of a history and a perception of successful environmental interactions. The *need* for competence implies that people intentionally and voluntarily strive to master their environments and to control the outcomes that happen to them. The need for competence motivates people to pay attention to and learn about the contingencies that exist between their behavior and the environment's reactions and outcomes. The need for competence also motivates people to develop their interests in life domains in which their skills are immature and poorly developed. Even in the face of a critical or rejecting environment (because one's skills are ineffective), the need for competence promotes strivings for mastery. Competence as a need adds the proactive face of challenge seeking to the mostly reactive nature of effectance motivation, as depicted in Figure 4.1.

Involving the Need for Competence: Optimal Challenge

The principal environmental condition that involves the need for competence is optimal challenge. The principal environmental condition that satisfies the need for competence is competence-affirming (i.e., positive) feedback.

OPTIMAL CHALLENGE AND FLOW. To determine the conditions that help produce a feeling of fun and enjoyment, Csikszentmihalyi (1975, 1982, 1990) interviewed and studied hundreds of people he presumed knew what it felt like to have fun: rock climbers, surgeons, dancers, chess champions, basketball players, and others. Later, he studied more representative samples, including working professionals, high school students, assembly line workers, groups of the elderly, and people sitting at home watching television. Irrespective of which sample he studied, Csikszentmihalyi found the essence of the enjoyment experience could be traced to *flow*.

Flow is a state of concentration that involves a holistic absorption in an activity. In flow, action is effortless, and the performer focuses attention narrowly on the task at hand, which provides an optimal challenge to his or her current skills and abilities. Flow is such a pleasurable experience that the person often repeats the activity with the hope of experiencing flow again (Csikszentmihalyi & Nakamura, 1989). Maximal enjoyment with holistic involvement (or flow) arises when the person perceives that the challenges offered by the task equal, or match, his or her task-related skills and competencies. That is, optimal challenge to the performer's current level of ability causes flow.

Figure 4.2 illustrates the relationship between task challenge and personal skill by showing the emotional consequences that arise from the different pairings of challenge and skill. When challenge outweighs skill (skill is low, challenge is high), performers worry about having the demands of the task overwhelm their skills. Being overchallenged threatens competence, and that threat manifests itself emotionally as worry (if moderately overchallenged) or anxiety (if extremely overchallenged). When challenge matches skill (challenge and skill are both average or high), concentration,

FIGURE 4–2
Model of Intrinsic Motivation and Flow

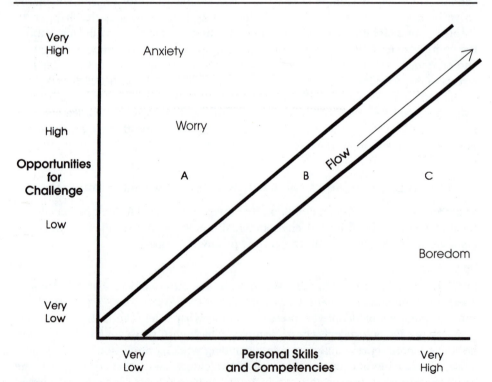

SOURCE: Adapted from Csikszentmihalyi, M. (1975). *Beyond bordom and anxiety: The experience of flow in work and play.* San Francisco: Jossey-Bass.

involvement, and enjoyment rise. When challenge and skill are perfectly matched, concentration, involvement, and enjoyment rise to their maximums to collectively produce the psychological experience of flow. When skill outweighs challenge (skill is high, challenge is low), task engagement is characterized by reduced concentration, minimal task involvement, and an emotional state of boredom. Worry, anxiety, and boredom are all antithetical to flow.

Being overchallenged or overskilled produces emotional problems and suboptimal experience, but the worst profile of experience actually emanates from the pairing of low challenge and low skill (the lower left-hand corner of Fig. 4.2). With both challenge and skill at low levels, literally all measures of emotion, motivation, and cognition are at their lowest levels—the person does not care about the task (Csikszentmihalyi, Rathunde, & Whalen, 1993). Flow is therefore a bit more complicated that just the balance of challenge and skill, because balancing low skill and low challenge produces only apathy. A more accurate description of how challenge relates to skill is that flow emerges only in those situations in which both challenge and skill are average or better (Csikszentmihalyi & Csikszentmihalyi, 1988). With this qualification in mind, another way to look at Figure 4.2 is to divide it into four quadrants in which the upper-left quarter represents conditions for worry and anxiety, the lower-left quarter represents conditions for apathy, the lower-right quarter represents conditions for boredom, and the upper-right quarter represents conditions for flow.

Figure 4.2 also graphs the hypothetical case of three individuals, A, B, and C, as each performs a task that offers moderate opportunity for challenge. A, B, and C differ only in level of personal skill each brings to the task. A will worry, because his skills cannot match the tasks' demands and challenges; B will experience flow, because his skills nicely match with the task's demands and challenges; and C will be bored, because his skills exceed the task's demands and challenges. To alleviate his worry, A has two options: decrease task difficulty or increase personal skill. To alleviate his boredom, C has two options: increase task difficulty or decrease personal skill (through self-handicapping). To alter challenge, A and C can manipulate task difficulty by solving easier or harder math problems, choosing an easier or harder jigsaw puzzle, or selecting a more or less proficient partner in an athletic contest. A and C might also change the rules of the task, such as solving the jigsaw puzzle with help or within a time limit or allowing the baseball hitter additional or fewer strikes. As to manipulating skills, A and C can practice to increase skills or impose handicaps on skills, such as running a race with ankle weights or doing what my right-handed brother did when we played tennis together in our youth—play left-handed.

For a concrete example, consider three friends on a snow-skiing outing. Ski slopes offer different difficulty levels such that some slopes are relatively flat (beginner slopes), some are fairly steep (intermediate slopes), and others are downright death-defying (advanced slopes). If the skiers have different levels of skiing skill, Figure 4.2 predicts the emotional experience will vary for each skier on each slope. The novice skier will experience most enjoyment on the beginner slopes, but worry on the intermediate and feel anxiety on the advanced slopes. The average skier will experience flow on the intermediate slopes, but boredom on the beginner slopes and worry on the advanced slopes. The professional will experience flow on the advanced slopes, but intense boredom on the beginner slopes and moderate boredom on the intermediate slopes. Each skier, however, can experience flow on each slope by intentionally adjusting level of personal skill or level of slope difficulty. For example, a skier might increase and decrease personal skill through practice and handicapping; the skier might increase and decrease slope difficulty through confronting moguls or by going very slow. The fact that people can adjust both level of skill and level of task difficulty means that people can set up the conditions for optimal challenge.

The most important practical implication of flow theory is this: Given optimal challenge—the appropriate balance of skill and challenge—*any* activity can be enjoyed. Doing electrical work, writing papers, debating contemporary issues, sewing, analyzing a play, mowing the lawn, and other such activities do not necessarily make the top of anyone's list of must-do Saturday afternoon joys, but the balance of high skill with high challenge adds the spice of flow—concentration, absorption, enjoyment, and optimal experience. Consistent with the idea that optimal challenge gives rise to flow, Csikszentmihalyi found in a pair of studies that students enjoyed doing homework and working on part-time jobs more than they enjoyed viewing (challengeless) television programs (Csikszentmihalyi, Rathunde, & Whalen 1993) and people actually experience flow most often in work, rather than in leisure, settings (Csikszentmihalyi, 1982).

Under some conditions, people enjoy being overchallenged (Stein et al., 1995). With very high challenge, people sometimes see in a task a potential for gain, growth, and personal improvement. The perception of improvement and progress can be enjoyable, at least until the hope for gain gives way to the reality of being overwhelmed. Under other conditions, people enjoy very low levels of challenge (Stein et al., 1995). Generally speaking, people enjoy feedback that confirms that they have a skill level that is above and beyond the challenge of the task. Easy success can generate some level of enjoyment, especially in the early stages of task engagement when even the skilled performer harbors a bit of doubt as to how today's task performance will go. The quality of enjoyment that easy success breeds, however, is defensive and relief based. It is success in the context of optimal challenge that generates sincere, need-satisfying enjoyment.

THE INTERDEPENDENCY BETWEEN CHALLENGE AND FEEDBACK. Each of us is challenged every day. In school, teachers put examinations in front of us. At work, projects and assignments test our writing, creativity, and teamwork skills. On the drive home, the interstate challenges our driving skills. If the car breaks down, our automotive repair skills are put to the test. In the gym, an opponent challenges our athletic skills during a contest. These situations, like those Csikszentmihalyi used to test flow theory, set the stage for challenge but they do not create the psychological experience of being challenged until one additional ingredient is tossed into the equation—performance feedback. Having a test, project, or contest in front of us invites challenge, but we do not experience challenge per se until we begin to perform the task. As we engage in the task, we receive performance feedback information and it is at that point—during feedback in the context of being tested—that people report the psychological experience of being challenged (Reeve & Deci, 1996).

ERROR TOLERANCE, FAILURE TOLERANCE, AND RISK TAKING. The problem with optimal challenge, motivationally speaking, is that when faced with moderately difficult tasks, performers are as likely to experience failure and frustration as they are success and enjoyment. Thus, the dread of failure can diminish the need-involving qualities of optimal challenge. In fact, the dread of failure, if intense, can motivate avoidance behaviors so that people go out of their way to escape challenging tasks that would otherwise be potentially need involving. Before people will engage freely in and persevere at optimally challenging tasks, the social context must tolerate (and even value) failure and error making (i.e., adopt a performance climate rich in failure tolerance or error tolerance; Clifford, 1988, 1990). Optimal challenge implies that considerable error making is essential to optimize motivation (Clifford, 1990). Error tolerance, failure tolerance, and risk taking rest on the belief that we learn more from failure than we do from success, which suggests the constructive aspects of failure—identifying its causes, changing strategy, seeking advice and instruction, and so on—and provides an emotional green light to seek out and attempt to master optimal (rather than easy) challenges (Clifford, 1984, 1990).

Satisfying the Competence Need: Positive Feedback

Whether individuals perceive their performance to be competent or incompetent is often ambiguous. To make such an evaluation, a performer needs feedback. Feedback comes from one (or more) of the following three sources: the task itself, comparisons of current performance with past performances, and the evaluations of others (Boggiano & Ruble, 1979; Dollinger & Thelen, 1978; Grolnick, Frodi, & Bridges, 1984; Koestner, Zuckerman, & Koestner, 1987; Schunk & Hanson, 1989).

In some tasks, competence feedback is inherent in the performance of the task itself, as in successfully logging onto the computer (or not) or repairing a machine (or not). In most tasks, however, performance evaluation is more ambiguous than a right-versus-wrong performance outcome (for example, consider competence evaluations of social skills or artistic talents). In performances such as these, our own past performances and the evaluations of other people (rather than the task itself) supply the information necessary to make an inference of competence versus incompetence. As for our own past performances, the perception of progress is an important signal of competence (Schunk & Hanson, 1989) that gratifies the competence need. As for the evaluation of other people, positive feedback bolsters competence whereas negative feedback deflates it (Anderson, Manoogian, & Reznick, 1976; Blank, Reis, & Jackson, 1984; Deci, 1971; Dollinger & Thelen, 1978; Vallerand & Reid, 1984). To convey a message of competence in one experiment, some researchers gave participants bogus feedback such as, "You did better than the average student on these puzzles" (Harackiewicz, 1979, p. 1357). In another study, participants performed an unfamiliar task as experimenters offered repeated positive performance feedback ("It looks like you have a natural ability . . . and it shows in your performance") or negative performance feedback ("This is an easy task but your improvement is quite slow"). Such verbal praise increased perceived competence whereas verbal criticism decreased it (Vallerand & Reid, 1984). In summary, informative performance feedback in its various forms—task generated, self generated, and other generated—supplies the information necessary for individuals to formulate a cognitive evaluation of their perceived level of competence, and when that feedback signals high competence, activity participation provides an arena for competence-need satisfaction.

THE PLEASURE OF OPTIMAL CHALLENGE IN THE CONTEXT OF POSITIVE FEEDBACK. To confirm that people do indeed derive maximum pleasure from optimal challenge, Harter (1974, 1978b) gave school-aged children anagrams of different difficulty levels and monitored each student's expressed pleasure (through smiling) upon solving each anagram. (An anagram is a word or phrase such as *table*, with its letters rearranged to form another word or phrase, as in *bleat*. In general, anagram-solving success produced greater smiling and higher enjoyment ratings than did anagram-solving failure (Harter, 1974), suggesting than mastery gratifies the competence need. In addition, some anagrams were very easy (3 letters), some were easy (4 letters), others were moderately difficult (5 letters), and still others were very hard (6 letters). As the anagrams increased in difficulty, it took students longer and longer to solve them, as expected, but the critical measure in the study was expressed pleasure (through smiling) as a function of how difficult the solved anagram was (Harter, 1978b). A curvilinear inverted U pattern emerged in which smiling was least following success on the very easy problems, moderate following success on the easy and very hard problems, and greatest following success on the moderately difficult problems. The central point is that children experience the greatest pleasure following success in the context of moderate challenge. After solving the easy, moderate, and difficult anagrams, the children concluded, "The 5s were just right. They were a challenge, but not too much challenge." and "I liked the hard ones because they gave you a sense of satisfaction, but the really hard ones were just too frustrating." (Harter, 1978b, p. 796).

RELATEDNESS

We all need to belong. We desire frequent social interaction. As we interact with others, we want to form and maintain warm, close, affectionate ways of relating. We want those interactions to become relationships and perhaps become attachments as well, both with individuals and with groups or organizations. We like it when others are responsive to our needs and when they really hear what we are saying, and we feel alone and alienated when others ignore us. We like it most when our relationships are reciprocal, such that we not only want to form social bonds with others, we also want others to include us in their attachments, relationships, and groups. In other words, we have a need for relatedness.

Relatedness is the need to establish close emotional bonds and attachments with other people, and it reflects the desire to be emotionally connected to and interpersonally involved with significant others in warm relationships (Baumeister & Leary, 1995; Fromm, 1956; Guisinger & Blatt, 1994; Ryan, 1991; Ryan & Powelson, 1991; Sullivan, 1953). Because each of us has an organismic psychological need for relatedness, social bonds form easily (Baumeister & Leary, 1995). Given an opportunity to engage others in face-to-face interaction, people go out of their way to create relationships (Brewer, 1979). The emergence of friendships and alliances seems to require little more than proximity and spending time together (Wilder & Thompson, 1980). The more people interact and the more people spend time together, the more likely they are to form friendships, and once social bonds are formed, people are generally reluctant to break them. When we move, when we graduate from school, and when others take their leave of us, we resist the breakup of the relationship. We promise to write or telephone, we cry, we exchange addresses and phone numbers, we plan an occasion to get together in the future, and so on.

Involving the Need for Relatedness: Interaction with Others

People seek emotionally positive interactions and interaction partners, and they want these interactions to occur within a context of a stable, long-term relationship rich in warmth, care, and mutual concern. Interaction with others is the primary condition that involves the relatedness need, at least to the extent that those interactions take place in an environment of warmth, care, and mutual concern. In addition, starting new relationships especially involves the need for relatedness. Consider, for instance, the relatedness-involving potential of the following events, each of which promises an entry into new social relationships—first dates, falling in love, childbirth, fraternity or sorority pledging, and starting anew as in school or employment.

Satisfying the Need for Relatedness: Perception of a Social Bond

Although frequent interaction involves the relatedness need, relatedness-need satisfaction requires that the person perceives a social bond between self and another person or between self and a group of persons. To be satisfying, that social bond needs to be characterized by the perceptions that the other person (1) cares about the self's welfare and (2) likes the self (e.g., Baumeister & Leary, 1995).

Relationships that do not involve care and liking do not satisfy the need for relatedness. Researchers, for instance, routinely find that people who are lonely do not lack frequent social contact; rather, they lack close, intimate relationships (Wheeler, Reis, & Nezlek, 1983). Similarly, marriages, which are clearly close relationships, are not always emotionally satisfying. Some marriages are full of conflict, stress, criticism, and basically making the other person's life more difficult that it otherwise would be. Supportive marriages, those rich in mutual care and liking, are the emotionally satisfying relationships that lead people to feel happy (Coyne &

DeLongis, 1986). Further, youths' relationships with their parents follows the same pattern, such that to keep youths' depression at bay, parent-youth relationships not only need to exist but they also need to be supportive and nonproblematic (Carnelley, Pietromonaco, & Jaffe, 1994). So, whereas quantity of relationships sufficiently involves the relatedness need, quality in those relationships is necessary to satisfy it.

COMMUNAL VERSUS EXCHANGE RELATIONSHIPS. We all involve ourselves in many different relationships. Some of these relationships are more need satisfying than are others. The distinction between communal and exchange relationships captures the essence of relationships that do (communal) and do not (exchange) satisfy the relatedness need (Mills & Clark, 1982). Exchange relationships are those between acquaintances or between people who do business together. Communal relationships are those between persons who care about the welfare of the other, as exemplified by friendships, family, and romantic relationships. What distinguishes exchange from communal relationships are the implicit rules that guide the giving and receiving of benefits, such as money, help, and emotional support (Clark, Mills, & Powell, 1986). Exchange partners give benefits with the expectation of receiving comparable benefits in the near future. In exchange relationships, no obligation exists between interactants to be concerned with the other person's needs or welfare. Communal partners give benefits in response to the other person's needs or simply to please the other. In communal relationships, an obligation exists to care for the needs of the other and to support his or her welfare. Only communal relationships effectively satisfy the relatedness need. Exchange relationships satisfy many (quasi-) needs such as those for money or status, but the satisfaction of relatedness requires the perception of a social bond that is emotionally meaningful.

In communal relationships, people monitor and keep track of the other's needs, regardless of any forthcoming opportunities for reciprocity or material gain (Clark, 1984; Clark & Mills, 1979; Clark, Mills, & Powell, 1986; Clark et al., 1987). For instance, people involved in communal (as compared to exchange) relationships frequently check up on the needs of the other (Clark, Mills, & Powell, 1986), resist keeping track (or score) of individual inputs into their joint projects (Clark, 1984), provide help when the other feels distressed (Clark et al., 1987), and experience the receipt of tangible economic gifts as *detrimental* to how friendly, relaxed, fun, spontaneous, and smooth forthcoming interactions are (Clark & Mills, 1979). On this latter point, consider the emotional discomfort you would feel after providing a ride home to a close (communal) friend and, upon arrival, were handed ten dollars in payment of the favor (following Mills & Clark, 1982).

All of us do not make the distinction between exchange and communal relationships, and among those of us who do we do not make the distinction in the same way (Clark & Mills, 1979). Some people restrict their communal relationships to only a few confidants, whereas others extend their communal relationships into a wide network. Some people treat all their relationships in terms of exchange, even their family and romantic relationships. For this reason, people vary in the extent to which interacting with others is sufficient to involve and satisfy their organismic need for relatedness with others. Still, participation in communal relationships characterized by reciprocal care and mutual concern provides the social context that best satisfies the relatedness need.

Role of Relatedness in Internalization of Cultural Norms

Internalization refers to the process through which an individual transforms a formerly externally prescribed regulation or value into an internal one (Ryan, Rigby, & King, 1993). As a process, internalization reflects the individual's tendency to voluntarily adopt and integrate into the self the values and regulations of other people. It is an active, volitional process in which the person strives to acquire self-determined (i.e., chosen) values and regulatory styles and to move away from heteronomy and toward autonomy.

Relatedness to others provides the social context that supports internalization (Goodenow, 1993; Ryan & Powelson, 1991). When a person feels emotionally connected to and interpersonally involved with another, relatedness is high and internalization occurs willingly. When a person feels emotionally distant from and interpersonally neglected by another, relatedness is low and internalization does not occur willingly. Relatedness, however, does not make internalization an automatic process. For internalization to occur, the individual must also see the value, meaning, and utility in other people's prescriptions (do X, believe Y) and proscriptions (do not do X, do not believe Y). So, relatedness is a necessary (but not sufficient) condition for cultural transmission to occur. Internalization flourishes in relationships that provide a rich supply of both relatedness and information-laden rationale to make sense of the prescriptions and proscriptions.

EMOTION AND ORGANISMIC PSYCHOLOGICAL NEEDS

Interest and enjoyment are the primary emotional markers of organismic psychological needs. That is, when events allow the person to involve psychological needs, interest occurs; when events allow the person to satisfy psychological needs, enjoyment occurs. For illustration, Table 4.2 summarizes some prototypical events that reliably involve the three organismic psychological needs of self-determination, competence, and relatedness as well as some prototypical events that reliably satisfy these three needs. When involved in activities that offer opportunities for choice and initiative, optimal challenge, and frequent social interaction, the person typically experiences interest. When involved in activities that offer opportunities for autonomy-support, positive feedback, and communal relationships marked by care, liking, and mutuality, the person typically experiences enjoyment.

Interest is an emotion that flows from the relationship a person has with a particular activity. Both the person and the activity bring their unique characteristics into this relationship. The person, for instance, brings characteristics such as skills and psychological needs, while the activity offers unique opportunities, challenges,

TABLE 4–2

Factors That Involve and Satisfy Organismic Psychological Needs

ORGANISMIC PSYCHOLOGICAL NEED	INVOLVEMENT FACTORS	SATISFACTION FACTORS
Self-Determination	Choice, initiative	Autonomy-supportive environments
Competence	Optimal challenge	Positive feedback
Relatedness	Frequent social interaction	Communal relationships

and demands. Interest occurs whenever the needs and skills of the person fit or match the opportunities, challenges, and demands of a particular activity (Danner & Lonky, 1981; Deci, 1992b; Gibson, 1988). The tasks that people find most interesting are those that involve their needs, challenge the skills they possess (and care about), and demand they exercise and develop the capacities that are important to them. So, a person might find singing interesting because, for that person, singing involves the need for competence, challenges important skills, and develops valued musical talents. Another person might care little for singing, but might find partying on the weekend to be interesting because, for that person, partying provides an opportunity to involve their need for relatedness, to experience developmentally appropriate challenges, and to develop the social skills they care about most.

Enjoyment follows from need satisfaction rather than need involvement. Autonomy-supportive environments gratify the need for self-determination; positive performance feedback gratifies the need for competence; and communal relationships gratify the need for relatedness. Consider one in-depth study of the enjoyment experienced by elite figure skaters (Scanlon, Stein, & Ravizza, 1989). The researchers interviewed 26 national championship figure skaters (males and females) by asking each to think "back over the various aspects of your skating experience. . . . From the time you were a novice until your retirement, what do you remember being the major causes or sources of your enjoyment of that experience?" (Scanlan et al., 1989, p. 67). Figure 4.3 organizes the skaters' verbatim transcripts into emergent themes. The quotations are arranged from specific quotes (e.g., "Being close") to higher-order themes (e.g., "friendship opportunities through skating) and finally into four superordinate categories of enjoyment—social and life opportunities, perceived competence, social recognition of competence, act of skating, and special cases (the fifth category was not related to enjoyment). Although this analysis pertains to only one particular activity, it nonetheless succeeds in linking organismic psychological need satisfaction with enjoyment. For instance, friendships and relationships satisfy relatedness, mastery and achievements satisfy competence, and self-expression and creativity opportunities satisfy self-determination.

Whereas need involvement and need satisfaction produce positive emotions, need deprivation and frustration produce negative emotions. When people are told what to do and when they find themselves in controlling environments, the lack of

FIGURE 4–3
Classification of Sources of Enjoyment for Figure Skaters

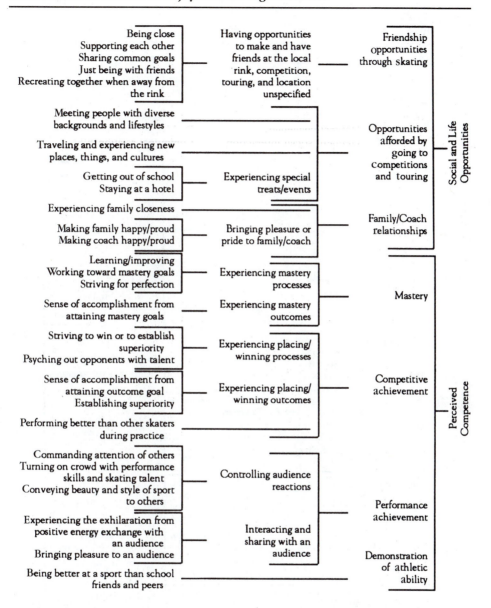

Note: The complete inductive content analysis showing all the emergent themes beyond the quote level. Examining the themes from the left to right depicts the inductive building process. Starting with the theme level on the far left, each successive theme level to the right represents a higher order theme comprising the themes on its left. Brackets indicate themes clustering together. Long lines represent themes that were carried directly into a higher inductive level. Please note that special cases is the only theme that is not a source of enjoyment. It is an organizational category to order two clustered themes.

SOURCE: Scanlan, T.K., Stein, G.L. & Ravizza, K. (1989). An in-depth study of former elite figure skaters: II. Sources of enjoyment. *Journal of Sport and Exercise Psychology, 11*, 65-83.

**FIGURE 4–3
(CONTINUED)**

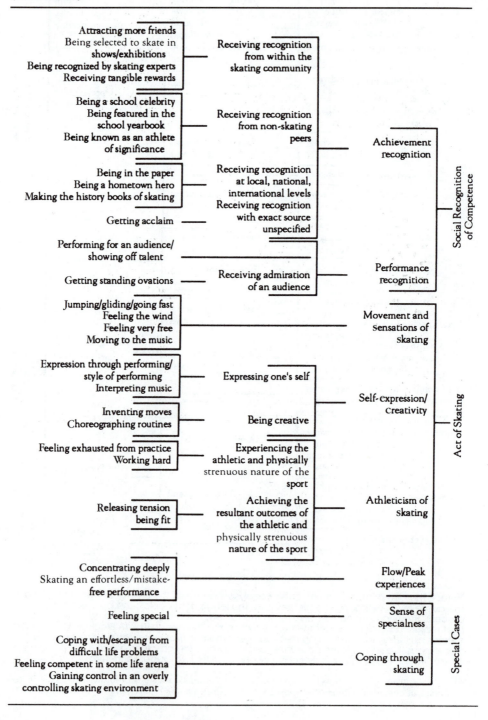

self-determination is generally associated with emotions like tension, pressure, and anger (Patrick, Skinner, & Connell, 1993; Ryan, 1982). When people are underchallenged, the inability of the task to involve their need for competence leads to boredom and apathy; when people are overchallenged, the task's tendency to overwhelm their sense of competence leads to worry, stress, and anxiety (Csikszentmihalyi, 1990). The absence of intimate social bonds to involve and satisfy the need for relatedness is associated with a host of negative emotions, including sadness, depression, jealousy, and loneliness (Baumeister & Leary, 1995; Williams & Solano, 1983).

SUMMARY

Two assumptions define an organismic approach to motivation: (1) Human beings are inherently active, and (2) differentiation and integration guide the development of internal structures such as the self. The organismic psychological needs provide the innate source of energy, referred to as intrinsic motivation, that allows human beings to be inherently active. These needs create the desire to seek out and interact with the environment. Differentiation involves elaboration and increased complexity, and it occurs as psychological needs motivate exploratory and mastery behaviors that allow people to expand their capacities and develop their interests. Integration involves synthesis that refines the individual's emerging complexity into an organized coherence. The picture that emerges from an organismic approach to motivation is that human beings possess a natural motivation to learn, grow, and develop in a way that is healthy and mature.

The self-determination need is the need to experience choice in the initiation and regulation of one's behavior, and it reflects the desire to have personal choices rather than environmental incentives or pressures determine one's actions. When self-determined, behavior feels free, emanates from an internal perceived locus of causality, and carries with it a phenomenological tone of play, leisure, and positive emotion. The more autonomy-supportive the environment is, the more likely the person's behavior will be self-determined. Autonomy-supportive environments emphasize the individual's point of view, encourage choice and self-initiative, communicate the rationale for any behavioral controls, and rely on a communication style that is rich in noncontrolling, positive feedback. People whose behavior is self-determined, as opposed to controlled, gain in perceived competence, sense of self-worth, and self-esteem; solve problems in ways that are flexible, conceptual, and creative; prefer optimal challenges over easy successes; and experience task-related emotions such as interest and enjoyment rather than tension and pressure. Such a self-determined way of thinking and feeling, in turn, produces behavioral gains in achievement, productivity, and self-regulated behavioral change.

The competence need is the need to be effective in interactions with the environment, it reflects the desire to exercise one's capacities and skills and, in doing so, seek out and master optimal challenges. Competence is basic to the understanding of human motivation because human beings possess a natural, intrinsic motivation to engage in environmental challenges. In the absence of a need for competence, one wonders why a child would practice her skateboard techniques, why a student would try to master a musical instrument, or an author would subject a manuscript to yet another revision. Of course, children, students, and authors often have strong extrinsic incentives to perform these tasks, and we will address such incentives in the next chapter. But, in the absence of strong extrinsic controls, competence supplies a reinforcement system to produce voluntary, active, and continuous refinement of personal skills and capacities (Harter, 1978a). When people exercise their skills, they seek out arenas of optimal challenge and they pay careful attention to the effects they produce on their environment so as to interpret its feedback as competence affirming or not. Hence, the motivational dynamics that organize the competence reinforcement system are challenge, feedback, and enjoyment. Optimal challenge is the principal environmental event that arouses, or involves, the competence need. Performance feedback supplies the objective information the performer uses to make a cognitive evaluation that the performance was competent and effective (versus incompetent and ineffective). Enjoyment serves as the emotional marker to signal that competence need satisfaction occurred.

The relatedness need is the need to establish close emotional bonds and attachments with other people, and it reflects the desire to be emotionally connected to and interpersonally involved with others in warm, caring relationships. Mere interaction with others is a sufficient condition to involve the need for relatedness. Relatedness need involvement brings with it emotional interest and an interpersonal desire to develop stable, caring, long-term relationships. To satisfy the relatedness need, however, requires that the emerging social bonds confirm that the other person (or persons) likes us and cares about our welfare. Communal relationships provide the social context that allows both the involvement and satisfaction of the relatedness need. Relationships that are not embedded within a context of liking and mutual care (i.e., exchange relationships) frustrate the relatedness need and leave us feeling distressed, sad, lonely, depressed, or jealous. When successfully achieved, relatedness to others provides the social context that supports internalization, which is the process through which one person takes in and accepts as their own a belief, value, or way of behaving of another person. When a person feels emotionally connected to and interpersonally involved with another, relatedness is high and internalization occurs willingly.

RECOMMENDED READINGS

Baumeister, R. F., & Leary, M. R. (1995). The need to belong: Desire for interpersonal attachments as a fundamental human motivation. *Psychological Bulletin, 117*, 497–529.

Clark, M., Mills, J., & Powell, M. C. (1986). Keeping track of needs in communal and exchange relationships. *Journal of Personality and Social Psychology, 51*, 333–338.

Csikszentmihalyi, M. (1982). Toward a psychology of optimal experience. *Review of Personality and Social Psychology, 3*, 13–36.

Deci, E. L., & Ryan, R. M. (1987). The support of autonomy and the control of behavior. *Journal of Personality and Social Psychology, 53*, 1024–1037.

Harter, S. (1978a). Effectance motivation reconsidered: Toward a developmental model. *Human Development, 21*, 34-64.

Harter, S. (1978b). Pleasure derived from challenge and the effects of receiving grades on children's difficulty level choices. *Child Development, 49*, 788-799.

Ryan, R. M., & Grolnick, W. S. (1986). Origins and pawns in the classroom: Self-report and projective assessments of individual differences in children's perceptions. *Journal of Personality and Social Psychology, 50*, 550-558.

Ryan, R. M., & Powelson, C. L. (1991). Autonomy and relatedness as fundamental to motivation and education. *Journal of Experimental Education, 60*, 49-66.

Shapira, Z. (1976). Expectancy determinants of intrinsically motivated behavior. *Journal of Personality and Social Psychology, 34*, 1235-1244.

Vallerand, R. J., & Reid, G. (1984). On the causal effects of perceived competence on intrinsic motivation: A test of cognitive evaluation theory. *Journal of Sport Psychology, 6*, 94-102.

Chapter 5

EXTERNAL EVENTS: EXTRINSIC AND INTRINSIC MOTIVATIONS

Each year more than a half-million Americans suffer injuries from automobile accidents, many of which are fatal. Riders can drastically reduce their probability of serious injury by wearing a seat belt. Despite convincing data that seat belts save lives and despite our society's consensus that wearing seat belts is a desirable behavior, all too many of us drive without buckling up. To reverse seat belt apathy, the government first tried national advertising campaigns to encourage riders to buckle up. Regrettably, such educational campaigns failed miserably. One study, for instance, reported that a nationwide multimedia advertising campaign increased seat belt usage by 0.1% of drivers (Robertson et al., 1974). Rather than relying on advertising campaigns, promoters have turned to a different means of seat belt persuasion—the offering of attractive extrinsic incentives to riders who buckle up (Elman & Killebrew, 1978; Geller, Casali, & Johnson, 1980; Rudd & Geller, 1985).

The logic behind incentive-based programs is that if people cannot find within themselves the motivation to buckle up, perhaps the offer of an attractive incentive to do so will give them reason enough. Consider the seat belt sweepstakes program tested at a Virginia university (Rudd & Geller, 1985). To conduct the sweepstakes, researchers placed posters like the one in Figure 5.1 on bulletin boards in campus classrooms and lecture halls. Campus radio also announced the seat belt sweepstakes. In the conduct of the sweepstakes, campus police recorded all license plate numbers of drivers seen wearing a shoulder seat belt. Those license plate numbers went into a raffle of weekly prizes, which ranged in value from $20 to $450. To be eligible to win the prizes, drivers therefore had to wear their seat belts. During the three weeks of the sweepstakes, campus seat belt usage doubled.

The offering of attractive incentives for compliant behavior represents only one strategy of extrinsic motivation. A second strategy is the use of an aversive incentive. Just as people will perform a behavior to attain attractive rewards, people will also perform a behavior to avoid or escape from an unattractive punishment. In regard to seat belt usage, the aversive stimulus is typically a harsh-sounding buzzer, bright panel lights, or an ignition interlock system (Geller, Casali, & Johnson, 1980). Almost all automobiles now offer one of these aversive stimuli, which continue until the driver fastens the seat belt. Buckling the seat belt prevents the aversive noise or light; failure to buckle the seat belt results in the persistence of the aversive stimulus. Thus, people buckle up not in the name of saving their lives, but to prevent or to escape from an obnoxious light or noise. Field studies show that drivers will indeed wear seatbelts if given a strong enough aversive incentive to do so (Geller, Casali, & Johnson 1980).

The discussion throughout this chapter follows the spirit of the seat belt sweepstakes and obnoxious buzzer studies by addressing how external events generate extrinsic sources of motivation. Practically every environment we find ourselves in discriminates between desirable and undesirable behaviors. Further, practically every environment we find ourselves in rewards us in one way or another for performing those desired behaviors and punishes us in one way or another for performing those undesired behaviors. As a result, we generally engage in those courses of action that we believe will reward us and prevent punishment. Over time, we learn to want to engage in a particular behavior such as buckling a seat belt because of that behav-

FIGURE 5–1
Campus Poster to Advertise Seat Belt Sweepstakes

SOURCE: Rudd, J.R. & Geller, E.S. (1985). A university-based incentive program to increase safety belt use: Towards cost-effective institutionalization. *Journal of Applied Behavior Analysis, 18*, 215-226.

ior's history of being associated with attractive consequences. We do not necessarily want to engage in any one particular behavior per se; instead, we want to do whatever we have learned the environment will reward us for doing.

In the two previous chapters on needs, motivation arose from inner sources—physiological needs and organismic psychological needs. These needs explained when people ate and drank, sought out optimal challenges and intimate relationships, and so on. To propose that people eat and drink and that people seek out challenges and relationships because of needs to do so, however, recognizes only half of the story. A person might also engage in such behaviors because of external reasons to do so. Some examples of external events that create extrinsic motivation include social customs or laws, advertising influences, peers and companions, praise, money, the approval of another person, and so on. A fruitful analysis of motivated behavior, according to the behavior theorists we will meet (e.g., Baldwin & Baldwin, 1986; Skinner, 1938, 1953, 1986), requires a careful analysis of the environmental incentives and consequences associated with a given course of action.

EXTRINSIC MOTIVATION

Needs energize and direct our behavior. Needs motivate us to seek out those situations we believe to be capable of involving and satisfying our needs. Causal observation of day-to-day behavior, however, suggests that our needs are sometimes silent. We are not always active, and we do not always want to engage our environment. In schools, students are sometimes apathetic and unwilling to put forth anything more than minimal effort. At work, employees are sometimes listless and unwilling or slow to apply themselves. In hospitals, patients sometimes feel little desire to exercise, take their medicines, or put away their cigarettes. Such observations point to the conclusion that people do not always generate their own motivation. Instead, people sometimes turn passive and look to the environment to supply motivation for them. In school, teachers use grades, stickers, praise, and special privileges to motivate their students; at work, employers use paychecks, bonuses, surveillance, and competitions to motivate their employees; and in the hospitals, doctors use orders, implicit threats, and appeals to pleasing loved ones to motivate their patients. Such are the external events that underlie extrinsic motivation.

Intrinsic and Extrinsic Motivations

Experience teaches us there are two ways to enjoy an activity—intrinsically or extrinsically. Consider activities like playing the piano, using the computer, or reading a book. On the one hand, the pianist may become interested and begin to enjoy piano playing because it is an opportunity to involve and satisfy psychological needs. The musician plays the piano to have fun and to exercise valued skills. On the other hand, the same piano-playing behavior can be enjoyed because it is an opportunity to make money, win accolades, and earn a scholarship. Any activity, in fact, can be approached with either an intrinsic or an extrinsic motivational orientation (Amabile, 1985; Pittman, Boggiano, & Ruble, 1983; Pittman, Emery, & Boggiano, 1982; Pittman & Heller, 1988).

Intrinsic motivation is the innate propensity to engage one's interests and exercise one's capacities, and in doing so, seek out and master optimal challenges (Deci & Ryan, 1985a). It emerges spontaneously from organismic psychological needs, personal curiosities, and innate strivings for growth. As such, intrinsic motivation provides a natural motivational force that fosters learning and development, and it can motivate behavior without the assistance of extrinsic rewards and pressures. For instance, even in the absence of rewards and pressures, curiosity can spark the desire to read a book, and the need for competence can involve a person in a challenge for hours. Functionally, intrinsic motivation provides us with an innate motivational force to engage our environments and to exert the effort necessary to exercise and develop our skills and capabilities.

Extrinsic motivation, on the other hand, arises from external contingencies. Whenever we act to gain a high grade, win a trophy, or to comply with a deadline, our behavior is extrinsically motivated. When employees work hour after hour to earn a bonus, make a quota, or impress their peers, their behavior is extrinsically motivated. In essence, extrinsic motivation is an environmentally created reason to initiate or persist in an action. Extrinsic motivation is a means to an end in which the means is the behavior and the end is some attractive consequence (or the prevention of an unattractive consequence). Children who study hard for school may work hard out of a strong desire to please their parents, and that desire provides an environmentally created reason to work hard. The desired end is parental approval, and working hard in school just happens to be the means to obtain the approval.

Often, intrinsically and extrinsically motivated behaviors look precisely the same—the person reads a book, paints a picture, or goes to school or work. The essential difference between the two types of motivation lies in the source that energizes and directs the behavior. With intrinsically motivated behavior, the source of the activity emanates from organismic needs; with extrinsically motivated behavior, the source of the activity emanates from incentives, rewards, and punishments that are contingent on the behavior.

Rewards, Punishments, and Incentives

The study of extrinsic motivation revolves around the three central concepts of reward, punishment, and incentive. A *reward* is an attractive environmental consequence of behavior that increases the probability that the behavior will recur. Approval, paychecks, and trophies are attractive environmental consequences that occur after saying thank you, working a 40-hour week, and practicing athletic skills. Further, the recipient of the approval, paycheck, or trophy is more likely to repeat the politeness, work, or practice than is the person who receives no such attractive environmental consequence.

A *punishment*, or *punisher*, is an unattractive environmental consequence of behavior that decreases the probability that the behavior will recur. Criticism, jail terms, and public ridicule are unattractive environmental consequences of dressing sloppily, stealing another's property, and endorsing antisocial attitudes. The person who receives criticism, a jail term, or public ridicule is less likely to repeat such behavior than is the person not offered such an unattractive environmental consequence. Thus, both rewards and punishments follow behavior and affect the probability of its recurrence.

An *incentive* is an environmental influence that attracts or repels the individual toward or away from certain behavior. Incentives precede behavior and give rise to an expectation that attractive or unattractive consequences are forthcoming. Positive incentives include a smile, a green light, an open door, and the presence of friends and colleagues; negative incentives include a grimace, a red light or stop sign, a locked door, and the presence of enemies or competitors. The chief differences between rewards and punishers and incentives are (1) when each occurs and (2) what the external event is supposed to do. Unlike rewards and punishments that follow behavior and increase or decrease its probability of recurrence, incentives precede behavior and excite or inhibit its initiation.

Operant Conditioning

The foundation for the study of operant conditioning began a century ago when a researcher placed animals (usually house cats) inside an upside-down wooden crate with a tempting morsel of fish lying outside (Thorndike, 1898). The crate had a door and a rope latch that, if pulled, opened the door. After placing the cat in the crate and filling the bowl with fish, the experimenter simply watched what the cat did. At first, the cat performed stereotypically—walking in circles, caressing the walls, sniffing the fish, pawing at the open spaces in the walls, and so forth. Eventually, one of these behaviors would trigger the rope latch quite by accident and open the door. The cat would then, of course, exit and eat. When placed back in the crate (with the bowl refilled with fish), the cat would eventually show goal-directed (e.g., pawing at the walls) rather than stereotypical behavior. In time, each cat performed the behavior necessary to escape from the crate and attain the attractive fish reward more quickly. After 40 or so placements, the cats escaped the crate and gained the reward within 20 seconds every time.

The cats' behavior began as stereotypical actions and quickly became an array of strategic acts. Pawing at the wall became a highly probable course of action, whereas spinning in circles became an improbable course of action (because it never triggered the latch). The consequences that followed each behavior eventually came to determine its likelihood of being expressed in the future. Behaviors that produced positive consequences (food) became more likely, whereas behaviors that produced negative consequences (confinement) became less likely. By paying attention to the consequences that followed specific behaviors, the cats learned how best to operate on their environments. The term *operant conditioning* refers to the process by which a person learns (i.e., is conditioned) how to operate effectively on the environment.

To communicate how rewards, punishments, and incentives work together to motivate behavior, proponents of operant conditioning (e.g., Baldwin & Baldwin, 1986) offer the following conceptualization of behavior:

$$S: R \rightarrow C$$

In this three-term model, *S, R,* and *C* stand for situational cue, behavioral response, and consequence, respectively. The colon between *S* and *R* shows that the situational cue sets the occasion for (but does not cause) the behavioral response; the arrow between *R* and *C* shows that the behavioral response causes particular consequences (Baldwin & Baldwin, 1986). Having the attention of a group of friends, for instance, does not cause a storyteller to recite jokes, but the group does serve as a situational cue to set the occasion for storytelling. Once told, the jokes cause the friends' reactions, such that the telling of the jokes causes the audience's laugh or perhaps its ridicule.

Incentives

Rather than causing behavior, a situational cue (an incentive) affects the likelihood of whether a response will be initiated. The incentive signals the likelihood that a behavior will or will not produce rewarding or punishing consequences, and this knowledge about a stimulus' incentive value is learned. The theater audience, for instance, does not cause anxiety in the novice actor. Rather, the actor has learned that aversive outcomes (e.g., ridicule, rejection) are likely consequences of poor performance in the presence of a theater audience. Thus, people learn that particular incentives signal that positive consequences are likely and set the stage for approach behavior, and they learn that particular other incentives signal that aversive consequences are likely and set the stage for avoidance behavior.

Precisely how people learn that one situational cue signals positive consequences whereas another signals negative consequences is a matter of discriminative learning via operant conditioning. Baldwin and Baldwin (1986) present the illustration of the neighborhood newcomers who have two grocery stores where they can shop. Without experience (i.e., without conditioning), the newcomers do not know which store produces positive consequences (e.g., fresh fruit, friendly personnel, double coupons) and which does not. At first, the newcomers visit each store indiscriminately, often switching back and forth between store X and store Y. After several visits and after learning which store has the fresher produce, friendlier personnel, and better value, the shoppers begin to discriminate between the two stores. Soon, the newcomers learn that store X signals more positive consequences than does store Y. From then on, store X functions as a positive incentive that energizes and attracts the shopper's attendance.

Consequences

There are three fundamental consequences that follow behavior—positive reinforcers, negative reinforcers, and punishers. Positive and negative reinforcers increase behavior; punishers decrease behavior.

POSITIVE REINFORCERS (REWARDS). A positive reinforcer is any environmental stimulus that, when presented, increases the probability of certain behavior. If giving a child an award for athletic participation increases the child's future athletic participation, then the award is a positive reinforcer. Similarly, if you smile in response to a stranger's conversation initiation and your smile makes the stranger more likely to converse the next time you meet, then the smile is a positive reinforcer. External consequences that most of us find rewarding—and therefore increase the probability of those behaviors that produce them—include money, praise, attention, grades, scholarships, approval, prizes, food, awards, trophies, public recognition, and privileges.

NEGATIVE REINFORCERS. A negative reinforcer is any environmental stimulus that, when removed, increases the probability of certain behavior. Like positive reinforcers, negative reinforcers increase the probability of certain behavior. Unlike positive reinforcers, negative reinforcers are aversive stimuli. The shrill ring of the alarm clock is an aversive stimulus. Stopping the ringing is negatively reinforcing when it increases the probability that the would-be sleeper will get out of bed. In the same way, medicine that removes the pain of a headache is a negative reinforcer that increases the sufferer's willingness to take aspirin or other such medicine. Some external events that most of us find negatively reinforcing—and that therefore function to increase those behaviors that remove them—include whining, crying, nagging, surveillance, deadlines or time limits, a pet's incessant meowing or barking, pain, and worrisome noises that come from our car.

It is easy to visualize the approach behavior positive reinforcers motivate, but a couple of examples will help show how negative reinforcers motivate escape and avoidance behaviors. (Escape involves the removal of aversive stimuli; avoidance involves preventing aversive stimuli; Iwata, 1987). Consider how people escape the sound of the alarm clock by getting out of bed, the car buzzer by buckling a seat belt, and the whining child by leaving the room. The alarm, buzzer, and whining are aversive stimuli that energize and direct escape behaviors. When we discover which behaviors remove us from hearing the alarm, buzzer, or whining, we tend to repeat them when the alarm, buzzer, or whining return. To prevent the aversive stimuli from occurring in the first place, people get out of bed early to avoid the alarm, buckle up before starting the car to avoid its buzzer, and stay away from the child to avoid hearing the whines.

One further illustration of how a negative reinforcer motivates escape and avoidance behaviors is the wearing of a postural harness (Azrin et al., 1968), shown in Figure 5.2. An automated shoulder harness to discourage postural slouching sends off a 55-dB tone whenever slouching at the shoulders occurs. To escape the tone, the wearer must adjust the posture accordingly. The termination of the noise negatively reinforces the escape behavior of thrusting one's shoulder blades back. To avoid hearing the tone, the wearer must maintain correct posture. The desire not to hear the noise negatively reinforces the avoidance behavior of keeping one's shoulder blades pinned back. For all 25 adults using such a postural harness in one study, a marked improvement in posture occurred, presumably because people would rather make the effort necessary for good posture than hear the 55-dB tone (Azrin et al., 1968).

Figure 5.2 illustrates a source of motivation that is clearly outside (i.e., extrinsic to) the individual. The obnoxious noise and its threat of forthcoming irritation or embarrassment motivate the person's change in posture. Motives are internal processes (needs, cognitions, emotions), but external events, as represented here by the signal box and its 55-dB noise, can also determine when the person's behavior becomes energized and directed.

PUNISHERS. A punisher is any environmental stimulus that, when presented, decreases the probability of a certain response. If a bite makes it less likely that a person will pet a dog, then the bite is a punisher that suppresses petting. A traffic ticket

FIGURE 5–2
Front and Rear View of Person Wearing Postural Harness

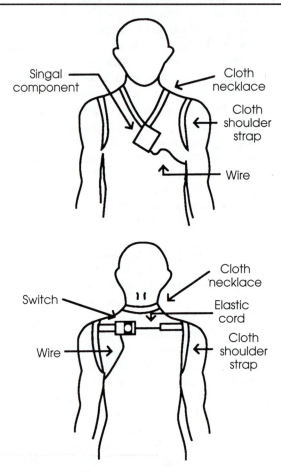

SOURCE: Azrin, N.H., Rubin, H., O'Brien, F., Ayllon, T., and Roll, D. (1968). Behavioral engineering: Postural control by a portable operant apparatus. *Journal of Applied Behavior Analysis, 2*, 39-42. Copyright © 1968 by the *Journal of Applied Behavior Analysis*. Reprinted by permission. NOTE: The front view in the upper sketch shows the signal component worn around the neck. A wire runs from the component, under the arm, and to the posture switch on the back, which is shown in the lower sketch. The posture switch is attached by the shoulder straps, which are adjusted for the desired posture. Outer garments are worn over the assembly and thereby conceal it from view.

for parking in a handicapped parking space, a reprimand for staying out past curfew, and a slap for suggesting intimate behaviors are examples of punishers—if the parking, staying out, and intimate suggestions are subsequently suppressed. Some potential confusion exists in discriminating punishment from negative reinforcement, because both are aversive stimuli, as when parents reprimand children for not cleaning their room. The reprimand is a punisher if its intent is to *suppress* behavior (e.g., suppress cluttering the room with toys). The reprimand is a negative reinforcer, however, if the children clean their room to *escape from* or *avoid* the reprimand. Punishers suppress behavior; negative reinforcers increase (escape and avoidance) behavior.

Actually, there are two types of punishment. The first type, as discussed, involves the administration of an aversive stimulus to suppress behavior. The second type involves the removal of positive consequences to achieve the same end. Punishment via removal of positive consequences constitutes essentially a *time-out* from positive reinforcers. Examples include having a driver's license taken away to suppress drunk driving, taking a toy away from a child to suppress a temper tantrum, or sending a child to bed without the privilege of watching a favorite television show. For reference, Figure 5.3 provides a 2×2 matrix to organize the four behavioral consequences discussed. Consequences can be pleasant or aversive, and they can be presented or removed. In Figure 5.3, the presentation of a pleasant stimulus is a positive reinforcer, the presentation of an aversive stimulus or the taking away of a pleasant stimulus is a punisher, and the removal of an aversive stimulus is a negative reinforcer.

What Is a Reinforcer?

From a practical point of view, defining a reinforcer is easy. It is any stimulus that increases behavior. From a theoretical point of view, however, the definition of a reinforcer is more difficult. Theoretically, a reinforcer must be defined in a manner that is independent from its effects on behavior. The problem with defining a positive reinforcer solely in terms of its effects on behavior is that the definition of a reinforcer becomes circular: The cause produces the effect, and the effect justifies the

FIGURE 5–3
Valence of Consequence as Function of Stimulus Presentation or Removal

	Valence of Consequence	
	Positive	**Negative**
Stimulus Presented	Positive Reinforcement	Punishment
Stimulus Removed	Punishment	Negative Reinforcement

SOURCE: Based on Kazdin, A.E. (1980). *Behavior modification in applied settings* (rev. ed.). Copyright © 1975 and 1980 by the Dorsey Press. Used with the permission of Brooks/Cole Publishing Corp., Pacific Grove, CA 93950.

cause (i.e., reinforcers increase behavior, and whatever increases behavior must be a reinforcer). For illustration, consider the theoretical quagmire researchers find themselves in by using the following circular definition of what a reinforcer is: "the pleasures, satisfactions, and gratifications the person enjoys" (Thibaut & Kelley, 1959, p. 12). If the only way to identify what is versus what is not a reinforcer is to give it and then wait to see whether it increases behavior or whether it produces pleasures and satisfactions, researchers have no means to identify a reinforcer before using it. The question then becomes, "Well, what is it that makes the reinforcer pleasurable, satisfying, or gratifying *in the first place*?" Or, the problem becomes figuring out ahead of time what will work (see Timberlake & Farmer-Dougan, 1991). To get out of the circular quagmire, the researcher needs to be able to pick out an object never used before (say, a candy bar or a trip to the zoo) and know a priori whether it will or will not increase the desired behavior.

In the history of motivation research, each of the following has been used to define a reinforcer theoretically and in a noncircular way: (1) a stimulus that decreases drive (e.g., food decreases hunger; Hull, 1943); (2) a stimulus that decreases arousal (e.g., a drug tranquilizes an anxious person; Berlyne, 1967); (3) a stimulus that increases arousal (e.g., rock concerts stimulate bored persons; Zuckerman, 1979); (4) an attractive environmental object (e.g., money increases going to work; Skinner, 1938); (5) hedonically pleasurable brain stimulation (e.g., brain stimulation of the medial forebrain bundle produces high rates of responding; Olds, 1969); (6) the opportunity to perform a high-frequency behavior (e.g., the opportunity to watch television increases the willingness to clean one's room; Premack, 1959); and (7) the opportunity to perform a prohibited behavior (e.g., the privilege of talking is especially reinforcing after being made to keep quiet for some duration of time; Timberlake, 1980; Timberlake & Allison, 1974). The advantage of these definitions of a reinforcer, as compared to the previous circular ones, is that the researcher can say, "Well, if a stimulus decreases drive, then it will increase behavior." Notice, a reinforcer is defined by its effect on drive, and this definition explains *why* the stimulus event will increase behavior.

To address the nature of reinforcing stimuli in a practical way, consider one study that used various potential reinforcers to encourage an 8-year-old to wear an orthodontic device (Hall et al., 1972). The parents observed that the child had little intrinsic motivation to wear the device, so they sought to create an extrinsic motivation to wear it. As shown in Figure 5.4, the parents kept track of the percentage of time their child wore the orthodontic device (five observations per day at random times, such as at breakfast, leaving for school, bedtime). In the first week of observation (with no positive reinforcer), the child wore the device 25% of the time. The parents then began to praise the child each time they saw the orthodontic gear being worn. With praise, the child wore the gear 36% of the time. For the next two weeks, the parents administered a delayed monetary reward for wearing the orthodontic device. Each time the parents saw the child wearing the gear, they promised 25 cents at the end of the month. With a quarter on the line, wearing the gear increased to 60%. Next, for a two-week period, the parents administered an immediate 25-cent reward for compliance. Orthodontic wearing increased to 97%. For the

FIGURE 5–4
Affect of Reinforcement on Use of Orthodontic Device

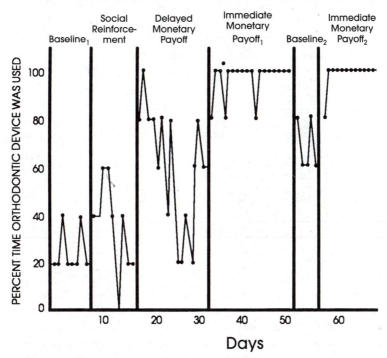

SOURCE: Hall, R.V., Axelrod, S., Tyler, L., Grief, E., Jones, F.C., & Robertson, R. (1972). Modification of behavior problems in the home with a parent as observer and experimenter. *Journal of Applied Behavior Analysis, 5*, 53-64. Copyright © 1972 by the *Journal of Applied Behavior Analysis.* Reprinted by permission.

next five days, the child received no positive reinforcers for wearing the gear. Wearing dropped to 64%. Finally, for two weeks, the parents reintroduced the immediate quarter reward, and the child's compliance increased to 100%.

This study highlights two important considerations in the attempt to understand the nature of reinforcers. First, reinforcers vary in their quality. Quarters worked better than praises. Second, the immediacy of delivery of a reinforcer partly determines how effective it is. Quarters given on the spot were more effective than quarters promised a month later.

In addition to quality and immediacy, four other characteristics speak to what is versus what is not a reinforcer. First, a reinforcer can be effective for one person but not for another, suggesting that the person/reinforcer fit is more important than any particular characteristic of the reinforcer per se. Attention and candy might prove effective for young children (and ineffective for adults), whereas social status and peer approval might prove effective for adults (and ineffective for young children). Second, the same reinforcer can be effective for a person at one time but ineffective at another. A cup of coffee might work early in the morning, but it may prove ineffective several hours later. Third, reinforcers vary in their intensity. Money is typically an effective reinforcer, but money comes in pennies, quarters, and dollars. Similarly, traffic fines can be $10 or $200. Lastly, the rewards that administrators (e.g., parents, teachers, employers, therapists, coaches) expect to function as reinforcers often do not correspond to what their recipients actually find to be reinforcing (Green et al., 1988; Pace et al., 1985; Smith, Iwata, & Shore, 1995). For example, a parent might give a child a big hug, thinking the child highly values hugging, though the child might rather have a bowl of chocolate pudding. Thus, six considerations determine how effective a positive reinforcer will be: (1) its quality; (2) its immediacy; (3) the person/reinforcer fit; (4) the recipient's need for that particular reward; (5) its intensity; and (6) the recipient's valuing of the reinforcer.

HIDDEN COSTS OF REWARD

The research on intrinsic and extrinsic motivation began with an interesting question: "If a person is involved in an intrinsically interesting activity and begins to receive an extrinsic reward for doing it, what happens to his or her intrinsic motivation for that activity?" (Deci & Ryan, 1985a, p. 43). For example, what happens to the motivation of the student who reads for the fun of it after getting money from parents for reading? One might suppose that rewarding students' reading behavior with a $20 bill would add to their motivation. That is, if a student enjoys reading and is also extrinsically rewarded to read, the intrinsic (enjoyment) and extrinsic (money) motivations should summate and produce a supermotivation to read. Typically, supermotivation does not occur. Rather, the imposition of an extrinsic reward for an intrinsically interesting activity undermines (has a negative effect on) future intrinsic motivation (Condry, 1977; Lepper, Greene, & Nisbett, 1973). The reward's adverse effect on intrinsic motivation is termed the *hidden cost of reward* (Lepper & Greene, 1978), because our society typically regards rewards as positive contributors to motivation.

Extrinsic rewards can have positive effects on motivation and behavior, as discussed earlier. But extrinsic rewards and controls also produce serious detrimental effects on motivation and behavior. The concept of self-determination (chapter 4) provides one way to understand the hidden costs of reward (e.g., Deci & Ryan, 1987). When experiment participants are paid (Deci, 1972), promised an award (Lepper, Greene, & Nisbett 1973), promised a toy (Lepper & Greene, 1975), threatened with a punisher (Deci & Casio, 1972), given a deadline (Amabile, DeJong, & Lepper, 1976), subjected to surveillance (Pittman et al., 1980), or experience other such extrinsic rewards and constraints, they gradually lose their perception of self-determination and show decreased intrinsic motivation. In other words, coercing individuals to do a task, even with the promise of an attractive reward, instigates a shift in their understanding of why they choose to engage in that task from one of self-determination to one of reward determination, from origin to pawn, from an internal to an external perceived locus of causality.

Experiments by Lepper and his colleagues nicely illustrate the hidden costs of extrinsic rewards (Greene & Lepper, 1974; Lepper & Greene, 1975, 1978; Lepper, Greene, & Nisbett, 1973). Preschool children with a high interest in drawing were grouped under one of three experimental conditions: expected reward, no award, and unexpected award. In the *expected reward* group (extrinsic motivational orientation), children were shown an extrinsic reward, a Good Player certificate, and asked if they wanted to draw in order to win the certificate. In the *no award* group (intrinsic motivational orientation), children were simply asked if they wanted to draw. In the *unexpected reward* group, children were asked if they wanted to draw, but unexpectedly received the Good Player certificate after they finished. One week later, the experimenters provided the children with another opportunity to draw or not, at their choice. During this week, children who initially drew in order to win the certificate (expected reward group) spent significantly less time drawing than did children in the other two groups. Relative to preexperiment interest levels, children in the expected reward group showed a significant decrease in subsequent interest in the drawing activity. The no award and unexpected reward groups showed no such interest decline. The interest maintenance of the unexpected reward group is important because it shows the extrinsic motivational orientation (rather than the reward per se) was the causal agent that decreased the children's interest in drawing. It was not the reward that undermined interest, but rather, the loss of self-determination, the seduction from being an origin to being a pawn, and the shift from internal to external perceived locus of causality.

In interpreting these findings, one might muse over the fact that the sample included preschoolers, the experimental task was drawing, and the reward was a certificate, and conclude that the findings therefore have little to do with more complex adult motives. These findings, however, have been replicated using adults with different tasks (e.g., puzzles, anagrams) and different rewards (e.g., money, public recognition) (Condry, 1977; Deci, 1971; Greene & Lepper, 1974; Lepper, 1981; Lepper & Greene, 1975, 1978; Ross, 1975; Swann & Pittman, 1977). In accepting the generality of the negative effects of an extrinsic motivational orientation (Deci & Ryan, 1985a; Kohn, 1993; Lepper & Greene, 1978; Rummel & Feinberg, 1988; Sutherland, 1993), one might ask whether rewards *always* and *inevitably* decrease intrinsic motivation. This is precisely what psychologists did question. After two decades of research, it is clear that rewards do not always decrease intrinsic motivation (e.g., see Cameron & Pierce, 1994). In particular, three factors affect the degree to which rewards decrease subsequent intrinsic motivation: expectancy, salience, and tangibility.

The *expectancy* of a reward is one factor in whether a reward decreases intrinsic motivation. As mentioned earlier, the study by Lepper, Greene, and Nisbett (1973) suggests that extrinsic rewards decrease intrinsic motivation only if the individual engages in the task with an expectation that a reward will follow participation. If the individual expects no task-contingent reward, whether or not one is later given, the reward will not decrease intrinsic motivation. The telltale sign that a person expects a reward for task participation is an if-then or in-order-to orientation, such as "If I eat my vegetables, then I can watch TV" or "I read the textbook in order to pass the test." For eating vegetables, the child expects TV privileges; for reading the book, the student expects a good grade.

A second factor is the *salience* of the reward. Ross (1975, 1976) suggested that for expected extrinsic rewards to decrease intrinsic motivation, the reward must be prominent in the individual's experience during the activity. In his experiment, children expected to receive an attractive food reward for engaging in an interesting activity. The experimenter requested that each child either (1) think continually about the food reward as they performed the activity (high salience group), (2) think continually about a nonfood topic (low salience group), or (3) simply engage in the activity for the food reward (control group). Relative to the children in the low salience group, children in the high salience and control groups showed a significant decrease in task engagement in a free-choice opportunity with the activity. These findings indicate that if the reward is not salient, it will not decrease intrinsic motivation.

A final factor concerns whether the reward is a *tangible* one. Tangible rewards, such as money, awards, and food, tend to decrease intrinsic motivation, whereas intangible rewards, such as praise and verbal encouragement, do not (Anderson, Manoogian, & Reznick, 1976; Cameron & Pierce, 1994; Deci, 1972; Swann & Pittman, 1977). In other words, rewards that one can see, touch, feel, and taste generally decrease intrinsic motivation, whereas verbal, symbolic, or abstract rewards do not. These three limiting factors suggest the conclusion that rewards do not always decrease intrinsic motivation; rather, intrinsic motivation decreases when an individual's initial interest is high and he or she expects a salient, tangible reward for performing the activity.

Implications of Hidden Costs of Reward

The fact that not all rewards decrease intrinsic motivation is a sort of good news/bad news message. The good news is that extrinsic rewards can be used in a way that does not put intrinsic motivation at risk of decline. The bad news is that our society so often relies on expected, salient, and tangible rewards to motivate others. Money, bonuses, paychecks, prizes, trophies, scholarships, privileges, grades, gold stars, awards, honors lists, salesperson of the week, incentive plans, our name in the newspaper, food, frequent flyer miles, and so on are ubiquitous sources of motivation in Western societies (e.g., Kohn, 1993).

Another bad news message within the hidden costs of rewards is that more than just decreased intrinsic motivation is at risk when expected, salient, and tangible rewards are used as motivators (Condry, 1977, 1987; Condry & Chambers, 1978; Deci & Ryan, 1985a; Harter, 1978b; Shapira, 1976). Extrinsic reinforcers not only decrease intrinsic motivation; they also interfere with the *process* and *quality* of learning. During information processing, extrinsic rewards distract attention away from learning and toward its product (getting the reward). Rewards shift the learner's goals away from mastery and toward potential extrinsic gains. Compared to those who are intrinsically motivated, extrinsically motivated individuals choose to engage in easy tasks, because easy tasks maximize the probability of receiving quick rewards

(Harter, 1978b; Pittman, Boggiano, & Ruble, 1983; Shapira, 1976). Extrinsically motivated learners are also more prone to a negative emotional tone (e.g., frustration; Garbarino, 1975) and less prone to positive emotional experiences (e.g., enjoyment; Harter, 1978b; see also Ryan & Connell, 1989; Skinner & Belmont, 1993). Further, extrinsically motivated learners are relatively passive information processors (Benware & Deci, 1984). Rewards also narrow the learner's attention to focus more on rote factual information at the expense of conceptual understanding (Benware & Deci, 1984; Boggiano et al., 1993; Flink, Boggiano, & Barrett, 1990). Rewards further put at risk learners' flexibility in their way of thinking and problem solving (try for a right answer rather than an optimal solution; McGraw & McCullers, 1979). Rewards also undermine information processing because of their detrimental effect on creativity (Amabile, 1985; Amabile, Hennessey, & Grossman, 1986). And, when rewards are involved, learners typically quit information processing as soon as some reward criterion is attained (e.g., read the 100 pages required for the test); when rewards are not involved, learners generally persist until curiosity is exhausted or mastery is attained (Condry, 1977, Condry & Chambers, 1978). Thus, not only is intrinsic motivation potentially at risk with the use of expected, salient, and tangible rewards, but so are learning processes such as attention, preference for challenge, emotional tone, active information processing, conceptual understanding, cognitive flexibility, and creativity.

A Positive Note on Extrinsic Motivation

The motivational significance of extrinsic events is twofold: Extrinsic stimuli gain control over behavior by increasing its frequency and, when withdrawn, decrease intrinsic motivation and interfere with active information processing (Schwartz, 1990). Whether extrinsic events are desirable and useful or condemnable and harmful therefore depends on the relative salience of these two functions of extrinsic rewards and controls. One way to minimize the detrimental effects of rewards on intrinsic motivation, as discussed earlier, is to rely on rewards that are verbal, abstract, and symbolic (e.g., praise) rather than expected, salient, and tangible (e.g., a bribe). A second means of decreasing the salience of rewards' detrimental effects on intrinsic motivation is to limit the use of extrinsic motivators to tasks that have social importance but very little intrinsic appeal. That is, if a person has little or no intrinsic motivation to engage in a task in the first place, intrinsic motivation is not put at risk by extrinsic rewards because there is no intrinsic motivation to undermine.

Rewards can make an otherwise uninteresting task seem suddenly worth pursuing. So long as the reward is attractive enough, rewarded individuals will engage in almost any task. Not so with unrewarded individuals; without reward they engage in the task on the basis of its intrinsic appeal, which in many cases is quite low. Consider the value of extrinsic sources of motivation in the following instances in which researchers used rewards to increase socially important but intrinsically uninteresting tasks: developing daily living skills, such as dressing and making lunch (Pierce & Schreibman, 1994); teaching severely nearsighted children to wear contact lenses (Mathews et al., 1992); preventing drunk driving (Geller, Altomari, &

Russ, 1984); eating foods that reduce seizures (Amari, Grace, & Fisher, 1995); participating in recycling (Brothers, 1994; Austira et al., 1993); changing habits of young children with severe problems so they will start or complete their homework (Miller & Kelley, 1994); teaching children with autism to initiate conversations with their peers (Krantz & McClannahan, 1993); and preventing harmful behaviors such as biting and poking (Fisher et al., 1993). In each of these examples, an argument can be made that the concern of achieving and maintaining compliance outweighs the concern of preserving or protecting intrinsic motivation. That is, the positive motivational effects of rewards (increase positive behavior) outweigh their negative effects (undermine intrinsic motivation), at least under some conditions (when interest is already dismally low) and within one particular ideological way of thinking about motivation (e.g., acceptable in behaviorism, unacceptable in humanism).

So it is okay to use extrinsic motivators when another person's intrinsic motivation is low, right? Not necessarily. Consider the following four reasons not to use extrinsic motivators for even intrinsically uninteresting endeavors (from Kohn, 1993): (1) Extrinsic motivators still undermine the quality of performance and interfere with the process of learning; (2) it is naive to presume that one person can determine what another will find intrinsically interesting or uninteresting; (3) using rewards distracts attention away from asking the hard question of why we are asking another person to do an uninteresting task in the first place; and (4) there are better ways to encourage participation than extrinsic bribery (e.g., consider autonomy-supportive environments). When all is said and done, extrinsic motivators simply carry too high a psychological cost in the individual's intrinsic motivation, self-determination, quality of learning, emotional tone, conceptual understanding, cognitive flexibility, creativity, and preference for challenge.

COGNITIVE EVALUATION THEORY

When external events are used as positive reinforcers, negative reinforcers, and punishers, they create in people an extrinsic motivation to engage in (or cease) an activity. When people use such external events to affect other people's behavior, they influence or control what the other person is doing. Sometimes the attempt to control another person's behavior is obvious (e.g., using quarters to bribe a child to wear orthodontic gear; see Fig. 5.4), but other times the attempt at control is more seductive (e.g., giving free soft drinks at a bar to anyone agreeing to be a designated driver; Brigham, Maier, & Goodner, 1995). Thus part of the purpose of implementing almost any external stimulus is to control another person's behavior. But there is a second purpose because external stimuli also provide feedback on the person's level of competence at the task. Rewards such as monetary bonuses, letter grades of As, and praise not only encourage hard work (i.e., control behavior) but also communicate a message of a job well done (i.e., inform of competence).

Cognitive evaluation theory asserts that all external events have a controlling aspect and an informational aspect (Deci & Ryan, 1985a). The theory presumes that people have organismic needs for self-determination and competence (chapter 4) and that the event's controlling aspect relates to the need for self-determination whereas the event's informational aspect relates to the need for competence. Cognitive evaluation theory exists as a set of three propositions, as listed in Table 5.1.

Propositions 1 and 2 reflect the themes expressed in chapter 4. According to proposition 1, events that promote an internal perceived locus of causality (PLOC) promote intrinsic motivation because they involve or satisfy the need for self-determination; events that promote an external PLOC promote extrinsic motivation because they bypass the need for self-determination. Hence, relatively noncontrolling events promote self-determination, an internal PLOC, and intrinsic motivation, whereas relatively controlling events undermine self-determination, promote an external PLOC, and increase extrinsic motivation. According to proposition 2, events that increase perceived competence promote intrinsic motivation, whereas events that decrease perceived competence undermine intrinsic motivation. When external events communicate positive effectance information, they satisfy the need for competence and increase intrinsic motivation, but when external events communicate negative effectance information, they frustrate the need for competence and decrease intrinsic motivation.

According to proposition 3, the relative salience of whether an event is mostly controlling or mostly informational determines its effects on intrinsic and extrinsic

TABLE 5–1
Cognitive Evaluation Theory

Proposition 1
External events relevant to the initiation and regulation of behavior will affect a person's intrinsic motivation to the extent that they influence the perceived locus of causality (PLOC) for that behavior. Events that promote a more external PLOC will undermine intrinsic motivation, whereas those that promote a more internal PLOC will enhance intrinsic motivation.

Proposition 2
External events will affect a person's intrinsic motivation for an optimally challenging activity to the extent that they influence the person's perceived competence, within the context of some self-determination. Events that promote greater perceived competence will enhance intrinsic motivation, whereas those that diminish perceived competence will decrease intrinsic motivation.

Proposition 3
Events relevant to the initiation and regulation of behavior have three potential aspects, each with a functional significance. The informational aspect facilitates an internal PLOC and perceived competence, thus enhancing intrinsic motivation. The controlling aspect facilitates an external PLOC, thus undermining intrinsic motivation and promoting extrinsic compliance or defiance. The amotivating aspect facilitates perceived incompetence, thus undermining intrinsic motivation and promoting amotivation. The relative salience of these three aspects to a person determines the functional significance of the event.

SOURCE: Deci, E.L., & Ryan, R.M. (1985a). *Intrinsic motivation and self-determination in human behavior.* New York: Plenum.

motivation. When an extrinsic event is presented in a relatively controlling way, it effectively undermines intrinsic motivation (via its effects on self-determination); when an extrinsic event is presented in a relatively informational way, it effectively increases intrinsic motivation (via its effect on competence). It is in proposition 3 that the usefulness of cognitive evaluation theory becomes apparent—namely, that the reader can use cognitive evaluation theory to predict the effect that *any* extrinsic event will have on intrinsic and extrinsic motivations.

Two Examples of Controlling and Informational Events: Praise and Competition

Any event—praise, money, grades in school, a scholarship, surveillance, a deadline, interpersonal competition, or whatever—can be delivered from one person to another in a relatively controlling or a relatively informational way. For example, a boss might communicate to an employee in a controlling way by saying, "Excellent job, you did just as you should" or in an informational way by saying, "Excellent job." Tagging words or phrases such as *should, must, have to*, and *ought to* onto praise gives the positive feedback a tone of contingency, of pressure, and of doing the work of someone else (Ryan, 1982). In contrast, providing clear, specific, and descriptive task-related feedback typically gives praise a highly informative function (Brophy, 1981). For example, the praise, "Excellent job, I noticed that you greeted the customer warmly and with a sincere tone in your voice" speaks informatively to an employees' sense of competence and effectance in a way that a simple "Excellent job" does not. The conclusion is that praise can be used in a controlling way, and when people pick up on the fact that another is using praise to foster certain behavior, self-determination and intrinsic motivation decrease. Also, praise can be used in a noncontrolling, informational way, and when people hear a message of a job well done, perceived competence and intrinsic motivation increase (Kohn, 1993).

A second illustration of how an external event can be either relatively controlling or relatively informational is the case of interpersonal competition (Olson, 1985; Reeve & Deci, 1996). Under some conditions, people experience competition as a relatively controlling event. When the social context puts a good deal of pressure on winning (with its evaluative audience, coaches, peers, newspaper reporters, championship trophies, career implications), competitors usually compete with a sense of contingency, pressure, and a sense of doing the work of others. When experienced in such a controlling way, competition decreases intrinsic motivation, because competitors care relatively little about the task itself and much more about the outcome of winning (Deci, Betley, Kahle, Abrams, & Porac, 1981; Vallerand, Gauvin, & Halliwell, 1986). But all competitions are not embedded in a controlling context. When the social context places little emphasis on winning (recreational competition, no audience present, no trophy or scholarship for winning), then competition's informational aspect can become relatively salient. Through its outcome and through competitors' perceptions of progress, competitive situations can provide a useful arena to send a message of effectance to competitors. As you might expect, winning increases intrinsic motivation relative to losing (Reeve, Olson, & Cole, 1985), though it is the perception of high competence, rather than the reward of winning, that increases intrinsic motivation (McAuley & Tammen, 1989). Further, winning with an informational social context ("try to do your best") increases intrinsic motivation, whereas winning with a controlling social context ("focus all of your attention on winning; focus on beating the other person") does not (Reeve & Deci, 1996). Thus, for intrinsic motivation to flourish, both competence *and* self-determination must be high (see Fisher, 1978), and for both competence and self-determination to be high, an external event must be presented in a noncontrolling, informational way.

SELF-DETERMINATION THEORY

Recall that motivation varies not only in intensity but also in its type. This chapter distinguishes between intrinsic and extrinsic motivation. A dichotomy of intrinsic versus extrinsic motivation, however, is a bit simplistic because motivational states that lie on a continuum between intrinsic and extrinsic motivation can be identified (Rigby et al., 1992). The distinction between intrinsic and extrinsic motivation follows from the distinction between an internal PLOC and an external PLOC. But all extrinsically motivated behaviors do not necessarily emanate from an external PLOC. I can exercise, read a school book, or attend a psychology experiment for which I will receive extra credit points, and each of these behaviors could be extrinsically motivated yet self-determined. People can freely choose to pursue extrinsic rewards. Thus, types of extrinsic motivation exist, because any intentional act can be conceptualized along a continuum that extends from highly self-determined to not at all self-determined.

According to self-determination theory, distinct motivational states exist along a continuum of self-determination that ranges from motivation that is not at all self-determined to that which is fully self-determined (Deci & Ryan, 1985a, 1991; Rigby et al., 1992). Figure 5.5 shows the self-determination continuum of motivation. On the far right-hand side, intrinsic motivation reflects the individual's full endorsement

FIGURE 5–5
Self-Determination Continuum of Motivation

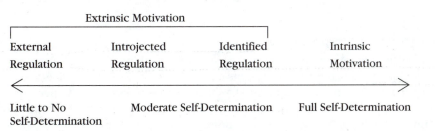

SOURCE: Based on Ryan, R.M., & Connell, J.P. (1989). Perceived locus of causality and internalization: Examining reasons for acting in two domains. *Journal of Personality and Social Psychology, 57,* 749-761.

of self-determination and pertains to all those instances in which a person's organismic psychological needs generate motivation to act. On the left-hand side are three types of extrinsic motivation that vary in degree of self-determination. These three types of extrinsic motivation are *extrinsic regulation* (not at all self-determined), *introjected regulation* (somewhat self-determined), and *identified regulation* (moderately self-determined).

Identifying types of motivation is important because the amount of self-determination in motivation has a substantial effect on what people think, how people feel, and what people do (Gottfried, 1985; Grolnick & Ryan, 1987; Ryan & Connell, 1989; Vallerand, Pelletier, Blais, Briere, Senecal, & Vallieres, 1992). For instance, Ryan and Connell (1989) asked school-aged children what motivated their academic behaviors (e.g., Why do you do your homework? Who do you do your classwork? Why do you try to do well in school?) and then measured the students' emotional states, level of effort, and academic performance in school. Students' reasons reflected various styles of extrinsic regulation (to make good grades, because its the rule), introjected regulation (because I would feel guilt if I didn't, I want the teacher to like me), identified regulation (because studying is meaningful and important), and intrinsic motivation (because it's fun, I enjoy it). The more self-determined students' motivation was, the more they enjoyed school, the more effort they put forth, and the more they achieved. School children with little self-determination felt mostly anxiety, put forth minimal effort, and achieved poorly.

Types of Extrinsic Motivation

EXTERNAL REGULATION. External regulation is the prototype of non–self-determined extrinsic motivation. For the person who is externally regulated, the appearance and disappearance of extrinsic events such as rewards, pressures, and constraints creates rises and falls in motivation. A person who is externally regulated typically has a difficult time beginning a task unless there is some external prompt to do so. A student, for instance, begins to study only when a test is upcoming or begins to write a term paper only when a deadline is near. Without the test or the deadline, the student lacks motivation to study or to write. With external regulation, the person has not internalized a voluntary willingness to perform. With no internalization, the person simply waits for incentives and pressures in the environment to provide a reason to act.

INTROJECTED REGULATION. Introjected regulation involves taking in, but not truly accepting, other people's rules or demands to think, feel, or behave in a particular manner. Introjection represents a partial internalization of beliefs and is characterized by self- and other-approval-based pressures. In essence, the person, *acting as a proxy for the environment*, emotionally rewards himself for performing other-defined good behavior and emotionally punishes himself for performing bad behavior. With introjected regulation, the person appears to be carrying the rules, commands and standards of another person (or society in general) inside the head to such an extent that the internalized voice generates the motivation. Notice, however, that introjected regulation does include the changing of internal structures, because the behavior is regulated not by explicit external contingencies but rather by internalized representations of those contingencies (i.e., mom's voice, cultural expectations). For instance, employees might come to work on time or may resist stealing supplies not because they choose to be punctual or honest, but because being late or dishonest produces feelings of guilt and shame (i.e., self-administered punishments), whereas being on time or honest produces feelings of pride and approval (i.e., self-administered rewards).

IDENTIFIED REGULATION. Identified regulation represents fully internalized extrinsic motivation. Identification represents an adoption of beliefs as personal values and is characterized by greater volition than is introjection. With identified regulation, the person voluntarily accepts the merits of a belief or behavior, because that way of thinking or that way of behaving seems important and useful. Thus, if a student comes to believe that extra work in mathematics is important (e.g., for a career in science), or an athlete comes to believe that extra practice on the backhand is important (e.g., to become a professional tennis player or to keep a college scholarship), the motivation to study and to practice is extrinsic, *but freely chosen*. Extra work in mathematics or tennis is extrinsic because these behaviors are instrumental to other aims (a career as a scientist or tennis pro), yet they are freely chosen because they are perceived to be useful and valuable for one's life. Exercise and being polite to others provide two additional examples of identified regulation; many people exercise religiously and go out of their way to be helpful, not because they enjoy jogging, lifting weights, giving strangers money, or fixing misbehaving automobiles, but because they value what such behaviors can do for them and for their relationships with others. So, identified regulation involves substantial internalization of societal norms, values, ideals, priorities, and practices to such an extent that these are integrated into and become a part of the self. At first glance, intrinsic motivation and identified extrinsic motivation seem similar, but the distinction is this: The regulatory process underlying identified regulation asks is the activity *important?* whereas the regulatory process underlying intrinsic motivation asks is the activity *enjoyable?* (Deci, 1992a).

One important practical implication of self-determination theory in understanding motivation and emotion is that it highlights the existence of at least three ways to motivate self and others. The first two are fairly obvious—extrinsic motivation and intrinsic motivation. But identified regulation adds a third route to generate motivation. (Introjected regulation would be a fourth means to motivation, but it is associated with poor adjustment and development and thus leaves little to recommend it; Ryan & Connell, 1989.) Hence, essentially three reasons exist to engage in a task—because it is fun (intrinsic motivation), because it leads to an attractive extrinsic event (extrinsic motivation), or because it is an important and personally useful thing to do (identified regulation). Identified regulation gives practitioners such as teachers and managers a useful alternative to extrinsic regulation on those tasks that are not intrinsically motivating to students and workers. The benefit of identified regulation, as compared to external regulation, is that it avoids the hidden costs of rewards by preserving the person's sense of self-determination.

SUMMARY

Extrinsic motivation arises from an environmentally created reason to initiate or persist in an action. It is a means to an end in which the means is the behavior and the end is some attractive consequence (or the prevention of an unattractive consequence). The study of extrinsic motivation revolves around the three central concepts of reward, punishment, and incentive. A *reward* is an attractive environmental consequence of behavior that increases the probability that the behavior will recur (e.g., approval, paychecks, and trophies). A *punisher* is an unattractive environmental consequence of behavior that decreases the probability that the behavior will recur (e.g., criticism, jail terms, and public ridicule). An *incentive* is an environmental influence that attracts or repels the individual toward or away from certain behavior. The chief differences between consequences and incentives are (1) when each occurs, and (2) what the extrinsic event is supposed to do. Incentives precede behavior and give rise to an expectation that attractive or unattractive consequences are forthcoming, they therefore excite or inhibit action. Consequences follow behavior and increase or decrease its future probability of occurrence.

Consequences and incentives are ubiquitous external events that motivate behavior, and extrinsic events can have positive effects on motivation and behavior. Extrinsic events can also, however, produce serious detrimental effects termed the hidden costs of reward. Expected, salient, and tangible (and often superfluous) extrinsic reasons to engage in a task typically undermine motivation by decreasing self-determination and undermine learning by interfering with attention, preference for challenge, emotional tone, activity level, conceptual understanding, cognitive flexibility, and creativity. That is not to say that extrinsic events are always motivationally problematic, because they not only have their hidden costs they also have their obvious benefits—namely, energizing behavior (incentives) and increasing its frequency (consequences). Cognitive evaluation theory provides a way of predicting the effects extrinsic events will have on motivation. The theory explains how any extrinsic event—money, grades, a deadline, or whatever—affects intrinsic and extrinsic motivations, as mediated by the external event's effect on the organismic psychological needs for competence and self-determination. When an extrinsic event is presented in a relatively controlling way (i.e., given to gain compliance), it undermines intrinsic motivation because of its detrimental effects on self-determination. When an extrinsic event is presented in a relatively informational way (i.e., given to communicate a message of a job well done), it increases intrinsic motivation because of its favorable effect on competence. Hence, whether an extrinsic event is motivationally beneficial or motivationally harmful depends on the relative salience of its controlling and informational aspects.

Self-determination theory extends the intrinsic versus extrinsic motivation dichotomy into a continuum of motivational states that exist along a continuum of self-determination. External regulation reflects the least self-determination type of extrinsic motivation and involves no internalization and much dependence on the presence of external events to generate (extrinsic) motivation. Introjected regulation reflects some self-determination, because it involves an internalization (but not truly accepting) of social rules, demands, priorities, and ways of behaving. With introjected regulation, motivation appears as if the person were carrying others' rules and commands inside the head to such an extent that the internalized voice generates self-administered rewards and punishments. Identified regulation refers to volitionally internalized extrinsic motivation. With identified regulation, the person willfully accepts the merit or usefulness of an externally prescribed way of thinking or behaving. Identified regulation is carried out to accomplish extrinsic aims (get a job, improve one's health) but the person's willfulness (rather than the extrinsic event per se) generates the motivation to act. Lastly, intrinsic motivation represents the prototype of self-determined motivation. When intrinsically motivated, the person relies not at all on extrinsic incentives and consequences for motivation but, instead, on the organismic need-satisfying interest and enjoyment that participation in the activity brings.

RECOMMENDED READINGS

Amabile, T. M., DeJong, W., & Lepper, M. R. (1976). Effects of externally-imposed deadlines on subsequent intrinsic motivation. *Journal of Personality and Social Psychology, 34,* 92–98.

Cameron, J., & Pierce, W. D. (1994). Reinforcement, reward, and intrinsic motivation: A meta-analysis. *Review of Educational Research, 64,* 363–423.

Deci, E. L., & Ryan, R. M. (1980). The empirical exploration of intrinsic motivational processes. In L. Berkowitz (Ed.), *Advances in experimental social psychology* (Vol. 13, pp. 39–80). New York: Academic Press.

Elman, D., & Killebrew, T.J. (1978). Incentives and seat belts: Changing a resistant behavior through extrinsic motivation. *Journal of Applied Social Psychology, 8,* 73–83.

Hall, R. V., Axelrod, S., Tyler, L., Grief, E., Jones, F. C., & Robertson, R. (1972). Modification of behavior problems in the home with a parent as observer and experimenter. *Journal of Applied Behavior Analysis, 5,* 53–64.

Hom, Jr., H. L. (1994). Can you predict the overjustification effect? *Teaching of Psychology, 21,* 36–37.

Koestner, R., Ryan, R. M., Bernieri, F., & Holt, K. (1984). Setting limits on children's behavior: The detrimental effects of controlling versus informational styles on intrinsic motivation. *Journal of Personality, 52,* 233–248.

Lepper, M. R., & Greene, D. (1975). Turning play into work: Effects of adult surveillance and extrinsic rewards on children's intrinsic motivation. *Journal of Personality and Social Psychology, 31,* 479–486.

Rigby, C. S., Deci, E. L., Patrick, B. P., & Ryan, R. M. (1992). Beyond the intrinsic-extrinsic dichotomy: Self-determination in motivation and learning. *Motivation and Emotion, 16,* 165–185.

Ryan, R. M., & Connell, J. P. (1989). Perceived locus of causality and internalization: Examining reasons for acting in two domains. *Journal of Personality and Social Psychology, 57,* 749–761.

Chapter 6

ACQUIRED PSYCHOLOGICAL NEEDS

Acquired Needs
- Quasi-Needs
- Social Needs
- Thematic Apperception Test
- Acquiring the Social Needs for Achievement, Affiliation, Intimacy, and Power
- How Social Needs Motivate Behavior

Achievement
- Origins of the Need for Achievement
- Atkinson's Model of Achievement Behavior
- Dynamics-of-Action Model
- Achievement for the Future
- Conditions that Involve and Satisfy the Need for Achievement

Affiliation and Intimacy
- Conditions that Involve and Satisfy the Need for Affiliation and Intimacy

Power
- Conditions that Involve and Satisfy the Need for Power
- Leadership Motive Pattern

Imagine driving down the interstate as the sun begins to set. Hour after hour after hour you drive; the monotony multiplies. To alleviate the boredom, you stop at every other exit and you listen to the radio. Still you continue, mile after mile, and your mind and imagination begin to wander. You daydream.

Glancing at the passing countryside, you see houses and farms. Horses run outside one farm, and you imagine what it would be like to race in the Kentucky Derby. You imagine racing and going neck and neck with the best jockeys in the world. Of course, you win and the crowd goes wild. Having conquered the racing world, your thoughts turn to the examination you took before leaving town. You performed well below your expectations and aspirations; that failure feedback gnaws at you, and you plan ways that you might do better. You decide to study harder and budget your time more efficiently. Hopeful in your plan, your imagination turns to what life will soon be like when you graduate and become a physician. You think about working in the laboratory, making important scientific advancements, and perhaps discovering the cure for cancer or aids. Yours will be a grand career!

The driving and its monotony continue. A song on the radio drives home the fact that you just left friends 600 miles behind. You feel a sense of loss; the pain of separation stirs you to recall a trivial argument with your partner just before you left. You imagine all the things that you could do to make things right again—make a telephone call, write a letter, or turn the car around and surprise your partner with an impromptu visit. You pass a high school and suddenly remember your high school friends and how comfortable it was to hang out. As you recall the best of times, you smile and laugh. Your laughing draws the attention of a passerby and, for a moment, you wonder what it would be like to get to know her—to learn about her life and what interests her. What does she do? Where is she going? What does she believe? What makes her tick?

The driving continues deep into the night, and another car zooms by at 90 miles per hour. For some reason, you feel that the other driver has somehow made you look bad, as they drive so fast and you so slow. Also, they dart in front of you and that somehow seems aggressive, in a posturing sort of way. Offended, you feel an impulse to yell at them and flash your bright lights in their rearview mirror. To restrain yourself, you mutter some tough name-calling words, turn up your shirt collar, and put on your sunglasses to look cool. Since it's dark, you put the sunglasses away; your thoughts wander to imaging what it would be like to drive down the road in a convertible and to have others see you talking on a car phone. Maybe you could drive one of those high-sitting, all-terrain, megapower vehicles. You like the thought of being rich and well respected, maybe with a reputation of leadership and of being a shrewd deal maker.

Fantasies of winning a race, doing well in competition, becoming a better student, and discovering a cure for an incurable disease are achievement-related thoughts. Thoughts of separation and goals to make amends for a broken relationship, be with close friends, and establish new friendships are affiliation- and intimacy-related thoughts. Impulses to assertiveness and concerns over status and reputation arise from power-related thoughts. As the mind wanders, our needs have a way of working their way into consciousness to affect our thoughts, emotions, and desires.

ACQUIRED NEEDS

This chapter discusses two categories of acquired psychological needs—social needs and quasi-needs. None of us is born with psychological needs for achievement, power, money, a 4.0 GPA, or a new car that will impress our friends. Yet each of us develops many such strivings, at least to some degree. Personal experience, socialization opportunities and pressures, and our unique developmental history teach us to expect positive emotional experiences in certain situations but not in other situations. We associate positive emotional experience with some situations, organize our goals around these situations, and make plans that incorporate them. Over time, we acquire preferences for situations, hobbies, and careers that involve and satisfy the constellation of needs we acquire. Some of us learn to prefer situations that challenge us with explicit standards of excellence (i.e., achievement needs). Others learn to prefer situations that afford plentiful opportunities for relationships (i.e., affiliation needs). This chapter reviews four such acquired psychological needs—achievement, affiliation, intimacy, and power. The review of each need traces its social origins and discusses how social needs, once acquired, change and manifest themselves in thoughts, emotions, and actions. An analysis of social needs constitutes the bulk of the chapter's content, but another class of acquired psychological needs also energizes and directs behavior—quasi-needs.

Quasi-Needs

A need describes a deficiency-replenishing or growth-promoting condition that produces energy and behavioral direction (chapter 3). People harbor a multitude of needs, many of which are psychological in origin. Chapter 4 discussed the organismic psychological needs that originate from human nature and healthy development. This chapter focuses on socially acquired psychological needs that originate from preferences gained through experience, socialization, and development. People further harbor a multitude of quasi-needs, including needs for money, self-esteem, an umbrella when it rains, an item in a store window, marriage before the age of 30, and so on. Quasi-needs are situationally induced wants and desires that are not actually full-blown needs in the sense that physiological, organismic and social needs are. Quasi-needs are so called because they resemble true needs in some ways.

Quasi-needs affect how we think, feel, and act (i.e., affect cognition, emotion, and behavior). But quasi-needs originate not from any condition of the person (as do physiological, organismic, and social needs) but, instead, from demands and pressures in the environment. Whenever the person satisfies the situational demand or pressure, the quasi-need fades away. To place an order at the restaurant we need money, after being rejected we need self-esteem, during a downpour we need an umbrella, upon seeing an item in the store window we need to possess it, as we age into our late 20s we need to get married, and so on. Once we get the money, self-esteem, umbrella, item, or wedding, however, the situation is such that we no longer need more money, self-esteem, umbrellas, items, or proposals.

Quasi-needs originate from situational events that promote a psychological context of tension, pressure, and urgency. Hence, quasi-needs are largely deficiency oriented. For example, when the situation pressures them in one way or another, people say they need a vacation, need to make a good grade on a test, need to get a haircut, need to find their lost car keys, need a piece of paper to write on, need a friend to talk to, need to take a bath, need to get a job, and so on. It is this situationally induced psychological context of tension, pressure, and urgency that supplies the motivation of a quasi-need.

Sometimes pressuring environmental conditions endure over time. As situational pressures endure, the quasi-needs they produce also endure. Enduring situational demands typically come in conflict with a person's other needs and feelings. If the situational demand (and hence the quasi-need) is strong enough (e.g., I just *have to* do well in school so my parents will be proud and so I can earn a well-paying job), then the person must ignore other needs and interests to minimize conflict and anxiety (Deci, 1980). In school, for instance, students might feel pressured by circumstances to pursue a business major. That is, parents might endorse a major in business and the job market might promise the big bucks only to business majors. If the parents and job market reward business studies and deny rewards for pursuing art, then college students might over time ignore their interest in art to please their parents and gain the well-paying job. Not being allowed to pursue an interest in art will be frustrating, but the pressures of the situation are such that people are not allowed to do what they otherwise want or feel. Quasi-needs often have a sense of urgency that dominates consciousness and may overwhelm other needs. Over time, the need to please parents and the need for a well-paying job carry the potential to replace or cover up a self-determined need for art studies. Hence, in practice, quasi-needs carry the potential to act and function like the full-blown (physiological, organismic, and social) needs by energizing and directing day-to-day behavior.

Social Needs

Early personality theorists debated whether personality was best described structurally in terms of traits (e.g., Allport, 1961) or more dynamically in terms of needs and motives (e.g., Murray, 1938). From Murray's point-of-view, a core set of universal human needs governed much (but not necessarily most) behavior. For Murray, any individual could be regarded as having a particular constellation of basic needs that energized and directed behavior toward satisfaction of those particular needs central to the personality. One person, for instance, might have needs for achievement and order and, as a consequence, spend much time pursuing an entrepreneurial business career. Another might be low in these needs but high in others, such as affiliation and nurturance, and therefore spend much time building and repairing relationships.

If universal human needs govern human behavior, a top priority becomes identifying those needs. Not knowing exactly where to start to compile such a list, Murray decided to investigate all motives that previous personality theorists (e.g., Freud, Jung, McDougall) had suggested were important. Table 6.1 lists Murray's (1938) compilation of human needs and briefly describes each. The pairing of needs was also important to Murray's system because he believed that needs coordinated with one another, at least to some degree. Some needs are opposites (e.g., dominance and deference), one need might conflict with another (e.g., autonomy versus affiliation), other needs might fuse (e.g., aggression and dominance), while still other needs might facilitate one another (e.g., achievement and counteraction).

TABLE 6–1
Murray's List of Human Needs

NEED	DESCRIPTION
Abasement	Self-depreciation. To seek and enjoy injury, blame, criticism, punishment.
Achievement	To overcome obstacles. To attain a high standard. To strive and master.
Affiliation	To form friendships. To cooperate, join, and converse sociably with others.
Aggression	To injure another. To belittle, harm, blame, accuse, or depreciate another.
Autonomy	To be independent and free to act according to impulse.
Counteraction	To master or make up for a failure by striving. To overcome a weakness.
Defense	To defend oneself against blame, criticism, belittlement. To offer excuses.
Deference	To cooperate with a leader. To praise, honor, and follow a superior other.
Dominance	To influence or control others. To persuade, prohibit, dictate, or command.
Exhibition	To attract attention or make an impression. To stir, shock, and thrill others.
Harm avoidance	To escape or avoid injury and danger. To take precautionary measures.
Infraavoidance	To avoid shame, humiliation. To refrain from action because of a fear of failure.
Nurturance	To nourish, aid, or protect a helpless other. To help, support, comfort.
Order	To arrange, organize, put away objects. To be precise and tidy.
Play	To seek diversion and be merry. To act for fun without further purpose.
Rejection	To snub or exclude. To remain aloof and indifferent. To discriminate.
Sentience	To seek and enjoy sensuous impressions.
Succorance	To seek aid, protection, or sympathy. To be dependent, to seek support.
Understanding	To analyze experience. To discriminate concepts. To synthesize ideas.

Murray sought to measure these social needs in a multitude of ways, because needs expressed themselves in many ways. Needs expressed themselves through approach behavior, through avoidance behavior, through selective attention, through strong emotional reactions, and so forth. To measure human needs, Murray decided to use as many techniques as possible—questionnaires, interviews, free association, dream analysis, diaries, autobiographical statements, observation of behavior in group settings and various laboratory experiments, and reactions to frustration, music, and humor. Most important, he developed the Thematic Apperception Test (TAT; Murray, 1943; Morgan & Murray, 1935).

Thematic Apperception Test

The TAT presents a series of pictures and asks the test taker to write short stories about the events portrayed in each picture (Bellak, 1993; Smith, 1992). *Thematic* refers to the content, or theme, expressed in each story. For example, one test item shows a person looking into a microscope, a story about efforts to work one's way through medical school, become a doctor, and discover the cure for an incurable disease reflects an achievement theme. *Apperception* refers to the human tendency to perceive more than is actually present in the stimulus object (to apperceive). A person's apperception fills in the picture's ambiguous aspects with personal interpretations to make sense of the scene. Seeing a pattern like a mushroom in a randomly shaped cloud is an example of apperception. In taking the TAT the test taker looks at a series of between 4 and 21 pictures, one at a time. Recently, researchers have successfully substituted sentences (e.g., "Ann is sitting on a chair with a smile on her face") to replace the pictures (for one illustration of using verbal cues as fantasy-based stimuli to assess needs, see Jenkins, 1987, p. 925).

Some of Murray's needs interest contemporary researchers more than do others. In particular, four needs have received the bulk of attention—achievement, affiliation, intimacy, and power (or what Murray called *dominance*). As we shall see throughout the chapter, most empirical studies use the TAT to assess individual differences, but the TAT has been criticized on the basis of its poor reliability (Entwistle, 1972; Fineman, 1977). Fineman (1977) observed that TAT scores were neither stable over time nor correlated with other measures of the social needs. Entwistle (1972) showed that the TAT had low reliability on several indices, including retest reliability, split-half reliability, equivalent forms, and internal consistency. Defenders of the TAT acknowledge that the fantasy-based measure has low reliability, but they do not see low reliability as such a stumbling block (Atkinson, Bongort, & Price, 1977; McClelland, 1980). The TAT test taker writes short stories for many different pictures (or sentences) that are meant to arouse different motives. Some scenes, for instance, typically arouse achievement themes (e.g., "At the end of the day, Mark is going back to the office"), whereas other scenes typically arouse affiliation themes (e.g., "A young man is talking about something important with an older person"). When one considers that the TAT pictures constantly change, low reliability is to be expected, because by design the test changes the stream of the test taker's imagination. The real test of the TAT's usefulness concerns its validity—can the TAT predict what people do and how people behave (e.g., McClelland, 1980)? This chapter shows that it can.

A second troublesome aspect of the TAT (besides low reliability) is that it is a labor-intensive job to score the story protocols written by the test takers (i.e., imagine scoring 5 protocols for 100 individuals). Excellent scoring manuals do exist, however, and I recommend the following: for achievement, see McClelland et al. (1958); for affiliation, see Heyns, Veroff, and Atkinson (1958); for intimacy, see McAdams (1980); for power, see Winter (1973); and for additional social needs, see Smith (1992). In the attempt to measure social needs in a way that is reliable and more convenient to administer and score, researchers have developed many self-report measures (e.g., see Edwards, 1959; Gough, 1964; Hermans, 1970; Jackson, 1974; Lindgren, 1976; Mehrabian, 1968; Mehrabian & Bank, 1975). The self-report measure that is particularly reliable, valid, and well constructed is Jackson's measure (Anastasi, 1982; Clarke, 1973; Harper, 1975; Wortruba & Price, 1975). Like the TAT, Jackson's scales are based on Murray's theory of needs, and the scales have proven themselves useful as an empirical measure of social needs (e.g., Costa & McCrae, 1988; Harackiewicz, Sansone, & Manderlink, 1985). The TAT defenders counterargue that social motives are largely unconscious and people therefore necessarily have difficulty in reporting these strivings accurately on a questionnaire. Rather than reporting actual social motives on a questionnaire, test takers often report a distorted view of themselves, a view of self that is more socially desirable than it is accurate.

Acquiring the Social Needs for Achievement, Affiliation, Intimacy, and Power

Human beings acquire social needs through experience, development, and socialization. In an extensive investigation, one group of researchers sought to determine the child-rearing antecedents of adult needs for achievement, affiliation, and power (McClelland & Pilon, 1983). Raters initially scored the parental practices of mothers and fathers of 78 five-year-old boys and girls. When the children grew to age 31, the researchers administered a TAT to each to assess their social needs as adults. Only a few child-rearing antecedents emerged as significant, but the few that did emerge illustrate some of the early origins of social needs. Adults high in the need for achievement generally had parents who used a strict feeding schedule and severe toilet training practices. Adults high in the need for affiliation generally had parents who used praise (rather than authority or coercion) as a socialization technique. Adults high in the need for power generally had parents who were permissive about sex and aggression (i.e., permissive about masturbation, sex play, fighting with siblings, fighting back with parents).

In adulthood, social contexts continue to shape the development and change of the social needs. For instance, some occupations are more congenial to achievement than are others, because they provide opportunities for moderate challenges, independent work with personal responsibility, and rapid performance feedback. People in achievement-congenial occupations (e.g., entrepreneurs) show marked increases in their achievement strivings over the years compared to people in achievementnoncongenial occupations (e.g., nursing; Jenkins 1987). As to developing power strivings, workers in jobs that require assertiveness (e.g., sales) show increases in the need for power over the years (Veroff et al., 1980).

Social needs are acquired emotional and behavioral potentials that are activated by particular situational incentives (Atkinson, 1982; McClelland, 1985). That is, when an incentive associated with a particular need is present (e.g., a date is an intimacy incentive, an inspirational speech is a power incentive), the person high in that particular social need experiences emotional and behavioral activation. These activation potentials are learned early in childhood (e.g., McClelland & Pilon, 1983) and continue to change throughout adulthood by virtue of training (McClelland & Winter, 1969), occupational demands and opportunities (Jenkins, 1987), and other socializing forces. Acquired experience socializes each of us to experience positive emotional reactions in response to some incentives rather than others. An opportunity for objective performance feedback might make the achievement-needing individual feel hope and seek challenges whereas a person high in the need for affiliation might experience positive emotion and approach behavior not in response to performance feedback incentives but, instead, to an opportunity to establish a close relationship.

Each social need becomes associated with a particular environmental incentive that arouses emotional and behavioral potentials. The environmental incentive that activates each of the four social needs is as follows (from McClelland, 1985):

- For achievement, the need-activating incentive is doing something well to show personal competence.
- For affiliation, the need-activating incentive is an opportunity to please others and gain their approval.
- For intimacy, the need-activating incentive is a warm, secure attachment.
- For power, the need-activating incentive is having impact on others.

How Social Needs Motivate Behavior

Social needs energize behavior differently from other needs. Physiological and organismic psychological needs energize the individual to seek out and interact with need-satisfying opportunities in the environment. Hunger (a physiological need) initiates an exploratory search for food. Competence (an organismic psychological need) initiates an exploratory search for optimal challenges. Social needs, in contrast, produce motivation that is more reactive than proactive. Social needs produce an energetic (emotional and physiological) reaction when need-satisfying incentives appear. With social needs, people learn the incentive value (positive or negative) of objects and events in the environment, and when these objects and events appear, individuals react to them to different degrees. For one person a test might bring fear and avoidance whereas a school dance might bring hope and approach; yet another person might fear and avoid the dance but not the test. The person's socialization, or developmental history, teaches the incentive value of environmental events and objects, and social needs energize a reactive motivational force either to approach or avoid them.

Social needs are mostly, but not exclusively, reactive sources of motivation.

People learn rather quickly which incentives are associated with what sort of environments and situations. That is, people learn that particular occupations, organizations, recreational events, and so on are primarily opportunities to do well and demonstrate personal competence, or to please others and gain their approval, or to participate in a warm and secure relationships, or to have an impact on others. Thus, people rely on knowledge of their social needs to interact with the environment in a proactive way. The person high in achievement strivings enters business as an entrepreneur, the person high in power strivings takes up a hobby that permits influencing others, and so on.

ACHIEVEMENT

The need for achievement is the desire to do well relative to a standard of excellence. It motivates people to seek "success in competition with a standard of excellence" (McClelland et al., 1953, pp. 110–111). *Standard of excellence* is, however, a broad term, as standards of excellence encompass competitions with a task (e.g., solving a jigsaw puzzle or writing a persuasive essay); competitions with the self (e.g., running a race in a personal best time or improving one's GPA); or competitions against others (e.g., winning a competition or becoming the class valedictorian) (Heckhausen, 1967). While including task-related, self-related, and other-related standards of excellence, achievement situations have in common those instances in which the person knows that his or her performance will lead to either a favorable or unfavorable evaluation that can serve as the basis of an evaluation of personal competence.

When facing standards of excellence, people's emotional reactions vary. Individuals high in the need for achievement generally respond with approach-oriented emotions such as hope, pride, and gratification from a job well done. Individuals low in the need for achievement generally respond with avoidance-oriented emotions such as anxiety, defensiveness, and the fear of failure. People's behavioral responses to standards of excellence also vary. When confronted with an opportunity to engage in a task featuring a clear standard of excellence, people show differences in choice (to engage the task or not), latency (how long before they begin the task), effort (intense vs. lackadaisical), persistence (how long performance continues once begun), and the willingness to take personal responsibility for successes and failures (e.g., Cooper, 1983). High-need achievers, compared to low-need achievers, choose moderately difficult to difficult versions of tasks instead of easy versions (Kuhl & Blankenship, 1979; Slade & Rush, 1991); quickly engage in achievement-related tasks rather than procrastinate or avoid them (Blankenship, 1987); show more effort and better performance on moderately difficult tasks (because pride energizes high-need achievers whereas fear debilitates low achievers; Karabenick & Yousseff, 1968; Raynor & Entin, 1982); persist more in the face of difficulty and failure on moderately difficult tasks (Feather, 1961, 1963); and take a personal responsibility for successes and failures (rather than seeking help or advice from others; Weiner, 1980).

Origins of the Need for Achievement

As discussed earlier, researchers set out decades ago on a journey to discover the roots of children's need for achievement in parenting style and in social learning opportunities. The hope was to explain the social determinants of the high- versus low-need achiever's personality. As research progressed, it became increasing clear that the need for achievement was a multifaceted phenomenon steeped not in a single process but in a host of social, cognitive, and developmental processes.

1, **SOCIALIZATION INFLUENCES.** Part of the development of achievement strivings revolves around the contribution that parental and social influences play in socializing a child toward a strong need for achievement (Heckhausen, 1967; McClelland & Pilon, 1983). Research on socialization influences showed that children develop relatively strong achievement strivings when their parents provide independence training (e.g., self-reliance, autonomy), high performance aspirations, realistic standards of excellence (Rosen & D'Andrade, 1959; Winterbottom, 1958), high ability self-concepts (e.g., "This task will be easy for you"), endorse a positive value for achievement-related pursuits (Eccles-Parsons, Adler, & Kaczala, 1982), explicit standards for excellence (Trudewind, 1982), a home environment rich in stimulation potential (e.g., books to read), a wide scope of experience such as traveling, and exposure to children's readers rich in achievement imagery (e.g., *The Little Engine That Could*; deCharms & Moeller, 1962). In the end, however, this effort to identify the childhood socialization practices of high-need achievers was only partly successful, largely because longitudinal findings began to show that achievement strivings change a great deal from childhood to adulthood and that adult achievement strivings were mostly unreliable from one decade to the next (Jenkins, 1987; Maehr & Kleiber, 1980).

2. **COGNITIVE INFLUENCES.** Some (but certainly not all) researchers have given up on the idea that people develop enduring achievement-related personalities and, instead, have turned their attention to the study of the cognitive underpinnings of what appears to be an achievement-based way of thinking. Researchers soon found that some ways of thinking are more achievement related than are others—namely, perceptions of high ability, adoption of a mastery orientation, high expectations for success, strong valuing of achievement tasks, and an optimistic attributional style. Perceptions of high ability facilitate both task persistence (Felson, 1984; Phillips, 1984) and competent performances on those tasks (Hansford & Hattie, 1982; Marsh, 1990). A mastery orientation (compared to a helpless orientation; chapter 8) leads people to choose moderately difficult tasks and to respond to difficulty with increased rather than with decreased effort (Dweck, 1986; Elliot & Dweck, 1988). Expectations for success breed approach-oriented behaviors such as seeking out and participating in optimal challenges (Eccles, 1984a) and performing well (Eccles, 1984b; Volmer, 1986). Valuing achievement in a particular domain predicts displays of achievement-related persistence in that domain (Eccles, 1984b; Ethington, 1991). An optimistic attributional style (attributing success to the self and attributing fail-

ure to outside causes; chapter 10) fosters the positive emotions of hope and pride following successes and keeps at bay the negative emotions of fear and anxiety (Weiner, 1985, 1986). Thus, conditions in the home, school, gymnasium, workplace, and therapeutic setting that work to promote high perceptions of ability, a mastery orientation, expectations for success, valuing of achievement, and an optimistic attributional style of achievement-related outcomes provide the cognitive soil to cultivate strong and persistent achievement behavior.

3. **DEVELOPMENTAL INFLUENCES.** The effect of different ways of thinking on achievement behavior led researchers to study how these cognitive differences develop over the life span. Hence, researchers focused their attention on the developmental components of the cognitive underpinnings of the need for achievement (Heckhausen, 1982; Parsons & Ruble, 1977; Ruble et al., 1992; Stipek, 1984; Weiner, 1979). One such framework is that of Stipek (1984), who outlined the developmental course of (1) achievement-related beliefs, (2) valuing of achievement-related activities, and (3) achievement-related emotions of pride and shame.

As to the developmental course of achievement-related beliefs, young children are notoriously amateur in estimating their actual abilities; they hold unrealistically lofty ability beliefs (Nicholls, 1979; Stipek, 1984), do not lower their ability beliefs following failures (Parsons & Ruble, 1977), and ignore their poor performance in relation to the strong performance of others (Ruble, Parsons, & Ross, 1976). Throughout middle childhood, children increasingly compare their performance to the performance of others, and by late childhood children rely on the full gamut of information that allows them to construct realistic perceptions of their abilities: self-evaluations, peer evaluations, teacher evaluations, and parental evaluations (Felson, 1984; Nicholls, 1978, 1979; Rosenholtz & Rosenholtz, 1981; Ruble et al., 1992; Stipek, 1984). As to the developmental course of valuing achievement-related endeavors, young children care much about approval (being thought good), but they care little about achievement per se (Stipek, 1984). The three strongest sources of developing a valuing of achievement for its own sake emanate from parental attitudes that place a high value on achievement (Eccles-Parsons, Adler & Kaczala, 1982), occupational utility that gives a sense of meaning or purpose to work-related achievements (Waterman, 1988), and an internalization of the importance or significance of a particular task or skill (Ryan & Connell, 1989). As to the developmental course of pride and shame, children are not born with pride or shame as innate emotions. Instead, each emerges from social experiences and consequences. Pride arises from the social implications of the tendency to approach success and from environmental mastery episodes; shame arises from the social implications of the tendency to avoid failure and from being ridiculed for it (Stipek, 1983).

Atkinson's Model of Achievement Behavior

Atkinson (1957, 1964) argued that the need for achievement only partly predicts achievement behavior. Achievement behavior depends not only on the need for achievement but also on the probability of success at a task and the incentive value for succeeding at that task. For Atkinson, probability of success and incentive value for succeeding were situationally determined. That is, some tasks had high probabilities for success whereas others had low probabilities, and some tasks offered greater incentive for success than did others. For instance, consider the classes you are presently taking. Each course has its own probability of success (e.g., a senior-level advanced calculus course is generally harder than an introductory-level physical education class) and its own incentive for success (e.g., doing well in a course in your major would be more important than doing well in a course irrelevant to your major).

Atkinson's theory features four variables: achievement behavior, the need for achievement, probability of success, and incentive for success. Achievement behavior is defined as the tendency to approach success, abbreviated as Ts. The three determining factors of Ts are (1) the strength of the person's achievement motive (Ms, motive to succeed), (2) the strength of the perceived probability of success (Ps), and (3) the incentive value of success at that particular activity (Is). Atkinson's model is expressed in the following formula: $Ts = Ms \times Ps \times Is$.

TENDENCY TO APPROACH SUCCESS. The first variable in the equation, Ms, corresponds to the person's score on the TAT and represents the strength of the person's need for achievement. Ps is estimated from the perceived difficulty of the task and from the person's perceived ability at that task, such that the Ps of defeating a master at chess is very low whereas the Ps of defeating a child is very high. Atkinson defined Is as equal to $1 - Ps$. If the probability of success is .25, the incentive for success at that task is .75 $(1.00 - .25)$. Thus, the incentive value of beating the chess master is very high (because Ps is low), and the incentive value of beating a child is very low (because Ps is high).

Perhaps an example will help explain Atkinson's theory. Consider two teammates on a high school wrestling team getting ready for a weekly match. One wrestler, who has a strong achievement motive (TAT score = 8), is scheduled to wrestle last year's state champion (Ps = .1) and consequently has a strong incentive to beat the champ (Is = .9). The second wrestler, who has a relatively weak achievement motive (TAT score = 1), is scheduled to wrestle an opponent who is his equal (Ps = .5) and consequently has a moderate incentive to achieve victory (Is = .5). According to Atkinson, the first wrestler's tendency to approach success (Ts) is 0.72 $(8 \times .9 \times .1)$, and the second's tendency to approach success is 0.25 $(1 \times .5 \times .5)$. If the two teammates had equal achievement strivings—say TAT score = 1 for both—Atkinson's theory predicts the greater achievement motivation for the second wrestler (Ts = 0.25 versus Ts = 0.09), because optimal challenge (Ps = .5) provides the richest motivational combination of expectancy of success and incentive for success whereas expecting defeat (Ps = .1) is amotivating despite its strong incentive value.

TENDENCY TO AVOID FAILURE. Atkinson (1957, 1964) assumed that achievement behaviors were guided not only by a tendency to approach success but also by a tendency to avoid failure. For Atkinson, just as people bring a motive to achieve success (Ms) into the achievement setting, so too do they bring a motive to avoid failure (Maf). The tendency to avoid failure motivates the individual to defend against the loss of self-esteem, the loss of social respect, and the fear of social punishment and embarrassment (Birney, Burdick, & Teevan, 1969). Atkinson measured Taf with the Test Anxiety Questionnaire (TAQ, Sarason, 1977), a 23-item self-report questionnaire with questions such as, "During tests I find myself thinking of the consequences of failing." The TAQ assesses anxiety-based avoidance motivations such as evaluation apprehension, defensiveness, and fear. The tendency to avoid failure, abbreviated Taf, is calculated with a formula that parallels that for Ts: Taf = Maf × Pf × If. Maf represents the motive to avoid failure (as scored by the TAQ), Pf represents the probability of failure (which by definition is 1 − Ps), and If represents the negative incentive value for failure (i.e., 1− Pf). Thus, if an individual has a moderate motive to avoid failure (Maf = 5), the tendency to avoid failure against an expert opponent or a difficult task (Pf = .9) can be calculated as 0.45 (i.e., Maf × Pf × If = 5 × .9 × .1 = 0.45).

COMBINED APPROACH AND AVOIDANCE TENDENCIES. Atkinson conceptualized Ms as a force within the person to prefer and to seek out achievement situations, and Maf as a force within the person to escape from (or be anxious and uncomfortable about) achievement situations. Thus, to engage in any achievement task is to enter into a risk-taking dilemma in which the person struggles to find a balance between the attraction of pride, hope, and social respect versus the repulsion of shame, fear, and social humiliation. When Ts is greater than Taf, the person eagerly approaches the opportunity to involve and satisfy the need for achievement. When Taf is greater than Ts, the person bypasses the opportunity to involve and satisfy the need for achievement because other needs (e.g., approval) are more important. Atkinson's complete formula to predict achievement-related behaviors (i.e., choice, latency, effort, persistence) is as follows:

$$T = Ts - Taf = Ms \times Ps \times Is - (Maf \times Pf \times If)$$

Dynamics-of-Action Model

In the dynamics-of-action model, achievement behavior occurs within a "stream of behavior" (Atkinson & Birch, 1970, 1974, 1978). The stream of behavior is determined largely by three forces: instigation, inhibition, and consummation. *Instigation* causes a rise in approach tendencies and occurs by confronting environmental stimuli associated with past reward. Instigation is the same as Ms (and the same as Ts if Ps is held constant). *Inhibition* causes a rise in avoidance tendencies and occurs by confronting environmental stimuli associated with past punishment. Inhibition is the same as Maf (as the same as Taf, if Pf is held constant). *Consummation* refers to the fact that performing an activity brings about its own cessation (e.g., running, eating). Consummation adds a new wrinkle to the understanding of achievement behavior and allows it to be understood as dynamic (changing over time) instead of episodic or static. For instance, your achievement strivings in this course change as the course progresses and as you do well or poorly on tests, study many hours or neglect to study much at all, get interested in other activities, go on vacation, feel depressed, learn something new and exciting about motivation, and so on. The dynamics-of-action model seeks to capture the rise and fall of achievement strivings over time.

The four panels in Figure 6.1 portray achievement behaviors over time (adapted from Blankenship, 1987). Each panel shows the individual's behavioral preference for an achievement task (a task that arouses hope for success and fear of failure) and a nonachievement task. The four panels correspond to different levels of instigatory and inhibitory forces. Panel 1 shows behavior with high instigation and low inhibition (Ms > Maf), panel 2 shows behavior with high levels of both instigation and inhibition (Ms = Maf, and both are high), panel 3 shows behavior with low levels of both instigation and inhibition (Ms = Maf, and both are low), and panel 4 shows behavior with low instigation and high inhibition (Ms < Maf). The panels show that the Ms > Maf individual is the quickest to engage the achievement task, the Ms = Maf (both high) second, the Ms = Maf (both low) third, and the Ms < Maf the slowest.

Once the activity is engaged, that behavioral tendency persists until acted on by

FIGURE 6–1
Streams of Behavior for High and Low Ms and Maf

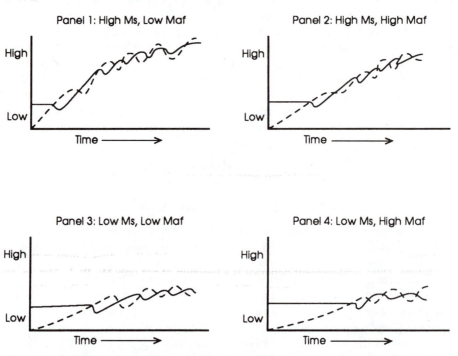

Panel 1: High Ms, Low Maf

Panel 2: High Ms, High Maf

Panel 3: Low Ms, Low Maf

Panel 4: Low Ms, High Maf

SOURCE: Blankenship, V. (1987). A computer-based measure of resultant achievement motivation. *Journal of Personality and Social Psychology, 53,* 361–372. Copyright © by the American Psychological Association. Adapted by permission.
NOTE. Dashed line represents tendency strength to engage the achievement-related task; solid line represents tendency strength of nonachievement task.

some psychological force that either increases or decreases its strength. A psychological force that might increase the achievement tendency would be an extrinsic incentive towards achievement (e.g., a prize); a psychological force that might decrease it would be the aforementioned consummatory force. The four panels in Figure 6.1 show how, in the dynamics-of-action model, the tendencies to pursue the achievement-related and non-achievement-related tasks rise and fall, depending on motive profiles (strengths of Ms and Maf). What is most important are the ideas that (1) latency to initiate an achievement task varies with motive strengths, (i.e., a quick latency is associated with a high MS), (2) persistence on an achievement task varies with motive strengths (i.e., long persistence is associated with a low Maf), (3) tendencies to pursue achievement and nonachievement tasks rise and fall, because of extrinsic incentives and consummatory forces, and (4) achievement behavior occurs within a continual stream of behavior rather than at any one particular time.

Achievement for the Future

Not all achievement situations are alike. Some achievement situations have implications that affect one's future achievement efforts whereas other achievement situations have implications only for the present (Raynor, 1969, 1970, 1974). For example, a track athlete tries to win a race not only to experience the pride of accomplishment for the day, but also to open up opportunities to win races in the future. A win in today's race might lead to invitations to other important track meets, such as the Olympic trials. Further, if the runner can win an invitation to the Olympic trials, there might be the opportunity to win a race in the Olympic games. Thus, the future possibility of being invited to Olympic trials and the future possibility of winning an Olympic race add to the runner's motivation to win today's race.

Future achievement orientation refers to an individual's psychological distance from a long-term achievement goal (e.g., winning a race in the Olympics). According to Raynor, psychological distance is a negative function of the probability of reaching that future goal. Perceived psychological distance from a long-term goal is determined by two factors (Gjesme, 1981): (1) the time (in hours, days, years) between the present and the future attainment of the goal and (2) a personality disposition. Thus, as the goal approaches, arousal of the achievement motive increases; and some individuals find greater incentives in the future while others find greater incentives in the present. The importance of Raynor's future orientation is that, other things being equal, any achievement goal perceived far away in time receives less weight than does a goal in the very near future. Thus, achievement behavior is a function of not only Ms, Ps, Is, Maf, Pf, and If, but also whether the achievement will lead toward some future goal. From this point of view, achievement behavior is a series of steps in a path (Gjesme, 1981).

Conditions That Involve and Satisfy the Need for Achievement

Four situations are particularly noteworthy for their ability to involve and satisfy the need for achievement: moderately difficult tasks, failure, competition, and entrepreneurship (e.g., McClelland, 1985).

PEAK PERFORMANCE AT MODERATELY CHALLENGING TASKS. High-need achievers outperform low-need achievers on tasks that they are told are of intermediate difficulty. Highs do not, however, outperform lows on tasks designated as either easy or difficult (Karabénick & Yousseff, 1968; Raynor & Entin, 1982). Performance on a moderately difficult task offers the high achiever a set of positive emotional and cognitive incentives that the low achiever does not experience. Emotionally, moderately difficult tasks provide an arena that best tests the high achiever's skill and ability and therefore best cultivates emotions like pride and a feeling of a job well done. Cognitively, moderately difficult tasks provide an arena for the high-need achiever to diagnosis level of ability. The stronger a person's need for achievement, the stronger the tendency to seek information about one's abilities (Trope, 1983). Increased information about our abilities effectively decreases uncertainty about achievement outcomes (Trope, 1975; Trope & Brickman, 1975). Hence, moderately challenging tasks provide an inviting mixture of pride from success and diagnosticity of important abilities.

FAILURE. High-need achievers are generally motivated by failure, whereas low-need achievers are generally motivated by success (Feather, 1961, 1963; Littig, 1963). This is so because high-need achievers prefer to engage in moderately difficult challenges whereas low-need achievers prefer to avoid them. Thus, following success, especially repeated success at the same task, high-need achievers quit the task because it can no longer provide them with much of an arena for positive emotions or skill diagnosis (i.e., it is no longer an opportunity to involve and satisfy their need for achievement). In contrast, low-need achievers find success a relatively safe, nonthreatening situation so they willingly persist so long as the success feedback persists. Following failure, especially repeated failure at the same task, high-need achievers show enduring persistence as their expectations for success fall from high ("Sure, I can solve that puzzle") to more moderate ("I'm not so sure I can solve it; it's a 50/50 chance"). Low-need achievers, who start off with lower expectancies for success in the first place, find failure amotivating as expectancies for success fall from moderate to low.

COMPETITION. Interpersonal competition is a situational event that captures much of the risk-taking dilemma involved in achievement settings. It generally promotes positive emotion and approach behavior in high-need achievers, but negative emotion and avoidance behaviors in low-need achievers (Covington & Omelich, 1984; Epstein & Harackiewicz, 1992; Reeve, Olson, & Cole, 1987). High-need achievers enter competitive situations because they welcome the opportunity to test their skills and see doing well as a personally important thing to do, relative to low-need achievers (Epstein & Harackiewicz, 1992; Harackiewicz, Sansone, & Manderlink, 1985). High-need achievers also focus on competition's potential to diagnose their abilities and on the positive feedback a favorable outcome can provide, whereas the competitive situation's inherent evaluative pressures outweigh such potential benefits for low-need achievers (Epstein & Harackiewicz, 1992). These findings suggest that competition represents the sort of task that high-need achievers respond to in a positive way. Consider that high achievers seek diagnostic ability assessment and feedback (Trope, 1975), value competence for its own sake (Harackiewicz & Manderlink, 1984), are attracted to activities that allow for self-evaluation (Kuhl, 1978) and opportunities to demonstrate or prove their ability (Harackiewicz & Elliot, 1993). Competition often offers all these attributes and is therefore attractive to high-need achievers (Harackiewicz & Elliot, 1993).

ENTREPRENEURSHIP. McClelland (1965, 1987) finds that high-need achievers often display the behavioral pattern of entrepreneurship. McClelland assessed the need for achievement in a group of college students and checked their occupational choices 14 years later. Each occupation was classified as either entrepreneurial (e.g., founder of own business, sales, stockbroker) or not entrepreneurial (e.g., office manager, service personnel). Eighty-three per cent of the entrepreneurs had scored as high-need achievers years earlier; 79% of the nonentrepreneurs had scored as low-need achievers. Entrepreneurship appeals to the high-need achiever because it requires certain achievement-oriented behavior: for example, taking moderate risks and assuming responsibility for one's successes and failures. Also, entrepreneurship provides concrete, rapid performance feedback (e.g., costs and profits, gains and losses, and daily changes in the stock market, which are attractive to the high-need achiever) and opportunities to show high initiative and exploratory behavior.

Beyond entrepreneurship, some occupations are more congenial to involving and satisfying the need for achievement than are other occupations (Jenkins, 1987). High-need achievers prefer occupations that offer challenge, personal responsibility, and rapid performance feedback, because these aspects of work combine to define an explicit standard of excellence for the worker in which to best diagnose skills, abilities, and rates of improvement (Atkinson, 1981; Jenkins, 1987; McClelland, 1961, 1980; Trope & Brickman, 1975). On the other side of the coin, low-need achievers do not necessarily enjoy occupations rich in challenge, personal responsibility, and rapid feedback, as such ego-involving conditions are more likely to conjure up more anxiety and behavioral avoidance than hope and behavioral approach (Covington & Omelich, 1984).

AFFILIATION AND INTIMACY

In its early study, the need for affiliation was defined as manifesting itself via "establishing, maintaining, or restoring a positive, affective relationship with another person or persons" (Atkinson, Heyns, & Veroff, 1954). According to these authors, the need for affiliation is not the same construct as extraversion, friendliness, or sociability. In fact, the early investigators noted that persons high in the need for affiliation were often less popular than persons low in affiliative strivings (Atkinson, Heyns, & Veroff, 1954; Crowne & Marlowe, 1964; Shipley & Veroff, 1952). Rather than being rooted in extraversion and popularity, the need for affiliation has its roots in a fear of interpersonal rejection (Heckhausen, 1980). High-need affiliators interact with others to avoid negative emotions such as fear of disapproval and loneliness and typically experience much anxiety in their relationships. As they try to calm their anxieties, high-need affiliators monitor whether others disapprove of them and they spend time seeking reassurance from others, a pattern of behavior that unfortunately tends to make them rather unpopular. The need for affiliation, then, can be thought of as the need for approval, social acceptance, and security in interpersonal relations.

The more contemporary view of affiliative strivings is that the social need has two facets—the need for approval and the need for intimacy. The contemporary dual view of affiliative strivings answers the criticism that the former conceptualization of need for affiliation was too heavy on rejection anxiety and too light on affiliative interest, the more positive aspect of the need for affiliation (Boyatzis, 1973; McAdams, 1980).

McAdams (1980, 1982a, 1982b; McAdams & Constantian, 1983; McAdams, Healy, & Kraus, 1984) answered Boyatzis' call for a more positive conceptualization of affiliative strivings by focusing attention on the intimacy motive, the social motive to engage in warm, close, positive interpersonal relations that hold little fear of rejection. The intimacy motive reflects a concern for the quality of one's social involvements. It is not so much the need to be with others as it is a willingness to "experience a warm, close, and communicative exchange with another person" (McAdams, 1980). Table 6.2 shows a profile of high intimacy motivation. An individual with high intimacy motivation thinks frequently about friends and relationships; writes imaginative stories about the positive affect in relationships; engages in self-disclosure, intense listening, and frequent conversations; names love and dialogue as especially meaningful life experiences; is rated by others as warm, loving, sincere, and nondominant; and tends to remember episodes of interpersonal interactions.

The full picture of affiliative strivings includes a theoretical conceptualization that includes both its positive aspects—the need to engage in warm, close, positive

TABLE 6–2

Profile of High Intimacy Motivation

CATEGORY	DESCRIPTION
Thoughts	Of friends, of relationships
TAT Themes	Relationships produce positive affect, reciprocal dialogue between two people, expression of relationship commitment and union, and expression of interpersonal harmony
Interaction Style	Self-disclosure Intense listening habits Many conversations
Autobiography	Themes of love and dialogue are mentioned as personally significant life experiences
Peer Ratings	Individual is judged to be warm, loving, sincere, nondominant
Memory	Enhanced recall with stories involving themes of interpersonal interactions

relations—and its negative aspects—the anxious need to establish, maintain, and restore interpersonal relations. These positive and negative aspects of affiliative strivings affect the extent to which people live happy, well-adjusted lives. One group of researchers, for instance, assessed young adults' needs for affiliation and intimacy (with the TAT) and found that almost two decades later the men previously high in the need for intimacy were better adjusted—happier and better-adjusted in work, marriage, and so on—than were men low in the need for intimacy (McAdams & Vaillant, 1982). The need for affiliation did not predict who was or was not well adjusted nearly two decades later. There seems to be a real growth quality to the need for intimacy, a quality that is mostly absent in the need for affiliation.

Conditions That Involve and Satisfy the Need for Affiliation and Intimacy

Depriving people of the opportunity for interaction with others is the principal condition that involves the need for affiliation (McClelland, 1985). Conditions such as loneliness, rejection, and separation raise people's desire or need to be with other people. Hence, the need for affiliation expresses itself as a deficiency-oriented motive (the deficiency being a lack of opportunity for social interaction). Intimacy involvement centers around conditions that allow opportunities for interpersonal caring and concern, interpersonal warmth and commitment, emotional connectedness, reciprocal dialogue, joy and congeniality, and love (McAdams, 1980). The need for intimacy expresses itself as growth-oriented motive (the growth opportunity being progress toward enriching relationships). In the words of Maslow (1987), involvement and satisfaction of the need for affiliation revolves around "deprivation-love," whereas involvement and satisfaction of the need for intimacy revolves around "being-love."

FEAR AND ANXIETY. Social isolation and fear-arousing conditions are two situations that increase a person's desire to affiliate with others (Baumeister & Leary, 1995; Schachter, 1959). Under conditions of isolation and fear, people report being jittery and tense, feel as if they are suffering and in pain, and see themselves as going to pieces. To reduce or eliminate such anxiety and fear, human beings typically adopt the strategy of seeking out others (Rofé, 1984). When afraid, people desire to affiliate for emotional support and to see how others handle the emotions they feel from the fear object. For example, imagine camping out in the wilderness and hearing a sudden loud noise in the middle of the night. The sudden, unexplained noise might produce fear, and you would likely seek out others for physical and emotional support and to see if they seemed as afraid of the potential danger as you.

Schachter (1959) tested the proposed fear-affiliation relationship. He created two experimental conditions, one of high anxiety and one of low anxiety. All participants were told that they were about to receive some electric shocks (the fear object) as part of an experiment. The experimenter told participants in the high-anxiety group that they were going to receive intense shocks: "These shocks will hurt, they will be painful"; the experimenter told participants in the low-anxiety group that they were going to receive very mild shocks that "will not in any way be painful" and would feel more like a tickle than a shock. After alerting the participants that they would soon be shocked, the experimenter announced that there would be a 10-minute wait; the participants were asked if they (1) preferred to wait alone, (2) preferred to wait with another participant, or (3) had no preference. The study's dependent variable was whether the participant preferred to wait alone or to affiliate with others, and, of course, no participant was ever shocked. Two-thirds of the high-anxiety participants preferred to affiliate during the wait period, whereas only one-third of the low-anxiety participants sought affiliation. A second investigation found that anxious people's desire to affiliate applied only to those instances in which the cohort shared the cause of the anxiety. Hence the old adage misery loves company must be qualified as misery loves miserable company. The popularity of mutual support groups for alcoholics, unwed mothers, patients suffering a particular illness, and people facing particular adjustment problems provides some confirming testimony to the human tendency to seek out similar others when troubled or anxious. Simply talking to similar others, being exposed to calm role models, and being distracted from thinking about the fear object (e.g., telling a joke) are strategies by which affiliating with others can reduce anxiety (Epley, 1974). Interestingly, if others cannot be expected to reduce our anxiety, we prefer to be alone (Rofé, 1984).

The reason threat, and therefore feelings of fear and anxiety, increases the desire to affiliate is partly an emotional sharing function (misery loves miserable company), but mostly affiliation desires serve cognitive clarity purposes (Kulik, Mahler, & Earnest, 1994). A cognitive clarity explanation argues that people facing threat desire to affiliate with others to get information that will allow them the opportunity to interpret the situation and to faciliate their coping strategies and responses (Kirkpatrick & Shaver, 1988).

EMBARRASSMENT. Whereas anxiety increases affiliative strivings, embarrassment decreases them. Imagine a study in which participants were told that they would be asked to disclose their innermost private feelings, personal inadequacies, and fears to strangers while their truthfulness was monitored by a lie detector (Teichman, 1973). Participants in a second group were told that they were to engage in normal, natural conversation on enjoyable topics. In addition to this high versus low anxiety manipulation, the study added a high versus low embarrassment manipulation. Participants in the high-embarrassment group were asked to use objects of oral gratification such as baby bottles, pacifiers, breast shields, and lollipops so the experimenter could ostensibly determine their physiological responsiveness to oral gratification. Participants in the low-embarrassment group were given essentially the same story, except the objects of oral gratification were neutral and not embarrassing, such as a whistle and a balloon. When made to feel anxious, people generally preferred to wait with another person (90% versus 75%), but when made to feel embarrassed, fewer people preferred to wait with another (60% versus 77%). Thus, anxiety increased and embarrassment decreased affiliative strivings.

DEVELOPMENT OF INTERPERSONAL RELATIONSHIPS. In an apparent effort to initiate new friendships, persons with a high need for intimacy join more social groups, spend more of their time interacting with others, and, when friendships are started, form more stable, long-lasting relationships than do persons with a low need for intimacy (McAdams & Losoff, 1984). As relationships develop, individuals with a high need for intimacy come to know more personal information and history about their friends (McAdams & Losoff, 1984; McAdams, Healy, & Krause, 1984). In addition, as relationships develop (e.g., roommates or teammates meet and might or might not become friends), individuals with a high need for intimacy report being more and more satisfied as their relationships progress whereas individuals with a low need for intimacy report being less and less satisfied with their developing relationships (Eidelson, 1980). Individuals with a high need for intimacy perceive the tightening bonds of friendships as satisfying whereas those with a low need perceive the tightening bonds of friendship as stifling and as emotional entrapment.

MAINTAINING INTERPERSONAL NETWORKS. Once a relationship has been established, individuals with a high need for affiliation (but not necessarily for intimacy) make an effort to maintain those relationships by making more telephone calls, writing more letters, and paying more visits to their friends than do those with a low need for affiliation (Lansing & Heyns, 1959). They also spend more time in telephone conversations (Boyatzis, 1972). Those with a high need for intimacy spend more time writing letters and participating in face-to-face conversations, compared to those with a low need for intimacy (McAdams & Constantian, 1983).

One study asked persons with high and low needs for intimacy to keep a logbook that described ten 15 to 20 minute friendship episodes that occurred over a two-month period (McAdams, Healy, & Krause, 1984). Those with a high need for intimacy reported more dyadic (versus larger group) friendship episodes, more self-disclosure, more listening, and more trust and concern for the well-being of their friends. Such a finding underscores the high-intimacy-need person's want of a warm and personal (i.e., intimate) friendship pattern. Even when thinking and talking about strangers, high-intimacy-need persons treat others differently from lows in that they use more positive adjectives when describing others and they avoid talking about others in negative terms (McClelland, Constantian, Pilon, & Stone, 1982). In the area of values, persons with a high need for affiliation give higher ratings to the values of a world at peace and true friendship than do lows, values that express a need for interpersonal harmony (Rokeach, 1973). In regard to how satisfying they find their interpersonal relations, high-intimacy-need persons laugh, smile, and make eye contact with others during interaction more frequently than do low-intimacy-need persons (McAdams, Jackson, & Kirshnit, 1984). Such laughing, smiling, and eye contact behaviors lead others to rate high-intimacy-need persons as relatively warm, sincere, and loving human beings (McAdams & Losoff, 1984). Gender also moderates the relationship between the need for affiliation and its satisfaction. Highly affiliative boys and girls both report wishing to be with their friends, but girls actually spend more time with their friends than do boys such that highly affiliative girls generally report a positive day-to-day mood whereas highly affiliative boys generally report a negative (need-frustrated) day-to-day mood (Wong & Csikszentmihalyi, 1991).

SATISFYING THE NEED FOR AFFILIATION. Because it is largely a deficit-oriented motive, the need for affiliation when satisfied brings emotions of relief rather than joy. When interacting with others, people high in the need for affiliation go out of their way to avoid conflict (Exline, 1962), avoid competitive situations (Terhune, 1968), are unselfish and cooperative (McAdams, 1980), avoid talking about others in a negative way (McClelland, 1985), and they resist making imposing commands on others to do certain things for them (McAdams & Powers, 1981). Highly affiliative individuals also prefer careers that provide positive relationships and support for others (the helping professions; Sid & Lindgren, 1981), and they perform especially well under conditions that support their need to be accepted and included (McKeachie, Lin, Milholland, & Issacson, 1966). When told that others will be evaluating them, people high in the need for affiliation experience relatively high levels of anxiety via a fear of rejection (Byrne, 1961). Social acceptance, approval, and reassurance, then, constitute the need-satisfying conditions of people high in the need for affiliation.

SATISFYING THE NEED FOR INTIMACY. Because it is largely a growth-oriented motive, people satisfy the need for intimacy through achieving closeness and warmth in a relationship. Hence, people high in the need for intimacy more frequently touch others (in a nonthreatening way; McAdams & Powers, 1981), successfully cultivate deeper and more meaningful relationships (McAdams & Losoff, 1984), find satisfaction in listening and in self-disclosure (McAdams, Healey, & Krause, 1984), and participate in more looking, laughing, and smiling during interaction (McAdams, Jackson, & Kirshnit, 1984). Achieving a high-quality relationship, then, constitutes the need-satisfying condition of people high in the need for intimacy.

POWER

The essence of the need for power is desire to make the material and social world conform to one's personal image or plan for it (Winter & Stewart, 1978). People high in the need for power desire to have "impact, control, or influence over another person, group, or the world at large." (Winter, 1973). Impact allows power-needing individuals to initiate and establish power, control allows for power to be maintained, and influence allows them to expand or restore power. Such power strivings often center around a need for dominance, reputation, status, or position. When asked to recall the peak experiences in their lives, for instance, individuals high in the need for power report so-called power peak experiences, life events associated with strong positive emotions that occurred as a result of their impact on others, such as being elected or receiving applause from an audience (McAdams, 1982b).

Winter (1973) provides two scenarios that illustrate power strivings. In one scenario, research participants watched a film of a power figure giving an influential speech (John F. Kennedy's presidential inaugural address), and in the second they watched a powerful figure in action—a hypnotist ordering students to behave in particular ways as an audience watched. After having his participants view one of these two scenarios, Winter asked each to complete a TAT to score for the arousal of power strivings. These participants scored higher in power strivings than did a comparison group who did not view the scenarios of leadership and influence (Winter, 1973). Others have performed experiments that essentially replicated this procedure, but in addition to measuring power strivings they added measures of mood and physiological arousal (Steele, 1977). As power-needing research participants listened to inspirational speeches, their moods became significantly more lively and energetic and their physiological arousal (measured by epinephrine, or adrenaline) showed a striking increase. Based on these findings, the opportunity to involve one's power strivings fills the power-needing individual with a vigor that can be measured via mood and psychophysiological activation (Steele, 1977).

Conditions That Involve and Satisfy the Need for Power

Four conditions are particularly noteworthy in their capacity to involve and satisfy the need for power: leadership, aggressiveness, influential occupations, and prestige possessions.

LEADERSHIP AND RELATIONSHIPS: RECOGNITION IN SMALL GROUPS.

Persons with a high need for power seek recognition in groups and find ways to make themselves visible to others, apparently in an effort to attain power or influence (Winter, 1973). Power-seeking college students, for example, write more letters to the university newspaper, and power-seeking adults willingly take risks to achieve public visibility (McClelland & Teague, 1975; McClelland & Watson, 1973). They are also more likely to put in hours at a public radio station, presumably in pursuit of an impact on an audience of listeners (Sonnenfield, 1974, cited in McClelland, 1985). They are also more willing to argue with a professor and relatively eager to get their points across in the classroom (Veroff, 1957). In selecting their friends and co-workers, power-striving individuals generally prefer others who are not well known and are thus in a position to be led (Fodor & Farrow, 1979; Winter, 1973). When hanging out with their friends, they prefer small groups over dyads and an interpersonal orientation that takes on more of a tone of influence and organization than it does intimacy (McAdams, Healey, & Krause, 1984). In dating relationships, power-striving men generally fare poorly (Stewart & Rubin, 1976). In marriage, power-striving men generally make poor husbands, at least from the spouse's point of view (McClelland et al., 1978). In both dating and marriage, power-striving women do not suffer the same poor outcomes that men do, apparently because they resist using interpersonal relationships as an arena to satisfy their power needs (Winter, 1988).

To test the influence of the need for power on tendencies toward leadership, experimenters arranged to have a group of strangers interact with each other for a short time (after completing the TAT to identify individual needs for power; Fodor & Smith, 1982; Jones, 1969, cited in McClelland, 1985; Winter & Stewart, 1978). Power-seeking individuals talked more, were judged to have influenced the others the most, and were rated as those who most encouraged the others to participate. However, the power-seeking individuals were not the best liked, nor were they judged to have contributed the most to getting the job done or for coming to a satisfactory conclusion. In fact, groups that had power-seeking leaders were the ones that produced the poorest decisions. These groups exchanged less information, considered few alternative strategies, and reached poorer final decisions than did groups with a leader low in the need for power. These findings suggest that power-seeking leaders attempt to make others follow their personal plan, though their assertiveness and leadership style can sometimes be detrimental to group functioning.

AGGRESSIVENESS. If power strivings revolve around desires for impact, control, or influence over others, aggression ought to be a means to both involve and satisfy power needs. To some extent the relationship between power strivings and aggression holds true, as men high in power strivings get into more arguments and participate more frequently in competitive sports (McClelland, 1975; Winter, 1973). However, the relationship between power strivings and aggression is diluted because society largely controls and inhibits people's acts of overt aggression. For this reason, aggressive manifestations of the need for power largely express themselves as impulses to (rather than acts of) aggression. Individuals with a high, compared to low, need for power, both males and females, report significantly more impulses to act aggressively (McClelland, 1975). Also, consider the question, "Have you ever felt like carrying out the following: yelling at someone in traffic, throwing things around the room, destroying furniture or breaking glassware, or insulting clerks in stores?" Power-seeking individuals report significantly more impulses to carry out these acts (Boyatzis, 1973). When asked if they had actually carried out such behaviors, those with a high need for power did not act on their impulses any more or less than did those with a low need.

Societal inhibitions and restraints largely constrain the power-seeking person's expression of aggression, but when societal inhibitions are forgone, power-seeking men are more aggressive than men with a low need for power (McClelland, 1975; McClelland, Davis, Kalin, & Wanner, 1972; Winter, 1973). Alcohol is one means of a socially acceptable release from societal inhibitions, and power-seeking men do indeed act relatively more aggressively after drinking (McClelland et al., 1972). Alcohol likely contributes to individuals' aggressiveness, however, by making them feel more powerful. Similarly, because men get feelings of power from drinking, men with the highest need for power drink the most (McClelland et al., 1972). This research suggests that people can not only increase power through reputation, prestige, and leadership, but they can also create the illusion of increased power through strategies such as drinking alcohol and also risk-taking, gesturing and posturing, using abusive language, using drugs, and driving very fast. In short, people drink alcohol to regu-

late the quality of their emotional experience, and power-striving individuals seek alcohol as a means to enhance their expectancies of successful coping via an inflated sense of control (Cooper et al., 1995). Negative life events can build stress and frustration that can work as an emotional trigger to release aggressive displays as a means of conflict resolution. For instance, power-seeking men, but not women, frequently respond to negative life events and stress by inflicting abuse on their intimates (Mason & Blankenship, 1987).

INFLUENTIAL OCCUPATIONS. People high in the need for power are attracted to certain occupations; they may want to be a business executive, teacher or professor, psychologist, journalist, cleric, or international diplomat, for example (Winter, 1973). Each can direct the behavior of other people in accordance with some preconceived plan (Winter & Stewart, 1978). People in some of these professions speak to and influence audiences (teachers, journalists, clergy), others have inside information they use to influence others (psychologists, diplomats), and others have professional status that allows them to tell others what to do (business executives). Further, these careers equip the individual with the rewards and punishments necessary to sanction others' behavior. The teacher, cleric, and diplomat, for instance, all have the means to sanction the behavior of other people if they comply with prescribed plan (through grades, heavenly rewards, and deals). The journalist can sanction the behavior of others through editorial means. The business executive administers orders and schedules to employees and enforces them through salaries and wages, bonuses, and job security. Thus, people can involve and satisfy their power strivings through the job they choose.

PRESTIGE POSSESSIONS. Persons high in the need for power tend to amass a collection of symbols of power, or "prestige possessions" (Winter, 1973). Among college students, power-seeking individuals are more likely than others to have a car, wine glasses, television set, boom box, wall hangings, carpeted floor, and so on. They are also more likely to put their name on their dormitory room door. Older power-seeking individuals are more likely to own a rifle or pistol, a convertible car, or a truck that exudes status, power, or both (McClelland, 1975). Power-seeking individuals also tend to have significantly more credit cards than do others (McClelland, Davis, Kalin, & Wanner, 1972; Winter, 1973). Winter and Stewart (1978) suggest that credit cards provide financial power because they can gratify any whim with only a signature, much like that of royalty, presidents, and the very rich (all persons of immense power).

Leadership Motive Pattern

A special variant of the need for power is the leadership motive pattern (McClelland, 1975, 1985; McClelland & Burnham, 1976; Spangler & House, 1991). Leadership motivation consists of the threefold pattern of (1) above average need for power, (2) below average need for intimacy/affiliation, and (3) above average activity inhibition (operationally determined by the number of times the word *not* appears in a TAT protocol, usually signifying inhibition of action; McClelland, 1982). Thus, the leadership motive pattern features individuals who are interested in exercising influence, are not concerned with being liked, and are well controlled. Such a constellation of needs with an internally controlling regulatory style generally results in effective leaders or managers (Spangler & House, 1991). The characteristic of an internally controlling style (i.e., high activity inhibition) is important because managers who are high in power, low in affiliation, and high in inhibition are generally productive, successful, and rated highly by workers (McClelland & Burnham, 1976). In contrast, managers who are high in power, low in affiliation, but low in inhibition are often unproductive, unsuccessful, and rated lowly by workers. Apparently, an internally controlling style is the difference between an effective manager and a Don Juan (McClelland, 1985). In addition, power-striving managers showing leadership motivation, as opposed to a Don Juan syndrome, internalize characteristics associated with effective management: respect for institutional authority, discipline, self-control, and a concern for just rewards (McClelland, 1975).

The leadership motive provides a framework to assess the effectiveness of U.S. presidents (Spangler & House, 1991; Winter, 1973, 1987). Winter coded the thematic content of each president's inaugural address for the social needs of achievement, affiliation, and power and used these scores to predict presidential effectiveness. Presidents generally considered strong by historians—Kennedy, Truman, Wilson, and both Roosevelts—scored relatively high on power needs and relatively low on affiliative needs. Spangler and House (1991) rated presidential effectiveness with the following five variables—direct presidential actions (e.g., enter or avoid war), perceived greatness, social performance, economic performance, and international relations performance. To assess each president's needs for power, affiliation, and activity inhibition, the researchers coded their inaugural speeches, presidential letters, and other speeches. The presidential leadership syndrome of high power, low affiliation, and high inhibition correlated significantly with all five measures of effectiveness.

The leadership motive pattern also predicts when leaders will engage in war and when leaders will pursue peace (Winter, 1993). Of course, war has many nonpsychological causes, but on the psychological side historical research is consistently clear that when leaders express a motive profile of high power and low affiliation, the probability of subsequent war increases. As to power motivation, when it rises war is likely, when it falls war is less likely and ongoing wars are more likely to end. When affiliation motivation rises, war is less likely; when it falls, war is more likely to begin (Winter, 1993).

SUMMARY

Acquired psychological needs include both quasi-needs and social needs. Quasi-needs are situationally induced wants and desires such as wanting a 4.0 GPA or desiring money. Such situational pressures produce a psychological context of tension that supplies the motivation to interact with the environment. Social needs are more en-during and arise from the individual's personal experiences and unique develop-mental, cognitive, and socialization history. Once acquired, social needs act as emo-tional and behavioral potentials that are activated by situational incentives. For achievement, the need-activating incentive is doing something well to show personal competence. For affiliation, the need-activating incentive is an opportunity to please others and gain their approval. For the intimacy need, the need-activating incentive is a warm, secure attachment. For power, the need-activating incentive is having im-pact on others.

To measure social motives researchers typically administer the Thematic Apperception Test (TAT), which presents a series of pictures or sentences to the test taker, who writes short stories to make sense of the events portrayed in each picture or sentence. As a psychometric instrument, the TAT suffers from low relia-bility and is difficult to administer and score, but over 1000 studies using the TAT have confirmed its validity by predicting thoughts and behaviors related to the needs for achievement, affiliation, intimacy, and power.

The achievement motive is the desire to do well relative to some standard of ex-cellence. When facing standards of excellence, people's emotional reactions vary. Compared to low-need achievers, high-need achievers generally perform well on moderately difficult tasks, persist longer at moderately difficult tasks, respond to fail-ure with increased effort, enjoy competitions, enjoy situations that allow them to di-agnose their skills, and show entrepreneurial behaviors. According to Atkinson's model, achievement behavior is a multiplicative function of the individual's achieve-ment motive, probability of task success, and incentive for success (i.e., $Ts = Ms \times Ps \times Is$), as well as fear of failure, probability of task failure, and incentive to avoid failure (i.e., $Taf = Maf \times Pf \times If$).

Affiliative strivings have two sides—the need for approval based in rejection anx-iety and the need for intimacy based in affiliative interest. The need for affiliation in-volves establishing, maintaining, and restoring relationships with others, mostly to avoid negative emotions such as fear of disapproval and loneliness. The need for in-timacy is the social motive to engage in warm, close, positive interpersonal rela-tionships that cause positive emotions and hold little threat of rejection. Depriving people of the opportunity for interaction with others is the principal condition that involves the need for affiliation, and situational conditions that threaten the oppor-tunity to interact are particularly involving—conditions such as fear and anxiety and social embarrassment. Developing and maintaining warm, close relationships in-volves and satisfies the need for intimacy, and individuals with high intimacy needs are more likely to join social groups, spend time interacting with others, and form stable, long-lasting relationships that are characterized by self-disclosure and positive affect expressed through looking, laughing, and smiling.

The need for power is the desire to make the material and social world conform to one's personal image or plan for it. Power-seeking individuals strive for leader-ship and recognition in small groups, experience frequent impulses to aggression, prefer influential occupations, and seek to amass prestige possessions. Situational factors further enhance the power motive, particularly situations in which the person has some degree of control or influence over another. A special variant of the need for power is the leadership motive pattern, which consists of the threefold pattern of (1) above average need for power, (2) below average need for intimacy, and (3) above average activity inhibition. Such a constellation of needs with an internally controlling regulatory style generally results in effective leaders, managers, or presidents.

RECOMMENDED READINGS

Atkinson, J. W. (1964). A theory of achievement motivation. In *An introduction to motivation* (Chpt. 9, pp. 240-268). Princeton, NJ: D. Van Nostrand.

Atkinson, J. W., Bongort, K., & Price, L. H. (1977). Explorations using computer simulation to comprehend TAT measurement of motivation. *Motivation and Emotion, 1*, 1-27.

Lansing, J. B., & Heyns, R. W. (1959). Need affiliation and frequency of four types of communication. *Journal of Abnormal and Social Psychology, 58*, 365-372.

McAdams, D. P., Jackson, R. J., & Kirshnit, C. (1984). Looking, laughing, and smiling in dyads as a function of intimacy motivation and reciprocity. *Journal of Personality, 52*, 261-273.

McAdams, D. P., & Losoff, M. (1984). Friendship motivation in fourth and sixth graders: A thematic analysis. *Journal of Social and Personal Relations, 1*, 11-27.

McClelland, D. C. (1965). Achievement and entrepreneurship: A longitudinal study. *Journal of Personality and Social Psychology, 1*, 389-392.

Spangler, W. D., & House, R. J. (1991). Presidential effectiveness and the leadership motive profile. *Journal of Personality and Social Psychology, 60*, 439-455.

Steele, R. S. (1977). Power motivation, activation, and inspirational speeches. *Journal of Personality, 45*, 53-64.

Teichman, Y. (1973). Emotional arousal and affiliation. *Journal of Experimental Social Psychology, 9*, 591-605.

Winter, D. G. (1988). The power motive in women—and men. *Journal of Personality and Social Psychology, 54*, 510-519.

PART TWO

Cognition

Chapter 7

p. 158-9
164-72

DISCREPANCIES

The Nature of Cognition
Pioneer Theorists in the Cognitive Approach to Motivation
    Edward Tolman
    Kurt Lewin
Plans
    Corrective Motivation
Goals
    Goals and Performance
    Goal Acceptance
    Long-Term Goal Setting
    Criticisms of Goal Setting
Dissonance
    Dissonance-Arousing Situations
    Does Dissonance Produce an Aversive Motivational State?
    Dissonance Processes
    Self-Perception Theory

They say mirrors do not lie. Lately, your mirror has been telling you that you added a few pounds. It is time, you decide, to lose 10 pounds and get back on the road to physical fitness. You want to take action, but what? You decide to start jogging. It is easy, new, even a bit fun, as you jog along and enjoy the outdoors. A week goes by, but you do not lose much weight; you wonder how much exercise is enough exercise. Another week goes by and the pressures of everyday living increase and distract your attention away from exercise. Each day you find it more difficult to mobilize the effort and to find the time to exercise. After a month, jogging is history.

Later, you stroll through a used bookstore and come upon *Aerobics* (Cooper, 1968). You still think exercise and getting into shape are important, so you flip through the book. The critical feature of the book is a point system. Page after page, the book lists several different aerobic activities, such as running, swimming, and cycling. For each exercise, the system lists a distance, a performance time, and a number of aerobics points earned for that particular distance and time. For example, under running, joggers who run one mile in 8:00 earn 5 aerobics points. A few pages later, the book provides a personal progress chart with space to write in the date, the exercise, its distance and duration, number of points earned, and, for each week, cumulative points earned. According to *Aerobics*, a person needs to earn 30 points per week to increase physical fitness and decrease weight.

Now you have a goal. No longer are you going to just do your best; now you are going to earn 30 aerobic points per week. You start the week bent on earning 30 points, but your body protests that 20 is enough. Because you cannot quite earn 30 points, you find yourself devising point-increasing strategies (e.g., exercise in the morning rather than evening). By the end of the third week, you earn the 30 points and feel the warm glow of accomplishment. After a month, you boldly decide to try for 40 points per week. This new goal will take a little more effort, a bit more persistence, and perhaps a new and improved exercise strategy. You add racquetball to your weekly routine.

This chapter asks how and why mental events such as goals mobilize effort and increase commitment to a long-term course of action. It discusses three mental entities that have motivational properties—plans, goals, and dissonance—and illustrates how cognitive discrepancies energize and direct behavior. The three chapters that follow discuss expectancies (chapter 8), attributions (chapter 9), and self-concept (chapter 10). Before plunging forward into the motivational significance of cognitive discrepancies, consider first the nature of cognition.

THE NATURE OF COGNITION

A cognitive perspective on motivation focuses on mental processes, or thoughts, as causal determinants to action (e.g., Gollwitzer & Bargh, 1996). Among the more heavily researched cognitive motivators in the cognition → action sequence are the following: plans (Miller, Galanter, & Pribram, 1960), goals (Locke & Latham, 1990), dissonance (Cooper & Fazio, 1984), appraisals (Lazarus, 1991a), schemas (Ortony, Clore, & Collins, 1988), expectancies (Peterson, Maier, & Seligman, 1993), attributions (Weiner, 1986), and self-concept (Markus & Nurius, 1986).

Figure 7.1 illustrates a typical sequence of events in the cognitive view of motivation. Events in the external environment affect the human senses and supply information to be processed and interpreted by the brain. Seeing a friend beckoning to us or hearing the telephone ring initiates active information processing. Such sensory information is attended to, transformed, organized, elaborated on, and held in mind while relevant information is retrieved from memory to assist in the information processing flow. Based on our understanding of the meaning of the information processed, we build up expectancies (e.g., of what our friend wants to talk about), construct goals (e.g., to invite our friend to lunch), formulate plans (e.g., of what to talk about), and so forth. These cognitive events energize and direct behavior toward a particular course of action. Once the behavioral activity is carried out, outcomes occur (e.g., success, failure, improvement, rejection) that are attended to, appraised, and explained. These behavioral outcomes add further to the active information processing flow and, hence, contribute to the ongoing regulation of behavior.

The concern of cognitive psychology is twofold. First, cognitive psychology is the study of how people understand the world in which they live, as indicated on the left in Figure 7.1 (sensory experience affecting active information processing). Pertinent questions address the issue of how human beings take incoming sensory information (by watching, reading, touching, and so on) and transform, reduce, organize, elaborate, store, retrieve, and eventually use that acquired information (Anderson, 1980; Neisser, 1967). The second concern of cognitive psychology is

FIGURE 7–1
Sequence of Events in the Cognitive View of Behavior

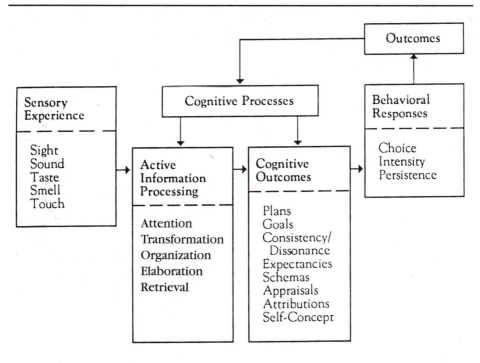

how cognition aids our effort to adapt successfully to the environment and therefore regulate behavior (cognitive outcomes affecting behavioral responses). From a motivational point of view, cognition is a spring to action, a moving force that instigates behavior. For cognitive theorists, motivation is primarily a function of a person's thoughts, rather than a product of a person's needs, drives, or states of arousal (Ames & Ames, 1984).

PIONEER THEORISTS IN THE COGNITIVE APPROACH TO MOTIVATION

This chapter illustrates how plans, goals, and dissonance function as springs to action. First, however, the chapter will introduce two pioneers of a cognitive approach to motivation, Edward Tolman and Kurt Lewin.

Edward Tolman

Tolman was an early- to mid-1900s behaviorist whose observations led him to conclude that behavior "reeks of purpose." Tolman (1925, 1932, 1959) meant that behavior was perpetually goal directed. People are always approaching or avoiding goal objects. People drive to particular places and librarians search for particular books. Once the goal is attained, that behavior ceases. Hence, behavior is fundamentally purposive. Behavior further exudes knowledge, or cognition. To attain goals and avoid obstacles, people depend heavily on hypotheses, expectations, and strategies. The librarians' book searches, for instance, are entrenched in cognition because they know where to look and what they will find when they look there, and because the direction of their behavior reflects their hypotheses of where the book might be (Tolman, 1938; Tolman, Ritchie, & Kalish, 1946a, 1946b).

Tolman's terms for purpose and cognition are demand and expectation, respectively. Demand emanates from the desire for relief from a bodily demand (hunger, thirst, sex, sleep, and so on), and therefore purpose constitutes the desire to obtain a demand-satisfying environmental object (food, water, and so on). Given a bodily demand, potential demand-satisfiers are given selective attention and become sought-after environmental goals. Expectations arise as people search for appropriate environmental goals and, as they become familiar with their environments through repetition, learn what leads to what as they build up a cognitive map of their surroundings. As bodily demands arise, people use their cognitive maps to search for demand-satisfying objects. As an illustration, consider how you learn your way about campus. First you learn the general location of a major building, such as a dormitory. Then you learn what buildings are near that building, perhaps the student union and the administration building. Soon, after several exposures to the dormitory's surroundings, you develop a cognitive map of how far away and in what direction the athletic fields, library, parking lot, and cafeteria are. First you form a rudimentary cognitive map, and as demands arise (to register, meet with an advisor, check out a book, find a cup of coffee), you continue to interact with the environment and continue to build up an increasingly accurate cognitive map of the campus. Thus, when a demand arises, you need only rely on your cognitive map to elicit effective demand-satisfying behaviors.

TOLMAN'S INFLUENCE ON CONTEMPORARY MOTIVATION THEORY. In Tolman's era, the dominant learning theories were stimulus-response (S-R) conceptualizations (e.g., Hull, Guthrie); in contrast, Tolman advocated mental events (or cognitive expectancies) as intervening variables between S and R. Tolman showed how expectancies are acquired and how expectancies, once acquired, motivate behavior. In doing so, Tolman popularized the cognitive approach to motivation and behavior. The fruits of Tolman's approach manifest themselves in each concept discussed—plan, goal, and the rest. Each represents a mental construct right out of the Tolman intervening-variable approach. Throughout part 2, the reader should not lose sight of Tolman's general intervening-variable model in which mental events (not environmental stimuli) motivate action: S $\rightarrow$ cognitive event $\rightarrow$ R. This model is the basis for all cognitive interpretations of motivation.

Kurt Lewin

Lewin's (1935) cognitive view of motivation, like Tolman's, portrays the individual as a goal-seeking organism; the person is always approaching or avoiding something. Lewin sees the individual as constantly influenced by a constellation of many different needs, not only from bodily demands but also from psychological needs and desires ("I need to do well on this test today"; "I want to get to work on time"). Needs lead to intentions. Thus, "I need a new pair of shoes" creates the intention to go to the shoe store. Once an intention is made, tension remains until that intention is fulfilled through consummatory action. Thus, for Lewin, needs create intentions, intentions produce tensions, and tensions motivate approach and avoidance consummatory behavior.

Lewin's cognitive construct is valence, which refers to the positive or negative value environmental objects have for an individual. Attractive and tension-reducing objects acquire positive valence; threatening and tension-producing objects acquire a negative valence. Hence, given the need $\rightarrow$ intention $\rightarrow$ tension $\rightarrow$ goal-directed behavior sequence, the person searches the environment selectively to find positive goal objects capable of satisfying the intention and thereby reducing tension and gratifying the need.

For Lewin, human behavior is a continuous and perpetually repeating cycle of equilibrium, need, intention, tension, goal-directed behavior, and relief that returns the individual to equilibrium. Consider the motivational dynamics, the intentions and valences, of the child who peers into the department store window and eyes a wished-for toy. The sight of the toy arouses a toy-desiring need (the toy has a positive valence), which arouses an intention to own the toy. The child engages in a great deal of cognitive activity (e.g., expectancies, problem solving) to satisfy the toy-possessing intention. If the child lacks the money to purchase the toy, any number of strategies may be initiated to obtain the wished-for toy, including asking father for money, contriving a plan to swipe the toy, fantasizing what it would be like to play with the toy, or planning for the future (by saving allowances). The point is that (1) a need, once aroused, produces a great deal of cognitive and behavioral activity, and (2) a goal object becomes attractive as a function of the person's need for it.

LEWIN'S INFLUENCE ON CONTEMPORARY MOTIVATION THEORY. For Lewin, individuals locomoted through a psychological space, and that locomotion was constantly pushed by inherent tensions and pulled by environmental valences. Lewin conceptualized human beings as bodies in motion that moved in certain directions because of forces pushing and pulling them at any given moment. Traditional theorists (including Tolman) emphasized the long developmental learning history of individuals that created individual motivations. Lewin, on the other hand, emphasized the here-and-now influences that gave rise to contemporaneous motivations and behaviors (e.g., Jones, 1985). Together, then, Lewin and Tolman constructed the theoretical foundation for understanding how our thoughts from one moment to the next (Lewin) and our expectancies acquired over an extended time (Tolman) contribute to motivated action.

PLANS

In one of the earliest models to illustrate how cognitive processes energize and direct behavior, a trio of psychologists studied how plans motivate behavior (Miller, Galanter, & Pribram, 1960). According to Miller and his colleagues, people have cognitive representations of the ideal states of their behavior, of environmental objects, and of events. In other words, people have in mind what an ideal tennis serve looks like, what an ideal term paper is, and what happens during an ideal night on the town. People are also aware of the present state of their behavior, environment, and events. That is, people have the knowledge of what their current tennis serve, term paper, and evening plans are. When people find a mismatch, or incongruity, between their ideal state and their present state, they adopt a plan of action that will result in a match, or congruity, between the two states (Miller, Galanter, & Pribum, 1960; Newell, Shaw, & Simon, 1958). Hence, people develop a plan as to how to improve their present term paper and they act on that plan. The incongruity between present and ideal is motivational (a spring to action), and the plan is the cognitive event that acts as a motivational bridge from the present state to the ideal.

The cognitive mechanism by which plans energize and direct behavior is the test-operate-test-exit (TOTE) model, as illustrated in Figure 7.2 (Miller, Galanter, & Pribram, 1960). *Test* means to compare the present state against the ideal. A mismatch between the two (incongruity) causes the individual to *operate* via a sequence of action. By operating on the environment, the person strives to realize the ideal state. After a period of time, the person again tests the present state against

FIGURE 7–2
Schematic of the TOTE model

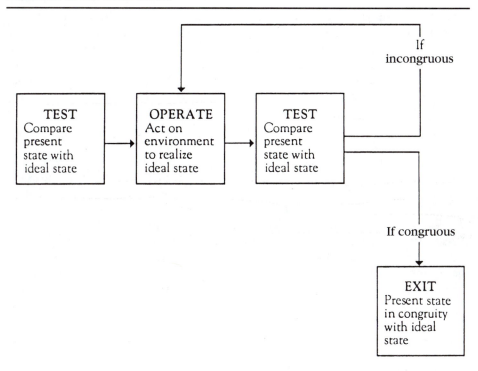

the ideal. Given incongruity, the person continues to operate on the environment (T-O-T-O-T-O, and so on). If the present matches the ideal, however, the person *exits* the plan.

Consider the following example of how the TOTE model links plans to motivated action. A painter takes an easel to a waterfall, paints the scenery, compares the canvas to the waterfall, and notices that the two are quite dissimilar. Because the canvas does not yet show a satisfactory representation of the waterfall, the painter operates on the painting to realize on the canvas the ideal picture in her mind. The painter continually compares (tests) the painting on the canvas to its ideal in her mind. As long as incongruity persists, the painting continues (T-O-T-O-T-O, and so on). Only when the actual and ideal paintings match one another does the painter exit the plan and cease to paint.

Corrective Motivation

The plan-action sequence portrays individuals as (1) detecting present-ideal inconsistencies, (2) generating a plan to eliminate the incongruity, (3) instigating plan-regulated behavior, and (4) monitoring feedback as to the extent of present-ideal incongruity that remains. Contemporary researchers (e.g., Campion & Lord, 1982;

Carver & Scheier, 1981, 1982, 1990), however, no longer view plans as so fixed, static, and mechanical. Rather, plans are adjustable and subject to frequent modification. Given an incongruity between present and ideal, the individual's plan is as likely to change as is his or her behavior. The emphasis on modifiable plans is important because it presents human beings as active decision makers who choose which process to follow: act to achieve an ideal or change an ineffective plan (Carver & Scheier, 1981, 1982). From this point of view, any present-ideal incongruity does not create an automatic discrepancy-motivated action sequence. Rather, incongruity gives rise to a more generalized corrective motivation (Campion & Lord, 1982).

Corrective motivation activates a decision-making process in which the individual considers many ways to reduce the present-ideal incongruity: Change the plan, increase behavioral effort, or withdraw from the plan altogether. That is, plan-directed behavior is a dynamic process in which corrective motivation energizes the individual to pursue the most adaptive course: by cognitive change of plan, behavioral change of effort, or task disengagement.

People are not always successful in fulfilling their plans. Sometimes events in the situation interfere and sometimes personal inadequacies interfere. Facing difficulty, people put their plans and coping efforts on hold and assess the likelihood that further effort will accomplish the plan's objective. This reassessment affects emotional processes (Carver & Scheier, 1990). When people progress toward their ideal at a rate equal to their expectations, they feel little emotion. When people progress toward their ideal slower than expected, a negative discrepancy produces negative emotions such as anxiety, frustration, or despair. When people progress toward their ideal faster than expected, a positive discrepancy produces positive emotions such as enthusiasm, hope, excitement, and joy or elation (Carver & Scheier, 1990).

GOALS

A goal is whatever an individual is striving to accomplish (Locke et al., 1981). When people strive to earn $100, make a 4.0 GPA, sell 100 boxes of Girl Scout cookies, or go undefeated in an athletic season, they engage in goal-directed behavior. Like plans, goals generate motivation by focusing people's attention on the discrepancy (or incongruity) between their present level of accomplishment (As of today, I have sold 0 boxes of cookies) and their ideal level of accomplishment (By the end of the month, I want to have sold 100 boxes of cookies). Researchers refer to this discrepancy between present and ideal accomplishments as a *goal-performance discrepancy* (Locke & Latham, 1990).

There are two types of goal-performance discrepancies (Bandura, 1990). The first type is discrepancy reduction, which is based on feedback. Some element in the environment (e.g., a boss, scholarship, athletic opponent) provides feedback that informs the person that current performance differs from an ideal level of accomplishment. For instance, at work, competition from another business might cause the boss to raise the standards and tell each salesperson to sell 15 products this month instead of the usual 10. Or a 2.0 GPA student might read in a brochure that a 3.0 GPA is required this semester to be eligible for an honor's club. The idea underlying discrepancy reduction is that energized and directed behavior is reactive to and created by environmental feedback.

The second type is discrepancy creation, which is a feedforward-based model in which the person proactively sets a new, higher goal. The person deliberately sets a personal higher goal and does not require feedback from a boss or an honor's club to impose it. For instance, the salesperson might, for whatever reason, decide to try for 15 sales this week instead of the usual 10, and the student might decide to try for a 3.0 GPA rather than the usual 2.0. Thus, the person raises the goal, past performance is seen as inadequate, and the goal therefore pulls up performance.

The important distinctions between discrepancy reduction and discrepancy creation are that (1) discrepancy reduction corresponds to plan-based corrective motivation whereas discrepancy creation corresponds to goal-setting motivation, and (2) discrepancy reduction is reactive, deficiency oriented, and revolves around a feedback system whereas discrepancy creation is proactive, growth oriented, and revolves around a feedforward system. Goal-setting motivation supplements the motivational significance of plans to help explain motivated action. Goal setting is first and foremost a discrepancy-creating process (Bandura, 1990).

Goals and Performance

Generally speaking, people with goals outperform people without goals (Locke & Latham, 1990). And, generally speaking, the same person performs better with a goal rather than without a goal. Consider one study in which high school students did sit-ups for 2 minutes (Weinberg et al., 1988). Some students set a goal for themselves of how many sit-ups they would accomplish during the 2 minutes (goal-setting group), and others simply completed sit-ups without a predetermined goal (no-goal group). The goal-setting students finished significantly more sit-ups than did the no-goal students. In this study, the presence of a goal motivated exercisers more than did the absence of a goal.

In addition to the mere presence of goals, the type of goals one sets is also important. Goals vary in difficulty and how specific they are. Goal difficulty refers to how hard a goal is to accomplish. As goals increase in difficulty, performance increases linearly (Locke & Latham, 1990; Mento, Steel, & Karren, 1987; Tubbs, 1986). Relative to goals such as score 80 on a test, run a mile in 10 minutes, and don't blow it with a new acquaintance, more difficult goals would be to score 90 on a test, run a mile in 8 minutes, and make a new friend. The more difficult the goal, the more it energizes the performer. Goal specificity refers to how clearly a goal informs the performer precisely what to do. Telling a performer to "do your best" sounds like goal setting, but is an ambiguous statement that does not make clear precisely what the person is to do (Locke & Latham, 1990). On the other hand, telling a writer to have a first draft by week 1, a revised draft by week 2, and a final manuscript by week 3 specifies precisely what the writer is to do.

WHICH GOALS FACILITATE PERFORMANCE? Goals do not always enhance performance. Only those goals that are (1) difficult and (2) specific facilitate performance (Locke et al., 1981). The reason difficult, specific goals increase performance is a motivational one. Difficult goals *energize* the performer, specific goals *direct* him or her toward a particular course of action (Earley, Wojnaroski, & Prest, 1987).

Goals energize behavior; they motivate the performer's effort and persistence. Output of effort is directly proportional to the perceived demands of the task (Bassett, 1979; Locke & Latham, 1990). The harder the goal, the greater the effort expended to accomplish it (Earley, Wojnaroski, & Prest, 1987; Bandura & Cervone, 1983, 1986). Goals increase persistence because effort continues until the goal is reached (Laporte & Nath, 1976; Latham & Locke, 1975). Goals also decrease the probability that the performer will be distracted from the task or will give up prematurely (Laporte & Nath, 1976). With a goal in mind, performers quit the task when the goal is accomplished, not when they get bored, frustrated, tired, or distracted.

Goals direct the performer's attention and strategic planning. Goals direct the individual's attention toward the task at hand and therefore away from tasks that are incidental (Kahneman, 1973; Locke & Bryan, 1969; Rothkopf & Billington, 1979). Specific goals clearly tell the performer where to concentrate and what specifically to do (Klein, Whitener, & Ilgen, 1990; Latham, Mitchell, & Dossett, 1978; Locke et al., 1989). In studies with students reading texts, for instance, readers with specific goals spend significantly more time looking at their text during a study session than do readers with ambiguous goals (Locke & Bryan, 1969; Rothkopf & Billington, 1979). Specific goals also prompt performers to plan a strategic course of action (Latham & Baldes, 1975; Terborg, 1976). With a specific goal in mind, a performer who is unable to accomplish a goal on a first attempt will tend to drop that strategy and create an improved strategy (Earley & Perry, 1987; Earley, Wojnaroski, & Prest, 1987).

Difficult, specific goals provide a positive motivational effect on behavior, but performance depends on nonmotivational factors as well—factors such as ability, training, coaching, and resources (Locke & Latham, 1984). Because these factors also contribute to performance outcomes, no one-to-one correspondence exists between goals and performance. This is an important practical point because when difficult, specific goals fail to enhance performance, one might be well advised to increase ability (via instruction, practice, role models, and videotaped performance feedback) or to increase resources (via supplying equipment, books, tutors, computers, or money). When such nonmotivational factors are held constant, however, difficult and specific goals generate the motivation that enhances performance.

THE IMPORTANCE OF FEEDBACK. Difficult, specific goals enhance performance by energizing and directing performance. One additional variable is crucial to make goal-setting effective: feedback (Erez, 1977). Goal setting translates into increased performance only in the context of timely feedback that documents the performer's progress in relation to the goal (Locke et al., 1981). In other words, a performer needs both a goal *and* performance feedback to maximize performance attainments

(Bandura & Cervone, 1983; Becker, 1978; Erez, 1977; Strang, Lawrence & Fowler, 1978; Tubbs, 1986).

Without feedback, performance can be emotionally unimportant and uninvolving (I performed at level X, so what?). The combination of goals with feedback produces an emotionally meaningful mixture, such that goal attainment breeds emotional satisfaction while goal failure breeds emotional dissatisfaction (Bandura, 1991). Emotional satisfaction contributes to the discrepancy-creating process, whereas emotional dissatisfaction contributes to the discrepancy-reducing process. When performers feedback shows the individual is performing at or above goal level, the individual feels satisfied and competent, competent enough perhaps to create a higher, more difficult goal (the discrepancy creation process; Wood, Bandura, & Bailey, 1990). When performance feedback shows the individual is performing below goal level, the individual feels dissatisfied and becomes keenly aware of the goal-performance discrepancy, enough perhaps to marshal greater effort to eliminate the goal-performance incongruity (the discrepancy reduction process; Bandura & Cervone, 1983, 1986).

Goal Acceptance

In addition to goals needing to be difficult and specific and combined with feedback, a third condition must be met before goals increase performance outcomes—goal acceptance (Erez & Kanfer, 1983). Goal acceptance involves the person's decision either to accept or reject the goal and varies on a continuum from total acceptance to total rejection (Erez & Zidon, 1984). Only internalized goals improve performance (Erez, Earley, & Hulin, 1985). Erez and Zidon (1984) have shown that if the person accepts a performance goal, a positive relationship exists between task difficulty and performance—as goal difficulty increases, so does performance. If the goal is rejected, a negative relationship exists between task difficulty and performance—as goal difficulty increases, performance declines, such that the person puts forth little or no effort in the face of a difficult, rejected goal.

Four factors affect the goal acceptance process:

- Goal difficulty
- The goal assignee's level of participation in the goal-setting process
- The goal assigner's perceived credibility
- Extrinsic incentives

Goal difficulty is inversely related to goal acceptance. Easy goals generally breed ready goal acceptance whereas difficult goals breed goal rejection (Erez, Earley, & Hulin, 1985). Before a person accepts a goal, he or she evaluates its level of difficulty. When the parent tells the child to bring home all As, the child evaluates the likelihood of attaining such a goal before accepting it. Perhaps for this child a B average is a difficult goal, while a C average is an easy goal. As the goal changes from a C average ("that's reasonable; I'll try") to a 3.0 ("that will take my best effort; I'll probably try") and perhaps to a 4.0 GPA ("that's impossible; I won't even try"), the child's willingness to accept the parent's goal decreases accordingly.

Participation in the goal-setting process refers to how much say the performer has in the goal being pursued. If the performer sets the goal, it is readily accepted. However, the goal may originate from a teacher, manager, parent, coach, friend, or society in general. With an external goal origin, an interpersonal negotiation process ensues in which the performer's goal acceptance versus rejection is at stake. In general, performers reject assigned goals that others try to force on them (Latham & Yukl, 1975). In contrast, performers accept assigned goals when others listen carefully to their point of view, provide a clear rationale for the goal, and support the performer's autonomy and self-determination (Latham, Erez, & Locke, 1988; Latham & Saari, 1979).

Credibility of the goal assigner refers to how trustworthy, supportive, knowledgeable, and likeable the performer perceives the goal assigner to be. A goal assigner with little credibility may be characterized as being authoritarian, manipulative, and pejorative. All other things being equal, performers are more likely to accept and internalize goals assigned to them by credible others as opposed to suspicious or manipulative others (Locke & Latham, 1990; Oldham, 1975).

When extrinsic incentives and rewards are contingent on goal attainment, a performer's goal acceptance increases in proportion to the perceived benefit associated with goal attainment (Locke & Latham, 1990). Incentives such as money, public recognition, scholarships, and the like add to a performer's willingness to accept a goal regardless of the goal's difficulty, the goal's origin, and the credibility of the goal assigner. Overall, then, goal acceptance is highest when goals are easy or moderately difficult, are self-set, or at least negotiated to the performer's satisfaction, are assigned by credible and trustworthy others, and are associated with personal benefit. When these conditions are met, goal acceptance occurs and goals, through feedback, enhance performance.

Long-Term Goal Setting

SHORT-TERM AND LONG-TERM GOALS. The student who wants to become a doctor or the athlete who wants to win an Olympic event exemplify individuals involved in long-term goal setting. To accomplish such distant goals, the performer first has to attain several requisite short-term goals. Would-be doctors first have to make a high GPA as undergraduates, get accepted into a medical school, raise a great deal of money, probably move to a different city, graduate from medical school, complete an internship, and so forth, all before they can begin their careers as doctors. Thus, goals can be short term (to understand this chapter), long term (to understand human motivation), or a series of short-term goals linked together into one long-term goal (understand chapter 1, understand chapter 2, and so on). No significant difference in performance enhancement emerges among performers with short-term, long-term, or a mixture of short- and long-term goals (Hall & Byrne, 1988; Weinberg, Bruya, & Jackson, 1985; Weinberg et al., 1988). Instead of affecting performance per se, goal proximity affects goal-attaining persistence and intrinsic motivation.

As for goal persistence, many would-be doctors and Olympians forfeit their long-term goal strivings in the face of a lack of positive reinforcement for that goal along the way. The long-term goal striver is at risk of insufficient opportunities for performance feedback and positive reinforcement and might therefore benefit from setting a series of short-term goals that chain together to eventually end in the long-term target goal. Transforming one long-term goal into a series of short-term goals yields two benefits. First, short-term goals provide repeated opportunities for reinforcement on goal attainment that long-term goals cannot. Positive reinforcement for short-term goal attainment generally increases the individual's commitment to the long-term goal (Latham, Mitchell, & Dossett, 1978). Second, short-term goals provide repeated opportunities for relevant performance feedback that allows the performer to evaluate performance as being at, above, or below the goal. An athlete trying for a long-term goal such as to win the state championship receives little day-to-day feedback, as compared to the athlete trying for a short-term goal such as to win a contest each week.

GOAL SETTING AND INTRINSIC MOTIVATION. Several researchers assessed the impact of goal setting on intrinsic motivation (Bandura & Schunk, 1981; Harackiewicz & Manderlink, 1984; Mossholder, 1980; Vallerand, Deci, & Ryan, 1985). In an early study, participants worked on an interesting puzzle, and goal-setting participants performed better than no-goal participants (Mossholder, 1980). This performance boost from goal setting is a reliable finding; however, the goal-setting participants also showed significantly less intrinsic motivation for the activity than did the no-goal participants. Thus, goal setting improved performance but depressed intrinsic motivation.

Two later experiments had performers complete an enjoyable task with either (1) several short-term goals, (2) one long-term goal, or (3) no goals ("do your best"); intrinsic motivation was assessed after participation. Short-term goals enhanced performance, while long-term goals enhanced intrinsic motivation (Manderlink & Harackiewicz, 1984). On an unenjoyable task, short-term goals increased both performance and intrinsic motivation (Bandura & Schunk, 1981). Thus, some studies find that goals decrease intrinsic motivation, other studies find that short-term goals increase intrinsic motivation, and still other studies find that a long-term goal increases intrinsic motivation. Vallerand, Deci, and Ryan (1985) integrated these contradictory findings by suggesting that the performer's initial level of intrinsic motivation toward the task is the key variable determining how goal setting affects intrinsic motivation. On uninteresting tasks, short-term goals enhance intrinsic motivation by enhancing the performer's sense of competence. Short-term goals increase competence when they function as opportunities for positive feedback via attaining a series of short-term goals (Vallerand, Deci, & Ryan, 1985). On interesting tasks, long-term, but not short-term, goals facilitate intrinsic motivation. For the highly interested performer, short-term goals are experienced as superfluous, intrusive, and controlling. People who enjoy an activity typically already feel competent at that task, so their sense of competence is not in question. Hence, the only effect a short-term goal can have on an interesting task is a negative one (because pretask interest and competence are already high). Generally speaking, people prefer to pursue long-term goals in their own way (Manderlink & Harackiewicz, 1984; Vallerand, Deci, & Ryan, 1985).

GOALS AS COMPLEX COGNITIVE STRUCTURES. Goals can be thought of as specific targets, such as to lose 5 pounds, get a job, or make 10 consecutive free throws. Sometimes, however, goals cannot be identified so categorically. It is typically more accurate to think of goals as cognitive lattice structures (Ortony, Clore, & Collins, 1988). Figure 7.3, for example, represents an aspiring concert pianist's cognitive goal lattice (from Ravlin, 1987). At the top of the lattice are the pianist's most abstract (and long-term) aspirations and at the bottom are the most concrete (and short-term) aspirations. Each abstract or concrete aspiration is interconnected with every other in the sense that each shares in the musician's overall goal of becoming a concert

FIGURE 7–3
Complex Lattice Structure of Long-Term Goal

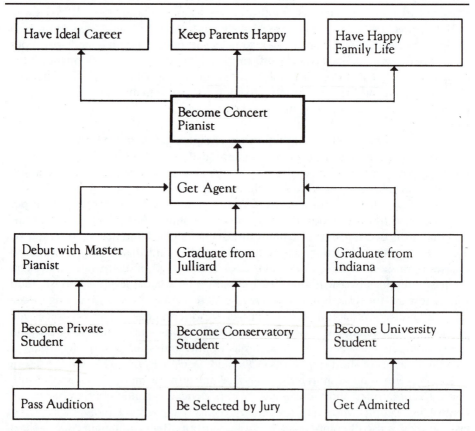

SOURCE: Adapted from Ravlin, S. B. (1987). A computer model of affective reactions to goal-relevant events. Unpublished Master's thesis, University of Illinois-Urbana-Champaign. As cited in A. Ortony, G. L. Clore, & A. Collins (Eds.) *The cognitive structure of emotions*, Cambridge University Press.

pianist. Further, each aspiration is connected in a causal flow in which the achievement of one goal increases the probability of attaining another, whereas the failure to achieve one goal decreases the probability of attaining another.

Criticisms of Goal Setting

Goal setting has its advantages, but it also has its fair share of dangers and pitfalls (Locke & Latham, 1984). The following paragraphs present two cautions and three concerns.

Goal setting theory (Locke & Latham, 1990) developed within the fields of business and management, in the world of work, productivity, sales, and the bottom line (profit). Goal setting theory is therefore more about enhancing performance (worker output) than it is about enhancing motivation per se. This then is a first caution: The purpose of goal setting is to enhance performance rather than motivation for its own sake. The second caution is that goal setting works best when tasks are relatively uninteresting and require a straightforward procedure (Wood, Mento, & Locke, 1987), as shown by studies of tasks such as adding numbers (Bandura & Schunk, 1981), typing (Latham & Yukl, 1976), proofreading (Huber, 1985), assembling nuts and bolts (Mossholder, 1980), and performing sit-ups (Weinberg, Bruya, & Jackson, 1985). On these tasks, goal setting often generates motivation (through challenge, competence feedback) that the task itself cannot (Bandura & Schunk, 1981). On tasks that are inherently interesting and lend themselves to a more creative, problem-solving approach, goal setting does not enhance performance (Earley, Connolly, & Ekegren, 1989). In fact, when tasks are interesting and require cognitive flexibility and creativity, goal setting generally undermines both performance (Bandura & Wood, 1989; McGraw, 1978) and task interest (Mossholder, 1980; Vallerand, Deci, & Ryan, 1985). This then is the second precaution: Goal setting is concerned more with the quantity of performance than it is with the quality of performance (Deci, 1992a).

Three concerns are particularly noteworthy—increasing stress, creating opportunities for failure, and putting intrinsic motivation at risk. The logic behind goal setting is to increase performance demands from underchallenging to optimally challenging so the performer's effort, persistence, attention, and strategy development improve from lackluster to optimal. Sometimes, however, overchallenging goals are set that ask performers to put forth a level of effort, persistence, attention, and strategic planning that exceeds their capabilities. Overchallenging goals open the door to stress and negative emotions in general (Csikszentmihalyi, 1990; Lazarus, 1991). Goals, especially overchallenging ones, also create an explicit performance standard and therefore open the door to the possibility of failure and negative feedback. Failure often has consequences that extend beyond the task itself, as failure often brings consequences that are emotional (e.g., feelings of inadequacy), social (e.g., loss of respect), and tangible (e.g., financial). Like other external events (chapter 5), goals can be delivered from one person to another in a way that is controlling, intrusive, and annoying and thus undermine intrinsic motivation by interfering with performers' sense of self-determination (Harackiewicz & Manderlink, 1984; Mossholder,

1980; Vallerand, Deci, & Ryan 1985). When goals are presented in a controlling way they put performers' intrinsic motivation at risk.

These cautions and concerns limit the practice of goal setting, but they do not speak against the cognitive understanding of motivation and emotion. With a goal in mind, and when accepted as one's own, goal-performance discrepancies energize action via increased effort and persistence and direct that action via attention and strategies. Such motivated action produces performance feedback that the person uses to diagnose whether performance is below, at, or above goal level. Goal attainment generally leads performers to create new goals (discrepancy creation), whereas goal failure generally leads performers to continue efforts to reduce the goal-performance discrepancy. The whole goal-performance scenario echoes nicely the information processing flow so central to the cognitive perspective on motivation (recall Fig. 7.1).

DISSONANCE

Dissonance theory begins with a reasonable assumption: Human beings dislike inconsistency and therefore strive for consistency among their mental structures, such as their attitudes, beliefs, opinions, and values (Aronson, 1969, 1988; Festinger, 1957). Dissonance arises whenever two thoughts contradict one another (e.g., I believe that smoking causes cancer; I think it is OK to allow cigarette advertisements on television) or when behavior contradicts one's beliefs (e.g., I believe school is important; I skipped school today). It is psychologically disturbing to hold contradictory beliefs or to believe one thing yet do another. Inconsistency generates an emotional discomfort that acts as an affective signal that the individual is not coping adequately and that consistency needs to be restored or established (Kellman & Baron, 1968). It is this negative affective state that has motivational properties, as it energizes coping behavior and it directs that behavior toward the goal of eliminating, or at least reducing, the inconsistency.

Imagine the following scenario of an environmentally minded individual who believes in clean water, clean air, and clean land. Suppose our environmentalist turns on the radio and hears an announcement that automobile exhaust fumes are rapidly depleting the ozone layer and that used tires are polluting our waterways and crowding our landfills. Further, suppose that our environmentalist needs to drive to and from work. Beliefs that exhaust damages the ozone layer and that used tires litter our rivers and crowd our landfills stand in stark contradiction to driving to and from work. Our environmentalist experiences dissonance, and its resulting emotional upset energizes and directs thinking and coping.

Believing one thing and doing another has an air of hypocrisy that causes dissonance (Fried & Aronson, 1995). Believing in but not using condoms (Aronson, Fried, & Stone, 1991) and believing in but not acting on water conservation (Dickerson, Thibodeau, Aronson, & Miller, 1992) illustrate hypocrisy in everyday life. For dissonance to occur, we need to be reminded that we are not using condoms or conserving water. Hypocrisy puts pressure on the consistency of a person's belief system. How much pressure is felt depends on the importance of our beliefs, the number of complementary (supportive) beliefs we endorse, and the number of additional hypocrisy-implying dissonant beliefs we hold. The most important determinant of how much dissonance we experience is the importance of our beliefs involved in the inconsistency, because beliefs that are central to the self or its valued goals arouse the highest degree of dissonance (Simon, Greenberg, & Brehm, 1995; Thibodeau & Aronson, 1992).

When dissonance is great enough to motivate the person to action, cognitive dissonance theory predicts that dissonance-suffering individuals will pursue one of five courses of action: (1) change the inconsistent belief, attitude, or opinion; (2) change the inconsistent behavior; (3) change some aspect of the environment; (4) seek out new information to effectively add new cognitive elements to resolve the inconsistency, as through justification; or (5) decrease the importance of the inconsistent belief via trivializing it (Festinger, 1957; Simon, Greenberg, & Brehm, 1995). Our environmentalist, for example, might (1) change the original belief to "the purpose of landfills is to hold old tires and such," (2) change behavior by using a bicycle, (3) change the environment by lobbying for bike trails or by installing an emissions control device on the car, (4) talk to friends who claim that a tiny amount of exhaust will not hurt the global condition or listen to a television show that suggests that science will find a solution to the problem, or (5) trivialize the inconsistency by saying, "In the grand scheme of things, my driving to work is no big deal." The important idea is that dissonance energizes one to reestablish cognitive consistency, and it directs that energy in one or more of the following five ways—changing beliefs, changing behaviors, altering the environment, adding new cognitive elements, or trivializing the importance of the inconsistency.

Dissonance-Arousing Situations

Human beings are frequently exposed to information dissonant with their beliefs and values, and they sometimes engage in behavior dissonant with their beliefs and values. Four specific situations illustrate such dissonance-arousing circumstances: choice, insufficient justification, effort justification, and new information. In reading through the paragraphs that follow, notice how circumstances pressure people to change their attitudes, beliefs, or values.

CHOICE. People often have to choose between two alternatives: two dates, two apartments, two jobs, or two routes of travel. In some cases, the choice between alternatives is easy, as the merits of one alternative far outweigh the merits of its rival. In other cases, the choice is not so easy, as both alternatives offer a number of advantages and disadvantages. In the apartment choice, one might be in a convenient location but expensive while the other might in an inconvenient location but less expensive. Once such a difficult choice is made, people experience dissonance. As soon as the choice for apartment A is made, the decision maker must face the fact that apartment B was cheaper. Given dissonance (or postdecision regret), the person engages in cognitive work to manipulate the relative desirability of the two alternatives. Some researchers refer to coping with the postdecision regret as the "Monty Hall problem," because it asks people to choose one door rather than another (Gilovich, Medvec, & Chen, 1995). To deal with the postdecision regret that follows difficult decisions and choices, the decision maker appreciates the chosen alternative and simultaneously depreciates the rejected alternative with a choice-justifying bias. (Brehm, 1956; Knox & Inkster, 1968; Younger, Walker, & Arrowood, 1977). For instance, ask a person both *before* and *after* acting on a difficult choice, "How sure are you that your selection is the correct one?" Postchoice decision makers are invariably more confident in the wisdom of their choices than are those still in the decision process because postchoice individuals engage in dissonance-motivated cognitive work to appreciate their chosen alternative and depreciate their rejected alternatives. My favorite illustration of this phenomenon is the often heard (yet absurd) quote from a person looking back on life, "If I had to live my life over again, I wouldn't change a thing—not where I lived, what school I attended, who I married, which career I pursued, nor anything I said or did."

INSUFFICIENT JUSTIFICATION. Insufficient justification addresses how people explain their actions for which they have little or no prompting. For example, people might ask themselves why they donated money to a charity or why they stopped to pick up litter. In an experiment, researchers ask participants to engage in a terribly dull and pointless task (Festinger & Carlsmith, 1959). Afterwards, an experimenter asked each participant to help him out by telling the next hour's participant that the task was really quite entertaining. Half of the participants received $1 for the telling (insufficient justification for lying) while the other half received $20 (sufficient justification for lying). After the participants complied (and they all did), a different experimenter asked each participant to rate how interesting the task was. Deceivers with insufficient justification ($1) reported liking the task significantly more than deceivers with sufficient justification ($20). Those paid the larger amount had little dissonance to wrestle with ("I know why I lied, I earned the big bucks!"), but those paid a measly dollar had to wrestle the dissonance brought on by deceiving another without good reason. To the extent that the $1 participants were able to add a new cognition—that the task was truly interesting—they reduced their dissonance.

EFFORT JUSTIFICATION. During initiation rituals in the military, fraternities, sororities, athletic teams, gangs, and other groups, recruits often exert great effort and perform extreme behaviors that must later be justified. Consider the military private who parachutes out of an airplane as part of boot camp training. For novice recruits parachuting is an extreme behavior. To justify why in the world they would put their lives on the line like this, privates typically endorse a rather extreme liking for the behavior. Extreme behaviors breed extreme beliefs: If I did *that*, then I must *really love* this place! In other words, dissonance theory proposes that the attractiveness of a task increases as a direct function of the magnitude of effort expended in completing it. In an experiment, researchers asked college-aged women to join a weekly discussion group on the topic of the psychology of sex (Aronson & Mills, 1959). All the women underwent either a mild initiation ritual (recite a list of sexual but not obscene words) or a severe initiation ritual (recite aloud a list of obscene words from sexually explicit novels). After completing one initiation ritual or the other, all women participated in a rather dull discussion on an unrelated topic and rated how interesting that second discussion was. Women in the severe initiation group reported significantly more interest in the discussion than did women in the mild initiation group. Other researchers have found essentially the same result (Rosenfeld, Giacalone, & Tedeschi, 1984). The conclusion is that people who engage in extreme behaviors need extreme attitudes or values to justify their otherwise dissonance-arousing behaviors (Aronson, 1988).

NEW INFORMATION. As we listen to the radio, watch the television, attend lectures, and interact with others, we expose ourselves to opportunities to have our beliefs and opinions contradicted. One group of researchers followed the Seekers, a cultlike group convinced that their city and the entire western coast of the Americas would be destroyed by a great flood on a specific day (Festinger, Riecken, & Schachter, 1956, 1958). The specific day of cataclysm came and passed rather uneventfully, so the Seekers found their cherished belief of doom unequivocally disconfirmed. Given belief disconfirmation, what were the dissonance-suffering Seekers to do? They must have felt like the child who watches as his baseball hero strikes out (How could that be?). Some Seekers dropped out of the group, rejecting their previously held beliefs. Other Seekers, however, responded with strong, more persistent attempts at proselytizing. They reasoned that the belief disconfirmation must be a test of their sincerity and commitment to the cause (they added a new cognitive element). By proselytizing to gain new members, the latter group of Seekers attempted to resolve their dissonance by finding other people who would agree with and support their beliefs (i.e., change the environment). For an overview, Figure 7.4 summarizes the Seekers' dissonance-based motivational plight and lists the four options different Seekers chose as a means of dissonance resolution. The fifth option, trivialization, was little used because these beliefs were clearly core beliefs of the Seekers' sense of self.

Does Dissonance Produce an Aversive Motivational State?

Dissonance manifests itself as an aversive physiological state of psychological arousal. The negative affective state that arises from the physiological arousal is both motivationally aversive (people desire to reduce it) and a psychological warning signal (coping responses are needed). Critics, however, question whether cognitive inconsistency actually produces an aversive motivational state (Cooper & Fazio, 1984; Higgins, Rhodewalt, & Zanna, 1979). Critics argue that participants in dissonance experiments are aroused not by cognitive inconsistency but by arousing experimental manipulations, such as discussions of sex (Kiesler & Pallak, 1976) or by experimental engineered embarrassments (Abelson, 1983). To answer these criticisms, Cooper and

FIGURE 7–4
Dissonance-Motivated Strategies of the Seekers

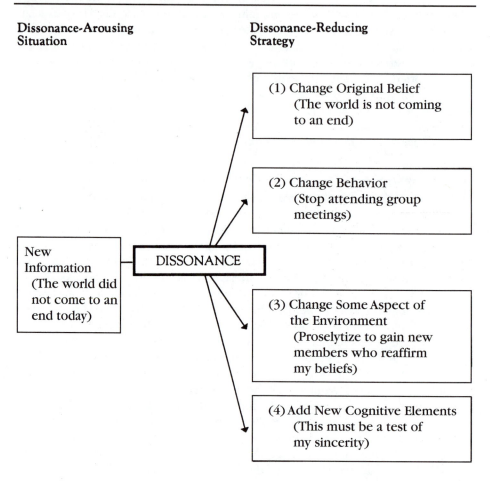

Dissonance-Arousing
Situation

Dissonance-Reducing
Strategy

New
Information
(The world did
not come to an
end today)

DISSONANCE

(1) Change Original Belief
(The world is not coming
to an end)

(2) Change Behavior
(Stop attending group
meetings)

(3) Change Some Aspect of
the Environment
(Proselytize to gain new
members who reaffirm
my beliefs)

(4) Add New Cognitive Elements
(This must be a test of
my sincerity)

his colleagues (Croyle & Cooper, 1983; Fazio & Cooper, 1983; Zanna & Cooper, 1976) tested whether cognitive inconsistencies produce autonomic nervous system arousal. The investigators asked college students to write an essay that argues for the merits of tuition increases; one group could choose not to write the essay, while another group had little choice (Croyle & Cooper, 1983). The high-choice group showed high physiological arousal by displaying a significantly greater number of galvanic skin responses (GSRs) than did the students with low choice. Hence, believing one thing but doing another without sufficient reason is indeed physiologically arousing (for additional empirical evidence, see Elkin & Leippe, 1986; Losch & Cacioppo, 1990).

Cognitive inconsistency does produce a negative affective state with motivational properties, a physiological dissonance motivation that operates at a psychological level (Elliot & Devine, 1994). The negative affective state dissipates rather quickly (Elkin & Leippe, 1986). Thus, dissonance motivation decays over time. The problem in daily life, however, is that circumstances frequently remind us of our cognitive inconsistencies via talking to friends, explaining our attitudes and values to others, listening to the news, hearing lectures, reading the paper, keeping a diary, and so forth. Dissonance decays in time, but life in the modern information age has a way of reminding us of our cognitive inconsistencies.

Dissonance Processes

Dissonance theory has generated over 1000 published studies (Cooper & Fazio, 1984), but it has also generated controversy. In the last decade or so, researchers have responded to criticisms with a diligent effort to delineate precisely those conditions that do or do not produce dissonance. Two processes emerged as necessary conditions for the generation of dissonance arousal (Rajecki, 1990). For dissonance to occur,

1. The persons counterattitudinal behaviors must produce aversive consequences.
2. The person must accept responsibility for those aversive consequences.

Figure 7.5 summarizes the necessary conditions under which dissonance arousal occurs (follow the double-line arrows). If the individual performs a counterattitudinal behavior, dissonance arousal occurs *if* the individual (1) assesses the consequences of his or her behavior to be aversive (e.g., driving my automobile will damage the environment and that is a bad thing) *and* (2) accepts personal responsibility for freely choosing to perform the behavior (e.g., I freely chose to drive my automobile instead of riding the bus). Without the assessment of the aversive consequences and without a perception of free choice, little or no dissonance arousal occurs (Goethals, Cooper, & Naficy, 1979; Johnson, Kelly, & LaBlanc, 1995).

Consider an empirical illustration of the proposition that perceived responsibility for aversive consequences from a counterattitudinal behavior is necessary for dissonance arousal (Johnson, Kelly, & LeBlanc, 1995). The researchers asked young college students to try to persuade another person to raise the legal drinking age. For

FIGURE 7–5
Sequence of Events Leading to Dissonance Arousal

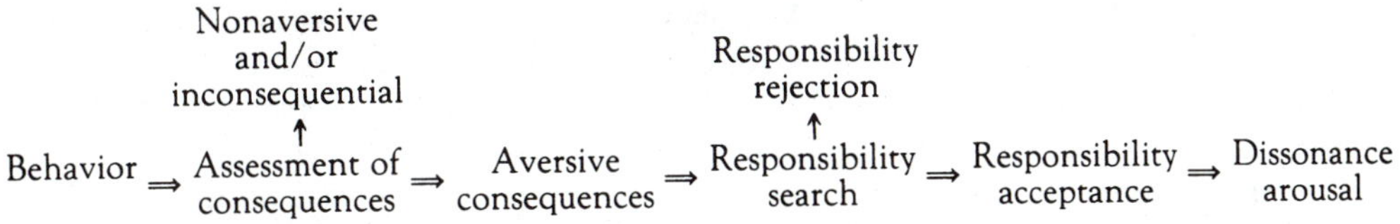

SOURCE: Cooper, J., & Fazio, R. H. (1984). A new look at dissonance theory. In L. Berkowitz's (Ed.), *Advances in experimental social psychology* (Vol. 17, pp. 229-266). New York: Academic Press.

perceived responsibility, the student persuaders were either asked (high choice/responsibility) or told (low choice/responsibility) to persuade the listener. For foreseeable harm, the listener had an opportunity to sign a petition to raise the legal drinking age. The only group of students to change their opinions in the direction of raising the drinking age were those who made counterattitudinal arguments under conditions of high choice/responsibility to a listener would could cause harm (by signing the petition).

Self-Perception Theory

An alternative interpretation of cognitive dissonance is that people develop their attitudes based not on an aversive physiological arousal (dissonance) but, rather, on self-observations of their behavior. That is, we eat squid for whatever reason (maybe we did not know it was squid) and after doing so presume that since we ate squid, we must therefore like it. Acquiring or changing attitudes via self-observations of one's own behavior is the basic tenet to self-perception theory (Bem, 1967, 1972; Bem & McConnell, 1970).

To test his ideas, Bem (1967) replicated the Festinger and Carlsmith (1959) study on insufficient justification (discussed earlier). Participants listened to a tape recording of another student (Bob) who performed the tedious task and received either $1 or $20 to lie, telling the next participant that the experimental task was an interesting one. The participant rated how interesting the task was either from his or her own perspective (one in which lying would produce dissonance motivation) or from Bob's perspective (one in which lying would not include dissonance motivation). From both perspectives—from their own as well as from Bob's—participants compensated with $1 reported significantly more task interest than did participants compensated with $20. Bem concluded that attitudes and beliefs have their roots in behavior and the stimuli that control that behavior ($1 and $20) and not in an aversive motivational state.

The dissonance versus self-perception debate led to a great deal of research (Fazio, Zanna, & Cooper, 1977, 1979; Ronis & Greenwald, 1979; Ross & Shulman, 1973; Snyder & Ebbesen, 1972). The conclusion was that both cognitive dissonance and self-perception theories are correct, but apply best to different sets of circumstances. Self-perception theory is more applicable to situations in which peoples' attitudes are initially vague, ambiguous, and weak. In such cases, people do indeed draw inferrences from their behavior. For example, suppose you go to the supermarket to buy hand lotion, but have little or no brand preference. After you pick brand X instead of brand Y, by chance or because of a coupon or whatever, the next time you buy lotion you tend to think, "Well, last time I picked brand X; therefore I must like brand X more than brand Y." Dissonance theory is more applicable to situations in which peoples' attitudes are initially clear, salient, and strong. In those cases, people tend to sense aversive motivation following counterattitudinal behavior.

The dissonance versus self-perception debate indirectly invited other theoretical explanations to compete against dissonance theory. Some dissonance behaviors have been explained as impression management (Gaes, Kalle, & Tedeschi, 1978; Tedeschi, Schlenker, & Bonoma, 1971), self-esteem protection (Greenwald & Ronis,

1978), or ego-based need for a positive self-image (Steele, 1978; Steele & Liu, 1983). The essence of these rival explanations is that people are not so concerned with cognitive consistency as they are with looking consistent and maintaining a favorable image to others and to themselves (Abelson, 1983; Greenwald & Ronis, 1978; Wickland & Brehm, 1976). In other words, consistency is often as much of a social concern as it is an aversive physiological state. These alternative explanations are as much additions to cognitive dissonance theory as they are theoretical rivals (Aronson, 1988). For example, the impression-management interpretation tells us that people wish to behave consistently to themselves and to others. Cognitive dissonance theory's basic idea that people strive for cognitive consistency and behave in ways that maintain or restore consistency is alive and well (Cialdini, Petty, & Cacioppo, 1981; Cooper & Croyle, 1984).

SUMMARY

The cognitive perspective on motivation focuses on mental processes as causal determinants to action. Thus, the cognitive study of motivation is interested in the cognition → action sequence, and this chapter discussed the motivational significance of three elements in the cognition-action sequence: plan, goal, and dissonance. Each concept of plan, goal, and dissonance assumes an internal process in which ongoing behavior is compared to an ideal, a goal, or a belief. Each concept contributes to a motivational analysis of behavior in that each functions to energize and direct ongoing coping behavior so that a discrepancy can be removed or reduced.

Plans exemplify the early cognitive models of motivation. People have a cognitive representation of ideal behavior, environment, and event. People are also aware of their present behavior, environment, and event. When a mismatch is thought to exist between the ideal and the actual, the incongruity motivates the individual to engage in plan-directed behavior that will produce a match between ideal and actual. Researchers now extend the concept of *plan* to correction motivation, a revision that allows present/ideal discrepancies to initiate either plan-directed behavior or plan-revising cognitive work. Corrective motivation also has emotional implications, as slower than expected progress generates negative emotions whereas faster than expected progress generates positive emotions.

Goals are those objectives people strive to accomplish. Like plans, goals generate motivation by focusing people's attention on the discrepancy between their present level of accomplishment and their ideal level of accomplishment. Two types of goal-performance discrepancies exist: discrepancy reduction and discrepancy creation. Discrepancy reduction captures the essence of plans, whereas discrepancy creation captures the essence of goals and the goal-setting process. Goals that are both difficult and specific generally improve performance, and they do so by producing four motivational consequences: Difficult goals mobilize effort and increase persistence, whereas specific goals direct attention toward the task and promote ongoing strategy development and revision. Two conditions are necessary for goals to enhance performance—feedback and goal acceptance. With feedback, a performer can evaluate his or her performance as being at, above, or below the level of the goal standard. Performing below goal level generates incongruity and a desire to improve future performance; performing above goal level generates competence and the setting of more difficult goals. Goal acceptance refers to the process in which the performer accepts an assigned goal as his or her own. Goal setting theory has a number of dangers and pitfalls. Specifically, its purpose is to increase productivity rather than motivation per se. Also, goals work best with simple and relatively uninteresting tasks, and goals potentially increase stress, open the door to the possibility of failure, and put intrinsic motivation at risk.

Cognitive dissonance theory focuses on the motivational implications of contradictions. Its basic tenet is that human beings dislike inconsistency and therefore strive for consistency in their thoughts, beliefs, attitudes, opinions, values, and behaviors. Cognitive inconsistencies arise in four types of situations—choice, insufficient justification, effort justification, and new information—provided that the behavior produced under these circumstances is voluntarily and potential harm is foreseeable. Dissonance motivation, when intense enough to motivate the person to action, gives rise to one or more of the following five dissonance-reducing coping strategies: changing original belief, changing behavior, changing some aspect of the environment, adding new beliefs, or trivializing the cognitive elements involved in the inconsistency.

RECOMMENDED READINGS

Becker, L. J. (1978). Joint effect of feedback and goal setting on performance: A field study of residential energy conservation. *Journal of Applied Psychology, 63,* 428–433.

Campion, M. A., & Lord, R. G. (1982). A control systems conceptualization of the goal-setting and changing process. *Organizational Behavior and Human Performance, 30,* 265–287.

Cooper, J., & Fazio, R. H. (1984). A new look at dissonance: A current perspective. In L. Berkowitz (Ed.), *Advances in experimental social psychology* (Vol. 4, pp. 1–34). New York: Academic Press.

Earley, P. C., Wojnaroski, P., & Prest, W. (1987). Task planning and energy expended: Exploration of how goals influence performance. *Journal of Applied Psychology, 72,* 107–113.

Erez, M., Earley, P. C., & Hulin, C. L. (1985). The impact of participation on goal acceptance and performance: A two-step model. *Academy of Management Journal, 28,* 50–66.

Goethals, G. R., Cooper, J., & Naficy, A. (1979). Role of foreseen, foreseeable, and unforeseeable consequences in the arousal of cognitive dissonance. *Journal of Personality and Social Psychology, 37,* 1179–1185.

Knox, R. E., & Inkster, J. A. (1968). Postdecision dissonance at post time. *Journal of Personality and Social Psychology, 8,* 319–323.

Locke, E. A., Shaw, K. N., Saari, L. M., & Latham, G. P. (1981). Goal setting and task performance: 1969–1980. *Psychological Bulletin, 90,* 125–152.

Simon, L., Greenberg, J., & Brehm, J. (1995). Trivialization: The forgotten mode of dissonance reduction. *Journal of Personality and Social Psychology, 68,* 247–260.

Tubbs, M. E. (1986). Goal setting: A meta-analytic examination of the empirical evidence. *Journal of Applied Psychology, 71,* 474–483.

Chapter 8   p. 182-3
              188-91

EXPECTANCIES

What Is an Expectancy?
  Two Kinds of Expectancy
  Efficacy Expectations
  Outcome Expectations
Self-Efficacy
  Effects of Self-Efficacy on Motivated Behavior
Expectancy × Value Theory
  Expectancy
  Value
  Force
Learned Helplessness
  Applications to Humans
  Components
  Effects
  Critical Research Issues
  Criticisms and Alternative Explanations of Helplessness
  Learned Laziness
Reactance Theory
  Reactance and Learned Helplessness

What do you expect will happen to you? Will you graduate from college? Do you expect next semester's classes to be interesting? If you raise your hand to speak in class, will the professor acknowledge you? Will your classmates support your initiative? This winter, will you catch the flu? When you apply for your next job, will you get it? Do you expect that the interviewer will be impressed? If you were to go on a blind date, would your date like you? Will you ever find someone to share your life with, as in marriage? When you drive to school or work tomorrow, will you get stuck in traffic? Receive a parking ticket? Have a flat tire? Have an accident? When you turn the car's ignition key, do you expect the car to start? Will you win the lottery this year? Will you live to see your 50th birthday?

How competent and expert do you expect your performances to be? In academics, can you make the dean's list? Can you use a computer to write and print out a term paper? Can you make an A in this course? If you were to fail the first exam, could you come back and do well? Could you explain the themes of chapter 7 to your roommate? What do you expect would happen if you tried to surf the internet? What would happen if you tried to surf a wave on the ocean? If you tried to recite the names of all your classmates, how many names could you recall? If you were to start reciting the 50 U.S. states and their capitals, how many could you name? In relationships, can you make another person laugh? Could you cheer up a friend who was depressed? Can you defuse arguments as they arise? In the next party you attend, could you be the life of the party? If a bully insults and pesters you, could you cope effectively? If you saw someone steal one of your possessions, could you get it back? In athletics, can you become a professional? Can you run a mile in 6 minutes or less? Could you run 3 miles without stopping to rest? How about 1 mile? Could you hit a golf ball on your first try? What if an audience was watching, could you hit it then?

What does it matter what you expect to happen, and what does it matter what you expect you can or cannot do? Imagine how motivationally problematic your college experience would be if you expected not to graduate, not to pass the course, not to get a job, not to understand the professor, and if you expected your classes to be dull and computers to be unresponsive? Imagine how motivationally problematic your interpersonal relationships would be if you expected others not to like you, not to care about your welfare, or to show only hostility? What if you expected that everyone you met would reject you? Imagine how motivationally problematic your athletic participation would be if you expected only to fail and to embarrass yourself in front of others? Imagine how difficult it would be to muster the motivation to run 3 miles if you knew beforehand that you could not do so.

WHAT IS AN EXPECTANCY?

Expectancy is a subjective prediction of how likely it is one can achieve a particular goal or successfully execute a course of action. It is a knowledge structure, based on past experience, that allows the individual to estimate the probable occurrence of some event or outcome. When politicians enter an election or athletes enter a competition, they appraise the likelihood that they will win. Before people leap across a creek or tell a risqué joke, they appraise the likelihood of landing on solid ground, literally and figuratively. In anticipating election and athletic outcomes and in anticipating jumping and joking, people make predictions of the probability of attaining their goals, and those expectancies have motivational properties and consequences.

Two Kinds of Expectancy

There are two types of expectancies: efficacy expectations and outcome expectations (Bandura, 1977, 1986; Heckhausen, 1977). An efficacy expectation, shown in Figure 8.1, is a judgment of one's ability to execute a particular act or course of action. An outcome expectation, also shown in Figure 8.1, is a judgment that a given action, once performed, will cause a particular outcome. Efficacy expectations pertain to estimates of the likelihood that the individual can perform an act; outcome expectations pertain to estimates of how likely it is that certain consequences will follow once the action is accomplished.

Both efficacy and outcome expectations are independent causal determinants to the initiation and ongoing regulation of behavior. Imagine the medical doctor considering performing open-heart surgery on a patient. The extent to which the doctor initiates the surgery and persists until its completion is a function of two expectations: (1) the doctor's efficacy expectation that he or she can successfully perform the surgery and (2) the doctor's outcome expectation that the surgery, once completed, will produce certain physical and social ends for the patient or certain professional and financial ends for the doctor.

Both efficacy and outcome expectations must be reasonably high before behavior becomes energetic and directed. Thus, understanding people's reluctance to engage in activities such as public speaking, dating, athletics, and job interviews becomes more understandable. To address a group, date, compete, or interview, the person must overcome doubt over executing these actions and expect that effective performance will pay off by leading to desired outcomes.

FIGURE 8–1
Efficacy and Outcome Expectations

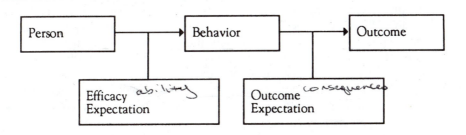

Efficacy Expectations

Efficacy expectations concern how confident the individual is of the ability to execute a specific act or a sequence of action. Generally speaking, the more people expect that they can adequately perform an action, the more willing they are to engage in activities requiring such actions, to put forth the effort necessary to master challenges, and to persist in the face of obstacles (Bandura, 1989; Bandura & Cervone, 1983; Weinberg, Gould, & Jackson, 1979). In contrast, when people expect that they cannot successfully perform the required task, they are not willing to engage in activities requiring such behavior; they slacken their effort, prematurely settle for mediocre outcomes, and quit in the face of obstacles (Bandura, 1989).

Efficacy expectations do not just occur out of the blue; they have causes. Efficacy expectations arise from (1) past performance history in trying to execute that particular task, (2) observations of others as they try to execute the task, (3) verbal persuasions (pep talks) from others, and (4) physiological states such as a racing heart.

PERSONAL BEHAVIOR HISTORY. Personal history in trying to execute a particular course of action provides the performer with firsthand performance-mastery information (Bandura, Reese, & Adams, 1982). Of the four sources of efficacy expectations, personal history is the most influential (Bandura, 1986). Performances judged as competent raise efficacy expectations whereas performances judged as incompetent lower them. For instance, if a person resolves to ride a bicycle or to sing in public, his or her expectations before the next ride or song grow out of a personal history of riding and singing. How important any one performance is to future efficacy expectations depends on the strength of the performer's expectation. After repeated successful experiences have produced a strong expectation of efficacy, an occasional failure will not change the previous efficacy expectation very much. Or, after repeated unsuccessful experiences have produced low efficacy expectations an occasional success will do little to raise them. If the performer is less experienced, each new success or failure will have greater effect on future efficacy expectations.

VICARIOUS EXPERIENCE. Seeing others perform masterfully raises an observer's own efficacy expectations (Bandura et al., 1980; Kazdin, 1979). Seeing others perform the action in question permits comparison (if they can do it, so can I). Of course, vicarious experience works the other way too. Observing someone performing incompetently lowers our own efficacy expectation (If they can't do it, what makes me think I can?) (Brown & Inouye, 1978). The extent to which another's performance affects our own efficacy expectations depends on two factors. First, the greater the similarity between the model and the observer, the greater the impact the model's performance has on the observer's expectation (Schunk, 1989a). Second, the less experienced the observer is at the activity (more novice than expert), the greater the impact of the vicarious experience (Schunk, 1989b). Thus, vicarious experience is a potent source of efficacy expectations for inexperienced observers who watch similar others perform.

VERBAL PERSUASION. Coaches, parents, teachers, employers, therapists, peers, spouses, friends, audiences, authors of self-help books, infomercials, inspirational posters, and songs on the radio often attempt to convince us that we can competently execute a given task or action, despite our entrenched inefficacy. Effective pep talks persuade the performer to focus more on potentials, competencies, and personal strengths and less on deficiencies, past failures, and personal weaknesses. If the persuasion is successful, then the individual is likely to expect an efficacious performance and put forth greater and more sustained effort. But verbal persuasion goes only so far if it is soon contradicted by direct experience. Its effectiveness is limited by the boundaries of the possible (in the mind of the performer) and depends on the credibility, expertise, and trustworthiness of the persuader. Individuals also give themselves pep talks, often in the form of self-instruction that can boost efficacy expectations (Schunk & Cox, 1986). Verbal persuasion is the third most influential source of efficacy expectations (Schunk, 1989a). The importance of verbal persuasions can be found in (1) providing the performer with enough of a temporary efficacy boost to initiate task engagement (Schunk, 1991) and (2) counteracting the occasional setback that might otherwise cultivate sufficient doubt in the performer to interrupt task persistence (Schunk, 1992).

PHYSIOLOGICAL STATE. Fatigue, windedness, pain, muscle tension, mental confusion, and trembling hands are physiological cues that the demands of the task currently exceed the performer's ability (Taylor et al., 1985). An abnormal physiological state is a private message that contributes to expectations of inefficacy. An absence of tension, fear, and stress, on the other hand, heightens efficacy expectations by providing firsthand bodily feedback that one can indeed cope adequately with task demands (Bandura & Adams, 1977). The causal direction between inefficacy and physiological arousal is bidirectional: inefficacy heightens arousal and heightened arousal signals inefficacy (Bandura et al., 1988). Like vicarious experience and verbal persuasion, physiological states are a relatively minor source of information in determining efficacy expectations. A physiological state contributes mostly when initial efficacy is uncertain (one is performing a task for the first time). When efficacy expectations are relatively certain, people generally reinterpret (Boy, am I pumped!) or discount their physiological cues (Carver & Blaney, 1977).

Outcome Expectations

Whereas efficacy expectations involve the person's judgment of how masterfully he or she can execute a particular course of action, outcome expectation involves the judgment of whether that course of action will produce a desirable outcome. The essence of an outcome expectation is the question, "If I perform behavior X adequately, will I get outcome Y?" (If I run a mile every day this week, will I lose two pounds? and If I can muster the courage to ask him to the dance, will he reject me?). All other things being equal (efficacy, needs, incentives), high effort and strong persistence are more likely for those outcomes for which individuals estimate a high probability of attainment; that is, they have a high outcome expectancy. There are four determinants of outcome expectancies: history of outcome feedback, task difficulty, social comparison information, and personality differences.

OUTCOME FEEDBACK. As individuals involve themselves in a task, they invariably assess whether their task engagements produce mostly successes or mostly failures. Success and failure appraisals can be subjective (I did better than I thought I would do, therefore I succeeded) or, more typically, objective (I won the trophy, therefore I succeeded). Figure 8.2 illustrates the effect of objective outcome feedback on an individual's future outcome expectancy (from Feather, 1966). Participants worked on a series of 15 anagrams in which the first five anagrams were either very difficult or very easy. Thus, half of the participants were set up for initial failure, whereas the other half were set up for initial success. Then, on trials 6 to 15, all participants worked on the same set of anagrams, all of which were of the same moderate difficulty. As illustrated, expectations of success in trials 6 to 15 were significantly biased by the initial outcome feedback. Success feedback on trials 1 to 5 positively biased outcome expectancies on trials 6 to 15, while initial failure outcomes negatively biased subsequent outcome expectancies (Feather, 1966; Feather & Saville, 1967). These data are especially noteworthy because participants in the initial failure and initial success groups actually performed about the same on trials 6 to 15.

FIGURE 8–2
Relationship between Performance Feedback and Outcome Expectations

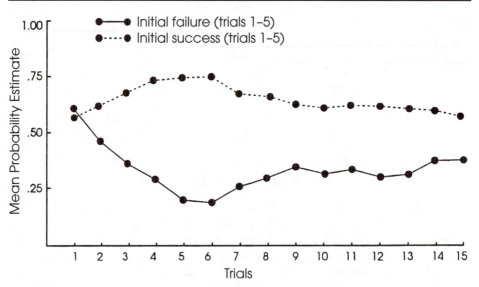

SOURCE: Feather, N. T. (1966). Effects of prior success and failure on expectations of success and subsequent failure. *Journal of Personality and Social Psychology, 3,* 287–298. Copyright © 1966 by the American Psychological Association. Reprinted by permission.

TASK DIFFICULTY. Task difficulty appraisals depend on the specific salient characteristics of the task that signal how easy or hard it is. Thus the hiker notices the very steep cliff, the programmer scans the complex computer program, and the student flips through the 500-page book. The steepness of the rock, the complexity of the program, and the length of the book are evaluated as difficult task characteristics. In contrast, the hiker might notice a gently sloping hill, the programmer might scan a basic computer program, and the student might flip through a three-page article (easy task characteristics). Generally speaking, difficult task characteristics yield low expectancies of success whereas easy task characteristics yield high expectancies of success.

SOCIAL COMPARISON INFORMATION. A third determinant of outcome expectancies is the observation of the outcomes others receive on the same task (DeVillis, DeVillis, & McCauley, 1978). A performer is almost always aware of some group norm of how people succeed and fail at the task. If the performer is aware of others' past outcomes, then his or her outcome expectancy will be based, in part, on this information. For example, a college student who enrolls in a particular course is often aware of the outcomes experienced by previous students in this class. The student consequently does not enter the course naively. Rather, the student enters the class with an outcome expectation that coincides with the typical outcomes others have previously attained (this is an easy course, so I expect to get an A). Similarly, if an athletic team plays a team that everyone else has previously defeated, the team will expect a victory.

PERSONALITY. The final determinant of outcome expectancies is the individual's personality. Need for achievement predisposes people to overestimate their chances for success prior to task participation (Weiner, 1974). High-need achievers generally have overly optimistic outcome expectations, whereas low-need achievers generally have relatively pessimistic outcome expectancies (they underestimate their chances for success). The same pattern holds for individuals with high and low self-esteem (McFarlin & Blascovich, 1981).

The variables that affect the acquisition and change of both efficacy and outcome expectations are summarized in Table 8.1, which implies separate therapeutic strategies for persons with low expectations. To alter efficacy expectations, direct mastery experience, vicarious experience, verbal persuasion, and physiological

TABLE 8–1

Sources of Efficacy and Outcome Expectations

SOURCES OF EFFICACY EXPECTATIONS	SOURCES OF OUTCOME EXPECTATIONS
Personal behavior history	Outcome feedback
Vicarious experience	Task difficulty
Verbal persuasion	Social comparison information
Abnormal physiological state	Personality

state are promising routes. To alter outcome expectations, attention is best directed toward outcome feedback, perceptions of task difficulty, social comparison information, and personality differences.

SELF-EFFICACY

Efficacy expectations center on questions such as, "Can I successfully perform a particular task?" Self-efficacy centers on the self's capacity to cope successfully with the demands presented by tasks or situations. The capacity to use one's resources well under diverse circumstances characterizes self-efficacy, which is defined as the individual's judgment of how well (or poorly) they will perform given the skills they possess and the circumstances they face (Bandura, 1986, 1993).

Self-efficacy concerns the difference between possessing skills and using them well. Competent functioning requires not only ability, but also the capacity to translate abilities into effective performance, especially under trying circumstances. Self-efficacy is just as important a determinant of performance as is ability, because performance situations often are stressful, ambiguous, and unpredictable and, as one performs, circumstances often change. Most of us can drive rather well on the interstate, as most of us rate very high on abilities such as steering, braking, negotiating traffic, reciting traffic laws, and finding our destinations. But self-efficacy is put to the test when driving in an unreliable car on an unfamiliar road with poorly marked streets during a heavy winter snowstorm as monster trucks whiz by. Highly skilled drivers sometimes perform dismally because circumstances change in stressful ways. Under trying circumstances, the driver must be able to plan before the trip begins, relax to keep arousal level in check, decide between options, avoid perils, and perhaps negotiate or show leadership to enlist the assistance of the passenger.

The opposite of self-efficacy is self-doubt. For the driver who doubts his abilities, unwelcomed surprises, setbacks, and difficulties create anxiety (Bandura, 1988), confusion (Wood & Bandura, 1989), negative expectations (Bandura, 1983), and aversive physiological arousal and bodily tension (Bandura et al., 1985). Imagine the unfolding of events that might occur when the self-doubt of an otherwise skilled driver comes face-to-face with surprises, setbacks, and difficulties. Perhaps an unexpected storm begins (surprise), or the windshield wipers fail (setback), or ice forms on the surface of the road (difficulty). Under such trying conditions, doubt can interfere with effective thinking, planning, and decision making to cause anxiety, confusion, arousal, tension, and distressing anticipations that spiral performance toward disaster. Of course, surprises, setbacks, and difficulties may not produce poor performance, just as skill, talent, and ability may not produce excellent performance. Rather, self-efficacy (or self-doubt) determines the extent to which a performer copes successfully when skills are stressed.

Consider a second example—the challenge of a first date. In a self-efficacy analysis, the skills involved in dating and the demands of the dating situation are complex and multidimensional. The following lists describe an adolescent on a first date (from Rose & Frieze, 1989) by listing some task demands (left) as well as the skills needed to meet those demands successfully (right).

Dating Demands	Dating Skills
Ask for a date	Assertiveness
Make a plan for what to do	Planning, creativity
Arrive on time at date's house	Punctuality
Meet parents or roommates	Sociability
Get to know date	Perception
Joke, laugh, and talk	Sense of humor
Try to impress date	Salesmanship
Be polite	Social etiquette
Understand how the other feels	Empathy
Kiss goodnight	Romance

As the adolescent contemplates the date, he or she must ask what specific task-related events will take place? What specific skills will be needed to perform well? If things go unexpectedly wrong, can he or she make necessary corrective adjustments? How does he or she expect to feel during the date, and during each specific event? In this hypothetical situation, the dater expects that the overall task at hand—going on a first date—will require a dozen or so skills, such as assertiveness, planning, punctuality, sociability, perception and so on. The adolescent also has some expectation of how effectively he or she can execute each of these skills on the date, and those expectancies probably range from terrible to excellent. These expectations of anticipated performance effectiveness—will I perform well or will I perform poorly?—represent the essence of self-efficacy beliefs. The adolescent also has some expectation that, if things go wrong, he or she can get the evening back on track by initiating the necessary corrective adjustments. These expectations affect the extent and persistence of the adolescent's coping efforts to enact corrective adjustments (discussed in the next section). Finally, the dater expects to feel a certain way as he or she executes specific skills. The expected emotions center around a continuum that ranges from confidence and hope to doubt and fear.

Effects of Self-Efficacy on Motivated Behavior

Efficacy beliefs exert diverse effects on motivational aspects of behavior (Bandura, 1986). Self-efficacy beliefs affect (1) choice of activities and selection of environments, (2) extent of effort and persistence put forth during performance, (3) the quality of thinking and decision making during performance, and (4) emotional reactions, especially those related to stress and anxiety.

CHOICE. People continually make choices about what activities and what environments to pursue. In general, people seek out and approach with excitement activities and situations they feel capable of adjusting to or handling, while people shun and actively avoid activities and situations they see as likely to overwhelm their coping capacities (Bandura, 1977, 1989). In a self-efficacy analysis, choice is frequently a self-protective action designed to ensure against the possibility of being over-whelmed by the demands and challenges of the task. If the student expects a math class or a foreign language class to lead to confusion and emotional frustration, self-doubt produces avoidance decisions such as withdrawing from class discussions or not enrolling in the first place. The same doubt-plagued avoidance choices apply to avoiding social opportunities, not participating in sports or music, and dropping out of organizations and careers. Such avoidance choices can exert a profound, long-term effect on development (Bandura, 1986). Weak self-efficacy beliefs set the stage for people to shun participating in activities and therefore contribute to arrested de-velopmental potentials (Holahan & Holahan, 1987). When people shun an activity out of doubt over personal competence, they participate in the self-destructive process of retarding their development. Further, the more they avoid such activities, the more entrenched self-doubt becomes—because doubters never give themselves a chance to prove themselves wrong. Tragically, such a pattern of avoidance pro-gressively narrows people's range of activities and settings (Bandura, 1982; Betz & Hackett, 1986; Hackett, 1985).

EFFORT AND PERSISTENCE. As people perform, self-efficacy beliefs influence how much effort they exert as well as how long they put forth that effort in the face of adversity (Bandura, 1989). Strong self-efficacy beliefs produce effortful and persis-tent coping efforts aimed at overcoming setbacks and difficulties (Salomon, 1984). The doubt from weak self-efficacy beliefs, on the other hand, leads people to slacken their efforts when they encounter difficulties or to give up altogether (Bandura & Cervone, 1983; Weinberg, Gould, & Jackson, 1979). Self-doubt also leads perform-ers to settle prematurely on mediocre solutions. In trying to master complex activi-ties, learning is always fraught with difficulties, obstacles, setbacks, frustrations, re-jections, and inequalities. Bandura (1989) argues that self-efficacy plays the pivotal role it does in facilitating effort and persistence not because it silences self-doubt fol-lowing failure and rejection (because these are expected, normal emotional reac-tions), but because self-efficacy leads to a *quick recovery* of self-assurance following such setbacks. Using examples of persistent writers, scientists, and athletes, Bandura argues that it is the resiliency of self-efficacy in the face of being pounded by unin-terrupted failure that provides the motivational support necessary to continue the persistent effort needed for competent functioning.

THINKING AND DECISION MAKING. People who believe strongly in their effi-cacy to solve problems remain efficient in their analytic thinking during episodes of complex decision making, whereas people who doubt their problem-solving capac-ities think erratically (Bandura & Wood, 1989; Wood & Bandura, 1989). To perform their best, people must use memories of past events to generate hypotheses about the most effective course of action to take, they must analyze feedback to assess and reassess the merit of their plans and strategies, and they must reflect upon perfor-mance and remember which courses of action were effective and which were not.

A strong sense of efficacy allows the performer to remain task involved, even in the face of situational stress and problem-solving dead ends. In contrast, self-doubt deteriorates and distracts such thinking and decision-making processes.

EMOTIONAL REACTIONS. Before performers begin an activity, they typically spend time thinking about how they will perform. Persons with a strong sense of efficacy attend to the demands and challenges of the task, visualize success scenarios for forthcoming performances, and react to task challenges and feedback with enthusiastic effort, optimism, and interest. Persons with a weak sense of efficacy dwell on personal deficiencies, visualize the formidable obstacles they face, and react to challenges and feedback with pessimism, anxiety, and depression (Bandura, 1986). When things go wrong, strong and positive self-efficacy beliefs keep anxiety at bay. People who doubt their efficacy, however, are quickly threatened by difficulties, react to setbacks with distress, and see their attention drift away from performing the task per se and toward their personal deficiencies and the potential consequences of failure. Life brings any number of potentially threatening events (e.g., examinations, public performances) and the extent of a person's self-efficacy plays a central role in determining how much stress and anxiety such events bring. Threat is not a fixed property of events, however, as threat always depends on the relationship a person has to the event at hand (Folkman & Lazarus, 1985; Lazarus & Folkman, 1984). Performers cope with potentially aversive demands, experiences, and consequences. Knowing that one's coping abilities cannot handle an event's perceived threats conjures up thoughts of disaster, emotional arousal, and feelings of distress and anxiety (Bandura, 1983; Bandura, Reese, & Adams, 1982; Bandura et al., 1985; Lazarus, 1991a). More optimistically, when people plagued with self-doubt undergo therapy-like conditions to enhance their coping capabilities, the once intimidating event that conjured up such an avalanche of doubt, dread, and distress no longer does so (Bandura & Adams, 1977; Bandura et al., 1980; Bandura, Reese, & Adams, 1982; Ozer and Bandura, 1990). As self-efficacy increases, fear and anxiety slip away.

EXPECTANCY × VALUE THEORY

According to expectancy × value theory, the tendency to approach or to avoid an event is the product of two factors: expectancy and value. The tendency to approach or avoid an environmental object is termed force.

Expectancy

In the expectancy × value framework, expectancy is means outcome expectancy. Expectancy is expressed on a scale of probability (p) from 0 to 1. Suppose a student considers which actions he expects to most successfully lead to a passing grade in the course; his expectancies can be expressed as follows: reading the textbook (p = .85), studying lecture notes (p = .60), going to class every day (p = .80), and becoming close friends with the teacher (p = .25). A probability near 1 represents a strong outcome expectancy that a particular behavior will lead to a particular outcome, while a probability near 0 represents a strong doubt as to whether the behavior will produce the outcome.

Value

Value expresses anticipated satisfaction toward something (Vroom, 1964). An object has positive value when a person prefers attaining it to not attaining it; an object has negative value when a person prefers not attaining it to attaining it. Value is expressed on a scale ranging from −10 to +10. When a child is at school, for instance, he is in an environment rich in stimuli of varying value that might be expressed as follows: recess, +9, best friend Johnny, +10, teacher, +5, principal, −1, reading time, −2, spelling bees, −10, art, +2, and dodgeball, −4. Though value is relatively straightforward, its determinants are many (Ortony, Clore, & Collins, 1988). First, an object can have *intrinsic value* derived from pleasure gained in the mere performance of the activity, as in hobbies and sexual activity. Second, an object can have a *difficulty value* stemming from the pleasure one feels from succeeding at a skill-demanding activity, such as climbing mount Everest or becoming the class valedictorian. Third, an object can have *instrumental value* from pleasure gained in accomplishing a subtask necessary to obtain a larger future goal, such as passing a driver's license test or a job interview. Fourth, an object can have *extrinsic value* gained from the pleasure derived from rewards, such as a paycheck or trophy. Finally, an object can have *cultural value* that stems from being esteemed by the society, such as honor felt after enlisting in the armed forces or helping a person in need.

Values exist not only as beliefs about what in life is valuable and what is not but also as motives (Feather, 1995). Though values and needs can be distinguished on a number of grounds, values function like needs in that they too influence goal-directed action. Value strength, like need intensity, predicts the person's invested effort, persistence, choices, and emotional reactions (Feather, 1992, 1995).

Force

Expectancies and values combine to produce a motivational tendency to approach or avoid situations. That motivational tendency is force (Vroom, 1964). Intensity of force is a product of expectancies and values, such that force equals expectancy × value. The greater the expectation of success times the value of the outcome obtained (or avoided), the more energetic will be the motivation to approach that environmental object. Conversely, the lower the expectation of success times the value of the goal object, the more energetic will be the motivation to avoid that environmental object. If either expectancy or value is zero, force will be zero. For a person who has no expectancy of success or values the environmental object as neutral (V = 0), then Force to approach or avoid will be zero. The expectancy × value = force conceptualization predicts approach/avoidance performances rather well (Feather & Newton, 1982; Mitchell, 1974; Schwab, Olian-Gottlieb, & Heneman, 1979).

TABLE 8–2

Expectancy × Value Framework Applied to Pursuing a Career

CAREER	EXPECTANCY	VALUE	(E × V) FORCE
Physician	.40	+7	+2.80
Teacher	.70	+5	+3.50
Astronaut	.01	+10	+0.10
Volunteer aide	.95	−1	−0.95
Politician	.25	−6	−1.50
Professional athlete	.10	+9	+0.90
Executive secretary	.45	−4	−1.80
Factory worker	.75	+4	+3.00
Nurse	.50	+7	+3.50

Expectancy = 0 to 1; value = −10 to +10.

Consider the motivational quandary of the high school student contemplating a career decision. Table 8.2 lists the student's career options; each career option can be assigned both an expectation for success as well as a value. The expectation represents the student's probability of entering that vocation. The value represents the student's estimate of how satisfying such a vocation would be (based on its intrinsic, difficulty, instrumental, extrinsic, and cultural values). Because each career option can be assigned an expectancy (of success) and a value, the student's motivation (force) to pursue each can be calculated. The careers of teacher (3.50) and nurse (3.50) have relatively high forces, while the careers of executive secretary (−1.80) and politician (−1.50) have relatively low forces. Table 8.2 illustrates a fundamental proposition of the expectancy × value framework, namely that for an individual to be energized to pursue a goal, both expectancy of success and value must be relatively high. If only expectancy is high (volunteer aids and factory worker) or if only value is high (astronaut and professional athlete), the tendency to approach that goal remains relatively low.

A second example is illustrated by a young woman deciding whom to invite to the Sadie Hawkins dance. The numbers for the four potential dates in Table 8.3 are the same as those of the first four career options in Table 8.2. According to the expectancy × value formula, the woman will probably ask Kurt Zoeller to the dance because he is the stimulus associated with the greatest force, or approach motiva-

TABLE 8–3

Expectancy × Value Framework Applied to Choosing a Date

POTENTIAL DATE	EXPECTANCY	VALUE	(E × V) FORCE
John Smothers	.40	+7	+2.80
Kurt Zoeller	.70	+5	+3.50
Billy Ray Johnson	.01	+10	+0.10
James Hatcher	.95	−1	−0.95

Expectancy = 0 to 1; value = −10 to +10.

tion. Billy Ray Johnson is highly valued as a potential date, but he is not asked because of the woman's expectancy that he would not accept. James Hatcher is expected to accept the invitation, but he is not invited because of his relatively low value.

LEARNED HELPLESSNESS

When people consider engaging in a task, they typically know what outcome is at stake, so the chief dimension on which outcome expectancies vary is the extent of how personally controllable the outcome is. The strongest outcome expectancy comes from a one-to-one relationship between behavior (what I do) and outcomes (what happens to me); the weakest comes from a random relationship between behavior and outcomes. When people expect that desired outcomes (e.g., making friends, getting a job) are independent of their behavior and when people expect that they are helpless to influence the undesired outcomes (e.g., preventing illness, being fired from a job), they start to develop a *learned helplessness.* Learned helplessness is the psychological state that results when an individual expects that life's outcomes are uncontrollable (Mikulincer, 1994; Seligman, 1975).

Consider the following experiment with three groups of dogs that were given (1) inescapable shock, (2) escapable shock, or (3) no shock (control group) (Seligman & Maier, 1967). Dogs in the two shock groups were placed into a sling and given mild 5-second electric shocks once a day for 64 days. In the inescapable shock group, the shocks occurred randomly and no response could terminate the shock. Whether the dog barked, howled, or thrashed about frantically, the shock continued for its full 5 seconds. In the escapable shock group, the dogs could push a button that terminated the shock. The dogs therefore had a response available to escape the shock. In the no-shock control group, dogs were placed into a sling but received no shocks.

Exposure to inescapable, escapable, or no shock constituted the first phase of the two-phase experiment. In the second phase, the dogs from each group were all treated the same. Each dog was placed into a two-way shuttle box in which two compartments were separated by a wall partition of shoulder height. The two compartments were the same size and similar in most respects, except the first compartment had a grid floor through which a mild electrical shock could be delivered. To illustrate the procedure, Figure 8.3 shows a dog in the sling (A, phase 1 of the experiment) and in the shuttle box (*B*, phase 2 of the experiment, from Carlson, 1988). On each trial, the dogs were placed into the grid floor compartment and a mild shock was delivered. The onset of the shock was always preceded by a signal (a dimming of the light on the wall). After the lights were dimmed, the electric shock followed 10 seconds thereafter. If the dog jumped over the partition, it could escape the shock. If the dog failed to jump over the partition within 10 seconds, the electric shock started and continued for either 60 seconds or until the dog jumped over the partition.

Table 8.4 summarizes the study's procedure and results (Seligman & Maier, 1967). The dogs in both the escapable shock and no shock groups quickly learned

FIGURE 8–3
Apparatus for Seligman and Maier Experiment on Learned Helplessness

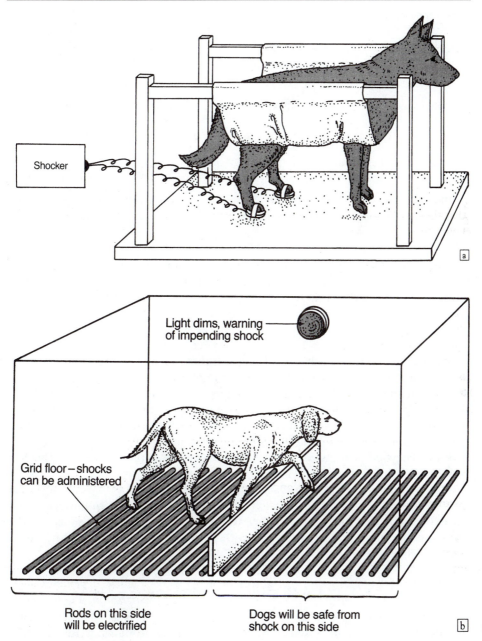

SOURCE: Carlson, N. C. (1988). *Discovering psychology*. Copyright © 1988 by Allyn and Bacon. Adapted by permission.

TABLE 8–4

Results of a Prototypical Learned Helplessness Study

EXPERIMENTAL CONDITION	PHASE 1	PHASE 2	RESULTS
Inescapable Shock	Received shock, no coping response could terminate the shock	Received an escapable shock	Failed to escape from the escapable shock
Escapable Shock	Received shock, pressing nose against button could terminate shock	Received an escapable shock	Quickly learned to escape shock by jumping over barrier
Control, No Shock	Received no shocks	Received an escapable shock	Quickly learned to escape shock by jumping over barrier

how to escape the shock when put into the shuttle box. When shocked, these dogs ran about frantically at first and rather accidentally climbed, fell, scrambled, or jumped over the barrier. That is, through trial and error, the dogs learned that if they somehow over-stepped the barrier they could escape the shock. After only a few trials, these dogs jumped over the barrier to safety as soon as the warning light dimmed. The dogs in the inescapable shock group, however, behaved very differently. When shocked, the dogs at first behaved as the other dogs did by running about frantically and howling. However, unlike the dogs in the other two groups, these dogs soon stopped running around and quietly whimpered until the trial (and shock) terminated. After only a few trials, these dogs gave up and passively accepted the shock. On subsequent trials, they failed to make any escape movements at all. What these dogs learned in the sling—that the onset, duration, intensity, and termination of the shock was beyond their control—had a carry-over effect in the shuttle box: The dogs perceived escape as beyond their control.

The startling generalization that emerged from this study is that whenever animals are placed in a situation in which they have little or no control, they develop the expectation that their future actions will have little effect on the situation. This learned expectation that behavior will not effect desired outcomes is the heart of learned helplessness.

Applications to Humans

The early experiments on learned helplessness used animals as subjects but later studies tested the extent to which helplessness applied to humans (Hiroto, 1974; Hiroto & Seligman, 1975; Mikulincer, 1994; Peterson, Maier, & Seligman, 1993). In Hiroto's (1974) experiment, noise, rather than electric shock, constituted the aversive, traumatic stimulus event. College students participated by wearing a set of earphones capable of sending a rather aversive blast of noise. For the inescapable noise group, the noise was programmed to be random; terminating the noise was therefore independent of whatever actions the participant tried. Those in the escapable noise group could terminate the loud noise by manipulating a lever (a toggle switch) from one side to the other. For the no noise control group, participants wore the headphones but heard no loud noise. In the second phase of the study, all participants heard an escapable series of noise bursts. The results with humans paralleled the results with dogs in that participants in the inescapable noise group sat passively and were unwilling to attempt an escape from the aversive noise in the second phase of the experiment. Participants in the escapable and no noise groups learned quickly to escape the noise by operating the lever in the second phase of the experiment.

Components

Learned helplessness theory relies on three fundamental components to explain the motivational dynamics that occur whenever experience leads people to expect that the events in their lives will be beyond their personal control. Those three components are contingency, cognition, and behavior (Peterson, Maier, & Seligman, 1993).

CONTINGENCY. Contingency refers to the relationship between people's behavior and outcomes in that environment—home, classroom, workplace, or psychology laboratory. Contingency exists on a continuum that ranges from outcomes that occur on a random, noncontingent basis (i.e., uncontrollable outcomes) to outcomes that occur in perfect synchronization with a person's voluntary behavior (i.e., controllable outcomes). Take a moment to ask yourself what your own experience has taught you about contingency in the following situations: getting a traffic ticket on the highway, getting a job in your hometown, winning a tennis match against a rival, winning the state lottery, catching the flu during the winter, getting cancer from smoking cigarettes, gaining weight during the winter, and graduating from college. To characterize the contingency inherent in each of these situations, ask yourself, "To what extent does voluntary, strategic behavior influence the outcomes that occur in these settings?" That is, how much influence does voluntary coping behavior exert on avoiding a traffic ticket, avoiding the flu, getting a job, winning a contest, winning the lottery, escaping cancer, preventing weight gain, and obtaining a college degree? I suspect that contingency varies across these eight situations in that some are controllable outcomes, some are uncontrollable, and others are somewhere in between controllable and uncontrollable.

COGNITION. A good deal of cognitive intervention takes place between actual, objective environmental contingencies and a person's subjective understanding of personal control in such environments. Mental events dilute the relationship between objective contingencies and subjective understandings of personal control, and they therefore create some margin of error between objective truth and subjective understanding. Three elements are particularly important: perceptions, attributions, and expectancies. When we find ourselves on the highway, job hunting, or competing against an opponent, perceptions are inherently incomplete, biased, and distorted, attributions (explained in the next chapter) vary from one person to the next, and outcome expectations arise from a host of factors unique to each individual (recall Table 8.1). To illustrate the importance of cognition, ask two people who experience the same environmental contingency why they were unable to avoid a traffic ticket, avoid the flu, get a job, and so on. People's outcome beliefs (and hence replies to these questions) stem not only from the objective information about the world but also from their unique perceptions, attributions, and expectancies. Hence, to understand learned helplessness, we need to pay attention not only to objective environmental contingencies but also to subjective personal control beliefs.

BEHAVIOR. As contingency exists on a continuum, voluntary behavior to prevent or avoid outcomes also exists on a continuum. In a traumatic event, people's voluntary coping behavior varies as to how active or passive it is. Coping responses can be active and assertive, or coping responses can be passive as the individual is quick to give up and withdraw. Passivity, giving up, and withdrawing typify a listless, demoralized effort that characterizes the behavior of the helpless individual (recall the passive behavior of the dogs in the inescapable shock group). Again, consider the situations listed earlier (driving on the highway, job hunting, competing against an opponent) and consider your own passive-to-active coping behaviors in the face of such situations and potential outcomes. The job hunter who quits reading newspaper advertisements, word processing the resumé, telephoning prospective employers, and waking up early in the morning manifest the listless coping behavior that characterizes helplessness.

Effects

Learned helplessness occurs when people expect that their voluntary behavior will produce little or no effect on the outcomes they strive to attain or avoid. Once it occurs, learned helplessness produces three kinds of deficits: motivational, learning, and emotional (Alloy & Seligman, 1979). Motivational deficits consist of a decreased willingness to initiate voluntary coping responses. Learning deficits consist of an acquired pessimistic learning set that interferes with the ability to learn new response-outcome contingencies. Emotional deficits consist of affective disruptions in which lethargic, depressive emotional reactions occur in situations that call for active, agenetic emotion.

MOTIVATIONAL DEFICITS. Motivational deficits become apparent when a person's willingness to emit voluntary coping responses decreases or disappears altogether. Typically, when people care about an outcome and when the environment is responsive in delivering those outcomes, they act in ways to bring about those outcomes. For instance, at the first of a season an athlete might practice diligently and persistently, but after a series of athletic defeats (victory becomes an uncontrollable outcome) willingness to practice wanes. In one learned helplessness experiment, the experimenters asked participants why they did not try to terminate an unpleasant noise in the second phase of the study (Thornton & Jacobs, 1971). Approximately 60% of the participants (from the inescapable noise group) reported that they felt little control over the noise, so why try? The so why try? verbalization is the prototypical representation of motivational deficit in learned helplessness.

LEARNING DEFICITS. Over time, exposure to uncontrollable environments cultivates a pessimistic learning set in which people believe that outcomes are generally independent of their actions. Once expectancies take on a pessimistic tone, the person has a difficult time learning that a new response can effect future outcomes. This pessimistic set interferes with, or retards, the learning of future response-outcome contingencies (Alloy & Seligman, 1979). When students first learn the results from learned helplessness experiments, they frequently wonder why dogs or humans in the group that cannot escape do not learn in the second phase of the experiment that jumping over the barrier or flipping the lever terminates the shock or noise blast. Consider, however, what the subjects learn during the first phase of the earphone session with the inescapable noise. The first time they hear the noise, they jump, and the second time they manipulate the lever or shift their weight from side to side. Perhaps they perceive that on some trials turning the head or shifting weight coincides with the turning off of the noise. But, on later trials, they again turn the head or shift weight, but the noise persists for its programmed 5 seconds. Gradually, they learn that no response turns off the noise in a reliable way. Consequently, when they enter the second phase of the experiment and happen to move the now working lever, this behavioral outcome appears to be a successful accident and unworthy of being tried again (as were head turning, weight shifting, and so forth earlier). The participant in the control group, who has no such interfering expectation, is quick to learn that lever turning works. Likewise, the participant in the escapable shock group learns that some responses work while others do not, and the trick is to discover *which* response, rather than *if any* response, works.

EMOTIONAL DEFICITS. The emotional deficit in learned helplessness manifests itself through lethargic, depressive affect in situations that normally would call for energy-mobilizing emotionality. In the face of trauma, the typical human response is one of highly aroused fear, assertiveness, anger, or frustration. When afraid, people struggle vigorously to overcome, escape, counteract, or do whatever is necessary to cope effectively. Over time, however, an unrelenting onslaught of environmental unresponsiveness leads people to see coping as futile. Once fear-mobilized responses are believed to be unproductive, depression-related behavior takes their place. Once the person becomes fully convinced that there is nothing that they can do to escape the trauma, the resulting expectation makes energy-mobilizing emotions less and less likely and makes energy-depleting emotions such as listlessness, apathy, and depression more and more likely.

SUDDEN DEATH. One catastrophic affective consequence of helplessness is sudden death, death based on a psychological rather than physiological cause. Physiologist Curt Richter began to research sudden death after he repeatedly observed that rats died as he held them in his glove-protected grasp. Apparently, rats held captive in the mouths of predators learn, after struggling, that their escape efforts are futile. The perception of futility breeds expectations of hopelessness, and the rats psychologically give up and actually die. According to Ritcher, sudden death is most likely whenever an animal (1) perceives a strong threat to life, (2) gives up attempts to escape from the threat and accepts its fate, and (3) goes into a depressed, quiescent state stemming from hopelessness.

To test his ideas, Ritcher (1957) developed an experiment. In one group, wild rats were placed into a vat of 3-feet-deep warm water. These rats swam for some 60 hours (swimming for survival and struggling for escape), or until they drowned from exhaustion (but the experimenter had a hidden net that would catch them before they drowned). In a second group, the experimenter first held the wild rats in his gloved hand until each rat stopped struggling, about 30 minutes. Once the rat had stopped struggling, it was placed into the same 3-foot-deep warm water vat. These rats swam excitedly for only a few minutes and then drowned, sinking with little effort to struggle for escape (again, there was a protective net to catch them). In a third group, the experimenter held the wild rats in his gloved hand until each stopped struggling, just as in group 2. After the rats stopped struggling, however, they were set free on the ground. Later, the experimenter again held the rats until they stopped struggling, and then set them free again. He repeated this process a third time. Finally, these rats were placed into the vat of water. He expected these rats would have "hope" to escape, because their coping efforts had set them free. The rats in group 3 behaved just as did the rats in group 1; they swam about excitedly for as long they physically could.

These sudden death findings offer profound implications. Consider, for instance, that susceptibility to death during bereavement, the time following the loss of one's spouse, is 40% greater than expected without bereavement (Parkes, Benjamin, & Fitzgerald, 1969). Helplessness also relates to susceptibility to cancer (Schmale & Iker, 1966), as psychological helplessness suppresses the cells in the human immune system that fight off foreign invaders, such as natural killer cells and T lymphocytes (Sklar & Anisman, 1979; Visintainer, Volpicelli, & Seligman, 1982). Sudden death does not have to be a product of such extremities as capture by a predator, bereavement, or cancer, however, as shown in a study that divided elderly nursing home residents into two groups (after matching the residents on physical health status; Langer & Rodin, 1976; Rodin & Langer, 1977). The experimental group of residents received enhanced control over their daily lives. These residents planned their schedules, took responsibility to care for room plants, and so forth. The control group of residents had a schedule assigned to them, were given a plant but told that the nurse, not they, would care for it, and so on. In other words, the experimental group had high personal control over the events in their lives, whereas the control group had low personal control. A year and a half later, significantly more low-control residents had died than high-control residents.

Critical Research Issues

DO MOTIVATIONAL, LEARNING, AND EMOTIONAL DEFICITS OCCUR BE-CAUSE OF EXPOSURE TO TRAUMA? Helplessness results from the individuals' learned expectation that their responses are independent of desired outcomes (Peterson, Maier, & Seligman 1993). The cause of learned helplessness is therefore a cognitive one—an expectation of response-outcome independence. One might reasonably argue, however, that helplessness deficits are a function of physical trauma rather than psychological expectation. Put another way, traumatic experience might produce dramatic physical changes, and these physical changes might in turn produce motivational, learning, and emotional deficits. After all, participants in learned helplessness are usually subjected to trauma—electric shocks, noise blasts, and so forth.

Researchers addressed this criticism through a strategic experimental design, referred to as triadic (after Weiss, 1972). To illustrate the triadic design consider the arrangement of three rats (one rat in controllable shock, one rat in uncontrollable shock, and one rat in the control (no shock) group) participating in a learned helplessness study (see Fig. 8.4). All three rats participated in the first phase of the experiment simultaneously. Notice also that all three rats have both a paddle wheel placed in front of them and a wire attached to their tails. The rat on the left (subject to escapable shock) has a small current of electricity sent to its tail; to terminate the shock the rat must rotate the paddle wheel. The turning of the wheel terminates the shock. The rat in the middle (subject to inescapable shock) has the same current of electricity sent to its tail, but it cannot terminate the shock by rotating the wheel. Rather, there is no rat response that will terminate the shock. The shock is terminated only if the rat on the left rotates its paddle wheel. Then both the rat on the left and the rat in the middle have their shock terminated. The rats are yoked together. Yoking is important because it ensures that both rats receive exactly the same number and duration of electric shock (i.e., the same traumatic experience). (The control rat, on the right, has a wire attached to its tail but no current passes through it, so the rat never gets shocked.)

The triadic design provides a test of the hypothesis that it is the expectation of uncontrollability and not the physical trauma itself that produces helplessness. The finding that animals in the escapable shock group learn to escape shock in the second phase of the experiment while the animals in the inescapable shock group do not support the hypothesis that a cognitive, rather than a physical, change causes helplessness.

DO DEFICITS OCCUR BECAUSE OF PERCEIVED FAILURE? A second concern in interpreting learned helplessness research is whether helplessness deficits arise from the expectation of uncontrollability or from the experience of failure. Many of the studies of learned helplessness with humans use an unsolvable anagram task to induce helplessness (Hiroto & Seligman, 1975; Dweck, 1975; Mikulincer, 1988). Participants are given a series of either solvable (e.g., PAPYH = HAPPY) or unsolvable (e.g., PAPYT = ?) anagrams in the first phase of the experiment. In the second

FIGURE 8–4
Triadic Design in Learned Helplessness Experiment

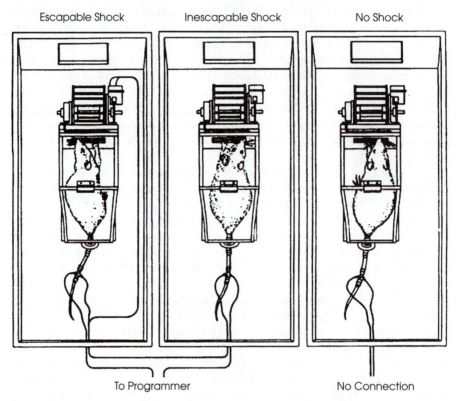

SOURCE: Weiss, J. M. (1972). Psychological factors in stress and disease. *Scientific American, 226,* 104–113. Copyright © 1972 by Scientific American. Adapted by permission from the illustration by Eric Mose.

phase all participants are given a series of solvable anagrams. The typical finding is that participants given the unsolvable anagrams in the first phase solve fewer anagrams in the second phase than do participants given the solvable anagrams (a helplessness effect).

In these studies it is not possible to tell whether an expectation of uncontrollability or an expectation of failure degrades performance. It seems just as reasonable to suppose that the participants given the unsolvable anagrams developed a sense of incompetence and quit as it does to suppose they perceived the situation as uncontrollable and felt helpless. (Alternatively, the participants given the solvable anagrams might develop an enhanced sense of mastery and try harder.) To address this confusion, researchers designed an experiment with independent variables of prior exposure to uncontrollability and success-failure feedback (Winefield, Barnett, & Tiggemann, 1985). In the first phase of the experiment participants heard a buzzer through headphones and understood that the purpose of the experiment was to learn to turn off the buzzer as quickly as possible by producing a particular sequence of button presses. For half of the participants there was no sequence of button presses that terminated the buzzer (uncontrollable noise), and for the other half a sequence of button presses could terminate the buzzer (controllable noise). The experimenter also gave success or failure feedback to each participant. The experimenter randomly told participants that they had done either significantly better than (success condition), significantly worse than (failure condition), or about the same as (control condition) others. In the second phase of the experiment all participants had a similar (but different) button-pressing task to learn to escape the buzzer.

Controllability of the outcome affected performance more than did success-failure feedback. In fact, there was a slight tendency for the participants in the failure group to outperform participants in the success and control groups. Failure actually provided positive motivation (a phenomenon we will discuss in the next section under *reactance theory*). From such results, the conclusion is that the expectation of uncontrollability, not the expectation of failure, causes the observed deficits.

DO DEFICITS OCCUR BECAUSE OF UNPREDICTABILITY? A methodological problem in a great number of learned helplessness experiments with humans is that uncontrollable events are also unpredictable events (Winefield, 1982). An outcome (e.g., shock, noise, natural disaster) is unpredictable when it is independent of all signaling stimuli. What is needed is an experiment in which an outcome's uncontrollability and unpredictability are experimentally manipulated and separated to see if uncontrollability, unpredictability, or both produce helplessness. Unfortunately, it is exceptionally difficult to arrange an outcome that is controllable yet unpredictable. In fact, the task of disentangling the effects of uncontrollability and unpredictability is "next to logically impossible" (Seligman, 1975, p. 128).

But psychologists are a persistent bunch, and one group of researchers tested the effect of predictability on learned helplessness deficits using the following four experimental conditions (Tiggemann & Winefield, 1987): controllable predictable (C-P), uncontrollable unpredictable (UC-UP), uncontrollable predictable (UC-P), and a no-treatment (NT) control group. (There was no controllable-unpredictable condition.) In the first phase of the experiment, all participants sat at a computer terminal and understood that "from time to time a buzzer will come on." Participants were to try to find a way to stop the buzzer, using a switch in front of them. Participants in the C-P group could terminate the buzzer by pressing the switch four times. Participants in the UC-UP group heard random buzzer noises (but yoked to those in the C-P condition). Participants in the UC-P condition knew when the buzzer was going to sound and how long it would continue (2.03 seconds) but they had no means to terminate it. In the second phase of the experiment, all participants were given 20 controllable test trials of the buzzer. The critical dependent measure was how long it took the participants in each group to learn to terminate the buzzer by operating the switch. Learned helplessness deficits emerged only for the participants in the UC-UP condition. Participants in the UC-P condition learned to terminate the buzzer much as did the participants in the C-P and NT conditions.

Based on these results, Tiggemann and Winefield concluded that predictability does mitigate the learned helplessness deficit. Findings from a second study confirmed these results, showing that both controllability and predictability were necessary to produce helplessness (Burger & Arkin, 1980). Thus, uncontrollability is necessary but not sufficient to induce learned helplessness deficits. For sufficiency, uncontrollability needs to coincide with unpredictability.

RELATIONSHIP BETWEEN HELPLESSNESS AND DEPRESSION. Some view learned helplessness as a model of naturally occurring unipolar depression (Rosenhan & Seligman, 1984; Seligman, 1975). Learned helplessness and depression are similar in that the same expectations cause both: The individual expects that bad events will occur and there is nothing he or she can do to prevent their occurrence (Rosenhan & Seligman, 1984). Learned helplessness and depression also share causes (the general belief that responding will be ineffective), symptoms (passivity, low self-esteem, loss of appetite), and therapeutic strategies (time, cognitive behavior modification). Where the two differ is that depression is a broader concept than is helplessness, as depression includes biochemical, somatic, psychodynamic, emotional, and cognitive causes and symptoms that are not necessarily associated with learned helplessness.

Using the learned helplessness model to understand the etiology of depression touched off a flurry of research. The idea of using the learned helplessness model to understand the dynamics of depression met both strong criticism (Depue & Monroe, 1978; Costello, 1978) and strong support (Seligman, 1975). Nonetheless, one of the most exciting findings to emerge from this body of research is that depressed individuals sometimes see the events in their life as less controllable than do nondepressed individuals. Such a finding led researchers to wonder whether the depressive tendency to see their world as an uncontrollable place might be a core cause of depression. A consistent body of research documents that people very often misjudge their control over life events (Abramson & Alloy, 1980; Alloy & Abramson, 1979, 1982; Langer, 1975; Nisbett & Ross, 1980). Perhaps the root of depression lies in depressed individuals' inability to see that they have more control over life outcomes than they know.

Depressed and nondepressed college students (as assessed by a questionnaire) performed a task in which they were asked to push a button on some trials and not push it on other trials (Alloy & Abramson, 1979). With a button push, a green light sometimes came on. The point of the study was for the participant to estimate what proportion of time the green light came on. The experimenters controlled the light, so they could determine whether each participant overestimated or underestimated control over whether the light came on. For one group, button pressing flashed the green light 75% of the time and never flashed when the participant did not push the button. This was the high-control group. For a second group, button pressing flashed the green light 75% of the time, but the light also came on 50% of the time the participants did not push the button. This was the low-control group. In a final group, button pressing flashed the green light 75% of the time, but it also came on 75% of the time when the participants did not push the button. This was the no control group.

As shown in Figure 8.5, the results were most surprising. The depressives accurately judged how much control they had over each situation, as did the nondepressives except in the no-control situation (Alloy & Abramson, 1979). The depressives saw reality more accurately than the nondepressives.

A second study tested the idea that nondepressives have an *illusion of control* (Alloy & Abramson, 1982). An illusion of control is evident whenever individuals overestimate the extent of their control over life events (Langer, 1975). In the experiment's first phase, participants completed a button-pressing task and were told that a buzzer noise was either controllable or uncontrollable. In the experiment's second phase, participants either succeeded (were given a monetary payment for the number of trials controlled) or failed (lost money for each trial they did not control) at a task. In actuality, outcomes in the second phase of the experiment occurred randomly so that the participant had no control over their outcomes whatsoever. The experiment tested depressives' versus nondepressives' judgments of control on the win and lose noncontingency problems. Results appear in Figure 8.6. Depressives in all groups and nondepressives in the controllable-noise groups accurately judged the extent of their control over the win and lose problems. The interesting group was the nondepressives who received positive feedback over the uncontrollable

FIGURE 8–5
Perceived Control for Depressives vs. Nondepressives

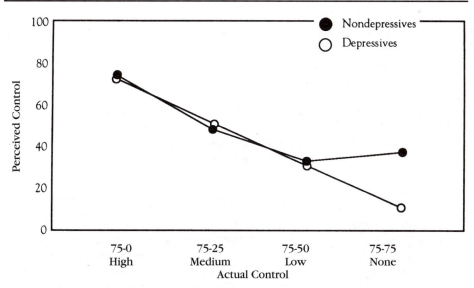

SOURCE: Alloy, L. B., & Abramson, L. T. (1979). Judgments of contingency in depressed and nondepressed students: Sadder but wiser? *Journal of Experimental Psychology: General, 108,* 441–485. Copyright © 1979 by the American Psychological Association. Adapted by permission.

FIGURE 8-6

Perceived Control for Depressives and Nondepressives after Winning and Losing

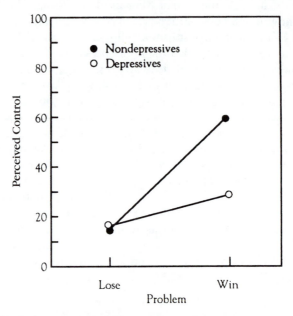

SOURCE: Alloy, L. B., & Abramson, L. T. (1979). Judgments of contingency in depressed and nondepressed students: Sadder but wiser? *Journal of Experimental Psychology: General, 108,* 441–485. Copyright © 1979 by the American Psychological Association. Adapted by permission.

noise outcomes. The nondepressives showed a strong illusion of control by overestimating the degree of control they exerted in the win problem.

The most interesting conclusion to draw from the Alloy and Abramson (1979, 1982) program of research is that depressed people are not more prone to learned helplessness deficits because they perceive little personal control. Rather, it is the nondepressives who sometimes believe that they have more personal control than they actually have (Taylor & Brown, 1988, 1994). We will continue the discussion on the relationships among depression, learned helplessness, and the illusion of control in chapter 9 by adding the attributional perspective to our analysis.

Criticisms and Alternative Explanations of Helplessness

The learned helplessness model is not without its critics (Costello, 1978; Weiss, Glazer, & Pohorecky, 1976; Wortman & Brehm, 1975). One alternative explanation for the fact that people give up in the face of uncontrollable outcomes is that people are actually motivated to remain passive. People are motivated to be passive if they are under the impression that active responding will only make matters worse (Wortman & Brehm, 1975). In the face of a hurricane (an uncontrollable, unpredictable event), for example, it is possible that people are passive and helpless because they believe that negative outcomes will be more likely when they respond compared to when they do not respond. If this is the case, passivity is an enlightened strategic coping response that minimizes the trauma incurred. For a second example, imagine the socially anxious person who does not voluntarily engage in social interaction because of a belief that they will only makes matters worse by initiating conversations. By intentionally not initiating interactions, the anxious person may very well avoid making circumstances worse (by keeping secret his lack of social skill). Thus, looked at in a different light, passivity can be, in some circumstances, a strategic coping response rather than a motivational deficit.

A second interpretation of helplessness argues that helplessness might fundamentally be a physiological, rather than a cognitive, phenomenon (Weiss, 1972). When animals experience inescapable shock, they invariably are significantly decreased in the neurotransmitter norepinephrine (Weiss, 1972, Weiss, Glazer, & Pohorecky, 1976; Weiss, Stone, & Harrell, 1970). Exposure to a traumatic event such as a shock is certainly stressful, and a physiological response to stress includes many physiological changes, including elevated levels of epinephrine and norepinephrine. As animals cope with a stressor over time, norepinephrine continues to be discharged while epinephrine does not. For animals in the escapable shock conditions, levels of epinephrine and norepinephrine return to a stable level as the animal copes successfully with the stressor. For the animals in the inescapable shock conditions, however, only epinephrine returns to a stable level, and these animals are severely depleted in brain norepinephrine. Depletion of brain norepinephrine has been repeatedly associated with helplessness and giving-up responses (Weiss, Glazer, & Pohorecky, 1976).

In one of Weiss' experiments, rats were placed into a vat of either cold or warm water for 6 minutes. Both groups of rats were placed in equal amounts of water, but exposure to cold water depletes norepinephrine whereas exposure to warm water does not. Thirty minutes after swimming, both groups of rats were placed into a shuttle box. The rats in the cold water (those experiencing a substantial decrease in brain norepinephrine) showed helplessness-like effects in the shuttle box. The rats placed in the warm water, however, did not. From this brief review, a case can be made to understand helplessness as a physiological phenomenon. Hence, a full understanding of helplessness requires a parallel understanding of both cognitive and physiological changes that occur as the individual faces environments that are unresponsive, demoralizing, and uncontrollable.

Learned Laziness

When thinking about uncontrollable events, the outcomes that come to mind are typically aversive ones—shocks, loud noises, migraine headaches, accidents, family deaths, and other causes of grief. But the phenomenon of *learned laziness* questions whether any uncontrollable event, aversive or pleasant, produces helplessness deficits (Engberg et al., 1972). That is, do people who receive random (uncontrollable) rewards on a continual basis show motivational, learning, and emotional deficits? To test their idea, the experimenters placed pigeons in one of three experimental groups. Some were trained so that a food pellet was given if they made an appropriate response (industrious group). Other pigeons received the same number of food pellets as the first group, but their pellets were administered on a schedule that was independent of their behavior (learned laziness group). The last group received no training in the first phase of the experiment (control group). In the second phase, all pigeons performed the same task. To attain a food pellet reward in this new situation, each pigeon had to learn a new response.

The experiment measured how many trials it took each pigeon to learn the behavior necessary to get the food reward. The pigeons in the learned laziness group learned the response-outcome relationship the slowest while the pigeons in the industrious condition learned the new response-outcome relationship the fastest. When rewards were free and the pigeons had little reason to work for them, their latency to learn the appropriate response-outcome relationship was significantly retarded (i.e., a helplessness-based learning deficit).

Consider some speculative illustrations. Children who are showered with attention, toys, and treats may begin to develop learned laziness. If rewards are given randomly and with no correspondence with behavior the children may adopt a so-why-try? orientation in initiating effort to obtain rewards on tasks such as homework, chores, yard work, or cleaning a room. Spoiled children know that they will still get attention and toys whether or not they do their homework, chores, or yard work or clean their room. A second (equally presumptuous) illustration might apply to people who are very attractive, very competent, or very intelligent. Very attractive people get free and continual attention and praise from other people. Attention and praise often come independent of any behavioral effort on their part (people notice me whether or not I'm polite, whether or not I cheat on examinations, and so on). If very attractive people perceive that environmental reinforcement is independent of their behavior, then they might seemingly ask, so why try? (why work for attention, why work to be accepted, why be polite). No matter what they do, other people reward them.

REACTANCE THEORY

Why do people sometimes do the opposite of what they are told? Why do people sometimes resist another person's favor? Why is propaganda often ineffective and sometimes backfires? These are the questions posed by reactance theorists (Brehm, 1966; Brehm & Brehm, 1981). According to Brehm, human beings want the freedom to make up their own mind in deciding which behavior they will pursue at any given time. Any instruction, any favor, any advice, no matter how well intended, has the potential to interfere with people's freedom to make up their own mind. When children do precisely what they were told not to do, when gift recipients are more hostile than thankful, and when the targets of propaganda do the opposite of the source's intention, each performs a countermaneuver aimed at reestablishing a threatened sense of freedom (Brehm, 1966). The term *reactance* refers to the psychological and behavioral attempt to reestablish an eliminated or threatened freedom.

Reactance and Learned Helplessness

The perception of a threat to personal freedom often coincides with the perception of an uncontrollable outcome. Reactance theory predicts that people experience reactance only if they expect to have some control over what happens to them. And people react to a loss of control by becoming more active, even hostile and aggressive. Both reactance and learned helplessness theories focus on people's reactions to uncontrollable outcomes, but they suggest that human beings act in two very different ways when exposed to uncontrollable outcomes. Recognizing this discrepancy, Wortman and Brehm (1975) proposed an integrative model of reactance and learned helplessness, which is shown in Figure 8.7.

If a person expects to be able to control important outcomes, exposure to uncontrollable outcomes should arouse reactance (Wortman & Brehm, 1975). Thus, in the first few trials in a learned helplessness experiment, the person or animal should show vigorous opposition to the uncontrollable environment. Recall that the dogs in the inescapable shock group in the Seligman and Maier (1967) study first howled, kicked, and generally thrashed about before becoming helpless. The lines graphed between point "A" point "B" in Figure 8.7 represents reactance responses. Over time,

FIGURE 8–7
Integrative Model of Reactance and Learned Helplessness

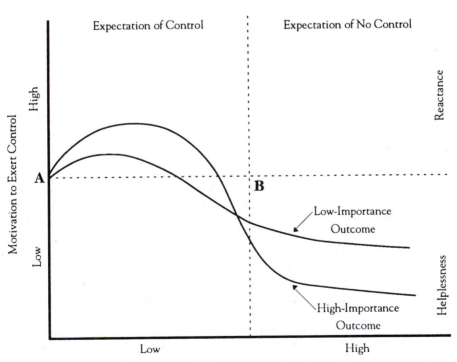

SOURCE: Wortman, C. B., & Brehm, J. W. (1975). Responses to uncontrollable outcomes: An integration of reactance theory and the learned helplessness model. In L. Berkowitz (Ed.), *Advances in experimental social psychology* (Vol. 8, pp. 277-336). New York: Academic Press.

however, if individuals repeatedly experience uncontrollable situations, they will learn that all attempts at control are futile. Once they become fully convinced that reactance behaviors exert little or no influence over the uncontrollable situation, they show the passivity of helplessness. The lines graphed after point "B" represent helplessness responses.

The critical difference in predicting whether an individual will show reactance or helplessness is the equivocal status of the uncontrollable outcome. As long as the person perceives that coping behavior can effect outcomes, reactance behaviors persist. It is only after the person perceives a response-outcome independence (or the unequivocal loss of a freedom) that he or she demonstrates helplessness. As an illustration, consider the following experiment (Mikulincer, 1988). One group of undergraduates was given one unsolvable problem, a second group was given four unsolvable problems, and a third group was given no problems (control group). Mikulincer reasoned that exposure to one unsolvable problem would produce reactance and performance improvement while exposure to four unsolvable problems would produce helplessness and performance impairment. In the second phase of the experiment, all participants worked on the same set of solvable problems. Participants who had been given one unsolvable problem performed the best, participants who had been given four unsolvable problems performed the worst, and participants who had been given no problems performed between these two groups. This finding provides strong support for the ideas that (1) amount of previous exposure to unsolvable problems is associated with both reactance and helplessness and (2) reactance promotes performance enhancement whereas helplessness promotes performance decrement.

SUMMARY

Expectancies come in two forms: efficacy expectations and outcome expectations. Efficacy expectations are subjective predictions of the capacity to execute successfully a particular course of action. Outcome expectancies are subjective predictions that a particular outcome will be achieved (or prevented) once a given action is adequately executed. Both efficacy and outcome expectancies must be reasonably high if certain behavior is to be initiated and to persist.

Expectancy × value proposes that the motivation to approach or avoid an event is the product of expectancy (E) that an action will produce an outcome and the anticipated satisfaction, or value (V), of that outcome. The expectancy × value framework applies best to those situations in which an individual must choose between competing events or objects. The chapter used career and dating choices to illustrate how the expectancy × value framework simulates choice behavior.

The practical lesson that emerges from the study of self-efficacy is that competent performance requires not only physical, cognitive, social, and behavioral skills (ability), but also the capacity to use those skills well. People have high self-efficacy when they believe that they can act effectively, even when they face circumstances that are difficult and unpredictable. People have low self-efficacy when they worry about and expect to struggle in their performances. Of course, we often experience worry, anxiety, and self-doubt in our performances, but self-efficacy beliefs and expectations can reduce or prevent the worry, anxiety, and doubt that might otherwise interfere will skillful performance. Self-efficacy arises from (1) past performance history in trying to execute a particular course of action, (2) observations of similar others as they execute the same actions, (3) verbal persuasions from others, and (4) physiological states such as an abnormal heartbeat. Self-efficacy affects (1) choice of activities and selection of environments, (2) extent of effort and persistence, (3) the quality of thinking and decision making during performance, and (4) emotional reactions, especially those related to stress and anxiety.

Learned helplessness is the psychological state that results when an individual expects that events in his or her life are uncontrollable. More generally, learned helplessness theory relies on three fundamental components to explain helplessness effects: contingency, cognition, and behavior. Contingency refers to the relationship between a person's behavior and positive or negative outcomes. Cognition is a general term that includes all those mental processes (e.g., perceptions, attributions, expectancies) that the individual relies on to understand environmental contingencies. Behavior refers to the person's voluntary coping behavior, and it varies in terms of how active and energetic or passive and withdrawing it is. Once it occurs, helplessness can produce profound disruptions in motivation, learning, and emotion. The motivational deficit is a decreased willingness to engage in voluntary coping responses; the cognitive deficit is a pessimistic learning set that interferes with learning of new response-outcome contingencies; and the emotional deficit involves the emergence of energy-depleting emotions such as depression in place of energy-mobilizing emotions such as frustration. In the two decades of research since learned helplessness was first proposed, several critical questions have emerged, including how learned helplessness relates not only to expectations of uncontrollability but also to (1) trauma, (2) perceived failure, (3) unpredictability, (4) clinical depression, and (5) physiological conditions.

Reactance theory, like the learned helplessness model, examines how people react to uncontrollable life events. According to reactance theory, an individual's initial reaction to uncontrollable outcomes is a psychological and behavioral attempt to reestablish control over the environment. Wortman and Brehm offer a model to integrate learned helplessness and reactance. When control is expected people show reactance. When control is not expected people show helplessness.

RECOMMENDED READINGS

Alloy, L. B., & Abramson, L. V. (1982). Learned helplessness, depression, and the illusion of control. *Journal of Personality and Social Psychology, 42*, 1114-1126.

Bandura, A. (1988) Self-efficacy conception of anxiety. *Anxiety Research, 1*, 77-98.

Bandura, A. (1989). Human agency in social cognitive theory. *American Psychologist, 44*, 1175-1184.

Bandura, A. (1993). Perceived self-efficacy in cognitive development and functioning. *Educational Psychologist, 28*, 117-148.

Brown, I., Jr., & Inouye, D.K. (1978). Learned helplessness through modeling: The role of perceived similarity in competence. *Journal of Personality and Social Psychology, 36,* 900-908.

Mikulincer, M. (1988). Reactance and helplessness following exposure to unsolvable problems: The effects of attributional style. *Journal of Personality and Social Psychology, 54,* 679-686.

Ozer, E. M., & Bandura, A. (1990). Mechanisms governing empowerment effects: A self-efficacy analysis. *Journal of Personality and Social Psychology, 58,* 472-486.

Schunk, D. H. (1989). Self-efficacy and achievement behaviors. *Educational Psychology Review, 1,* 173-208.

Wortman, C. B., & Brehm, J. W. (1975). Responses to uncontrollable outcomes: An integration of reactance theory and the learned helplessness model. In L. Berkowitz (Ed.), *Advances in experimental social psychology* (Vol. 8, pp. 277-336). New York: Academic Press.

Zimmerman, B. J., & Ringle, J. (1981). Effect of model persistence and statements of confidence on children's self-efficacy and problem-solving. *Journal of Educational Psychology, 73,* 485-493.

Chapter 9

ATTRIBUTIONS

Finally, spring has arrived! The melting of the snow and the greening of the grass mean one thing to you: It's tennis season! Imagine that you and your roommate are on the university's varsity tennis team and doubles partners. Both of you are first-year players, so neither knows quite what to expect in the upcoming matches in terms of winning and losing. You are both good tennis players. In fact, you and your roommate/partner are as well matched as any two players you know.

As the season starts, you both have rather conservative expectations of winning. For the first match, you both guess that your chances of winning are 50/50. The first match comes and goes, and the two of you win a close one. Reviewing the match that evening, you suggest the win simply and obviously went to the better team. Your partner, however, suggests that you won because of a fortuitous run of luck and good breaks at the end of the match. Reflecting on the victory, you feel pride while your partner feels mostly relief at the good fortune. The second match comes and goes, but this time, alas, you lose. This time, you are sure the outcome was a fluke; the two of you just could not get the break you needed at any critical point in the match. Your partner is not so sure. She thinks you lost because both of you are very much out of shape and simply did not have the stamina necessary to win. Reflecting on the loss, you feel angry at the bad luck while your partner feels shame at her incompetence.

Today is the third match and the conversation again turns to your chances of winning. You are confident and predict a high chance of victory; your partner is less confident and predicts only a small chance of victory. You cannot wait to get started and play the match while your partner has little difficulty concentrating on her biology textbook. Your partner's pessimism surprises you, and you wonder what happened to her confidence. After all, the two of you clearly earned your victory and the loss was a fluke. Your partner explains the outcomes differently; the victory was the fluke and the loss was caused by incompetence. The present chapter examines the motivational significance of people's explanations for why they succeed and fail at life events. As was true for the tennis players, the attributions we make affect our emotions, our predictions for future outcomes, and our eagerness to pursue similar events in the future. Even when people experience identical outcomes, as the tennis players did, different attributions produce different emotional, cognitive, and motivational states.

EXPLAINING OUTCOMES

The principle assumption of attribution theory is that people actively seek to discover *why* events occur (Heider, 1958; Jones & Davis, 1965; Kelley, 1967, 1973; Weiner, 1980, 1985, 1986). We seek to understand the causes that lie behind our successes and failures, our triumphs and tragedies, our invitations and rejections. Following life's outcomes, we ask questions such as, Why did I fail that chemistry examination? Why did the Braves win the World Series? Why did Suzy drop out of school? Why is that person poor? Why did Carter lose the 1980 presidential election? and Why didn't Frank return my telephone call?

We do not always engage in a causal analysis to explain what happens, as most outcomes require no special explanation. If a person expects a particular outcome to occur and, sure enough, it occurs, there is little reason to labor through a causal analysis. If, for example, you expect the 4:00 bus to be on time and, sure enough, the bus is on time, then there is little need to spend cognitive effort trying to figure out this favorable turn of events. Predictable outcomes fail to instigate causal analysis. Success when success was expected and failure when failure was expected are predicted outcomes. Unexpected outcomes, on the other hand, arrest our attention and prompt us to engage in cognitive activity to discover their cause or causes. Failure when success was expected or success when failure was expected are unpredicted outcomes. Unexpected success and unexpected failure prompt explanations: Why did the underdog politician win? Why did I fail a test in my best subject? Why was I passed over for my sure-thing promotion? and Why did she reject my innocent invitation for a pleasant night on the town?

In addition to unexpected outcomes, people often search for reasons when outcomes are negative or important (Weiner, 1985). Thus, causal analysis occurs following those outcomes that are (1) unexpected, (2) negative, or (3) important. People attribute reasons after these types of outcomes for two reasons. First, the attributor seeks information about why a particular outcome occurred. Second, the attributor seeks to improve life management skills or interactions with the environment (Weiner, 1985). By searching for the cause of unexpected, negative, and important outcomes, the attributor attempts to guide future courses of action. The student who fails an examination, for instance, and analyzes the cause is more apt to do better on the next examination than the student who does not look for a reason for failure. If the first student blames the failure on his lackluster effort, he is likely to take the steps necessary to remedy the failure's cause. In contrast, the second student may well repeat the earlier failure.

Attributions have important implications for a number of motivational phenomena discussed in other chapters. For example, attributions affect learned helplessness in that some understandings of why an aversive event is uncontrollable lead to helplessness deficits whereas other understandings (or explanations) do not. The present chapter discusses how attributions affect learned helplessness and other motivational phenomena such as the illusion of control, intrinsic motivation, and emotions. Figure 9.1 presents a general overview of the attribution process and its motivational effects.

Causal Attributions

A causal attribution is an explanation of why a particular outcome occurred (Weiner, 1985, 1986). It is whatever reason a person believes explains why he or she won or lost, was accepted or rejected, was rewarded or punished, and so on. The interpretation that he accepted my invitation for a date because I am such a charming person specifies an outcome (the date was accepted) and its causal attribution (because I am so charming). Of course, a hundred rival attributions are also possible to explain why he accepted the date, but attribution theory concerns

FIGURE 9–1
Attribution Process and Motivational Effects

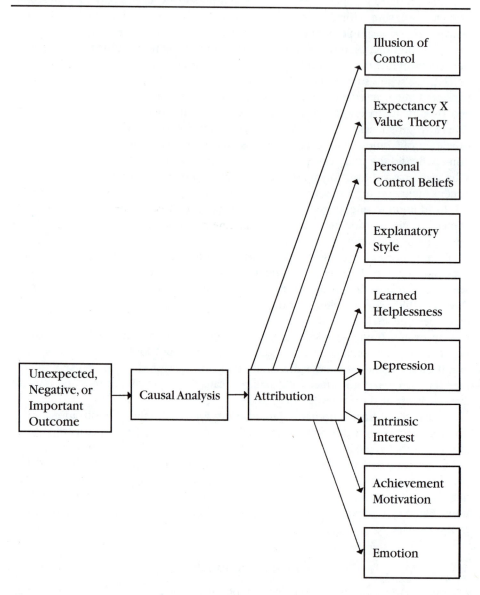

the individual's attribution and how that attribution affects motivation and emotion (Weiner, 1986).

   Think about a recent outcome you experienced in your own life, and take a moment to brainstorm reasons that might explain it. You will probably think of many reasons, and any such list can quickly become cumbersome. Consider an athlete who has just lost an important contest. Her defeat might be attributed to a lack of ability, lack of effort, the proficiency of an opponent, fatigue, biased referees, an injury, ineffective strategy, lazy teammates, a hostile crowd, equipment failure, an incompetent coach, or just plain bad luck. Perhaps in considering your own outcome, you thought of additional attributions beyond the dozen listed here, attributions such as intelligence, cleverness and cunning, physical attractiveness, mood, illness, the weather, a personality characteristic, the daily horoscope, biorhythms, and the help, hindrance, or bias of others.

In explaining your recent outcomes, you probably experienced another attributional phenomena, namely economy or simplicity of causal analysis (Weiner, 1985). While hundreds of attributions are possible, the most salient and frequent are ability and effort, at least in explaining achievement (i.e., high ability and hard work generally cause success; low ability and a lack of trying generally cause failure; Weiner, 1985). While ability and effort are relatively common attributions, many others are both possible and regularly claimed; therefore researchers organize all possible attributions into three primary causal dimensions.

Causal Dimensions of Attributions

The potential array of all possible causes begins with the differentiation between those located inside the person (e.g., personality, intelligence, skill, effort, strategy, and physical beauty) and those located in the environment (e.g., weather, influence of another person, or difficulty of the task). The internal-external (or person-environment) attributional dimension is referred to as *locus*.

Potential causes also vary in their consistency, or *stability*, the second dimension. Some attributions are relatively long lasting (e.g., intelligence, skill, and personality) while others fluctuate from time to time and are relatively ephemeral (e.g., mood, effort, luck, and the weather). Causal attributions that are consistent over time and across many situations are stable causes whereas those that change over time and across situations are unstable causes (Weiner et al., 1971; Weiner, 1986).

A third attributional dimension, *controllability*, distinguishes between controllable and uncontrollable causes (Weiner, 1979, 1986). Some examples of controllable causes include personal effort, laziness, and strategy, while some examples of uncontrollable causes include the weather, physical coordination, equipment failure, and the proficiency, help, hindrance, or bias of others (e.g., teammates, employers, opponents). Notice, however, that whether or not a cause is controllable depends largely on individual interpretation, as ability or an injury might be a controllable cause to one person yet be an uncontrollable cause to someone else.

The three fold classification scheme for causal attributions is therefore as follows:

Locus	Internal versus external
Stability	Stable versus unstable
Controllability	Controllable versus uncontrollable

The benefits of the three-dimensional classification are that (1) any attribution can be categorized as a *type* of attribution (e.g., mood is an internal–unstable–uncontrollable attribution) and (2) causal dimensions reveal the common denominator among otherwise diverse attributions. For instance, ability, intelligence, physical attractiveness, and personality all share a common classification (internal-stable-uncontrollable), and it is that common denominator that motivation psychologists use to predict the effects an attribution will have on motivation and emotion. Thus, attribution theorists talk little about how specific attributions affect motivational processes and, instead, talk much about how dimensions of attribution affect motivational processes (i.e., stable attributions have this effect, controllable attributions have that effect, and stable–uncontrollable attributions have this other effect).

Attributional Errors and Biases

Attributional decision making generally proceeds via logical information processing. After witnessing a car wreck, for example, we scan for possible causes—the slippery road surface, obstructions and defects in the road, bad weather, distracted drivers, dense traffic, and so forth—and choose one or more explanations that best fit the observed evidence. One of the more interesting aspects of the attributional process, however, is that several biases cloud that otherwise rational information processing (Harvey & Weary, 1981). In other words, if you provide people with sufficient information to make accurate causal attributions, what you find is that people all too often arrive at the wrong answer (Funder, 1987). Those wrong answers are predictable, however, because the following three biases or errors pervade the attributional process.

FUNDAMENTAL ATTRIBUTION ERROR. When we explain other people's outcomes, we rely heavily on internal factors such as personality characteristics (he won because he is so talented). The tendency to use internal factors in explaining another person's outcomes is so pervasive that it is referred to as the *fundamental attribution error* (Ross, 1977). Think about the last time one of your friends was late in meeting you for an appointment. In accordance with the fundamental attribution error, you were probably more willing to think that your friend was late because of some personality factor (e.g., irresponsibility, laziness) rather than some external situational factor (e.g., traffic, telephone call). The fundamental attribution error applies not only to inferring faults onto others, it also applies to positive characteristics. When a salesperson smiles at us and treats us politely, we generally explain such behavior as a personality factor (he is nice) rather than a situational factor (he is trying to make a buck). The fundamental attribution error is reversible. When an observer is instructed to pay close attention to how the situation influences the behavior of the other person, the observer is as likely to attribute the person's outcomes to an external factor as an internal factor (Quattrone, 1982). Hence, the fundamental attribution error emanates from a perceptual, not a motivational, bias.

ACTOR-OBSERVER ERROR. A second pervasive shortcoming of the attributional process is the *actor-observer error* (Jones & Nisbett, 1971). As demonstrated in several experiments, individuals tend to explain personal outcomes by external causes but explain another's outcomes by internal causes (Eisen, 1979; Monson & Snyder, 1977; Taylor & Fiske, 1978). Inevitably, the actor and observer have different perspectives in any situation (Jones & Nisbett, 1972). Suppose, for example, that Mark stumbles and trips over an ill-positioned chair. Mark will tend to explain the trip on the basis of the intrusive chair (external cause), but an observer will tend to explain Mark's stumble on the basis of his clumsiness (internal cause). Each explains the event using whatever evidence is most salient. Mark sees and pays attention mostly to the chair; the observer sees and pays attention mostly to Mark. Knowledge of the actor-observer error provides one explanation as to why therapists working with alcoholics find their patients more willing to take personal responsibility for their drinking behavior after watching a videotape of their intoxicated behavior (Dworetzky, 1988). By watching their videotaped alcohol-influenced behavior, the alcoholics gain the opportunity to see themselves rather than the situation. By focusing attention on themselves, the alcoholics become increasingly likely to see themselves as the cause of their drinking behavior. As this study suggests, the actor-observer error, like the fundamental attribution error, is reversible. If an observer actively empathizes with the actor, then the observer, like the actor, will attribute the actor's behavior to situational causes (Gould & Sigall, 1977). Thus, both the fundamental attribution error and the actor-observer error are perceptual rather than motivational phenomena.

SELF-SERVING BIAS. A third attributional shortcoming is the *self-serving bias* (Arkin, Cooper, & Kolditz, 1980; Miller & Ross, 1975; Miron Zuckerman, 1979), by which people favor internal attributions following success but external attributions following failure. After failure or rejection, perhaps the first question that comes to mind is whether the cause was due to me or the situation. In general, people see success as internally caused and failure as externally caused. Unlike the previous two errors, the self-serving bias is a motivational phenomenon (Zuckerman, 1979). Studies in sports confirm that competitors make more internal attributions for success than for failure (Gill, Ruder, & Gross, 1982; Iso-Ahola, 1977; Lau & Russell, 1980; Riss & Taylor, 1984; Riordan, Thomas, & James, 1985). Following a victory by high school basketball players, for instance, internal attributions (ability and effort) are more common than are external attributions (task difficulty and luck) (Spink, 1978). Following a loss, however, the players used external rather than internal attributions (but only slightly so). The self-serving bias also underlies coaches' explanations for winning and losing (Lau & Russell, 1980). In interviews, coaches explained victories by talking about their players' ability or heroic efforts, but they explained defeats by talking about unexpected injuries or poor luck. Other research shows that the self-serving bias operates in areas other than sports (Van Der Pligt & Eiser, 1983). A prototypical display of the self-serving bias occurs when the successful businessperson believes that she is rich because of her personal ability rather than because of her good luck, privileged status, or convenient circumstances (O'Malley & Becker, 1984).

The self-serving bias is a motivational phenomenon rooted in the desire to protect self-esteem (Dunning, Leuenberger, & Sherman, 1995; Greenberg, Pyszcynski, & Solomon, 1982). To the extent that performers internalize success and externalize failure, they maintain a positive self-concept. Consider the destructive consequences to a performer's self-esteem following internalized failures but externalized successes. Imagine the motivational consequences for a student who explains academic successes or marital happiness via good luck and outside assistance and academic and marital setbacks via personal inadequacies. Attributing negative outcomes (failures) to personal deficiencies has been linked to depression (Peterson & Seligman, 1984). The self-serving bias therefore serves as a motivational buffer against feelings of unworthiness, apathy, and feelings of despair (Abramson, Seligman, & Teasdale, 1978).

EFFECTS OF ATTRIBUTION ON MOTIVATIONAL PHENOMENA

Figure 9.1 introduced the motivational consequences of attribution. This section relates attributional analysis to expectancy × value theory, personal control beliefs, explanatory style, illusion of control, motivational orientations, achievement motivation, learned helplessness, depression, intrinsic interest, and emotion.

Implications for Expectancy × Value Theory

Chapter 8 introduced expectancy × value theory. An attributional analysis adds to the theory by showing how causal stability produces changes in expectancies while causal locus produces changes in value (Weiner, 1974).

EXPECTANCY. Recall that expectancy refers to the individual's perceived probability of success or failure at a task. The attributional dimension of stability explains changes in expectancy over time, according to Weiner's expectancy principle (1985, p. 559) and its corollaries.

> *Expectancy Principle*. Changes in expectancy of success following an outcome are influenced by the perceived stability of the cause of the event.
> *Corollary 1*. If the outcome of an event is ascribed to a stable cause, then that outcome will be anticipated with increased certainty, or with an increased expectancy, in the future.
> *Corollary 2*. If the outcome of an event is ascribed to an unstable cause, then the certainty or expectancy of that outcome may be unchanged or the future may be anticipated to be different from the past.

Following an outcome, an attribution to a stable cause increases the person's expectancy that the same outcome will recur. Unstable attributions leave expectancies unchanged, because the cause of the outcome fluctuates and cannot be expected to recur. For instance, failure ascribed to bad luck (an unstable cause) leaves the performer with little reason to believe that failure will recur. If the bad luck is unstable, the failure outcome should also be unstable.

VALUE. Outcomes generate emotional reactions. Success and inclusion lead to joy whereas failure and rejection lead to frustration or sadness (Weiner, Russell, & Learman, 1978, 1979). In addition, however, the locus attributional dimension generates specific emotions (Weiner, 1982, 1986). Internal attributions (e.g., ability, effort) produce pride following success and shame following failure, emotions that affect the individual's perceived value of a particular activity. Following pride from a success, the individual values the activity more; following shame from a failure, the individual values the activity less. External attributions leave value unaffected, because the cause of the outcome lies outside the self. Because externally-caused outcomes have little or no bearing on the self, they do not produce pride and shame.

INTEGRATION OF ATTRIBUTION AND EXPECTANCY × VALUE THEORIES. According to expectancy × value theory, a person's motivation to approach or avoid a particular goal is a product of the expectancy of success and the value assigned to that particular goal. Attribution theory provides a cognitive mechanism by which expectancies and values change over time. Consider the example shown in Table 9.1 for a high school junior contemplating a list of courses for the coming semester. The left side gives the student's first semester expectancies of passing each course and the value for each course; the force to approach each course is calculated (expectancy × value = force). The center columns list hypothetical outcomes (pass or fail) for each course along with the student's attributions and their consequences. The right side lists the student's (new) second semester expectancies of passing each course and new values; the table lists a calculated force to approach each course.

In the first semester the student is expected to approach (i.e., study for, attend, read the text) the courses with the highest forces (English, art) and to avoid the courses with the lowest forces (physical education, mathematics). By semester's end, the student succeeds in some courses and fails in others. (Succeeding and failing are subjectively defined; failing could be an F or making any grade under an A.) The student sees course grades as especially important and thus assesses why each success or failure occurred. Suppose the student explains successes in English by high ability, Spanish by effort, history by how easy it was, and physical education by good luck. Similarly, suppose the student explains failures in art by low ability, science by low effort, and mathematics by bad luck. Each attribution affects the student's future expectancies and values via its locus and stability. Table 9.1 shows the specific effect of each of the seven attributions. Notice what happens to the student's expectancy and value for each course as the second semester begins. Success attributed to internal and stable reasons (e.g., ability) increases both expectancy for success and the value of each course, respectively. Failure attributed to internal and stable causes, however, decreases expectancy for success and the value of each course. Success and failure attributed to external and unstable reasons (e.g., luck) affects neither subsequent expectancy for success nor value of that course. The stu-

TABLE 9–1

Integration of Attribution and Expectancy × Value Theories

Class	Before First Semester			Outcome (Grade)	Attribution Category	Attribution Consequences	Between First Semester and Second Semester		
	Expectancy at Time 1	Value at Time 1	Force E × V				Expectancy at Time 2	Value at Time 2	Force E × V
English	.8	6	4.8	Success	High Ability	Expectancy: Increases Value: Increases	1.0	8	8.0
Art	1.0	4	4.0	Failure	Low Ability	Expectancy: Decreases Value: Decreases	.8	2	1.6
Science	.4	9	3.6	Failure	Low Effort	Expectancy: No change Value: Decreases	.4	7	2.8
Spanish	.7	4	2.8	Success	High Effort	Expectancy: No change Value: Increases	.7	6	4.2
History	.7	2	1.4	Success	Low Task Difficulty	Expectancy: Increases Value: No change	.9	2	1.8
Physical Education	1.0	1	1.0	Success	Good Luck	Expectancy: No change Value: No change	1.0	1	1.0
Mathematics	.3	2	0.6	Failure	Bad Luck	Expectancy: No change Value: No change	.3	2	0.6

dent begins the second semester with revised expectancies and values for each course. Notice that the student now has a different arrangement of forces to approach each of the seven courses. English and Spanish now rank first and second in force.

Personal Control Beliefs

Personal control is the degree to which an individual believes he or she causes desirable outcomes and prevents aversive outcomes (Peterson, Maier, & Seligman, 1993). When personal control is believed strong and resilient, the individual perceives a strong causal link between actions and outcomes. When personal control is believed weak and fragile, the individual feels helpless and perceives that desirable and aversive life outcomes are independent of personal initiatives and actions. As discussed in the next section, positive personal control beliefs cultivate a *mastery orientation* whereas negative personal control beliefs cultivate a *helpless orientation*.

Explanatory Style

Explanatory style is a relatively stable cognitive personality variable that reflects the way people explain why bad events happen to them (Peterson & Barrett, 1987; Peterson & Seligman, 1984). Bad events happen to everyone, but people explain their setbacks with attributions that vary in their locus, stability, and controllability. An *optimistic explanatory style* manifests itself as the tendency to explain bad events with attributions that are external, unstable, and controllable (I lost the contest because my coach called the wrong plays at the wrong time). A *pessimistic explanatory style* manifests itself as the tendency to explain bad events with attributions that are internal, stable, and uncontrollable (I lost the contest because I am just not physically coordinated enough).

To understand the effect of explanatory style, imagine you have been looking for a job unsuccessfully for some time. What is the one major cause of this misfortune? Take a moment to identify a likely cause, then rate that cause on the following three questions (based on Seligman et al., 1979):

1. Is the cause of your unsuccessful job search due to something about you or something about other people or circumstances?
2. In the future when looking for a job, will this cause again be present?
3. Is the cause something that you can do something about, or is this cause something over which you have little or no control?

These three questions pertain to the attributional dimensions of locus, stability, and controllability, respectively. These questions, based on the Attributional Style Scale (Seligman et al., 1979; also see the Attributional Style Questionnaire, Peterson et al., 1982; Peterson & Villanova, 1988) produce a profile of the person's attributional style. The optimistic attributor explains bad events with external, unstable, and uncontrollable causes. The pessimistic attributor explains bad events with internal, stable, and controllable causes.

PESSIMISTIC STYLE. Academic failures, poor physical health, and subpar job performance are common. Some of us react to such failures by trying harder whereas others react by giving up. A pessimistic style predisposes people toward the latter giving up. Consider the following three examples of how a pessimistic explanatory style decreases motivation and affects emotions following academic failure, health problems, and poor job performance.

Disappointing grades, uncompleted assignments, confusing and misplaced textbooks, writer's block, locked library doors, unintelligible lectures, and unprepared presentations are part of many academic careers, at least from time to time. When students with a pessimistic style face such educational frustrations and failures, they respond and cope in a passive, fatalistic manner (Peterson & Barrett, 1987). Attributional pessimists trace the cause of such failures to causes that are pervasive, far-reaching, and from the self (i.e., internal, stable, and uncontrollable). To document that pessimistic students acted in a passive, fatalistic manner, researchers measured how frequently each student sought out academic advising during the year. Attributional pessimists tended not to go to an advisor, and avoiding an advisor was, in turn, associated with poor grades and performance (Peterson & Barrett, 1987).

Now consider the relationship between pessimistic explanatory style and physical health (Peterson, Seligman, & Vaillant, 1988). These researchers studied 99 college graduates from 1944 through 1980. Each person completed a survey of explanatory style at age 25, and the researchers rated health status at five-year intervals. Table 9.2 lists the correlation between pessimistic explanatory style and poor physical health over time. Pessimistic explanatory style correlated significantly with poor physical health starting at age 45, and that relationship remained significant through age 60. Again, the explanation seems to be that attributional pessimists react to life's setbacks in a passive, fatalistic manner.

As a final example, consider poor job performance. One vocation that has more than its share of frustrations, failures, and rejections is life insurance sales, as only a

TABLE 9–2

Correlation between Pessimistic Explanatory Style and Poor Physical Health

POOR HEALTH: AGE	R
30	.04
35	.03
40	.13
45	.37****
50	.18*
55	.22**
60	.25***

N = 99; r = coefficient of partial correlation.
*p < .10; **p < .05; ***p < .01; ****p < .001.
SOURCE: Peterson, C., Seligman, M.E.P., & Vaillant, G.E. (1988). Pessimistic explanatory style is a risk factor for physical illness: A thirty-five year longitudinal study. *Journal of Personality and Social Psychology,* 55, 23–27. Copyright © 1988 by American Psychological Association. Adapted with permission.

small percentage of potential clients ever buy a policy. One pair of researchers assessed life insurance agents' explanatory style and recorded which agents stayed on the job and which quit; the researchers also recorded job performance to determine which agents did relatively well and which did relatively poor (Seligman & Schulman, 1986). The attributionally pessimistic agents were more likely to quit and, for those who persevered, to perform worse than their more optimistic peers.

Overall, the pessimistic explanatory style is associated with academic failure (Peterson & Barrett, 1987), social distress (Sacks & Bugental, 1987), physical illness (Peterson, Seligman, & Vaillant, 1988), impaired job performance (Seligman & Schulman, 1986), depression (Beck, 1976), and even electoral defeat in presidential elections (Zullow et al., 1988). Individuals with a pessimistic explanatory style generally make lower grades in college, react to nonresponsive (uncontrollable) partners by speaking less, quit work, and consider depression and suicide. Care must be exercised in interpreting these correlational data, however. It certainly could be the case that poor grades, nonresponsive partners, and failed work lead individuals toward pessimistic styles. Thus, one can say that a pessimistic style and mental and physical well-being correlate negatively, but one *cannot* say assertively that a pessimistic style causes mental and physical distress. Research continues to investigate the causal status of a pessimistic explanatory style in coping with life's setbacks (Peterson, Maier, & Seligman, 1993).

OPTIMISTIC STYLE. The illusion of control is an attributional phenomenon that, over time, fosters an optimistic explanatory style. People with an optimistic style tend to take substantial credit for success but accept little or none of the blame for failure. As you might expect, depressives rarely have an optimistic style, as depressives are not vulnerable to the illusion of control (Alloy & Abramson, 1979) and do not make self-serving attributions (Alloy & Abramson, 1982). The illusion of control, and thus an optimistic style more generally, function to protect self-esteem. Equipped with the self-serving bias and optimistic style, people readily ignore negative self-related information, impose filters on incoming information to distort it in a positive direction, and impose self-protecting interpretations on the positive and negative outcomes that happen to them. Attributing failure to an external cause allows the individual to discount the self-related meaning of the failure. In the same spirit, negative life outcomes are blamed on others, bad luck, and the environment in general. Externalizing failure therefore immunizes the individual against any detrimental effect of failure. Thus, a history of internalizing success and externalizing failures breeds a belief that one has more control over one's outcomes than is actually the case, even if one needs to maintain a full repertoire of excuses, denials, and self-deceptions (Lazarus, 1983; Sackeim, 1983; Tennen & Affleck, 1987). But, functionally, an optimistic explanatory style is not so bad in the long run, because a "mentally healthy person appears to have the enviable capacity to distort reality in a direction that enhances self-esteem, maintains beliefs in personal efficacy, and promotes an optimistic view of the future" (Taylor & Brown, 1988, p. 204).

Motivational Orientations—Mastery versus Helplessness

Over time, explanatory styles foster increasingly distinct motivational orientations. A pessimistic style cultivates a motivational orientation toward helplessness whereas an optimistic style cultivates a motivational orientation toward mastery. Optimists expect their future holds good outcomes; pessimists expect their future holds bad outcomes (Scheier & Carver, 1985). Helplessness-oriented individuals tend to quit in the face of failure and avoid difficult problems because of their pervasive tendency to explain failure with a low ability attribution (i.e., internal–stable–uncontrollable); optimistic mastery-oriented individuals generally persist in the face of failure and try to solve difficult problems (Diener & Dweck, 1978; Dweck & Repucci, 1973). Mastery-oriented individuals resist attributing failure to low ability; instead they engage in self-instructions that function as strategies to overcome the failure feedback. Unlike their helplessness-oriented counterparts, they see failure as controllable (by increased effort, improved strategies) and therefore not as an insurmountable problem. Diener and Dweck (1978) concluded that helplessness-oriented children focus on the cause of failure (low ability) whereas mastery-oriented children focus on remedies for failure.

Diener and Dweck (1980) also studied how helplessness- and mastery-oriented children differ during and following success outcomes. After experiencing a series of successes, helplessness-oriented children underestimated the number of times that they had succeeded, did not attribute their successes to ability, and did not expect their success to continue in the future. Such a pattern of findings suggests that helplessness-oriented children tend to find reasons to discount, deny, or otherwise excuse their successes. A developmental pattern emerges that obviously favors the mastery-oriented individual. Mastery-oriented children, for instance, show more initiative in problem solving, approach problems with a task involvement, expect to do well, persist in the face of failure feedback, seek out challenges, and make controllable attributions in trying to understand the causes of their successes and failures.

Learned Helplessness

The original explanation for learned helplessness proposed that people show motivational, learning, and emotional deficits when they realize that their voluntary behavior has little or no effect on the outcomes they seek to obtain or to avoid (chapter 8; Peterson, Maier, & Seligman, 1993; Seligman, 1975). Attribution research, however, shows that people do not *always* develop helplessness after learning that there is little they can do about an aversive event (Tennen & Eller, 1977). In the attributional analysis of learned helplessness, the causal attribution individuals make following a bad event is an additional crucial determinant of their expectations of future uncontrollability and helplessness. The perception that the world is a nonresponsive, uncontrollable place (response-outcome noncontingencies are the rule) is the first requirement of helplessness. The second is the individual's pessimistic analysis of the cause of the noncontingency (Abramson, Seligman, & Teasdale, 1978;

Peterson, Maier, & Seligman, 1993). For helplessness to occur, individuals must (1) perceive the world as nonresponsive and uncontrollable and (2) believe they lack the capacity to overcome the nonresponsive, uncontrollable world. The person who sees the world as a nonresponsive, uncontrollable place but believes future control is possible does not develop helplessness. It is only when expectancies turn pessimistic and people view the world as nonresponsive and uncontrollable that they experience helplessness.

REFORMULATED MODEL OF LEARNED HELPLESSNESS. In the reformulated model of learned helplessness (Abramson, Seligman, & Teasdale, 1978), the individual's causal analysis of why outcomes are uncontrollable is just as important as the uncontrollability itself. Internal, stable, and uncontrollable attributions to explain a lack of personal control put people at risk of learned helplessness. For example, suppose a job applicant's phone calls are not returned for a week (an unresponsive environment); the applicant who attributes the unreturned calls to an internal-stable-uncontrollable cause stands most at risk of reacting in a passive, listless manner. Another job applicant who attributes the same unreturned calls to an external-unstable-controllable cause is likely to respond in an assertive, active manner. What the reformulated (attributional) model adds to the original (nonattributional) model of learned helplessness is that, given uncontrollable events, people think Okay, the world is an uncontrollable place, but is this lack of control my fault? Will my lack of control continue in the future? Is there anything I can do to overcome it? External-unstable-controllable attributions for a lack of control send the message that failures and setbacks are surmountable and the appropriate response is therefore assertive coping. Internal-stable-uncontrollable attributions send the message that failures and setbacks are insurmountable and the appropriate response therefore is to give up and accept fate.

Depression

Learned helplessness can be viewed as a model of environment-based unipolar depression (Seligman, 1975). Helpless people, like depressives, tend to view an aversive situation as both an uncontrollable event and one caused by internal, stable factors. Just as the perception of uncontrollable outcomes fosters helplessness, a perception of a loss of control over important events and outcomes in the person's life can foster depression. From an attributional perspective, both learned helplessness and depression share a common feature: the negative expectations that emanate from a pessimistic attributional style.

Everybody experiences negative life outcomes, but not everyone is depressed. Following failure, depressives gravitate toward either an internal, internal-stable, or internal-stable-global attribution (Rizley, 1978; Seligman et al., 1979). Depressive also attribute the good things that happen to them pessimistically as from external-unstable-uncontrollable causes. Thus, depressives generally hold a lopsided view of positive and negative outcomes that is a bit on the dark side, as they hold in memory the pains of failure but fail to remember the joys of success (Seligman et al., 1979). The mixture between bad events and a pessimistic style for both bad and good events opens the door to depression. In general, research supports the co-variation between attributional style and depression (Abramson, Metalsky, & Alloy, 1989; Brewin, 1985; Robins, 1988; Sweeney, Anderson, & Bailey, 1986). To say that attributions cause depression, however, is an overstatement because depression fol-lows not only from pessimism but also from bad events. So, the safest conclusion to draw is that a pessimistic attributional style makes the individual more vulnerable to depression (Peterson & Seligman, 1984).

Intrinsic Interest

Consider a brief list of activities that many people find to be intrinsically interesting or enjoyable: engaging in recreational sports, showing out-of-town guests the local sites, playing a musical instrument, and creating a three-course meal. People gener-ally find these activities interesting for various reasons, such as opportunities to in-volve and satisfy the needs for competence, relatedness, and self-determination (chap-ter 4). A curious effect occurs, as discussed in chapter 5, when the person is compensated for engaging in these behaviors—publicly recognized for playing sports, paid money for entertaining, promised a scholarship for playing a musical in-strument, and praised lavishly for preparing three–course meals. Now the person has two reasons for performing the activity: (1) because it is interesting and (2) be-cause they are compensated. To the extent that individuals engage in an activity without thought of any external reward or pressure to do so, attribution theorists argue that they will attribute high intrinsic interest (Bem, 1972). If you ask the am-ateur athlete or the recreational cook why they hit tennis balls or prepare extrava-gant meals, they will more than likely answer, "because it's fun; it's an interest of mine." If external reasons for doing that task are added, the attribution, "because I get paid good money for doing it" begins to compete against the intrinsic interest attribution. The predictable outcome is that intrinsic interest is discounted, or un-dermined, by the external reason (i.e., by extrinsic interest). Generally speaking, the more salient the extrinsic incentive or compensation, the more the intrinsic reason is discounted or undermined (Ross, 1975). In effect, increases in extrinsic interest decrease intrinsic interest. This attributional phenomenon is termed the *overjustifi-cation effect* (Boggiano & Main, 1986; Greene & Lepper, 1974; Higgins et al., 1995; Lepper & Greene, 1978; Lepper, Greene, & Nisbett, 1973; Newman & Layton, 1984; Ross, 1976).

The term *overjustification* connotes that the intrinsic reason to do the task is jus-tification, while the added extrinsic reason amounts to overjustification. Given over-justification, college students do not generally say that they read a textbook because of its interest *and* because they have a test tomorrow; rather, students generally pro-vide only a single explanation for why they do what they do. Given both intrinsic and extrinsic reasons, students generally go with the external reason, saying "I'm reading my textbook because I have a test tomorrow." The discounting of intrinsic interest oc-curs with a variety of external factors, including money (Deci, 1972), prizes (Kruglanski et al., 1975), awards (Lepper, Greene, & Nisbett, 1973), food (Ross, 1975), deadlines

(Amabile, DeJong, & Lepper, 1976), and another person's surveillance (Lepper & Greene, 1975). Thus, the overjustification effect applies to external reasons in general.

For the overjustification effect to occur, two conditions must be met (Newman & Layton, 1984):

1. High initial intrinsic interest.
2. Extrinsic inducement potent enough to justify task participation by itself.

In their experiment, for instance, children played at an intrinsically interesting or uninteresting activity and received either a large or small inducement for doing so (Newman & Layton, 1984). Children playing at the interesting activity who received a strong external inducement (a fistful of M&M candies) lost much of the intrinsic interest in the task. Children playing at the interesting activity who received a small external inducement (a single M&M candy) lost only a little of their intrinsic interest. Children playing at the uninteresting activity had little intrinsic interest to lose and the inducements, large or small, therefore did not affect their intrinsic interest. Thus, overjustification occurs in those activities for which initial intrinsic interest is high and after the individual receives an attention-getting external inducement. When these two conditions are met, intrinsic interest is put at risk.

External incentives and rewards do not inevitably decrease intrinsic interest. After all, some (but certainly not all) professional athletes, musicians, artists, and actors continue to maintain high intrinsic interest in their activities despite ridiculously large extrinsic rewards. There are two qualifications to the overjustification effect. First, external rewards are less likely to undermine intrinsic interest if individuals continually keep in mind their initial level of intrinsic interest (Fazio, 1981). Second, extrinsic rewards that involve and satisfy the need for competence do not decrease intrinsic interest. In fact, rewards that reflect competence (e.g., praise) often increase intrinsic interest (Rosenfield, Folger, & Aldeman, 1980). Recall from cognitive evaluation theory (chapter 6; Deci & Ryan, 1985a) that rewards used to control behavior undermine intrinsic interest whereas rewards that communicate information of a job well done increase intrinsic interest. This second qualification helps explain how some athletes, musicians, artists, and actors preserve intrinsic interest, as money, applause, and public praise can involve and satisfy the competence need and thus promote, rather than undermine, intrinsic interest. Notice, however, that money, applause, and banner headlines are also highly salient extrinsic rewards that can promote extrinsic interest and threaten intrinsic interest. The conclusion is that salient and superfluous extrinsic rewards undermine intrinsic interests via the overjustification process, unless the performer consciously recalls intrinsic interest and interprets extrinsic rewards as information of a job well done.

Emotion

People respond emotionally to life's successes and failures, acceptances and rejections. Following success people generally feel happy, and following failure people generally feel sad or frustrated. Joy and distress occur irrespective of the cause of the outcome (Weiner, 1986). Attribution theory, however, proposes that in addition to these primary emotional reactions to life outcomes, people go on to explain why they succeeded or failed. Some (but not all) emotions occur as a function of the attributional information-processing flow. The locus dimension contributes to pride; the controllability dimension contributes to anger, guilt, pity, shame, and gratitude; the stability dimension contributes to hope and hopelessness (Weiner, 1985, 1986). Chapter 12 details the specific process by which attributions produce emotional reactions. What follows here is an introduction of the relationship between attributional information processing and the six specific emotional reactions of pride, anger, pity, guilt, shame, and hope.

Pride occurs when the individual attributes a positive outcome to the self (I won the contest because of my outstanding ability). Anger occurs when the individual attributes a negative outcome to the will of another (I lost because my opponent cheated). Pity occurs as the individual attributes a negative outcome to an uncontrollable deficit (I (or someone else) lost because I am short). Guilt occurs as the individual attributes a negative outcome to an uncontrollable deficit for which he or she is personally responsible (I lost because I was unprepared and just didn't know what to do). When the uncontrollable deficit is the person's fault, guilt occurs; when the uncontrollable deficit is not the person's fault, pity occurs. Shame occurs when the deficit is controllable and one's fault (I lost because of a lack of effort). Gratitude occurs as the individual attributes a positive outcome to the will of another (I won because my teammates helped me so much). Hope and hopelessness follow outcomes attributable to stable causes (My outstanding ability gives me hope for future success). The individual who expects the future will be as good as the past feels hope; the individual who expects the future will be as bad as the past feels hopelessness.

ATTRIBUTIONAL TRAINING AND RETRAINING

People learn attributions. Experience teaches us how to interpret the causal structure of the world around us. We learn how to make sense of academic failure, interpersonal rejection, financial loss, unreturned phone calls, disappointing performances, automobile accidents, and so on. The conclusions we come to in interpreting the causal structure of our environmental interactions produce habitual ways of thinking, and when our habitual way of explaining life's outcomes become pessimistic, we become vulnerable to academic failure, poor health, poor job performance, learned helplessness, and depression.

Because attributions and attributional styles are learned ways of thinking, the reformulated (attributional) model of learned helplessness stresses that helplessness (and other expectancy-based problems) is both *preventable* (Altmaier & Happ, 1985; Hirt & Genshaft, 1981; Jones, Nation, & Massad, 1977) and *reversible* (Klein & Seligman, 1976; Miller & Norman, 1981; Orbach & Hadas, 1982). Though still somewhat preliminary in its endorsement, clinical psychology sees attributional training and retraining as a promising cognitive approach to therapeutic intervention in helplessness-related emotional and behavioral problems (Cotton, 1981; Forsterling, 1985; Peterson, Maier, & Seligman, 1993). Attributional retraining has been effective in the treatment of unipolar depression (Person & Rao, 1985; Seligman et al., 1988), interpersonal aggression (Hudley & Graham, 1993), and poor academic performance (Wilson & Linville, 1982).

Preventing Helplessness

To prevent helplessness, one must prevent its causes, which are (1) a belief that behavioral initiatives have little or no control over environmental outcomes and (2) a pessimistic explanatory style. These causes suggest two strategies to preventing helplessness: Change the responsiveness of the environment from uncontrollable to controllable and develop an optimistic style.

CHANGE ENVIRONMENT FROM NONRESPONSIVE TO RESPONSIVE. Sometimes people feel helpless because their environments at home, at work, in school, in relationships, and on the athletic field are truly outside their realm of influence and control. In such situations, the person's efforts are best directed not so much at changing attributions as at changing either the environment itself or interactions with the environment. Responses to nature and circumstances (e.g., hurricanes, cars that won't run) are difficult or impossible to change except by moving, purchasing a new car, and other such measures. But other situations (e.g., whether the salesperson makes the sale) are somewhat or even mostly controllable; the person could benefit by brushing up on social skills, developing a social support network, refining communication skills, developing new athletic techniques, getting performance advice from a coach or an instruction book, or perhaps by improving personal hygiene. In addition, the responsiveness of other people (e.g., whether or not they harbor prejudices, whether or not they are willing to cooperate) can be changed or restructured through negotiation, bargaining, confrontation, help-seeking, coalition formation, and the like. In these examples, it is not the individual's pessimism that underlies vulnerability to helplessness; rather, the uncontrollability is quite real, and one's attention is best directed at changing the environment either directly (or indirectly, as through how one interacts with it).

IMMUNIZATION AND ATTRIBUTION TRAINING. Even if the environment is at least somewhat responsive and controllable, many people still sometimes react to failures and frustrations in a helpless way. People who are optimistic are to some extent immunized against the demoralizing effects of life's failures (Seligman, 1990). Immunization is an attempt to prevent helplessness before it occurs (Jones, Nation, & Massad, 1977; Seligman & Maier, 1967; Ramirez, Maldonado, & Markus, 1992). It is a developmental process in which the person is raised to experience early control and mastery over the environment, typically by giving the individual small doses of early failure experiences that are quickly followed up by (1) training and coaching that enables the person to cope successfully and (2) cognitive intervention that enables the person to interpret obstacles and setbacks in an optimistic way (more external, unstable, controllable). So, immunization is one part prior experience (with controllable failures) and one part cognitive or attributional interpretation (forthcoming setbacks explained in an optimistic way). The focus of immunization via prior experience is to encourage people to see connections between their behaviors and their outcomes (Klein & Seligman, 1976). Its logic is to foster strong and resilient personal control beliefs that prevent the onset of learned helplessness. The cognitive/attributional approach to immunization is to encourage people to see the situationally specific and external causes of failure instead of just its internal causes (Ramirez, Maldonado, & Markus, 1992). Providing people with early experiences of controllability and of optimistic interpretation biases immunizes them against the detrimental effects of uncontrollable environments (Altmaier & Happ, 1985; Eckelman & Dyck, 1979; Hirt & Genshaft, 1981; Jones, Nation, & Massad, 1977; Ramirez, Maldonado, & Markus, 1992; Thornton & Powell, 1974).

Reversing Helplessness

When people face life's difficulties, they sometimes make pessimistic attributions that leave them vulnerable to helplessness. In the face of a pessimistic style, attributional retraining programs act as therapeutic attempts to reverse existing helplessness. To reverse helplessness, research suggests a two-part retraining strategy: (1) extend the range of possible attributions to explain a lack of control and (2) persuade the person to exchange the original pessimistic attribution for a more optimistic one (Peterson, Maier, & Seligman, 1993).

EXTENDING THE RANGE OF POSSIBLE ATTRIBUTIONS. The first step in the attempt to reverse helplessness is to extend the range of attributions that might explain the problematic setback or failure. For instance, in the face of a frustrating turn of events such as having a job application rejected, applicants might pessimistically conclude that they just don't have what it takes to get a good job. Given such a pessimistic attribution (internal–stable–uncontrollable), another person might suggest the job applicant consider alternative, yet equally valid, rival attributions, such as lack of proper experience, lack of preparation, ineffective interview strategy, tough economy, high odds against any single applicant getting a job with 100 applicants (high task difficulty), and so on. In his cognitive therapy of depression, Beck (1967, 1984) documents that depressives often jump to their negative thoughts about the self and the future on the basis of a single fact (a process referred to as *arbitrary inference*). An effective means of countering arbitrary inference is to encourage the individual to extend the limited range of possible attributions for a setback.

CHANGING UNNECESSARILY PESSIMISTIC ATTRIBUTIONS. The fundamental objective in attributional retraining is to encourage a person to rethink the merits of unstable, controllable attributions for a setback. Stable, uncontrollable attributions lead to the conclusion that the setback is part of a permanent, irreversible condition. Unstable, controllable attributions, on the other hand, lead to the conclusion that a setback is a temporary, reversible condition. Thus, the first goal in attributional retraining programs is to alter the individual's perception of why failure occurred (Andrews & Debus, 1978; Dweck, 1975; Zoeller, Mahoney, & Weiner, 1983). One likely attribution for failure is, of course, a lack of ability (stable–uncontrollable), but ability attributions leave the person asking, why try? Fortunately, other attributions are equally valid, including lack of effort (Dweck, 1975), lack of an effective strategy (Anderson & Jennings, 1980), and lack of experience (Wilson & Linville, 1982). Each of the attributions of effort, strategy, and experience are unstable and under volitional control; hence, failure's cause becomes interpreted as an unstable and volitional outcome. Failure therefore loses its stigma as an insurmountable, uncontrollable obstacle. Attributing failure to poor effort, ineffective strategy, or insufficient experience, rather than to a lack of ability, enhances both performance and persistence (Anderson & Jennings, 1980; Dweck, 1975; Wilson & Linville, 1982).

Consider a rather extended example of one of these attributional retraining studies (Wilson & Linville, 1982). College freshmen whose fall semester's work was worse than expected were asked why they performed so poorly. Most of the students attributed their perceived failure to a lack of ability. Wilson and Linville reasoned that many of these students were at risk of dropping out of college (because a stable-uncontrollable cause of failure could be expected to persist throughout their college careers). In the study, half of the students were told that most students attain higher grades as they progress through college. These students watched testimonial videotapes of juniors and seniors who confirmed their own steady year-by-year improvement in academic performance. The other half of the students, who constituted a control group, received no such attributional retraining, showed no increase in their grade point average over the next year and had, as the researchers feared, a 25% dropout rate. The retrained students, on the other hand, showed a significant improvement in their grade point average and showed only a 5% dropout rate. Explaining the students' failure with an unstable cause resulted in positive, significant improvements in performance (GPA) and persistence (dropout rate).

Forsterling (1985) reviewed the procedures used in 15 different attributional retraining programs and concluded that researchers accomplish retraining in one of three ways: persuasion, behavior modification, and information. Each method has proved successful, but it remains an open question whether one technique works better than another. The three methods are as follows:

1. *Persuasion.* A person performs a task, and then an expert commentator verbalizes the desired attribution (Zoeller, Mahoney, & Weiner, 1983). A trustworthy expert attempts to convince the performer of the validity of the desired attribution.
2. *Behavior modification.* In the attributional retraining version of behavior modification, desired attributions are reinforced while undesired attributions are ignored. A therapist first encourages the performer to verbalize a range of attributions to explain failures and rejections, and then verbally and nonverbally reinforces only those attributions that are both unstable and uncontrollable (e.g., equipment failure, bad luck; Andrews & Debus, 1978).
3. *Information.* Information can lead performers to make more optimistic at-

tributions than they otherwise might. Naive students might be quick to attribute the cause of their academic difficulties to themselves; in contrast, more
informed students experience fewer academic problems and make better
grades by acknowledging the influence of factors that are unstable and more
controllable (learning the ropes or the system, how to use the library's resources, and so on; Wilson & Linville, 1982, 1985).

CRITICISMS OF THE ATTRIBUTIONAL APPROACH

Attribution theory is not without its critics. Nisbett and Wilson (1977) present two
criticisms. First, they argue that people do not typically make attributions to explain
the events and outcomes in their lives. Rather, people devote more attention to the
outcome per se but relatively little attention to diagnosing why it occurred. Further,
even when people do make causal attributions, their attention quickly turns to other
more pressing matters, such as the consequences (rather than the cause) of the outcome. After being rejected for a job, applicants often worry more about what they
will do without a job (consequences) than about why they were rejected (attributions).

Nisbett and Wilson (1977) also argue that psychologists often artificially force
attributions by asking their research participants such questions as, How important
was your ability in determining your outcome? People readily answer such questions,
but it remains a fair question to ask whether people spontaneously ask themselves
how important their ability was in determining why they succeeded or failed. Nisbett
and Wilson's first criticism is that people just do not think about attributions of ability, effort, task difficulty, and luck all that much. Attribution theorists counter such
criticism by conceding that people do not always make spontaneous attributions.
Rather, attribution theorists argue that people make attributions following unexpected, negative, and important outcomes. Thus, attributions occur only some of
the time.

Second, Nisbett and Wilson (1977) report that there is little evidence for the
proposition that attributions produce any direct effect on the individual's behavior.
In fact, the two critics report an inability to find *any* evidence in the research literature that attributions influence behavior. This second criticism levied against attribution theory is especially disturbing in light of the fact that psychology often defines itself as "the scientific study of behavior." Several attribution and cognitive
theorists in general have responded to the Nisbett and Wilson analysis (Smith &
Miller, 1978), but this criticism remains valid. If attributions do not influence behavior, it seems reasonable (even crucial) to ask what attributions do influence.
Attributions affect the information-processing flow and, by affecting the content of
thought, attributions affect cognitive, motivational, and emotional processes. This
chapter described some of these processes, including expectancy, value, personal
control beliefs, explanatory style, learned helplessness, depression, intrinsic interest,
and emotion (recall Fig. 9.1). These processes, rather than attributions per se, affect
behavior.

Summary

The principal assumption of attribution theory is that people actively seek to discover why they succeed and fail at important life events. We want to discover and understand the causes for the events and outcomes that happen to us. When people make attributions, they do so for two reasons. First, people seek knowledge and information. Second, an attributional analysis may improve the way the person interacts with the environment by replacing ineffective ways of thinking or behaving with better ways of thinking and acting. But people do not always engage in an active causal analysis. Rather, attributions follow outcomes that are unexpected, negative, and important, such as failure at an important event when success was expected. Once made, attributions may affect a variety of cognitive, motivational, and emotional states including expectancies, values, personal control beliefs, explanatory style, learned helplessness, depression, intrinsic interest, and emotion.

Hundreds of attributions are possible to explain why any particular outcome occurred. So, attribution researchers generally use attributional dimensions, rather than attributions per se, to understand how attributions affect thinking, feeling, and wanting. The three attributional dimensions that categorize practically all possible attributions are locus (internal versus external), stability, and controllability. Attributions are subject to two errors and one bias. When making attributions to explain another person's outcome, the fundamental attribution error documents that people overestimate the importance of internal or personality factors. The actor-observer error describes how actors typically explain their own behavior as externally caused but explain other people's behavior as internally caused. Self-serving bias means that people tend to ascribe success internally and failure externally. Self-serving bias helps the illusion of control in that people more readily ignore negative self-related information, distort negative outcomes in a favorable light, and develop self-protective strategies that allow them to interpret outcomes favorably.

Attribution theory is a cognitive model that extends into an impressive array of emotional and motivational processes. Attribution theory applies to expectancy $\times$ value theory by proposing that expectancies change over time through stable versus unstable attributions while values change over time through internal versus external attributions. The habitual tendency to explain setbacks with external-unstable-controllable explanations cultivates an optimistic explanatory style whereas the habitual tendency to explain setbacks with internal-stable-controllable attributions cultivates a pessimistic style. The reformulated learned helplessness model depends as much on making a pessimistic attribution as it does on perceiving that the environment is an uncontrollable, nonresponsive one. Models of unipolar depression assert that a pessimistic explanatory style makes the individual more vulnerable to depression whereas the illusion of control makes the individual less vulnerable to depression. The overjustification effect demonstrates that when intrinsic and extrinsic attributions compete to explain task engagement, the intrinsic reason is discounted in favor of the extrinsic justification. Different attributional dimensions explain the cognitive roots of pride (locus), anger, pity, guilt, and shame (controllability), and hope (stability). Learned helplessness deficits can be prevented (through immunization or increased environmental responsiveness) or reversed (through extending the range of possible attributions and attributional retraining techniques).

For all its merits, attribution theory is susceptible to two major criticisms. According to Nisbett and Wilson, (1) people do not spontaneously make attributions to explain their life outcomes and instead pay more attention to the consequences of what happens to them and (2) attributions seem to have very little direct effect on behavioral responses. Thus, people only sometimes make attributions (when outcomes are unexpected, negative, and important) and attributions affect behavior only indirectly through their effects on cognitive, motivational, and emotional processes.

RECOMMENDED READINGS

Abramson, L. Y., Seligman, M. E. P., & Teasdale, J. (1978). Learned helplessness in humans: Critique and reformulation. *Journal of Abnormal Psychology, 87,* 49–74.

Anderson, C. A., & Jennings, D. L. (1980). When experiences of failure promote expectations of success: The impact of attributing failure to ineffective strategies. *Journal of Personality, 48,* 393–407.

Diener, C. I., & Dweck, C. S. (1978). An analysis of learned helplessness: Continuous changes in performance, strategy, and achievement cognitions following failure. *Journal of Personality and Social Psychology, 36,* 451–462.

Greenberg, J., Pyszcynski, T., & Solomon, S. (1982). The self-serving attributional bias: Beyond self-presentation. *Journal of Experimental Social Psychology, 18,* 56–67.

Newman, J., & Layton, B. D. (1984). Overjustification: A self-perception perspective. *Personality and Social Psychology Bulletin, 10,* 419–425.

Peterson, C., Seligman, M. E. P., & Vaillant, G. E. (1988). Pessimistic explanatory style is a risk factor for physical illness: A thirty-five year longitudinal study. *Journal of Personality and Social Psychology, 55,* 23–27.

Taylor, S. E., & Brown, J. D. (1988). Illusion and well-being: A social psychological perspective on mental health. *Psychological Bulletin, 103,* 193–210.

Weiner, B. (1979). A theory of motivation for some classroom experiences. *Journal of Educational Psychology, 71,* 3–25.

Weiner, B. (1985). An attributional theory of achievement motivation and emotion. *Psychological Review, 92,* 548–573.

Wilson, T. D., & Linville, P. W. (1982). Improving the academic performance of college freshman: Attribution theory revisited. *Journal of Personality and Social Psychology, 42,* 367–376.

Chapter 10

THE SELF

How have you been lately? Looking back over the last two weeks, how many days have you felt happy? How many days have you felt blue or depressed? How satisfying is your time at school or work? How about your relationships? Consider the following six questions and, first, decide whether you agree or disagree; second, indicate whether you agree or disagree slightly or strongly:

1. Many of my personal qualities trouble me enough that I wish I could change them.
2. I feel somewhat isolated and frustrated in interpersonal relationships.
3. When making the important decisions in my life, I prefer to rely on the judgments of others.
4. Often I am unable to change or improve my life circumstances.
5. My life lacks a sense of meaning or purpose.
6. I have a sense of personal stagnation that leaves me bored and uninterested in life.

These six questions represent separate dimensions of psychological well-being. These six dimensions are *self-acceptance*, or positive evaluations of oneself; *positive interpersonal relations*, or close, warm relationships with others; *autonomy*, or self-determination; *environmental mastery*, or the capacity to manage surrounding challenges and events; *purpose in life,* or the conviction that life offers purpose and meaning; and *personal growth*, or a sense of forward-moving development (Ryff, 1989, 1995; Ryff & Keyes, 1995). Each of these dimensions, and thus each of your responses, reflects a distinct contour of self-functioning and psychological well-being. To be well psychologically is to possess positive self-regard, positive relationships with others, autonomy, mastery, purpose, and a sense of growth and development (Ryff, 1995). Possessing these qualities is the province of the self.

THE SELF

Three problems occupy the self: (1) defining or creating the self; (2) relating the self to society, and (3) discovering, developing, and fulfilling personal potential (Baumeister, 1987). In the quest to define or create the self, we wonder about who we are, how others see us, how similar or different we are to others, and whether we can become the person we want to be. In the quest to relate the self to society, we contemplate how we want to relate to others, what place we wish to occupy in the social world, and what societal roles are available to us. In the quest to discover, develop, and fulfill the self, we explore what does and does not interest us, we experiment with our surroundings to discover our talents and skills, we develop some skills but ignore others, and we pay attention to what our culture values as important and worthwhile.

Each of the self's three basic tasks has motivational implications. Defining or creating the self shows how *self-concept* energizes and directs behavior. Some aspects of self-definition are simply ascribed to us (e.g., gender). Other aspects, however, must be gained through achievement and acts of choice (e.g., career, friends, beliefs, values), which makes our struggle to define and create the self a motivational one. Relating the self to society shows how *identity* energizes and directs behavior. In some respects, society is rigid in the roles it encourages or even allows individuals to pursue. In other respects society is flexible in that it gives the individual some degree of choice and personal responsibility in determining relationships to others and to society (e.g., partners, careers), which makes the struggle to relate the self to society a motivational one. Discovering, developing, and fulfilling the potential of the self is also a motivational struggle, one that reflects the *agenetic self*. Agency provides the self with inherent motivational and developmental processes that energize and direct discovering, developing, and fulfilling behaviors in a way that moves the self toward greater complexity and a higher-order organization.

SELF-FUNCTIONING AND THE PROBLEM WITH SELF-ESTEEM

Before discussing self-concept, identity, and agency, I would like to pause and challenge a cornerstone belief that many people endorse—that the best way to increase motivation in another person is to increase his or her self-esteem. The teachers, employers, and coaches I have talked to over the years invariably and assertively tell me that if you want to motivate students, workers, and athletes, then here is what you do: increase their self-esteem! Make them feel good about who they are and then watch as all sorts of wonderful things happen. Increasing self-esteem is a fine objective, but the problem with boosting self-esteem in the name of motivation is that "there are almost no findings that self-esteem causes anything at all. Rather, self-esteem is caused by a whole panoply of successes and failures. . . . What needs improving is not self-esteem but improvement of our skills [for dealing] with the world" (Seligman, quoted in Azar, 1994, p. 4). Notice the causal relationship between self-esteem and achievement/productivity: Increases in self-esteem do not produce increases in achievement; rather, increases in achievement produce increases in self-esteem (Byrne, 1984; Harter, 1993; Marsh, 1990; Scheier & Kraut, 1979; Shaalvik & Hagtvet, 1990). So, changes in self-esteem do *not* cause changes in achievement but, rather, changes in achievement cause changes in self-esteem.

Inflated self-esteem has a dark side. People with an inflated self-view are prone to aggression and acts of violence when that favorable self-view is threatened (Baumeister, Smart, & Boden, 1996). For these two reasons—gains in self-esteem do not cause anything good and threats to an inflated self-view is a prelude to violence—the crusade to boost self-esteem in the name of motivation is overrated. The function of self-esteem is that it is an anxiety buffer (Solomon, Greenberg, & Pyszczynski, 1991). People low in self-esteem tend to be anxious, threats to self-esteem make people feel anxious, and increases in self-esteem (as through success) quiet anxiety (Greenberg et al., 1992).

The conclusion is not that self-esteem is the royal road to high motivation, but, rather, that esteem is an end product of other self-related functions. Self-esteem is like happiness or morale in that trying to be happy or enthusiastic does not get you very far. Rather, happiness and morale are emotional by-products of life's satisfactions, triumphs, and positive relationships (Izard, 1991). Likewise, self-esteem is an emotional by-product of successfully measuring up to culturally mandated norms (Josephs, Markus, & Tafarodi, 1992). The same holds true, though to a lesser degree, for the six aspects of positive psychological well-being introduced in the first paragraph—self-acceptance, positive interpersonal relationships, autonomy, environmental mastery, purpose in life, and personal growth. Each is less of an end product than it is a by-product of other pursuits. This chapter is about those other pursuits, which are (1) defining or creating the self (self-concept); (2) relating the self to society (identity); and (3) discovering, developing, and fulfilling the self's potential (agency).

SELF-CONCEPT

Self-concepts are individuals' mental images of themselves. People pay close attention to the feedback they receive in their day-to-day affairs that reveals their personal attributes, characteristics, and preferences. Most of the self-related information comes from specific life experiences: During the group discussion, I felt uncomfortably self-conscious; On the weekend field trip, I did not talk very much; At lunch I avoided sitting and talking with others. But people do not remember the thousands of individual life experiences. Rather, people aggregate their experiences into general conclusions. Over time, people translate their multitude of specific experiences into a general representation of self such as, For the most part, I am shy. It is this general conclusion (I'm shy), rather than the specific experiences, that people readily remember and use as building blocks to define self-concept.

Self-Schemas

Self-schemas are cognitive generalizations about the self that are domain specific and learned from past experience. The earlier illustration, I'm shy, exemplifies a self-schema. In athletics, a high school student might look back on the week to recall finishing last in a 100 meter dash, quitting running from exhaustion during the mile, and repeatedly bumping the high jump bar at the track meet. In school, however, the student might recall scoring well on a test, answering all the questions the teacher asked, and having a poem accepted for a school publication. Eventually, if the experiences in athletics and in the classroom are consistent and frequent enough, the student will generalize a self that is, for the most part, incompetent in athletics but skillful in school. These generalizations (Athletically, I am inept; intellectually, I am smart) constitute self-schemas (Markus, 1977, 1983).

A self-concept is a collection of domain-specific self-schemas that extends into all major life domains that are important to that person (Markus, 1977). The major life domains in early childhood, for instance, typically include cognitive competence, physical competence, peer acceptance, and behavioral conduct (Harter & Pike, 1984). In adolescence, the major life domains generally include scholastic competence, athletic competence, physical appearance, peer acceptance, close friendships, romantic appeal, and behavioral conduct or morality (Harter, 1990). By college, the major life domains include scholastic competence, intellectual ability, creativity, job competence, athletic competence, physical appearance, peer acceptance, close friendships, romantic relationships, relationship with parents, morality, and sense of humor (Harter, 1990; Neemann & Harter, 1986). What this litany of life domains shows is the general variety and range of self-schemas a person likely possesses at different stages in the life cycle. The specific life domains vary from one person to the next, but the domains just mentioned illustrate the typical age-related structure of self-concept. This collection of self-schemas forms a general self-concept (Harter, 1988; Kihlstrom & Cantor, 1984; Markus & Sentisk, 1982; Scheier & Carver, 1988).

Motivational Properties of Self-Schemas

Self-schemas generate motivation in two ways. First, self-schemas, once formed, direct the individual to behave in ways that ensure social feedback that is consistent with established self-schemas. The basic idea behind self-schema consistency is that if someone tells me that I am introverted when I think I am extraverted, that contradictory feedback generates a motivational tension. The motivational tension acts as cognitive dissonance (chapter 7) to motivate the self to restore consistency. For instance, in response to feedback that another person sees me as an introvert, a tension arises that creates a desire to prove that I am actually an extravert. Second, the self acts to generate motivation to move the present self toward a desired future self. Much like goal setting's discrepancy-creating process (Chapter 7), an ideal possible self initiates goal-directed behavior. Thus, the student who wants to become an actor initiates whatever actions seem necessary to graduate from being a student to becoming an actor.

CONSISTENT SELF: STABILITY VERSUS CHANGE IN A SELF-SCHEMA. Once individuals establish a well-articulated self-schema in a particular domain, they generally act to preserve that self-view. Hence, once established, self-schemas become increasingly resistant to contradictory information (Markus, 1977, 1983). People preserve their established self-schemas by actively seeking out information consistent with their self-concept and by ignoring information that contradicts their self-view (Swann, 1983, 1985; Tesser, 1987). It is psychologically disturbing to believe one thing is true about the self yet be told that the reverse is actually the case. Imagine the turmoil of the career politician who loses a local election or the turmoil of the star athlete who does not get drafted into the professional ranks. Inconsistency and contradiction generate an emotional discomfort that signals that consistency needs to be restored. It is this negative affective state that produces the motivation to seek self-confirmatory and to avoid self-disconfirmatory information and feedback.

To ensure that other people see us as we see ourselves, we adopt self-presentational signs and symbols. Through external appearances, we announce our self-view to others. Examples include the appearance we try to convey through clothes, dieting and weightlifting, cosmetic surgery, room fixtures and arrangements, and so forth. For instance, the person wearing a Green Bay Packers jacket sends messages to others such as "talk to me about football" and "treat me as an athlete." Further, in the name of self-schema preservation, we intentionally choose to interact with others who treat us in ways that we want to be treated. For example, when given a choice to interact with either a person who just evaluated them favorably or a person who just evaluated them unfavorably, high-self-esteem persons choose to interact with the positive evaluator while low-self-esteem individuals choose the negative evaluator (Robinson & Smith-Lovin, 1992). By choosing friends who confirm our self-view, we make self-confirmatory feedback more likely and we make self-disconfirmatory feedback less likely.

Despite preventive efforts, self-discrepant feedback does sometimes occur (as it did for the career politician and star athlete). The first line of defense is to distort that information until it loses its status as discrepant information. In the face of discrepant self-schema feedback, the individual asks, "Is the feedback valid? Is the source of the feedback trustworthy? How important or relevant is this feedback?" (Crary, 1966; Markus, 1977; Swann, 1983). For example, a student with a self-view of intelligence who fails a college course might discredit that feedback by arguing against its validity (I scored as unintelligent because I was just so busy and distracted), against the professor's judgment (Oh, Mr. Barnes, what does he know—he's a nitwit), and against its importance or relevance (It's not what you know, it's who you know). People also counter disconfirming feedback with compensatory self-inflation (Greenberg & Pyszczynski, 1985) and self-affirmation techniques (I may have lost the election, but look at all the wonderful support these people gave me!) (Steele, 1988). The effectiveness of such reactions to self-discrepant feedback depends on whether convincing counterexamples are readily available so the person can reinforce his existing self-view (Eisenstadt & Leippe, 1994).

In those domains in which experience is relatively rich and consistent, self-schemas are relatively stable; in those domains in which experience is sparse or contradictory, self-schemas exist in a state of flux and are therefore susceptible to change (Swann, 1983, 1985). Individuals' confidence that their self-schemas are valid and true constitutes *self-concept certainty* (Harris & Snyder, 1986). In effect, self-concept certainty *anchors* stable self-schemas. When self-concept certainty is high, discrepant feedback rarely changes a self-schema, but rather, leads only to a slight lowering of self-schema certainty (Swann, 1983). When self-concept certainty is low, discrepant feedback can instigate self-schema change. Conflict between an uncertain self-schema and discrepant feedback instigates a "crisis self-verification" (Swann, 1983): "How do I verify the accuracy of my self-view, given this contradictory feedback?" People go about the task of resolving the self-verification crisis by seeking out additional domain-relevant feedback (Swann, 1983), a sort of best two out of three to break the tie approach to understanding the self.

Figure 10.1 illustrates the self-verification process. Individuals start with a representation of self (a self-schema). Three types of social feedback are possible: self-confirmatory, mildly self-disconfirmatory, and strongly self-disconfirmatory (Swann, 1983). People handle self-confirmatory and mildly self-discrepant information rather well (Swann & Hill, 1982). Figure 10.1 illustrates the effect of potent self-disconfirming feedback. The effect of strongly disconfirming feedback on self-schema change depends on self-concept certainty. When self-concept certainty is

FIGURE 10–1
Process of Self-Verification and Self-Concept Change

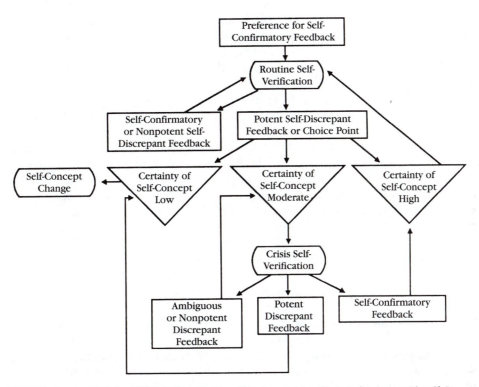

SOURCE: Swann, W. B. Jr. (1983). Self-verification: Bringing social reality into harmony with self. In J. Suls & A. Greenwald (Eds.), *Psychological perspectives on the self* (Vol. 2, pp. 33–66). Hillsdale, NJ: Lawrence Erlbaum.

low, potent feedback overwhelms the self-schema and instigates the crisis self-verification process. When self-concept certainty is high, potent feedback is evaluated as one piece of information in the context of a lifetime of historical information—Well, I was outgoing this time, but I was not outgoing on 1000 occasions in the past; therefore I still think I am shy, all things considered. So, before self-schemas change, (1) self-concept certainty must be low and (2) self-discrepant feedback must be unambiguous, potent, and consistent—that is, difficult to discredit (Swann, 1983, 1985, 1987). The fact that social feedback can change a self-schema leads to a portrait of the self that is, in part, an architect of its own design (via self-verification processes) and, in part, a consequence of the feedback of others and the social world (McNulty & Swann, 1994).

POSSIBLE SELVES: GOAL-DIRECTED BEHAVIOR. Self-schemas change through reacting to discrepant feedback and also by a second more proactive means. Self-schema change occurs through an intentional and deliberate effort to advance the present self toward a desired future possible self. Possible selves represent individuals' ideas of what they would like to become, what they might become, and what they are afraid of becoming (Markus & Nurius, 1986). Some hoped-for selves might include, for instance, the successful self, the creative self, the rich self, the thin self, or the popular self; some feared selves might include the unemployed self, the disabled self, the overweight self, or the rejected self. Possible selves are mostly social in their origin, as the individual observes others and makes inferences such as, what she is now, I could soon become (Markus & Nurius, 1986). For instance, a child might watch performers in a musical and say, Hey, I could become a singer myself. Possible selves are not always positive, though, as a person might read of massive job layoffs in the newspaper and say, I too could become unemployed.

Self-schemas represent the present state of the individual, whereas the hoped-for self represents the future, desired state (or the future, dreaded state). The motivational function of a possible self, like that of a goal, is to provide the individual with an attractive incentive for which to strive. A possible self can therefore act as potent impetus for action by energizing effort and persistence and by directing attention and strategies (recall chapter 7).

Possible selves add an important piece of the puzzle to the role of the self in development. Possible selves are essentially mental representations of attributes, characteristics, and abilities that the self does not yet possess (e.g., I would like to become a physician, though I don't know how to perform surgery and I know the names of only about three bones of the human body). When the self does not have the evidence or feedback to confirm the emerging possible self, one of two outcomes will follow (Markus, Cross, & Wurf, 1990). On the one hand, an absence of supportive evidence or the presence of disconfirming feedback will lead the self to reject the possible self and abandon it. On the other hand, the possible self can energize and direct action so that the attributes, characteristics, and abilities of the self as a physician are attained (Cross & Markus, 1994; Nurius, 1991; Oyserman & Markus, 1990). Thus, the possible self's motivational role is to link the present self with ways to become the possible self. Hence, an individual pursuing a possible self relies less on the present self-schema than on the hoped-for self: If I am going to become my possible self, then how should I behave, what activities should I pursue, and what education do I need? (Cantor, Markus, Niedenthal, & Nurius, 1986; Markus & Nurius, 1986; Markus & Wurf, 1987).

The notion of possible selves negates the self as a product of past experience only, but sees the self as a dynamic entity with a past, present, and future (Cantor et al., 1986; Day et al., 1994). The individual without a possible self in a particular domain lacks an important cognitive basis to develop and use abilities and skills in that domain (Cross & Markus, 1994). On the other hand, an individual who can envision a possible self in the domain engenders feelings of competence and acts to attain the future view of self (Cross & Markus, 1994; Markus, Cross, & Wurf, 1990). Perhaps, the reader can look back at his or her own effort devoted to college courses and ask, to what extent did a possible self relate to each course I completed or dropped, each book I have or have not read, and each lecture I attended or skipped? The presence of a possible self creates a proactive source of motivation to develop toward a particular goal.

IDENTITY

A second aspect of self is *identity*. Identity is the means by which the self relates to society, and it captures the essences of who one is within a cultural context (Deaux et al., 1995; Gecas & Burke, 1995). Of course, people have unique personality traits, but people also are members of social groups and assume roles that provide a basis for social identity. There are five parameters of social identity—relationships (friend, grandfather), vocations (musician, salesperson), political affiliations (republican, liberal), stigma groups (smoker, homeless person), and ethnic groups (Catholic, Southerner) (Deaux et al., 1995). People find themselves in a host of roles such as student, mother, jogger, and poet. These social roles assign culturally-based meaning to that individual. These roles have motivational properties.

Roles

A role consists of cultural expectations for behavior from persons who hold a particular social position (Gross, Mason, & McEachern, 1958). Each of us holds a number of different social positions (roles), and which role we inhabit at any given time depends on the situation we are in and on the people with whom we are interacting. For instance, in a college classroom you probably assume the role of student as you interact with other students and with a professor. When you leave the classroom and go to your job at the psychology clinic, you assume the role of counselor as you interact with clients. At home you assume the role of partner who interacts with another partner and perhaps a daughter.

While assuming one role rather than another, you change how you act—the topic of your conversation, the vocabulary you use, the tone of your voice, and so forth. Behavior varies to such an extent from one role to the next that it makes sense to speak of identities rather than identity. Individuals have many identities, and they present to others the particular identity that is most appropriate for the situation and relevant others. For instance, if you telephone an office, the person who answers is likely to assume roles such as secretary, salesperson, or boss. This places a burden on you (and the person answering) to figure out who you are and who the other person is. Perhaps that sounds silly, but deciding how to act and what to say is actually quite difficult when the identities of the self and others remain in question. Knowing what roles the self and others hold in a given situation tells you which behaviors and which ways of interacting are most and least appropriate (Foote, 1951). Sociologists refer to this process as the "definition of the situation" (Goffman, 1959; Gonos, 1977). Would you act differently if the person answering was a secretary instead of boss or if you presented yourself as a client instead of as a friend? Whenever you participate socially, your first task is to define the other person's role and your role. Then social interaction can proceed to the extent that you both agree on your identities and the definition of the situation.

Affect Control Theory

According to affect control theory (Heise, 1979, 1985; MacKinnon, 1994; Smith-Lovin & Heise, 1988), people act differently from one situation to the next because they use different identities. In affect control theory, identity is rated numerically along the three dimensions of evaluation (E, how good), potency (P, how powerful), and activity (A, how lively?) (EPA, after Osgood, May, & Miron, 1975; Osgood, Suci, & Tannenbaum, 1957). For instance, how good, how powerful, and how lively is a teacher? A lawyer? A drug addict? EPA scores generally range from -3 to $+3$ and are described as follows: evaluation, bad to good; potency, weak to strong; and activity, quiet to lively. Ratings are defined as 0, neutral; 1, slightly; 2, quite; 3, extremely.

According to U.S. citizens (the reference culture), the EPA score or profile for a teacher is 1.5, 1.4, -0.6; that is, teachers are considered slightly to quite good, slightly powerful, and slightly quiet. The EPA score/profile for a lawyer is 1.0, 1.7, 0.2 (someone who is slightly good, quite powerful, and neither lively nor quiet). The EPA score/profile for a drug addict is -2.0, -1.7, 0.7 (someone who is quiet bad, quite weak, and slightly lively). Consider the EPA (evaluation, potency, and activity) scores for the following 10 identities:

Alcoholic,	EPA = -1.6, -1.6, -0.5	Musician,	EPA =	1.3, 0.4, 0.3
Baby,	EPA = 2.5, -2.3, 2.3	Newcomer,	EPA =	0.9, -0.8, 0.2
Beggar,	EPA = -1.0, -2.1, -1.3	Slob,	EPA =	-1.6, -1.3, -0.2
Criminal,	EPA = -1.8, -0.3, 1.1	Superstar,	EPA =	1.0, 2.0, 1.8
Daughter,	EPA = 1.5, -0.3, 1.2	Teammate,	EPA =	1.4, 1.2, 1.4

Trying to represent an identity by a three-dimensional score might at first appear cumbersome, but doing so creates a common ground (how good, how powerful, how active) among all the identities in a culture.

Behaviors and emotions, like identities, have EPA meanings. That is, any action a person takes and any emotion a person expresses can be understood in terms of its cultural meaning—its goodness, its potency, and its liveliness. To assault someone is (according to United States citizens) extremely bad, slightly powerful, and quite active (EPA = -3.0, 1.2, 2.0). To hug someone is quite good, quite powerful, but not too lively (EPA = 2.3, 1.9, -0.2). The EPA profiles for five behaviors (on the left) and for five emotions (on the right) are as follows:

Amuse,	EPA = 1.9, 1.3, 1.3	Anger,	EPA = -0.8, 0.2, 0.7
Command,	EPA = -0.3, 2.0, 1.0	Disgust,	EPA = -1.1, -0.3, 0.2
Double-cross,	EPA = -2.5, 0.1, 1.0	Fear,	EPA = -0.8, -0.9, -0.2
Flee,	EPA = -0.2, -0.6, 1.3	Happiness,	EPA = 1.6, 0.9, 1.3
Work,	EPA = 0.1, 1.0, 0.5	Sadness,	EPA = -1.3, -1.1, -1.0

TERMINOLOGY AND DYNAMICS. Affect control theory labels culturally defined identities according to *fundamental sentiments*, the EPA scores for a particular iden-

tity. When identities participate in social interaction, the behaviors and emotions that occur create a *transitory impression* of who the person is. Thus, if a teacher (EPA = 1.5, 1.4, −0.6) coerces (EPA = −1.0, 1.4, 0.0) a student, the act of coercing creates a transitory impression of who the teacher is—is this person a teacher (someone with an EPA of 1.5, 1.4, −0.6) or is this person a coercer (someone with an EPA of −1.0, 1.4, 0.0)? The discrepancy between a culturally defined identity and a behaviorally implied identity creates a motivational state referred to as a *deflection*. Deflections range from nonexistent (identity-confirming behavior) to very large (identity-violating behavior). When they occur, deflections motivate behavior (MacKinnon, 1994) and, once energized, direct behavior in ways that restore the original, culturally defined fundamental sentiment (Smith-Lovin, 1990; Smith-Lovin & Heise, 1988.)

The affect control principle is this: People behave in ways that minimize affective deflection (MacKinnon, 1994). To minimize affective deflection, people act in ways that maintain their identities and restore those identities when deflections arise. This then is the vocabulary of affect control theory: Fundamental sentiments, transitory impressions, deflection, identity-confirming behaviors, and identity-restoring behaviors. These five constructs are the basis of the following five principles:

1. *Fundamental sentiments*: Society defines the fundamental sentiments associated with each of its identities (I am a teacher; the culture therefore see me as somewhat nice, somewhat strong, and neither active nor passive).
2. *Transient impressions*: Social interactions create transitory impressions of who the person is (a student brings the teacher an apple; this implies that the teacher is very nice, rather than only somewhat nice).
3. *Deflections*: Discrepancies between fundamental sentiments and transitory impressions create deflections (my identity suggests I am somewhat nice, but the student's gift suggests I am very nice).
4. *Identity-confirming behaviors*: People behave as the culture expects them to for each identity (a person with an identity corresponding to an EPA score of 2, 2, 1 behaves in ways consistent with that profile).
5. *Identity-restoring behaviors*: Whenever social interaction creates a discrepancy, people use a variety of means (discussed shortly) to counteract the transient impression and restore the identity.

Energy and Direction in Affect Control Theory

You may be wondering what EPA scores have to do with understanding motivation and emotion. Energy comes from affective deflections; direction comes from fundamental sentiments. Thus, in affect control theory, motivation and emotion express themselves through (1) identity-confirming and (2) identity-restoring behaviors and emotions (as each minimizes deflection and directs behavior toward a particular goodness, power, and activity).

IDENTITY-CONFIRMING BEHAVIORS. Human beings possess a wide range of potential behaviors, but as they enter a particular setting only a subset of those behaviors are appropriate and expected. In any situation, a person's identity activates and selects those behaviors and emotions than are most appropriate. That is, for a friend (EPA = 3.0, 1.5, 0.6) the behaviors that are most appropriate are those the culture assigns a similar EPA profile—help (2.2, 1.5, 0.3) and laugh with (2.2, 0.8, 1.0). For a pest (EPA = −1.8, −0.5, 1.7) the behaviors that are most appropriate are disrespect (−2.1, −0.2, 1.1) and annoy (−1.6, 0.0, 1.2). When the cultural meaning of an identity matches the cultural meaning of one's behavior, identity confirmation occurs and the person experiences little affective deflection.

The essence of affect control theory's behavioral predictions is this: Nice identities lead people to behave in nice ways, powerful identities lead people to behave in powerful ways, passive identities lead people to behave in passive ways, and so on. Identities motivate identity-confirming behaviors in the same way self-schemas motivate self-confirmatory behaviors. Affect control theory is an identity-maintenance theory (Robinson & Smith-Lovin, 1992).

IDENTITY-RESTORING BEHAVIORS. When events cause deflection from identity, the individual initiates restorative actions and cognitive revisions to bring affectively disturbing events back in line with established sentiments. Consider the EPA of a mother (2.7, 1.6, 1.0) versus the EPA of a mother who scolds her child (−1.4, 0.9, 1.0). Incidentally, the changes in numbers are generated by a computer program (Heise, 1991). A mother who scolds her child (without justification) becomes less good and somewhat less powerful. To restore the culturally understood meaning of mother, the scolding mother needs either to perform a good and powerful behavior or a good and powerful emotional reaction. Thus, the mother who scolds needs subsequently to cuddle (1.7, 1.0, −0.7) or educate (2.2, 2.2, 0.0) her child or show that she was pleased (1.5, 0.8, 0.8) or elated (1.5, 0.8, 1.1) with her child.

As this example shows, there are two primary ways people restore a deflected identity—through strategic emotion displays and through selective interaction. Consider first how people use strategic emotion displays to restore their identities (Robinson, Smith-Lovin, & Tsoudis, 1994). A teacher who ignores a student can look sorrowful to send an identity-restoring message that says to the student, "I ignored you, but since you can see that I am sorry, you should still see me as an overall nice person—that is, as a teacher." Emotion displays create transitory impressions just as behavior does, and these transitory impressions act as identity cues such that good people who act bad should show sorrow if they are truly good people (just as bad people who act bad should show no such sorrow if they are truly bad people).

Now consider how people restore their identities by selectively choosing those with whom they do and do not want to interact (Robinson & Smith-Lovin, 1992). In *selective interaction*, people seek those interaction partners they think are most likely to confirm, or verify, their identities and avoid those interaction partners they think are most likely to disconfirm their identities (McNulty & Swann, 1994; Robinson & Smith-Lovin, 1992; Swann, 1987, 1990; Swann, Hixon, & De La Ronde, 1992). Individuals who have a positive identity seek interaction partners (including friends, roommates, tutors, teachers, spouses, teammates, and so on) who will treat them in a positive way. Individuals with negative identities seek interaction partners who will treat them in a negative way. Similarly, individuals with powerful identities seek interaction partners who will treat them in a power-confirming way. That is, as a rule, people seek out interaction partners who confirm their identities, irrespective of whether that identity is a culturally valued one (Swann, Pelham, & Krull, 1989). You might ask, "How can this be?" and "Why would students with negative identities (bully or troublemaker) intentionally seek out and prefer to interact with others who will treat them in a negative and critical way?" The answer lies in the identity negotiation process in which people use others to provide social interactions that maintain their identities (Swann, 1987).

Why People Self-Verify

The self prefers feedback to verify its self-schemas and to verify its social roles. Self-verification theory (Swann, 1983, 1990, 1992a) assumes that the key to smooth interpersonal relationships is the individual's ability to recognize how other people and society in general perceive the self. The self notices how others respond to it and internalizes these social and cultural responses into self-concept and sense of identity. Stable self-concepts and identities play such a central role in the self's negotiation of social reality that the self comes to prefer social feedback that confirms its self-schemas and identities (Swann, 1992a, 1992b). People prefer self-verification feedback for both cognitive and pragmatic reasons. On the cognitive side, people self-verify because they seek to know themselves (to thine own self be true). On the pragmatic side, people self-verify because they wish to avoid interactions that might be fraught with misunderstandings and unrealistic expectations and performance demands; they seek interaction partners who know what to expect from them and therefore ensure smooth interactions (Swann, 1992a).

Consider the ramifications of self-verification in day-to-day social interaction (Swann, 1992b). Imagine the college student who was just dumped by his girlfriend; he heads back to his dormitory room devastated and is greeted by his roommate. If the roommate's view of him is favorable, the roommate will dismiss the rejection by denigrating the judgment or character of the lost love, thus stabilizing the rejected man's self-view. If the roommate's view of him is unfavorable, the roommate might reinforce the rejection theme in ways that are subtle or perhaps not so subtle ("and another thing . . ."), thus diminishing the rejected man's self-view. In this scenario, the roommate's interaction following potent self-discrepant feedback will exert a potentially profound influence on the college student's self-view, especially if repeated over time. Potent self-discrepant feedback given to a friend can either augment or buffer the friend's positive or negative self-view (Swann & Predmore, 1985). The bottom line is this: People with positive self-views prefer to hang out with friends who augment positive feedback and buffer negative feedback; people with negative self-views prefer to hang out with friends who buffer positive feedback and augment negative feedback (Robinson & Smith-Lovin, 1992; Swann, 1992a, 1992b; Swann, Hixon, Stein-Seroussi, & Gilbert, 1990; Swann, Pelham, & Krull, 1989; Swann, Wenzlaff, & Tafarodi, 1992).

AGENCY

The self presented thus far has been highly cognitive and social. But the self goes deeper than just cognitive structures and social relationships (Ryan, 1993). The self also has intrinsic motivation that gives it an agenetic quality. This section presents a view of self "as action and development from within, as innate processes and motivations" (Deci & Ryan, 1991, p. 277).

The self does not enter into the world as a tabula rasa, an empty slate, awaiting life experiences to endow it with a self-concept and cultural identities. Rather, the newborn possesses a rudimentary self characterized by inherent needs, developmental processes, preferences, and capacities to interact with the environment, which represent the roots of agency for the developing self. As the newborn taps into its inherent resources (e.g., walking, talking), the self begins the lifelong process of discovering, developing, and fulfilling its potential. In doing so, the self begins a lifelong task to advance away from heteronomy (a dependence on others) toward autonomy (a dependence on self) (Ryan, 1993).

Self as Action and Development from Within

Chapter 4 discussed the organismic psychological needs of self-determination, competence, and relatedness, needs that provide a natural motivational force that fosters agency. Intrinsic motivation is inseparably coordinated with the active nature of the developing self (Deci & Ryan, 1991). Intrinsic motivation is the innate propensity to pursue one's interests and exercise one's capacities and, in doing so, seek out and master optimal challenges.

It spontaneously energizes people to exercise and develop their skills. The newborn grasps, sucks, and makes facial expressions; the two-year-old walks, runs, carries objects, tosses objects, comprehends language, and speaks short sentences; the preschooler uses innumerable motor, language, and social skills; and the adolescent has a repertoire of skills and capacities too extensive to list (Gibson, 1988). Interacting with the environment not only develops skills and competencies, but also cultivates interests and preferences. Interests develop in those ways of interacting with the world that involve the person's needs; preferences develop from those ways of interacting with the world that satisfy those needs (Deci, 1992b). The child who finds that building a model airplane challenges (involves) the competence need develops an interest in doing so; completing the model satisfies the competence need and therefore builds a preference for such projects. Thus, agency emanates directly from inherent psychological needs and indirectly from acquired interests and preferences.

Differentiation and Integration

Differentiation and integration are two inherent developmental processes that guide the development of the self. Differentiation expands and elaborates the self into an ever-increasing level of complexity. Integration synthesizes that emerging complexity into a coherent whole, thereby preserving the sense of a single, cohesive self.

Differentiation proceeds as the individual exercises interests, preferences, and capacities in such a way that a relatively general understanding of self becomes specialized into more specific elements. For illustration, consider your own history in which you learned that not all computers are alike, not all sports are alike, not all politicians are alike, and not all religions are alike. Minimal differentiation manifests itself in simplicity in which the person has only a unidimensional understanding of a particular domain of knowledge; rich differentiation manifests itself in complexity in which the person understands fine discriminations and unique aspects of a particular domain of knowledge. Intrinsic motivation, interests, and preferences motivate the self to interact with the world in such a way as to set the stage for the self to differentiate into an ever-increasing complexity (the child with an interest in model airplanes skims through catalogues, attends club meetings, talks with peers about model building, subscribes to a relevant magazine, experiments with new materials and construction techniques, and basically develops specialized skills and learns a lot).

Integration is an organizational process that brings the self's differentiated parts together. Differentiation does not expand the complexity of the self unabated. Rather, there is a synthetic tendency to integrate the self's emerging complexity into a single sense of self, into a coherent unity. Integration occurs as the self's individual parts (self-schemas, identities, interests, and so on) are successfully interrelated and organized as mutually complementary. One example of the interplay between differentiation and integration can be found in a study that asked young and older adults to list their possible selves and what acts they took to realize them (Cross & Markus, 1990). The young adults listed many more possible selves than did the older adults (showing strong differentiation), while the older adults took more actions to realize specific possible selves (showing more integration). Thus, young adults explored and experimented with many possible selves, while the older adults, who had completed this experimental (differentiation) process, focused their attention on a more cohesive, well-defined self (integration).

Individuals differ in the extent to which their self is differentiated into several characteristics and identities versus the extent to which their self is integrated into a unitary, single self. The self develops through differentiation in ways that are growth oriented, stagnant, or regressive. Life challenges and new opportunities promote differentiation of the self as it changes and assimilates its new skills, interests, and preferences. Stagnation occurs when the self lives in a stable, unchanging environment that fails to ask the self to revise itself. A chaotic environment promotes such extreme differentiation that differentiation spills over into fragmentation. Fragmentation of the self is typically caused by multiple conflicts between identity from one situation to the next or from one relationship to the next (e.g., who I am with my parents versus who I am with my friends). Fragmentation is linked to poor psychological adjustment (Donahue et al., 1993). Integration, however, is associated with positive psychological well-being. So, both differentiation and integration have their positive sides, as differentiation fuels growth processes whereas integration fuels the sense of vitality that contributes to psychological well-being. But differentiation needs integration as a complementary way to direct agency motivation in ways that are healthy (Block, 1982).

DIFFERENTIATION, INTEGRATION, AND THE SOCIAL CONTEXT. With its inherent needs and emerging interests, preferences, potentials, and capacities, the self is poised to grow, develop, and differentiate. But behaviors, emotions, and ways of thinking originate not only within the self but within the social context and society as well. As people play, study, work, perform, and interact with one another, their friends, parents, teachers, coaches, employers, priests and rabbis, family, and others request that they comply with particular ways of behaving, feeling, and thinking. Thus, intentional acts sometimes arise from the self and sometimes arise from the guidance and recommendations of others.

Differentiation is a cognitive process linked to agency, whereas integration is a cognitive process linked to communion with others (Woike, 1994). Differentiation involves perceiving characteristics of the self as different, separate, and independent from those characteristics that exist in the social context. Integration involves perceiving characteristics of the self as similar, connected, and interdependent with those characteristics that exist in the social context. It is hoped that the discussion in the previous paragraph reminds the reader of self-determination theory and the intrinsic/extrinsic dichotomy discussed in chapter 5. The basic tenet of self-determination theory is that any intentional act can be described as emanating from somewhere along a perceived locus of causality and thus can be understood as more or less self-determined (Deci & Ryan, 1985a, 1991). Thus, all intentional acts involve some *degree of involvement of the self*. Intrinsically motivated behaviors (as well as intrinsically motivated ways of feeling and thinking) exemplify the prototype of self-determined behaviors. Activity that originates from the self is self-regulated or self-determined. Any extrinsically motivated behavior is more or less internalized and therefore more or less integrated into the self. The process through which individuals take in and accept as their own an externally prescribed way of thinking, feeling, or behaving is referred to as *internalization* (Ryan & Connell, 1989; Ryan, Rigby, & King, 1993).

Internalization is a natural outcome of organismic integration, as it occurs from the individual's desires to achieve meaningful relationships with friends, parents, teachers, coaches, employers, priests and rabbis, family, and others (via the relatedness need) and to interact effectively with the social world (via the competence need). In the process of internalization, behavior (and ways of thinking and feeling) typically proceeds through the following levels of integration into the self:

External regulation: Action motivated by social request, rule, pressure, or bribe.

Introjected regulation: Action motivated by internalized representations of social requests, rules, pressures, or bribes (that take the form of feelings of approval, pride, guilt, shame, and obligation).

Identified regulation: Action motivated by internal representations of those courses of action that are deemed to be important, useful, or valuable to the developing self.

Identified regulation represents the culmination of integrating a formerly externally prescribed behavior or value into the self-system. With identification, the self identifies the behavior's utility and consequently accepts it. Through internalization, external ways of thinking, feeling, and behaving become represented as internal ways of thinking, feeling, and behaving. Such internalization has adaptive value for the self both psychically and interpersonally as it promotes greater unity between the self and society, as in the close relationships between parent and child, teacher and student, and so on (Ryan, 1993).

The notions of agency (via intrinsic motivation), differentiation, and integration argue that the self possesses innate aspects. Psychological needs and developmental processes provide the starting point for the development of the self. As individuals mature, they gain increasing contact with the social context, and some of these aspects of the social world become assimilated and integrated into the self-system (interests, preferences, identifications). The motivational portrayal of self-development therefore argues strongly against the idea that the self is merely a passive recipient of the social world's feedback (self-schemas) and identities (places in the social order). An understanding of the developing self therefore begins by adopting the frame of reference of the individual rather than that of the society (Deci & Ryan, 1991; Ryan, 1993). The need for relatedness, however, keeps the individual close to societal concerns and regulations, and the self therefore develops both toward autonomy and toward internalization of society's concerns.

The contribution of agency and the self as action and development from within, as innate processes and motivations, is to recognize that (1) human beings possess a core self, one energized by organismic psychological needs and directed by differentiation and integration processes, and (2) not all internalized self-structures are equal in that some are qualitatively more authentic (reflecting the self rather than the society) than are others (Deci et al., 1994; Deci & Ryan, 1985a, 1991; Ryan, 1991, 1993; Ryan & Connell, 1989).

SUMMARY

Three basic problems occupy the self—defining the self, relating the self to society, and discovering, developing, and fulfilling its potential. This chapter presented these problems as self-concept (defining the self), identity (relating the self to society), and agency (discovering, developing, and fulfilling personal potential). The notions of self-concept, identity, and agency tell the story of how the self generates motivation. They also present a comprehensive view of the self, one characterized by cognitive structures, social relationships, and strivings from within.

A self-concept is knowledge used to conceptualize personal attributes and characteristics. It is a collection of domain-specific self-schemas, which are cognitive generalizations about the self that are learned from past experience. Self-schemas generate motivation toward the consistent self and the possible self. For the consistent self, self-schemas direct behavior toward ways that confirm the self-view and away from the disconfirmation of that self-view. Self-schemas also function as a view of the future self that a person would very much like to become. Possible selves generate a proactive source of motivation to develop and grow toward particular goals or aspirations.

Identity is the means by which the self relates to society. Affect control theory explains how identities motivate behavior such that cultural values (how good?, how powerful?, how active?) direct behavior while affective deflections (between fundamental sentiments and transitory impressions) energize behavior. Once people assume a social role, that identity directs their behavior in ways that express its cultural value. Thus, a physician is helpful and kind, rather than hostile or cruel, because these behaviors exemplify the identity of doctor; thus social interactions flow smoothly and as the culture expects. Affect control theory presents a model in which identities motivate the self to select a specific and somewhat narrow range of behaviors, whereas the affective deflections that occur during social interaction energize identity-restoring courses of action, such as emotion displays and selective interactions.

The self also possesses motivation of its own, or agency. Its activity emerges spontaneously from intrinsic motivation based in the inherent psychological needs of self-determination, competence, and relatedness, and its development proceeds through the processes of differentiation and integration. Intrinsic motivation spontaneously energizes the self to exercise and develop inherent capabilities. Differentiation of the self occurs as the individual exercises interests, preferences, and capacities in such a way that a relatively general understanding of self becomes divided into more specific elements. Integration of the self occurs as these differentiated parts are brought together into a sense of unity. The process is a dynamic one in which intrinsic motivation, social experience, differentiation, and integration all contribute to the ongoing development of the self. Conceptualizing the self as agent recognizes its innate aspects and inherent motivations. As individuals mature, they gain increasing contact with the social context, and some of these aspects of the social world become assimilated and integrated into the self-system. The self is therefore both the agent (initiator) of activity that promotes development as well as the internalizer of the cognitive and social structures that are integrated into self-concept and social identity. Thus the self defines itself, relates to society, and fulfills its potential.

RECOMMENDED READINGS

Baumeister, R. F. (1987). How the self became a problem: A psychological review of historical research. *Journal of Personality and Social Psychology, 52,* 163–176.

Deci, E. L., & Ryan, R. M. (1991). A motivational approach to self: Integration in personality. In R. Dienstbier (Ed.), *Nebraska symposium on motivation: Perspectives on motivation* (Vol. 38, pp. 237–288). Lincoln: University of Nebraska Press.

MacKinnon, N. J. (1994). Affect control theory. In *Symbolic interactionism as affect control* (Chpt. 2, pp. 15–40). Albany, NY: SUNY Press.

Markus, H. (1977). Self-schemata and processing information about the self. *Journal of Personality and Social Psychology, 35,* 63–78.

Markus, H., & Nurius, P. (1986). Possible selves. *American Psychologist, 41,* 954–969.

Robinson, D. T., & Smith-Lovin, L. (1992). Selective interaction as a strategy for identity maintenance: An affect control model. *Social Psychology Quarterly, 55,* 12–28.

Ryan, R. M. (1993). Agency and organization: Intrinsic motivation, autonomy, and the self in psychological development. In J. E. Jacobs (Ed.), *Nebraska symposium on motivation: Developmental perspectives on motivation* (Vol. 40, pp. 1–56). Lincoln: University of Nebraska Press.

Ryff, C. D. (1989). Happiness is everything, or is it? Explorations on the meaning of psychological well-being. *Journal of Personality and Social Psychology, 57,* 1069–1081.

Smith-Lovin, L. (1991). An affect control view of cognition and emotion. In J. A. Howard & P. L. Callero (Eds.), *The self-society dynamic: Cognition, emotion, and action* (pp. 143–169). New York: Cambridge University Press.

Swann, W. B., Jr. (1987). Identity negotiation: Where two roads meet. *Journal of Personality and Social Psychology, 53,* 1038–1051.

PART THREE

Emotions

Chapter 11

THE NATURE OF EMOTION

The telephone rings, so you answer it. A friend asks you to spend the weekend skiing with the group. You accept and your thoughts turn to traveling, snowcapped mountains, and racing down the slopes. Being included in the group's plans brings you a comfortable feeling of acceptance, and anticipating the adventure brings excitement and enthusiasm. Once you hit the slopes, however, the excitement changes to apprehension and then to full-blown fear. The sight of the mountain's omnipresent dangers—its steep slopes, many moguls, and thick-trunk trees—calls up a rather urgent need to flee from the dangers you face. Your fear expresses itself publicly in your face, voice, and hesitancy. Nonetheless, you begin to ski and, sure enough, you fall. Plowing through the snow with your face changes your feelings from fear to distress. To cope with and to alleviate the distress, you ask your friend for a quick lesson. When you begin to show signs of improvement and a hint of mastery, your distress turns into pride.

You experience a wide array of emotions, from excitement to fear to distress to pride. Whether skiing or doing any number of activities, emotion seems always with us, forever changing, and motivating us to act adaptively. We seem to have an emotion for every situation.

The three chapters in this section discuss the nature of human emotion. Emotions typically arise from situational or environmental events, express themselves uniquely, serve different functions and purposes, and produce a predictable set of related behaviors. In the example, for instance, the skier's sight of the steep slopes produced feelings of fear, expressive signals from the face and voice, motivation to flee, and fear-directed behaviors such as hesitancy and avoidance. To tackle the nature of emotion, we begin with the most fundamental of all questions, what is an emotion?

WHAT IS AN EMOTION?

Emotions are multidimensional. Emotions are subjective, biological, purposive, and social phenomena. In part, emotions are subjective feelings, as they make us feel a particular way such as angry or joyful. Emotions are also biological reactions, physiological responses to situations that prepare the body to cope effectively. When emotional, our bodies—heart, muscles, and so on—are active in different ways from when we are unemotional. Emotions are also purposive, much like hunger is functional and purposive. For instance, anger motivates us to want to fight an enemy whereas fear motivates us to want to flee a danger. Finally, emotions are social phenomena. When emotional, we send distinct facial and bodily signals that communicate the quality of our emotionality to others (e.g., the movements of our eyebrows, the tone of our voice).

Given the four-part character of emotion, it is apparent that the concept of emotion is going to elude a straightforward definition. The difficulty in defining emotion is puzzling to the student because emotions seem so straightforward in everyday experience. Everyone knows what it is like to experience joy and anger, so the student asks, what's the problem? The problem is, "Everyone knows what emotion is, until asked to give a definition" (Fehr & Russell, 1984, p. 414). None of the dimensions or aspects listed earlier—subjective, biological, purposive, expressive—adequately defines emotion. As we shall see, it is simply not defensible to equate a way of feeling with an emotion, any more that it is defensible to equate a posed facial expression with an emotion. Each aspect simply emphasizes a different contribution to the emotion process. To understand (or define) emotion, it is necessary to study each of emotion's four components and their interactions.

Table 11.1 summarizes emotion's four components. The subjective component gives emotion its feeling, a subjective experience that has both meaning and personal significance. In both intensity and quality, emotion is felt at a subjective, phenomenological level. The biological component includes the activity of the autonomic and hormonal systems as they participate in emotion to prepare and regulate our behavior in a given context. Neurophysiological activity is so intertwined with emotion that any attempt to imagine an unaroused angry person is nearly impossible. The functional component pertains to the question of how an individual benefits from emotion. The person without emotions would be at a substantial evolutionary disadvantage. Imagine, for instance, the physical or social survival potential of the person without the capacity for fear, interest, or love. Emotions are functional in that they create motivation to cope effectively with life situations. The expressive component of emotion is its social, communicative aspect. Through postures, gestures, vocalizations, and, especially, facial expressions, emotions are expressed and communicated to others. We send emotion-identifying signals to others, and we use these signals from others to infer their private feelings and affective states. Emotions engage our whole person—our feelings and phenomenology, our biochemistry and motor activity, our desires and purposes, and our communication and interaction with others.

TABLE 11-1

Multidimensional Aspects of Emotion

COMPONENT	CONTRIBUTION TO EMOTION	MANIFESTATION
Subjective (Cognitive)	Feelings Phenomenological awareness	Self-report
Biological (Physiological)	Arousal Physical preparation Motor responses	Brain structure activity Autonomic nervous system activity Endocrine (hormonal) system activity
Functional (Purposive)	Motivation Goal-directed desire	Selection of appropriate way of coping for the situation at hand
Expressive (Social)	Communication	Facial expressions Bodily postures Vocalizations

You probably noticed that I have not yet answered the question, What is an emotion? An emotion is not any of its individual components. After all, we can smile and yet not experience joy, as when greeting a stranger or trying to appease a person in authority. So, facial expressions are not synonymous with emotions (Russell, 1995), just as feelings are not synonymous with emotions. Emotion is the psychological construct that unites and coordinates the four aspects of affective experience into a synchronized pattern. Emotion choreographs the subjective, biological, functional, and expressive components into a reaction to an eliciting event. For instance, in the case of fear, the eliciting event might be the steep ski slopes while the reaction might include feelings, neurological reactions, particular motives and desires, and nonverbal communications to others. Thus, the skier feels scared (subjective aspect), experiences increased muscle tension (biological aspect), desires self-protection (functional aspect), and shows tensed lips (expressive aspect). These interdependent, synchronized elements form a pattern of reactivity to an environmental danger that is fear.

Emotion per se does not actually exist. That is, dangerous or threatening situations do not activate a fear emotion that, in turn, makes us feel and behave in a fear-congruent way. Rather, what exists is a synchronized anger system, a synchronized fear system, a synchronized sadness system, and so on for each of the specific emotions (LeDoux, 1989). For instance, there is a connection between what people feel and how they move the muscles of their face. As you view and smell rotten food, the way you feel and way you wrinkle your nose and scrunch your upper lip are integrated, as a coherent feeling-expressive system (Rosenberg & Ekman, 1994). Similarly, the way you move your face is integrated with your physiological reactivity, such that lowering your brow and pressing the lips firmly together coincides with increased heart rate and skin temperature (Davidson et al., 1990). These synchronized systems coordinate subjective, biological, functional, and expressive ways of reacting adaptively to events. Emotion is just the word psychologists use to name this coordinated process.

Relationship Between Emotion and Motivation

Emotions relate to motivation in two ways. First and foremost, emotions act as motives. Like needs and cognitions, emotions energize and direct behavior. Anger, for instance, energizes a person by mobilizing physiological, hormonal, and muscular resources and directs that activity to achieve a particular purpose, such as overcoming an obstacle.

Second, emotions provide a readout of the status of the person's ever-changing motivational states. Motivation and emotion exist as two sides of the same coin (Buck, 1988). Motives such as hunger and thirst energize the person to action, while emotions such as frustration and relief provide an ongoing progress report as to how well or how poorly these motives are being gratified. For instance, consider sexual motivation and how emotion readout provides an informative progress report that facilitates some behaviors and inhibits others. During attempts at sexual gratification (e.g., copulation, masturbation, looking at pornography), positive emotions such as interest and joy facilitate sexual conduct whereas negative emotion such as disgust, anger, and guilt inhibit it. Thus, given a readout of interest and joy, the person continues such activity; but given a readout of disgust, anger, or guilt, the person terminates such activity. With such an information emotional readout system, the person's motives and behaviors are nicely coordinated.

EMOTION AS A MOTIVATIONAL SYSTEM. Although all emotion researchers conceptualize the emotions as a type of motive, some argue that emotions constitute the *primary* motivational system (Tomkins, 1962, 1963, 1984; Izard, 1991). Throughout the history of psychology, the physiological drives (hunger, thirst, sleep, sex, pain) were assumed to be the primary motivators (Hull, 1943, 1952). As an illustration, consider air deprivation and the motivation such a biological emergency energizes. Air deprivation threatens the body's homeostasis, so it seems logical to conclude that air deprivation produces a homeostatic motive to do whatever is necessary to gain the air needed to reestablish homeostasis. Tomkins called this reasoning, this apparent truism, a "radical error" (Tomkins, 1970, p. 101). The loss of air produces a strong emotional reaction of fear or terror. The terror provides the motivation to act. Thus the terror, not the air deprivation or homeostasis threat, is the source of the panicked, grasping display of motivated behavior.

The position taken here, however, is that there are three primary motives—needs, cognitions, and emotions. Emotions are important motivators, but their status is equal to that of needs, cognitions, and external events. This section illustrates how discrete emotions, like needs and cognitions, motivate action.

WHAT CAUSES AN EMOTION?

One of the central struggles emotion researchers face is to understand the cause or causes of an emotion. Many viewpoints come into play in the causal analysis of emotional reactions, including those that are biological, psychoevolutionary, cognitive, experiential, developmental, psychoanalytical, social, sociological, cultural, anthropological, and perhaps others as well. Despite this diversity, understanding what causes an emotion begins with the biology versus cognition debate, which asks whether emotions are primarily biological or primarily cognitive phenomena. If emotions are largely biological, they should emanate from some causal biological core such as neurophysiological brain activity. If emotions are largely cognitive, they should emanate from causal mental events such as an appraisal of the benefit or harm of a particular event or an expectation that one can or cannot cope effectively with the event.

Let me relay what happened one fateful rainy day on a city street in the center of my local campus. On one side of the street is the psychology building, and on the other side are the residence halls. That morning, our research team planned to run a laboratory experiment. About 15 minutes before we were ready to begin, I happened to look out the window to see one of my research partners crossing the street toward the psychology building. As she crossed over the curb, a car sped by splashing a wave of dirty water that covered her from head to toe. Having dirty water splashed over your person on the way to an important meeting is certainly an opportunity for emotional experience. My partner reacted as you might expect— she cringed, threw her arms up, wiped the water off her face, and turned and walked rather quickly back to the residence hall. She looked distressed, angry, and, perhaps, a bit embarrassed. She never did make it to the laboratory that day.

I use this example as an opportunity to ask, what caused her emotional reaction? On the one hand, the abrupt sensation of splashing cold water, the sight of the mess, and having her clothes changed from white to brown might cause emotion. Perhaps the cringing, changed facial expressions, and reactive physiological changes (e.g., rapid heart rate) caused her emotionality. These are all biological causes. On the other hand, a moment's reflection of why the event happened and what caused the driver's rude behavior might cause emotion. Her reflection on the meaning of the drenching and her expectations of how the day's plans were now shot might cause her emotionality. These mental events are cognitive causes. In this example, there is a myriad of possible causes to my friend's emotion—sensory impressions, neuroendocrine activity, physiological reactions, facial feedback, appraisals of the splashing as good or bad, concerns of how she would present herself to others, and attributions of whether the driver splashed her on purpose.

Biology Versus Cognition

Together, the cognitive and biological perspectives provide a comprehensive picture of the emotion process. Nonetheless, acknowledging that both cognitive and biological aspects underlie emotion begs the question as to which is primary—biological or cognitive factors (Lazarus, 1982, 1984, 1991a, 1991b; Scherer & Ekman, 1984; Zajonc, 1980, 1981, 1984). Those who argue for the primacy of cognition contend that individuals cannot respond emotionally unless they first cognitively appraise the meaning and personal significance of an event—is it relevant to my well-being? Is it relevant to a loved one's well-being? Is it important? Beneficial? Harmful? Those who argue for the primacy of biology contend that emotional reactions do not necessarily require such cognitive evaluations. Events of a different sort, such as subcortical neural activity or spontaneous facial expressions, activate emotion. For the biological theorist, emotions can and do occur without a prior cognitive event, but emotions cannot occur without antecedent biological events. Therefore biology, not cognition, is primary.

BIOLOGICAL PERSPECTIVE. Izard (1989, 1991), Ekman (1992), Panksepp (1982, 1994), and Zajonc (1980, 1984) are outspoken representatives for the biological perspective. Izard (1984) finds that infants respond emotionally to certain events despite their cognitive shortcomings (limited vocabulary, lack of language, limited memory capacity). A three-week-old infant, for instance, smiles in response to a high-pitched human voice (Wolff, 1969), and the two-month-old infant expresses anger in response to pain (Izard et al., 1983). By the time the child acquires language and begins to use sophisticated long-term memory capacities, most emotional events involve cognitive processing. Nonetheless, despite the richness of cognitive activity in the emotion process, Izard (1989) insists that much of the emotional processing of external events remains noncognitive—automatic, unconscious, and mediated by subcortical structures.

Ekman (1992) points out that emotions have very rapid onset, brief durations, occur sometimes automatically and involuntary, and that we sometimes act emotionally even before we are consciously aware of our emotionality. For reasons such as these, Ekman argues that it is necessary to take an evolutionary (biological) point of view and understand that emotions evolved through their adaptive value in dealing with fundamental life tasks. Ekman, like Izard and others, recognizes the cognitive, social, and cultural contributions to emotional experience, but he concludes that biology rather than learning, social interaction, or socialization processes lie at the causal core of emotion.

For Panksepp (1982, 1994), emotions arise from genetically inherited neural circuits that coordinate brain activity such as biochemical and neurohormonal events. Panksepp acknowledges that it is more difficult to study the hidden recesses of genes and brain circuits than to study verbal interpretations and labels of our feelings, but he insists that genes and brain circuits provide the essential biological reason for emotional experience. For instance, we (and other animals) inherit a brain anger circuit, a brain fear circuit, a brain sadness circuit, and a few others. Zajonc provides some of the rationale to support Panksepp's biological perspective with three important findings. First, because emotional states are often difficult to verbalize, it seems logical to presume that they can have origins that are noncognitive (not language based). Second, emotional experience can be induced by noncognitive procedures, such as electrical stimulation of the brain or activity of the facial musculature. Third, emotions occur in both infants and nonhuman animals. For these reasons, Zajonc (1980, p. 192) concludes that "people do not get married or divorced, commit murder or suicide, or lay down their lives for freedom upon a detailed cognitive analysis of the pros and cons of their actions."

COGNITIVE PERSPECTIVE. Lazarus (1984, 1991a, 1991b), Scherer (1994a, 1994b), Weiner (1986), and Averill (1982, 1991) are outspoken representatives of the cognitive perspective. For each of these theorists, cognitive activity is a necessary prerequisite to emotion; take away the cognitive processing and the emotion disappears. Lazarus argues that, without an understanding of the personal relevance of the stimulus to one's well-being, there is no reason to respond emotionally. Stimuli appraised as irrelevant to one's well-being do not elicit an emotional reaction. For Lazarus (1991a, 1991b), the individual's cognitive appraisal of the meaning of an event (rather than the event itself) sets the stage for emotional experience. That is, a car passing me in traffic is not likely to call up my fear unless the car's passing threatens my well-being in some way. From this point of view, the emotion does not reside in either the event or my biophysiological reaction to it; rather, the emotion-generating process begins with the cognitive appraisal of the meaning of the event.

Scherer (1994a) points out that people continuously process information without necessarily experiencing emotions in every moment. Some encounters produce emotions whereas others do not. Those encounters that lead the person to one of the following five types of appraisals elicit emotional reactions—novelty, pleasantness, goal/need significance, coping potential, and norm compatibility. These five types of appraisal, Scherer contends, constitute the sort of cognitive processing that gives rise to emotions. Weiner (1986) emphasizes a different type of emotion-causing appraisal. In his attributional analysis of emotion, Weiner concentrates on the information processing that takes place not before interacting with an event but, instead, after outcomes occur such as success or failure, inclusion or rejection (recall chapter 9). In other words, people not only appraise what they see and hear as beneficial or harmful, but also evaluate why they experienced the benefit or harm (why was I rejected?). Attributions are different sorts of appraisals, but they are cognitive events that cause emotional reactions nonetheless.

For Averill (1982, 1985) emotions are best understood in a social or cultural context. People show emotion (become angry, fall in love) to produce social consequences. When angered, one can violate a social norm, deny responsibility for action (I couldn't help it, I was overcome by anger), and effectively communicate their intentions toward others. Consider the example of falling in love. According to Averill and Boothroyd (1977), the romantic ideal is a cultural standard by which people interpret their experiences of love. The romantic ideal holds that one is emotionally and unexpectedly overwhelmed by the (usually chance) appearance of another. Once the ideal is internalized into a belief system, people try to emulate that ideal in relationships, and they interpret their relationship behavior as conforming or not conforming to that ideal. The whole emotion process has little to do with biological states and much to do with social and cultural activity.

The most direct benefit one can extract from the cognition versus biology debate is that both sides clearly state the details of their respective positions. Once introduced to the theory of both sides, we can now ask, who is correct? Emotion psychologists have struggled for answers to settle the debate, and three of these answers are presented in the paragraphs that follow.

Two-Systems View

One answer to Who is correct? is, both! According to Buck (1984), human beings have two synchronous systems that activate and regulate emotion. One system is an innate, spontaneous, and primitive physiological system that reacts involuntarily to emotional stimuli. A second interactive, but distinct, system is a cortical, experience-based cognitive system that reacts interpretatively and socially. The physiological emotion system came first in humankind's evolution; the cognitive emotion system came later as human beings became increasingly cerebral and social. Together, the primitive biological system and the relatively contemporary cognitive system combine to provide a highly adaptive, two-system emotion mechanism.

Figure 11.1 presents a schematic of emotion as regulated by two distinct, separate systems (based on Buck, 1984). The first system is biological and traces its origins to the ancient evolutionary history of the species. Sensory information is processed rapidly, automatically, and unconsciously by subcortical (i.e., limbic) struc-

FIGURE 11-1
Buck's Two-System View of Emotion

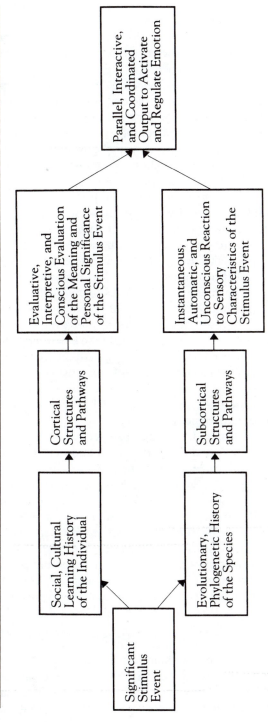

tures and pathways. The second system is cognitive and depends on the unique social and cultural learning history of the individual. Sensory information is processed
evaluatively, interpretively, and consciously by cortical pathways. The two emotion
systems are complementary rather than competitive and work together to activate
and regulate emotional experience.

To illustrate the two systems, Buck (1984) uses the example of how we tell another person that we are happy or pleased. One way we communicate joy is with
a spontaneous, reactive facial expression. The sight of our friend gives rise to a rapid,
automated experience and expression of joy. Without thinking, we smile. A second
way we communicate joy is with a symbolic, voluntary communication of happy
words or a practiced smile. The sight of our friend gives rise to an appraisal of who
this person is and what his or her presence means to us, and we then evaluate the
most appropriate way to respond. After interpretive deliberation, we smile.

Levenson (1994a) takes the two-system view of emotion a bit farther by hy-
pothesizing how these two systems interact. In his biocultural model of emotion, all
emotional situations are first cognitively appraised in terms of how they affect the
person's well-being, plans, and goals. Specific types of appraisals produce an emotion prototype (e.g., threat provokes fear, loss provokes sadness). Once activated,
the emotion prototype energizes biological systems, including facial expressions, vocal expressions, physiological activity, and emotion-specific behaviors. How these
biological systems express themselves overtly, however, depends on the individual's
cultural learnings and socialization history. In the biocultural model of emotion, stimuli lead to cognitive appraisals, cognitive appraisals energize biological reactions, and
social and cultural learning filter how one experiences, expresses, and labels the
emotion. So, while Buck argues that we possess two distinct emotion systems,
Levenson attempts to illustrate how these two systems interact with one another to
produce emotional experience.

Panksepp (1994) provides another perspective on the biology versus cognition
debate by positing that two categories of emotion exist such that some emotions
arise primarily from the biological system whereas other emotions arise primarily
from the cognitive system. Emotions such as fear and anger arise primarily from subcortical neural command circuits (from subcortical structures and pathways in Buck's
terminology). Other emotions cannot be well explained by subcortical neural circuits; they arise chiefly or perhaps fully from individual learning, social modeling,
and cultural contexts. This category of emotions arises primarily from appraisals, expectancies, and attributions (from cortical structures and pathways in Buck's terminology). Thus, some emotions are primarily biologically regulated, while other emotions are primarily cognitively, socially, or culturally regulated.

Chicken-and-Egg Problem

Plutchik (1985) sees the cognition versus biology debate as a chicken-and-egg
quandary. Emotion should not be conceptualized as cognitively caused or as biologically caused. Rather, emotion is a process, a chain of events that aggregate into
a complex feedback system. The elements in Plutchik's feedback loop are cognition,

arousal, feelings, preparations for action, expressive displays, and overt behavioral activity. Figure 11.2 illustrates one possible representation of Plutchik's emotion feedback loop. The feedback system begins with a significant life event and concludes with emotion. Mediating between life event and emotion is a complex interactive chain of events that produce emotion. Further, one can intervene at any point in the feedback loop to influence emotion. One can cognitively appraise a stimulus event as a threat and activate the emotion process. Alternatively, one can put an electrode to the brain and affect emotion, and a drug might do much the same as the electrode. One might further change bodily expression, such as the facial musculature or bodily posture, and influence the emotion process, and so on.

Figure 11.2 shows graphically that Plutchik's solution to the cognition-biology debate is to enter into the complex world of dialectics, in which each aspect of emotion is both cause and effect and the final outcome is due to the dynamic interplay of these six forces. The most important single theme to extract from Plutchik's chicken-and-egg analysis is that cognitions do not directly cause emotions any more than biological events do. Together, cognition, arousal, preparation for action, feelings, expressive displays, and overt behavioral activity constitute the cauldron of experience that gives rise to emotion. Other emotion researchers (e.g., Scherer, 1994b) echo this emotion-as-a-process view by emphasizing that all emotional experiences exist as episodes that occur over time in which the components of emotion move in synchronization with feedback and feedforward effects on one another.

Comprehensive Biology-Cognition Model

Emotions are complex (and interactive) phenomena. As with most complexities, it makes sense to work on one piece of the puzzle at a time. Generally speaking, bi-

FIGURE 11–2
Plutchik's Feedback Loop in Emotion

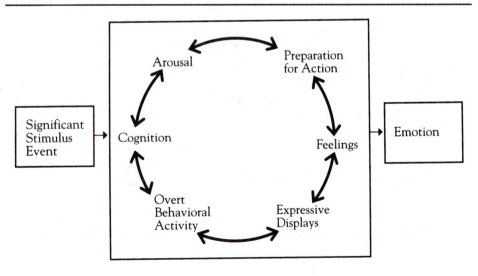

ologists, ethologists, and neurophysiologists focus mostly on the biological aspects of emotion, whereas cognitive psychologists, social psychologists, and sociologists focus mostly on the cognitive, sociocultural aspects. Consequently, emotion study offers biological theories of emotion and cognitive theories of emotion. What we do not as yet have, however, is a comprehensive model that integrates both cognitive and biological components. Such a comprehensive model will specify how biological and cognitive inputs influence and integrate with one another. What such a model will not discover, I suspect, is that one source (biology or cognition) is primary or more important than the other. In the meantime, some researchers study emotions from one perspective, others study emotions from another, and eventually, after researchers understand the biological and cognitive superstructures of the emotions, a coherent, integrated, comprehensive biology-cognition model will emerge.

The case of pain provides a nice analogy to underscore the need for a comprehensive biology-cognition model of emotion (from Clark & Watson, 1994). We have innate ways of knowing which environmental events produce pain and which do not. We also develop a cognitive appreciation of the danger value of environmental events. The innate ways of knowing what causes pain provide millisecond judgments to motivate avoidance behavior, while the acquired ways of knowing provide deliberate, reflective judgments to motivate avoidance and the preventing of future pain. Possessing only innate ways of knowing or only acquired ways of knowing about pain would leave human beings ill equipped to adapt to a dangerous, complex, and ever-changing environment. A dual system, however, takes advantage of both the immediacy and reliability of limbic response as well as the flexibility of cognitive processing. Emotions too operate with the immediacy of limbic responding, the flexibility of cognitive processing, and the integration of limbic and cognitive processing.

MULTIPLE MEANS OF EMOTION ACTIVATION. Emotion can be activated in many ways. As a final point on the biology-cognition debate, consider Izard's (1993) multisystem model of emotion activation. Izard categorized the causes of emotion as follows:

Neural Systems

- Emotion induction via changes in levels of neurotransmitters (e.g., decreased serotonin → depression)
- Emotion induction via electrical stimulation of the brain (e.g., artificial stimulation of the hypothalamus → rage)

Sensorimotor Systems

- Emotion induction via facial expression (e.g., nose contraction → disgust)
- Emotion induction via body posture (e.g., slumping posture → sadness)

Motivational Systems

- Emotion induction via taste, odor (e.g., sweet taste → interest)
- Emotion induction via pain (e.g., aversive stimulation → anger)

Cognitive Systems

■ Emotion induction via appraisal, evaluation, attribution (e.g., judging a harm as unjustified → anger)

■ Emotion induction via memory (e.g., recall of childhood experience → sentimentality)

Social Systems

■ Emotion induction via social contagion (e.g., another person's joy or anxiety "rubs off" on us)

■ Emotion induction via identity confirmation (e.g., a cheerleader role → excitement)

In his multisystem model of emotion activation, Izard (1993) actually lists only the first four systems, and I added the fifth category, social systems. Emotions sometimes arise from social interaction and cultural influences, and these processes are discussed in chapter 13. Izard argues, however, that social/interpersonal/cultural forces activate emotions through one of the other four systems. For example, social contagion is a process by which one person mimics the facial, vocal, and postural expressions of the other and therefore "catches" the emotional experience of the other. Hence, social systems affect the individual's sensorimotor systems, and socially induced changes in the face, voice, and posture actually activate the emotion. The benefit of the multisystem model of emotion activation is that it shows the variety of aspects in the emotion process.

How Many Emotions Are There?

The cognition-biology debate indirectly raises another interesting and important question: How many emotions are there? A biological orientation emphasizes basic emotions (e.g., anger, fear) and downplays the importance of acquired, or secondary, emotions. A cognitive orientation acknowledges the importance of the primary emotions, but stresses the richer variety of emotional experience that arises from individual, social, and cultural experience. The number of emotions ultimately depends on one's orientation. For this reason, we need to consider the number of emotions as viewed from each perspective.

Biological Perspective

The biological perspective typically emphasizes about a half-dozen primary emotions, with a lower limit of two (Solomon, 1980) or three (Gray, 1994) to an upper limit of ten (Izard, 1991). Each biological theorist has a very good reason for proposing a specific number of emotions, though each proposal is based on a different emphasis and line of research. Figure 11.3 presents eight major research traditions in the biological study of the emotions. The illustration also provides a reference for

FIGURE 11-3

Eight Research Traditions in Biological Study of Emotion

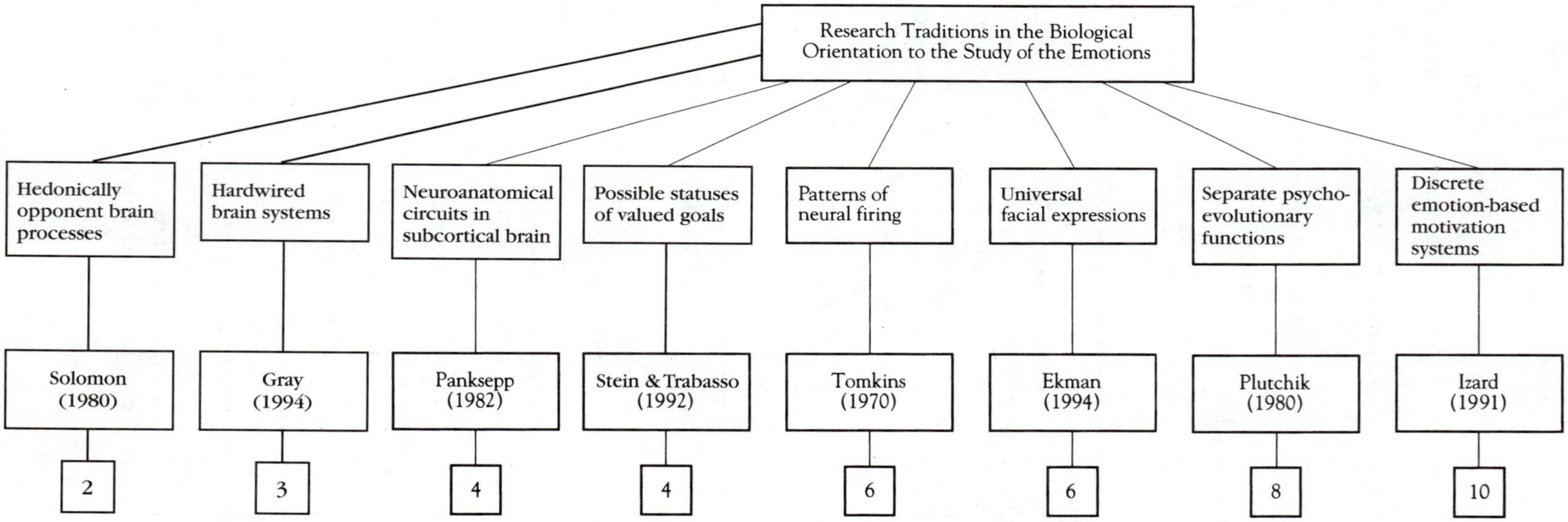

Research Traditions in the Biological Orientation to the Study of the Emotions

Tradition	Researcher	Number
Hedonically opponent brain processes	Solomon (1980)	2
Hardwired brain systems	Gray (1994)	3
Neuroanatomical circuits in subcortical brain	Panksepp (1982)	4
Possible statuses of valued goals	Stein & Trabasso (1992)	4
Patterns of neural firing	Tomkins (1970)	6
Universal facial expressions	Ekman (1994)	6
Separate psycho-evolutionary functions	Plutchik (1980)	8
Discrete emotion-based motivation systems	Izard (1991)	10

that tradition and includes the number of emotions suggested by the empirical findings within each tradition.

Solomon (1980) identifies the automatic, unconscious brain systems that exist such that any pleasurable experience is opposed by a counter aversion experience, and any aversive experience is opposed by a counter pleasurable process (e.g., fear countered by euphoria during parachute jumping). Gray (1994) proposed three basic emotion systems located within separate brain circuits—the behavioral approach system, the fight/flight system, and the behavioral inhibition system (i.e., joy, rage/terror, and anxiety). Panksepp (1982) proposes that there are four physiological emotions: fear, rage, panic, and expectancy, based on his finding of four separate neuroanatomical emotion-generating pathways within the limbic system. Stein and Trabasso (1992) stress the four emotions of happiness, sadness, anger, and fear, because these emotions reflect reactions to the four possible statuses of valued goals—attainment and maintenance, loss, obstruction, and uncertainty of goal attainment, respectively. Tomkins (1970) draws a distinction among six emotions—interest, fear, surprise, anger, distress, and joy—because six distinct patterns of neural firing produce different emotions (e.g., rapid increase in rate of firing instigates surprise). Ekman (1992, 1994a) proposes six distinct emotions—fear, anger, sadness, disgust, enjoyment, and contempt—because he finds that each of these emotions is associated with a corresponding clear, distinct, and universal (cross-cultural) facial expression. Plutchik (1980) lists eight fundamental emotions (anger, disgust, sadness, surprise, fear, acceptance, joy, and anticipation), with each emotion corresponding to one of eight emotion-behavior syndromes common to all living organisms (e.g., protection, affiliation). Finally, Izard (1991) lists ten emotions on the basis of his differential emotions theory—anger, fear, distress, joy, disgust, surprise, shame, guilt, interest and contempt.

Each of these eight research traditions shares the beliefs that (1) there exist a small number of basic emotions, (2) basic emotions are universal to all human beings, and (3) basic emotions are products of evolution. Where the traditions diverge is in their specification of the biological core that orchestrates emotional experience.

Cognitive Perspective

The cognitive perspective asserts firmly that human beings experience a much greater number of emotions than the two to ten highlighted by the biological tradition. Cognitive theorists grant that there are a limited number of bodily reactions (e.g., the fight-or-flight reaction), but they point out that several different emotions can arise from the same biological reaction. For instance, a single physiological response such as a rapid rise in blood pressure can serve as the biological basis for anger, jealousy, or envy. High blood pressure and an appraisal of an injustice produce anger; high blood pressure and an appraisal that another possesses an object that should be the self's produce jealousy; and high blood pressure and an appraisal that another is in a more favorable position than self produce envy. For cognitive theorists, human beings experience a rich diversity of emotion, because situations can be experienced and interpreted so differently (Shaver et al., 1987) and because emotion arises from a blend of language (Storm & Storm, 1987), personal knowledge (Linville, 1982), socializing agents (Kemper, 1987), and cultural influences (Leavitt & Power, 1989).

Figure 11.4 summarizes eight traditions of research within the cognitive study of the emotions, provides a reference for each research tradition, and shows that cognitive, social, and cultural variables determine emotions. Because of the many variations from one person to the next and from one culture to the next, the number of possible emotions is almost infinite.

Reconciliation of Numbers Issue

Answering the question of how many emotions there are is mostly a matter of perspective, as biologists stress a basic few emotions while cognitivists stress a great diversity. Because everyone agrees that there are many dozens of emotions, the debate therefore centers on whether some emotions are somehow more fundamental than others (Ekman & Davidson, 1994). A middle-ground perspective is to argue that each basic emotion is not a single affective state but, rather, is a *family* of related states (Ekman, 1994a). For instance, anger is a basic affective state, but anger is also a family of emotions that includes hostility, rage, fury, outrage, annoyance, resentment, envy, and frustration. Similarly, enjoyment is a basic emotion family that includes the affective states of amusement, relief, satisfaction, contentment, and pride in achievement. Each member of a family shares many of the characteristics of the prototypical emotion—its physiology, its subjective feeling state, its expressive characteristics, and so on. There are a limited number of these basic emotion families, and each emotion family features both a prototypical theme via evolution and biology and its variations via learning, socialization, and culture (Ekman, 1994a). Ekman (1992, 1994a) proposes that there are at least five such emotion families—anger, fear, disgust, sadness, and enjoyment.

From a cognitive perspective (rather than Ekman's biological perspective), Shaver and his colleagues' analysis of the English language (1987) led them to conclude that emotion knowledge involves five basic emotion prototypes—anger, fear, sadness, joy, and love. These are the most common emotions in everyday experience. People learn increasingly finer distinctions within the causes and consequences of these five basic emotions. Through experience and culture, people learn that different situations give rise to specific variations of fear: alarm, shock, fright, horror, terror, panic, hysteria, mortification, anxiety, nervousness, tension, uneasiness, apprehension, worry, dread, and perhaps others.

Basic Emotions

Any answer to the question of how many emotions there are forces one to commit to a level of specificity (Averill, 1994), which means that emotions can be conceptualized generally (at the prototype level, as in anger) or more specifically (at the situation level, as in hostility or envy). This chapter emphasizes emotions at their most general level. The so-called basic emotions are those that (1) are innate rather than

FIGURE 11–4
Eight Research Traditions in the Cognitive Study of Emotion

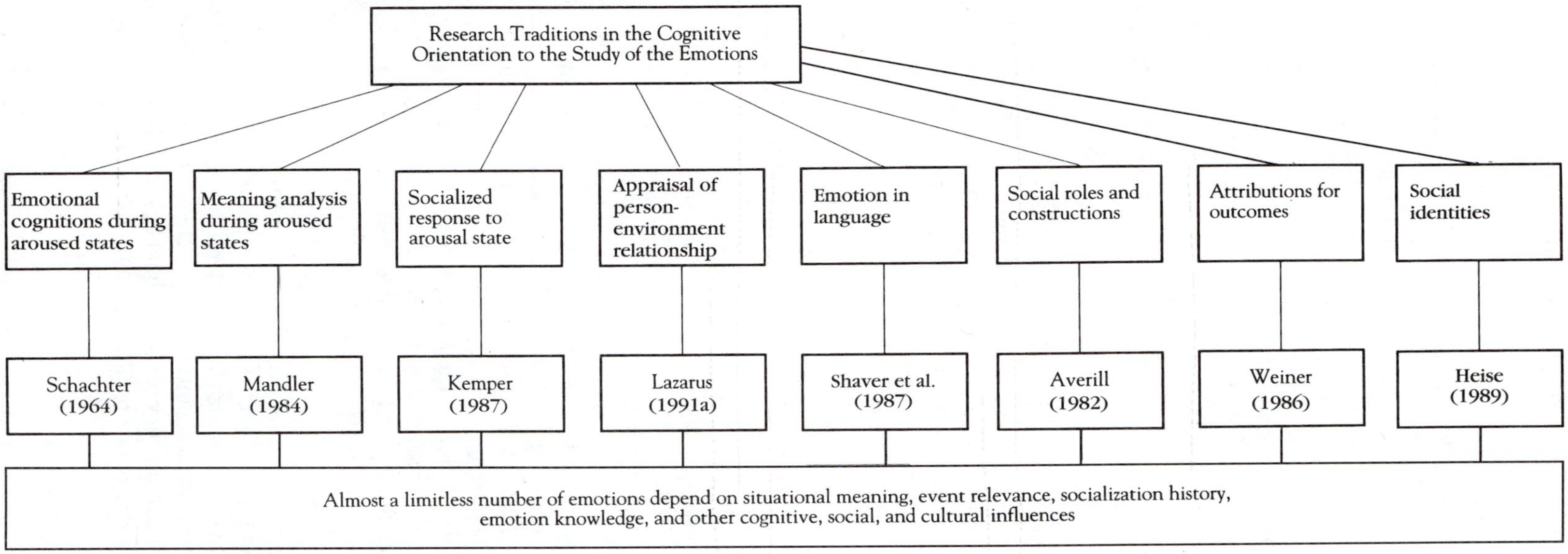

Research Traditions in the Cognitive Orientation to the Study of the Emotions

Emotional cognitions during aroused states	Meaning analysis during aroused states	Socialized response to arousal state	Appraisal of person-environment relationship	Emotion in language	Social roles and constructions	Attributions for outcomes	Social identities
Schachter (1964)	Mandler (1984)	Kemper (1987)	Lazarus (1991a)	Shaver et al. (1987)	Averill (1982)	Weiner (1986)	Heise (1989)

Almost a limitless number of emotions depend on situational meaning, event relevance, socialization history, emotion knowledge, and other cognitive, social, and cultural influences acquired from personal, social, or cultural experience, (2) arise from the same circumstances for all people (personal loss makes people sad irrespective of their age, culture, and so on), (3) are expressed uniquely and distinctively (as through a facial expression), and (4) evoke a distinctive physiological patterned response (Ekman & Davidson, 1994). Certainly, emotions develop and change throughout life, yet despite individual experience and cultures, we all share an emotion commonality of the basic emotions. Some researchers argue against the idea of basic emotions (e.g., Ortony & Turner, 1990). Other theorists offer a different list of basic emotions. Despite some diversity of opinion, no list varies very far from including the following six: fear, anger, disgust, sadness, joy, and interest. The following information that describes these six basic emotions comes from both cognitive and biological theorists (Ekman, 1992; Ellsworth & Smith, 1988a; Izard, 1991; Shaver et al., 1987; Weiner, 1986).

FEAR. Fear begins with the individual's interpretation of a situation as potentially dangerous and threatening. Perceived dangers and threats can be psychological or physical. The most common fear-activating situations are the anticipation of physical or psychological harm, the sense of vulnerability to danger, or an expectation that one's coping abilities fall short of stressful and overwhelming conditions. The perception that one can do little to cope with an environmental danger is at least as important a source of fear as is any actual characteristic of the threat itself (Bandura, 1983).

Fear is a defense motivation system. It functions as an emotional warning signal of forthcoming physical or psychological harm. Fear's warning signal manifests itself in autonomic nervous system arousal (as in the flight part of the fight-or-flight response). The individual trembles, perspires, looks around, and feels nervous tension to protect the self. The protection motivation is typically manifested either by escape and withdrawal from the object(s) or by coping responses to meet the object of fear face to face. Fleeing puts physical (or psychological) distance between the self and that which is feared. If escape is not possible, fear motivates the person to cope with the danger, as by being still or perhaps by acting courageously. On a more positive note, fear can facilitate the learning of new coping responses that remove the person from danger. Few highway drivers in a torrential rainfall need to be reminded to pay attention to the slippery road (fear activates coping efforts), and experienced drivers are better at coping with such a danger than are novice drivers (fear facilitates the learning of adaptive responses). Fear therefore activates coping efforts and facilitates the learning of coping skills.

ANGER. Anger arises from the experience of restraint, as in the interpretation that one's plans and goals have been interfered with by some outside force. Restraints come from physical barriers (locked doors), obstacles of interference (machines that don't work), or frustrating interruptions. The essence of anger is the individual's belief that the situation is not what it should be—that is, the restraint, interference, or interruption is illegitimate (deRivera, 1981). Anger also has a number of varieties that allow it to be expressed not only as a prototype (the offended person glares, clenches, and then lashes out violently) but also as specific and appropriate to a situation (anger as fury, hostility, vengefulness, rage, aggravation, wrath, and so on; Russell & Fehr, 1994).

Anger is the most passionate emotion. The angry person becomes stronger and more energized (as in the fight part of the fight-or-flight response). The fight is directed at overcoming or righting the illegitimate restraint, interference, or interruption. This attack can be verbal or nonverbal (yelling or slamming the door), direct or indirect (destroying the obstacle or just throwing objects about). Anger is potentially the most dangerous emotion, as its purpose is to destroy barriers in the environment. Sometimes anger produces needless destruction and injury, as when we push a child, curse at a teammate, or kick in the locked door. Other times, however, anger is productive, as when it energizes vigor, strength, and endurance in our efforts to cope with the world around us.

DISGUST. Disgust involves getting rid of or getting away from a contaminated, deteriorated, or spoiled object. Just what that object is depends on development and culture (Rozin, Haidt, & McCauley, 1993; Rozin, Lowery, & Ebert, 1994). In infancy, disgust is limited to the response to bitter tastes, but in childhood disgust reactions include a revulsion at the prospect of assimilating any offensive stimulus (Rozin & Fallon, 1987). Adult disgust elicitors include bodily contaminations (poor hygiene, gore, death), interpersonal contaminations (physical contact with undesirable people), and moral contaminations (child abuse, incest, infidelity). Cultural learning largely determines what the adult considers a bodily, interpersonal, or moral contamination.

The function of disgust is rejection; it is the self's way of rejecting some aspect of the environment physically or psychologically. Consider these environmental invasions that the person, through the disgust emotion, seeks to reject (examples from Rozin, Lowery, & Ebert, 1994)—eating something bitter (bad taste), smelling ammonia or rotten meat (bad smell), eating an apple with a worm in it (contaminated food), watching a medical dissection (body violation), thinking about a friend engaged in incest (moral violation), and sleeping in a hotel bed on which the linens have not been changed (interpersonal contamination). Because disgust is phenomenologically aversive, people learn coping behaviors designed to prevent creating or encountering conditions they suspect will produce the disgust emotion. So, people change personal habits and attributes, discard waste and sanitize their surroundings, reappraise their thoughts and values; they wash the dishes, brush their teeth, take showers, and exercise to avoid an out-of-shape or "disgusting" body.

SADNESS. Sadness (or distress) is the most negative, aversive emotion. Sadness arises principally from experiences of separation and failure. Separation, or the loss of a loved one through death, divorce, circumstances (e.g., travel), or argument, is distressing. One can also be separated from a valued job, position, or status. Failure also leads to sadness, as in failing an examination, losing a contest, or being rejected for a group's membership. Even failure outside of one's volitional control can cause distress, as in war, illness, accidents, and economic depression (Izard, 1991).

Sadness, because of its aversive phenomenology, motivates the individual to undertake whatever behavior is necessary to alleviate the distress-provoking circumstances. Sadness motivates the person to restore the environment to its predistress state. Following separation, and hence sadness, the rejected lover apologizes, sends flowers, or telephones in an effort to repair the broken relationship. Following a failure, and hence sadness, a performer practices to restore confidence. Unfortunately, many separations and failures cannot be restored to their preseparation or prefailure states. Under these hopeless conditions, the person behaves not in an active, vigorous way but in an inactive, lethargic way that essentially leads to withdrawing from the distressing situation.

Even sadness, however, has its beneficial aspect. Sadness indirectly facilitates cohesiveness of social groups (Averill, 1968). Because separation from significant other people causes sadness and because sadness is such an uncomfortable feeling, its anticipation motivates people to stay cohesive with their loved ones (Averill, 1979). If people did not miss others, then they would not be so motivated to go out of their way to maintain social cohesion. Similarly, if the student or athlete did not anticipate the possibility of failure-induced distress, they would be less motivated to prepare and practice.

FEAR, SADNESS, ANGER, AND DISGUST. Threat and harm are the themes that unite the negative emotions of fear, sadness, anger, and disgust. When bad events are forecast or anticipated, we feel fear. During the struggle to reject or fight off the threat or harm, we feel disgust and anger, respectively. Once the threat or harm has come to pass (i.e., once the bad event moves from the future through the present and into the past), we feel sadness. In response to threat and harm, fear motivates avoidance behavior to flee the threat. Disgust motivates rejection of the bad event or object. Anger motivates fighting and vigorous counterdefense. Sadness leads to inactivity and withdrawal and is effective when it leads us to give up our coping efforts in situations that we cannot flee from, reject, or fight against. This discussion confirms the functional aspect of emotion in that fear, sadness, anger, and disgust, as a collective emotion system, equip the individual to deal effectively with all aspects of threat and harm.

JOY. The events that bring us joy include desirable outcomes such as task success, personal achievement, progress toward a goal, or getting what we wanted; gaining esteem, respect, or praise; receiving love or affection or a wonderful surprise; or experiencing pleasurable sensations (Ekman & Friesen, 1975; Izard, 1991; Shaver et al., 1987). The causes of joy—desirable outcomes such as success and belongingness—are essentially the opposite of the causes of sadness (undesirable outcomes such as failure and separation or loss). How joy affects us also seems to be the opposite of how sadness affects us. When sad, we feel lethargic and withdrawn; when joyous, we feel enthuiastic and outgoing. When sad, we are often pessimistic; when joyous, we are often optimistic.

The function of joy is twofold. On the one hand, joy is a positive feeling derived from a sense of satisfaction and triumph. Being an intrinsically positive feeling, joy makes life pleasant. The pleasantness of joy therefore counteracts the inevitable life experiences of frustration, disappointment, and negative affect in general and allows us to preserve psychological well-being. On the other hand, joy facilitates our willingness to engage in social activities. Few social stimuli are as potent and as rewarding as are the smile and interpersonal inclusion. Expressed joy is therefore the social glue that bonds relationships, such as infant and mother, lovers, co-workers, and teammates.

INTEREST. Interest is the most prevalent emotion in the day-to-day functioning of human beings. Interest arises mostly from those situations that involve the person's needs or well-being significantly (Deci, 1992b), though some level of interest is ever present. At the neurological level, interest involves a moderate increase in the rate of neural firing. When a person is at a resting level of neural activity, environmental events—change, novelty, challenge, thoughts of learning or achieving, and acts of discovery initiate an increasing rate in neural activity (Izard, 1991). Increases and decreases in interest usually involve a shifting of interest from one event, thought, or action to another. In other words, we typically do not lose interest, but rather, we continually redirect it from one object or event to another.

Interest creates the desire to explore, investigate, seek out, manipulate, and extract information from the objects that surround us by turning things around, upside down, over, and about. Interest also underlies our desire to be creative, to learn, and to develop our competencies and skills (Renninger, Hidi, & Krapp, 1992). A person's interest in an activity is a predictor of that person's attention to it and how well that person processes, comprehends, and remembers relevant information (Hidi, 1990; Renninger, Hidi, & Krapp, 1992; Renninger & Wozniak, 1985; Schiefele, 1991; Shirey & Reynolds, 1988). Interest therefore enhances learning (Alexander, Kulikowich, & Jetton, 1994). It is difficult to learn a foreign language or to allocate time to read a book, for example, without emotional support from interest.

INTEREST AND JOY. Need involvement and need satisfaction are the themes that unite the positive emotions of interest and joy. When a beneficial event is forecast or anticipated, we feel interest. Once the need has been satisfied, we feel joy (or enjoyment). When a task or event involves one or more of our needs, interest motivates the approach and exploratory behavior necessary to promote contact with the potentially need-satisfying event. It is interest that prolongs our task engagement enough so we can experience need satisfaction. Joy (or enjoyment) replaces interest when need satisfaction occurs (Izard, 1991). Joy then promotes ongoing task persistence and subsequent reengagement behaviors with the need-satisfying event.

Together, interest and joy are the emotions that regulate a person being fully involved in a voluntary activity (Reeve, 1989).

WHAT IS THE DIFFERENCE BETWEEN EMOTION AND MOOD?

A fourth fundamental question on the nature of emotion concerns the difference between emotion and mood (Ekman & Davidson, 1994). Several distinguishing criteria can be listed (Goldsmith, 1994), but three seem especially telling. First, emotions and moods arise from different antecedents. Emotions emerge from significant life situations and from appraisals of their significance, whereas moods emerge from processes that are oftentimes unknown or at least not situation specific (Goldsmith, 1994). Second, emotions function mostly to bias behavior and select specific courses of action, whereas moods function mostly to bias cognition and what the person thinks (Davidson, 1994). Ekman argues that emotions emanate from neurochemical events that last for seconds or minutes whereas moods emanate from mental events that last for hours. Hence, the third distinguishing characteristic is time course such that moods are more enduring than emotions (Ekman, 1994a).

Everyday, Ongoing Affective Experience

Most people have about 1000 waking minutes in their day, but only a few of these actually include a prototypical emotion such as anger, fear, or joy (Clark, Watson & Leeka, 1989; Watson & Clark, 1994). In contrast, the average person generally experiences an ever-present stream of moods. People are always feeling something, but acute emotions are rare. What people typically feel is some level of positive affect and some level of negative affect (Watson & Tellegen, 1985; Watson, Clark, & Tellegen, 1988). Often these moods exist as aftereffects of episodes involving multiple emotions (Davidson, 1994). These two moods (positive and negative affect) are more independent of one another than they are mutually exclusive ways of feeling (Diener & Emmons, 1984; Diener & Iran-Nejad, 1986). For example, during a job interview, people often report feeling both positive and negative affect simultaneously.

Positive affect exists as a person's current level of pleasure, enthusiasm, and quick progress toward goals, whereas negative affect exists as a person's current level of displeasure, distress, and slow progress toward goals. Persons feeling high positive affect typically experience energy, alertness, and optimism, whereas persons feeling low positive affect typically experience apathy and boredom. Persons feeling high negative affect typically experience dissatisfaction, nervousness, and irritability, whereas persons feeling low negative affect typically experience calmness and relaxation. These feelings of alertness versus boredom (measure of positive affect) and irritability versus relaxation (measure of negative affect), rather than prototypical emotional states like joy and fear, constitute the essential nature of everyday, ongoing affective experience.

The Nature of Positive Affect

Positive affect refers to the everyday, low-level, general state of feeling good (Isen, 1987). It is the warm glow that so often accompanies everyday pleasant experiences such as walking in the park on a sunny day, receiving an unexpected gift or good news, listening to music, or making progress on a task. Although we focus on the park scenery, good news, music, or positive task feedback, the mild good feeling of positive affect often arises subconsciously. We may smile more, whistle while we walk, daydream about happy memories, or talk more excitedly, but the positive feelings typically remain outside our conscious attention. In fact, if someone brings the pleasant mood to our attention ("My, aren't we in a good mood today!"), such attention paradoxically is the beginning of the end of the positive affect.

This lack of awareness that characterizes positive affect stands in contrast to the more intense, attention-grabbing positive emotions, such as joy and love. The purpose of an emotion is to capture attention and direct coping behavior so the person can adapt to situational demands effectively. Positive affect is more subtle. Positive affect generally does not affect attention and behavior; instead, positive affect largely affects the information processing flow—what we think about, the decisions we make, creativity, judgments, and so on. The difference between positive affect and emotions illustrates *the fundamental differences between moods and emotions* (see Ekman & Davidson, 1994). Emotions arise from specific events, serve specific adaptive purposes, are short-lived, and motivate emotion-specific coping behaviors. Moods arise from ill-defined and often unknown sources, exert a general effect on the way we manage our affairs, are pervasive, and affect behavior only indirectly through their effects on cognitive processes.

Sources of Positive Affect

People have a difficult time explaining why they feel good. If pressed, they typically say that life is generally going well. But emotion researchers can create conditions that lead people to feel good, whether they are aware of the source of their good mood or not (Isen, 1987). Consider these experimental manipulations that produced mild positive affect states by giving a person a small gain, amusement, or pleasure: People feel good (experience positive affect) after finding money in the coin return of a public telephone (Isen & Levin, 1972), receiving a gift of a bag of candy (Isen & Geva, 1987; Isen, Niedenthal & Cantor, 1992), receiving a product sample (worth a quarter, Isen, Clark, & Schwartz, 1976), receiving a candy bar (Isen et al., 1985; Isen, Daubman, & Nowicki, 1987), learning that their task performance was successful (Isen, 1970), receiving a cookie (Isen & Levin, 1972), receiving refreshments such as orange juice (Isen et al., 1985), receiving positive feedback (Isen, Rosenzweig, & Young, 1991), thinking about positive events (Isen et al., 1985), experiencing sunny weather (Kraut & Johnston, 1979), watching an amusing film (Isen & Nowicki, 1981), or rating funny cartoons (Carnevale & Isen, 1986).

Once instigated by an eliciting event (e.g., receiving refreshments), the warm glow of positive affect continues for up to 20 minutes (Isen, Clark, & Schwartz,

1976). Because we enjoy feeling good, happy people make decisions and act in ways that maintain their good mood (Forest et al., 1979; Isen et al., 1978). More often than not, however, some rival event or life task distracts our attention away from the positive affect–inducing event. That is, we lose our positive mood by engaging in a neutral or aversive event (e.g., boring work, dense or congested traffic, bad news, a risk turned sour).

Effects of Positive Affect

Compared to people in a neutral mood, people exposed to conditions that allow them to feel good are more likely to help others (Isen & Levin, 1972), act sociably (i.e., initiate conversations, Batson et al., 1979), express greater liking for others (Veitch & Griffitt, 1976), be more generous to others (Isen, 1970) and to themselves (Mischel, Coates, & Raskoff, 1968), take greater risks (Isen & Patrick, 1983), act more cooperatively and less aggressively (Carnevale & Isen, 1986), solve problems more creatively (Isen, Daubman, & Nowicki, 1987), persist in the face of failure feedback (Chen & Isen, 1992), make decisions more efficiently (Isen & Means, 1983), and show greater intrinsic motivation towards relatively interesting activities (Isen & Reeve, 1996). The explanation as to *how* and *why* positive affect facilitates sociability, prosocial behavior, creativity, persistence, and so on is not as straightforward as it first appears. Positive affect affects cognitive processes, such as memories, judgments, and problem-solving strategies, and therefore influences the contents of working (short-term) memory by biasing what the individual thinks about and what memories and expectations come to mind (Isen, 1984, 1987). In brief, positive affect serves as a retrieval cue for positive material stored in memory (Isen et al., 1978; Laird et al., 1982; Nasby & Yando, 1982; Teasdale & Fogarty, 1979). As a result, people who feel good have greater access to happy thoughts and positive memories than do people who feel neutral. With happy thoughts and pleasant memories in mind, people show increased creativity, persistence in the face of failure, decision-making efficiency, and intrinsic motivation on interesting endeavors.

CREATIVITY. Positive affect facilitates cognitive flexibility (Isen, Niedenthal, & Cantor, 1992) and creative problem solving (Isen, Daubman, & Nowicki, 1987). Isen and colleagues (1987) induced positive or neutral affect in groups of college students and then asked them to solve one of two creative problem-solving tasks—the candle task (Dunker, 1945) or the Remote Associates Test (RAT; Mednick, Mednick, & Mednick, 1964). In the candle task, the participant receives a pile of tacks, a candle, and a box of matches and the instruction to attach the candle to the wall (a corkboard) so it can burn without dripping wax on the floor. In the RAT, the participant sees three words (soul, busy, guard) and is to generate a fourth that relates to the other three (body). Positive affect participants solved the creativity-demanding candle task and gave creative (unusual or remote) associates to the RAT (Isen et al., 1987). In contrast, the candle task stumped the neutral affect participants, and they gave routine, stereotypical responses to the RAT.

PERSISTENCE IN THE FACE OF FAILURE. Positive affect serves as a buffer against failure such that it encourages persistence rather than quitting (Chen & Isen, 1992). Chen and Isen (1992) induced positive or neutral affect in college students; had them experience either success, failure, or an ambiguous outcome; and then gave them an opportunity to persist or not at the task. Only the participants who received a small bag of candy (to induce positive affect) retried the problem after failure or after an ambiguous outcome. Happy and neutral participants persisted only after success. Thus, either past success or a good mood that buffers failure is sufficient to encourage persistence.

DECISION-MAKING EFFICIENCY. Positive affect enhances cognitive efficiency (Carnevale & Isen, 1986; Isen & Means, 1983; Isen, Rosenzweig, & Young, 1991). Feeling good biases people toward faster, more efficient, and less effortful decision-making performances. On tasks that are more structured and need to be double-checked for accuracy (e.g., geometry proofs, second drafts of a manuscript), however, positive affect individuals do not outperform their neutral affect counterparts (because their fast, efficient, effortless decision-making style makes them increasingly susceptible to error making).

INTRINSIC MOTIVATION. Positive affect enhances intrinsic motivation on interesting activities (Isen & Reeve, 1996). Isen and Reeve induced either positive or neutral affect in participants and introduced them to two experimental tasks, one that was interesting (a puzzle) and the other that was not (a clerical task). Nobody felt intrinsically motivated toward the uninteresting task, but the positive affect participants felt more intrinsically motivated toward the interesting task. Notice that positive affect does not increase intrinsic motivation toward *all* tasks, but rather, positive affect increases intrinsic motivation only toward relatively interesting tasks.

SUMMARY

This chapter addressed four questions central to emotion research: (1) What is an emotion? (2) Is emotion primarily a biological or a cognitive process? (3) How many emotions are there—a basic few or many? and (4) What is the difference between emotion and mood?

The first question, What is an emotion?, comes across as a rather curious one to most students, because everyone knows what an emotion is. But emotions are multidimensional phenomena that elude a straightforward definition. Emotions have a four-part character in that they feature distinct subjective, biological, functional, and expressive aspects. The subjective component gives an emotion its feeling state. The biological component gives an emotion its physiological reaction and bodily preparedness to cope with a specific situation. The functional component gives an emotion its motivational aspect as emotions create desires and purposes to channel behavior in appropriate ways. Finally, the expressive component gives emotion a social, communicative aspect. Emotion is the psychological construct that coordinates and unifies these four aspects of experience into a synchronized, adaptive pattern. Emotions relate to motivation in two ways. First, emotions act as a special type of motive. Like needs and cognitions, emotions too energize and direct behavior. Second, emotions serve as an information readout of ongoing motivational states.

The second question asked, What causes an emotion? and introduced the debate as to whether emotion is primarily a biological or a cognitive phenomenon. According to the biological perspective, emotions arise from bodily influences such as limbic neural pathways, patterns of neural firing, and facial feedback. According to the cognitive perspective, emotions arise from cognitive resources such as appraisals, knowledge, and memory as the individual interprets the personally relevant meaning of a stimulus event. Both sides of the biology-cognition debate marshaled an impressive array of evidence to support their position. Because events such as drugs, electrical brain stimulation, and facial feedback can activate emotion, it is clear that biological forces cause emotional experience, with or without cognitive participation. Because people can almost always interpret the self-relevance and personal significance of an event, it is clear that cognitive forces also cause emotional experience. In response to the biology-cognition debate, three solutions emerged. The first solution argues that human beings possess two parallel emotion systems. The biological system stems from the person's phylogenetic evolutionary history and functions as an innate, spontaneous, and primitive physiological emotion system; the cognitive system stems from the person's unique history and functions as an acquired, interpretive, and social emotion system. The second solution argues that the biology-cognition debate is fruitless, as emotion should be considered a dynamic process rather than the output of either the biological or cognitive systems. The third solution proposes that emotions include both cognitive and biological components, and it is simply a matter of perspective as to which set of variables one wishes to emphasize and investigate (you say toe-may-toes, I say ta-mott-ohs). Perhaps the most general conclusion is that emotions are complex, multifaceted response syndromes. A biological analysis provides a necessary but probably insufficient understanding of the emotions. An understanding of the cognitive contribution is required to include the secondary, situation-specific emotions. Both perspectives combined provides a comprehensive and more satisfactory perspective on the emotion process.

The third question asked, How many emotions are there? The answer depends on the perspective. According to the biological perspective, human beings possess about a half-dozen basic emotions—somewhere between two and 10. The fundamental biological research traditions for primary emotions stem from the following: hedonically opponent processes, hardwired limbic neural pathways; patterns of neural firing, universal facial expressions, evolutionary functions, and discrete patterns of facial feedback. In contrast, according to the cognitive perspective, human beings possess a much richer, more diverse emotional repertoire than the basic emotions. Secondary emotions are acquired as the individual learns to interpret situations differently, gains experience in emotional situations, learns new emotion words, learns to manage emotion expressions, and learns cultural display rules. This section concludes by discussing six basic emotions—fear, anger, disgust, distress, joy, and interest.

The fourth and final question asked, What is the difference between emotion and mood? Emotions arise from specific events, serve specific adaptive purposes, are short-lived, and motivate emotion-specific coping behaviors. In contrast, moods arise from ill-defined and often unknown sources, exert a general effect on the way we manage our affairs, are pervasive, and affect behavior only indirectly through their effects on cognitive processes. To illustrate the motivational significance of moods, the chapter focused on positive affect. Positive affect refers to the everyday, low-level, general state of feeling good. It is the warm glow that so often accompanies everyday pleasant experiences. When people feel good, they are more sociable, cooperative, creative, persistent despite failure, efficient in their decision making, and intrinsically motivated on interesting tasks. Positive affect exerts these effects by affecting cognitive processes such as memories, judgments, and problem-solving strategies. As a result, people who feel good have greater access to happy thoughts and positive memories and therefore behave in ways that are more sociable, cooperative, creative, persistent, efficient, and self-regulated.

RECOMMENDED READINGS

Ekman, P. (1992). An argument for basic emotions. *Cognition and Emotion, 6,* 169–200.

Isen, A. M., Daubman, K. A., & Nowicki, G. P. (1987). Positive affect facilitates creative problem-solving. *Journal of Personality and Social Psychology, 51,* 1122–1131.

Izard, C. E. (1993). Four systems for emotion activation: Cognitive and noncognitive processes. *Psychological Review, 100,* 68–90.

Kemper, T. D. (1987). How many emotions are there? Wedding the social and autonomic components. *American Sociological Review, 93,* 263–289.

Lazarus, R. S. (1991). Cognition and motivation in emotion. *American Psychologist, 46,* 352–367.

Levenson, R. W. (1994). Human emotion: A functional view. In P. Ekman & R. J. Davidson (Eds.), *The nature of emotion* (pp. 123–126). New York: Oxford University Press.

Oatley, K., & Duncan, E. (1994). The experience of emotions in everyday life. *Cognition and Emotion, 8,* 369–381.

Plutchik, R. (1985). On emotion: The chicken-and-egg problem revisited. *Motivation and Emotion, 9,* 197–200.

Watson, D., Clark, L. A., & Tellegen, A. (1988). Development and validation of brief measures of positive and negative affect: The PANAS scales. *Journal of Personality and Social Psychology, 54,* 1063–1070.

Zajonc, R. B. (1980). Feeling and thinking: Preferences need no inferences. *American Psychologist, 35,* 151–175.

Chapter 12

BIOLOGICAL ASPECTS OF EMOTION

You are in love and live a happy life with your spouse and child. Suddenly, boom, an accident takes the life of your spouse. In the face of death and loss, emotion overwhelms you and you cannot help but feel sadness and grief. Grief becomes a biological imperative—you cry, search frantically to find your lost love, and yearn for the spouse's return. Crying, searching, and yearning usually promote reunion following separation, as that is the function of these behaviors. But in death such attachment seeking must eventually give way to listlessness and withdrawal. Death has implications not only for you but for society as well: Will other people treat you differently as a single rather than as part of a couple? What will happen to your child? The social function of grief is to reestablish your social cohesion and inclusion, and society typically enacts some mourning ritual (a funeral) whose explicit function is to reaffirm your inclusion in the lives of others. These then are the biological and social functions of grief (Averill, 1968, 1979)—to overcome loss and to counteract separation.

FUNCTIONS OF EMOTION

What purpose, or purposes, do emotions serve—what good are the emotions? Work on the functional significance of emotion stems from Darwin's *The Expression of Emotions in Man and Animals* (1872), a less famous effort than his 1859 work. Darwin argued that expressive characteristics had a functional significance for the adapting organism much in the same way that physical characteristics such as height and the position of the eyes do. For example, the dog baring its teeth in defense of its territory and the human's flushed face with eyebrows drawn down and inward during a fight have functional significance. To the extent that the baring of the teeth or the intimidating face help the expresser cope with hostile situations (by warding off an opponent), these expressions are functionally significant and are therefore candidates for natural selection.

Coping Functions

Emotions do not just occur out of the blue; they occur for a reason. From a functional point of view, emotions evolved for their adaptive value in dealing with fundamental life tasks (Ekman, 1994). To survive, animals must explore their surrounding, vomit harmful substances, develop and maintain relationships, immediately attend to emergencies, avoid injury, reproduce, fight, and both receive and provide caregiving. Each of these behaviors is emotion produced, and each facilitates the individual's adaptation to changing physical and social environments.

Fundamental life tasks are universal human predicaments such as loss, frustration, achievement, and so on (Johnson-Laird & Oatley, 1992). The emotion during life tasks energizes and directs our behavior in evolution-benefitting ways (e.g., after separation, crying for help proved more effective than other courses of action). That is, emotion and emotional behavior provide us with coherent and ingrained ways of coping with the major challenges and threats to our personal welfare (Tooby

& Cosmides, 1990). According to Plutchik (1970, 1980), emotions serve eight distinct purposes: protection, destruction, reproduction, reunion, affiliation, rejection, exploration, and orientation. Thus, for the purpose of protection, fear prepares the body for withdrawal and escape. To destroy some aspect of the environment, such as an enemy or an obstacle to food, anger prepares the body for attack. To explore the environment, anticipation sparks a sense of curiosity and readies the body for investigation. For every major life task, human beings evolved a corresponding, adaptive emotional reaction. The function of emotion is therefore to prepare us to respond appropriately to the demands of life's fundamental tasks.

Table 12.1 pairs some fundamental situations with their responses. The table also lists the functional aspects of such emotional behavior. Thus, the table shows that, facing threat, animals run or fly away to serve the purpose of protection. Given an obstacle, animals bite and hit to serve the purposes of destruction, and so forth. Table 12.1 also lists related human emotions.

From a functional point of view, there is no such thing as a "bad" emotion. Joy is not necessarily a good emotion, and anger and fear are not bad emotions. *All* emotions are beneficial. Any statement that emotions can be dysfunctional, such as the clinical term *emotional disorder* is a misnomer (Izard, 1982), because emotions are fundamentally adaptive. Each emotion provides a unique readiness to a particular situation. The pounding heart and quickened breath optimize the bodily reaction to anger-eliciting and fear-eliciting situations. The calm heart that accompanies anticipation, on the other hand, prepares the body for optimal attention, information processing, and problem solving. From this point of view, fear, anger, disgust, sadness, and all specific emotions are good emotions, because fear facilitates protection, disgust facilitates repulsion of gruesome objects, and so forth. Plutchik's psychoevolutionary perspective of emotion allows us to consider emotions as positive, functional, purposive, and adaptive organizers of behavior.

Other biologically oriented emotion researchers stress greater flexibility in emotional readiness and ways of coping than is apparent from Table 12.1 (e.g., Frijda, 1994). That is, while fear essentially motivates protective behavior, it also readies us for additional action, including preventing the dangerous event from occurring in

TABLE 12–1

Functional View of Emotional Behavior

STIMULUS	RESPONSE	FUNCTION	EMOTION
Threat	Running, flying away	Protection	Fear
Obstacle	Biting, hitting	Destruction	Anger
Potential mate	Courting, mating	Reproduction	Joy
Loss of valued person	Crying for help	Reunion	Sadness
Group member	Grooming, sharing	Affiliation	Acceptance
Gruesome object	Vomiting, pushing away	Rejection	Disgust
New territory	Examining, mapping	Exploration	Anticipation
Sudden novel object	Stopping, alerting	Orientation	Surprise

SOURCE: Plutchik, R. (1980). Functional view of emotional behavior. In *Emotion:* A psychoevolutionary synthesis. New York: Harper & Row. Adapted with permission.

the first place and suppressing activity until the threat passes. Likewise, anger essentially motivates destructive action, but it also prepares us to enforce social norms and to discourage anger-causing events (e.g., discourage someone from insulting us). The point is that individual experience and cultural learning also contribute to how we express our emotional readiness to cope with fundamental life tasks.

Social Functions

Emotions serve social functions, at least four of which can be identified. Emotions (1) communicate our feelings to others; (2) regulate how others interact with us; (3) invite and facilitate social interaction; and (4) are pivotal in creating, maintaining, and dissolving relationships (Izard, 1989; Manstead, 1991).

COMMUNICATING OUR FEELINGS TO OTHERS. Emotional expressions are potent nonverbal communication messages. Through emotional expressions, infants nonverbally communicate what they cannot communicate verbally. At birth, infants are capable of expressing pain, joy, interest, and disgust; by two months, infants can express sadness and anger; and by six months, infants can also express fear (Izard, 1989). Equally important, each expression can be reliably recognized and interpreted by a caregiver (Izard et al., 1980). Huebner and Izard (1988) tested whether infant facial expressions functioned as specific communications signals by showing mothers pictures of infants expressing sadness, anger, physical distress, and interest. The experimenters asked the mothers to imagine that the infant in each slide was their own and respond to the question, "When my baby shows this expression, I tend to. . . ."

Table 12.2 lists the 13 behavioral responses asked of the mothers. When the infants expressed physical distress, the mothers were most apt to select the responses of Hurry/Pick up (8.3), Love/Cuddle (8.5), and Feel sad or sorry for baby (8.1). In response to anger expressions, mothers mostly selected Distract/Give change of scene (7.7) and Look around first (7.1). With sadness expressions, the mothers mostly selected the Talk/Play/Interact (7.5) and Distract/Give change of scene (7.1). When the infant expressed interest, the mothers selected Talk/Play/Interact (8.3) and Keep distance/Watch (7.6) or Feel good/Smile (7.6), but would not feel annoyed or angry (1.4) or enforce discipline/control (1.6). What these data suggest, at least for infant-mother relationships, is that emotional expressions communicate feelings to others.

REGULATING HOW OTHERS RESPOND TO US. The infant-mother study shows that the emotional expression of one person can prompt selective behavioral reactions from a second person. In addition, emotional expressions affect how others respond (Camras, 1977; Coyne, 1976a, 1976b; Frijda, 1986; Klinnert et al., 1983). For instance, in a conflict situation to retain a toy, the child who expresses anger or sadness is much more likely to keep the toy than the child who expresses no such emotional reaction (Camras, 1977; Reynolds, 1982). The emotional expression communicates to others what the expresser's probable forthcoming behavior is likely to

TABLE 12–2
Mothers' Responses to Infants' Facial Expressions

	INFANTS' FACIAL EXPRESSION			
WHEN MY BABY SHOWS THIS EXPRESSION, I TEND TO...	PHYSICAL DISTRESS	ANGER	SADNESS	INTEREST
1. Ignore/Turn away	1.9	3.4	3.4	4.1
2. Talk/Play/Interact	6.6	6.0	7.5	8.3
3. Hurry/Pick up	8.3	6.3	4.2	3.0
4. Feel good/Smile	1.4	1.6	2.7	7.6
5. Love/cuddle	8.5	6.5	6.9	6.9
6. Distract/Give change of scene	7.8	7.7	7.1	2.5
7. Look around first	6.9	7.1	7.0	5.1
8. Feel annoyed or angry	3.5	5.2	2.6	1.4
9. Take care of needs	7.1	7.0	6.0	2.7
10. Keep distance/Watch	2.4	4.2	5.9	7.6
11. Feel sad or sorry for baby	8.1	6.1	6.0	2.2
12. Discipline/Control	3.0	5.2	2.5	1.6
13. Not act	1.9	2.7	4.4	6.8

Range of scores, 0–10; standard deviations range from 0.8 to 2.8.
SOURCE: Huebner, R.R., & Izard, C.E. (1988). Mother's responses facial expressions of sadness, anger, and physical distress. *Motivation and Emotion,* 12, 185–196.

be. If the toy is taken away, the anger-expressing child communicates a probable forthcoming attack whereas the sadness-expressing child communicates a probable barrage of tears. The signal that one is likely to attack or cry soon often succeeds in regaining the lost toy (or in preventing the toy being taken in the first place). Hence emotions expressed in a social context serve both an informative (how I feel) and directive (what I want you to do) function (Schwartz & Clore, 1983).

Sometimes strategic emotional expressions backfire (Coyne, 1976a). Depressed persons, for instance, present their emotional state to others to gain support and re-assurance. Unfortunately, such depressive communication frequently arouses nega-tive affect in others that leads to rejection rather than to the hoped-for support and reassurance. It communicates a sad mood, low self-esteem, hopelessness, and fatigue to others (Winer et al., 1981). Because sad moods are intrinsically unpleasant and something to be avoided, people tend to reject expressers of sad moods, and the tendency to reject a sadness expresser increases with repeated encounters (Winer et al., 1981). Thus, although expressions of distress sometimes solicit nurturant be-haviors from others (see Table 12.2), communication of depression seems counter-productive, especially when repeated over time.

INVITING AND FACILITATING SOCIAL INTERACTION. Emotional expressions are often socially, rather than biologically, motivated. This assertion sounds strange because it is generally assumed that people smile when they feel joy, frown when they feel sad, and so forth. Nonetheless, people frequently smile when they do not feel joy. People sometimes smile when they wish to facilitate social interaction.

Ethologists studying smiling in primates find that chimpanzees use the voluntary smile expression to deflect potentially hostile behavior from dominant animals (van Hooff, 1962) and to maintain or increase friendly interactions (van Hooff, 1972). Just as primates smile (bare their teeth) to appease dominants, young children frequently smile when approaching a stranger, and children are more likely to approach a stranger who smiles than a stranger who does not smile (Connolly & Smith, 1972). Adults who make mistakes or who are embarrassed socially are also likely to smile, apparently in an effort to rectify a faux pas (Kraut & Johnston, 1979). In addition, the smile is a universal greeting display (Eibl-Eibesfeldt, 1972; van Hooff, 1972) that seems to say, nonverbally, "I am friendly" and "I would like us to be friendly, at least for a while." In each of these instances, the individual's smile is socially, rather than emotionally, motivated.

The idea that a smile can be socially motivated leads to the question of whether smiling evolved as an emotional expression of joy or as a social expression of appeasement and friendliness (Fernandez-Dols & Ruiz-Belba, 1995; Kraut & Johnston, 1979). To test the latter hypothesis, Kraut and Johnston observed people smiling while bowling, while watching a hockey match, and while walking down the street. The researchers wondered whether people smiled more often when engaged in social interaction or when experiencing a joy reaction to a positive event (a good bowling score, a goal for their hockey team, sunny weather). Generally speaking, bowlers, spectators, and pedestrians were more likely to smile when engaging in social interactions than when experiencing joy from these positive outcomes.

CREATING, MAINTAINING, AND DISSOLVING INTERPERSONAL RELATIONSHIPS. Joy, sadness, and anger all work to affect the social fabric of relationships. Joy promotes the establishment of relationships, sadness maintains relationships in times of separation, and anger takes the action necessary to break off an injurious relationship. Sadness and grief also motivate us to behave so as to prevent losing our relationships in the first place. Other emotions help preserve social order. Shame and guilt, for instance, motivate prosocial behaviors such as conforming to groups (to prevent shame) or being careful to show respect to others and cultural standards of right and wrong (to prevent guilt).

Emotions are intrinsic to interpersonal relationship processes. Most emotions arise not from impersonal encounters with the environment, but from the actions of those around us. If you kept track of what events caused your emotional reactions—another person's action, an action of your own, something you read or saw, et cetera—you would probably find that interpersonal encounters triggered most of your emotional reactions (Oatley & Duncan, 1994).

BIOLOGICAL ASPECTS OF EMOTION

Emotions are, in part, biological reactions to important life events. There are at least five biological aspects of emotion, as follows:

1. autonomic nervous system
2. endocrine system
3. neural brain circuits
4. rate of neural firing
5. facial feedback

Emotions mobilize the body for specific actions, such as running or fighting, by activating (1) biological systems that arouse and regulate the heart, lungs, and muscles (autonomic nervous system); (2) glands, hormones, and organs (endocrine system), (3) limbic brain structures such as the hypothalamus (neural brain circuits), (4) increases and decreases in the pace of information processing (rate of neural firing), and (5) discrete patterns of the facial musculature (facial feedback).

Emotion study began 100 years ago by asking what role the autonomic nervous system played in the subjective experience of emotion. The first theory of emotions, the James-Lange theory, asked whether individual emotions had particular patterned bodily reactions associated with them. For illustration, consider the activities of the autonomic nervous system in fear. In fear, predictable bodily changes occur—the heart races, palms sweat, and breathing quickens. People in love experience similar bodily changes. There is little doubt that fear and love feel different, but it is an interesting question whether fear and love have unique bodily reactions. Do our heart, spleen, eyes, and stomach behave one way when we are afraid yet other way when we are in love?

James-Lange Theory

Personal experience suggests that we experience an emotion and the emotional experience is quickly followed by bodily changes. As soon as we see and hear the flashing red lights and siren of the police car, fear arises and makes our heart race and our palms sweat. That is, the order of events seems to be stimulus leads to emotion, which leads to bodily reaction. James (1884, 1890, 1894) argued against this common view. He suggested that our bodily changes do not follow the emotional experience; rather, emotional experience follows and depends on bodily and behavioral responses to the flashing lights and siren. Hence, bodily changes cause emotional experience: stimulus leads to bodily reaction, which leads to emotion.

James' theory rests on two assumptions: (1) the body reacts discriminately to different emotion-eliciting stimuli and (2) nonemotional stimuli elicit no bodily changes. To appreciate James' hypothesis, think of the physiological responses to an unexpectedly cold shower. The physiological reaction—the increased heart rate, quickened breath, and wide eyes—begins before we have time to think about why our heart is racing and our eyes are widening. James argued that such instantaneous bodily reactions occur in discernable patterns, and emotional experience is our making sense of such bodily reactions. When such physiological changes do not occur, people do not feel emotion. Perhaps, one can imagine a stoic John Wayne not feeling fear, even while 100 violent desperados are galloping directly toward him. Like John Wayne, the person who does not experience bodily changes does not feel fear.

At the same time James presented his ideas, a Danish psychologist, Carl Lange (1885), proposed essentially the same (but more limited) theory of emotion. For this reason, the idea that emotions emanate from our interpretation of patterns of physiological arousal is traditionally called the James-Lange theory (Lange & James, 1922).

The James-Lange theory of emotions quickly became popular, but it also met criticism (Cannon, 1927). Cannon argued that the sort of bodily reactions James talked about were actually part of the body's general mobilizing fight-or-flight response that did not vary from one emotion to the next. He also argued that emotional experience was quicker than physiological reactions. That is, while a person feels anger in a tenth of a second, it takes our nervous system a full second or two to activate important glands and to send excitatory hormones through the bloodstream. It seems that some kind of emotional experience occurs almost instantaneously, and that the complete emotion is augmented, rather than caused by, later bodily changes (Newman, Perkins, & Wheeler, 1930). Cannon further noted that people continue to experience emotion even after surgery or an accident makes it impossible for the brain to monitor the body's visceral activities. Cannon also questioned whether a person would become emotional after taking a stimulant drug known to increase heart rate, stop gastrointestinal activity, and dilate the bronchioles. Rather, drug-induced visceral stimulation led to bodily changes that people felt "as if afraid" or "as if I were going to weep without knowing why" rather than afraid or sad per se. Cannon concluded that the contribution of physiological changes to emotional experience was small, supplemental, and relatively unimportant.

Contemporary Perspective

Cannon's remarks are tough criticisms, tough enough to lead emotion researchers to question the validity of James' notion that different emotions were associated with unique patterns of physiological activity. James' idea faded out of favor in the face of rival theories of emotion (e.g., Schachter & Singer, 1962), but his ideas continue to guide and inform contemporary motivation study (Ellsworth, 1994; Lang, 1994). Contemporary research finds support for some of James-Lange's postulates (Levenson, 1992). Ekman, Levenson, and Friesen (1983), for example, studied whether each emotion does or does not have a unique pattern of bodily changes. In contrast to Cannon's procedure of artificially manipulating bodily changes to see if emotion occurred, Ekman and his colleagues had participants experience the emotion first and then measured for patterned physiological changes. These researchers recruited people who could experience different emotions on command (professional actors) and asked each to relive five different emotions—anger, fear, sadness, joy, and disgust—while the researchers measured for emotion-specific patterns of physiological activity. Distinct differences in heart rate (HR) and skin temperature (ST) emerged among the emotions, as follows: with anger, HR and ST both increased; with fear, HR increased while ST decreased; with sadness, HR increased while ST was stable; with joy, HR was stable while ST increased; and with disgust, both HR and ST decreased.

The contemporary perspective on whether emotions have distinctive patterns of physiological activity is that a few emotions do while most do not. Persuasive evidence exists for distinctive autonomic nervous system (ANS) activity associated with anger, fear, disgust, and sadness (Ekman & Davidson, 1993; Ekman, Levenson, & Friesen, 1983; Levenson, 1992; Levenson et al., 1991; Levenson, Ekman, & Friesen, 1990). These patterns of ANS activity emerged because they recruit patterns of behavior that proved to be adaptive. For instance, in a fight that arouses anger, increased heart rate and skin temperature facilitate adaptive aggressive behavior. But not all emotions have distinct associated patterns of ANS activity. If no specific pattern of behavior has survival value for an emotion, there is little reason for the development of a specific pattern of ANS activity (Ekman, 1992, 1994a). For instance, what is the most adaptive behavioral pattern to jealousy? To envy? Joy? Hope? For these emotions, no single adaptive activity seems universally most appropriate. Hence, there is little reason to expect a single pattern of ANS activity to evolve.

When one juxtaposes the criticisms of Cannon and the support of Ekman and his colleagues, the emerging question is whether the physiological arousal causes or follows emotion. This question is important because, if arousal causes emotion, the study of physiological arousal becomes the cornerstone for the study of emotion. But if arousal merely follows emotion, physiological activity is therefore much less important. Contemporary researchers generally agree that physiological arousal accompanies, regulates, and sets the stage for emotion, but it does not cause it directly. The modern perspective is that emotions recruit physiological support for adaptive behaviors such as fighting, fleeing, and nurturing. Hence, the physiological function of emotion is to create the optimal physiological milieu to support the particular action tendency (behavior) called for by a life situation (Levenson, 1994).

NEURAL CIRCUITS AND SPECIFIC PHYSIOLOGICAL STATES. Some researchers search for emotion-specific patterns in the central nervous system (the brain; Gray, 1994; LeDoux, 1987; Panksepp, 1982, 1986). For instance, Gray's (1994) neuroanatomical findings (with nonhuman mammals) document the existence of three distinct brain systems, each of which regulates a distinctive pattern of emotional behavior: (1) a behavioral approach system that readies the animal to seek out and interact with attractive environmental opportunities and events, (2) a fight/flight system that readies the animal to flee or escape some aversive environmental events and to defend aggressively against others, and (3) a behavioral inhibition system that readies the animal to freeze in the face of aversive environmental events. These three systems cause the four distinct emotions of joy, fear, rage, and anxiety and therefore correspond to unique and specific physiological states.

Overall, the conclusion is that four emotions possess distinct patterns of peripheral (autonomic nervous and endocrine systems) physiological activity (namely, anger, fear, disgust, and sadness) whereas three emotion systems possess distinct patterns of (subcortical) central nervous system physiological activity (joy, rage, fear, and anxiety).

NEURAL ACTIVATION. Another physiologically based answer to the question of what causes an emotion is neural activation, namely, that different emotions are activated by different rates of cortical neural firing (Tomkins, 1970). Neural firing refers to the pattern of electrocortical activity at any given time in the neocortex. According to Tomkins, there are three basic patterns: activity (or rate of neural firing) increases, activity decreases, or activity remains constant. Whether the rate of neural firing is increasing, decreasing, or constant depends mostly on environmental events. For example, if you are sleeping (a low rate of neural firing, as measured by the electroencephalogram, or EEG) and the cat jumps on your face (a stimulating event), the rate of neural firing will increase. If you are at a rock concert (another stimulating event) and then exit to relative quiet, the rate of neural firing will decrease. Other times, neural activity is constant, as in persistent cognitive effort while reading the newspaper.

With these three basic patterns of neural firing, the person is equipped for virtually every contingency in terms of cortical activity. If neural firing suddenly increases, the person experiences one class of emotions—surprise, fear, or interest, with the specific emotion depending on the suddenness of the increased rate of neural firing. A very gradual increase in neural firing activates interest, a gradual increase activates fear, and a sudden increase activates surprise. If neural firing reaches and maintains a high level, then the constant (and high) neural firing activates either distress or anger, depending on the magnitude of the neural stimulation. Rapid neural firing activates distress, whereas very rapid neural firing activates anger. Finally, if neural firing decreases, joy is activated, as the individual laughs and smiles with the relief and neural relaxation. Figure 12.1 illustrates each specific emotion as activated from these changes in the rate of neural firing.

FIGURE 12–1
Emotion Activation as Function of Changes in Rate of Neural Firing in the Cortex

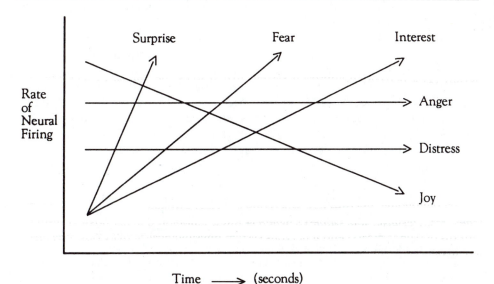

SOURCE: Tomkins, S. S. (1970). Affect as the primary motivational system. In M. B. Arnold (Ed.)., *Feelings and Emotions* (pp. 101–110). New York: Academic Press.

Consider the neural activity of an audience watching a horror movie. First, the audience is slowly introduced to the characters, setting, and circumstances of the plot. All this new information gradually increases neural firing and the audience becomes interested. Suddenly, the crazy man with an axe jumps out from behind the bushes, an event that drastically increases the audience's neural firing. The audience feels surprised, at least for a fleeting second. Later, the audience watches the protagonist move through the dark forest, hearing unfamiliar noises and seeing strange sights. The audience's neural firing quickens and arouses a feeling of fear. Of course, the hero and heroine conquer the crazy man in the end, a resolution that lessens the audience's rate of neural firing and activates joy.

FACIAL FEEDBACK HYPOTHESIS

Proponents of the facial feedback hypothesis assert that human beings possess innate, genetically wired, emotion-specific programs in the subcortical brain. When activated, these programs generate discrete facial expressions and a particular pattern of changes in the ANS and endocrine system (respiratory rate, cardiovascular activity, vocalizations). Supposedly, then, our evolutionary past equipped our subcortical brains with emotion-specific programs for anger, for fear, and so on, and when the anger program is activated, our facial muscles and bodies change in predictable ways. What is most controversial about the facial feedback hypothesis, however, is the definition of emotion as an awareness of proprioceptive feedback from facial behavior. According to the facial feedback hypothesis, the subjective aspect of emotion stems from feelings arising from (1) movements of the facial musculature, (2) changes in facial temperature, and (3) changes in glandular activity in the facial skin. Therefore, emotions are "sets of muscle and glandular responses located in the face" (Tomkins, 1962, p. 243).

Consider the following sequence of events to understand how sensations from the face feed back to the cortical brain to produce emotional experience. A quick increase in neural firing activates a subcortical emotion program (e.g., fear), and the facial musculature quickly displays a fear expression. Within microseconds, the brain interprets the facial feedback from drawn back corners of the mouth, decreased facial temperature, and activated glandular secretions, and this particular pattern of facial feedback gives rise to the feeling of fear. Once fear is activated, the whole body typically becomes involved. The glandular-hormonal, cardiovascular, and respiratory systems, for example, are aroused and their activity amplifies and sustains the fear experience.

Facial feedback does only one job: emotion activation (Izard, 1989, 1994). Facial feedback instantaneously activates an emotion program. The emotion program, not the facial feedback, then arouses cognitive and bodily participation to continue the emotional experience beyond activation. Thus, following emotion activation from facial feedback, people monitor not their facial feedback but their changes in heart rate, respiratory rate, muscle tonus, and how much they perspire. People also monitor their posture and gestures. These bodily changes maintain the emotional experience over time. Nonetheless, it is the facial feedback that activates the chain of events that underlie the emotion experience.

Figure 12.2 illustrates the sequential process of emotional activation, according to Izard (1991). Internal (memory) or external (e.g., a loud firecracker) events change the gradient in neural firing (see Fig. 12.1). Impulses from the neocortex are directed to the limbic system. The limbic system plays a key role in emotion differentiation by determining which particular facial expression will be effected. From the limbic system, impulses go to the basal ganglia, which organize the neural message for facial expression and send excitatory impulses to the motor cortex. Impulses from the motor cortex travel through the facial nerve (cranial nerve VII) and produce a specific facial expression. In the facial musculature, specific muscles are contracted and relaxed and changes in blood flow and glandular secretions occur. The trigeminal nerve (cranial nerve V) relays the changing proprioceptive stimulation to the sensory cortex. Finally, cortical integration of the proprioceptive stimulation generates the subjective experience of emotion. It is in the frontal lobe of the neocortex that

FIGURE 12–2
Sequence of Neurological Events in Facial Feedback Hypothesis

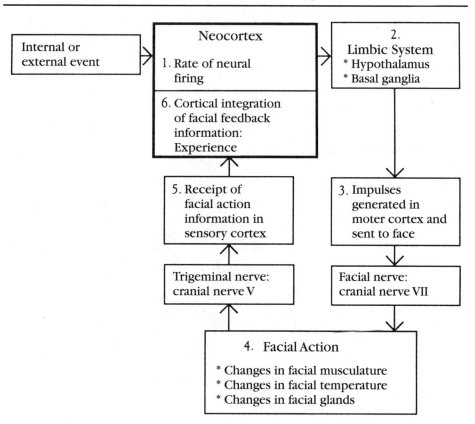

the individual eventually becomes aware of the emotional experience at a conscious level.

Musculature of the Face

Descriptions of facial expressions rely on the particular muscles that produce them (Ekman & Friesen, 1978). There are 80 facial muscles, three dozen of which are involved in facial expression. For purposes of exposition, however, eight facial muscles are sufficient to differentiate among the basic emotions. Figure 12.3 shows the eight major muscles underlying human facial expressions (for more information, see Ekman & Friesen, 1978; Izard, 1971). The upper section of the face (the eyes and forehead) has three major muscles—the frontalis, corrugator, and orbicularis oculi. The frontalis covers the forehead, the corrugators lie beneath each eyebrow, and the orbicularis oculi is the circular muscle surrounding each eye. The middle section of the face has two major muscles, the zygomaticus and nasalis. The zygomaticus extends from the corner of the mouth to the cheekbone, and the nasalis wrinkles the nose. Finally, the lower section of the face has three major muscles—the

FIGURE 12–3
Eight Major Facial Muscles

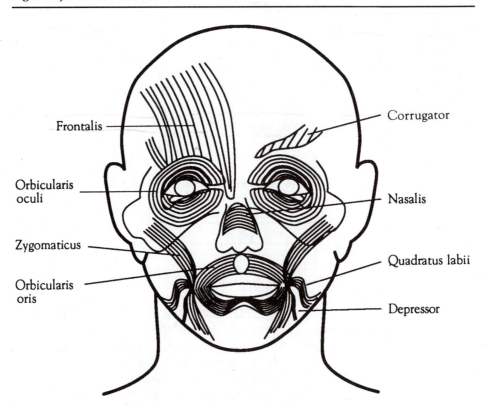

FIGURE 12–4
Facial Expressions for Five Emotions

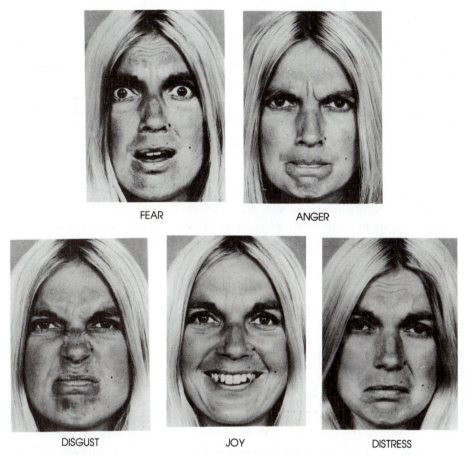

FEAR   ANGER

DISGUST   JOY   DISTRESS

SOURCE: Ekman, P., & Friesen, W. V. (1975). *Unmasking the face.* Englewood Ciffs, NJ: Prentice Hall.

depressor, orbicularis oris, and quadratus labii. The depressor draws the corner of the mouth downward, the orbicularis oris is the circular muscle surrounding the lips, and the quadratus labii draws the corners of the mouth backward.

Particular patterns of facial behavior produce discrete emotional signals. Anger, fear, disgust, distress, and joy, for instance, are each associated with a particular pattern of facial behavior (Ekman & Friesen, 1978), as shown in Figure 12.4. For anger, the corrugators draw the eyebrows inward and downward, the orbicularis oculi tenses the lower eyelid upward so the eyes have a hard stare appearance, and the orbicularis oris presses the lips firmly together. For fear, the corrugators raise the inner corners of the eyebrows, the contracted frontalis produces horizontal wrinkles, the orbicularis oculi raises the upper eyelid and tenses the lower eyelid, and quadratus labii pulls the lips tightly backwards. For disgust, the orbicularis oris raises the upper lip, the nasalis wrinkles the nose, and the zygomaticus raises the cheeks. For sadness, the corrugators raise and draw together the inner corners of the eyelids, the orbicularis oculi raises the upper eyelid inner corner, and the depressors pull the corners of the lips down. For joy, the corners of the lips are pulled back and slightly up by the zygomaticus quadratus labii, and the cheeks raise and push the lower eyelid up. Recent research also supports the conclusion that two additional emotions are associated with a particular pattern of facial behavior—interest (Reeve, 1993) and contempt (Ekman & Friesen, 1986).

Test of the Facial Feedback Hypothesis (FFH)

Pause for a moment and look sad. As you do, pay close attention to the changing sensations of your facial musculature. If you have just moved your mouth by pulling down the depressors and pushing out the lower lip (orbicularis oris) in a pout, you probably did not feel too sad. Now try to produce another sad face, but this time move your eyebrows inward as well. Pretend that you have a couple of golf tees attached to the inner corners of the eyebrows (about an inch apart and pointing outward such that the base of the tee rests on the eyebrow and the tip of the tee extends out perpendicularly from the face; Larsen, Kasimatis, & Frey, 1992, p. 328). Now, move your corrugators inward until the tips of the golf tees touch. Hold your eyebrows this way, and move your lower face as before (orbicularis oris pouts the lower lip, depressors pull down the corners of the lips). Feel the sensory changes. Do you sense a hint of a sad feeling? If so, the feeling will be mild because a posed facial expression is not as authentic and feeling producing as is a spontaneous one. But, the mild sad feeling via a patterned facial expression is a good way to introduce empirical tests of the facial feedback hypothesis.

Feedback from facial behavior, when transformed into conscious awareness, constitutes the experience of emotion (Laird, 1974; Tomkins, 1962, 1963). Much energy has been devoted to the test of Tomkins' facial feedback hypothesis (FFH). The studies relevant to the FFH use one of two general methodologies, because it is generally accepted that there are two testable versions of the FFH (Rutledge & Hupka, 1985). The two variations are termed its strong and weak versions. In its strong version, the FFH proposes that manipulating one's facial musculature into a pattern that corresponds to an emotion display will activate that emotional experience. In other words, smiling will activate joy, and frowning will activate distress.

To test the strong version of the FFH, an experimenter instructs a participant to contract and relax specific muscles of the face (as with the imaginary golf tees on the brow) and, with the pattern of facial musculature common to a specific emotion activated, complete a questionnaire to assess emotional experience. For example, in one study, participants were instructed to (1) "raise your brows and pull them together," (2) "now raise your upper eyelids," and (3) "now also stretch your lips horizontally, back towards your ears" (Ekman, Levenson, & Friesen, 1983). So posed, the participants were asked about their emotional state. In this case, in accordance with the hypothesis, the participant would express feelings of fear on a questionnaire rating scale. Research has both supported (Laird, 1974, 1984; Larsen, Kasimatis,

& Frey, 1992; Rutledge & Hupka, 1985; Strack, Martin, & Stepper, 1988) and refuted (McCaul, Holmes, & Solomon, 1982; Tourangeau & Ellsworth, 1979) the strong version of the FFH. One area of consensus among these researchers is that a posed facial musculature produces reliable changes in physiological reactions, such as changes in cardiovascular and respiratory rates (Tourangeau & Ellsworth, 1979; Ekman, Levenson, & Friesen, 1983). It is still debated whether the posed facial musculature produces emotional experience, but most studies suggest that it does, though the facial feedback effect is small (see Adelmann & Zajonc, 1989; Izard, 1990; Laird, 1984; Matsumoto, 1987; Rutledge & Hupka, 1985). Perhaps the conclusion from the research on the strong version is that posed expressions can activate emotions, but the experience is short-lived and seems to produce a more discernable effect on bodily states (Izard, 1981).

In its weaker, more conservative version, the FFH proposes that facial feedback modifies the intensity of ongoing emotion. Thus, managing one's facial musculature into a particular emotional display will augment (exaggerate) but not necessarily activate the emotional experience. In other words, if you intentionally smile *when you are already joyful,* then you will feel relatively intense joy. Consider an early experimental test of the weak version of the facial feedback hypothesis (Zuckerman, Klorman, Larrance, & Spiegel, 1981). Participants either exaggerated or suppressed their spontaneous facial expressions while watching a video. The videos depicted either a pleasant (Carol Burnett show), neutral (apple harvest scenes), or unpleasant (traffic fatalities) scenario. Results indicated that exaggerating the facial expressions did augment emotional and physiological experience, and suppressing the facial expressions moderated the intensity of the emotional and physiological experience. In a similar experiment, participants exaggerated or suppressed their facial expressions during a series of electric shocks (Lanzetta, Cartwright-Smith & Kleck, 1976). As before, the exaggeration of spontaneous facial expressions led participants to experience the shocks as significantly more painful than did the suppression of facial expressions.

Unlike its stronger version, the weaker version of the FFH has received a consensus of support. Facial management does moderate emotional experience, and human beings can intensify or reduce naturally occurring emotional experience by exaggerating or suppressing facial actions. The central issue in the debate is not, however, whether facial behavior contributes to emotional experience. Rather, the question is the degree to which facial expressions cause emotional experience (Matsumoto, 1987). Proponents of the facial feedback hypothesis highlight the two-way street between the emotions we feel and the emotions we express: Emotions activate facial expressions and facial expressions, in turn, feed back to exaggerate and suppress the emotions we feel. Critics of the FFH contend that the contribution of such facial feedback is small and therefore trivial. Matsumoto (1987), for example, used a sophisticated quantitative technique for summarizing evidence from a number of studies (meta-analysis) to demonstrate that the effect of feedback from facial behavior on emotional experience was small to moderate. Critics such as Matsumoto argue that factors other than facial feedback are more important and therefore more worthy of serious attention.

Voluntary and Involuntary Facial Expressions

Before 18 to 24 months of age, the facial expressions of the human infant are largely involuntary. When infants are distressed by hunger, the face reflects this inner state. Similarly, when infants are surprised or joyous, the facial expression reflects these internal states. Infants make woeful actors. As infants acquire language, undergo rapid cognitive development, and become increasingly social beings, they acquire an increasing ability to control facial expressions voluntarily. By the preschool years, children can mask (inhibit) most inner states. With increased cognitive development, children become increasingly capable of voluntary control of the facial musculature.

IS FACIAL BEHAVIOR LEARNED OR INNATE? There are two major motor systems in the nervous system, one that regulates the voluntary musculature and one that regulates the involuntary musculature. The pyramidal system controls precise and voluntary control of localized movements (Rinn, 1984; Weil, 1974). For example, the pyramidal system controls the muscles involved in the intentional, socially polite smile. The nonpyramidal system regulates nonspecific and involuntary control of general muscle tonus and facial behaviors under involuntary control. The nonpyramidal system produces the spontaneous smile, as in the automatic reaction to a funny joke. The significance of the distinction between the pyramidal and nonpyramidal systems is that it addresses the question of whether facial expressions are innate and automated or learned and modifiable. Much facial behavior is surely learned. It is a rare individual who has not learned the polite smile and the inhibition of the angry face while talking with the boss. But the fact that some facial behavior is learned (and therefore under voluntary control) does not rule out the possibility that facial behavior also has a genetic, innate component, as proposed by the proponents of the FFH.

A series of cross-cultural investigations tested the proposition that human beings display similar facial expressions regardless of differences in environmental or cultural backgrounds (Ekman, 1972, 1994b; Izard, 1994). In each of these studies, representatives from diverse nationalities looked at three photographs, each of a different facial expression (Ekman, 1972, 1993; Ekman & Friesen, 1971; Ekman, Sorenson, & Friesen, 1969; Izard, 1971, 1980, 1994). From the three photographs, participants chose, via a multiple-choice format, the photograph that best expressed a particular emotion. For example, participants were shown photographs of three faces, one expressing anger, one expressing joy, and one expressing fear. The participants selected the picture they thought showed anger (or fear or joy, as the case may be). The research question is whether persons from different cultures agree on which facial expressions correspond with which emotional experiences. The finding that persons from different cultures match the same facial expressions with the same emotional experiences is evidence that facial behavior is cross-culturally universal, which is supportive evidence that facial behavior has an innate, unlearned component (Ekman, 1994b).

Glance at the photographs shown in Figure 12.5 to test yourself as the participants in the cross-cultural experiments were tested. The photographs show four dif-

FIGURE 12–5
Which Facial Expression Shows Disgust?

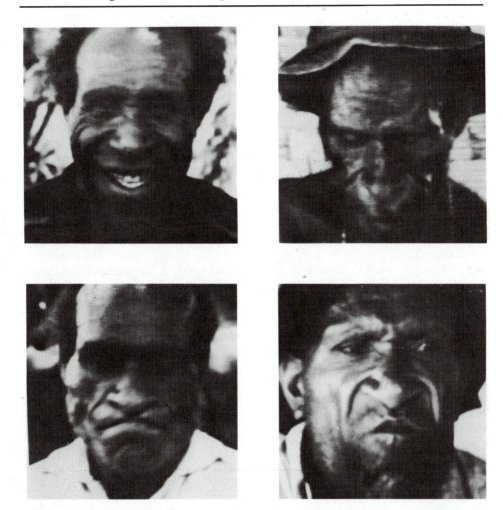

The photograph of the New Guinea native expressing disgust appears in the lower right corner.
Clockwise from the bottom left are expressions of anger, joy, and distress.

SOURCE: Ekman, P. (1972). Universal and cultural difference in facial expression of emotion. In J. R. Cole's
(Ed.), Nebraska symposium on motivation (Vol. 19, pp. 207–283). Lincoln: University of Nebraska Press.

ferent expressions of a New Guinea native. Your task is to identify the photograph
of the man who feels disgust. Ekman and Friesen (1971) conducted an experiment
such as the one described in Figure 12.5 with people from five different cultures:
Brazil, United States, Argentina, Chile, and Japan. They found substantial cultural
agreement in emotion expressions. Izard (1971) also presented the expression-
emotion matching test to people from the United States, Great Britain, Germany,
Sweden, France, Switzerland, Greece, and Japan. Participants from each of these

eight cultures correctly matched emotions with expressions at much greater than chance, suggesting an innate, universal component to facial expressions.

Research with infants supports the idea that facial behavior has a strong innate component (Izard et al., 1980) in that infants show distinct, identifiable facial expressions in response to particular emotion cues. Blind children, who lack opportunity to learn facial expressions from others through modeling and imitation, show the same recognizable facial expressions as do sighted children of the same age (Goodenough, 1932). Severely mentally handicapped children also show full expressions of the emotions (Eibl-Eibesfeldt, 1971). Because severely mentally retarded children frequently find it difficult to perform the behaviors necessary to control a fork, one would think that the learning of facial expressions would be even more difficult, unless facial expressions were innate and required little or no learning.

The involuntary (nonpyramidal) and voluntary (pyramidal) motor systems typically work together to produce moment-to-moment facial expressions of emotion. Almost any facial expression is the product of both systems, though the contributions of each system are rarely equal (Rinn, 1984). In unconstrained circumstances (when we are alone), facial expressions are relatively more automated, and emotional experience corresponds highly to expression. In constrained circumstances (when we are in public), facial expressions are relatively more managed, and emotional experience corresponds only roughly to expression. Hence, the pyramidal motor system typically dominates in social situations, whereas the nonpyramidal motor system typically dominates in nonsocial settings.

Just because facial expressions such as a smile can be produced by voluntary or involuntary muscles does not necessarily mean that the two smiles are interchangeable (Frank, Ekman, & Friesen, 1993). Spontaneous, enjoyment-motivated smiles show a more even duration and smoothness than intentional, socially motivated smiles. And we can distinguish an enjoyment-motivated (involuntary) smile from a socially-motivated (voluntary) smile. Further, we rate people who smile spontaneously more positively than we rate people who smile intentionally (Frank, Ekman, & Friesen, 1993).

Can We Voluntarily Control our Emotions?

One of the more intriguing questions in emotion research asks, can we voluntarily control our emotions? (Ekman & Davidson, 1994). The difficulty in providing a definitive answer emerges when you recall that emotions have four aspects—subjective, physiological, functional, and expressive. Emotion's multidimensional nature begs the question whether feelings are controllable, whether heart rate and other physiological states are controllable, whether our motivational desires are controllable, and whether our facial expressions are controllable (as discussed earlier). In trying to answer the more general question, however, some emotions plainly happen to us, and we therefore cannot be held responsible for the involuntary feelings, physiology, desires, and behaviors that ensue (Ekman, 1992, 1994a). Consistent with the idea that emotions happen to us (i.e., emotions are involuntarily), we all have difficulty conjuring up an emotion at will—courage, love, optimism, interest, and so on. Instead, we need an emotion-generating event to conjure up an emotion. Emotions are reactions, and we need something to react to before conjuring up an emotion.

Daily experience confirms that we can voluntarily regulate emotions once they happen to us, at least to some extent. Intentionally, we mask and hide our fear before bungee jumping, and we suppress our boredom while listening to another's conversation. Because we can regulate our emotions, through inhibition mostly (Levenson, 1994), we are somewhat responsible for our emotionality (e.g., how angry or sad we get and how long we stay that way). Therefore, emotional onsets are difficult to control, but our capacity for emotional regulation allows us control over the rise, fall, and intensity of our emotions (Averill, 1994; Ekman, 1992; Levenson, 1994).

If emotions are largely biological phenomena that are governed by subcortical structures and pathways, it makes sense that much of an emotion will escape our voluntary control. If, however, emotions are largely cognitive phenomena that are governed by thoughts, beliefs, and ways of thinking, it makes sense that a good deal of emotional experience can be controlled (at least to the point that thoughts, beliefs, and ways of thinking can be controlled).

DIFFERENTIAL EMOTIONS THEORY

Differential emotions theory takes its name from its emphasis on basic emotions serving unique, or different, motivational forces (Izard, 1991, 1992, 1993; Izard & Malatesta, 1987). The theory endorses the following five core assumptions (after Izard, 1991):

1. Ten discrete emotions constitute the principal motivation system for human beings.
2. Each discrete emotion has a unique subjective, phenomenological quality.
3. Each discrete emotion has a unique facial-expressive pattern.
4. Each discrete emotion has a specific rate of neural firing that activates the emotion into consciousness.
5. Each discrete emotion leads to different behavioral consequences.

Each of the ten discrete emotions, therefore, is defined in terms of its unique subjective feeling, facial expression, rate of neural firing, and behavioral consequences. The central assertion of differential emotions theory (assumption 1) is that emotions are essentially motivational systems that prepare the individual to act in adaptive ways (Izard, 1989, 1991, 1992). Each emotion is inherently adaptive and each emotion has its own unique organization and motivational properties. Of the 10 discrete emotions, listed in Table 12.3, two are phenomenologically positive (interest and joy), seven are phenomenologically negative (fear, anger, disgust, distress, contempt, shame, and guilt), and one is phenomenologically neutral (surprise).

TABLE 12–3

Izard's 10 Fundamental Emotions

POSITIVE	NEGATIVE	NEUTRAL
Interest	Fear	Surprise
Joy	Anger	
	Disgust	
	Distress	
	Contempt	
	Shame	
	Guilt	

Emotion Combinations

Students' typical first reaction to a list of the 10 basic emotions is, where are the emotions of love and hate, of anxiety and depression? Differential emotions are fundamental emotions, in part because they produce distinct facial expressions. Because love, hate, anxiety, and depression do not produce distinct facial expressions, these affective states are not basic emotions per se. According to Izard, if two or more of the fundamental emotions are experienced in rapid succession, the individual experiences a "pattern of emotion." Emotion patterns are combinations of successive basic emotions. For instance, love is an emotion pattern resulting from the combination of interest that is repetitively followed by joy. If this emotion pattern of interest-joy is concurrent with the sex drive, then romantic love is experienced. (Izard acknowledges, however, that love also has a substantial cognitive component featuring expectations, goals, and memories.) Hate (or hostility) is an emotion pattern derived from the combination of anger, disgust, and contempt. According to Izard (1975, 1977), the prominence of each of these emotions within the hate pattern gives hate its particular characteristics. The predominance of anger characterizes hate as aggression; the predominance of disgust characterizes hate as an active avoidance of the hated object; and the predominance of contempt characterizes hate as acts associated with prejudice. Anxiety is an emotion pattern that combines fear with two or more of the following emotions: distress, anger, shame, guilt, and interest (Izard, 1975). Depression is an emotion pattern involving a complex combination among all of the negative emotions (Izard, 1972).

Ekman (1992) has several answers to explain why biologically minded theorists do not count jealousy, hope, love, smugness, and so on among the basic emotions. Consider Ekman's seven answers to explain why there are really only a small number of basic emotions and why emotions such as jealousy, hope, and love are not counted among them:

1. Emotion families exist, such that many nonbasic emotions are experienced-based derivatives of a single basic emotion (e.g., anxiety is a derivative of fear).
2. Many emotion terms really describe moods (e.g., apprehension, irritation).
3. Many emotion terms really describe attitudes (e.g., love, hatred).

4. Many emotion terms really describe personality traits (e.g., hostile).
5. Many emotion terms really describe disorders (e.g., depression, anxiety).
6. Some nonbasic emotions are blends of basic emotions (as discussed).
7. Many emotion words refer to specific aspects of a basic emotion (e.g., what elicits the emotion (homesickness) or how a person behaves (gaiety, aggression).

OPPONENT-PROCESS THEORY

Experience suggests that we react to situations with a single emotion. For example, during an examination students feel afraid, and that fear fades after the exam is over. Opponent-process theory argues against this commonsense description (Solomon, 1980). Instead, a hedonically opposite (or opponent) emotional experience replaces the original emotion immediately on the removal of the emotion-generating event. It is the opponent emotion, not the original emotion, that gradually decays. To continue the example, the student feels afraid during the examination but also a rebound of joy after it is over. Joy, not anxiety, is the emotion that eventually decays (Craig & Siegel, 1980). Figure 12.6 shows the difference between common experience and the opponent-process theory.

The fundamental assumption driving opponent-process theory is that mammalian brains resist any departure from emotional neutrality, regardless of whether that departure is pleasurable or aversive. Any emotional response, because it displaces emotional neutrality, activates a brain-triggered opposing process to counter, or neutralize, that departure (Solomon, 1977a, 1977b, 1980, 1982; Solomon & Corbit, 1973, 1974). These brain-triggered countermechanisms are fully automatic and unconscious. Automatically, the brain generates an aversion process to counter any pleasure, and the brain generates a pleasurable process to counter any aversion. These counter (rebound) emotional processes serve as the brain's attempt to restore emotional neutrality.

FIGURE 12–6
Two Views of Emotional Experience

Before Stimulus	During Stimulus	After Removal of Stimulus
	Common Experience View	
Baseline	→Emotion	→ Gradual Return to Baseline
	Opponent-Process View	
Baseline	→Emotion	→ Hedonically Opposite Emotion → Gradual Return to Baseline

Baseline equals emotional neutrality.

Time Course of Affective Reaction to Stimulus

Figure 12.7 illustrates the standard pattern of affective dynamics. Panel 1 presents five distinct phases produced by exposure to an emotion-generating stimulus. The first phase is the peak of the primary hedonic emotional state (A), which follows immediately after the presentation of the stimulus. As the stimulus continues, the primary emotion declines somewhat in a short period of adaptation. As long as the stimulus endures, the primary emotion settles into a steady level. The removal of the stimulus initiates the rise of a hedonically opposite emotion (B), the fourth phase in opponent-process theory. Lastly, the opposite emotion begins to decay and subsequently disappears.

Panel 3 of Figure 12.7 presents these same five phases—(1) peak of primary emotion, (2) adaptation, (3) maintenance of primary emotion, (4) peak of opposite emotion, and (5) decay of opposite emotion—applied to a frequently repeated stimulus. With repeated exposure, the brain gradually acquires the capacity to counteract the original emotional reaction. The opponent process gains strength and builds up over time to suppress (neutralize) the original emotion.

Panel 2 of Figure 12.7 illustrates how these brain mechanisms integrate over time. The primary emotion (state A) remains a constant, while the opponent emotional reaction (state B) grows in intensity. The A state is a stable emotional reaction and is fully a function of the properties of the emotion-generating stimulus in its intensity and duration. A mild shock, for example, produces a weak fear, whereas a potent shock produces a strong fear. The opponent B state, on the other hand, is aroused by the A state (not by the stimulus). The B state strengthens with use and weakens with disuse. A comparison of panel 1 and panel 3 shows that only the opponent process changes with time. With repeated use, the B state grows by acquiring a (1) shorter latency of onset, (2) greater intensity, and (3) longer decay time.

Opponent-process theory offers three fundamental principles: affective contrast, affective habituation, and affective withdrawal (Solomon, 1980). *Contrast* refers to the emergence of an emotion opposite to the original stimulus-caused emotion. Contrast explains why we feel relief (or even joy) following the termination of events that make us suffer. *Habituation* refers to a tolerance effect in which the brain's emotional reaction is progressively less intense to any repeated stimulus event. For example, the novice coffee drinker experiences an unpleasant bitter taste, but the veteran drinker gets use to it. Lastly, *withdrawal* refers to the lingering effects of an opponent-process emotion. For example, after a person takes a euphoria-inducing drug several times, its absence produces a long-lasting craving. The craving is the affective withdrawal. The principles of contrast, habituation, and withdrawal explain how opponent processes regulate emotional experience.

Costs of Pleasure and Benefits of Pain

The consequences of the brain's buildup of a strong B state have been called the "costs of pleasure" and the "benefits of pain" (Solomon, 1980). That is, the brain produces aversion to counter pleasurable experiences (the costs of pleasure) and pleasure to counter aversive experiences (the benefits of pain).

FIGURE 12–7
Affective Dynamics of Opponent-Process Theory

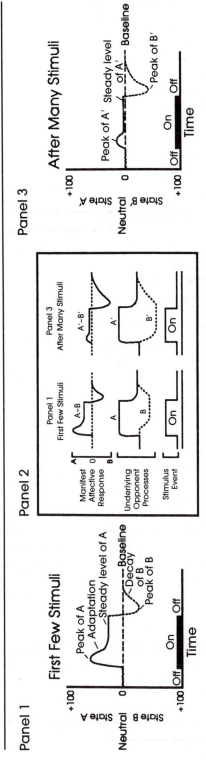

SOURCE: Solomon, R. L., & Corbit, J. D. (1974). An opponent-process theory of motivation. *Psychological Review, 81,* 119–145. Copyright © 1974 by American Psychological Association. Adapted with permission.

COSTS OF PLEASURE. According to opponent-process theory, repeated pleasures lose much of their pleasantness over time. In fact, repeated pleasures make the person susceptible to new sources of suffering. Consider two examples presented in Table 12.4: opiate drug usage and dating.

The emotional experience produced by the first few exposures to each attractive stimulus brings pleasure and reward. Taking opiate drugs and entertaining dates produce positive emotion in the form of a rush, euphoria, and feelings of excitement. When the drug wears off or the date ends, there is, at first, a mild craving for the return of the positive emotion-generating event. This mild craving quickly dissipates, and the person returns to emotional neutrality. Repeated encounters, however, soon give rise to the cost of pleasure, as illustrated on the right in Table 12.4. The emotional experience before the often-repeated stimulus event is no longer a baseline neutral state (as it was for early stimuli). Rather, because the opponent B state persists for a long time after the last stimulus exposure, the before-stimulus emotional state is one of a mild craving for the absent stimulus. During stimulus presentation, the emotional experience is only modest pleasure (because of affective habituation). When the stimulus is again removed (the drug wears off, the date ends), the individual experiences the strongest of sufferings (the strong B state).

BENEFITS OF PAIN. As repeated pleasures lose much of their pleasantness, repeated aversive events lose much of their unpleasantness. In fact, repeated aversive experiences make the person capable of new sources of pleasure. Table 12.4 provides two examples of the benefits of pain: parachuting and sauna bathing.

The emotional experience produced by a first exposure to parachuting and sauna bathing brings pain and aversion in the form of physical and emotional suffering. When the parachutist lands and the bather exits the sauna, there is, at first, a sense of relief and mild satisfaction. This mild satisfaction quickly abates and the individual returns to emotional neutrality. The benefits of repeated pain emerge on the right in the table. Following repeated encounters with an aversive event, the experience before the stimulus presentation is not emotional neutrality (baseline). Rather, the veteran parachutist and the veteran sauna bather feel a mild eagerness to begin, a remnant of the residual, long-lasting B state. During stimulus presentation, the emotional experiences occasioned by each of these aversive stimuli habituates to mild anxiety. When the stimulus is again removed (the parachutist lands, the bather exits), they experience the strongest of pleasures (a strong B state): a rush, euphoria, and excitement.

ACQUIRED MOTIVATION. Opponent-process theory illustrates how pleasure and aversion can be learned or acquired. Consider the example of opiate usage once more. Initially, the motivation to take the drug is the pursuit of pleasure. With repeated usage, the individual builds up a tolerance, and the B state grows in intensity and its presence continues for a longer and longer time; the drug soon gives little pleasure but much aversive after effect. Because the aftereffect is so aversive and because it takes so long to decay, the opiate drug user begins to acquire a motiva-

TABLE 12–4
Costs of Pleasure and Benefits of Pain Applied to Four Stimuli

	First Few Exposures			After Many Exposures		
	Before Presentation	During Exposure	After Removal	Before Presentation	During Exposure	After Removal
Pleasurable Stimuli						
Taking Opiate Drugs	Baseline emotion	Rush, euphoria, excitement	Mild craving for drug	Mild craving for drug	Contentment, satisfaction	Intense craving, withdrawal syndrome
Dating	Baseline emotion	Rush, euphoria, excitement	Mild craving for boyfriend/girlfriend	Mild craving for boyfriend/girlfriend	Contentment, satisfaction	Intense grief, loneliness
Aversive Stimuli						
Parachuting	Baseline emotion	Fear, anxiety	Relief, mild satisfaction	Mild eagerness	Mild anxiety	Rush, euphoria, excitement
Sauna Bathing	Baseline emotion	Fear, anxiety	Relief, mild satisfaction	Mild eagerness	Mild discomfort	Rush, euphoria, excitement

tion to escape from the aversive, long-lasting B state. The motivation to take the drug becomes less and less the pursuit of pleasure (because the B state has neutralized the A state) and more and more the avoidance of pain (because the B state is aversive and long lasting). Hence, for the repeat opiate drug user, there are now two motivations for taking the drug: (1) to experience the drug-induced feeling of pleasure and (2) to avoid or escape from the brain-triggered acquired feeling of agony from the absence of the drug. The drug abuser is first motivated by curiosity, then by pleasure, and finally by the escape from pain and a desire to feel normal (Zuckerman, 1987a, 1987b).

Opponent-process theory helps explain some of the apparent masochism of everyday life, as people come to enjoy many initially aversive experiences. People enjoy having their lungs collapsed on a roller coaster, being brought to tears by a chili pepper, feeling utter fear jumping out of an airplane, suffering through donating blood, tasting coffee or alcohol, crying at sad movies, breast-feeding their infants, feeling exhausted after a marathon run, or diving into near-freezing water (Meyers & Siegel, 1985; Piliavin, Callero, & Evans, 1982; Rozin & Schiller, 1980). But opponent-process theory does not presume that *all* initially aversive experiences will eventually produce acquired pleasure, nor does it presume that *all* initially pleasurable experiences will eventually produce acquired aversion (Sandvik, Diener, & Larsen, 1987). Rather, opponent-process theory applies best to acquired pains from addiction-related phenomena and acquired pleasures from physical, sensory stimuli that produce fear and distress reactions (Mauro, 1988).

SUMMARY

Emotions serve a purpose. From a functional point of view, emotions evolved as biological reactions that help us adapt successfully to fundamental life tasks such as facing a threat or an obstacle. The emotion that arises during a life task energizes and directs behavior in a way that the course of evolution proved to be most effective. Hence, emotions possess an inherent coping function. In addition, emotions serve social purposes. Emotions communicate our feelings to others, affect how others interact with us, invite and facilitate social interaction, and play a pivotal role in creating, maintaining, and dissolving interpersonal relationships.

The coping function of an emotion revolves around its capacity to prepare and involve the body's autonomic nervous system, endocrine system, neural brain circuits, rate of neural firing, and facial feedback in the coping process. Emotions energize and direct bodily actions (e.g., running, fighting) by affecting the autonomic nervous system and its regulation of the heart, lungs, and muscles; by affecting the endocrine system and its regulation of glands, hormones, and organs; by affecting neural brain circuits such as those in the limbic system; by affecting the rate of neural firing and hence the pace of information processing; and by affecting facial feedback and discrete patterns of the facial musculature.

Tomkins' facial feedback theory of emotion asserts that the subjective aspect of emotion is actually the awareness of proprioceptive feedback from facial action.

Facial feedback is so rapid and reflexive that it escapes conscious awareness, but facial feedback does activate emotion. Once activated, other factors, such as external stimuli and physiological arousal, maintain the emotion over time. The facial feedback hypothesis appears in the research literature in two forms, weak and strong. According to its strong version, posed facial expressions activate specific emotions such that a full smile activates joy. According to its weak version, exaggerated and suppressed facial expressions augment and attenuate naturally occurring emotion. Although research is mixed on the strong version, considerable evidence confirms the validity of the weaker version of the facial feedback hypothesis. Facial management does moderate emotional experience, and human beings can intensify or reduce naturally occurring emotional experience by exaggerating or suppressing facial actions.

According to differential emotions theory, there are 10 fundamental emotions. For Izard, an emotion is basic if it (1) has a unique subjective quality, (2) has a unique facial expression, (3) has a unique pattern of neural firing, and (4) leads to a unique set of behavioral consequences. Differential emotions theory's central assertion is that each basic emotion is inherently adaptive and has its own organizational and motivational properties. The basic emotions according to this theory are interest, joy, fear, anger, disgust, distress, contempt, shame, guilt, and surprise.

According to opponent-process theory, emotions of pleasure and pain can be acquired. In this theory, a hedonically opposite (rebound) emotion follows immediately after and replaces the initial stimulus-elicited emotion. Such a portrayal of brain functioning offers a promising framework in which to understand the costs of pleasure and the benefits of pain. In respect to the costs of pleasure, positive events such as opiate drugs, dating, and social attachments lose much of their initial pleasure and eventually give rise to an acquired source of suffering (intense cravings, grief, loneliness). In respect to the benefits of pain, aversive events such as parachuting, sauna bathing, marathon running, and donating blood lose much of their initial pain and eventually give rise to new, acquired sources of pleasure (rush, euphoria, excitement).

RECOMMENDED READINGS

Ekman, P. (1993). Facial expression and emotion. *American Psychologist, 48*, 384–392.

Izard, C.E. (1989). The structure and functions of emotions: Implications for cognition, motivation, and personality. In I.S. Cohen (Ed.), *The G. Stanley Hall lecture series* (Vol. 9, pp. 39–73). Washington, DC: APA.

Kraut, R.E., & Johnston, R.E. (1979). Social and emotional messages of smiling: An ethological approach. *Journal of Personality and Social Psychology, 37*, 1539–1553.

Laird, J.D. (1974). Self-attribution of emotion: The effects of expressive behavior on the quality of emotional experience. *Journal of Personality and Social Psychology, 29*, 475–486.

Larsen, R.J., Kasimatis, M., & Frey, K. (1992). Facilitating the furrowed brow: An unobtrusive test of the facial feedback hypothesis applied to unpleasant affect. *Cognition and Emotion, 6*, 321–338.

Levenson, R.W. (1992). Autonomic nervous system differences among emotions. *Psychological Science, 3*, 23-27.

Plutchik, R. (1970). Emotions, evolution, and adaptive processes. In M.B. Arnold (Ed.), *Feelings and emotions* (pp. 3-24). New York: Academic Press.

Rinn, W.E. (1984). The neuropsychology of facial expression: A review of the neurological and psychological mechanisms for producing facial expressions. *Psychological Bulletin, 95*, 52-77.

Solomon, R.L. (1980). The opponent-process theory of motivation: The costs of pleasure and the benefits of pain. *American Psychologist, 35*, 691-712.

Tooby & Cosmides (1990). The past explains the present: Emotional adaptations and the structure of ancestral environment. *Ethology and Sociobiology, 11*, 375-424.

Chapter 13

COGNITIVE ASPECTS OF EMOTION

Imagine that you are going downtown to enjoy a night on the town. Being environmentally conscious, you and your good mood hop on the metro bus and take a seat just behind a woman. Politely, you ask her for the time. She does not respond. You ask again, but this time with a sweet, more inviting tone of voice. Again, no response. At this point, you feel really blown off, your good mood is slipping away, and you are a bit hurt and socially embarrassed. Under your breath, you question her moral character; she is cold, uptight, and probably classist and racist too. Aggravated and feeling that you have some unfinished business to clear up, you tap the woman on the shoulder, with a hint of a bitter scowl. This time she responds. To your surprise, she begins to communicate with her hands. Her sign language tells you she simply never heard your request. In the blink of an eye, your anger is gone. She could not have acted any differently; you feel compassion. Instantly, a sociable cheerfulness rushes in to replace your irritation.

This interaction was, for you, an emotional event. With each turn of events, your anger grew and differentiated itself into aggravation, bitterness, and irritation. Experiences of being slighted, sensing self-esteem injury, and blaming the woman for her rebuffs are the sort of events that activate and regulate anger. Change the event, or the way it is interpreted, or the way you reacted to it, or the attribution you used to explain the rebuff, and you change the emotional experience—be it enjoyment, anger, aggravation, irritation, bitterness, compassion, or cheerfulness. This chapter explores the intricate and interdependent relationship between the way we think and interpret events and the way we feel. Emotion follows cognition.

COGNITIVE THEORIES OF EMOTION

For those who study emotional processes from a cognitive, social, or cultural point of view, biological contributions are not necessarily the most important aspects of emotion. Emotions also emerge from information processing, social interaction, and cultural contexts. For instance, a purely biological analysis that highlights subcortical brain circuits, autonomic and endocrine system activity, and facial expressions does not get the researcher very far when it comes to understanding emotions such as hope, pride, alienation, and romantic love. In fact, emotions such as these arise less from biological sources than from social and cultural origins. This chapter begins with a cognitive analysis of emotion and concludes with a discussion of how social and cultural factors influence emotion.

Appraisal

The central construct in a cognitive understanding of emotion is appraisal (Frijda, 1993; Smith et al., 1993). All cognitive emotion theorists endorse two interrelated beliefs: (1) Emotions do not occur without an antecedent appraisal (cognition) of the stimulus event and (2) the appraisal, not the stimulus event, causes the emotion (Frijda, 1986; Lazarus, 1991a; Ortony, Clore, & Collins, 1988; Roseman, 1984; Scherer, 1984a, Smith & Ellsworth, 1985; Weiner, 1986). Consider a child who sees a person approaching. Immediately and automatically, the child appraises the approach of the person as probably good or probably bad. The appraisal is based on the salient characteristics of the approacher (gender, facial expression, pace of approach), expectations of who might be approaching, beliefs of what approaching people typically do, and memories of people approaching her in the past. It is not the approaching man per se that leads to her emotional reaction, but, rather, how the child thinks the approaching man will affect her well-being. If she sees the approaching person smiling and waving and if she remembers the approacher is her friend, she will likely appraise the event as a good one. If she sees the approaching person ranting and raving and if she remembers the approacher is the neighborhood bully, then she will likely appraise the event as a bad one. These appraisals lead the child to experience emotion (and physiological bodily changes too).

In this illustration, the child's immediate appraisal of the stimulus as good or bad is the causal cognitive mechanism to emotional experience. If the child did not appraise the approaching person, she would not have had an emotional reaction to the approacher, because events that are irrelevant to personal well-being do not generate emotions (Lazarus, 1991a; Ortony & Clore, 1989; Ortony, Clore, & Collins, 1988). Therefore, appraisal, and not the situation itself, determines the quality of the emotional experience. For instance, consider the counterintuitive finding that Olympic bronze medalists experience more happiness than do Olympic silver medalists, a phenomenon explained by the fact that the athlete's appraisal of what might have been is at least as important as what has been (Medvec, Madey, & Gilovich, 1995). The silver medalist might have won the gold medal while the bronze medalist might have won no medal at all. The same sort of cognitive construal also works in emotions such as shame (if only I weren't . . .) and guilt (if only I hadn't . . .) (Niedenthal, Tangney, & Gavanski, 1994).

One of the earliest cognitive theories of emotion that established appraisal as a central mechanism was that of Magda Arnold (1960, 1970). This theory specified how cognition, neurophysiology, and arousal work together to produce the experience and expression of emotion. Arnold focused on three questions: (1) how the perception of an environmental object or event produces a good or bad appraisal; (2) how the appraisal generates emotion; and (3) how a felt emotion manifests itself in expression and action.

FROM PERCEPTION TO APPRAISAL. According to Arnold, people categorically appraise stimulus events and objects as positive or negative. To substantiate her ideas, Arnold paid particularly close detail to the neurological pathways in the brain. In all encounters with the environment, limbic system brain structures (the amygdala) automatically appraise the hedonic tone of sensory information. For instance, a harsh pitch instantaneously is appraised as intrinsically unpleasant (bad) while the smell of a rose is appraised as intrinsically pleasant (good). Recent neuroanatomical research confirms Arnold's claim that the limbic system (and amygdala in particular) is the focal brain center that appraises the emotional significance of sensory stimuli (LeDoux, 1992a, 1992b). In addition, most stimuli are further appraised cortically by adding information processing and hence expectations, memories, plans, beliefs, goals, judgments, and attributions. Full appraisal therefore draws on both subcortical (limbic system) and cortical interpretations and evaluations.

FROM APPRAISAL TO FELT EMOTION. According to Arnold, once an object or event has been appraised as good or bad (as beneficial or harmful), an experience of liking or disliking follows immediately and automatically. The liking or disliking is, for Arnold, the felt emotion.

FROM FELT EMOTION TO ACTION. Liking generates a motivational tendency to approach the emotion-generating object or event; disliking generates a motivational tendency to avoid it. During appraisal, the individual relies on memory and imagination to generate a number of possible courses of action to deal with the liked or disliked object. When a particular course of action is decided upon, the hippocampal brain circuit activates the motor cortex, which leads to behavioral action. Contemporary research adds that the limbic system also has direct access to the muscles that control facial expressions (Holstedge, Kuypers, & Dekker, 1977), autonomic and endocrine system reactions (Kapp, Pascoe, & Bixler, 1984; LeDoux et al., 1988), and general arousal systems (brain stem; Krettek & Price, 1978).

One important feature of Arnold's theory is that emotion is defined in terms of motivation. The tendency to approach or avoid gives the emotion a directional force, while the physiological changes in the muscles and viscera give emotion its energy. A second important feature of Arnold's theory is a tendency to treat emotion as a unitary construct, as she preferred to talk about emotion forces of approach and avoidance, of attraction and repulsion, of liking and disliking, more than she did of the specific emotions such as anger, sadness, or pride. Contemporary emotion researchers, however, mostly reject this undifferentiated view of emotions (Solomon's opponent-process theory is one exception, as discussed in chapter 12). This oversimplified view of emotion was soon expanded upon by the cognition-oriented emotion researchers who followed, such as Richard Lazarus.

Primary and Secondary Appraisal

Like Arnold, Lazarus emphasized the cognitive processes that intervene between environmental conditions and the behavioral and physiological reactivity they enliven, but he supplemented Arnold's general good/bad appraisal with a more complex conceptualization (Lazarus, 1968, 1991a; Lazarus & Folkman, 1984). First, people evaluate whether the situation they face has personal relevance for their well-being. When well-being is at stake, people then evaluate the potential harm, threat, or benefit. For Lazarus (1991a), the appraisals include, "Is this situation relevant to my well-being?," "If relevant, is this situation congruent or incongruent with the goals I seek?," and "How deeply does this event touch my self-esteem?" Given these three appraisals of relevance, goal congruence, and extent of ego involvement, people appraise situations as a particular kind of harm, as a particular kind of threat, or as a particular kind of benefit. Table 13.1 lists primary appraisals people make (Lazarus, 1991a, 1994).

TABLE 13–1

Types of Appraisals and Related Emotions

PRIMARY APPRAISAL CATEGORY	EMOTION
Type of Harm:	
Being demeaned by a personal offense	Anger
Transgressing against a moral imperative	Guilt
Failing to live up to an ego ideal	Shame
Experiencing an irrevocable loss	Sadness
Taking in or being too close to an indigestible object or idea	Disgust
Type of Threat:	
Facing uncertainty or a nonspecific threat	Anxiety
Facing immediate overwhelming physical danger	Fright
Wanting what someone else has	Envy
Resenting a rival	Jealousy
Types of Benefit:	
Making progress toward a goal	Happiness
Taking credit for a valued object or achievement	Pride
Removing or improving a distressing condition	Relief
Feeling confident of desired outcome	Hope
Sharing affection	Love
Being moved by another's suffering and wanting to help	Compassion

SOURCE: Lazarus, R. S. (1991). *Emotion and adaptation.* New York: Oxford University Press. Adapted with permission.

Coping abilities alter how people interpret (appraise) situations they face (Folkman & Lazarus, 1990; Lazarus, 1991a, 1991b). For instance, once insulted and thus potentially harmed, people cope by (1) taking action to change the harmful relationship, (2) denying its importance (psychological avoidance), or (3) changing the appraisal itself (that comment is not harmful; it's actually beneficial because I'll learn from it). Thus, coping changes the way a situation is appraised, and a changed appraisal leads to a changed emotion. People also evaluate the extent to which other people are to be blamed or credited for the situation, and they estimate future expectancies of their well-being given their potential coping resources. Overall, then, people first appraise their relationship to the situation (primary appraisal) and then appraise their coping potential (secondary appraisal).

PRIMARY APPRAISAL. Primary appraisal, the automatic evaluation of the relevance of an event, involves an estimate of whether one has anything at stake in the encounter (Folkman et al., 1986). The following are potentially at stake in primary appraisal: (1) physical well-being, (2) self-esteem, (3) a goal, (4) financial state, (5) respect for another person, and (6) the well-being of a loved one. In other words, primary appraisals ask whether one's physical or psychological well-being, goals and financial status, or interpersonal relationships are on the line during this particular encounter with the environment. For instance, when driving and the car swerves on the ice, the cognitive system immediately generates the primary appraisal that much is now at stake—personal health, reputation as a skillful driver, getting to work on time, a valuable possession (the car), and the physical and psychological well-being of one's passenger. Not all primary appraisals involve such high stakes, but the example communicates the essence of primary appraisal. Also, all emotional experiences are not as intense, and the extent to which each involves the person's self-esteem seems to explain which situations lead to the most intense emotions.

In some encounters, nothing related to well-being is at stake (e.g., hearing today's weather forecast for Sydney, Australia; participating in an athletic contest after the championship has been ensured). Events appraised as irrelevant do not cause emotions. Only events relevant to goals and well-being lead to emotion, and which specific emotion the person experiences depends on the particular kind of harm, threat, or benefit one expects during the encounter (Table 13.1).

SECONDARY APPRAISAL. Secondary appraisal, which occurs after some reflection, involves the person's assessment of how to cope with the emotion-generating event (Folkman & Lazarus, 1990). Coping involves the person's cognitive, emotional, and behavioral efforts to manage specific external and internal demands. Personal strategies, skills, and abilities are the resources that enable a person to effect a change in the environment or to manage their emotional, cognitive, and physiological reactions to it. For instance, imagine the coping options for a musician scheduled to perform for an audience. The musician might solicit advice from a friend, practice throughout the previous night, become uncommunicative, make a plan of action and follow it, copy another musician's style, make light of the event's significance, and so forth. Whichever strategy seems most adaptive for that situation will likely be used.

APPRAISAL MODEL OF EMOTION. Figure 13.1 summarizes Lazarus' overall emotion model. Given an encounter with the environment, the individual first makes a primary appraisal pertaining to the personal significance and its meaning in terms of physical, psychological, or social well-being. Personally significant stimulus events are evaluated either as a threat, harm, or benefit, which causes autonomic nervous system (ANS) discharge in the form of sympathetic activation, as the individual prepares to adapt to the stimulus (Tomaka et al., 1993). Sympathetic activation, in turn, prompts secondary appraisal. Voluntary coping responses follow secondary appraisals. If the coping responses are successful, the emotion-generating stimulus event is apt to lose its status as a potential threat, harm, or benefit. If coping responses are unsuccessful, the ANS activation continues until either the stressor goes away, the coping responses are successful, or the ANS fails from exhaustion.

MOTIVATION. Lazarus' portrayal of emotion is a motivational one. A person brings personal motives (goals, well-being) into a situation and appraises the situation's relevance. When motives are at stake, emotions follow. Further, emotions constantly change as the situation changes. The process is characterized not so much by the sequence of situation → appraisal → emotion as it is by the ongoing change in the status of motives. Lazarus labels his ideas as a cognitive-motivational-relational the-

FIGURE 13–1
Lazarus' Conceptualization of Emotion as a Process

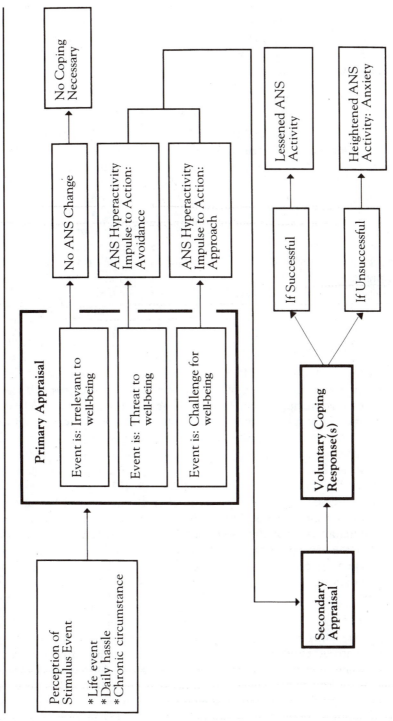

ory of emotions (Lazarus, 1991b). *Cognitive* communicates the importance of appraisal, *motivational* communicates the importance of goals and well-being, and *relational* communicates a recognition that emotions arise from environment situations. Hence, emotions are processes that change in response to the person's goals and relationship with the environment.

Appraisal Process

Following the work of Arnold and Lazarus, a number of cognition-minded theorists developed somewhat different models of emotion (Frijda, 1986; Johnson-Laird & Oatley, 1989; Ortony, Clore, & Collins, 1988; Roseman, 1984, 1991; Smith & Ellsworth, 1985; Scherer, 1984; Weiner, 1986). Each theorist embraces the stimulus event → appraisal → emotion sequence, but they differ on how many dimensions of appraisal are necessary to explain emotional experience. Arnold explained two emotions (like and dislike), Lazarus' primary and secondary appraisals explain about 15 emotions (see Table 13.1), yet cognitive emotion theorists seek to explain every emotion because they believe that each emotion can be described by a unique pattern of appraisal. That is, a researcher who knew the full pattern of appraisals a person made could then correctly predict the person's specific emotion.

In one study, researchers asked people how they appraised certain situations and attempted to predict their emotions (Oatley & Duncan, 1994). Their success rate was quite good, such that usually when people experienced a loss they felt sadness (50%) but sometimes they experienced anger (20%), fear (15%), disgust (10%), or happiness (5%) instead. Evidently, additional appraisals are needed to explain why people experience an emotion other than sadness following loss (e.g., an appraisal of loss plus a second appraisal of blaming someone for that loss would lead to anger).

To explain the full complexity of emotions, theorists have argued for the importance of additional dimensions of appraisal. One such list begins with goal significance and coping potential (Lazarus' primary and secondary appraisals) but also adds appraisals of the stimulus event's (1) novelty, (2) intrinsic pleasantness, and (3) compatibility with internalized standards (Scherer, 1984). Another such list features certainty, anticipated effort to goal, attention, pleasantness, and legitimacy (Smith & Ellsworth, 1985). It is difficult to say how many dimensions of appraisal exist or which appraisals are most fundamental and which are of only a peripheral importance. The following list of appraisals, however, is representative of those of most cognition-minded emotion theorists (these dimensions are a combination of those proposed by Roseman, 1984, 1991; Smith & Ellsworth, 1985; Scherer, 1984):

- Pleasantness   Arnold's primary appraisal
- Goal/Need at stake   Lazarus' primary appraisal
- Coping ability   Lazarus' secondary appraisal
- Anticipated effort   Appraisal whether effort is needed in a situation
- Certainty   The predictability of the situation or its events
- Control/responsibility   Who causes the events—self, others, or circumstances?

- Legitimacy   Whether the outcome was deserved
- Norm/self compatibility   Appropriateness of thoughts or behaviors to a private or public standard
- Novelty   Appraisal of change in the environment or situation

For instance, a combination of the following four appraisals produces anger: (1) Need/goal is at stake in the encounter, (2) the need/goal was lost (unpleasantness), (3) someone else blocked the goal or need fulfillment (control/responsibility), and (4) the personal loss was undeserved (illegitimate). An event that leads to the appraisals of high goal relevance, high coping potential, high familiarity (low novelty), high intrinsic pleasantness, and compatibility with standards produces sentimentality. Change one dimension of appraisal and the emotion changes. That is, change high coping potential to low (while keeping the other appraisals constant) and sentimentality changes to longing. The ultimate goal of adding new appraisal dimensions is to construct a decision tree that leads to a single emotion (Scherer, 1993). That is, if the person makes appraisals X, Y, and Z, then emotion A must follow.

There is no consensus on how many or which dimensions are needed to specify the appraisal decision tree driving cognitive emotional experiences. It is doubtful that an appraisal decision tree will ever predict specific emotions 100% correctly, for the following reasons (after Fischer et al., 1990; Reisenzein & Hofmann, 1993):

1. Processes other than appraisal contribute to emotion.
2. Developmental differences exist among people such that children generally experience basic, general emotions, whereas socialized adults generally experience a richer variety of situation-specific emotions.
3. Much cognitive elaboration and information processing follows the initial emotion-generating appraisal.

First, the idea that processes other than appraisal contribute to emotion was the theme of chapter 12. Second, developmental differences manifest themselves as people gain experience with the situations that cause emotions, and these differences lead people to experience different emotions even in the same situation. That is, given an identical situation, a person with relatively little experience will experience a general emotion (e.g., joy) whereas a person with much relevant knowledge will experience a more specific emotion (e.g., pride). The next section on emotion knowledge discusses these developmental differences. Third, postappraisal information processing manifests itself in many ways, including an attribution of why outcomes occurred and predictions about forthcoming consequences. The section on attributional analysis of emotion discusses these ongoing appraisals.

Emotion Knowledge

Infants and young children understand and distinguish between only a few basic emotions. They learn to name the few basic emotions of anger, fear, sadness, joy, and love (Kemper, 1987; Shaver et al., 1987). As people gain experience with different situations, they learn to discriminate shades of the same emotion. The shades of joy, for instance, might be understood as happiness, relief, optimism, pride, contentment, gratitude, and so on (Smith & Ellsworth, 1988). The shades of anger might be understood as fury, hostility, vengefulness, rage, aggravation, wrath, and so on (Russell & Fehr, 1994). These distinctions are stored cognitively in hierarchies of basic emotions and their derivatives. Thus, the number of different emotions that can be distinguished is limited by our *emotion knowledge* (Shaver, Schwartz, Kirson, & O'Connor, 1987). Through experience, we construct a mental representation of the different emotions and how each relates to the other emotions and to the variety of situations that produce them.

Figure 13.2 presents an example of emotion knowledge. One level includes basic emotion categories—love, joy, surprise, anger, sadness, and fear. With experience, the individual learns types of these basic emotions. The individual depicted in Figure 13.2 understands three types of love—affection, lust, and longing (the asterisk denotes the prototype emotion) and six types of sadness—suffering, depression, disappointment, shame, neglect, and sympathy.

Much of the diversity of emotion experience comes from learning fine distinctions among emotions and specific situations that cause them. There are as many emotions as there are cognitive appraisal possibilities of a situation (Ellsworth & Smith, 1988; Smith & Ellsworth, 1985, 1987). For example, an individual who has just lost out to a rival might experience distress, anger, fear, disgust, and jealousy (Hupka, 1984). Further, one learns that these emotions can coincide and are therefore related to one another (as in the jealousy complex, Hupka, 1984; White, 1981). One also learns that other emotions (e.g., love, joy) are far removed from this cluster of emotion experience. Finally, one learns the difference between types of anger—jealousy, hate, irritation, and so on. Eventually, such learning produces a highly personal emotion knowledge, which enables the individual to appraise situations with high discrimination and therefore, respond with situationally-appropriate emotions.

Knowledge in the more general sense is also important to emotional experience (Clore, 1994). We use our knowledge of the world to endow events with positive or negative values (primary appraisal). We also use our knowledge of the world to predict the probable effects of our coping efforts (secondary appraisal). While driving in traffic as snow starts falling, for instance, our knowledge of having new tires and four-wheel drive allows us to ward off the thought of potential harm and consider the snow's potential benefits (scenery, skiing). Without new tires or four-wheel drive, our knowledge of the difficulty of driving on the curvy road, how poorly we have driven in snow in the past, and how serious an accident can be further affect our emotions. Knowledge, in fact, plays such an intricate role in practically all our environmental interactions that some researchers conceptualize emotions themselves as mental states (e.g., Clore, 1994; Clore, Ortony, & Foss, 1987). From this point of view, emotions are cognitions invested with a motivating force (Sabini & Silver, 1987).

FIGURE 13–2
Typical Emotion Categories

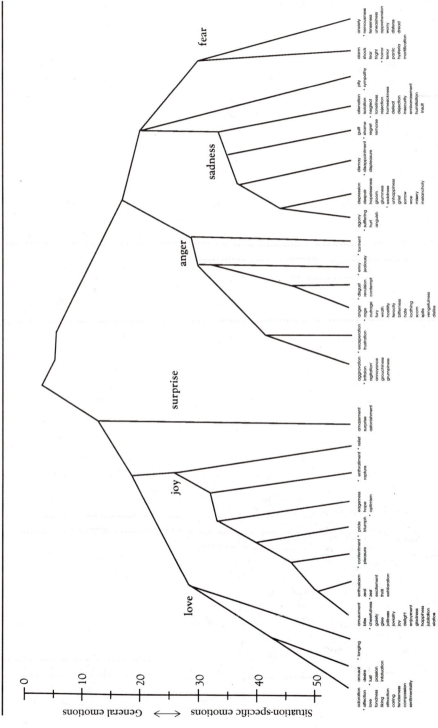

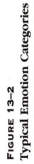

SOURCE: Shaver, P., Schwartz, J., Kirson, D., & O'Connor, C. (1987). Emotion knowledge: Further exploration of a prototype approach. *Journal of Personality and Social Psychology, 52,* 1061–1086. Copyright © 1987 by American Psychological Association. Adapted with permission.

Attributional Analysis of Emotion

Appraisal theorists begin their analysis with relatively simple appraisals, such as whether an event signifies harm, threat, or danger (Lazarus, 1991a), and continue with progressively more complex appraisals (Ellsworth & Smith, 1988) and then add the emotion knowledge to explain how people make fine-tuned appraisals. In his attributional analysis, Weiner (1982, 1986) adds yet another type of appraisal to the experience and regulation of emotion. People make appraisals not only before (primary) and during (secondary) their interactions with the event, but also following an event's outcome. In other words, people further evaluate why they experienced harm (why was I fired from my job?), threat (why did this person want to belittle me?), or benefit (why did I win the contest?). This postoutcome appraisal is termed an attribution (recall chapter 9).

Fundamental to attribution theory is the postulate that people search for explanations for the favorable and unfavorable events that happen to them (Weiner, 1985, 1986). The emotion-generating sequence is situation → outcome → attribution → emotion. The attribution to explain why an outcome occurred is the cognitive mechanism that produces emotion. Hence, after winning a contest and attributing the victory to talent and ability, the individual experiences pride. If the attribution for winning were different, the emotion following the victory would also be different. If the victory were attributed to help from a teammate, for instance, the emotion would be gratitude, not pride. Notice that people can experience different emotions in response to the same situation, even to the same outcome in that situation. It is the attribution, the cognitive event, rather than the situation or its outcome that causes the specific emotion.

Weiner refers to the outcome-dependent emotional response as a primary appraisal of the outcome. One simply interprets whether the outcome was beneficial or harmful, good or bad, and the emotions that follow are the basic emotions of happiness or sadness (Weiner, Russell, & Learman, 1978, 1979). Then attributions constitute a secondary appraisal of the outcome. Attributions differentiate the general happy-sad initial emotional reaction into more specific secondary emotions. Figure 13.3 shows the sequence of events in Weiner's attribution theory of emotions.

As discussed in chapter 9, three attributional dimensions explain why an outcome occurred: (1) locus (internal or external); (2) stability (stable or unstable); and (3) controllability (controllable or uncontrollable). These dimensions can explain the positive outcome emotions of pride, gratitude, and hope and the negative outcome emotions of anger, pity, shame, and guilt (Weiner, 1985, 1986; Weiner & Graham, 1989).

Following success, three attribution-based emotions are possible. Attributing success to internal factors enhances self-esteem and leads to pride; attributing success to an external locus leads to gratitude. In other words, gratitude follows success caused by another (the matchmaker sets up a date). Hope follows an attribution of success to stable factors (irrespective of its locus), as one expects success to continue in the future.

Following failure, locus and controllability produce four specific emotions: anger,

FIGURE 13-3
Cognition-Emotion Process according to Attribution Theory

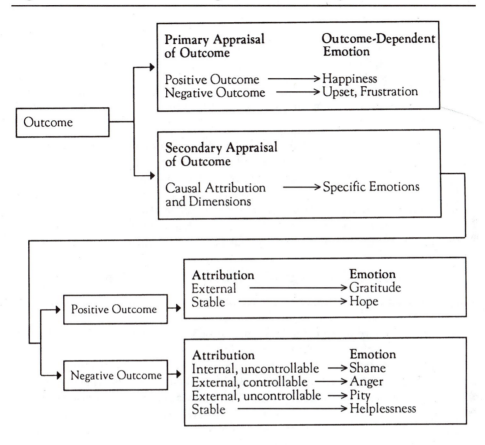

pity, shame, and guilt. As shown in Table 13.2, guilt occurs when failure is self-generated and controllable (the student fails because of insufficient study effort). Shame occurs when failure is self-generated and uncontrollable (the student fails because of a lack of intelligence). Anger occurs when failure is other-generated and controllable by the other (the teacher attributes the student's failure to not trying). Lastly, pity (or sympathy) occurs when failure is other-generated and not controllable by the other (the teacher attributes the failure to the student's low intelligence).

These examples all apply to achievement-related situations. Guilt, shame, anger, and pity also apply to interpersonal failure outcomes. Consider the teenager who has a first date, and for various reasons the date fails to materialize. If the failed date is self-caused and controllable (the teenager remembers a prior commitment and cancels), she feels guilt. If the failed date is self-caused and uncontrollable (the teenager suffers from severe allergies and cancels), she feels shame. If the failed date is caused by the other and is controllable (the other remembers a prior commitment and can-

TABLE 13–2
Attributional Antecedents of Four Failure Emotions

	ATTRIBUTION	
	LACK OF EFFORT	LACK OF ABILITY
Self-generated emotion	Guilt	Shame
Other-generated emotion	Anger	Pity

SOURCE: Weiner, B. (1986). *An attributional theory of motivation and emotion.* New York: Springer Verlag. Reprinted with permission.

cels), she feels anger. If the failed date is caused by the other and is uncontrollable (the other suffers from severe allergies and cancels), she feels pity.

To summarize, together, primary appraisals, situational appraisals (including secondary appraisals), and postoutcome attributions constitute the three core cognitive events in the emotion process. Primary appraisals, secondary appraisals, and attributions all add a unique contribution to the understanding of discrete emotions such as anger, guilt, fear, anxiety, sadness, hope, challenge, and happiness (Smith et al., 1993).

Emotional Significance of Interruptions

Human behavior is largely under cognitive control: Behavior routinely follows a well-programmed scenario. When we go to a restaurant, for example, we expect to be seated, to wait before placing an order, to wait before receiving food, to eat, to pay the waiter, and finally, to walk to our car and find it exactly where we parked it. The whole restaurant-going process follows a well-programmed scenario. If circumstances prevent us from completing the scenario, emotions arise (Mandler, 1975, 1982, 1984; MacDowell & Mandler, 1989). If no one is there to seat us or if the wait is excessive, we get upset. If the bill is not what we expected, we are surprised. If our car is not where we left it, we feel anxiety and frustration. Such interruptions in the program form the core of emotional behavior. Interruptions get us aroused, and that arousal demands our attention and readies us for action. Once aroused, we have words with the staff, question our bill, and frantically search the parking area for our vehicle. Interruptions in the program cause emotion.

Two types of interruptions get us aroused: (1) events that occur unexpectedly (the closed-road sign that interrupts the drive to work) and (2) expected events that do not occur (the engine that does not start when the car key is turned). In these cases, well-organized cognitive activity is interrupted. An interrupted plan is typically repeated—we turn the key again, redial the busy phone number, or knock once more on the unopened door. When the plan fails a second time, interruption is unambiguous. Autonomic nervous system (ANS) discharge follows the interruption, and the situation is evaluated emotionally. Interruptions turn on the arousal switch. Arousal (1) puts the individual into a state of physiological readiness to perform the behavior necessary to cope with interruption and (2) signals the cognitive system for increased alertness and prompts a scanning of the environment to determine why the interruption occurred.

Interruptions generate arousal, but arousal is not emotion. Rather, the quality of the emotional experience depends on the person's cognitive evaluation of the situation. Situations are interpreted as being pleasant, awe inspiring, sexy, funny, frustrating, disgusting, and so forth, and these cognitive appraisals guide corresponding emotional experience and expression (Dutton & Aron, 1974; Mandler, 1984; Schachter, 1964).

SCHEMA INCONGRUITY. A schema is an abstract, mental representation of an environmental regularity (Mandler, 1982), that is, a well-organized plan of action. Through experience, we build up a set of expectations of what fancy restaurants, sporting events, teenagers, and people from other countries are like. That is, by repeated visits to sporting events and restaurants and by repeated interactions with teenagers and people from other countries, we organize our knowledge into schemas, sets of expectancies about these events and people. When an experience matches our expectancy (or script), schema congruity follows. When experience contradicts what was expected to happen, schema incongruity follows. Figure 13.4 shows how schema congruity and incongruity produce emotional reactions.

Schema congruity is emotionally positive. But schema congruity is only mildly positive because when events occur as expected, there is little or no ANS discharge to give the felt emotion an intensity. Schema incongruity can be emotionally positive or negative. When slight, schema incongruity is mildly positive. When we read a book on an unfamiliar topic or travel to a foreign city, we gain new and somewhat unexpected knowledge and feel curiosity (Loewenstein, 1994) or interest (Berlyne, 1966). Severe incongruity, on the other hand, is an emotional negative. When an event catches us fully by surprise, the expectancy disconfirmation is unsettling and aversive. Sometimes, severe schema incongruity is quickly followed by matching an alternative schema to the incongruous event such that initial schema incongruity is followed by a delayed congruity. The final emotional experience of delayed congruity is a positive one (as in problem solving). Delayed congruity is typically more emotionally positive than immediate congruity, because delayed congruity involves interruption and therefore more intense ANS arousal. Severe incongruity that remains incongruous is both negative and intense. In assimilation and accommodation, schema incongruity is replaced by schema congruity. Assimilation applies to situations in which our thinking needs adjustment to correspond with the evidence. Accommodation applies to those situations in which our thinking about the world is so inadequate that we need to forfeit our present schema and adopt a different schema.

SCHEMA INCONGRUITY APPLIED TO RELATIONSHIPS. Consider how Mandler's ideas might apply to close interpersonal relationships, which involve a multitude of shared plans and well-coordinated behavioral sequences. Together, a husband and wife eat, raise children, work around the house, play tennis, and take vacations. Together, they aspire to common goals such as buying a home, entertaining friends, and sending their children to college. Similarly, roommates, brothers and sisters,

FIGURE 13–4
How Schema Congruity and Incongruity Produce Emotional Reactions

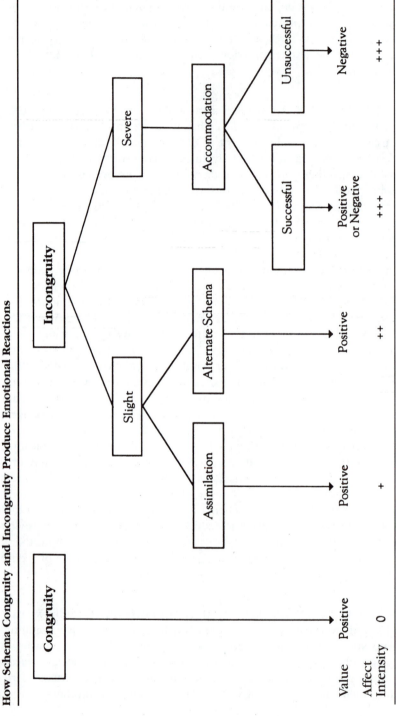

SOURCE: Mandler, G. (1982). The structure of value: Acounting for taste. In M. S. Clark & S. T. Fiske (Eds.), *Affect and cognition*. Hillsdale, NJ: Laurence Erlbaum.

teammates, co-workers, and others share common goals and interdependent behaviors. When the individual plans and behaviors of two people become intertwined, their combined plans and behaviors form a unit—together the couple entertains, recreates, and travels; together the basketball team practices, copes with opponents, and deals with the coach.

Berscheid (1982) studied the emotional consequences when the couple's joint plans and behaviors were interrupted, as in argument, separation, divorce, death, and so forth. Highly meshed behavioral sequences occur when each person in the relationship facilitates and augments the performance of the other's sequence of behavior. For example, if the husband cooks breakfast while the wife awakens the children, the morning chores pass quickly and uneventfully. Or, if the basketball player screens the opponent, the teammate has a clear shot at the basket. Like schema congruities, meshed sequences result in little arousal. Hence, meshed behavioral sequences are not the occasion for emotional experiences in close relationships (except for mild positives from schema congruities). Nonmeshed behavioral sequences, on the other hand, occur when the behavior of one person in the relationship prevents or interferes with the behavior of the other person. Like schema incongruity, nonmeshed sequences prompt intense arousal. With nonmeshed couples, interruptions occur frequently and therefore so do arousal and unpleasantness. To relieve the distress, the couple will try a second time to mesh their behaviors, presumably through promises, apologies, and reassurances of future behavioral intentions. The promises, apologies, and reassurances prompt new expectancies in the relationship. Through a perpetual cycle of disconfirmed (interrupted) expectancies followed by promises and reassurances and followed again by disconfirmed expectancies, the couple experiences considerable emotional turmoil, and the relationship is emotionally hot.

SOCIAL AND CULTURAL CONSTRUCTION OF EMOTION

As appraisal contributes to a cognitive understanding of emotion, social interaction contributes to a social and cultural understanding of emotion. Social psychologists, sociologists, anthropologists, and others challenge the idea that emotion is necessarily a private, biological, intrapsychic phenomenon by arguing that most emotions originate in social interaction (e.g., Averill, 1980, 1983; Kemper, 1978; Manstead, 1991). Social interaction puts people into particular identities such as high and low status, and it is within the context of social interaction that events such as exchange, reciprocity, and equity stir us to emotion. Consider, for instance, the emotions that arise in a soup kitchen situation that features interactants with different statuses (staff, volunteers, clients) who participate in events such as exchange and reciprocity (Stein, 1989). Staff and volunteers (high-status people) expend a good deal of effort preparing and serving food to people who are in need of assistance (low-status people). Such a relationship makes some emotions likely (low-status people should express gratitude). Occasionally, beneficiaries show not gratitude but attitude (e.g., a snide remark, "Is that all?"). Complaints lead volunteers, in turn, to feel anger and indignation ("How dare they complain?"). Such emotions arise from who is interacting with whom and the types of interpersonal exchanges that take place.

Those who study the social construction of emotion point out that if you changed the situation, emotions would change. Think about the typical emotions experienced at a playground, at work, at a weekend party, at the theater, on a blind date, at a sporting event, playing tennis at the country club, cleaning the bathroom, attending a church or synagogue, watching the late-late movie, and so on. Situations define what emotions are most appropriate and expected, and because people know which emotions go with which settings, they can select a setting and therefore "construct" a particular emotional experience. If you want to construct joy, you go to a weekend party; if you want to construct disgust, you clean the bathroom. Also, think about the typical emotions experienced while interacting with someone with superior status (boss, parent), with someone of equal status (friend, spouse), or someone of inferior status (child, new employee). Status differences between interactors define what emotions are appropriate and expected, and because people know which emotions go with which interactors, they can select an interactor and therefore "construct" a particular emotional experience.

Social Interaction

Other people are our most frequent source of day-to-day emotion (Oatley & Duncan, 1994). Other people not only cause emotions directly but also indirectly, as through *emotional contagion* (Hatfield, Cacioppo, & Rapson, 1993a, 1993b). Emotional contagion is "the tendency to automatically mimic and synchronize expressions, vocalizations, postures, and movements with those of another person and, consequently, to converge emotionally" (Hatfield, Cacioppo, & Rapson, 1993a). The three propositions of mimicry, feedback, and contagion explain how the emotions of others create emotions in us through social interaction (Hatfield, Cacioppo, & Rapson, 1993b, pp. 97–99):

Mimicry: "In conversation, people automatically and continuously mimic and synchronize their movements with the facial expressions, voices, postures, movements, and instrumental behaviors of other people."

Feedback: "Subjective emotional experience is affected, moment to moment, by the activation of and feedback from facial, vocal, postural, and movement mimicry."

Contagion: "Consequently, people tend, from moment to moment, to 'catch' other people's emotions."

Social interaction also provides the context to reexperience and relive a past emotional experience. People frequently reactivate an emotional experience through conversation with another person, a process referred to as "the social sharing of emotion" (Rimé et al., 1991). Social sharing of emotion is not an uncommon event, as people are at least as likely to tell others about the emotional events in their lives as they are to keep these experiences private. These conversations usually take place later in the day or week with intimates (close friends, love partners). When people share their emotions, they typically do so by "giving the other person a full account of what happened," "telling the other person what the event had meant," and "telling the other person how the subject had felt" (Rimé et al., 1991, p. 448). It is in these times of sharing our emotions that we build and maintain the relationships that are central to our lives, such as the marital relationship (Noller, 1984). And the act of sharing emotion is itself important to the development of close relationships, as we find it relatively easy to feel close to others who generate positive feelings in us and relatively difficult to feel close to those who do not (Edwards, Manstead & McDonald, 1984).

Social sharing of emotions pays off in several ways. An empathic other person can offer support or assistance, divert the person's attention, help the person relax, provide tips about impression management, help the person work their way through the emotional experience, and so on (Lehman, Ellard, & Wortman, 1986; Thoits, 1984). Thus, through social sharing, people can use the assistance of others to reconfirm their self-concepts and facilitate and strengthen their coping responses.

Emotional Socialization

Emotion socialization occurs as adults tell children what they ought to know about emotion. Emotion socialization certainly occurs among adults as well, but the process is best illustrated when adults interact with children for the explicit purpose of socializing them (Pollak & Thoits, 1989). Adults tell children about the situations that cause emotions, about how emotion expresses itself, and about emotion words or labels. In turn, children learn that a basic emotion can be differentiated into more specific emotional states (emotion knowledge; Shaver et al., 1987), that certain expressive displays can and should be controlled (expression management; Saarni, 1979), and that negative emotions can be manipulated deliberately into neutral or positive emotions (emotion control; McCoy & Masters, 1985).

Consider the socialization that occurs in settings such as daycare centers, preschools, and elementary schools (Pollak & Thoits, 1989). During an emotional episode, a caretaker or teacher might explain the child's feelings, point out their causes, and instruct the child about which expressive displays are appropriate, as follows. Consider an example of how adults tell children about the causes of feelings (Pollak & Thoits, 1989, p. 26):

GIRL (SEVERAL TIMES): *My mom is late*.
STAFF MEMBER: Does that make you *mad*?
GIRL: Yes.
STAFF MEMBER: Sometimes kids get *mad* when their *moms are late to pick them up*.

Consider an example of how adults tell children about expressing emotions through behaviors (from Pollak & Thoits, 1989, p. 26):

STAFF MEMBER, WHILE HOLDING A KICKING, SCREAMING BOY IN TIME-OUT: Robert, I see you're *very angry*.

Consider also how adults teach children that they can control their emotional displays (from Pollak & Thoits, 1989, p. 30):

DURING CIRCLE, ALEC TRIED TO CLIMB ALL OVER JOHN, A VOLUNTEER.

JOHN: If you want to *be close*, there are some things you could do. . . . You could *sit next to me and we could hold hands*, or I could put my arm around you, or *you could sit on my lap*.

Clearly, limits exist as to how much a culture can socialize particular emotions into its constituents. Consider the claim that in some cultures people exchange intimate partners without jealousy. Evolution-minded and biology-minded theorists (chapter 12) argue that sharing a sexual partner would surely produce jealously, and appraisal theorists might make a similar argument (see Table 13.1). But can people be socialized against jealousy and toward other feelings under these circumstances? In short, no. In every study, the claim that people can share intimate partners without jealousy turned out to be false (Reis, 1986). Cultures do vary as to which behaviors signal jealousy, which signs of affection justify jealousy, and how people express jealousy, but sexual jealousy occurs in all cultures (Reis, 1986). Jealousy is universal, though some of its nuances (causes, expression) vary from one culture to the next. The lesson is that social constructivists do not argue that all emotions are socially constructed; rather they strive to illustrate the role that social processes play in the emotion process. Some of these processes include instruction in the cause of the emotions (emotion knowledge), instructions in the expression of the emotions (expression management), and instruction in how to control emotions (emotion control).

Managing Emotions

Consider the emotional socialization pressures placed on professionals such as physicians (Smith & Kleinman, 1989), airline flight attendants (Hochschild, 1983), and hairdressers (Parkinson, 1991). Physicians, for instance, are not supposed to feel either attraction or disgust for their patients. Therefore physicians learn affective neutrality, a detached concern for their patients, during their medical school training. They learn to manage their emotions so desires, attraction, disgust, and the like are appropriately controlled.

Imagine being a medical student asked to conduct pelvic, rectal, and breast examinations and perform surgery, dissections, and autopsies. The problem of learning affective neutrality while performing these and other tasks was studied by a group of sociologists (Smith & Kleinman, 1989). For two years, the researchers interviewed medical students to identify their emotion management strategies, including (1) transforming the contact, (2) accentuating the positive, (3) using the patient, (4) laughing about it, and (5) avoiding the contact. Transforming the contact involves mentally transforming intimate contact with the body into something qualitatively different such as a step-by-step academic procedure. Accentuating the positive involves identifying with the satisfaction of learning or with the opportunity to practice medicine. Using the patient involves shifting awareness of uncomfortable feelings onto the patient, as in projection or in blaming the patient. Laughing about it exempts the doctor from admitting weakness. Avoiding contact involves keeping the patient covered, looking elsewhere, or hurrying through a procedure. These five emotion management strategies illustrate part of the culture that is Western medicine. When students rely on that culture for guidance in managing their emotions, they in effect reproduce that culture for the next generation of students (Smith & Kleinman, 1989).

Consider also trainee hairdressers (Parkinson, 1991). To be professionally successful, hairdressers need to develop an open communication style that is characterized by expressiveness, affect intensity, empathy, poise, frequent positive facial expressions, and a concealment of negative emotions. Further, the more natural and spontaneous the hairdresser appears to clients, the better the job goes. How do hairdressers learn to manage their emotions? The problem is how to be open with clients who are often uptight and socially remote. The solution is to develop an open interaction style, because emotional expressiveness and control are acquirable social skills (Straub & Roberts, 1983). Interestingly, the hairdressers who have or develop this skill report high job satisfaction, whereas those hairdressers who do not report feeling deceptive and experience low job satisfaction.

Flight attendants need to adopt an emotional style similar to that of the hairdressers. To do so, they frequently use "deep-acting" methods in which they replace their natural and spontaneous emotional reactions with constant courtesy to clients (Hochschild, 1983). In all these cases, medical students, hairdressers, and flight attendants learn to merge their private, spontaneous feelings into public, scripted feelings and ways of acting. The merger both facilitates and emanates from social life (Manstead, 1991).

Inferring Identities from Emotional Expressions

People react to the events in their lives emotionally, and how people react emotionally tells us something about what kind of people they are. For instance, weeping has traditionally communicated weakness whereas laughter has communicated health (Labott et al., 1991). According to affect control theory (chapter 10), emotional displays confirm or disconfirm our identities (Heise, 1989). For instance, a man who disparages a woman and shows joy disconfirms his identity as a man. His joy leads us to believe his identity is something closer to an assassin. What if a man who disparages a woman remains calm? The calm expression leads us to believe his identity is something like an ogre or a monster. Or, what if a man who disparages a woman shows disgust? His disgust leads us to believe his identity is something like a boss or supervisor (identities from Heise, 1989).

Recall that affect control theory expresses identities, behaviors, and emotions in terms of EPA (evaluation, potency, activity) profiles. For instance the identity of a man is slightly good, slightly powerful, and a bit active (EPA = 1.1, 1.1, 0.6), and the behavior of a kiss is quite good, slightly powerful, and slightly active (EPA = 2.3, 1.0, 0.8). Given these cultural perceptions of who a man is and what a kiss is, consider the consequences of a man kissing a woman and then expressing either joy, calm, or disgust (data from Heise, 1989):

After kissing, he expresses:	His new EPA profile is:	Therefore, his new identity is:
Joy	3.4, 0.3, −0.1	gentleman, or mate
Calm	1.0, 1.5, −1.1	grown-up, or advisor
Disgust	−2.4, 0.8, −0.5	snob, or killjoy

The brief table implies that a joy expression raises the man's goodness and lowers his power and liveliness a bit so that he appears to be a gentleman. The calm expression slightly increases his power and rather dramatically decreases his liveliness so that he appears to be an advisor. The disgust expression drastically decreases the man's goodness and somewhat decreases his liveliness so that he appears to be a snob.

During social interaction, each person uses the emotional expressions of the other to infer the other's identity and likely future behaviors. Legal trials provide an excellent illustration of this process, as judges and jurors must observe a person they know little about (the defendant), infer his or her character (identity), and predict what the defendant's likely future behavior will be so that they can make sentencing recommendations (see Robinson, Smith-Lovin, & Tsoudis, 1994). Consider the different impressions criminals make when they show (1) visible distress over the deed or (2) show no signs of remorse. When people engage in bad acts and show no signs of remorse, the observer infers that this is a bad person; but when people engage in bad acts and do show remorse, the observer infers that this person is not so bad after all (Robinson, Smith-Lovin, & Tsoudis, 1994).

When people speak of their deviant acts (as does a defendant in a court case), they are given an identity such as thief, murderer, or freeloader. The person's emotional expressions signal confirmation or disconfirmation. The sobbing, remorseful thief somehow is a regular sort of guy who got involved in an unfortunate accident, while the relaxed, affectively neutral thief somehow is a devilish rogue who performed a heinous crime (Robinson, Smith-Lovin, & Tsoudis, 1994, p. 186).

SUMMARY

The central construct in a cognitive understanding of emotion is appraisal. Two types of appraisal, primary and secondary, regulate the emotion process. Primary appraisal is the automatic evaluation of whether the person has something at stake in a situation—physical well-being, self-esteem, a goal, financial state, respect for another person, or the well-being of a loved one. Events appraised as a potential harm, threat, or benefit arouse emotion, but events appraised as unrelated to well-being do not arouse emotion. Secondary appraisal occurs after some reflection and revolves around the person's assessment of how to cope with the harmful, threatening, or beneficial situation.

Additional information processing guides the emotion process. People rely on their acquired emotion knowledge and on their attributions for events and outcomes. Emotion knowledge involves learning the fine distinctions among the basic emotions and which situations cause which emotions. Sophisticated emotion knowledge enables the individual to appraise situations with high discrimination and therefore respond with appropriate emotions. Weiner's attributional analysis adds the important cognitive activity that follows an individual's interpretation of why outcomes are successful or unsuccessful. An attributional analysis clarifies how explanations for favorable outcomes produce the emotions of pride, gratitude, and hope and how explanations for unfavorable outcomes produce the emotions of guilt, shame, anger, and pity. Primary appraisals, situational appraisals (including secondary appraisals), and postoutcome attributions are the three fundamental cognitive elements in the emotion process.

Social interaction contributes a social and cultural aspect to emotion. Other people are our richest source of emotional experience, as most day-to-day emotions arise from social interaction. Other people also show us how to interpret, experience, and express emotions as they instruct us about the cause of our emotions (emotion knowledge), how we should express our emotions (expression management), and how and when we should control our emotions (emotion management). Through social interaction, influences such as language, ideology, cultural values, and socialization pressures contribute to the emotion process.

RECOMMENDED READINGS

Averill, J. A. (1983). Studies on anger and aggression. *American Psychologist, 38*, 1145–1160.

Hatfield, E., Cacioppo, J. T., & Rapson, R. L. (1993). Emotional contagion. *Current Directions in Psychological Science, 2*, 96–99.

Lazarus, R. S. (1991). Progress on a cognitive-motivational-relational theory of emotion. *American Psychologist, 46*, 819–834.

Lazarus, R. S., & Smith, C. A. (1988). Knowledge and appraisal in the cognition-emotion relationship. *Cognition and Emotion, 2*, 281–300.

Pollak, L. H., & Thoits, P. A. (1989). Processes in emotional socialization. *Social Psychology Quarterly, 52*, 22–34.

Scherer, K. R. (1993). Studying the emotion-antecedent appraisal process: An expert system approach. *Cognition and Emotion, 7*, 325–355.

Shaver, P., Schwartz, J., Kirson, D., & O'Connor, C. (1987). Emotion knowledge: Further exploration of a prototype approach. *Journal of Personality and Social Psychology, 52*, 1061–1086.

Smith, III, A. C., & Kleinman, S. (1989). Managing emotions in medical school: Students' contacts with the living and the dead. *Social Psychology Quarterly, 52*, 56–69.

Smith, C. A., & Ellsworth, P. C. (1985). Patterns of cognitive appraisal in emotion. *Journal of Personality and Social Psychology, 48*, 813–838.

Weiner, B., & Graham, S. (1989). Understanding the motivational role of affect: Life-span research from an attributional perspective. *Cognition and Emotion, 3*, 401–419.

PART FOUR

Individual Differences

Chapter 14

PERSONALITY CHARACTERISTICS

It is Monday morning again and time for another humdrum psychology class. You stroll in, take a seat, and listen halfheartedly as the professor introduces the day's events. To begin, the professor hands out a questionnaire assessing your preferences and tendencies in a variety of categories. Glancing over the questionnaire, you realize that these items are not your typical run-of-the-mill psychology questions. The first dozen ask about sex. One item asks about open-mouth kissing, two items ask about number of partners and affairs, another asks about your frequency of sexual contact in the last year, still another about homosexual experience. The next few items asks about drug experience. Consecutive items ask for your experience with LSD, amphetamines, marijuana, hashish, cocaine, and opium. Three more ask about cigarette smoking, coffee drinking, and alcohol consumption (from Zuckerman et al., 1972). This questionnaire seems to have some potential, so you eagerly turn to the second page. The second page offers the Figure Preference Test that displays 40 figures like those in Figure 14.1. For each figure, you simply indicate whether you like or dislike it.

You finish the questionnaire, but you wonder what such questions have to do with personality and motivation. The professor announces that the day's topic addresses the personality characteristic *sensation seeking*, which corresponds to an uninhibited, nonconforming, impulsive disposition. The professor says the sensation-

FIGURE 14–1
Sample Figures from the Figure Preference Test

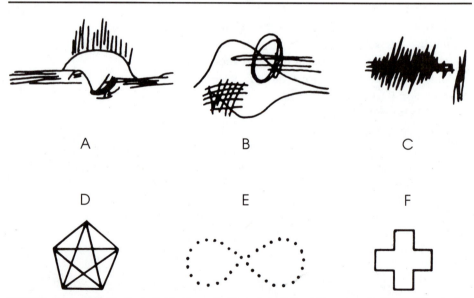

SOURCE: Zuckerman, M., Bone, R. N., Neary, R., Mangelsdorff, D., & Brustman, B. (1972). What is the sensation seeker? Personality trait and experience correlates of the Sensation Seeking Scale. Journal of Clinical and Counseling Psychology, 39, 308–321. Copyright © 1972 by American Psychological Association. Adapted with permission.

seeking trait goes a long way in predicting what sort of stimuli (figures) and activities (sex, drug experience) you prefer and actively seek out.

This chapter explains why (1) the sensation seeker is relatively uninhibited, nonconforming, and impulsive; (2) sensation seekers, as a group, report more varied and frequent experiences with sex and drugs; and (3) sensation seekers prefer figures that are complex and sketchlike (drawings A, B, and C in Fig. 14.1) to figures that are simple and symmetrical (drawings D, E, and F). The chapter also discusses extraversion and affect intensity. Sensation seekers, extraverts, and affectively intense individuals seek out and prefer arousal-increasing activities, while sensation avoiders, introverts, and affectively stable individuals seek out and prefer arousal-decreasing activities. The second half of the chapter examines individual differences related to personal control beliefs with an emphasis on causality orientations and desire for control.

A Caution in the Study of Individual Differences

One important caution pertains throughout the chapter. When the discussion refers to specific individual differences, such as sensation seeking, the reader should remember that relatively few people lie at either extreme of the characteristic. *Most people score in the middle, rather than toward the extremes, of each characteristic*. Figure 14.2, top, describes the distribution graphically. As illustrated, about 15% of the population score between 15 and 21, the high end of the sensation seeking scale; about 15% score 0 to 7, the low end; and about 70% score between 7 and 15 (the middle). Also beware of typologies, shown in the lower part of Figure 14.2, which categorize people (e.g., sensation seeker or sensation avoider). Typologies are both simplistic and misleading.

TEMPERAMENT AND PERSONAL CONTROL BELIEFS

Temperament refers to those psychological qualities that emanate from inherited physiological potentials and processes. Thus, temperament concerns the day-to-day excitability of an individual's brain, autonomic nervous system, and endocrine system. Such individual differences exist because of inherited differences in genetic makeups. Temperament differences are therefore largely biological differences, differences that play a large part in accounting for why people react differently to events such as taking an examination, speaking in public, and entertaining friends.

The three ideas that link temperament, personality, and motivation are as follows:

1. People differ in their genetic physiological make-up.
2. Differences in physiology correspond to relatively stable personality traits.
3. Differences in personality give rise to different motives among individuals.

These three ideas argue that genetic differences produce differences in temperament, temperament differences produce differences in personality, and differences

Figure 14-2
Individual Differences as Normal-Distribution and as Typology

Normal Distribution Curve

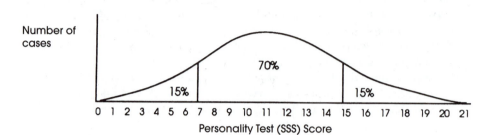

Typology

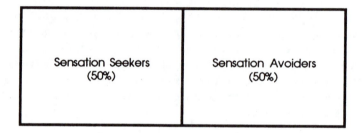

in personality produce differences in motivation. Temperament therefore has motivational implications. Buss and Plomin (1984) use the acronym EAS to argue that we
all have different genetic propensities to express different emotionalities (E), activity levels (A), and sociabilities (S). Thus, because we differ in our inherited potentialities, we differ in expression of distress and fear (E), behavioral tempo and vigor
(A), and affinity for social interaction (S). Research confirms that each of these separate aspects of temperament has a significant genetic basis (Saudino et al., 1995).

As a case in point, infants display different temperaments through irritability,
smiling, motor activity, and adaptability to new situations (Kagan, 1989). When infants are placed in an unfamiliar situation, some are naturally quiet and restrained
while others act with little restraint (Kagan et al., 1984). The quiet children have inhibited temperaments, whereas the unrestrained children have uninhibited temperaments. Inhibited children are quiet in the company of an unfamiliar adult, shy
with unfamiliar peers, cautious and reserved in risk-taking opportunities, and show
motor restraint in general (Kagan, 1989). These behavioral differences exist, in part,
because children inherit differing threshold levels of reactivity in their limbic system
structures, particularly the hypothalamus and amygdala. Inhibited children have
higher and more stable heart rates, larger pupil diameters, greater tension in the

skeletal musculature, and higher cortisol (steroid) levels (Kagan, Reznick, & Snidman, 1988).

From this quick overview of inhibited and uninhibited infants, an introductory picture begins to emerge in how people differ in temperament and how these differences form the foundation for differences in personality and motives. Infants with overly reactive limbic systems tend to have inhibited personalities and to avoid overly arousing, risky situations. Infants with less reactive limbic systems tend to have uninhibited personalities and to approach arousing, risky situations. Hence, infants inherit different temperaments; these different threshold levels of limbic system reactivity orient them toward personality characteristics in childhood; and personality characteristics like shyness give rise to distinct desires, wants, and fears (motivations).

Human beings do not inherit the personality traits of shyness, sensation seeking, extraversion, or affect intensity. Rather, people inherit temperamental dispositions that produce and regulate neurotransmitters and hormones that contribute a physiological basis to motivation, emotion, and behavior. We are born with different temperaments that provide us with different ways of reacting to external stimuli, and these different ways of reacting affect our choices. These choices interact with our developmental history, social influences, and cultural pressures to build in us the preferences and response dispositions that make up personality (Zuckerman, 1995).

Personal control beliefs are people's assessment of their ability to interact effectively with the world. When personal control beliefs are strong, the individual's sense of self-determination and sense of mastery over life's outcomes are strong. When personal control beliefs are weak, individuals feel that impersonal forces regulate their behavior and they feel helpless in controlling life's outcomes. Chapter 8 discussed personal control beliefs from self-efficacy, learned helplessness, and reactance theories. This chapter discusses personal control beliefs from a personality perspective.

Many personality characteristics could be included in the category of personal control beliefs, including locus of control (Levenson, 1981), causality orientations (Deci & Ryan, 1985b), explanatory style (Peterson & Seligman, 1984), desire for control (Burger, 1992), type A behavior pattern (Strube et al., 1987), self-esteem (Janis & Field, 1959), personal strivings (Emmons, 1996; Emmons & McAdams, 1991), depression (Beck & Beamesderfer, 1974), and others. Two of these adequately capture most of the sense of control beliefs: *causality orientations* and *desire for control.* Causality orientations concern differences in people's understanding of what causes their behavior—what forces cause them to read a book, go to college, or lose weight. Desire for control concerns differences in the extent to which people strive to make their own decisions, influence others, assume leadership roles, and enter situations overly prepared (Burger, Oakman, & Bullard, 1983).

AROUSAL

Arousal is a hypothetical construct representing a variety of processes that govern alertness, wakefulness, and activation (Anderson, 1990). The processes are cortical, behavioral, and autonomic mechanisms. Thus, the activity of the brain, skeletal muscular system, and autonomic nervous system together give meaning to the general motivational construct of arousal. Three principles explain arousal's contribution to motivation:

1. Arousal level is mostly a function of how stimulating the environment is.
2. People engage in behavior to increase or decrease their level of arousal.
3. When underaroused, increases in environmental stimulation are pleasurable and decreases are aversive; when overaroused, increases in stimulation are aversive and decreases are pleasurable.

Figure 14.3 relates psychological arousal to (1) performance efficiency and (2) affect, which is experienced as reward (positive affect) or aversion (negative affect). The inverted-U curve illustrates that a low level of arousal produces relatively poor performance (lower left). As arousal level increases from low to moderate, performance quality improves and performance intensity increases. As arousal level continues to increase from moderate to high, performance quality and efficiency (but not intensity) decrease (lower right). To make sense of the arousal-performance relationship, recall your personal performance efficiency while doing something important—public speaking, competing in athletics, job interviewing, or whatever. When nonchalant and underaroused or when anxious and overaroused, performance tends to be subpar. When moderately aroused—alert but not too tense—performance tends to be optimal.

FIGURE 14–3
Relationship between Performance Efficiency, Affect, and Arousal Level

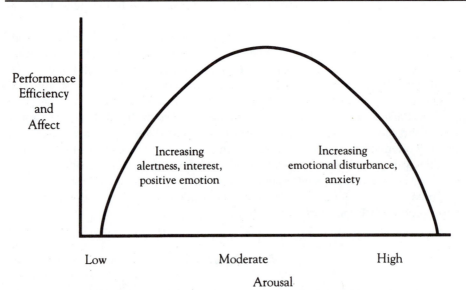

SOURCE: Adapted from Hebb, D. O. (1955). Drive and the C. N. S.—Conceptual nervous system. *Psychological Review, 62,* 245–254.

Arousal as Reward and Aversion

The inverted-U curve is of great importance to the understanding of human motivation (Berlyne, 1967; Duffy, 1957; Hebb, 1955; Lindsley, 1957; Malmo, 1959). A moderate level of arousal coincides with the experience of pleasure (Berlyne, 1967). Low stimulation tends to produce boredom and restlessness; high stimulation tends to produce states of tension, apprehension, and stress. Both boredom and stress are aversive experiences, and people strive to escape from each. When underaroused and experiencing negative affect, people seek out activities that offer increased stimulation and perhaps risk taking. When arousal is less than some optimal level, environmental stimulation invites exploration. On the other hand, when arousal is greater than some optimal level, the individual avoids and is repulsed by further increases in environmental stimulation. When overaroused, increased stimulation and risk taking create negative affect—stress, frustration, and hassle. The overaroused person experiences positive affect with decreased stimulation and is therefore attracted to environmental calm—a vacation, a casual reading of the newspaper, going for a quiet walk, and so on. Thus, the inverted-U curve predicts when increases and decreases in stimulation will lead to positive affect and approach behavior or to negative affect and avoidance behavior.

INSUFFICIENT STIMULATION AND UNDERAROUSAL. The psychological consequences of being underaroused for a long time are best illustrated by research on sensory deprivation (Bexton, Heron, & Scott, 1954; Heron, 1957; Zubek, 1969). Sensory deprivation refers to an individual's sensory and emotional experience in a rigidly unchanging environment. In his studies, Heron (1957) paid male college students a substantial amount of money per day to lay on a comfortable bed for as many days as they cared to stay. Figure 14.4 shows the sensory deprivation chamber. The participant's task was simply to stay in the unchanging environment, with time out for meals and visits to the restroom (note the door off the participant's right shoulder). To restrict sensory information from touch, participants wore cotton gloves with long cardboard forearm cuffs. They wore a special translucent visor that restricted their visual information. To restrict auditory information, an air conditioner put out a steady hum that masked most sounds.

During the first day, nearly all participants reported an inability to think clearly. In the beginning, participants planned to sleep or to think about their work, studies, or personal problems, and, at first, this is what they did. Hours later, most participants reminisced and thought about movies, traveling, and other experiences. As the deprivation continued, participants found it increasingly difficult to focus their concentration. Many reported experiencing blank periods ("I just ran out of things to think of"), and others just let their minds wander. Many of the wandering minds began to see images, and nearly everyone reported dreams and visions while awake. Hallucinations were common. Participants also reported little control over what came to mind or how long the hallucination lasted. For example, one participant who reached for a pen first "saw" an inkblot, then a pencil, then a green horse, and finally a pen. Another participant could see nothing but dogs, no matter how hard he tried to change what he "saw."

FIGURE 14–4
Sensory Deprivation Chamber

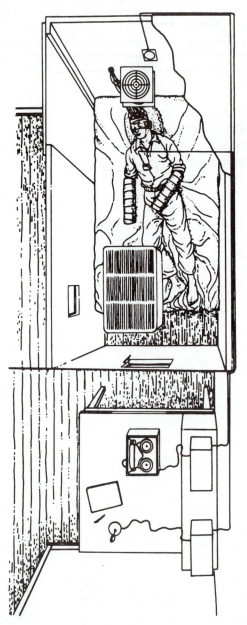

SOURCE: Heron, W. (1957). The pathology of boredom. *Scientific American,* 196, 52–56. Copyright ©
1957 by Scientific American. Adapted with permission from the illustration by Eric Mose.

To obtain a more objective measure of participants' mental processes, Heron administered a series of arithmetic, anagram, and word association tests after 12, 24, and 48 hours of deprivation. As the length of sensory deprivation increased, performance on these once-simple tasks depreciated accordingly. After 48 hours, participants had difficulty with even the most basic mathematic computations (16 times 6 = ?). The participants became increasingly irritable. In fact, Heron found it difficult to keep his irritated participants in the experiment for more than two or three days, despite the large financial incentive to stay. After a day or two, participants welcomed events that normally held no interest for them (e.g., recordings of stock market reports). When the experiment was over, participants were quick to seek out stimulation. They talked, sang, whistled, and recited poetry. Presumably, the freed participants were seeking out opportunities to increase their arousal.

Sensory deprivation studies underscore the fact that the brain and nervous system prefer a continual and at least moderate level of arousal generated by environmental stimulation. Imagine the emotional experiences of zoo animals in cages, inmates in prison cells, the elderly in nursing homes, political prisoners in solitary confinement, long-term patients in hospital wards, and students enduring monotonous lectures. Each experiences some measure of unvarying stimulation. But human beings are not simply passive recipients of whatever stimulation the environment offers. When understimulated, people rely on various cognitive and behavioral means to increase arousal level, such as mental imagery and social interaction. Hence, human beings have motives to counteract insufficient stimulation and underarousal.

EXCESSIVE STIMULATION AND OVERAROUSAL. Life is often stressful. The primary sources of stress include *major life events* such as divorce, physical injury, and unemployment (Holmes & Rahe, 1967; Iversen & Sabroe, 1989); *daily hassles* such as misplacing or losing things, cleaning up the house, and traffic (DeLongis, Folkman, & Lazarus, 1988; Lazarus & DeLongis, 1983); and *chronic circumstances* such as inadequate child care, overcrowding, or repetitive relationship difficulties (DeLongis et al., 1982; Eckenrode, 1984). Major life events stimulate and sometimes jolt the body's nervous and endocrine systems, whereas daily hassles and chronic circumstances occur frequently and thus build to produce a cumulative taxing effect on bodily systems.

In the absence of major life events, daily hassles, and chronically poor circumstances, our emotional state, thinking efficiency, and physiological functioning are basically at their normal, baseline levels. Overstimulating, stressful environments, on the other hand, upset emotion states, impair cognitive activity, and accelerate physiological processes such as blood pressure. Emotional disruption manifests itself in feelings of anxiety, irritability, and anger (Horowitz et al., 1980). Cognitive disruption manifests itself in confusion, forgetfulness, and impaired concentration (Broadbent et al., 1982). Physiological disruption manifests itself in sympathetic nervous system hyperactivity, as through hyperactive hormones and viscera (Seyle, 1956). As a case in point, recall the last time your term paper was due in two hours and was nowhere near completion. Your amiability was probably decidedly nega-

tive (few overly stressed individuals smile, laugh, and tell jokes), your mental efficiency was probably disturbed ("I can't think straight"), and your heart rate, muscle
tone, and vulnerability to a headache were probably high.

Researchers have concluded that overstimulation leads to stress, strain, and frustration. Because these are aversive ways of thinking and feeling, people want to escape from overstimulating environments. When unable to do so, day-to-day and year-
to-year functioning is characterized by negative affect, cognitive confusion,
performance impairment, and health problems. Fortunately, human beings have motives to counteract excessive stimulation and overarousal.

Credibility of the Inverted-U Hypothesis

The validity of the inverted-U curve (see Fig. 14.3) is not without debate. Neiss (1988)
levied four criticisms against the credibility of the inverted-U hypothesis, two of
which are relevant to motivation and emotion; all of which began some beneficial
discussion (see Anderson, 1990). Neiss's first criticism is that the inverted-U curve
is descriptive rather than explanatory; that is, it summarizes the relationship betwen
arousal and performance/affect but does not explain *how* arousal facilitates or im-
pairs performance/affect.

Neiss's second criticism is that the inverted-U hypothesis, if true, is trivial. In
other words, the inverted-U hypothesis applies only when arousal levels are
extreme—such as in sensory deprivation studies. Neiss concludes that the inverted-
U hypothesis does not apply to everyday affairs in which arousal level changes relatively little. This second criticism, however, has been nicely answered by inverted-
U defenders. To illustrate how the inverted-U hypothesis applies to mundane changes
in arousal, college students completed a pair of vocabulary tests under different conditions (Revelle, Amaral, & Turriff, 1976). Students completed the first vocabulary
test at their leisure—"spend as much time as necessary." Students completed the
second test under a 10-minute time pressure. In addition, before taking the tests, all
students took either a 200-mg caffeine pill (caffeine equivalent to two cups of coffee) or a placebo (pill with no caffeine). The purpose of the time pressure and caffeine administration was to create high stimulation; the purpose of the relaxed condition and placebo was to create low stimulation. The experiment had one more
important variable, as each student completed a personality survey to differentiate
introverts (people who are chronically overaroused) from extraverts (people who
are chronically underaroused). In summary, overaroused (introverts) or underaroused
(extroverts) individuals took a vocabulary test under conditions of either low (no
time pressure, no caffeine) or high (time pressure, caffeine) stimulation. Based on
the inverted-U hypothesis, the experimenters predicted that (1) introverts would perform better when relaxed and worse when stressed, whereas (2) extroverts would
perform worse when relaxed and better when stressed. Results confirmed the predictions. Relaxed introverts scored better than stressed introverts, and stressed extroverts scored better than relaxed extroverts. Perhaps most important, the experiment showed that the inverted-U hypothesis applies nicely to everyday sources of
stimulation—time pressures and a routine level of caffeine.

EXTRAVERSION

Personality psychologists generally agree that the introversion-extraversion characteristic is hereditary, meaning that differences in people's genes are largely responsible for introverted and extraverted tendencies (Eaves, Eysenck, & Martin, 1989; Pedersen et al., 1988; Shields, 1976; Viken et al., 1994). For instance, twins reared apart score similarly in terms of their disposition toward introversion or extraversion, suggesting that extraversion is based more on genetic factors than it is on environmental factors (Pedersen et al., 1988).

In assessing extraversion, researchers routinely use the Eysenck Personality Inventory (EPI, Eysenck & Eysenck, 1968), a self-report questionnaire with items such as "Do you stop and think things over before doing anything?" and "Can you easily get some life into a rather dull party?" Figure 14.5 shows the subtraits that make up the supertrait of extraversion (from Eysenck, 1986).

The most popular and widely accepted theory of extraversion is Eysenck's (1967). According to Eysenck, genetic differences produce physiological differences between individuals in the ascending reticular activating system (ARAS), the brain structure responsible for diffuse cortical arousal in response to an external stimulus (Eysenck, 1967; Eysenck & Eysenck, 1969, 1985). The ARAS's insensitivity to low levels of stimulation and reactivity at high levels of stimulation characterizes extraversion. Extraverts need strong external stimuli to arouse their ARAS. The ARAS's sensitivity and reactivity to low levels of stimulation and intolerance to high stimulation levels characterizes introversion. Introverts need less intense external stimuli to arouse their ARAS. Based on this line of reasoning, introverts are perpetually and inherently more cortically aroused than are extraverts.

Figure 14.6 illustrates schematically the basic tenets of Eysenck's neurophysiological theory of extraversion (Gale & Edwards, 1986). The ARAS mediates arousal level (A). The ARAS and neocortex have reciprocal relations in which each can ex-

FIGURE 14–5
Traits That Define Extraversion

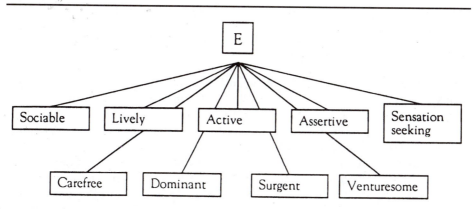

SOURCE: Eysenck, H. J. (1986). Can personality study ever be scientific? *Journal of Social Behavior and Personality,* 1, 3–19. Reprinted with permission.

FIGURE 14–6
Schematic Description of Eysenck's Theory of the Neurophysiological Basis of Extraversion-Introversion

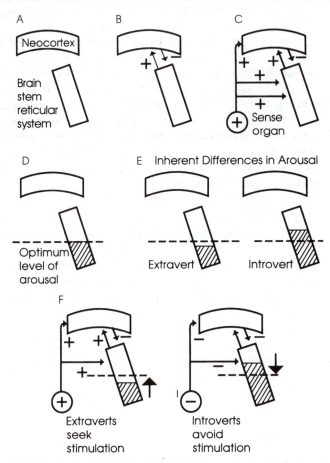

SOURCE: Gale, A., & Edwards, J. A. (1986). Individual differences. In M. G. H. Coles, E. Donchin, & S. W. Proges (Ed.), Psychophysiology: Systems, processes, and applications (pp. 431–507). New York: The Guilford Press. Adapted with permission.

cite or inhibit the other (*B*). Sense organs send axons into both the ARAS and cortex (*C*). There is an optimal level of arousal for the ARAS (*D*). Extraverts genetically inherit a below-optimum level of arousal, whereas introverts inherit an above-optimum level of arousal (*E*). Lastly, extraverts behave to increase external stimulation (by actively stimulating their sense organs), whereas introverts behave to decrease external stimulation (by avoiding stimulation to their sense organs) (*F*).

Temperament relates to introversion and extraversion through optimal level of arousal (Eysenck, 1967, 1971). Introverts attain an optimal level of arousal at relatively low levels of stimulation and therefore shun strong stimulation. Extraverts attain an optimal level of arousal at relatively high levels of stimulation and thus seek out and approach stronger forms of stimulation (Derryberry & Rothbart, 1988). Figure 14.7 graphically illustrates the relationship between external stimulation and hedonic tone for introverts, ambiverts, and extraverts. An ambivert is somewhere between an introvert and an extravert; most people are ambiverts rather than introverts or extraverts (recall Fig. 14.2). Introverts attain optimal level of arousal at relatively low levels of external stimulation (OL_I); ambiverts at moderate levels (OL_P); and extraverts at high levels (OL_E) (Derryberry & Rothbart, 1988).

A series of psychophysiological and pharmacological studies supports the basic idea of Eysenck's ARAS arousal theory of extraversion. In most, but not all, situations introverts show greater cortical (as measured in the brain by the electroencephalograph, EEG) and electrodermal (as measured in the finger tips by the galvanic skin response, GSR) reactivity than do extraverts (Gale, 1973, 1983). One situation, for instance, involves placing introverts and extraverts into a soundproof room and asking them to look at a black visual field (to minimize sensory stimulation) while the experimenter obtains EEG records (Gale, Coles, & Blaydon, 1969). In such a setting, introverts show greater cortical arousal than do extraverts (greater beta, alpha, and theta waves on the EEG). Hence, introverts are inherently more cortically aroused than are extraverts. Drugs also affect extraverts and introverts differently. Because introverts are inherently more aroused than extraverts, introverts are less affected by sedatives and depressants than are extraverts. Introverts feel and function better after taking a depressant; extraverts feel and function better after taking a stimulant. In the same spirit, introverts and extraverts show different sensitivities to conditions

FIGURE 14–7
Relationship between External Stimulation and Hedonic Tone for Introverts, Ambiverts, and Extraverts

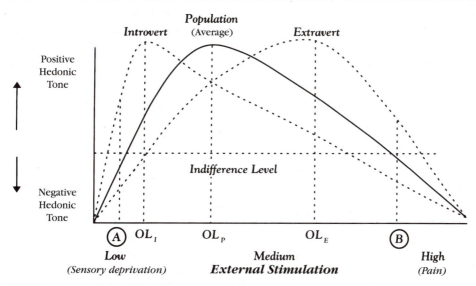

SOURCE: Eysenck, H. J. (1963). *Experiments with drugs: Studies in the relation between pesonality, learning, theory, and drug action.* New York: Pergamon Press.

that produce positive affect. Given the same enjoyment-producing circumstances, extraverts experience greater joy than introverts (Larsen & Ketelaar, 1991).

Because they prefer a lower level of external stimulation, introverts typically outperform extraverts in tasks of vigilance. In low-stimulation tasks, extraverts are more susceptible to performance impairments from boredom. Further, because persistence has its rewards, introverts tend to do better in school and achieve higher academic grades than do extraverts. Extraverts, on the other hand, show a greater social intelligence, they are better able to relate to people and anticipate their social responses. Extraverts are also generally happier, as they report more positive affect and day-to-day pleasant mood than do introverts (Costa & McCrae, 1980; Emmons & Diener, 1986; Watson et al., 1992; Williams, 1990). Extraverts are generally a happier bunch than introverts for two reasons. First, extraverts are more likely to engage in frequent social interaction, and the act of socializing is itself a source of positive emotionality (Watson et al., 1992). Second, extraverts also engage in more active participation events such as dating, partying, and social drinking, and this difference in lifestyle leads extraverts to more experiences of positive affect (Larsen & Ketelaar, 1991).

Because of their perpetually higher levels of cortical arousal, introverts must continually exert more cortical control over their lower brain centers (e.g., reticular formation). Consequently, the introvert exhibits more restrained, inhibited patterns of behavior than does the extravert. Many of the behavioral differences between introverts and extraverts can therefore be attributed to different patterns of self-regulation (the capacity to actively control arousal by managing exposure to external stimulation). For example, introverts avoid competitive situations more than do extraverts (Graziano, Feldesman, & Rahe, 1985) because they expect competitive situations to be arousing, anxiety provoking, and potentially punishing (Wolfe & Kasmer, 1988) and therefore highly stimulating. Extraverts also anticipate that competitive situations will be arousing, anxiety provoking, and potentially punishing, but are attracted to (rather than repulsed by) such an opportunity. Thus, introverts see competition as a negative stimulus event, whereas extraverts see it as positive.

SENSATION SEEKING

Sensation seeking is also based on temperament and arousability. A high sensation seeker prefers a continual external supply of brain stimulation, becomes bored with routine, and is continually in search of ways to increase arousal through exciting experiences. A low sensation seeker prefers less brain stimulation and tolerates routine relatively well. The sensation seeking construct pertains to the extent to which a person's central nervous system (brain and spinal cord) requires change and variability, as sensation seekers prefer to change activities, change television viewing from moment to moment, change drugs, change sexual and marital partners, and so on (Zuckerman, 1994).

"Sensation seeking is a trait defined by the seeking of varied, novel, complex, and intense sensations and experiences, and the willingness to take physical, social, legal, and financial risks for the sake of such experience" (Zuckerman, 1994, p. 27). Zuckerman (1994) uses the example of driving very fast after heavy drinking to illustrate sensation seekers' willingness to take physical risks (injure self or others), social risks (being exposed as a drunken driver), legal risks (being arrested and jailed), and financial risks (being fired from work). Such risks are the price sensation seekers are willing to take to receive the sensations and experiences they seek.

Research suggests that the sensation seeking construct is a set of interrelated components (like extraversion, see Fig. 14.5) rather than a unitary construct. Table 14.1 lists the four components of sensation seeking with a sample item from each scale of the Sensation Seeking Scale (SSS). Each item on the SSS offers the test taker two situations or activities from which to choose the more preferable alternative (see Zuckerman, 1978, 1994, for the SSS questionnaire). One alternative is a high-stimulation activity (the A alternative), while the second is a low-stimulation activity (the B alternative).

Thrill and adventure seeking (TAS) expresses a desire to engage in physical risk-taking. These activities include outdoor, noncompetitive activities that involve danger, personal challenge, and risk, such as flying, parachute jumping, scuba diving, motorcycle riding, speeding in a car, and mountain climbing. *Experience seeking* (ES) expresses the desire to pursue new experiences through the mind and senses. Art, music, travel, and certain types of drugs express the pursuit of experience through the senses, whereas a spontaneous, nonconforming lifestyle, especially with unusual people, typifies experience seeking through the mind. *Disinhibition* (Dis) pertains to a desire to disinhibit oneself in social situations in the pursuit of pleasure. The use of alcohol as a means of disinhibition and participation in gambling, sexual variety, and wild parties define disinhibition. *Boredom susceptibility*

TABLE 14–1

Sample Items from Sensation Seeking Scales

Directions: For each sentence pair, pick the one option that is most true for you.
General Sensation Seeking (SS-G)
  A: A good painting should shock or jolt the senses.
  B: A good painting should give one a feeling of peace and security.
Thrill and Adventure Seeking (TAS)
  A: I sometimes like to do things that are a little frightening.
  B: A sensible person avoids activities that are dangerous.
Experience Seeking (ES)
  A: I would like to hitchhike across the country.
  B: Hitchhiking is too dangerous a way to travel.
Disinhibition (Dis)
  A: Keeping the drinks full is the key to a good party.
  B: Heavy drinking usually ruins a party because some people get loud and boisterous.
Boredom Susceptibility (BS)
  A: I get bored seeing the same old faces.
  B: I like the comfortable familiarity of everyday friends.

SOURCE: Zuckerman, M. (1978). Sensation seeking. In H. London & J.E. Exner, Jr. (Eds.), Dimensions of personality (pp. 487–559). Copyright © 1978. Reprinted by permission of John Wiley & Sons, Inc.

(BS) expresses an aversion for any type of routine—monotony in work, repetition of experience, or exposure to boring people. When circumstances are unchanging, the boredom-susceptible person becomes restless and intolerant (Zuckerman, 1978).

Sensation seeking and extraversion correlate weakly with one another (Zuckerman, 1979a). Though both traits have their roots in temperament and the search for stimulating environments, Zuckerman (1994) illustrates the difference between the two constructs. Extraverts enjoy the company of many people and enjoy parties more than do introverts, but sensation seekers are susceptible to boredom such that the stimulation value of the other person is more important than the sociability afforded in social interaction. Instead of sociability, the sensation seeker is interested in (1) the search for new experience, (2) risk taking, and (3) novel and unusual activities.

Search for New Experience

The sensation seeker continually searches for novel experiences—spicy foods (Terasaki & Imada, 1988), switching television programs frequently (Schierman & Rowland, 1985), listening to music with some punch (Litle & Zuckerman, 1986), and so on. One manifestation of the search for new experience is sex. Compared to sensation avoiders, sensation seekers report a greater frequency and variety (number of partners) in sexual activity (Zuckerman et al., 1972; Zuckerman, Tushup, & Finner, 1976). Further, as parents, high sensation seekers set more permissive standards for their children's sexual activity (Zuckerman, Tushup, & Finner, 1976). Sensation seekers have more permissive attitudes toward sexual relations, as they report that less of a relationship and less emotional involvement are necessary prerequisites for participation in sexual relations than do the sensation avoiders (Hendrick & Hendrick, 1987; Zuckerman, 1976).

Drugs can also provide the means for a quick arousal elevation. Drugs open the door to variety and new experience (hallucinations), release inhibitions against risky behavior, and serve as an escape from boredom. Through any or all of these means of altering experience, drug use functions as a form of sensation seeking (Zuckerman, 1978, 1994; Zuckerman et al., 1972). To substantiate these claims, Zuckerman and his colleagues (1972) asked college students to complete the SSS and a questionnaire on the variety of drug use and frequency of alcohol use (recall the chapter's opening vignette). Table 14.2 lists the correlations between the SSS and the questionnaire on drug and alcohol use (as well as sexual frequency and variety). Several scales correlated with alcohol and drug use, especially for males.

The search for new experience can sometimes extend beyond drug and alcohol use and sexual precocity into deviance such as vandalism, acts of aggression, stealing, and criminality (Newcomb & McGee, 1991; White, Labourvie, & Bates, 1985). Experience seeking leads to the desire to experience novel and unconventional activities. Boredom susceptibility explains some of this attraction to adolescent thrill. Interestingly, sensation seeking's effect on adolescents' drug use explains the relationship between sensation seeking and general deviance, as sensation seeking predicts drug use and drug use predicts general deviance (Newcomb & McGee, 1991).

TABLE 14-2
Correlations between SSS, Sexual Activity, and Drug Use

SSS SCALE	MALES (N = 38)				FEMALES (N = 60)			
	SEXUAL ACTIVITY	NUMBER OF SEX PARTNERS	DRUG USE	ALCOHOL USE	SEXUAL ACTIVITY	NUMBER OF SEX PARTNERS	DRUG USE	ALCOHOL USE
SS-G	.51**	.40**	.42**	.27	.15	.27	.36**	.18
TAS	.44**	.47**	.42**	.39*	.16	.20	.28*	.15
ES	.37*	.35**	.47**	.10	.32*	.28*	.55**	.26*
Dis	.33*	.42**	.08	.47**	.43**	.29*	.43**	.43**
BS	.36*	.25*	.34*	-.09	.29*	.20	.32*	.12

*p < .05; **p < .01.

SOURCE: Zuckerman, M. Bone, R.N., Neary, R., Mangelsdorff, D., & Brustman, B. (1972). What is the sensation seeker? Personality trait and experience correlates of the Sensation Seeking Scale. Journal of Clinical and Counseling Psychology, 39, 308–321. Copyright ©1972 by American Psychological Association. Adapted with permission.

Such a finding suggests the interesting intervention strategy to prevent adult deviance is to provide adolescents high in sensation seeking with substitutes for the excitement of licit drugs (Zuckerman, 1979).

Risk Taking

No one likes risk per se, which is essentially the perception of the probability that a behavior will produce aversive consequences. The risks related to sensation seeking involve those that are physical, social, legal, or financial. It is not that sensation seekers are attracted to such risks; rather, sensation seekers see sensations and experiences being *worth* their risks while sensation avoiders do not. Thus, risk accepting seems a more appropriate term than risk taking.

High sensation seekers voluntarily engage in physically risky hobbies, such as motorcycling (Brown et al., 1974), parachuting and skydiving (Hymbaugh & Garrett, 1974), adventuresome travel (Jacobs & Koeppel, 1974), immigration (Winchie & Carment, 1988), cigarette smoking (Zuckerman, Ball, & Black, 1990), downhill skiing (Calhoon, 1988), and gambling (Kuhlman, 1975). In contrast, low sensation seekers show phobiclike reactivity to risky sources of stimulation such as snakes, heights, and darkness (Mellstrom, Cicala, & Zuckerman, 1976). Gambling illustrates some of the sensation-seekers motivation for risk taking, as excitement, rather than money, motivates most people's gambling (Anderson & Brown, 1984). Sensation seekers are attracted to the large increase in heart rate people experience as they place a wager (Anderson & Brown, 1984). High, compared to low, sensation seekers make larger bets and experience more pronounced heart rate spikes when they do so.

Zuckerman (1978) extracted a quotation from the *New York Times* in the 1970s to illustrate the feelings of the sensation seeker during a popular risk-taking fad of the day, streaking.

> Like other participants they discovered the heady exhilaration that is said to accompany streaking; first the sense of daring, then the nervous anticipation as you undress, the last fleeting moment of fear before you start, the wet grass underfoot, the pounding heart during the dash, the smiles of spectators flashing by, the wind brushing against your cheeks and the warm sense of accomplishment as you dress—uncaptured—at your goal.

To test whether sensation seekers were more willing to participate in streaking than sensation avoiders, Bone (1974, personal communication reported in Zuckerman, 1978) asked college students to complete both the SSS and a questionnaire on their desire to participate in a streaking episode. For both males and females, sensation seeking correlated significantly with the desire to streak.

Risk taking manifests itself in many areas of life, and sensation seeking relates positively to risk taking in areas such as criminal behavior (shoplifting, selling drugs), minor violations (traffic offenses), finances (gambling, risky businesses), and sports (scuba diving) (Horvath & Zuckerman, 1993). Fast driving offers potential physical, social, legal, and financial risks. Compared to sensation avoiders, sensation seekers report driving fast (well over the posted speed limit) under normal conditions (Arnett,

1991; Clement & Jonah, 1984; Zuckerman & Neeb, 1980). In addition, high sensation seekers do not perceive tailgating (driving close behind the car in front) as risky as sensation avoiders do. During simulated tailgating, sensation avoiders report high risk and much heart rate variability whereas sensation seekers report less risk and calmer hearts (Heino, van der Molen, & Wilde, 1992, as reported in Zuckerman, 1994).

Volunteering for Unusual Activities

Suppose several experimenters visited your psychology class to recruit volunteers for their experiments in learning, social psychology, sleep research, sensory deprivation, ESP, hypnosis, and drug research. For which experiments would you be most willing to participate? Such a study was made by Bone, Cowling, and Choban (as reported in Zuckerman, 1978, pp. 521–522; see also Trice & Ogdon, 1986). High sensation seekers were no more willing than lows to volunteer for usual experiments, such as learning and social psychology. Sensation seekers were, however, significantly more willing than their counterparts to volunteer for the unusual experiments, such as hypnosis and drug research.

U. S. Army personnel had a chance to volunteer for a high-risk or low-risk activity (or neither) after filling out the SSS questionnaire (Jobe, Holgate, & Sorapanshy, 1983). The high-risk activity involved setting off a dynamite explosive, while the low-risk activity involved filling out personality questionnaires. Sensation seekers volunteered more frequently for the high-risk activity than did the sensation avoiders. Sensation seekers and avoiders did not differ in how frequently they volunteered for the low-risk activity, thereby confirming that sensation seekers volunteer for high-risk activity and not for *any* type of activity. Volunteering for unusual activities therefore involved the search for new and intense experiences with the potential to be very interesting or arousing (Zuckerman, 1994).

Biological Bases of Sensation Seeking

Because sensation seeking is temperament based, researchers look for physiological differences between high and low sensation seekers (Neary & Zuckerman, 1976; Zuckerman, 1984; Zuckerman, Buchsbaum, & Murphy, 1980). The sensation seeker in not chronically underaroused, but instead seeks out and is excited by intense sources of stimulation (Zuckerman, 1994). For example, sensation seekers prefer stimuli that cause a sudden orientation reaction (Neary & Zuckerman, 1976), a rapid, 5- to 10-second drop in heart rate and a tensing of the musculature—a physiological jolt to the ANS—on encountering novel, complex, or personally significant stimuli. The sensation seekers' preference for stimuli that produce orienting reactions helps explain why they prefer activities like motorcycle riding, parachuting, and streaking. But sensation seekers do not just get high on physiological jolts to the nervous system. Instead, when intense stimuli lead to the orientation reflex, sensation seekers react by approaching the sense-jolting stimulation opportunities; the sensation avoiders react defensively by avoiding the jolting source (Zuckerman, 1994).

Sensation seekers respond positively to varied, novel, complex, and intense environmental events. Biochemical events in the brain determine how people react to environmental stimulation, so researchers have investigated the linkages between the sensation-seeking trait and biochemical events in the brain. The most reliable finding is that sensation seekers have low levels of monoamine oxidase (MAO) (Schooler et al. 1978). MAO is a limbic system enzyme involved in breaking down brain neurotransmitters such as dopamine, serotonin, and norepinephrine. Dopamine contributes to the experience of reward toward biologically significant events such as food and sex and therefore facilitates approach behaviors (Stellar & Stellar, 1985). Serotonin contributes to a biological inhibition, or stop system, in the brain and therefore inhibits approach behaviors (Panksepp, 1982). Sensation seekers tend to have relatively high levels of dopamine; hence, their biochemistry favors approach over inhibition (Zuckerman, 1994). Though the neurobiological basis of sensation seeking is not perfectly clear (Zuckerman, 1994), these three conclusions can be offered: Sensation seekers have lower levels of MAO; MAO enzymes regulate in part brain availability of dopamine, serotonin, and other biochemical agents relevant to sensation seeking (norepinephrine, cortisol); brain dopamine regulates approach tendencies whereas brain serotonin inhibits it (reviewed in Zuckerman, 1994).

There is also indirect evidence that sensation seeking has a genetic basis. Zuckerman and his colleagues (1980) reported that monozygotic (MZ, or identical) twins show greater similarity of SSS scores than do dizygotic (DZ, or fraternal) twins, presumably because MZ twins share the more similar genetic structure.

Affect Intensity

Affect intensity is a third measure of human temperament, as it concerns people's emotionality and arousability. Affect intensity is defined in terms of the strength with which individuals typically experience their emotions (Larsen & Diener, 1987). Affect-intense individuals experience their emotions strongly and show emotional reactivity and variability across many different emotion-eliciting situations. Affect-stable individuals experience their emotions only mildly and show only minor fluctuations in their emotional reactions from moment to moment or day to day. Affect intensity is significantly related to extraversion (Diener et al., 1985) and with activity level, arousability, and emotionality (Larsen & Diener, 1987). Affect intensity is not correlated, however, with any of the sensation seeking scales (Larsen, Diener, & Emmons, 1986).

Researchers measure affect intensity with a self-report questionnaire with 40 items, such as "When I feel happy it is a strong type of exuberance" and "When I am nervous I get shaky all over" (see Larsen & Diener, 1987). Originally, researchers assessed affect intensity in an interesting, although laborious, way (Larsen, 1988). Over a period of 80 or 90 consecutive days, respondents completed a daily mood questionnaire that featured positive (e.g., happy, joyful) and negative (e.g., depressed, worried) mood items. To compute affect intensity, the individual's daily score on the negative mood words was totalled and subtracted from the daily score on the positive mood words total to yield a daily mood. On each consecutive day, the overall daily mood score was plotted on a graph, as in Figure 14.8, which shows the daily mood graphs for three persons. The daily mood of the affect-intense individual (subject 23) rises and falls rather substantially, whereas the daily mood of the affect-stable individual (subject 21) hovers continuously around the neutral zone. How much the person's daily mood score deviated from neutral (0) defined affect intensity.

For example, imagine that each of the following events, some good and some bad, recently occurred: You received a scholarship you desperately needed or you received a letter from a friend from whom you have not heard in a while (positive life events); your automobile had a flat tire or you saw your ex-boyfriend/girlfriend with a new flame (negative life events; from Larsen, Diener, & Emmons, 1987). Suppose further that you were asked to rate precisely how good or how bad each event was immediately after it occurred. For example, how good did you feel when you received a letter from your long-lost friend? Figure 14.9 shows how affect-intense and affect-stable individuals (as measured by the 40-item self-report questionnaire) reacted to events classified by objective raters as slightly good, moderately good, and very good and to events classified as slightly bad, moderately bad, and very bad. As shown, affect-intense individuals react more positively to all categories of good events and more negatively to all categories of bad events. In other words, whereas an affect-stable individual feels slightly good about receiving a letter in the mail, an affect-intense individual feels moderately good about the same event. Affect-intense individuals therefore *augment* (intensify) the emotional effects of an event.

Originally, researchers presumed that affect-intense individuals were physiologically underaroused, relative to affect-stable individuals (Larsen & Emmons, 1986). Follow-up research, however, found that affect-intense individuals were neither less aroused than their affect-stable counterparts nor experienced greater arousal spikes in arousal-generating situations such as exercise or cognitive challenge (Blascovich et al., 1992). Instead of differing at the physiological level, affect-intense individuals are simply more psychologically sensitive to changes in arousal than are affect-stable individuals. It is almost as if affect-intense persons have a sensitive arousal thermostat monitoring their arousal increases whereas affect-stable individuals have an insensitive arousal thermastat (Blascovich et al., 1992).

Affect intensity contributes to arousability as an emotional route by which underaroused individuals seek out sources of stimulation. Just as extraverts and sensation seekers seek out stimulating activities to increase their arousal to an optimal level, affect-intense individuals use emotional reactivity to increase their arousal to an optimal level (Larsen & Diener, 1987). Affect-intense individuals in fact seek out and prefer opportunities for emotional arousal, whereas affect-stable individuals avoid emotional stimulation (Basso, Schefft, & Hoffmann, 1994; Larsen, Diener, & Cropanzano, 1987).

Temperament and Arousal Regulation

Human beings differ in their genetic baseline level of arousal and in their reactive arousability to intense environmental stimuli. The baseline level of arousal is the level

FIGURE 14.8
Daily Mood Reports Graphed over 80 Consecutive Days

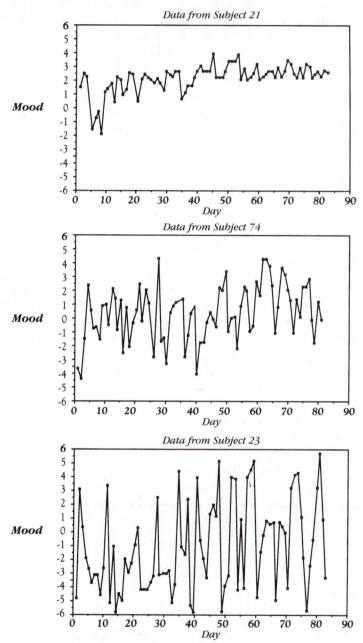

SOURCE: Larsen, R. J. (1988). Individual differences in affect intensity. Paper presented at the annual meeting of the Motivation and Emotion Conference at Nags Head, Nags Head, NC.

FIGURE 14–9
Affective Reactions to Good and Bad Events

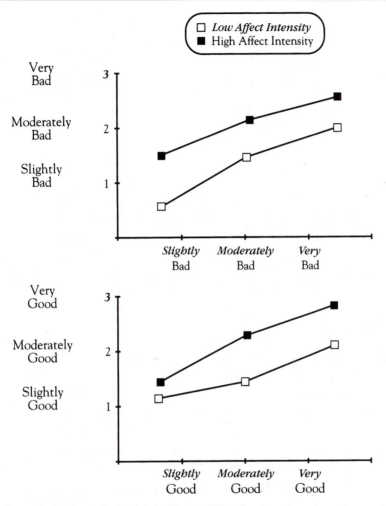

SOURCE: Larsen, R. J., Diener, E., & Emmons, R. A. (1987). Affect intensity and reactions to daily life events. Journal of Personality and Social Psychology, 51, 803-814. Copyright © 1987 by American Psychological Association. Adapted with permission.

without external stimulation. Arousability refers to the degree of reaction to external stimulation.

To illustrate how temperament differences lead to differences in self-regulation, consider Figure 14.10. Extraverts, sensation seekers, and affect-intense individuals have three modes of affect regulation (Larsen & Diener, 1987). One means of arousal increase is seeking out stimulating sensory experience. For example, sensation seekers seek out drugs, alcohol, sex, and unusual activities, all sources of stimulation. A second means of arousal increase is engagement in stimulating behavior. For exam-

FIGURE 14–10
Mechanisms of Arousal Regulation

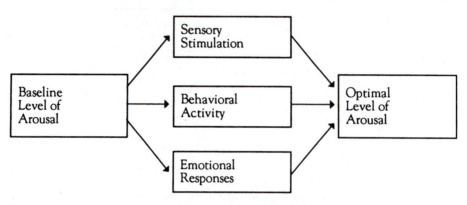

SOURCE: Larsen, R. J., & Diener, E. (1987). Affect intensity as an individual difference characteristic: A review. *Journal of Research in Personality,* 21, 1-39. Reprinted with permission.

ple, extraverts socialize with friends, accept dares, and play practical jokes. A third means of arousal increase is emotional hyperreactivity. For example, the affect-intense individual increases arousal through exaggerated emotional reactions, both to common situations such as holding a puppy and to severe situations such as taking college board examinations.

From this point of view, sensory stimulation, extraverted behavior, and emotional reactivity are all means of regulating arousal and arousability toward an optimal level. Thus, much temperament-motivated behavior can be understood as an attempt to self-regulate baseline level of arousal or situationally reactive arousability toward a preferred level (Derryberry & Rothbart, 1988). The preference for shocking art (sensory stimulation), going to parties (extraverted behavior), and overreacting to a compliment (emotional responsiveness) are means to augment arousal. The preference for calming art (sensory avoidance), vacationing for solitude (introverted behavior), and a nonchalant reaction to a compliment (emotional unresponsiveness) are means to attenuate arousal.

CAUSALITY ORIENTATIONS

People vary in their understandings of the forces that cause their behavior. Some people adopt a general orientation that their behavior is caused primarily by inner guides and self-determined forces; others adopt a general orientation that their behavior is caused primarily by social incentives and environmental forces. To the extent that individuals rely on internal guides such as needs and interests, they have an autonomy causality orientation. To the extent that individuals rely on external guides such as social cues, they have a control causality orientation.

The autonomy orientation involves a high degree of experienced choice with respect to the initiation and regulation of behavior (Deci & Ryan, 1985b). When autonomy oriented, people's behavior proceeds with a full sense of choice, volition, freedom, and an internal perceived locus of causality. Needs, interests, and personally valued goals initiate the behavior, and needs, interests, and goals regulate the decision whether to persist or quit. Behavior follows spontaneously from inner guides, such that decisions of what to major in and which career to pursue represent expressions of personal needs, interests, and goals. External factors such as salary and status are not irrelevant to these decisions, but autonomy-oriented individuals pay closer attention to their needs and feelings than they do environmental contingencies and pressures.

The control orientation involves a relative insensitivity to inner guides, as control-oriented individuals prefer to pay closer attention to behavioral incentives, cues, and pressures that exist either in the environment or inside themselves (Deci & Ryan, 1985b). When control oriented, people make decisions in response to the presence and quality of incentives such as extrinsic rewards or a concern over attaining some outcome, such as pleasing others. A central ingredient in the determination of control-oriented people's ways of thinking, feeling, and behaving is a sense of tension and pressure. Behavior is in response to feelings of tension and pressure, compliance to what is demanded, and a sense of "I have to" or "It's what I should do." Environmental factors such as pay and status are very important. When researchers ask control-oriented individuals what they aspire after, their goals center around financial and material success (Kasser & Ryan, 1993).

Religious beliefs and behaviors provide one example of the difference between autonomy-oriented and control-oriented ways of thinking, feeling, and behaving (Ryan, Rigby, & King, 1993). Based on their experience, some people commit to religious beliefs and behaviors with a relatively extrinsic orientation ("attending services is something I have to do") whereas others commit to religious beliefs and behaviors with an intrinsic orientation ("attending services is something I choose to do") (Donahue, 1985). Education and prosocial behavior provide two additional examples, as some people go to school and help others for extrinsic reasons whereas others do so for intrinsic reasons (Ryan & Connell, 1989). Autonomy-oriented persons' ways of thinking, feeling, and behaving in areas such as religion, education, and helping others flows from a sense of choice, freedom, and volition, and is associated with psychological adjustment. Control-oriented persons pay closer attention to incentives, social demands, and the feelings of tension and pressure to do what is expected or rewarded and are associated with psychological maladjustment (Ryan & Connell, 1989; Ryan, Rigby, & King, 1993).

The *General Causality Orientations Scale* (Deci & Ryan, 1985b) measures causality orientations by presenting a series of 12 vignettes (short stories). Each vignette presents a situation and lists responses to that situation, one of which is autonomy oriented and the other of which is control oriented. (A third scale to assess the impersonal orientation is not discussed here.) For instance, one of the vignettes presents the following situation:

> You have been offered a new position in a company where you have worked for some time. The first question that is likely to come to mind is:
> I wonder if the new work will be interesting? (Autonomy)
> Will I make more at this position? (Control)

Causality orientations reflect self-determination in personality. Hence, self-determination theory explains the origins and dynamics of causality orientations (Deci & Ryan, 1985a). The autonomy-oriented personality is characterized by intrinsic motivation and identified regulation, as the forces that cause behavior are personal needs and interests (intrinsic motivation) as well as beliefs and values that have been freely internalized into the self system (identified regulation). The control-oriented personality is characterized by extrinsic motivation and introjected regulation, as the forces that cause behavior are environmental rewards and constraints (extrinsic motivation) and beliefs and values that have been forced onto the self (introjected regulation). Because of these origins and therefore its close relationship to self-determination in personality, the autonomy orientation correlates positively with measures of positive functioning, including self-actualization, ego development, self-esteem, openness to experience, and acceptance of one's true feelings (Deci & Ryan, 1985b; Koestner, Bernieri, & Zuckerman, 1992; Scherhorn & Grunert, 1988).

Attitude-Behavior Consistency and Inconsistency

Because autonomy-oriented persons pay closer attention to needs and feelings than they do to controlling contingencies, they are able to maintain a high degree of consistency and harmony among their needs, thoughts, feelings, and behaviors. By contrast, control-oriented individuals are more alert to external contingencies and to internal imperatives than they are to their own needs and feelings. The consequence is a lack of consistency or harmony among needs, thoughts, feelings, and behaviors. Hence, control-oriented individuals are more affected by social persuasions, such as advertising appeals (Scherhorn & Grunert, 1988; Zuckerman, Gioioso, & Tellini, 1988).

Attitude-behavior consistency and inconsistency are expressed in several ways. In a typical intrinsic motivation study, for instance, people engage in a task that they find interesting or uninteresting with or without external incentives such as praise or a reward. Autonomy-oriented individuals engage in the task according to how interesting they find it to be. Control-oriented individuals engage in the task when praised or rewarded but do not when praise or reward is absent. Hence, autonomy-oriented persons follow their interests closely, whereas control-oriented persons behave in ways that do not correlate with their (intrinsic) interests (Koestner, Bernieri, & Zuckerman, 1992).

In another study, researchers assessed college students on conscientiousness (how dependable, organized, and hard-working they were) and then presented an opportunity to test that trait. The researchers gave the students a questionnaire, asked them to complete it later, and then return it one week later. All students agreed to return the questionnaires, but external factors also affect behavior such as the weather, how much they like the experimenter, whether they get paid for doing so, and so on. The autonomy-oriented students who were high in conscientiousness generally returned the questionnaire whereas those low in conscientiousness did not. Knowing whether the control-oriented student was conscientious or not did not predict their questionnaire-returning behavior (Koestner, Bernieri, & Zuckerman, 1992).

Maintenance of Behavior Change

When people seek to change their behavior, they typically rely on either internal guides (goals) or external guides (a rule) to do so. To lose weight, for instance, people can rely on inner guides ("I believe it's the best way to help myself") or on outer guides ("I want others to see that I am really trying to lose weight") (Williams et al., 1996). While involved in a weight-loss program, people can generally rely on both internal and external support for assistance and motivation to change their behavior. After the program ends, people lose much of their external support (the staff, the structure of the program) for changing their behavior. These researchers therefore reasoned that the more autonomy oriented the participants were, the more likely it was that they would stay in the program week to week, lose weight during the program, and, most important, maintain their weight loss after the program ended (maintain behavior change).

Figure 14.11 graphs the findings of how autonomy-oriented individuals succeeded in maintaining their behavior change (Williams et al., 1996). The more autonomy oriented the participants were (and the more autonomy supportive the staff-patient interactions were), the more they relied on relatively autonomous reasons

FIGURE 14–11
Model of Self-Determined Weight Loss

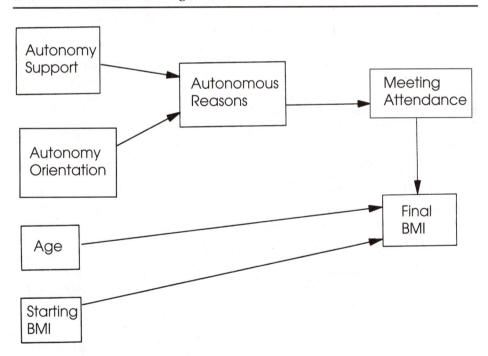

BMI body mass index.
SOURCE: Williams, G. C., Grow, V. M., Freedman, E. R., Ryan, R. M., & Deci, E. L. (1996). Motivational predictors of weight loss and weight-loss maintenance. Journal of Personality and Social Psychology, 70, 115–126. Copyright © 1996 by American Psychological Association. Adapted with permission.

to lose weight. Rooting weight loss motivation in autonomous reasons promoted week-to-week attendance at meetings. And the more frequently they attended meetings, the more successful they were in losing weight and maintaining that weight loss (final BMI means change in body mass index 20 months after the start of the program). Overall, the figure shows that the autonomy-causality orientation promoted self-determination in the personality (autonomous reasons for behaving), and self-determined reasons for acting led to the volitional behaviors (attendance) to maintain that behavior change in the future.

DESIRE FOR CONTROL

Desire for control (DC) reflects the extent to which individuals are motivated to establish control over the events in their lives (Berger, 1992; Berger & Cooper, 1979). Desire for control is not a desire for self-determination (as for the autonomy orientation). Instead, desire for control is rooted more in the struggle to establish a sense of mastery over events and outcomes. High DC individuals approach situations by asking themselves whether they will be able to control what happens; they are not content to take whatever life throws their way but instead are motivated to influence life and what happens (Burger, 1992). High DC persons prefer making their own decisions, prepare for situations in advance, avoid dependence on others, and assume leadership roles in group settings. Low DC persons tend to avoid responsibilities and feel comfortable having others make decisions for them (Burger & Cooper, 1979). They prefer to take life as they find it, to wing it (Burger, 1992).

The scale to assess the desire for control is the DC scale (the Desire for Control scale: Burger, 1992; Burger & Cooper, 1979). Three typical items from the DC scale are "I prefer a job where I have a lot of control over what I do and when I do it." "I like to get a good idea of what a job is all about before I begin." and "I am careful to check everything on an automobile before I leave for a long trip." Desire for control relates to a variety of experiences and behaviors that are fundamental to personal control beliefs, including learned helplessness, depression, illusion of control, hypnosis, gambling, achievement, perceived crowding, stress and coping, interpersonal style with friends, health habits and health-related behaviors, and even the elderly's choice of a place to die—in control at home or managed by experts in a hospital (Burger, 1984, 1992; Burger & Arkin, 1980; Burger & Cooper, 1979; Burger, Oakman, & Bullard, 1983; Burger & Schnerring, 1982; Smith et al., 1984). The common links between desire for control and these behavioral manifestations of personal control are the high desire to (1) establish control and (2) restore control when it is threatened or lost.

Establishment of Control

Control is often an issue in our daily conversations and interactions with others. To establish some measure of control over our interpersonal conversations (what will be talked about, what attitudes the other holds, what plans will be made), high DC individuals speak loudly, explosively, and rapidly; respond quickly to questions and comments; and interrupt and talk over their partners (Dembroski, MacDougall, & Musante, 1984). High DC persons also tend to end conversations when they want to, usually after having finished saying whatever it was they wanted to or after having successfully persuaded the other person (after establishing control; Burger, 1990, 1992).

Often, high DC individuals perceive control over events when in fact their outcomes are chance determined. For example, many gambling opportunities such as slot machines, lottery games, bingo, roulette, and coin tosses are clearly chance determined. These are games of chance, and the odds for these games are set in favor of the house. Nonetheless, high DC individuals tend to perceive that they can control such outcomes through personal effort. The *desire* for control tends to feed into the *illusion* of control (Burger, 1986, 1992). Consider one experimental demonstration. Participants signed up for a gambling experiment, received 50 poker chips, and bet whether a pair of thrown dice would add to a number between 2 and 12. For one group (the "bet before" group), the experimenter picked a number, asked the participants to make a bet, and then had the participants try to roll that number to win. In a "bet after" group, the participants first rolled the dice while the number was hidden under a cup; after the roll, the participant made a bet. The logic of the first (bet before) condition is that it sets up in the gambler's mind an illusion of control. If you know what number you are trying to roll, shouldn't the way you roll the dice matter and therefore affect your control over whether you win? Of course, the answer is no, but high DC individuals in the bet before group wagered significantly more chips than did participants in any of the other three groups with the magnitude of the bet serving as an expression of their personal control beliefs (Burger & Cooper, 1979).

Achievement situations provide another illustration of high DC individuals' desire to establish control (Burger, 1985). High DC individuals typically interpret a difficult task as a challenge to their ability to control. Thus, when confronted with a difficult task, the high DC individual should persist longer than the low DC individual in an effort to solve and therefore control the task. To give up on a difficult task is to admit that the task is beyond personal control. To test his idea, Burger gave students a series of insoluble cryptoquote puzzles and observed how long the high and low DC individuals persisted at this impossible task. As predicted, high DC individuals persisted longer at the puzzles than did the low DC individuals. The means by which high DC individuals attempt to exert control in achievement situations extend beyond persistence. Burger (1985) proposed a four-step model to illustrate the multidimensional nature of the high DC individual's quest to establish control in achievement situations, as shown in Figure 14.12. High DC persons select hard tasks because they generally have higher aspirations and standards, put forth unusually high effort when challenged to demonstrate their mastery, persist at difficult tasks longer and are slow to give up and move on, and make self-serving and control-enhancing attributions such as taking credit for success but attributing failure to an external or unstable cause (Burger, 1985, 1992).

Figure 14.12 also outlines the counterproductive side of the relationship between the desire for control and achievement-related behavior. Because high DC in-

FIGURE 14–12

Role of Desire for Control in Achievement-Related Performance

	Aspiration Level	Response to Challenge	Persistence	Attributions for Success and Failure
High DC Compared with Low DC	Select harder tasks; set goals more realistically	React with greater effort	Work at difficult task longer	More likely to attribute success to self and failure to unstable source
High DC Benefit	Higher goals are achieved	Difficult tasks are completed	Difficult tasks are completed	Motivation level remains high
High DC Liability	May attempt goals too difficult	May develop performance-inhibiting reactions	May invest too much effort	May develop an illusion of control

SOURCE: Burger, J. M. (1985). Desire for control and achievement-related behaviors. Journal of Personality and Social Psychology, 48, 1520–1533. Copyright © 1985 by American Psychological Association. Reprinted by permission.

dividuals strongly desire control, they sometimes attempt overly difficult goals, exhibit a hostile reactance effect (Brehm, 1966) in response to failure, persist too long on unsolvable tasks, and develop an illusion of control. The desire for control biases thought processes and approaches to achievement-related tasks. It leads people to overestimate how well they will perform, overexert their efforts when challenged, overpersist on difficult tasks, and interpret success and failure feedback in a way that confirms their perceptions of control. Sometimes the desire for control causes a person to struggle against an outcome that is only partially controllable (because nonpersonal factors such as task difficulty and luck also determine achievement outcomes).

Reactions to Loss of Control

Whether gambling or achieving, high DC individuals desire to establish control even in situations that are either chance determined or influenced little by personal effort. People often face situations where little control is possible. In circumstances such as overcrowding, military structure, nursing homes, hospitals, prison, and living next door to an offensive dump, little control is possible; such situations present an obvious plight for the high DC individual. When their control is threatened or lost altogether, high DC individuals exhibit distinct reactions to loss of control such as distress, anxiety, depression, dominance behavior, and assertive coping (Burger, 1992).

Visiting the dentist office is one of these low-control situations (Law, Logan, & Baron, 1994). When people with a high DC visit the dentist, the idea of another person using tools on their teeth causes unusually high levels of anxiety, expected pain, and expected distress. Interestingly, a 20-minute stress inoculation training session immediately before the dental visit can give high DC individuals the control coping strategies and responses they seek (Law, Logan, & Baron, 1994).

Crowding is another of these low-control situations. Crowding, defined by the number of people per square foot, decreases perceived control because one cannot move about freely (Stokols, 1972). Having a lot of other people around often interferes with our ability to get things done, as in dense traffic, overpopulated sidewalks, and long supermarket checkout lines. High DC individuals are more vulnerable to perceptions of being crowded, and they therefore do what they can to avoid such distressing situations (Burger, 1992). In an experiment, college students worked on a series of mathematical puzzles for 20 minutes in a six-foot-by-six-foot room (Burger, Oakman, & Bullard, 1983). Each student worked on problems and traveled from one side of the room to the other to accomplish the task. The small room had either three (low crowding condition) or six (high crowding condition) participants working individually on the problems at the same time. After the participants moved through either a crowded (six person) or uncrowded (three person) environment and solved as many problems as they could, the experimenters asked participants to report how much crowding and discomfort they felt during the 20 minutes. Table 14.3 shows these results. High DC individuals reported more crowding and greater discomfort than low DC individuals in both the high and low crowded environments. Notice also the similarity between high DC individuals' felt stress in the three-person room and the low DC individuals' felt stress in the six-person room. As they moved about, both high and low DC individuals recognized that they could exert little control over the situation. The crowding presence of others, however, affected the high DC individuals more than it affected the low DC individuals.

TABLE 14–3

Crowding and Discomfort Ratings versus Desire for Control (DC)

RATING SCALE	HIGH CROWDING (6 PERSONS)		LOW CROWDING (3 PERSONS)	
	HIGH DC	LOW DC	HIGH DC	LOW DC
Crowding	6.2	4.9	4.8	3.6
Discomfort	5.6	4.2	4.0	3.2

The higher the number, the more crowding and discomfort on a 9-point scale.
SOURCE: Burger, J.M., Oakman, J.A., & Bullard, N.G. (1983). Desire for control and the perception of crowding. Personality and Social Psychology Bulletin, 9, 475–479. Copyright © 1983. Reprinted by permission of Sage Publications.

Consider the implications for the high DC individual in situations in which their desire for control exceeds their ability to exert control, as in those situations mentioned earlier such as being in the military, a hospital, prison, or nursing home, living adjacent to an airport, and so on. Wondering what effect such low control environments have on high DC individuals, Burger and Arkin (1980) asked high and low DC individuals to participate in a typical learned helplessness experiment in which they were exposed to a harsh, uncontrollable, unpredictable noise. Compared to low DC persons, high DC persons reported higher levels of post-task depression. This brief overview of the DC construct demonstrates that high DC individuals seek to exert control over chance-determined and achievement-related situations and suffer discomfort and depression as emotional reactions to the loss of control. When people desire control and the environment refuses to afford it, the person becomes vulnerable to learned helplessness and depression. Further, the magnitude of the helplessness and depression vary with how important control is for that person in that situation, such that losing one's job calls up helplessness and depression more than does getting stuck in traffic (Wortman & Brehm, 1975).

SUMMARY

Including personality study within a motivational analysis allows us to address questions posed in chapter 1: For which motives are there individual differences? How do such motivational differences between people arise? And what are the implications of such individual motivational differences? This chapter identified three personality characteristics related to temperament and two more that are related to personal control beliefs, outlined how these personality differences arise to create individual differences between people, and pointed out the implications of such personality characteristics for motivation and everyday life (e.g., task preferences, career choices).

The three temperament-based personality characteristics reviewed were extraversion, sensation seeking, and affect intensity. Extraversion is a supertrait that includes several subtraits, including sociability, activity level, and venturesomeness. Differences in introversion-extraversion stem from physiological differences in the ascending reticular activating system (ARAS). Because of a chronically underaroused ARAS, extraverts need strong external stimulation to reach an optimal level. Introverts, because of a chronically overaroused ARAS, need and prefer less intense external stimulation. These genetic differences lead extraverts to seek out arousing, potentially anxiety-provoking situations such as competition and social activity and introverts to seek more restrained, inhibited behavior. Sensation seeking is the need for varied, novel, complex, and intense sensations and experiences and the willingness to take physical, social, legal, and financial risks for the sake of such experience. Strivings towards these experiences lead the sensation seeker to (1) the search for new experience, as in sex and drugs, (2) risk-taking behavior, as in gambling, and (3) volunteering for unusual activities, such as experiments on hypnosis. Psychophysiological, biochemical, and pharmacological studies generally support

Zuckerman's conceptualization of the sensation-seeking construct as physiologically based. Affect intensity is the strength with which individuals typically experience their emotions. Affect-intense individuals experience emotions strongly and show emotional hyperactivity across many different emotion-eliciting situations. Affect-stable individuals experience their emotions only mildly and show only minor fluctuations in their emotional reactions. To increase their low level of arousal to a more optimal level, affect-intense individuals exaggerate their emotionality by responding overly joyously to positive life events and overly depressively to negative life events.

Personal control beliefs concern the capacity to initiate and regulate behavior that comes from the self and that is effective in gaining desirable outcomes and preventing undesirable ones. Causality orientations concern differences in people's understanding of what causes their behavior. For the person with an autonomy causality orientation, behavior is in response to needs, interests, feelings, and goals with a full sense of choice, volition, and freedom. For the person with a control causality orientation, inner guides are relatively ignored; instead, behavior is in response to feelings of tension and pressure, compliance to what is demanded, expected, or rewarded, and a sense of "have to." Causality orientations reflect the extent of self-determination in personality and therefore arise from internalized reasons for acting. Autonomy-oriented individuals rely on intrinsic motivation and identified regulation, whereas control-oriented individuals rely on introjected regulation and extrinsic motivators. Autonomy-oriented individuals show a strong attitude-behavior consistency such that their behavior reflects a harmony with their attitudes and traits, and they maintain behavior changes over time such that autonomous reasons for acting produce lasting behavior change. Desire for control reflects the extent to which people are motivated to attempt to control the events in their lives. High DC individuals approach life situations by asking whether they will be able to control what happens to them. Typical life situations that involve control include interpersonal interactions, achievement behavior, health, gambling, hypnosis, and crowding. The common links between desire for control and these behavioral manifestations of personal control are the high DC individual's strivings to (1) establish control and (2) restore it when control is lost or threatened. To establish control, high DC individuals entertain high standards and aspirations, put forth high effort when challenged, overly persist at difficult tasks, and interpret success/failure feedback in a self-serving and control-enhancing way. When control is threatened or lost altogether (e.g., crowding), high DC individuals exhibit distinct reactions such as distress, anxiety, depression, dominance, and assertive coping.

RECOMMENDED READINGS

Anderson, K. J. (1990). Arousal and the inverted-U hypothesis: A critique of Neiss's "Reconceptualizing arousal." *Psychological Bulletin, 107,* 96–100.

Heron, W. (1957). The pathology of boredom. *Scientific American, 196,* 52–56.

Kagan, J. (1989). Temperamental contributions to social behavior. *American Psychologist, 44,* 668–674.

Koestner, R., Bernieri, F., & Zuckerman, M. (1992). Self-regulation and consistency between attitudes, traits, and behaviors. *Personality and Social Psychology Bulletin, 18,* 52-59.

Larsen, R. J., & Diener, E. (1987). Affect intensity as an individual difference characteristic: A review. *Journal of Research in Personality, 21,* 1-39.

Law, A., Logan, H., & Baron, R. S. (1994). Desire for control, felt control, and stress inoculation training during dental treatment. *Journal of Personality and Social Psychology, 67,* 926-936.

Watson, D., Clark, L. A., McIntyre, C. W., & Hamaker, S. (1992). Affect, personality, and social activity. *Journal of Personality and Social Psychology, 63,* 1011-1025.

Wilson, G. (1978). Introversion/Extraversion. In H. London & J. E. Exner, Jr. (Eds.), *Dimensions of personality* (pp. 217-261). New York: John Wiley.

Zuckerman, M. (1978). Sensation seeking. In H. London & J. E. Exner, Jr. (Eds.), *Dimensions of personality* (pp. 487-559). New York: John Wiley.

Zuckerman, M., Bone, R. N., Neary, R., Mangelsdorff, D., & Brustman, B. (1972). What is the sensation seeker? Personality trait and experience correlates of the Sensation Seeking Scale. *Journal of Clinical and Counseling Psychology, 39,* 308-321.

Chapter 15

GROWTH MOTIVATION

Extraversion, sensation-seeking, and affect intensity are biologically based individual differences that predispose individuals to act in temperament-consistent ways. But families and cultures sometimes have other ideas about how a person should behave, saying, in essence, "Oh no, you shouldn't be introverted and emotionally bland; you should be extraverted and emotionally expressive and entertaining!" When biological disposition contradicts socialization pressure, here is the problem: What happens when our inner nature is rejected and a more socially acceptable style is substituted in its place?" Such a state of affairs might be okay, as the individual becomes enculturated and socially adjusted. Humanistic psychology, however, argues that such conditions put personal growth and psychological well-being at risk.

Imagine yourself in the following experiment (from Ford, 1991a). The experiment begins by asking you to self-report your temperament, using questionnaires such as those discussed in the previous chapter for extraversion, sensation-seeking, and affect intensity. The experimenter also asks for permission to send identical questionnaires to one of your parents (whoever was your primary caretaker) to ask him or her to complete each in terms of how you behaved during the preschool ages of 3 to 5 years (old enough for temperament to express itself, young enough to precede heavy socialization). The prediction is that adults who express something other than their natural temperament will show maladjustment. To index maladjustment, the experimenter also asks you to complete questionnaire measures of anxiety, depression, hostility, feelings of inadequacy, and physical/somatic troubles. To test the humanistic hypothesis, the experimenter computes a discrepancy score of the difference between your expressed temperament as an adult and your parent's rating of your temperament as a child. Results showed the greater the discrepancy, the greater the adult's maladjustment. These findings introduce the theme of this chapter: "If this essential core (inner nature) of the person is frustrated, denied, or suppressed, sickness results" (Maslow, 1968, p. 193). And, if the essential core of the person is supported, realized, and nurtured, health results.

HOLISM

Human motives can be understood from many different perspectives, ranging from the most objective viewpoints of objectivism (Diserens, 1925), behaviorism (Watson, 1919), and logical positivism (Bergmann & Spence, 1941) to the most subjective viewpoints of existentialism (May, 1961), Gestalt psychology (Goldstein, 1939; Perls, 1969), and holism (Aristotle, *On the Soul*). Along with existentialism and gestalt psychology, holism asserts that a human being is best understood as an integrated, organized whole, rather than as a series of differentiated parts. It is the whole organism that is motivated rather than just part of the organism, such as the stomach or brain. In holism, any event that affects one system affects the entire person. To borrow a phrase from Maslow, it is John Smith who desires food, not John Smith's stomach.

Holism derives its name from "whole" or "wholeness" and therefore concerns itself with personality study of what is healthy, or unbroken. A broken view of personality, according to the holistic approach, emphasizes human beings as fragmented sets of structures or forces that oppose one another. For instance, a broken view speaks of the conflict between an ideal self and an actual self, or the conflict between the biological desire for food and the social demand for a slim figure. In psychoanalytic theory, a broken self manifests itself in a sort of psychological competition among the three personality structures of id, ego, and superego. Another salient aspect of holism, and of humanistic psychology in particular, is the view of self as a constantly growing, changing, and fluid process. Hence, holism emphasizes the self's processes of becoming (something in the future) rather than the person's past or present self or identity (e.g., chapter 10).

Humanism, a movement in psychology that identifies strongly with the holistic perspective, stresses inherent potentials within the organism and the notion of self and its strivings toward fulfillment. The notions of the self and its strivings are holistic forces that bind the individual into a unified motivational system. The self-actualizing tendency, for instance, is a sovereign motive system that organizes all other motives (e.g., hunger, sex, competence) toward holism. As we shall see, this master motive organizes the individual's inherent potentials into a striving "to be the self which one truly is"; the humanistic perspective concerns strivings toward growth, development, and self-realization and away from facade, self-concealment, and pleasing and fulfilling the expectations of others (Rogers, 1966).

Humanistic psychology is about discovering human potential and encouraging its development. This chapter provides guidance in the process, based on the ideas of Maslow and Rogers.

SELF-ACTUALIZATION

Self-actualization refers to the full realization and use of one's talents, capacities, and potentialities (Maslow, 1987). The process of realizing and using one's potentialities cultivates a climate for optimal psychological growth and health and for progress toward being a fully functioning human being. Self-actualization is the process of developing in a way that leaves behind infantile heteronomy, defensiveness, cruelty, and timidity, and moves toward autonomous self-regulation, realistic appraisals, compassion toward others, and the courage to create and to explore. The two fundamental directions for healthy development are autonomy and openness to experience. *Autonomy* means moving away from heteronomy (dependence on others) and toward an ever-increasing capacity to depend on one's self and to regulate one's own behavior (Deci & Ryan, 1987). *Openness* means a way of receiving information and feelings such that neither is repressed, ignored, filtered, nor distorted by wishes, fear, or past experiences (Mittelman, 1991).

Hierarchy of Human Needs

The cornerstone of Maslow's understanding of motivation is the proposition that human beings possess needs at the organismic level. Maslow proposed that one cluster of interrelated needs, those toward growth, govern and organize all other needs into a hierarchy featuring five clusters ranging from relatively potent survival needs to relatively weak growth needs. The arrangement of these needs, Maslow felt, was best communicated visually by a hierarchy, as illustrated in Figure 15.1. The first set of needs contains those physiological needs necessary for bodily homeostasis, quiescence, and survival. All the other needs in the hierarchy (safety and security, love and belongingness, esteem, and self-actualization) are psychological needs.

The hierarchical presentation conveys three fundamentals about the nature of human needs (Maslow, 1943, 1987). First, basic needs arrange themselves in the hierarchy according to strength. Thus, the physiological needs at the bottom of the hierarchy dominate as the strongest, whereas the self-actualization needs at the top are weak needs, quiet urges that are often confused and easily overlooked in day-to-day affairs. Second, the lower the need is in the hierarchy, the sooner it appears in development in terms of both phylogenetic (species) and ontological (individual) development. Thus, safety and security characterize typical needs of nonhuman animals and children whereas esteem needs pertain to adults and are uniquely human. Third, needs in the hierarchy are fulfilled sequentially, from lowest to highest, from the base of the pyramid to its apex. Thus, before people seek esteem and peer respect, they must first have physiological, safety, and belongingness needs sufficiently gratified.

DEFICIENCY NEEDS. Physiological disturbances and needs for safety, belongingness, and esteem are collectively referred to as the deficiency needs. Deficiency needs are like vitamins; we need them because their lack inhibits growth and development. For Maslow, human beings are constantly wanting and rarely reaching a state of satisfaction, except for only a brief time. Fulfillment of one set of deficiency needs typically gives rise to another set of needs. The physiological needs, for ex-

FIGURE 15–1
Maslow's Need Hierarchy

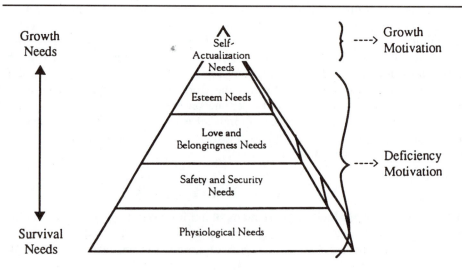

ample, dominate consciousness until gratification submerges them and allows the next, higher cluster of needs to emerge. Once emerged, the safety and security needs then dominate consciousness and occupy the individual's attention. Thus, gratification of hunger, thirst, and sleep not only submerge these needs, it in effect opens the door for the individual's desire to secure a predictable, orderly, and safe environment. The presence of any of the deficiency needs indicates that the individual is in a state of deprivation, whether for food, job security, group membership, or social status. Maslow (1971) characterized such deprivation as human sickness, a term he used to connote a failure to move toward growth and actualization.

GROWTH NEEDS. Given satisfaction rather than deprivation of the deficiency needs, growth needs surface and render the person restless and discontented. The person no longer feels hungry, insecure, isolated, or inferior, but he or she instead feels a need to fulfill personal potentialities, to become that person he or she is specifically suited to be. Self-actualization is the desire to become more and more of what one is, to become everything that one is capable of becoming: "A musician must make music, an artist must paint, a poet must write, if he is to be ultimately happy. What a man can be, he must be. This need we may call self-actualization" (Maslow, 1943, p. 382). It is difficult to pinpoint precisely what self-actualization needs are and are not. One can understand physiological needs by thinking of hunger and thirst, but self-actualization is a more abstruse term. It is actually a summary term that coalesces

TABLE 15–1
Maslow's Metaneeds and Their Pathogenic Deprivations

METANEED	PATHOGENIC DEPRIVATION
1. Truth	Dishonesty
2. Goodness	Evil
3. Beauty	Ugliness
4. Unity, Wholeness	Chaos, atomism, loss of connectedness
5. Dichotomy Transcendence	Black and white dichotomies, loss of gradations
6. Aliveness, process orientation	Deadness, mechanizing of life
7. Uniqueness	Sameness, uniformity, interchangeability
8. Perfection, necessity	Imperfection, sloppiness, poor workmanship
9. Completion, finality	Incompleteness
10. Justice	Injustice
11. Order	Lawlessness, chaos, breakdown of authority
12. Simplicity	Confusing complexity, disconnectedness
13. Richness, totality, comprehensiveness	Poverty, constricture
14. Effortfulness	Effortlessness
15. Playfulness	Humorlessness
16. Self-sufficiency	Contingency, occasionalism
17. Meaningfulness	Meaninglessness

SOURCE: A Theory of Metamotivation, pp 290–340, from The Farther Reaches of Human Nature by Abraham H. Maslow. Copyright © 1971 by Bertha G. Maslow. Used by permission of Viking Penguin, a division of Penguin Books USA Inc.

17 metaneeds (or higher-order needs). Table 15.1 lists Maslow's metaneeds. The table also provides the related deprivations.

RESEARCH ON THE NEED HIERARCHY. Maslow's need hierarchy (see Fig. 15.1) has been embraced as a modus operandi in education, business, management, the work place, psychotherapy, and the health professions of medicine, nursing, and geriatrics (Cox, 1987). Research has actually found very little empirical support for the need hierarchy despite its popularity (Wahba & Bridwell, 1976).

One research strategy to test the hierarchy's validity is the rank order method (Blai, 1964; Goodman, 1968; Mathes, 1981). Typically, test takers rank the needs in the order of their desirability or importance. In general, the ranking of the needs from least to most important does not conform to Maslow's predicted order. For instance, a group of service workers ranked safety/security needs as most important while the esteem needs ranked as least important (Blai, 1964). In a similar study, the experimenter paired one need against another and asked college students which need they would rather do without, as in "If from now on you have to do without *friends* (belongingness) or *respect from your peers* (esteem), which would you choose?" (Mathes, 1981, p. 70). Participants ranked physiological satisfaction as most basic, belongingness satisfaction as next, but the order thereafter deviated substantially from Maslow's predictions in that self-actualization needs were third most basic, security needs were fourth, and esteem satisfiers were weakest or most superfluous (Mathes, 1991).

A second research strategy is to investigate changes in motivation related to age (Goebel & Brown, 1981). According to Maslow, the young tend to be occupied with physiological and safety needs while older adults tend to be occupied with esteem and actualization needs, generally speaking. Goebel and Brown (1981) had children, adolescents, young adults, middle-aged adults, and old adults complete the Life Motivation Scale (LMS); one of the items appears in the upper part of Table 15.2.

Results appear in the lower part of Table 15.2. Looking across each row, you see that the children rated the physiological needs as more important than did the other four groups, just as Maslow would predict. However, all five populations rated safety as equally important. In fact, the age group rating safety as most important was the old adults. The same pattern appears to be true for the belongingness need, except that children rate this need as less important than do the other four groups. Adolescents rated esteem needs as relatively more important than did the other age groups. Self-actualization is ranked highest by the young adults and middle-aged adults and ranked lowest by the children and old adults. Overall, the weight of the evidence casts considerable doubt on the hierarchy's validity.

The one finding that is supported by empirical research is the conceptualization of a dual-level (rather than a five-level) hierarchy. In a dual-level hierarchy, the only distinction is between deficiency and growth needs (Wahba & Bridwell, 1976). In the studies just reviewed, a difference between *maintenance* and *growth* needs emerges. Thus, the conclusion from research on Maslow's need hierarchy is to reject the five-level hierarchy but to continue to make the two-level distinction.

TABLE 15–2
Life Motivation Scale Items and Rated Responses

Directions: Rank in order the five statements listed below in terms of how important each is to you.

_____ I like doing things that make other people look up to me. (Esteem)

_____ I like doing things with my family and friends. (Belongingness)

_____ I like doing things that fill my physical needs. (Physiological)

_____ I like doing things that let me develop my talents or interests. (Self-Actualization)

_____ I like doing things that are planned ahead. (Safety)

NEED HIERARCHY	CHILDREN (N = 22)	ADOLESCENTS (N = 21)	YOUNG ADULTS (N = 24)	MIDDLE ADULTS (N = 22)	OLD ADULTS (N = 22)
Physiological	22.59	14.24	14.50	13.14	14.82
Safety/Security	19.77	19.14	19.25	20.00	22.50
Belongingness	29.68	32.14	34.21	33.14	33.73
Esteem	17.50	19.33	13.63	15.73	15.36
Self-actualization	20.50	25.14	28.60	27.91	23.59

SOURCE: Goebel, B.L., & Brown, D.R. (1981). Age differences in motivation related to Maslow's need hierarchy. *Developmental Psychology*, 17, 809–815. Copyright © 1981 by American Psychological Association. Adapted with permission.

Encouraging Self-Actualization

Maslow estimated that less than 1% of the population ever reached self-actualization. Because the self-actualization needs were supposedly innate, one is left to wonder why everyone does not ultimately self-actualize. In some cases, Maslow reasoned, people fail to reach their potential because of a nonsupportive environment (e.g., not enough food or shelter to gratify basic needs). In other cases, the person was responsible for the lack of growth (we fear our own potential, which he termed the "Jonah complex"). Maslow recognized the contradiction between his proposition that self-actualization was innate (and therefore operative in all human beings) and his observation that few among us gratify self-actualization needs. Maslow (1971), ever the counselor and clinician, therefore offered several everyday behaviors to encourage self-actualization, as listed in Table 15.3.

Maslow also stressed that people could not directly bring about peak experiences in their lives (Hardeman, 1979). Instead, peak experiences were more of a byproduct of psychological health. By making growth choices (as in Table 15.3), by being honest, and by setting up supportive and honest conditions, people can make peak experiences more likely, but that is not the same as creating a peak experience directly. The closest prescription to setting up conditions that make peak experiences probable can be found, I think, in Csikszentmihalyi's (1990) flow model (recall chapter 4) that identifies the pairing of optimal challenge and level of skill to

TABLE 15–3

Eight Behaviors That Encourage Self-Actualization

1. See life as a series of choices, forever a choice toward progression and growth versus regression and fear. The progression-growth choice is a movement toward self-actualization, whereas the regression-fear choice is a movement away from self-actualization.
2. Dare to be different, unpopular, nonconformist.
3. Set up conditions to make peak experiences more likely. Get rid of false notions and illusions. Find out what you are not good at, and learn what your potential is by learning what your potentials are not.
4. Identify defenses and find the courage to give them up.
5. Be honest rather than not, especially when in doubt. Take responsibility for your choices and the consequences of those choices.
6. Let the self emerge. Perceive within yourself and see and hear the innate impulse voices. Shut out the noises of the world.
7. Experience fully, vividly, selflessly with full concentration and total absorption. Experience without self-consciousness, defenses, or shyness.
8. Use your intelligence to work toward doing well the thing one wants to do well, be it the work of physician, parent, pianist, scholar, or athlete.

generate the flow experience. Maslow also stressed the important role of relationships—beautiful, intimate, and fulfilling relationships rather than the all-too-common superficial ones—as the soil to cultivate peak experiences (Hardeman, 1979). Setting up conditions to make peak experiences likely often means involving oneself in relationships that are open and mutually autonomy supportive.

THE ACTUALIZING TENDENCY

Rogers' emphasis on holism and self-actualization is best represented by an oft-cited quotation: "The organism has one basic tendency and striving—to actualize, maintain, and enhance the experiencing self" (Rogers, 1951, p. 487). Fulfillment of physiological needs maintains and enhances the organism, as does the fulfillment of needs for belongingness and social status. Further, a motive like curiosity enhances and actualizes the person via greater complexity and understanding. Overall, Rogers (1959, 1963) recognized the existence of particular human motives, but he emphatically stressed the holistic proposition that all human needs serve to maintain, enhance, and actualize the person.

Rogers, like Maslow, believed that the actualizing tendency was innate, a continual presence that pushes the individual toward genetically determined potentials. The locus of that push toward potential is internal, not external or social. Rogers saw the actualizing tendency's forward-moving development as characterized by "struggle and pain," and offered the following illustration to communicate the path toward development and growth. The nine-month-old infant has the genetic potential to walk, but must struggle to advance from crawling to walking, to make those first steps. Such a struggle inevitably includes episodes of falling and feelings of frustration, of being hurt and disappointed. Despite the struggle and pain, the child persists toward walking and away from crawling. The pain and disappointment decrease the child's willingness to try to walk, but the actualization tendency, "the forward thrust of life," pushes the child ever forward. The actualizing tendency is the source of energy that motivates "development toward autonomy and away from heteronomy" (Rogers, 1959, p. 196).

All experiences within the struggle and pain of actualizing are evaluated in accordance with an "organismic valuation process," an innate capability to judge for oneself whether a specific experience promotes or debilitates growth. Experiences perceived as maintaining or enhancing the person are positively valued. Such growth-promoting experiences are subsequently maintained and approached. Experiences perceived as regressive and negating the enhancement of the person are valued negatively. Such growth-blocking experiences are subsequently terminated and avoided. In effect, the organismic valuation process provides a feedback system that allows the individual to coordinate life experiences in accordance with the actualization tendency.

Emergence of the Self

The actualizing tendency characterizes the individual as a whole. Self-perceptions are the raw material through which the self-concept is constructed (chapter 10). With the emergence of the self, the human being grows in complexity, and the organismic valuation process begins to apply not only to the organism as a whole but also to the self. Hence, experiences evaluated as satisfying for the self are approached, while experiences evaluated as unsatisfying for the self are avoided.

The most important motivational implication of the emergence of the self is that the actualizing tendency begins to express itself in part toward that portion of the organism conceptualized as the self. This means that the individual gains a second major motivational force in addition to the actualizing tendency, namely the *self*-actualizing tendency. Actualization and self-actualization are not the same thing (Ford, 1991b). Further, the actualizing tendency and the self-actualizing tendency can work at odds with one another, as explained in this chapter and as portrayed in Figure 15.2.

The emergence of the self prompts the emergence of the need for positive regard. Positive regard includes approval, acceptance, and love from others. The need for positive regard is of special significance because it makes the individual sensitive to the feedback of others (criticisms and praises). Other people (and their attitudes, evaluations, and perspectives) assume a greater importance in one's life. As the self emerges, the need for positive regard differentiates into both a need for positive regard from others and a need for positive self-regard. Over time, evaluating the self from other people's points of view becomes a rather automated process. By attending to the criticisms and praises of others, the individual internalizes societal feedback, and the person's sense of self becomes an increasing reflection of other people's perspectives.

FIGURE 15–2
Rogerian Model of the Process of Self-Actualization

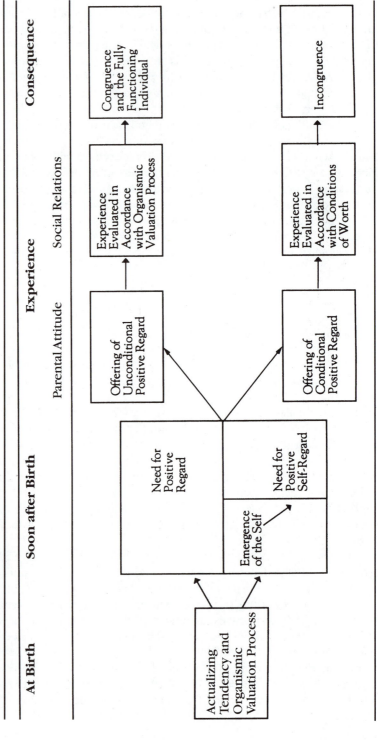

Conditions of Worth

Soon after the delivery room, children begin to learn the "conditions of worth" on which their behavior and personal characteristics (the self) are judged as either positive and worthy of acceptance or negative and worthy of rejection. Eventually, because the need for positive regard sensitizes the individual to attend to the acceptances and rejections of others, the child internalizes parental conditions of worth into the self structure. Throughout development, the self structure expands beyond parental conditions of worth to include societal conditions of worth as well. By adulthood, the individual learns from parents, friends, teachers, ministers and rabbis, coaches, employers, and others what behaviors and which characteristics are good and bad, right and wrong, desirable and undesirable.

All of us live in two worlds—the inner world of the organismic valuing process and the outer world of the conditions of worth. As a consequence of internalizing conditions of worth, notice what happens. Acquired conditions of worth substitute for the innate organismic valuation process. When governed by conditions of worth, individuals necessarily divorce themselves from their inherent means of coordinating experience with the actualizing tendency. No longer is experience judged in accordance with the innate organismic valuation process. Rogers viewed the child's movement toward socialized conditions of worth and away from organismic valuation as antithetical to the development of the actualizing tendency. When the developing individual adheres to conditions of worth, he or she moves farther and farther away from an inherent ability to make the behavioral choices necessary to actualize the self. Introjected social conditions of worth tend to become rigid and unchanging laws for social conduct. The result is an expression of socially endorsed attitudes, values, and actions. Figure 15.2 summarizes the overall process and consequences of adherence to either the organismic valuation process or socialized conditions of worth.

The way not to interfere with organismic valuation is to provide "unconditional positive regard," rather than the "conditional positive regard" that emanates from conditions of worth. If given unconditional positive regard, a child has no need to internalize societal conditions of worth. If parents approve of, love, and accept the child for who he or she naturally is rather than for who the parents wish him or her to be, then the child and the child's self structure will be a relatively transparent representation of his or her inherent preferences, talents, capacities, and potentialities.

In the absence of salient conditions of worth, conflict between the actualizing tendency and the self-actualizing tendency does not exist, and the two motivational tendencies remain unified (Rogers, 1959). Conditions of self-worth, however, create the potential for motivational conflict. With conditional self-regard, conflict between the actualizing and self-actualizing tendencies creates a tension and internal confusion since some aspects of behavior are regulated by the actualizing tendency while other aspects of behavior are regulated by the self-actualizing tendency (Ford, 1991b; Rogers, 1959). Self-actualization, when evaluated and directed via conditions of worth rather than organismic valuation, can paradoxically lead the person to develop in a way that is incongruent, conflicting and maladaptive (Ford, 1991b). Thus, self-actualization does not necessarily mean health and growth and can sometimes lead to maladjustment (when conditions of worth define and direct self-actualization processes). Health and growth occur only when the actualizing tendency and the self-actualizating tendency are in synchronization with one another and experiences are evaluated internally within the framework of organismic valuation.

Notice the difficult position parents are placed in when their child expresses a somewhat socially undesirable characteristic, such as shyness or irritability. Socially appropriate conditional positive regard implies rejection and retraining for the child's temperament, in the name of promoting social inclusion and popularity. But, unconditional positive regard implies acceptance of and support for the child's natural temperament. The difficult position the parents face manifests itself in the dilemma of avoiding psychological costs (e.g., depression) versus social costs (e.g., peer rejection) to the developing child.

Congruence

Congruence and *incongruence* describe with extent to which the individual denies and rejects personal characteristics, abilities, desires, and beliefs (incongruence) or accepts the full range of his or her personal characteristics (congruence). Psychological incongruence is essentially the extent of discrepancy or difference between "the self as perceived and the actual experience of the organism" (Rogers, 1959, p. 203). The individual might perceive himself as having characteristics a, b, and c and experiencing feelings d, e, and f, but then publicly expresses characteristics u, v, and w and feelings x, y, and z. Independence between experience and expression reveals incongruence; overlap between experience and expression reveals congruence.

When people move toward identifying with external conditions of worth, they adopt facades. A facade is essentially the social mask a person wears, and it relates to ways of behaving that have little to do with inner guides and much to do with a front to hide behind (Rogers, 1961). Consider the unauthentic smile. People vary in their extraversion and sociability, yet culture varies little in its preference for people who are outgoing and entertaining. Hence introverts often find themselves wearing the facade of the unauthentic smile. Consider the consequence of wearing a sociability facade on a regular basis (e.g., at a social gathering, "I've had this smile glued on my face for two hours. How much longer can I keep it on?"; Ford, 1995, p. 66). Relying on social facades predicts proneness to maladjustment, including high anxiety, depression, low self-assertiveness, and both a history and an expectation of negative experience in social interaction. Adopting socially desirable facades carries its psychological costs.

Fully Functioning Individual

The fully functioning individual allows the full range of his or her experiences to nurture the actualizing tendency. When fully functioning, the individual lives in close and confident relationship to the organismic valuation process, trusting that inner direction. Further, the fully functioning individual spontaneously communicates inner impulses both verbally and nonverbally. Figure 15.3 illustrates the process of the actualizing tendency—featuring the sequential process of a motive's emergence, acceptance, and expression.

Motivational Implications of the Self-Actualizing Tendency

INTERPERSONAL RELATIONSHIPS. The extent to which individuals develop toward congruence and adjustment depends greatly on the quality of their interpersonal relationships. At one extreme, relationships take on a controlling tone as others force their agendas on us, pushing us toward heteronomy and a commitment to conditions of worth. Such relationships oppress the actualizing tendency. At the other extreme, relationships take on a supportive tone as they promote self-determination and progress affording us the opportunity and support necessary to move from heteronomy toward autonomy. Such relationships support the actualizing tendency.

In humanistic therapy, clients move toward health and psychological congruence when the therapist brings the following characteristics into the relationship: warmth, genuineness, empathy, interpersonal acceptance, and confirmation of the other person's capacity for self-determination (Kramer, 1995; Rogers, 1973, 1980, 1995). *Warmth* essentially means caring for and nurturing the development of the other person. *Genuineness* acknowledges that each person must be fully present in the relationship's here and now, offering no pretense of emotional distance—no professional facade of being a therapist, expert, teacher, or professional, but instead openly himself or herself. Genuineness means authenticity and courage to reveal spontaneous (rather than socially expected) feelings, thoughts, and behaviors. *Empathy* relates to listening not only to hear clearly all the messages the other is sending but also to adopt the other's perspective on experience. Empathy strives for a genuine understanding of the other person, and it occurs as one person gains the capacity to enter the private perceptual world of the other and becomes thoroughly at home in it. *Interpersonal acceptance* means that each person in the relationship experiences a basic acceptance and trust from the other (unconditional positive regard); that is, each person must honor and prize the uniqueness and difference of the other without conditions or contingencies. Finally, *confirmation of the other*

FIGURE 15–3
Process of Actualizing Tendency

Emergence	Acceptance	Expression
Onset of innate desire, impulse, or motive	Desire, impulse, or motive is accepted "as is" into consciousness	Unedited communication of desire, impulse, or motive

person's capacity for self-determination acknowledges that the other is essentially competent and possesses an inherently positive developmental direction. These five characteristics affect the quality of the relationship and its capacity to support self-determination in each person.

HELPING OTHERS. Interpersonal relationships become helping relationships when one person, by virtue of his or her contact with another person, becomes better informed, more independent, more open to experience, better integrated, and more mature (Rogers, 1995). In trying to communicate how interpersonal relationships become helping (growth-promoting) relationships, Rogers (1995) offers the following four insights:

> 1. In my relationships with persons I have found that it does not help, in the long run, to act as though I were something that I am not. (P. 9)

Here, Rogers presents the antithesis of conditional positive regard and conditions of worth. The goal in helping is not to manipulate the other (into conforming to conditions of worth) but, instead, to understand the other. The facade of being loving or polite or interested or alert does not help the other person, if the helper actually feels hostile or critical or bored or tired; this was Roger's first insight.

> 2. I have found it effective, in my dealings with people, to be acceptant of myself. (P. 10)

Self-acceptance sets the stage for the relationship to move past the superficial and into the real. When people relate to each other, the interpersonal climate nurtures change, flexibility, and openness to experience. Rogers considered it a "very paradoxical thing" that the more willing the helper is to be herself and the less willing she is to try to manipulate the other person "the more change seems to be stirred up" (Rogers, 1995, p. 20).

> 3. I have found it of enormous value when I can permit myself to understand another person. (P. 11)

Typically, when we interact with people who hold different opinions (e.g., on the death penalty), different ideologies (e.g., how to best discipline our children), and different conclusions (e.g., whether I am inadequate as a human being), we counterargue and debate the other's opinion, ideology, or conclusion from our own perspective. Rogers argued that such an orientation forces us to pay more attention to our own frame of reference than we pay to the other person's frame of reference. To help, the helper must instead identify with the other person's frame of reference and therefore understand why he believes and feels whatever it is he believes and feels.

> 4. The more I am able to understand myself and others, the more I accept myself and others, the more I am open to the realities of life, the less I find myself wishing to rush in. (P. 20)

Helping, in the humanistic tradition, does not involve an expert rushing in to solve the problem—to fix things, to mold people, to advise them, or to manipulate and push them in a direction of the expert's choosing. Instead, helping involves letting the other person be herself. In this last insight perhaps the reader can best hear the antithesis of conditions of worth.

FREEDOM TO LEARN. Rogers continually lamented contemporary educational practices. He did not like the idea of a "teacher," because he felt that the only learning that really mattered was self-initiated (actualizing tendency–initiated) learning (Rogers, 1969). As a teacher looking back at the results of his own efforts, Rogers felt that he was responsible for more damage than good. Little of consequence occurs when a teacher gives out heaps of information for students to digest. Instead of "teacher," Rogers prefers "facilitator," a term that describes the classroom leader as one who creates and supports an atmosphere conducive to students' learning. Learning does not follow teaching; learning follows having one's interests facilitated and supported. Learning takes place when the student participates fully and responsibly in the learning process. Self-discovery and self-evaluation are of prime importance, while criticism and evaluation by teachers are inconsequential or harmful. Thus, education is not something a teacher can give to (or force on) a student; it must be acquired by the student by investing his or her energies and interests. On this point, I am reminded of golfer Ben Hogan's reply to the inquiry as to why he had not written another instructional book. Hogan, in a Rogerian spirit, quipped, "Golf is a game that cannot be taught; it must be learned."

In practice, humanistic education typically manifests itself in three themes: The facilitator (i.e., teacher) functions as a structuring agent in an open classroom, students learn cooperatively and in a context of the peer group, and students take the responsibility for initiating their own learning (Allender & Silberman, 1979). A facilitator relies on setting up learning centers or stations in the classroom to encourage students' choices and initiatives, and the facilitator focuses most of his or her attention on identifying students' needs, desires, feelings, and interests (McCombs & Pope, 1994). Peer-based cooperative learning facilitates individual learning by allowing students to communicate their ideas to others as well as to learn from the feedback, modeling, and insight of their peers (Johnson & Johnson, 1985). Personal responsibility for their own learning moves students out of the role of passive receivers of knowledge and into the role of active learners who construct their own ways of understanding. When classrooms support students' self-initiatives, students gain academic confidence, show greater mastery motivation, and participate with more involvement (deCharms, 1976; Ryan & Grolnick, 1986).

CREATIVITY. A distinction needs to be made between "special talent creativeness" and "self-actualization creativeness" (Hardeman, 1979; Maslow, 1971). Inventive poems, theories, novels, paintings, and the inborn talent of Mozart characterize special talent. But creativity rooted in self-actualization (i.e., universal creativity) springs directly from the whole personality and manifests itself in the ordinary affairs of life. This is the kind of creativity and spontaneity that is inherent in all human beings, the sort of day-to-day creativity that expresses itself in cooking, recreation, parenting, and all aspects of life. Self-actualization creativity entails a fresh, open kind of perceptiveness, a spontaneity of expression that has a bit of a childlike quality and an affinity for the unknown, mysterious, and puzzling. It is an openness to experience.

Humanistic psychology strives to discover how best to develop the human potential. In that spirit, Hale (1995) searched for the factors that foster creativity, and his research into the life circumstances of literary geniuses led him to emphasize the following creativity-fostering characteristics:

- Tendency to challenge and question traditional ways of thinking
- Risk taking in the face of profound inner uncertainty
- Flexible cognition or divergent thinking
- Compulsive discipline and hard work
- Tolerance for ambiguity, shades of grey, and contradiction
- Extreme concentration and immersion in the present moment
- Intellectual diversity and rich background knowledge
- An internal locus of evaluation
- Deep reflection on concerns related to the human condition

All too often, enculturation undermines or suppresses, rather than fosters, creativity. Amabile proposed that creativity can be suppressed by external evaluations or pressures to test (Amabile, 1979, 1985). In one experiment, college students wrote a short poem of five lines (Amabile, 1985). Before writing the poem, however, half were asked to think about intrinsic reasons for writing (e.g., pleasure, self-expression, relaxation, playing with words), and half were asked to think about extrinsic reasons (e.g., financial benefits, public recognition, impressing others, pleasing teachers). After the participants composed their poems, a panel of experienced poets rated each on its creativity. The creativity scores were lower for the writers thinking about extrinsic reasons for writing. Writers who focused on spontaneity of expression (the intrinsic reasons group) produced the more creative work.

Being given the opportunity to act in a creative way on one task enhances creativity on a second task (Conti, Amabile, & Pollak, 1995). Imagine getting ready to begin task A, but first doing task B, a task that either was or was not creativity involving. On task A, your creativity, intrinsic motivation, and long-term retention (quality of information processing) would all be enhanced by the prior creative experience. In short, creative activity produces a spillover effect of an active learning set and cultivates the kind of learning that leaves people with valuable knowledge and an eagerness to gain more information (Conti, Amabile, & Pollak, 1995).

Self-Definition and Social Definition

Self-definition and social definition are personality processes related to how individuals conceptualize who they are in terms of internal and external definitions (Jenkins, 1996; Stewart, 1992; Stewart & Winter, 1974). Socially defined individuals accept external definitions that pressure them to identify with stereotypical identities and ways of behaving that are appropriate for their social group. Self-defined individuals resist these external definitions and instead favor internal definitions of the self.

Self-definition and social definition processes are particularly instructive in the developing identity of women (Jenkins, 1996). Compared to their socially defined counterparts, self-defined women are more autonomous and independent in their interpersonal relationships (they depend less on others) and social roles (they may prefer nontraditional occupations or roles). They take decisive and successful goal-directed actions, as in occupational decisions and strategies for career development. They organize their goals around their own self-determined aspirations, including family goals such as whether to get married and how many children to have. They are also less invested in so-called traditional roles such as wife and mother.

Socially defined women prefer to work with and depend on others (Jenkins, 1996). They prefer traditional female roles both at home and at work. They are typically willing to compromise in terms of their plans, college degree aspirations, career persistence, and relationships in general. Decisions and experience flow not from the self but, instead, from the social support of others and the beliefs, abilities, and aspirations of those others. And, by depending on others, socially defined married women hope for husbands to provide them with a life that is stimulating and challenging.

Self-definition and social definition processes represent two ways for self-actualization to proceed, the first of which represents authentic self-actualization and the second of which represents commitment to conditions of worth to gain positive self-regard. These ways of actualizing the self affect the ways people think and behave, the decisions they make (e.g., career choices), the ways they relate to social pressures, and the interpersonal adjustment they make to achieve social/occupational outcomes.

AUTONOMY VERSUS COMPLIANCE: THE FUNDAMENTAL ANTITHESIS. One index of healthy psychosocial development is the extent to which the individual accepts social conventions, accommodates the self to the society, internalizes cultural values, cooperates with others, shows respect for others, and so on. What motivates the willingness to accommodate the self to others is the need for relatedness (Goodenow, 1993; Ryan & Powelson, 1991). Interpersonally, relatedness (chapter 4) refers to the quality of the relationship between socializer and socializee. When one person feels emotionally connected to, interpersonally involved with, liked by, respected by, and valued by the other person, then relatedness is high and internalization occurs willingly (Ryan & Powelson, 1991). But relatedness often comes with a price, a hidden agenda in which one person asks for compliance from the other before granting love or approval (Gruen, 1976). Conditions of worth, for instance, essentially mean that the other person's (or society's) love, approval, care, and emotional connectedness are contingent on compliance with socialization standards and norms. Maladjustment under such conditions is not always transparent, as the compliant individual might be held up as an exemplary "good boy." The maladjustment becomes clearer when socializing agents—family, school, church, coworkers, culture—supply contradictory values and contradictory conditions of worth. Facing contradictory conditions of worth, the self has a difficult time regulating its behavior in a way that gains approval and relatedness. It is hard to comply with a moving target.

Humanistic perspectives argue that there is another agent that capably guides development, namely the self (or the actualizing tendency in particular). And there is another type of relatedness between people besides a conformity-demanding conditional positive regard, namely, the degree to which each individual experiences the other as accepting and supporting in an unconditional way (Ryan, 1993). Consider relatedness in both childhood and adult development. The quality of relatedness in early attachments (infant and caretaker) depends on how sensitive and responsive caregivers are to the infant's needs and initiatives. The quality of relatedness in adult relationships depends on the mutuality of autonomy and involves an openness to each other's selves in an air of freedom rather than control. In both childhood and adulthood, relatedness requires understanding, accepting, and supporting the self as it expresses itself freely. Chapter 4 referred to this way of relating as "autonomy support" and documented several positive adaptive outcomes that emanate from autonomy-supportive relationships, including greater perceived competence, enhanced sense of self-worth and self-esteem, greater creativity, positive emotional tone, maintenance of behavioral change, and interpersonal relationships based on trust.

A final point is that autonomy is *not* independence, and autonomy is *not* interpersonal detachment (Ryan, 1993). Independence involves not relying on others for need fulfillment; detachment involves breaking ties with others. Neither foster the self's autonomy (Ryan, 1991, 1993; Ryan & Lynch, 1989). In fact, adolescents who detach themselves (from their family) become increasingly susceptible to conformity and decreasingly capable of mature relationships with others. The paradoxical conclusion that emerged from Ainsworth's classic program of research on infant attachment was that infants who received warm, need-satisfying, responsive, sensitive care from mothers did not become dependent or needy; instead, nurturing care enabled and even liberated the child's autonomy (Ainsworth, 1989). Relationships rich in relatedness paradoxically facilitate autonomy, at least when the relatedness occurs in a context of support rather than control. In contrast, when others provide contingent conditions of worth, then people often forego autonomy in order to preserve relatedness. In optimal development, neither autonomy nor relatedness is forgone (Ryan, 1993).

The Problem of Evil

Do we as a society dare trust a person to be self-determining? Freedom and self-determination are fine if human nature is benevolent, cooperative, and warm-hearted, but what if human nature is malevolent, selfish, and aggressive? What if human nature is evil, or at least partly evil? Recently, humanistic thinkers have become willing to wrestle with the nature of evil (Goldberg, 1995; Klose, 1995). The discussion typically takes one of two forms. On the one hand, the discussion asks *how much* of human nature is evil? This question asks, "If family, political, economic, and social institutions and systems were benevolent and growth-promoting, then would human evil be reduced to zero or would some residual ferociousness remain?" (Maslow, 1987). On the other hand, the discussion of the problem of evil tries to understand murderers and rapists who confess to enjoying what they do and express a willingness to continue doing such acts whenever the possibility of getting away with them presents itself (Goldberg, 1995).

Evil is the deliberate, voluntary, intentional infliction of cruel and painful suffering on another person without respect for his or her humanity or personhood. When people *desire* to act in ways that promote evil, they possess a malevolent personality (Goldberg, 1995). Rogers' conviction was that evil was not inherent in human nature. He argued that if caretakers provide enough nurturance and acceptance and if they establish a genuine connectedness and mutual presence with those they care for, people inevitably choose good over evil (Rogers, 1982). Other humanists see more ambiguity in human nature and assume that benevolence and malevolence are part of everyone, as are the impulses to do good or evil. In this view, under one set of social conditions, the actualizing tendency pairs itself with life-affirming values and adopts constructive ways of relating and behaving; but under another set of conditions, the actualizing tendency pairs itself with malicious values and leads to cruelty and destructive behavior (May, 1982). Thus, human beings need a value system (principles of law, justice, and judgments of right and wrong) to support the organismic valuation process, and if adults (parents) do not provide the child or adolescent with such, then the child will grab a value system wherever it is available, be it among equally confused peers on the street, the college fraternity world, or Wall Street (Maslow, 1971). In these views, the actualization tendency and organismic valuation process need a benevolent value system as a resource to express the actualizing tendency in ways that are benevolent and life-affirming.

The descent into evil is a slippery course of choices (Fromm, 1964). One portrayal of that slippery course proposes the following five developmental progressions toward a malevolent personality (as determined in clinical practice; Goldberg, 1995). First, the self is a child of scorn. Adults shame the child such that the child comes to the conclusion that he or she is flawed and incompetent as a human being. Second, the self incubates a negative self-view. To hide from his or her shame, the child comes to prefer lies and self-deceit over the critical self-examination that makes self-correction possible. Third, a transition occurs from being victim to becoming perpetrator. Insensitivity and disregard for others manifest themselves in the attempt to blame others for personal inadequacies and life failures. Fourth, the self initiates experimental malevolence. In manipulating others and in carrying out acts of cruelty, the self relies on denial and rationalization, such that rationalization provides a quasi-legitimate reason to justify cruel acts (and also blocks the developmental capacity for empathy). As to defenses, the personal dynamics that drive destructive behavior and the exploitation of others are ubiquitous lying, pretense of goodness, and blaming and scapegoating others. Finally, there is the forging of the malevolent personality through a rigid refusal to engage in critical self-examination. The self becomes unwilling to examine itself (e.g., scapegoating is used as a strategy to sacrifice others to preserve one's own self-image; Baumeister, Smart, & Boden, 1996).

The malevolent personality often possesses superior physical, social, or intellectual skills with which to intimidate others, and success in intimidation fosters the self-aggrandizement that counteracts the need for self-examination. In short, adult self-aggrandizement vanquishes childhood shame (Goldberg, 1995).

The consensus in humanistic thinking is that evil is not inherent in human nature. Within a supportive interpersonal climate, people's choices move them in the direction of greater socialization, improved relationships with others, and toward what is healthy and benevolent (Rogers, 1982). So, as murder, war, and prejudice continue, the culprit seems not to be the evil in human nature but the sickness in culture. Human beings behave malevolently only when they have been injured or damaged by their experience, as outlined previously. But culture is not the bad guy here, as cultures can promote either health and well-being *or* sickness and pathology, depending on the decisions of its individual members (May, 1982). As long as society offers people choices, the possibility remains that its members will internalize a pathological value system that makes possible the descent into evil and the forging of a malevolent personality. Human nature is not evil and culture is not evil; rather, the capacity for choice allows people to internalize and to resist the value system opportunities that come their way.

A final question asks whether human evil can be healed. One constant in humanistic thinking is that it never condemns without an affirmation of hope. But the malevolent personality is a tough one. Four reasons explain the difficulty in healing evil: (1) the malevolent personality's closed nature (unwillingness to engage in critical self-examination), (2) the rarity of the malevolent personality's genuine motivation to change, (3) the odds against the malevolent personality finding those supportive conditions in which motivation for personal change can take root and fulfill itself, and (4) the strong influence of the individual's self-determined choice to change or not to change (Klose, 1995).

CRITICISMS OF THE HUMANISTIC APPROACH

After spending a few hours reading the books of either Maslow or Rogers, it is difficult not to feel good and optimistic about yourself and about human beings in general. Still, one must square the optimism of humanism with the reality of observation and wonder if it is not overly naive to conceptualize human nature as intrinsically good. If humankind is good by nature and is something to be nurtured rather than constrained, then one must explain why hatred, prejudice, crime, exploitation, and war persist throughout human history without interruption (Geller, 1982). And, how are we to make sense of the classic studies carried out by Milgrim (1969) that showed that over 60% of normal people off the street were willing to obey an authority figure and turn up an electric current that they knew would kill another person in the next room? Perhaps people are not so intrinsically honorable, trustworthy, and kind. Perhaps people have within themselves not only positive human potentialities but also the potential to destroy themselves and others (May, 1982). One can image the potentially adverse consequences of a parent or a government who presupposes benevolent inner guides and therefore allows a permissive environment for their mis-behaving children or citizens. It seems that the humanistic view emphasizes only one part, although an important part, of human nature and is therefore somewhat limited in generalizability.

A second criticism is that both Maslow and Rogers use a full range of vague and ill-defined constructs. It is difficult to pinpoint precisely what an "organismic valua-tion process" and a "fully functioning individual" are, for example. Any theoretical construct that evades a precise operational definition must remain scientifically du-bious. For this reason, humanistic views on motivation have been harshly criticized (Daniels, 1988; Neher, 1991). The critics essentially recommend we drop unscien-tific concepts such as self-actualization and the organismic valuation process. But there is a middle ground that recognizes the relative infancy or newness of human-istic study (O'Hara, 1989). So far, in humanistic psychology's balance between method and topic, topic gets more attention, emphasis, and celebration than does method. As humanistic psychology matures, its study is slowly but surely leaving be-hind questionable scholarship and armchair speculation in favor of a more scientific approach and understanding of the origins, dynamics, and consequences of human potentiality.

"Feelingism" is a third criticism (Rowan, 1987). Humanism sometimes presents feelings as the royal road to the true self (to borrow a Freudian metaphor), such that feelings provide markers to identify the inner guides of the actualizing tendency and organismic valuation process. Feelingism becomes a problem when humanists afford feelings a conceptual status above all other aspects of experience, such as thinking, sensing, imagining, and so forth. This criticism is not so much against humanism per se as it is a branch or version of humanistic psychology, especially that practiced by some clinicians practicing group therapy. An exclusive focus on feelings can never reveal a satisfactory understanding of motivation and emotion because it neglects the contributions of needs, cognitions, and external events as well as the interaction among feelings (emotions) with needs, cognitions, and external events.

A fourth criticism questions how one is to know what is *really* wanted or needed by the actualizing tendency (Geller, 1982). For example, if a person is 100% confi-dent that abortion is bad, wrong, and something to be refused, then how is one to know, for sure, that such a preference is a product of the organismic valuation process rather than a product of internalization of socialized conditions of worth? People who are uncomfortable about a decision of right and wrong find it difficult to trace the origin of these feelings back to their true source. If standards of right and wrong are introjected from infancy, a person can be easily self-deceived into thinking their preference is their own rather than their parents'.

A fifth criticism is that humanistic psychology is a bit single-minded in its focus on the individual; it relatively neglects or underappreciates the contribution of so-cial, economic, political, and sociological forces on personal development (Greening, 1995). In its eagerness to promote individualism, humanistic study often "fails to ac-knowledge that our sense of personal autonomy, our sense of identity, our sense of stable personality, our sense of personhood *itself* comes to us from outside" (O'Hara, 1989, p. 271). Detaching the self from a society's shared values, meanings, beliefs, and ideals potentially exacts the serious cost on the individual of becoming vulnerable to suicide (Durkheim, 1951). Like inherited potentials, social forces too contribute to people's sense of autonomy, identity, personality, and personhood, and they do so in a way that is necessary, healthy, and productive. This criticism asserts that society and the standards of others are not necessarily a pair of corrupt bogeymen that seek to pollute the self. Only those social forces that demand conditions of worth threaten to fragment the self and set the stage for maladjustment. A future direction for humanistic theory is therefore the study of both how the society contributes to self-actualization and how the self-actualizing individual, in turn, becomes an advocate for transforming the society at large into one capable of materializing actualization goals (Bugental, 1970). An answer to this criticism will therefore illustrate how inherent potentials and social forces can be cooperative partners instead of antagonists.

SUMMARY

Humanistic psychology identifies strongly with the holistic perspective and in doing so, stresses the notions of inherent potentialities, the self, and strivings toward realization and fulfillment. In practice, humanistic psychology is about identifying and encouraging the development of human potential. The two outspoken proponents of the humanistic perspective on motivation are Maslow and Rogers.

For Maslow, self-actualization refers to the full realization and use of one's talents, capacities, and potentialities. Driving the process of actualization are urges or basic needs that exist at the organismic level. Five sets of needs—physiological, safety and security, love and belongingness, esteem, and self-actualization—are arranged hierarchically to communicate that the needs near the base of the pyramid are the relatively stronger needs, appear sooner in development, and must be fulfilled before other, higher needs can emerge. Despite its intuitive appeal and fit with common sense, research finds very little empirical support for the hierarchy. One finding that does gain empirical support, however, is the distinction between deficiency and growth needs. Developmental progress from a concern to satisfy deficiency needs to a concern to satisfy growth needs takes place only in a supportive social context. Maslow also offered a number of specific behaviors the person could engaging in to encourage progress toward self-actualization, including those listed in Table 15.3.

For Rogers, one fundamental need—the actualizing tendency—subsumes and coordinates all other motives to achieve organismic maintenance, enhancement, and actualization. With the onset of language, complex cognitive processes, and extensive social interaction, some aspects of experience lead to the emergence of the self. With the emergence of the self, the actualizing tendency differentiates part of its motivational force into the need for self-actualization. With socialization, children learn societal conditions of worth on which their behavior and personal characteristics are judged as either positive and valued or negative and rejected. As a consequence of becoming aware of and internalizing conditions of worth, all of us begin to live in two worlds—the inner world of the organismic valuation process and the outer world of conditions of worth. When people move away from organismic valuing and toward identifying with external conditions of worth, they adopt facades and become willing to reject or deny personal characteristics, preferences, abilities, desires, and beliefs. Rogers used the terms "congruence" and "incongruence" to describe the extent to which an individual denies and rejects personal characteristics and desires (incongruence) or accepts the full range of his or her personal characteristics and desires (congruence). The congruent, fully functioning individual lives in relatively close proximity to his or her actualizing tendency and therefore experiences a marked sense of freedom, creativity, spontaneity, and growth.

Four motivational implications of the self-actualizing tendency include interpersonal relationships, helping others, freedom to learn, and creativity. Interpersonal relationships characterized by warmth, genuineness, empathy, interpersonal acceptance, and confirmation of the other person's capacity for self-determination provide the social climate that supports self-determination in another person. Helping others revolves around the helper acting in a way that is honest, real, understanding, and nonauthoritarian. Freedom to learn concerns the educational relationship between teacher (or facilitator) and student and stresses the principles of autonomy support and learning over authoritarianism and traditional teaching. Creativity is inherent in all humans and is fostered by environmental forces such as openness to experience and suppressed by forces such as extrinsic contingencies. Two additional implications of the actualization tendency are the distinction between (1) personality processes that forge identity toward self-definition or social definition and (2) the problem of evil. The chapter concludes by offering a number of criticisms of a humanistic understanding of motivation, including Polyanna optimism, unscientific concepts, feelingism, unknown origins of inner motivational forces, and an underappreciation of the contribution of social, economic, political, and sociological forces on personal freedom and adjustment.

RECOMMENDED READINGS

Ford, J. G. (1991). Inherent potentialities of actualization: An initial exploration. *Journal of Humanistic Psychology, 31*, 65–88.

Geller, L. (1982). The failure of self-actualization theory: A critique of Carl Rogers and Abraham Maslow. *Journal of Humanistic Psychology, 22*, 56–73.

Hardeman, M. (1979). A dialogue with Abraham Maslow. *Journal of Humanistic Psychology, 19*, 23–28.

Jenkins, S. R. (1996). Self-definition in thought, action, and life path choices. *Personality and Social Psychology Bulletin, 22*, 99.

Maslow, A. H. (1943). A theory of motivation. *Psychological Review, 50*, 370–396.

May, R. (1982). The problem of evil: An open letter to Carl Rogers. *Journal of Humanistic Psychology, 22*, 10–21.

Rogers, C. R. (1959). A theory of therapy, personality, and interpersonal relationships, as developed in the client-centered framework. In S. Koch (Ed.), *Psychology: A study of science* (Vol. 3, pp. 184–256). New York: McGraw-Hill.

Rogers, C. R. (1969). Personal thoughts on teaching and learning. In *Freedom to learn: A view of what education might become* (Chpt. 6, pp. 151–155). Columbus, OH: Merrill.

Rogers, C. R. (1995). What understanding and acceptance mean to me. *Journal of Humanistic Psychology, 35,* 7–22.

Rowan, J. (1987). Nine humanistic heresies. *Journal of Humanistic Psychology, 27,* 141–157.

Chapter 16

UNCONSCIOUS MOTIVATION

Imagine watching as Sam undergoes hypnosis from a psychiatrist. Once hypnotized, the psychiatrist suggests that Sam brought a newspaper with him to the session and that once he awakes he will want to read it. In actuality, Sam brought no newspaper. Further, the therapist suggests that upon his awakening, he will look for the newspaper but will be unable to find it. The therapist tells Sam that, after this futile search, an idea will occur to him that another person has taken his newspaper, has in fact stolen it. The therapist also suggests that Sam's discovery of his loss will provoke him to anger and that he will direct that anger toward the thief. Unfortunately for you, the psychiatrist next tells Sam that you are that thief. The therapist tells Sam that, in his fit of anger, he will first insist and then will demand that you return his newspaper. To conclude the hypnosis session, the psychiatrist tells Sam that he will forget that the source of all this (mis)information was actually a suggestion given to him by the therapist during hypnosis.

Sam awakens. After a brief discussion of his daily schedule and other such chitchat, Sam remarks, "Incidentally, that reminds me of something I read in today's newspaper. I'll show you." Sam looks around, does not see his newspaper, and begins to search for it through a stack of magazines and books. Then, all of the sudden, he turns toward you with piercing eyes. Accusingly, Sam pronounces that he thinks you took his newspaper, and he now wants it back. You rather sheepishly say you know nothing of his newspaper, but Sam continues with his accusations and you notice that he is a bit ticked off. With his anger piqued, Sam forcefully accuses you of stealing his newspaper. He goes further. He says you took it because you are too cheap to buy one of your own. To substantiate his accusation, Sam says someone told him that they saw you steal his newspaper. At this point, this is no longer entertaining and your distress starts to rise. Sam *really* believes you stole his newspaper and he *really* wants it back, even though he never actually had a newspaper in the first place.

What does this hypnosis session, taken from Fromm (1941), illustrate? The scenario illustrates that human beings can have thoughts, feelings, and emotions which subjectively feel to be their own but, in fact, have been introjected from another source. Sam wanted something—to show us an item in the newspaper; Sam thought something—you stole his newspaper; and Sam felt something—anger against an alleged thief. But Sam's wants, thoughts, and feelings were not his own in the sense that they did not originate within him. Yet, Sam surely acted as if they were his own. Such a demonstration of the posthypnotic suggestion testifies to the paradox that while we can be sure of what we want, think, and feel, we can also have little idea as to the source of what we want, think, and feel.

PSYCHOANALYTIC PERSPECTIVE

In contrast to humanism (chapter 15), the psychoanalytic approach presents a deterministic, relatively pessimistic image of human nature. Psychoanalysis is deterministic in that it holds that the ultimate cause of motivation and behavior derives from a set of core biological drives. That is, we inherit biological drives that create in us motivational impulses that determine our desires, thoughts, feelings, and behaviors, whether we like it or not. Psychoanalysis is further deterministic in that personality changes very little after childhood. The personality of the 15-year-old is essentially the same personality at age 50; thus, many of the motivational impulses of the 50-year-old can be traced to events that happened many decades ago. Psychoanalysis is not only deterministic; it is also relatively pessimistic. The subject matter in psychoanalysis is a bit on the dark side, including sexual and aggressive urges, conflict, repression, defense mechanisms, unconscious desires, anxiety, and other such burdens and shortcomings of human nature. It sees anxiety as inevitable and the collapse of personality and mental health as a matter of degree rather than as an exceptional event that happens to only some of us. We are all dogged by guilt, by the most primitive of desires, and by distortions of reality. It is not a pretty picture, Freud said, but it is reality nonetheless. In his mind, Freud was not a pessimist; he was a realist.

Nevertheless, psychoanalysis is strangely appealing and wonderfully popular. Part of its appeal is that, in reading psychoanalytic theory, the reader comes face-to-face with some difficult aspects of human nature. As psychoanalysis portrays human nature, people "are more interested in getting sexual pleasure than they will admit" and people have "blind rages, wild lusts, and parasitic infantile longings, any of which may or may not be present as conscious desires" (Holt, 1989, pp. 172–173). These difficult aspects of human nature present us with a sort of psychological riddle or mystery that pulls in our curiosity. We question, we explore, we read. And when we read, it becomes increasingly apparent that the psychoanalytic approach to understanding motivation depends on the core concept of the *pathogenic secret* (Ellenberger, 1966), or the notion that secret impulses and thoughts need to be brought to consciousness to reverse their pathological effects. Who can resist a theory about the secrets of the heart and mind—secret crushes and jealousies, secret fantasies and desires, secret memories of things done and not done, and all sorts of hidden intrigue and despair? Another part of its appeal is that psychoanalysis makes the unconscious its subject matter. Thus psychoanalysis is unique and goes "where no theory has gone before" (to borrow an image from *Star Trek*)—into dreams, hypnosis, inaccessible memories, fantasy, and all the hidden forces that shape our motives and behaviors without our awareness or consent.

Sigmund Freud

A physician by training, Freud viewed motivation as regulated by physiological (i.e., biological) forces. For Freud, the human body was a complex energy system organized for the purpose of increasing and decreasing its energies through behavior. For example, by eating and breathing, the body increased its physical energy; by working and playing, the body decreased its physical energy. In addition to regulating physical energy, the body also regulated psychical (mental) energy. The mind needs psychical energy to perform its functions (thinking, remembering, and so forth) and draws its energy—its psychic force—from the body's physical energy. The driving force for both physical and mental energy in Freud's view of motivation is biological drive (or instinct). An instinct is a biologically rooted force "emanating within the organism and penetrating to the mind" (Freud, 1915, p. 64). Hence, motivation originates from instinctual bodily demands.

For Freud there were as many biological drives as there were different bodily demands, or needs. Some of the more obvious bodily needs are those for food, water, and sleep, but Freud recognized that there were too many different bodily needs to list. Instead of compiling a taxonomy of bodily drives, Freud (1920, 1923) emphasized two general categories: the instincts for life and the instincts for death.

EROS: THE INSTINCTS FOR LIFE. The first class of instincts—Eros, the life instincts—is the more easily defined of the two. Eros maintains life and ensures individual and collective (species) survival. Thus, instincts for food, water, air, sleep, temperature regulation, pain alleviation, and the like all contribute to the life and survival of the individual. Instincts for sex, nurturance, and affiliation contribute to the life and survival of the species, a reproductive emphasis Freud borrowed from Darwin (Ritvo, 1990). In his discussions of the life instincts Freud gave primary emphasis to sex, though he conceptualized sex quite broadly. He made a point of stressing the distinction between what is sexual and what is genital, and spoke mostly of the former. For Freud, the sex instinct manifests itself in a variety of behaviors that collectively mean pleasure seeking. Thumb sucking, tickling, rocking, rubbing, being caressed, being tossed in the air, rhythmic stimulation, masturbation, and sexual contact are all included as gratifications of the sex (or pleasure) instinct (Freud, 1905).

THANATOS: THE INSTINCTS FOR DEATH. The death instincts push the individual toward rest and energy conservation, toward inactivity and bodily equilibrium. Perfect equilibrium—no bodily disturbance, no imbalance, and unwavering homeostasis—can be achieved only through total rest, which is death. In discussing the death instincts, Freud gave primary emphasis to aggression. Aggression specifically compels the individual to destroy and kill. When aggression is focused on the self, it manifests itself in self-criticism, sadism, depression (or "melancholia"), suicide, masochism, alcoholism, drug addiction, and unnecessary risk taking. Even gambling is sometimes attributed to the aggression instinct directed against the self (Bergler, 1957). When aggression is focused on others, it manifests itself in anger, hate, prejudice, verbal insult, cruelty, rivalry, revenge, murder, and war. For example, a hostile joke about a disliked ethnic group represents a nonphysical expression of the thanatos (Freud, 1905).

These body-based instinctual drives toward life and death—sex and aggression—provide the energy that motivates behavior. Experience, however, not the drives themselves, directs behavior. Through experience (psychosexual development), the individual eventually learns defensive reactions to manage sexual and aggressive energies. One's habitual, learned manner of defense is much of what Freud meant by the ego. Thus, instinctual drives provided the energy for behavior, while the ego provided the direction for need satisfaction and for keeping itself from dangers (by means of anxiety). Essentially, the ego's task was to discover the most socially adaptive, socially appropriate, and least anxiety-provoking path to need satisfaction, taking into account the demands and constraints of the external world.

DRIVE OR WISH? Contemporary psychoanalysts review Freud's instinctual drives motivation theory and generally find it wanting (e.g., Holt, 1989). For instance, few contemporary psychoanalysts still endorse the idea of the death instincts (Berkowitz, 1962). After years of research, experimental psychologists testify that neither sex nor aggression conform nicely to a physiological model of drive (as hunger or thirst do, see chapter 3). For instance, notice how poorly aggression fits into Figure 3.2. Physiological deprivation rarely produces an urge to act aggressively, and the urge to do so does not intensify with its neglect. Further, consummatory behavior typically fuels rather than satiates aggressive desires. Because sex and aggression are so central to Freud's view of motivation, and because sex and aggression do not seem to fit the drive conceptualization of motives very well, contemporary psychoanalysts drop the idea of drive as their central motivational construct.

As a substitute motivational principle, sex and aggression are conceptualized as psychological wishes, rather than as physiological drives (Holt, 1989; Klein, 1967). The reformulated "wish model" proposes the following. At any time, individuals are aware, consciously or unconsciously, of their present state and, on encountering almost any situation, perceive some more potentially desirable state. For example, a man goes about his daily affairs without any disturbance from a physiological sex drive, but, upon encountering his scantily clad spouse, perceives a potentially more favorable state than his present one. Consequently, a perceptual-evaluative mismatch occurs. That discrepancy between present state and desired state gives rise to the wish. Using the concept of wish, rather than drive, contemporary psychoanalysts now propose that wishes, not instinctual drives, regulate and direct human behavior (Holt, 1989). The wish retains all the spirit of Freudian motivation as people wish all too frequently for desired states in the sexual and aggressive realms, but it discards the contradictory evidence that sex and aggression do not function much like physiological drives. The problem with the wish model is that it leaves open the question of the source of wishes. The source of motivation via physiological drives is clear—instinctual bodily demands. The source of motivation via psychological wish is less clear, so contemporary psychoanalysts spend much time wrestling with the cognitive, social, and personal sources of wishes (e.g., Wegner, 1989) that can explain phenomena such as suicide, alcoholism, masochism, binge eating, religious fanaticism, and other such ways of coping with life (Baumeister, 1991).

Psychodynamics

"The mind is an arena, a sort of tumbling-ground, for the struggle of antagonistic impulses" (Freud, 1917, p. 68). Freud conceptualized people as being of two minds, as it were. People have ideas and wills, but people also have counter ideas and counter wills. When the ego's conscious will and the id's unconscious counter will are of roughly equal strength, a sort of internal civil war ensues in which neither is completely satisfied. The armies of this civil war can be diagramed as follows:

$$\text{will} \to \; \leftarrow \text{counter will}$$

Freud's depiction of the human mind was one of conflict, of idea versus counter idea, will versus counter will, desire versus repression, excitation versus inhibition, cathexis (sexual attraction) versus anticathexis (guilt), and forces versus counter-forces. This clashing of forces is what is meant by the term *psychodynamics*.

At a general level, psychodynamics concerns the conflict between the personality structures of the id and ego (and superego, which is not discussed here). The motivations of the id are fully unconscious, involuntary, and fully consistent with hedonism, as the id obeys the pleasure principle: Obtain pleasure and avoid pain and do so at all costs and without delay. In the id there is no morality, no doubt about what is wanted, no learning from experience, and no distinction between reality and fantasy. The motivations of the ego are partly conscious and partly unconscious, and the ego obeys the reality principle: Hold pleasure seeking at bay until an appropriate, timely, and socially acceptable need-satisfying object can be found. The ego's delay of gratification and concerns for disapproving reactions from the social world counteract the id's demands for pleasure at all cost. Similarly, the pleasure principle counteracts the reality principle, as one cannot immediately fulfill hedonistic desires while taking time to say "please" and "OK, let's share."

REPRESSION. Repression refers to the process of forgetting information or experience by ways that are unconscious, unintentional, and automatic. Suppression (discussed in the next paragraph), in contrast, refers to the process of removing a thought from attention by ways that are conscious, intentional, and deliberate (Wegner, 1992). Repression is the ego's psychodynamic counterforce to the id's demanding desires. It is a defensive process to keep out of consciousness some otherwise distressing wish, desire, idea, or memory. Without repression, the ego's charge to coordinate the demands of the id, superego, and physical/social reality would be an impossible undertaking. When unconscious thoughts and impulses begin to surface, anxiety appears as a danger signal, and it is anxiety that moves the ego to action—to repression and perhaps to other ways of coping as well (Freud, 1926; Holmes, 1974, 1990). But repression is tremendously difficult to study empirically, sort of like trying to figure out whether the refrigerator light stays on when you close the door (to borrow an example from Wegner, 1989), because to study repression you have to ask people about things they don't remember. Research on repression has not yet produced impressive understandings (Erdelyi & Goldberg, 1979; Erdelyi, 1985, 1990), but research on a related process of mental control—suppression—has been enlightening.

Thought Suppression

The ability to stop a thought is beyond the human mind. When an unwanted thought or worry comes to mind, people generally try to control the intruder via suppression (the attempt to avoid a thought). Thought suppression does not work. When we try to suppress a thought, all we get for our efforts is a lesson that we have less control over our thoughts than we care to admit (Wegner, 1989). Consider the psychodynamics of the following: (1) do not think about something (try not to think about today's dental appointment); (2) do not do something (try to go all day without smoking a cigarette); (3) do not want something (try not to want to eat a certain food while on a diet); and (4) do not remember something (try to forget about a deeply humiliating experience). When such thoughts enter our consciousness, our thinking halts itself because the thought precedes something that we wish not to happen (the self-instruction of "don't think about that candy bar" precedes the undesired act of eating the candy bar). With the stream of thought halted, the unwanted thought just sort of sits out there in consciousness all by itself—with a spotlight on it. Perhaps we can suppress the thought for a few seconds, or perhaps for a few minutes, but there is a curious tendency for that thought to pop up again (Wegner, 1989; Wegner et al., 1987).

Consider a laboratory experiment in which college students were asked not to think of a white bear (Wegner et al., 1987). Each participant sat alone at a table with a bell on it (like those used in hotels for service). For the first 5 minutes the participant said whatever popped to mind. Everyone found free association to be easy. For the next 5 minutes, however, the participants were asked explicitly not to think of a white bear but, if they did, to ring the bell as a signal that the unwanted thought had popped to mind. The attempt at thought suppression was most difficult and a lot of bell ringing occurred during those 5 minutes. Finally, during a last 5-minute period, each participant was asked to think about a white bear. In this last period, participants experienced a rebound effect in which the thought of the white bear preoccupied their attention. Bell ringing was nearly constant. These results were quite paradoxical to what you might expect from common sense. Thought suppression not only failed, but it produced an obsessive preoccupation about those darn white bears (the rebound effect).

People rely on thought suppression to control their thoughts and actions in practically all areas of life. People rely on thought suppression for behavioral self-control, as in the effort to abstain from eating certain foods (Polivy & Herman, 1985) or consuming addictive substances (Marlatt & Parks, 1982). People rely on thought suppression for communication self-control, as in the effort to keep a secret (Pennebaker, 1990) or deceive another person (DePaulo, 1992). People rely on thought suppression for emotional self-control, as in the effort to silence pain (Cioffi, 1991) or fear (Rachman, 1978). And people use thought suppression to avoid making public the inner workings of their mind and its socially offensive wants, desires, and intentions (Wegner & Erber, 1993). People rely on thought suppression for seemingly good reasons. Many of our private thoughts would produce public confusion if allowed to be freely expressed, such as greeting a stranger and suppressing the first impression that he is extremely attractive—or worse, that he is extremely unattractive. Thought suppression turns potential social conflict into a private mental struggle of good thoughts versus bad (Wegner, 1992). We learn quickly that thought suppression can be a social ally when it allows us to avoid the dangerous social consequences that would otherwise follow if we did not suppress our thoughts, as sometimes happens when we are heavily stressed (Jacobs & Nadel, 1985) or tipsy from alcohol (Steele & Josephs, 1990) and just blurt out our thoughts.

All this makes for interesting psychodynamics. An unwanted thought appears, and suppression acts as a counterforce. With thought suppression, a curious problem emerges in that the act of suppressing produces a *rebound effect* of the unwanted thought. The unwanted thought returns a counterforce of its own against the suppression. Continued suppression builds a rather potent counterforce that drives the unwanted thought toward an obsession (e.g., the dieter who tries not to think of food is vulnerable to thinking only about food; Polivy & Herman, 1985). According to Wegner (1989, 1992), the way out of the quagmire of the suppression cycle (unwanted thoughts → thought suppression → obsession → unwanted thoughts, and so on) is to stop suppressing and, instead, focus on and think about the unwanted thought. Paradoxically, only those thoughts that we welcome are we able to forget (Frankl, 1960). Thought suppression makes intuitive sense as a strategy to clear the mind of traumatic memories, unpleasant emotions, hateful addictions, unwanted desires, and worries about the future, but psychodynamics explains why "you can't always think about what you want" (Wegner, 1992, p. 193).

The rebound effect makes for interesting psychodynamics, but is obsession the only possible outcome from thought suppression? The rebound effect (suppression → obsession intensifies → harder to suppress) does not occur with personally intrusive (self-defined) thoughts the way it does for thoughts given to the person by some outside force (Kelly & Kahn, 1994), like an experimenter saying not to think of a white bear (Wegner et al., 1987) or a friend asking you to keep a secret (Lane & Wegner, 1995). People's own intrusive thoughts are different from externally induced intrusive thoughts in that people have a good deal of experience trying to suppress the former. The number one strategy that works with intrusive thoughts is distraction (Wegner, 1989). With familiar intrusive thoughts, people generally have a rich network of thoughts they have used previously to distract themselves from their unwanted thoughts (Kelly & Kahn, 1994), such as when I fell the urge to smoke a cigarette (and don't want to) I learn to think about x, y, and z to take my mind off smoking.

Do the Id and Ego Personality Structures Actually Exist?

Now that we have laid out the basic personality structure that underlies psychodynamics, we will pause and ask what contemporary empirical research says about the scientific status of the id and ego. Is the human brain organized such that part exists as a cauldron of innate and impulsive biological desires while another part exists as an executive control center that perceives the world and learns and adapts to it? Actually, yes. Recall the metaphor of the onionlike structure of the brain from chapter 1. The limbic structures of the brain—the hypothalamus, thalamus, amygdala, medial forebrain bundle, and so on—are commonly referred to as pleasure-unpleasure brain centers. Limbic system brain structures are basic to the experiences of pleasure (Olds & Fobes, 1981; Stellar & Stellar, 1985; Wise & Bozarth, 1984).

Electrical stimulation of the brain reveals that some limbic areas are pleasure centers (i.e., septum, lateral hypothalamus, medial forebrain bundle) whereas other limbic areas are unpleasure centers (i.e., thalamus, amygdala, medial hypothalamus). As a side note, however, electrical brain stimulation in humans does not produce intense pleasure or rage-filled attack, but rather, only mild feelings of pleasure and unpleasure (Gloor, Oliver, & Quesney, 1981; Heath, 1964; Valenstein, 1973).

The neocortex qualifies as the brain structure that might correspond to the ego, as it performs all those functions that reflect learning, memory, information processing, and decision making. Further, the neural pathways and structures of the neocortex and the limbic systems are intricately interrelated. Even within the neocortex itself or the limbic system itself, the interrelationships of how one structure affects the other (e.g., how the amygdala excites and inhibits the hypothalamus) are so complex as to defy description here. The picture that emerges corresponds to a pattern of psychodynamics, of forces and counterforces, of cathexis and anticathexis, of excitations and inhibitions.

UNCONSCIOUS MOTIVATION

The division of mental life into what is conscious and what is unconscious is the fundamental premise of psychoanalysis (Freud, 1923). Freud rejected the idea that consciousness was the essence of mental life and therefore divided the structure of human personality into three components: conscious, preconscious, and unconscious. The conscious includes all the thoughts, feelings, sensations, memories, and experiences that a person is aware of at any given time; it is relatively unimportant to motivation study. The contemporary psychological term for the conscious is short-term, or working, memory. The preconscious stores all the thoughts, feelings, and so on that are absent from immediate consciousness but can be retrieved into consciousness with a little prompting. The contents of the preconscious are available for voluntary recall. For example, you are aware of (but are not currently thinking about) your name, today's date, or what color ink these words are. The most important and by far largest component of the personality is the unconscious. The unconscious is the inaccessible storehouse of instinctual impulses, repressed experiences, childhood (before language) memories, and strong but unfulfilled wishes. This mental storehouse of inaccessible desires and repressed impulses is fundamental to an understanding of the psychoanalytic view of human motivation (Freud, 1915, 1923).

Scientific psychology has a difficult time with the unconscious. After all, if the unconscious is hidden from both private consciousness and public observation, how can a researcher ever gain access to it? The problem is not an insurmountable one, however, any more than concepts such as (inaccessible) electrons are insurmountable to those who study physics. Freud believed that the individual must express strong unconscious urges and impulses, though often in a disguised form. The unconscious is therefore a "shadow phenomenon" that cannot be known directly but can be inferred from a variety of its indirect manifestations and signs (Erdelyi, 1985).

Methods of Tapping into the Unconscious

Freud and his fellow psychoanalysts found at least seven methods of tapping into the unconscious: hypnosis, free association, dream analysis, humor, projective tests, errors and slips of the tongue, and accidents. Examination of these methods cannot prove the existence of the unconscious, but a shadow of information is still better than total darkness. The first two methods—hypnosis and free association—are rather direct attempts to access the contents of the unconscious. The remaining five methods—dream analysis, humor, projective tests, slips of the tongue, and accidents—are indirect and require interpretation to transform the surface expression (e.g., the story line of a joke) into its deeper meaning (the contents of the unconscious).

HYPNOSIS. Under hypnosis, the psychoanalyst orders the individual to execute a given action at a specified time (e.g., get a drink of water when the watch alarm rings at 8:00 PM). Upon regaining consciousness (leaving the hypnotic state), the individual reports no recollection of the hypnotic experience. Nonetheless, precisely on hearing the watch alarm ring at 8:00 PM, the individual experiences a rush into his mind the impulse to drink water, and he does it consciously, though not knowing why. The behavioral execution of a posthypnotic suggestion is interesting because the person performs the action without knowing why. The person wants without knowing why. The motive, in the Freudian view, comes from the unconscious. Like no other technique in psychoanalysis, the performance of a posthypnotic suggestion demonstrates the ability of an unconscious motive to energize and direct behavior (recall the chapter's opening vignette).

Despite its potential, Freud questioned whether hypnosis could reveal the unconscious because not everyone could be hypnotized, and even those who could did not tend to show permanent improvement in therapy (Brill, 1938). Most important, however, Freud found that his attempts to hypnotize some clients with a "You are falling asleep; you are falling asleep" repetition actually did little more than ruin the clients' concentration. With these clients, Freud decided to give them more leeway to recall the events in their lives in their own way. After a while, Freud asked these clients simply to call out whatever crossed their mind, withholding nothing; his patients found this extremely difficult. The clients always held back, in effect censoring their thoughts. Such self-censorship and self-deception intrigued Freud, and the method of free association eventually replaced hypnosis.

FREE ASSOCIATION. In free association,[1] the individual daydreams aloud whatever thought or image comes to mind. Its aim is to uncover inaccessible desires or re-

---

[1]There are actually two variations of the free association technique, Freudian and Jungian. In Jungian free association (for Carl Jung), the psychoanalyst reads a list of words and the client is instructed to say the first thing that pops to mind. For example, the psychoanalyst might say, "mother," "rock," "school," "envelope." . . . at one second intervals and await the client's free association to each word. If the person pauses before responding verbally, fails to think of any word association, or repeats the stimulus word, the psychotherapist suspects that the particular stimulus word might tap into a significant emotional experience within the storehouse of the unconscious.

pressed memories. The individual is to report all associations spontaneously (in response to, "You mentioned your old high school friend. What comes to mind when you think of her?"), while the therapist intervenes with directed questioning or with interpretive hints. As the client freely associates, all efforts at self-censorship are to be abandoned. There must be no omitting, no rearranging, and no restructuring of the stream of consciousness. If there is, then what is not said is at least as important as what is said. Even if embarrassed, the person is to report all free-flowing ideas. Pauses in the stream of associations and disclaimers that particular information is unimportant are resistance against free association. In fact, the material most in need of overt expression is that which one resists making public. Free association, rather than self-censorship, permits the unconscious a relatively free and unrestricted expression. Free association in effect is a technique that attempts to raise the unconscious to the conscious. In practice, the client feels that each association emerges quite at random, but the therapist seeks to discover how superficially unrelated events are actually related and are in fact symptomatic of unconscious content. Because Freud found free association to be an effective procedure to uncover that which is disguised, he called free association without censorship or inhibition "the fundamental rule of psychoanalysis."

DREAM ANALYSIS. For Freud, dream analysis was "the royal road to a knowledge of the unconscious" and his book *The Interpretation of Dreams* was, according to his own standards, his finest achievement. Dream analysis begins by asking the individual to report the story line of his or her night's dream and ends with the therapist's interpretation of the underlying meaning of the dream. A dream's story line represents its *manifest content* (its face value), while the symbolic meanings underlying the events that occur in the story line represent its *latent content* (its underlying meaning). Because the explicit expression of unconscious wishes would be quite anxiety-provoking, the unconscious expresses its impulses through the latent and symbolic, rather than the obvious and manifest. Thus, to interpret a dream, the therapist puts aside the literal story line and, instead, uncovers its meaning through interpretation. Interpreting a dream, however, is a tricky business. Dream interpretation entails analysis of censorship and interpretation of symbols and usually proceeds with a sentence-by-sentence analysis of the dream's manifest content with free association (Erdelyi, 1985).

As one illustration, consider the dream reported by one of Freud's patients and analyzed with free association in Freud (1900): "A whole crowd of children—all of her brothers, sisters and cousins of both sexes—were romping in a field. Suddenly they all grew wings, flew away and disappeared." The patient first had this dream as a young child and continued to have this same dream repeatedly since. In the dream, all of the patient's brothers, sisters, and cousins flew away and she alone remained in the field. According to Freud, the dream does not make much sense at the manifest level, and to gain an understanding of its meaning and significance, the analysis must take place within the latent content. At the latent level, according to Freud (1900), the dream is (for this particular person) a death wish from the thanatos that her brothers, sisters, and cousins would all sprout wings and fly away like a butterfly (a child's view of the soul leaving the body upon death), leaving her to the full attention and affection of her parents.

The success of dream analysis depends fully on free association, so here is a second dream that adds more of the flavor of free association (from Stafford-Clark, 1966, p. 68). A woman dreamed she was strangling a little white dog. Her associations were that she liked cooking very much and that she sometimes had to kill animals to do so. She disliked that. She recalled that the way she strangled the dog in her dream was the same way she strangled chickens in real life. Her next association was capital punishment, then she next thought of how hangings were used in capital punishments. The therapist intervened at this point, asking if there was anyone she felt a particular grudge against. She said she did, her sister-in-law, saying, "She is trying to come between my husband and myself." Her next association was to recall a rather violent argument in which the woman kicked the sister-in-law out of the house saying, "Get out, I don't want a dog that bites in my house!" The interpretation of the dream, because of the success of the free associations, become clear.

HUMOR. Jokes and dreams are similar in that both are imagistic, both feature manifest and latent content, and both rely on similar modes of interpretation. The difference between the two is that jokes are voluntary and meant to be playful. According to Freud (1905), humor allows the expression of unconscious wishes in a socially approved manner. It is interesting to notice just how frequently the topic of a joke concerns sex, aggression, or rebellion against authority. Telling or hearing a joke about sex or aggression causes ego-generated anxiety to emerge. But with jokes, the ego (and superego) do not retaliate against the id as the joke teller has a sort of license to suspend social constraints that otherwise keep infantile wishes in check. But everybody does not find humor in the same sort of things, and Freud argued that what people laugh at can be used to reveal the contents of their unconscious. After the joke is told (or a practical joke is carried out), the psychic energy is discharged in the form of laughter. The laughter is a sign of pleasure, of catharsis. Indeed, in the Freudian interpretation of humor and laughter, a joke cannot be funny unless it is anxiety provoking. Thus, comedians insult audiences, talk frequently on taboo topics, draw attention to symbols of sexual anatomy, unleash verbal assaults against various ethnic groups, insult authority figures, and generally talk about "dangerous" material. But a joke that is too blatant fails to be humorous. A joke is too blatant when its latent content is insufficiently disguised from its manifest content (it comes across as bad taste). Sufficiently disguised humor, however, provides an audience with the opportunity to liberate themselves from sexual and aggressive repression (Freud, 1927).

PROJECTIVE TESTS. Projective tests expose individuals to a stimulus for which there is no culturally agreed on way to respond. Therefore the individuals must fill in the interpretive gaps by projecting their personal biases, wishes, and ways of perceiving and interpreting the world to make sense of what they see. The two best-known examples of projective tests include the Rorschach Inkblot Test (Exner, 1986; Exner & Exner, 1972) and the Thematic Apperception Test (TAT: chapter 6). The Rorschach, for instance, presents the test taker with a series of 10 symmetrical inkblots, and the test taker interprets what the inkblot looks like and then explains why that interpretation was made. The inkblot cards typically yield certain common interpretations such that many people interpret a particular inkblot in the same way. Occasionally, the test taker projects wishes into his or her interpretation of the inkblot and reports seeing blood, death, gore, and destruction on one card and sexual activity on another card. A psychotherapist presumes that what is projected is beyond volitional control and thus takes these interpretations of aggression and sex as leakages of the unconscious.

ERRORS AND SLIPS OF THE TONGUE. A sixth method of probing the unconscious is the "Freudian slip," such as saying "Sigmund Fraud" instead of "Sigmund Freud." Or, when talking with an uninteresting acquaintance, saying "shut the bore" instead of "shut the door." In one of his more entertaining (but difficult to read) works, *The Psychopathology of Everyday Life* (1901), Freud assembled dozens of examples (and analyses) of such slips of the tongue. As one illustration, consider Freud's report of a newspaper printer who was setting the type for a war correspondent's meeting with a general well known for his affinity for alcohol. Instead of typesetting "this battle-scarred veteran," the printer set "this battle-scared veteran." Embarrassed at such a slip of the hand, the printer carried the following correction in the next day's paper: "this bottle-scarred veteran."

ACCIDENTS. Freud strongly believed that *there were no accidents*. Freud was a strict determinist—every accident had its cause. All behavior, whether intentional or accidental, was motivated by some mental activity, conscious or unconscious. Thus, when a man loses his car keys just before an important meeting, such an "accident" is interpreted as a wish to avoid the meeting or, perhaps, as a wish to punish himself for a recent transgression. A missed or "forgotten" appointment with a "friend" or a momentary inability to recall the friend's name are additional examples of such accidents. Consider the anger and guilt expressed by a woman who is driving her husband's car, but stops suddenly in the street, therefore causing the car behind her to run into her car. Her anger expresses itself in the smashing of the automobile, and the guilt expresses itself in that she knows her husband will punish her, thus easing her guilt for being angry (Brenner, 1957). Freud (1920) relates the story of a woman who "accidentally" lost her wedding ring on her honeymoon. As you might guess, Freud was not at all surprised when the couple divorced soon thereafter. The woman's lost wedding ring, Freud reasoned, was an unconscious wish to "lose" the marriage and terminate the relationship. Other everyday slips and accidents that reveal our unconscious intentions, according to Freud, include getting on the wrong bus or train, dialing the wrong telephone number, misreading a sign by one letter, and other such bungled actions.

CRITICISMS OF THE
PSYCHOANALYTIC APPROACH

Despite its intrigue, Freud's contribution to the study of human motivation is plagued by (at least) five criticisms. The most devastating criticism against Freud is that many of his concepts are not scientifically testable (Eysenck, 1986). Without scientific test, such concepts are best taken with skepticism and understood metaphorically rather than as credible scientific constructs. Theoretical constructs that have not yet stood the test of empiricism and experimental rigor must remain guilty until proven innocent, invalid until proven valid. Consider repression and childhood amnesia. Freud argued that the reason we recall so little of our childhood is because we repress these experiences. That is a difficult idea to test (and disprove), but it is not difficult to generate an alternative explanation. For instance, the brain structures and pathways that allow us to encode and retrieve memories are simply not yet developmentally complete during early childhood, and the child therefore lacks the physical structures necessary for long-term memory encoding and retrieval (Jacobs & Nadel, 1985). Thus, immature neural pathways explain childhood amnesia, leaving us to wonder if we should put our faith in Freud's intuition or opt for recent findings in neurological development. In Freud's defense, however, hundreds of studies, perhaps a thousand, have been conducted on his theoretical constructs. Some (but certainly not all) of Freud's ideas have indeed stood the test of empirical validation (Fisher & Greenberg, 1977; Masling, 1983; Silverman, 1976). Other ideas and phenomena have been reinterpreted in ways that do not rely on psychoanalytic concepts (e.g., consider Brown's analysis of the tip-of-the-tongue phenomenon [1991] and Wegner's analysis of mental control [1994]).

Many of Freud's motivational concepts arose from case studies of disturbed individuals, and this is a second criticism. It is a difficult theoretical step to suppose that the motivational dynamics of a few adults from European background undergoing psychotherapy in the early 1900s represent the motivational dynamics of the human species in general. The criticism is one of external validity. It asks how appropriate it is to generalize the findings of a specific group to the general population. For example, how comfortable would you feel with a theory of motivation derived solely from the observation of men, or of adults? One is bound to wonder whether the motives of men apply equally to women, or to children.

A third criticism is that Freud placed a heavy emphasis on biological endowment, childhood experience, and the pessimistic aspects of personality. Freudian critics often point out that social and cultural influences shape our motives as much as does biology, that adult experiences are equally important as childhood experiences, and that the optimistic view of personality has as much to offer as does the pessimistic view. In other words, even if one sees value in Freud's view of motivation, one must at the same time recognize that there are many additional pieces of the theoretical puzzle left to be fitted before one understands human motivation.

A fourth criticism, a red flag of caution, arises with respect to Freud's methods of data collection. For empirical data, he used his own observations, his own dream diary, his memory of therapy sessions (rather than actual transcripts), and saw evidence for the death instinct from the devastation of the World Wars. Such methods of data collection inherently invite personal biases, skewed interpretations, omissions and distortions (even unconscious ones!), and a lack of consideration of alternative explanations. While Freud's insight was amazing, research shows that he was wrong about as often as he was right. Perhaps the most satisfying conclusion to a critical evaluation of Freud's ideas is echoed by the words of Henry Murray, a neo-Freudian: "There is no reason for going in blind and swallowing the whole indigestible bolus. . . . I, for one, prefer to take what I please, suspend judgment, reject what I please."

A final criticism is that although psychoanalytic theory is a wonderful interpretive device for events that occurred in the past, it is woeful as a predictive device. For instance, suppose a person has a dream about siblings dying (recall the section on dream analysis). For one person the dream might be best interpreted as a wish for her siblings to die. For a second person, however, the dream might be best interpreted (via reaction formation) as a wish for her siblings to survive. For yet another person, the siblings' death or survival might represent sentiments associated with a third party, say one's own children. All these post hoc (after the fact) interpretations make sense in psychoanalysis. But here is the problem: The theory is very poor at predicting a priori (before the fact) that a person will have a dream about siblings dying. For the theory to be predictive, the theory must allow us to anticipate when a person will or will not have a particular type of dream (or use a particular defense mechanism, or whatever). A scientific theory must be able to predict what will happen in the future. It is hard to trust a theory that explains only the past.

EGO PSYCHOLOGY: THE NEO-FREUDIANS

Freud postulated that all psychical energy originates in the id. At birth, the infant is all id; the ego is only in the beginning processes of formation (Freud, 1923). Throughout infancy, the ego develops from perceiving instincts to controlling them, from obeying instincts to curbing them. As an infant matures, id energies are distributed, in part, to the developing ego. How much energy is distributed to the id and ego during childhood determines the relative strengths of that personality. If the id has the greater energy, adult behavior is impulsive and pleasure oriented. On the other hand, if the ego has the greater energy, adult behavior is realistic and characterized by the timely gratification of needs and strategic avoidance of dangers. To describe the relationship between the id and ego, Freud (1923) wrote that "One might compare the relation of the ego to the id with that between a rider and his horse. The horse provides the locomotive energy, and the rider has the prerogative of determining the goal and of guiding the movements of his powerful mount towards it." In addition, the ego, "feels itself hemmed in on three sides and threatened by three kinds of danger. . . . Goaded on by the id, hemmed in by the superego, and rebuffed by reality, the ego struggles to cope with its economic task of reducing the forces and influences which work in it and upon it to some kind of harmony" (Freud, 1923, pp. 108–109). Thus, Freud saw the ego as a personality structure that arose from id energies to mediate between id impulses, superego demands, and the dangers of the environment. As mentioned earlier, the id is force and the ego becomes counterforce.

The neo-Freudians saw ego functioning as much more. Hartmann (1958), the "father of ego psychology," saw the ego involved in a process of maturation that made it increasingly independent from its id origins. For Hartmann, the ego, unlike the id, develops through learning and experience. Learning occurs because the child engages in a tremendous amount of manipulative, exploratory, and experimental activity (such as grasping, walking, crawling, and thinking), all of which provide the ego with information about itself and its surroundings. With feedback from its manipulative, exploratory, and experimental activity, the ego begins to acquire "ego properties"—language, memory, intentions, complex ideas, and so on—that facilitate its ability to adapt successfully to the realities, demands, and constraints of the world. Because of its ability to learn, adapt, and grow, Hartmann conceptualized the mature ego as mostly autonomous from the id. Neo-Freudians studied the motivational dynamics of the autonomous ego.

Ego Development

Defining ego is difficult, because the ego is not so much a thing as it is a developmental process. The essence of ego development is progression toward what is possible in terms of psychological growth, maturity, adjustment, competence, and autonomous functioning (Deci, 1980; Loevinger, 1976). From its infantile origins through its progression toward what is possible, the ego unfolds on the basis of a sequential trajectory that proceeds along the following developmental stages (Loevinger, 1976):

- Symbiotic
- Impulsive
- Self-Protective
- Conformist
- Conscientious
- Autonomous

During the (infantile) symbiotic stage, the ego is extremely immature, constantly overwhelmed by id impulses, and exists as wholly dependent on its caretaker. With language, the symbiotic ego begins to differentiate itself from the caretaker but remains extremely immature. In the impulsive stage, external forces (parental constraints, rules), not the ego per se, curb the child's impulses and desires. Self-control emerges when the child first anticipates consequences (i.e., punishments) and understands that rules exist, and the ego internalizes these consequences and rules to guide its self-protective defensive capabilities. During the conformist stage, the ego internalizes group-accepted rules, and the anxiety of group disapproval becomes a potent counterforce against id impulses. The conscientious ego has a "conscience," an internalized set of rules and a sense of responsibility to others, in which internal standards curb id impulses. The conscientious ego is the modal ego stage among adults (Loevinger, 1976). The autonomous ego is one in which thoughts, plans, goals, and behaviors originate from within the ego and its resources, rather than from other people and societal pressures (Ryan, 1993).

Each ego stage is more complex than the one that precedes it, and both cross-sectional studies that compare ego development in children, adolescents, and adults (Loevinger & Wessler, 1970) and longitudinal studies that compare the same individuals over the life course (Redmore, 1983; Redmore & Loevinger, 1979) confirm this progression of ego development. It is not known precisely when or why people achieve the maximum ego development, though social experiences such as going to college (Loevinger et al., 1985) and coping with divorce (Bursik, 1991) are important. What is clear is that most people stabilize their ego development much sooner than the autonomous stage (Holt, 1980; Loevinger, 1976).

Ego development centers around the effectiveness of acquired capacities such as ego strength, emotional stability, coping, emotional intelligence, competence or effectance, self-efficacy, hardiness, and autonomous self-regulation (Block & Kreman, 1996). To adapt successfully, unconscious impulses and desires need to be controlled. Impulse control occurs through development and largely reflects the extent to which the individual progresses from a personality based on the pleasure principle to a personality based on the reality principle. Strong impulse control allows the ego to inhibit aggression, experiment playfully with challenges in the environment, delay gratification, and reject inappropriate outlets for gratification. The ego-resiliency scale measures this characteristic; three items from this scale are as follows: I get over my anger at someone reasonably quickly. Daily life is full of things that keep me interested. I would be willing to describe myself as a pretty "strong" personality (Block & Kremen, 1996, Table 1, p. 352).

Ego Strength

Ego development does not happen automatically, and the day-to-day existence of the ego is one of vulnerability. To develop from immature status and from a susceptibility to being overwhelmed by unacceptable desires and environmental demands, the ego must gain resources, or strength. A mature, strong ego manifests itself in three ways: (1) Resilient defense mechanisms allow it to cope successfully with the inevitable anxieties of life; (2) a sense of effectance or competence provides it with a generative capacity to provide its own autonomous motivation; (3) a sense of identity provides it with a productive and fulfilling place within the society. These three attributes correspond to ego defense, ego effectance, and ego identity.

EGO DEFENSE. Through defense mechanisms, the ego buffers consciousness against potentially overwhelming levels of anxiety originating from conflict with id impulses (neurotic anxiety), superego demands (moral anxiety), and environmental dangers (realistic anxiety). Three signs provide evidence that an anxiety-reducing course of action is indeed a defense mechanism: (1) It is unconscious rather than deliberate, reflective, and intellectual; (2) its use is immediate (showing its defensive function);

and (3) it functions to deny, distort, or otherwise rearrange the person's understanding of reality so that it is less threatening. Table 16.1 lists 14 such defense mechanisms and provides a definition and example for each, borrowing rather liberally
from Anna Freud's *The Ego and Mechanisms of Defense* (1946).

These 14 defense mechanisms exist in an hierarchical ordering from least to
most mature, from least to most adaptive. The essential criterion for determining
how adaptive or mature a defense mechanism is depends on how much distortion
or blocking of reality the defense mechanism achieves. Denial and fantasy, for instance, are the defenses of psychosis, while sublimation and humor are relatively
mature ego defenses (Vaillant, 1977). The hierarchy is related to the concept of ego
strength, as a strong ego habitually relies on relatively mature defense mechanisms
that allow it to react to the realities of life with appropriate problem-solving coping
responses. In contrast, a weak ego relies on relatively immature defenses to sidestep
the realities of life in ways that prevent appropriate problem-solving coping responses.

Vaillant (1977) classified defense mechanisms into four categories of maturity.
At the most immature level, defense mechanisms, such as denial and fantasy, deny
reality or invent an imaginary reality. These defenses are the most immature because
the individual fails even to attempt to cope with external reality. The defenses of
projection and identification represent a second level of maturity. These defenses
recognize reality, but attempts to cope with it are accomplished by casting its disturbing aspects away from the self (as in projection) or reframing the stressor as a
harmless, nonthreatening life event (as in denial). With denial, for example, the executive refuses to acknowledge that the company is about to go bankrupt (which
lessens the anxiety but does not solve or remove the source of the stress). At the
third level of maturity are the most common defenses, including rationalization, regression, and reaction formation. Level three defenses deal effectively with short-

TABLE 16–1
Defense Mechanisms of the Ego

DEFENSE MECHANISM	DEFINITION (WITH *EXAMPLE*)
Denial	Unpleasant external realities are ignored or their acknowledgement is refused. *Preoccupation with work so there is no attention paid to the subtle messages of rejection coming from a problematic personal relationship.*
Fantasy	Gratifying frustrated desires by imaginary achievement. *Imagining oneself to be a courageous national hero who performs incredible feats and wins the admiration of all.*
Isolation	A form of self-censorship that prevents or keeps affect (emotion) out of consciousness while allowing the cold facts to register in consciousness. *Hearing the news of the death of a loved one and responding only cognitively (matter-of-factly) to the events that one is hearing.*

TABLE 16–1 (CONTINUED)

Defense Mechanisms of the Ego

DEFENSE MECHANISM	DEFINITION (WITH *EXAMPLE*)
Repression	Prevents and keeps anxiety-provoking thoughts out of consciousness. *Rejecting the desire to injure another person.*
Identification	Taking on the characteristics of someone viewed as successful. *Seeing the nation adore a celebrity and then adjusting one's appearance (hair style, mode of dress, walk) to be loved and treated like the celebrity.*
Projection	Attributing one's own unacceptable desire or impulse onto someone else, often producing a mild paranoia. *The anxiety of "I am failing this course because I am unintelligent" is expressed as "This textbook is stupid" or "The teacher is an idiot."*
Reaction formation	Adopting or expressing the strong opposite of one's true feelings or motives. *Expressing and endorsing strong optimism ("Everything will work out just fine") in the face of the grim realities of world hunger, nuclear war, or interpersonal rejection.*
Regression	Returning to an earlier stage of development when experiencing stress or anxiety. *Using baby talk to gain another's nurturance and sympathy and win an anxiety-provoking argument.*
Rationalization	Justifying a disturbing or unacceptable thought or feeling by selecting a logical reason to think or feel that way. *Producing an acceptable reason to justify one's hatred for a particular group of people, such as "because they lie and cheat all the time."*
Atonement	Undoing an anxiety-provoking thought or behavior by apology, repenting, or punishment. *The child-neglecting, world-traveling parent brings gifts home for children to make up for the neglect.*
Compensation	Covering up a weakness or inferiority by overemphasizing the importance of a desirable trait. *The physically unattractive person develops an exceptional athletic or musical skills, or a person with feelings of inferiority may brag frequently about the status of his or her ancestors.*
Displacement	Releasing one's anxiety against a substitute object when doing so against the source of the anxiety could be harmful. *Discharging pent-up aggressive impulses against a father figure (the boss) onto a more anxiety-manageable object, such as the household dog. The worker kicks the dog as a substitute for the father figure.*
Humor	Expression of unconscious wishes in a socially approved manner such that the person releases sexual and aggressive impulses and insults authority figures in a disguised form. *A newspaper editorial cartoon exaggerates an unflattering anatomical feature of a high-ranking politician that allows readers to laugh at the authority figure.*
Sublimation	A displacement that results in something advantageous to society. *Libidinal energy, such as a sexual impulse, is released through creative, scientific, or manual work.*

term anxiety but fail to accomplish any longer-term gain in adjustment (because reality is repressed rather than accommodated). Rationalization, for example, temporarily excuses unacceptable desires or characteristics, but it fails to provide the means to cope with the problem that produced the anxiety in the first place. Level four defense mechanisms are the most adaptive and mature and include defenses such as sublimation and humor. Sublimation, for instance, accepts (unconsciously) id impulses but effectively channels them into socially beneficial outlets, such as the creative energy that produces a painting or poem (making instinctual impulses both socially acceptable and personally productive). Consider also humor. All of us experience life stress, but people with a well-developed sense of humor suffer little maladjustment (e.g., depression) whereas people with little sense of humor suffer from stress (e.g., Lefcourt & Martin, 1986; Nezu, Nezu, & Blissett, 1988).

To test his ideas that the maturity level of one's defenses reflect ego strength and thus life adjustment, Vaillant (1977) followed the lives of 56 men over a 30-year period. He interviewed each man in his college-age years, and objective raters classified each man as using predominately mature (levels 3 and 4) or predominately immature (levels 1 and 2) defense mechanisms as a personal style against anxiety. The study asked how these two groups of men would fare in life, and the research assessed each man's life adjustment 30 years later in four categories—career, social, psychological, and medical. Table 16.2 reports the results. Ego strength, as indexed by maturity level of defense mechanisms, successfully discriminated men who had career, social, psychological, and medical problems from those who did not. Mature defense mechanisms allowed the men to live a well-adjusted life, find or keep a fulfilling job, develop a rich friendship pattern, avoid divorce, avoid the need for psychiatric visits and mental illnesses, and so on.

EGO EFFECTANCE. Ego effectance concerns the individual's competence in dealing effectively with environmental challenges, demands, and opportunities (White, 1959; Harter, 1981). Effectance motivation begins as an undifferentiated source of ego energy. With its diffuse energy, its ego properties (e.g., grasping, crawling, walking) and acquired skills (e.g., language, writing penmanship, social skills), the ego attempts to deal satisfactorily with the circumstances and stressors that come its way. In the process of adapting and developing, the undifferentiated ego energy begins to differentiate into specific motives such as the needs for achievement, affiliation, intimacy, and power (chapter 6). Thus begins the development of a variety of separate ego motivations, but the core ego motivation is effectance motivation, or the desire to interact *effectively* with the environment (also see chapter 4, especially Fig. 4.1).

Ego effectance develops into more than just a defensive, reactive coping response to life's demands. As the child exercises skills, he or she begins to learn how to produce successful change in the environment. The child learns how to use crayons, climb trees, cross streets, hold an adult's attention, feed itself, write letters, ride a bicycle, hit baseballs, and a hundred other tasks. When successful, such interactions produce a sense of efficacy, a perception of competence, and feelings of satisfaction and enjoyment. The ego aggregates these perceptions and feelings into

TABLE 16–2

Relationship between Maturity of Defense Mechanisms and Life Adjustment

| | PREDOMINANT ADAPTIVE STYLE (%) | | SIGNIFICANCE |
	MATURE (N = 25)	IMMATURE (N = 31)	(P)
Overall Adjustment			
1) Top third in adult adjustment	60%	0%	<.01**
2) Bottom third in adult adjustment	4%	61%	<.001*
3) "Happiness" (top third)	68%	16%	<.001
Career Adjustment			
1) Income over $20,000/year	88%	48%	<.01
2) Job meets ambition for self	92%	58%	<.001
3) Active public service outside job	56%	29%	<.05**
Social Adjustment			
1) Rich friendship pattern	64%	6%	<.001
2) Marriage in least harmonious quartile or divorced	28%	61%	<.01
3) Barren friendship pattern	4%	52%	<.001
4) No competitive sports (age 40-50)	24%	77%	<.001
Psychological Adjustment			
1) 10+ psychiatric visits	0%	45%	<.01
2) Ever diagnosed mentally ill	0%	55%	<.001
3) Emotional problems in childhood	20%	45%	<.05
4) Worst childhood environment (bottom fourth)	12%	39%	<.05
5) Fails to take full vacation	28%	61%	<.05
6) Able to be aggressive with others (top fourth)	36%	6%	<.05
Medical Adjustment			
1) 4+ adult hospitalizations	8%	26%	
2) 5+ days sick leave/year	0%	23%	<.05
3) Recent health poor by objective exam	0%	36%	<.05
4) Subjective health consistently judged excellent since college	68%	48%	<.05

*Very significant difference; would occur by chance only one time in a thousand.
**Significant difference.
***Probably significant difference.
SOURCE: Vaillant, G. E. (1977). *Adaptation to Life.* Boston: Little, Brown & Company, Copyright © 1977 by George E. Vaillant.

a general sense of competence. Eventually, the child's cumulative history of efficacious and inefficacious feedback yields a personal sense of competence, which is a synonym for ego strength. The greater the ego's effectance motivation, the greater the person's willingness to use ego properties *proactively*—not just reactively to cope—to intentionally change the environment. With each successful transaction with the environment (a friend is made, a tree house is constructed), the ego's pooled reservoir of effectance motivation increases. The greater the effectance motivation, the stronger is the desire to develop personal skills (ego properties) further and to seek out interactions with the environment in general.

With ego development, the mature individual has a repository of two sources of motives—id-based instinctual drives (wishes) and ego-based effectance motives. Id-based motivations are inherited and change little in the course of development. Ego-based effectance motives are acquired through environmental interactions and change markedly in the course of development (Harter, 1981). Together, these two sources explain human beings' energetic and directed behaviors in the psychoanalytic tradition.

EGO IDENTITY. A third aspect of ego development is an emerging sense of identity, the sense of being a distinct individual within a social framework (Erikson, 1959, 1963, 1964, 1968). A coherent sense of identity integrates the ego's physical, psychological, and social attributes and provides one's life course with both direction and effectiveness.

Erikson describes the lifelong quest to formulate and modify an identity by postulating an epigenetic sequence of eight developmental turning points, a theory of psychosocial life-span development that has received mostly empirical support and confirmation of its basic tenets (Whitbourne et al., 1992). In each turning point is the possibility for ego growth toward greater adjustment or ego decline toward greater maladjustment. A positive resolution (at each developmental turning point) empowers the ego's development toward growth, strength, and adaptation; a negative resolution fosters regression, fragility, and maladjustment.

During infancy, the ego is helpless and immature; it possesses literally no ego strength. Being helpless, the ego is fully dependent on its primary caregiver for need satisfaction and faces its first developmental turning point (trust versus mistrust of others). When caretakers prove themselves trustworthy, the ego gains the strength of hope, and begins to attend to exercising emerging skills such as locomotion and language in a positive way. In early childhood, the infant exercises his or her emerging competencies, initiates experiments on the world, and faces its second developmental turning point (autonomy versus doubt). Caretakers either support the child's emerging autonomy and endow the ego with strength of will or greet it with punishing shame. In the preschool years, the third developmental turning point arises in which the ego develops toward either initiative or guilt. With initiative support, the ego gains strength of purpose. During the elementary grades, the fourth developmental turning point arises in which the ego moves toward industry (effectance) or inferiority. The ego strength to be gained through industry is competence, or effectance. Industry involves competence-based development that is cognitive (development of skills and knowledge), behavioral (application of those skills and knowledge), and emotional (rewarding experiences during the acquisition and application of skills and knowledge) (Kowaz & Marcia, 1991). The developmental aggregate of an ego endowed with hope, will, purpose, and competence sets the ideal stage for the ego to face its fifth developmental turning point during adolescence: identity versus role confusion.

By adolescence, the emerging ego must prove itself relevant to an adult social system, to specific adult endeavors, and to available societal roles (Baumeister, 1986, 1987). Hence, occupational apprenticeship begins, and with it a sense of individuality and identity. When they search for, find, and eventually commit to a particular strategy for life, adolescents develop an identity; when they fail to search for, find, or commit to adult roles, adolescents develop role confusion and a sense of ego uncertainty (Marcia, 1966; Meilman, 1979). Whether the adolescent ego achieves a sense of identity therefore depends in part on his or her own developing ego strength and resources, including hope, will, purpose (self-determination), and effectance (competence), and in part on how relevant the ego's skills and talents are in the context of social opportunities, endeavors, and roles.

Four distinct identity statuses exist—achieved, in moratorium, foreclosed, and diffuse (Marcia, 1966). Classification of identity status follows the individual's pattern of exploration and commitment in socially relevant areas of life such as occupation and values. The adolescent with an achieved identity has explored actively and made personal commitments to a way of life. The adolescent with an identity in moratorium has explored actively but not made personal commitments (the identity crisis). The adolescent with a foreclosed identity has not explored but has committed to an identity (assimilated the parent's occupational role or values). The adolescent with a diffuse identity has neither searched, explored, nor committed to occupational choices or values.

Ego identity status explains how identity contributes to ego development by outlining the impact that each status has on ego development in general. Ego development (progress toward maturity and adjustment) occurs for two primary reasons: (1) the life path one follows and (2) the difficult, challenging experiences that are unique to the individual. Identity status reflects the personal dynamics that result from one's life path and life challenges. Achieved identity reflects both an integration of personal attributes and an acceptance of the social environment (i.e., the ego is characterized by independence, effectance, coherent values, and warm relationships with others); moritorium identity reflects a lack of integration of personal attributes and a questioning of the social environment (i.e., the ego values independence and is rebellious, anxious, introspective, and open to new ideas and change); foreclosed identity reflects an acceptance of the social environment (i.e., the ego is overcontrolled and relates to people in conventional ways); and a diffuse identity reflects poor integration in the personality (i.e., the ego is conflicted and its needs are difficult to reconcile into commitments) (Helson, Stewart, & Ostrove, 1995; Kroger, 1993; Marcia, 1966, 1980; Marcia et al., 1993; Waterman, 1982).

SUMMARY

Psychoanalysis makes for a strangely appealing study. By studying the unconscious and by embracing a rather pessimistic view of human nature, psychoanalysis opens the door to study topics such as traumatic memories, unwanted thoughts, unpleasant emotions, inexplicable addictions, anxieties about the future, dreams, hypnosis, inaccessible or repressed memories, fantasies, masochism, repression, self-defeating behaviors, thoughts of suicide, overwhelming impulses for revenge, and all the hidden forces that shape our needs, feelings, and ways of thinking and behaving. The father of the psychoanalytic perspective was Sigmund Freud. His view of motivation presented a biologically based physiological model in which the two instinctual drives of sex and aggression supplied the body with its physical and mental energies. Contemporary psychoanalysts, however, emphasize the motivational importance of psychological wishes (rather than biological drives) and cognitive information processing. The concept of wish retains all the spirit of Freudian motivation, but it discards all the contradictory evidence that sex and aggression do not function much like physiological drives. The study of suppression (rather than repression) also exemplifies how contemporary researchers study psychoanalytic processes. Because suppression, unlike repression, involves cognitive processes that are conscious, intentional, and deliberate, it can be studied empirically and objectively in the scientific laboratory.

Freud's division of mental life into what is conscious and what is unconscious is the fundamental premise of psychoanalysis. Freud paid the most attention to the id and the unconscious, and in doing so established seven methods of tapping into the unconscious: hypnosis, free association, dream analysis, humor, projective tests, errors and slips of the tongue, and accidents. Despite making contributions that are unparalleled in the history of psychology, Freud's psychoanalytic approach to motivation study can be criticized on at least five fronts, including problems involving whether his ideas are scientifically testable, the nonrepresentative samples he used to make his conclusions, his relative neglect of the contribution of adult experiences and social/cultural forces, his subjective data collection methods, and the post hoc nature of his theory.

For Freud, motivation emanated from the id, and the ego mostly directed (rather than energized) behavior. The neo-Freudians (Anna Freud, Hartmann, White, Erikson, and many others) saw ego functioning as much more and conceptualized the motivational significance of the autonomous ego. According to neo-Freudians, the ego developed motives of its own and it did so by moving through the following developmental progression: symbiotic, impulsive, self-protective, conformist, conscientious, and autonomous. But ego development does not happen automatically. To overcome its immaturity and to develop toward maturity, the ego must gain resources and strength. A mature, strong ego manifests itself in three forms: (1) resilient defense mechanisms that allow the ego to cope successfully with the inevitable anxieties of life (e.g., ego defense), (2) a sense of competence that provides a generative capacity to provide autonomous motives (e.g., ego effectance), (3) a sense of the ego's distinct individuality within the larger social context (e.g., ego identity). Mature defenses allow the ego to keep life's stresses and traumas at bay and prevent lapses into loneliness, unemployment, divorce, depression, and other indices of maladjustment. Effectance motivation is the ego's accumulated sense of whether it can interact competently in the world and provides the basis of distinct needs such as competence, affiliation, achievement, intimacy, and power. Identity represents the ego's struggle to discover, develop, and fulfill its potential and relate successfully to the larger society. Collectively, the ego's defenses, effectance, and identity provide the individual with a second source of motivation, as motivation derives not only from id-based drives and wishes but also from ego-based strivings and developmental energies.

RECOMMENDED READINGS

Freud, S. (1930). Civilization and its discontents. In *The standard edition of the complete psychological works of Sigmund Freud* (Vol. 21, pp. 64–145). London: The Hogarth Press and the Institute of Psychoanalysis, 1961.

Holt, R. R. (1989). Drive or wish?: A reconsideration of the psychoanalytic theory of motivation. In R. R. Holt, *Freud reappraised: A fresh look at psychoanalytic theory* (pp. 171–196). New York: Guilford Press.

Loevinger, J. (1976). Stages of ego development. In J. Loevinger, *Ego development* (Chpt. 2, pp. 13–28). San Francisco: Jossey-Bass.

Nezu, A. M., Nezu, C. M., & Blissett, S. E. (1988). Sense of humor as a moderator of the relation between stressful events and psychological distress: A prospective analysis. *Journal of Personality and Social Psychology, 54,* 520–525.

Rapaport, D. (1960). On the psychoanalytic theory of motivation. *Nebraska symposium on motivation* (Vol. 8, pp. 173–247). Lincoln: University of Nebraska Press.

Schiedel, D., & Marcia, J. (1985). Ego integrity, intimacy, sex role orientation, and gender. *Developmental Psychology, 21,* 149–160.

Silverman, L. H. (1976). Psychoanalytic theory: The reports of my death are greatly exaggerated. *American Psychologist, 31,* 621–637.

Wegner, D. M. (1992). You can't always think what you want: Problems in the suppression of unwanted thoughts. In M. P. Zanna (Ed.), *Advances in experimental social psychology* (Vol. 25, pp. 193–225). San Diego: Academic Press.

Wegner, D. M., Schneider, D. J., Carter, S., III., & White, L. (1987). Paradoxical effects of thought suppression. *Journal of Personality and Social Psychology, 53,* 5–13.

White, R. W. (1959). Motivation reconsidered: The concept of competence. *Psychological Review, 66,* 297–333.

Chapter 17

CONCLUSION

This is the final chapter, so I hope you feel confident of your understanding of motivation and emotion. Just how much confidence is appropriate depends to some extent on the degree to which you can (1) explain the reasons for behavior, (2) predict how various conditions will affect motivation and emotion, and (3) apply motivational principles to everyday situations. Let me ask you about each of these understandings in turn.

Explaining the reasons for behavior requires the ability to generate a psychologically satisfying answer to questions such as, "Why did he do that?" and "Why does she want to do that?" Answers to these questions lie in understanding the sources of motivation and how motives, once aroused, intensify, change, and weaken as they energize and direct behavior. Chapter 1 provided 30 or so theories of motivation, each of which provides a piece of the puzzle in the grand effort to explain human wants, desires, fears, and strivings. Working down the list of theories in Table 1.1, for instance, we can say that achievement motivation theory explains why people, when challenged, sometimes show positive emotion and approach behaviors but other times show negative emotion and avoidance behaviors. Achievement motivation theory best applies to those instances when people are challenged by a standard of excellence whereas the other 29 theories apply to a different set of conditions. Taken together, the collection of theories in motivation study provides the means to explain the reasons for behavior.

Motivation study pays close attention to the conditions that give rise to motivational and emotional states and asks, "Which antecedent conditions energize and direct behavior?" An understanding of motivation and emotion includes the ability to predict what effect environmental, interpersonal, intrapsychic, and physiological conditions will have on motivation and emotion. Successful predictions involve using motivation theories to predict how one or more variables will effect a person's motivation. Consider, for instance, that a teacher wants to know how giving report cards will effect students' motivation in the classroom. Cognitive evaluation theory (chapter 5) explains how any external event effects students' psychological needs, intrinsic motivation, and extrinsic motivation. In this example, the external event is a course grade, and cognitive evaluation theory explains that all external events have both an informational aspect, which affects perceived competence, and a controlling aspect, which affects self-determination. If the teacher presents the grades in a controlling way ("Read the textbook, because we'll have a test on the material next week"), they will decrease self-determination, decrease intrinsic motivation, and increase extrinsic motivation. If the teacher presents the grades in an informational way ("We'll have a test so you can get some feedback about how well you have mastered the material"), they will affect perceived competence such that a high grade will increase competence and intrinsic motivation whereas a low grade will decrease competence and intrinsic motivation. Motivation theories are based on past research findings but, once validated, they can be used to predict which conditions/variables will affect motivation and emotion. Theories tell us why those conditions have the effect they have.

An understanding of motivation and emotion also includes the ability to put theories into practice—to apply motivational principles in ways that promote optimal experience and human functioning. The effort to apply motivational principles asks, "How do I motivate myself, and how do I motivate others?" Improving human welfare involves the two complementary quests to (1) improve human functioning and (2) overcome motivational pathologies. Consider first the effort to improve human functioning—to increase effort in school, performance in athletics, productivity at work, wellness in therapy, personal growth in old age, environmental mastery, and so on. Each chapter provides some insight into the practical task of promoting the human welfare, and here are a few reminders in how to promote human functioning through the application of motivational principles:

- promote resilient self-efficacy beliefs (chapter 8)
- generate attractive possible selves (chapter 10)
- gain ego strength and effectance motivation (chapters 4 and 16)
- cultivate rich personal autonomy and self-determination (chapter 4)
- nurture self-actualization and the actualizing tendency's development toward becoming a fully functioning individual (chapter 15)
- set up conditions that promote the flow experience (chapter 4)
- develop and maintain warm interpersonal relationships (chapter 4)
- cultivate talent and high creativity (chapters 4 and 15)
- nurture growth needs (chapters 5 and 15)
- develop a mastery motivational orientation (chapters 4 and 9)
- promote intrinsic interest (chapter 4)
- adopt positive social identities (chapter 10)
- encourage differentiation and integration of the self (chapter 10)
- nurture mature ego development (chapter 16)
- improve decision-making efficiency (chapter 8)
- create conditions that allow the freedom to learn (chapters 4 and 15)
- promote consistency between attitudes and behaviors (chapter 7)
- promote self-definition over social definition (chapter 15)
- establish, maintain, and restore personal control beliefs (chapters 9 and 14)

Consider also how motivation study relates to overcoming motivational pathologies—student apathy, achievement anxiety, helplessness, depression, immature coping strategies, challenge avoidance, worker absenteeism, and breakdowns in regulation such as ignoring physiological cues to regulate eating or ignoring personal preferences in favor of conditions of worth. Each chapter provides insight into the practical task of overcoming motivational pathologies through the application of motivational principles, and here are a few reminders:

- reverse restraint release that leads to binge eating (chapter 3)
- avoid the hidden costs of reward (chapter 5)
- promote a constructive rather than destructive reaction to failure (chapters 8 and 9)
- channel acts of aggression into appropriate outlets (chapter 16)
- reverse decision making that is doubt plagued and fear dominated (chapter 8)
- prevent learned helplessness and its deficits (chapter 8)
- reverse pessimistic expectancies and explanatory styles (chapter 9)

- overcome addictions (chapters 3, 12, and 16)
- manage emotions and identities (chapter 13)
- deal with the problem of evil (chapter 15)
- solve the paradox of thought suppression (chapter 16)
- and identify immature defense mechanisms and find the courage to give them up (chapters 15 and 16)

Motivational principles offer the potential to improve the human condition. These principles are remarkable in their breadth, as they relate to all aspects of life including education, work, sports, therapy, and relationships.

THE SUBJECT MATTER OF CONTEMPORARY MOTIVATION STUDY

Motivation study is more than just the development and application of its theories. Specific phenomena—motivational agents—energize and direct behavior. Figure 17.1 presents the full range of motivational agents by organizing the sources of human motivation into four categories—needs, cognitions, emotions, and external events.

Motivation study is about explaining human wants, desires, wishes, strivings, hopes, goals, aspirations, longings, feelings, and emotions. The roots of such phenomena are needs, cognitions, emotions, or external events. As represented in Figure 17.1, physiological needs arise from biological processes, organismic psychological needs arise from inherent developmental processes, and socialization and learning experiences created acquired psychological needs. Cognitive information processing generates four distinct categories of motives—discrepancies, expectations, attributions, and the self. Emotions are also motives, as emotions arise from patterns of thinking, from biological processes, and their after-effects create moods and affective states. External events generate motivation too, and the two categories of external motivational agents include specific environmental stimuli like incentives and rewards and more general social contexts like the classroom milieu and the culture at large.

CENTRAL THEMES IN MOTIVATION STUDY

Theories (Table 1.1) and specific agents of motivation (Fig. 17.1) provide the nuts and bolts of motivation study. The assembly of these nuts and bolts into an organized construction allows the big picture of motivation study to emerge. Let me ask you to sit back for a moment, clear your mind, and ask yourself what you consider to be the big, grand themes that run throughout a motivational analysis. In other words, when all is said and done and read, what does motivation study boil down to for *you*? This section identifies the overriding, integrative themes that connect the 16 previous chapters into a coherent overview of what motivation study tells us about human beings.

FIGURE 17–1
Sources of Human Motivation

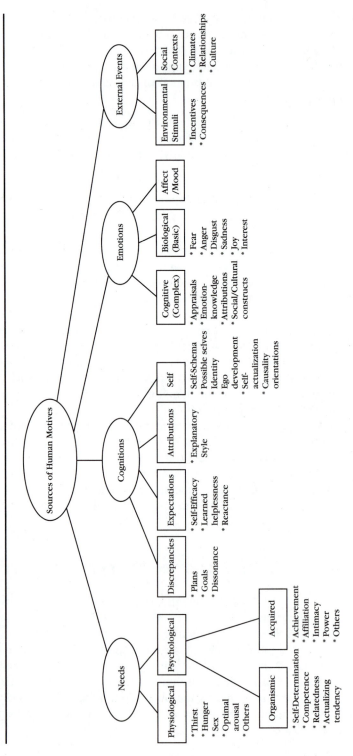

Basically, what do you think motivation study is all about? What themes run throughout the book and throughout the course that seem particularly fundamental or central to understanding motivation and emotion? What would your list look like? I have asked my colleagues and students to generate such a list from time to time, and I find that lists vary from person to person. Some themes pop up on a rather consistent basis, but mostly the lists have more variations than similarities. I think most of the variance can be attributed to different backgrounds, priorities, and philosophical orientations. Despite the diversity of opinions, here is why I find value in the exercise: It encourages students to focus on the big picture of motivation and define for themselves just what themes constitute the essential core of motivation study. Once generated, these are the themes you can take with you long after you have finished reading this book and placed it somewhere on the bookshelf.

As you might suspect, I have a list of my own. My list is admittedly a speculative and individualistic one that reflects my personal interests as much as it does objective motivational study. I encourage you to use my list as a supplemental aid in your own effort to generate a more personally relevant list. To spark your imagination, here are seven themes that I find to be particularly valuable and informative.

Reward and Aversion

Reward versus aversion, pleasure versus pain, hope versus fear, and approach versus avoidance converge on one fundamental theme. When motivated, people are always approaching or avoiding some event. Constructs like reward, pleasure, and hope constitute the essence of why people are approaching something, whereas constructs like aversion, pain, and fear constitute the essence of why people are avoiding something. Reward and aversion are particularly important in motivation study because these experiences can be investigated and understood at several different levels of analysis. Reward and aversion have their physiological underpinnings in electrical stimulation of specific brain sites, in neural circuits within the limbic system, in neurochemical pathways, and in hedonically opponent processes in the brain. Intrinsic motivation concerns inner sources of pleasure such as the competence-need satisfaction that emerges from a job well done. In a cognitive analysis, reward and aversion arise from mental events such as appraisals of benefit versus harm and attributions of why an outcome did or did not occur. Emotion researchers highlight joy, fear, and sadness as basic emotions, and they document the role of positive and negative moods on behavior. Pleasure and aversion also explain personality processes such as the reactions of the sensation seeker and avoider toward the prospect of jumping out of an airplane, and pleasure and aversion are basic to psychoanalytic thinking via the instincts toward pleasure (Eros) and unpleasure (Thanatos).

Competence

Competence serves as a second theme that runs throughout several approaches to motivation. As a need, competence generates the desire to seek out and master optimal challenges. As a reflected appraisal, competence generates perceptions of strong ability and efficacy that encourage persistence and future task reengagement. Competence ties together constructs such as effectance motivation/ego strength, intrinsic motivation, self-efficacy, mastery motivational orientation, and perhaps the need for achievement. Each of these constructs has in common the idea that pleasure and reward that is earned (through effective performance) is somehow qualitatively different from pleasure and reward that is not earned (a gift, a sunny day). The reason that earned competence generates greater vitality is that it involves and confirms some personal aspect such as self-concept, an organismic need, a personal identity, or ego strength.

Control

Control constitutes a third theme in motivation study (Skinner, 1996). Control beliefs enable people to shape their surrounding environment in a way that fits their particular needs and development potentials. Control beliefs therefore include motivational constructs such as self-efficacy, locus of causality, the desire for control, and the social need for power—all aspects of motivation that people rely on to seek out environmental opportunities and effect intentional changes in that environment. Control beliefs also include people's thoughts about the causal impact of their attempts to attain desirable outcomes and to prevent undesirable outcomes. Thus, the constructs of attribution, explanatory style, illusion of control, and locus of control have in common people's understanding of how much or how little control they have over what happens to them. The consequences of such personal control beliefs lead to motivational phenomena such as learned helplessness, depression, coping with stressors, optimism and pessimism, achievement motivation, and eating disorders such as anorexia and bulimia.

Discrepancy

Discrepancy, or incongruity, is a fourth theme in motivation study. A surprisingly large number of motivational phenomena conform to the following portrayal: Some present state of the individual is evaluated, it is compared with an ideal condition, the psychological distance between the present and ideal states produces a felt discrepancy, and discrepancy causes action that persists until the gap between the present and ideal condition is closed. In a cognitive analysis, discrepancy-based theories are plentiful, including plans, goals, dissonance, and self-concept consistency. The plan, in fact, represents the prototypical model of discrepancy. With hunger and thirst, the person undertakes goal-directed action to satisfy a physiological need in which homeostasis functions as the ideal state. In intrinsic motivation, a challenge sets up the discrepancy between present competence and some desired level of competence. With curiosity, encountering a novel environmental object creates a desired state of increased information. In personality motivation, extraverts, sensation seekers, and affect-intense individuals engage in behavioral, sensory, and emotional acts to achieve desired increases in physiological or psychological arousal. In contemporary psychoanalytic thinking, a wish is conceptualized as a perceived (actual) versus an evaluative (ideal) discrepancy. In attribution theory, discrepancy between expected and actual outcomes calls for the attributional analysis.

The Self

The self is a multidimensional phenomenon, and motivation study highlights four aspects of self—cognitive, social, agency, and ego—that motivate action. The cognitive aspects highlight the energizing and directing function of self-concept and possible selves. The social aspects highlight the energizing and directing function of social identities and roles. Agency in the self highlights its inherent potentialities, psychological needs, and developmental tendencies toward differentiation and integration. The ego, the psychoanalytic portrayal of the self, adds the contribution of ego development, which is essentially personality development toward stronger and more mature levels of defense, effectance, and identity. Overall, the self integrates motivational concepts such as self-schema, possible selves, strivings for consistency, introjected and identified regulatory styles, internalized shoulds and oughts, identity, ego, core self, facades, self-actualization needs, and organismic needs under a single explanatory concept of self. The self is also fundamental to emotion, as emotions that involve the self (and its well-being) generate richer, more intense experiences than do those that do not involve the self.

Motivating and Amotivating Environments

Motivation study identifies aspects of an environment that either promote or suppress motivation. It further explains why particular aspects of the environment promote or suppress motivation. Three central features of motivating environments are involvement, structure, and autonomy support (Connell, 1990; Connell & Welborn, 1991; Skinner & Belmont, 1993). Involvement refers to the quality of the interpersonal relationship between two or more people and each person's willingness to show care, warmth, interest, and psychological resources to the other. Involvement is a powerful motivator because human beings need relatedness or belongingness. Structure refers to the amount and clarity of information the environment provides to individuals about how to achieve desired outcomes; it includes features such as clear expectations, predictability and consistency of rules and regulations, clear goals, optimal challenges, and timely feedback. Structure is a powerful motivator because human beings need competence or effectance. Autonomy support refers to the amount of freedom the environment gives to a person so he or she can connect his or her behavior to personal goals, interests, and values; it expresses itself through the provision of choices and options, respect for others and their agendas, and support for personal initiatives. Autonomy support is a powerful motivator because human beings need autonomy or self-determination. When environments such as classrooms, work settings, sports arenas, home settings, and therapy rooms are rich in involvement, structure, and autonomy support, they exude a positive motivational climate; when these environments lack involvement, structure, and autonomy support (and are therefore characterized by neglect, chaos, and coercion), they exude a climate that is amotivational.

Human Nature

A final theme in the motivation literature is its perspective on the question of human nature—are people essentially good or evil, are people by nature active or passive, is psychological growth inherent in healthy development, and what do human beings really want, hope for, desire, and fear? Theories of motivation reveal what is common within the strivings of all human beings by identifying the commonalities among people with different cultures and experiences. All of us harbor physiological needs such as hunger, biological dispositions such as temperament, prewired neural circuits in the brain for pleasure and aversion, basic emotions such as anger and joy, psychological needs such as belongingness, intrinsic motivational processes, unconscious desires, and developmental tendencies to actualize our inherent potentialities. Motivation study also identifies those motivational forces that are learned and internalized (e.g., beliefs, expectations, explanatory styles, long-term goals, quasi-needs, social needs). Other motivational forces stem from environmental, social, and cultural forces that are clearly outside the realm of human nature (e.g., social identities, incentives, reinforcers, socially inspired possible selves). Motivation study informs us what part of want and desire stem from human nature and what part of want and desire arise from personal, social, and cultural experiences.

MOTIVATING OTHERS

Much of the appeal of motivation study is its potential to inform us as to how to motivate others. We want to promote effort, achievement, challenge seeking, and excellence in those people we care about, and we want to help them overcome or reverse their pessimistic expectations, anxiety and doubt, apathy and helplessness.

In practice, most attempts to motivate others take place in relationships that involves an interpersonal power differential between motivator and motivatee (Deci & Ryan, 1987). For example, consider the following interpersonal relationships in which the first person has some responsibility for motivating the other: teachers motivating students, parents motivating children, employers motivating employees, doctors motivating patients, coaches motivating athletes, clergy motivating parishioners, and therapists motivating clients. In each case, the first person has some influence over the second, whether the basis of that power or influence manifests itself in expertise, rewards, force, status, or position. Consequently, the person who is one down in the relationship is vulnerable to being controlled by the person who is one up in power.

Powerful people sometimes motivate others in a way that simply produces compliance (the desired behavior). To achieve compliance, an authority figure or an expert (teacher, coach, therapist) directs the other's way of thinking, feeling, or behaving by disseminating important information and by the effective use of extrinsic incentives that guide the person toward desirable (and away from undesirable) outcomes. I see this approach to motivating others manifest itself in some military leaders, authoritarian athletic coaches, controlling teachers, demanding parents, hardline politicians, patronizing doctors, most employers, and sometimes in myself as well. Of course, there is something appealing about this traditional viewpoint because others can be externally regulated and they will indeed work hard when they desire approval or seek rewards. A second approach to motivating others is to support their motivation from within. This more humanistic approach encourages others to move away from a dependence on authority figures and experts and to move toward an increased capacity for self-regulation in which the individual accepts personal responsibility for generating motivation from within. This approach resonates with what has been referred to in various chapters as the developmental course of moving away from heteronomy and toward autonomy.

I reject the idea that the way to motivate others is to manipulate them into doing whatever it is you think they should or ought to be doing. Motivating others does *not* mean controlling them. As an alternative, I ask you to consider that the fundamental rationale for motivating others is to cultivate in them inner motivational resources that allow them the greatest opportunity possible to develop, grow, and regulate their own behavior.

Inner motivational resources are the growth-promoting needs, cognitions, and emotions the person can rely on as a personal resource when facing a challenge or problem that is motivational. When people set goals, encounter failure feedback, or when they need to marshal great effort to face the challenges in their lives, it helps them tremendously if they have inner motivational resources to tap into to buffer stress, overcome doubt, maintain positive emotionality, initiate and direct their behavior, and maintain their effort and purpose over time. Consider the following list of needs, cognitions, and emotions that provide the foundation for self-regulation and personal growth: self-determination, competence, relatedness, self-efficacy, personal control beliefs, achievement strivings, optimistic explanatory style, goal setting, the self, curiosity, interest, and positive affect. I trust that the pages of the first 16 chapters provided you with the basis of information about nurturing in others strong and resilient inner motivational resources.

Most of us find the task of motivating others to be a challenging one, so we often use strategies that work and that work in a hurry. In other words, we use external motivational resources such as attractive rewards and incentives. On first glance, external motivational resources seem to work just fine—workers arrive on time, complete their projects, and act as employers request. On second glance, however, external motivational resources produce a number of side effects that are simply too damaging to ignore—they sometimes undermine intrinsic motivation and they risk leaving others motivationally empty after the removal of these external motivators. And pursuing the motivational agenda of another person is not all it is cracked up to be. Compared with those who pursue intrinsic goals such as personal growth, people who pursue extrinsic goals such as money, fame, and image have significantly less vitality and self-actualization and significantly more narcissism, negative emotionality, and physical distress (Kasser & Ryan, 1993, 1996).

In trying to motivate others, I find it useful to ask, "Who is motivating the person?" The motivator will be either the person or some outside force. This question is particularly central to the practice of motivating others because learning and achievement occur optimally when there is an intrinsic motivation to initiate self-determined contacts with the environment. Personal growth occurs optimally when there is active participation from the individual to take personal responsibility for his or her own ways of thinking, feeling, and behaving. For this reason, I find myself troubled when I perceive that another person's motivation is coming from me while I find myself assured when I perceive that I am helping that person generate motivation of their own.

Perhaps the best way to end this discussion is to ask a question. How does one go about the task of motivating others in a way that supports their motivation from within? I offer you 16 chapters to consider, but I also invite you to fall back on your own interests and beliefs about the importance of motivation study to generate answers of your own. The practitioner must identify inner motivational resources in others, such as interest, curiosity, autonomy, self-efficacy, and attractive possible selves; the practitioner must also identify inner motivational deficits such as apathy, fear, helplessness, doubt, and unattractive possible selves. Once identified, the practitioner must find the means to support other's inner motivational resources. By nurturing inner motivational resources, the practitioner has more than just behavioral compliance to look forward to; in addition, inner motivational resources cultivate in others a continuing motivation to learn, enhanced performance outcomes, positive developmental courses, positive emotionality, and the inner guides to achieve a successful, productive, and harmonious adjustment into society.

REFERENCES

Abelson, R. P. (1983). Whatever become of consistency theory? *Personality and Social Psychology Bulletin, 9*, 37-54.

Abramson, L. Y., & Alloy, L. B. (1980). Judgment of contingency: Errors and their implications. In A. Baum & J. Singer (Eds.), *Advances in environmental psychology* (Vol. 2). Hillsdale, NJ: Erlbaum.

Abramson, L. Y., Matalsky, G. I., & Alloy, L. B. (1989). Hopelessness depression: A theory-based subtype of depression. *Psychological Review, 96*, 358-372.

Abramson, L. Y., Seligman, M. E. P., & Teasdale, J. (1978). Learned helplessness in humans: Critique and reformulation. *Journal of Abnormal Psychology, 87*, 49-74.

Adelmann, P. K., & Zajonc, R. B. (1989). Facial efference and the experience of emotion. *Annual Review of Psychology, 40*, 249-280.

Adolph, E. F. (1980). Intakes are limited: Satieties. *Appetite, 1*, 337-342.

Ainsworth, M. D. S. (1989). Attachments beyond infancy. *American Psychologist, 44*, 709-716.

Alexander, P. A., Kulikowich, J. M., & Jetton, T. L. (1994). The role of subject-matter knowledge and interest in the processing of linear and nonlinear text. *Review of Educational Research, 64*, 201-252.

Allender, J. S., & Silberman, M. L. (1979). Three variations of student-directed learning: A research report. *Journal of Humanistic Psychology, 19*, 79-83.

Alloy, L. B., & Abramson, L. T. (1979). Judgment of contingency in depressed and nondepressed students: Sadder but wiser? *Journal of Experimental Psychology: General, 108*, 441-485.

Alloy, L. B., & Abramson, L. T. (1982). Learned helplessness, depression, and the illusion of control. *Journal of Personality and Social Psychology, 42*, 1114-1126.

Alloy, L. B., & Seligman, M. E. P. (1979). On the cognitive component of learned helplessness and depression. *The Psychology of Learning and Motivation, 13*, 219-276.

Allport, G. W. (1961). *Pattern and growth in personality*. New York: Holt, Rinehart, & Winston.

Altmaier, E. M., Happ, D. A. (1985). Coping skills training's immunization effects against learned helplessness. *Journal of Social and Clinical Psychology, 3*, 181-189.

Amabile, T. M. (1979). Effects of external evaluations on artistic creativity. *Journal of Personality and Social Psychology, 37*, 221-233.

Amabile, T. M. (1983). *The social psychology of creativity*. New York: Springer-Verlag.

Amabile, T. M. (1985). Motivation and creativity: Effect of motivational orientation on creative writers. *Journal of Personality and Social Psychology, 48*, 393-399.

Amabile, T. M., DeJong, W., & Lepper, M. R. (1976). Effects of externally-imposed deadlines on subsequent intrinsic motivation. *Journal of Personality and Social Psychology, 34*, 92-98.

Amabile, T. M., & Hennessey, B. A. (1992). The motivation for creativity in children. In A. K. Boggiano & T. S. Pittman (Eds.), *Achievement and motivation: A social developmental perspective* (pp. 54-76). New York: Cambridge University Press.

Amabile, T. M., Hennessey, B. A., & Grossman, B. S. (1986). Social influences on creativity: The effects of contracted-for reward. *Journal of Personality and Social Psychology, 50,* 14–23.

Amari, A., Grace, N. C., & Fisher, W. W. (1995). Achieving and maintaining compliance with the ketogenic diet. *Journal of Applied Behavior Analysis, 28,* 341–342.

Ames, C. A. (1987). Enhancing student motivation. In M. Maehr & D. Kleiber (Eds.), *Recent advances in motivation and achievement: Enhancing motivation* (Vol. 5, pp. 123–148). Greenwich, CT: JAI Press.

Ames, C. A., & Archer, J. (1988). Achievement goals in the classroom: Student learning strategies and motivational processes. *Journal of Educational Psychology, 80,* 260–267.

Ames, R., & Ames, C. (1984). Introduction. In R. Ames & C. Ames (Eds.), *Research on motivation in education: Student motivation* (Vol. 1, pp. 1–11). Orlando, FL: Academic Press.

Anand, B. K., Chhina, G. S., & Singh, B. (1962). Effect of glucose on the activity of hypothalamic "feeding centers." *Science, 138,* 597–598.

Anastasi, A. (1982). *Psychological testing* (5e). New York: Macmillan.

Andersen, B. L., & Cyranowski, J. M. (1994). Women's sexual self-schema. *Journal of Personality and Social Psychology, 67,* 1079–1100.

Anderson, C. A. (1989). Temperature and aggression: Ubiquitous effects of heat on occurrence of human violence. *Psychological Bulletin, 106,* 74–106.

Anderson, C. A., Deuser, W. E., & DeNeve, K. M. (1995). Hot temperatures, hostile affect, hostile cognition, and arousal: Tests of a general model of affective aggression. *Personality and Social Psychology Bulletin, 21,* 434–448.

Anderson, D. C., & Jennings, D. L. (1980). When experiences of failure promote expectations of success: The impact of attributing failure to ineffective strategies. *Journal of Personality, 48,* 393–407.

Anderson, G., & Brown, R. I. (1984). Real and laboratory gambling sensation seeking and arousal. *British Journal of Psychology, 5,* 401–411.

Anderson, J. R. (1980). *Cognitive psychology and its implications.* New York: W. H. Freeman.

Anderson, K. J. (1990). Arousal and the inverted-U hypothesis: A critique of Neiss's "Reconceptualizing arousal." *Psychological Bulletin, 107,* 96–100.

Anderson, R., Manoogian, S. T., & Reznick, J. S. (1976). The undermining and enhancing of intrinsic motivation in preschool children. *Journal of Personality and Social Psychology, 34,* 915–922.

Andreassi, J. L. (1986). *Psychophysiology: Human behavior and physiological response* (2e). Hillsdale, NJ: Lawrence Erlbaum.

Andrews, G. R., & Debus, R. L. (1978). Persistence and the causal perception of failure: Modifying cognitive attributions. *Journal of Educational Psychology, 70,* 154–166.

Appley, M. H. (1991). Motivation, equilibration, and stress. In R. A. Dienstbier (Ed.), *Nebraska symposium on motivation* (Vol. 38, pp. 1–67). Lincoln: University of Nebraska Press.

Arkin, R. M., Cooper, H., & Kolditz, T. (1980). A statistical review of the literature concerning the self-serving bias in interpersonal influence situations. *Journal of Personality, 48,* 435–448.

Arnett, J. (1991). Still crazy after all these years: Reckless behavior among young adults aged 23–27. *Personality and Individual Differences, 12,* 1305–1313.

Arnold, M. B. (1960). *Emotion and personality* (Vol. 1, 2). New York: Columbia University Press.

Arnold, M. B. (1970). Perennial problems in the field of emotion, In M. B. Arnold (Ed.), *Feelings and emotions* (pp. 169–185). New York: Academic Press.

Aronson, E. (1969). The theory of cognitive dissonance: A current perspective. In L. Berkowitz (Ed.), *Advances in experimental social psychology* (Vol. 4, pp. 1–34). New York: Academic Press.

Aronson, E. (1988). *The social animal* (5e). San Francisco: W. H. Freeman.

Aronson, E., Fried, C. B., & Stone, J. (1991). Overcoming denial and increasing the intention to use condoms through the induction of hypocrisy. *American Journal of Public Health, 81*, 1636-1637.

Aronson, E., & Mills, J. (1959). The effect of severity of initiation on liking for a group. *Journal of Abnormal and Social Psychology, 59*, 177-181.

Atkinson, J. W. (1957). Motivational determinants of risk-taking behavior. *Psychological Review, 64*, 359-372.

Atkinson, J. W. (1964). A theory of achievement motivation. In *An introduction to motivation* (Chpt. 9, pp. 240-268). New York: Van Nostrand.

Atkinson, J. W. (1981). Studying personality in the context of an advanced motivational psychology. *American Psychologist, 36*, 117-128.

Atkinson, J. W. (1982). Motivational determinants of thematic apperception. In A. J. Stewart (Ed.), *Motivation and society* (pp. 3-40). San Francisco: Jossey-Bass.

Atkinson, J. W., & Birch, D. (Eds.), (1970). *The dynamics of action*. New York: Wiley.

Atkinson, J. W., & Birch, D. (1974). The dynamics of achievement-oriented activity. In J. W. Atkinson & J. O. Raynor (Eds.), *Motivation and achievement* (pp. 271-325). Washington, DC: Van Nostrand Reinhold.

Atkinson, J. W., & Birch, D. (1978). *Introduction to motivation* (2e). New York: Van Nostrand.

Atkinson, J. W., Bongort, K., & Price, L. H. (1977). Explorations using computer simulation to comprehend TAT measurement of motivation. *Motivation and Emotion, 1*, 1-27.

Atkinson, J. W., Heyns, R. W., & Veroff, J. (1954). The effect of experimental arousal of the affiliation motive on thematic apperception. *Journal of Abnormal and Social Psychology, 49*, 405-410.

Austira, J., Hatfield, D. B., Grindle, A. C., & Bailey, J. S. (1993). Increasing recycling in office environments: The effects of specific, informative cues. *Journal of Applied Behavior Analysis, 26*, 247-253.

Averill, J. R. (1968). Grief: Its nature and significance. *Psychological Bulletin, 70*, 721-748.

Averill, J. R. (1979). The functions of grief. In C. Izard (Ed.), *Emotions in personality and psychopathology* (pp. 339-368). New York: Plenum.

Averill, J. R. (1980). A constructivist view of emotion. In R. Plutchik & H. Kellerman (Eds.), *Theories of emotion* (pp. 305-340). New York: Academic Press.

Averill, J. R. (1982). *Anger and aggression: An essay on emotion*. New York: Springer-Verlag.

Averill, J. R. (1983). Studies on anger and aggression. *American Psychologist, 38*, 1145-1160.

Averill, J. R. (1985). The social construction of emotion: With special reference to love. In K. Gergen & K. Davis (Eds.), *The social construction of the person* (pp. 89-109). New York: Springer-Verlag.

Averill, J. R. (1991). Emotions as episodic dispositions, cognitive schemas, and transitory social roles: Steps toward an integrated theory of emotion. In D. Ozer, J. M. Healy, Jr., & A. J. Stewart (Eds.), *Perspectives in personality* (Vol. 32, pp. 139-167). London: Jessica Kingsley.

Averill, J. R. (1994a). In the eyes of the beholder. In P. Ekman & R. J. Davidson (Eds.), *The nature of emotion: Fundamental questions* (pp. 7-14). New York: Oxford University Press.

Averill, J. R. (1994b). I feel, therefore I am—I think. In P. Ekman & R. J. Davidson (Eds.), *The nature of emotion: Fundamental questions* (pp. 379-385). New York: Oxford University Press.

Averill, J. R., & Boothroyd, P. (1977). On falling in love in conformance with the romantic ideal. *Motivation and Emotion, 1*, 235-247.

Azar, B. (1994, October). Seligman recommends a depression 'vaccine.' *APA Monitor, 27,* 4.

Azrin, N. H., Rubin, H., O'Brien, F., Ayllon, T., & Roll, D. (1968). Behavioral engineering: Postural control by a portable operant apparatus. *Journal of Applied Behavior Analysis, 2,* 39–42.

Bailey, J. M., Gavlin, S., Agyei, Y., & Gladue, B. A. (1994). Effects of gender and sexual orientation on evolutionary relevant aspects of human mating psychology. *Journal of Personality and Social Psychology, 66,* 1081–1093.

Bailey, J. M., Pillard, R. C. (1991). A genetic study of the male sexual orientation. *Archives of General Psychiatry, 48,* 1089–1096.

Bailey, J. M., Pillard, R. C., Neale, M. C., & Agyei, Y. (1993). Heritable factors influence sexual orientation in women. *Archives of General Psychiatry, 50,* 217–223.

Baldwin, J. D., & Baldwin, J. I. (1986). *Behavior principles in everyday life* (2e). Englewood Cliffs, NJ: Prentice-Hall.

Bandura, A. (1977). Self-efficacy: Toward a unifying theory of behavioral change. *Psychological Review, 84,* 191–215.

Bandura, A. (1982). Self-efficacy mechanism in human agency. *American Psychologist, 37,* 122–147.

Bandura, A. (1983). Self-efficacy mechanisms of anticipated fears and calamities. *Journal of Personality and Social Psychology, 45,* 464–469.

Bandura, A. (1986). Self-efficacy. In *Social foundations of thought and action: A social cognitive theory* (pp. 390–453). Englewood Cliffs, NJ: Prentice-Hall.

Bandura, A. (1988). Self-efficacy conception and anxiety. *Anxiety Research, 1,* 77–98.

Bandura, A. (1989). Human agency in social cognitive theory. *American Psychologist, 44,* 1175–1184.

Bandura, A. (1990). Conclusion: Reflections on nonability determinants of competence In R. J. Sternberg & J. Kolligian, Jr. (Eds.), *Competence considered* (pp. 315–362). New Haven, CT: Yale University Press.

Bandura, A. (1991). Self-regulation of motivation through anticipatory and self-regulatory mechanisms. In R. A. Dienstbier (Ed.), *Nebraska symposium on motivation: Perspectives on motivation* (Vol. 38, pp. 69–164). Lincoln: University of Nebraska Press.

Bandura, A. (1993). Perceived self-efficacy in cognitive development and functioning. *Educational Psychologist, 28,* 117–148.

Bandura, A., & Adams, N. E. (1977). Analysis of self-efficacy theory of behavioral change. *Cognitive Therapy and Research, 1,* 287–308.

Bandura, A., Adams, N. E., Hardy, A. B., & Howells, G. N. (1980). Tests of the generality of self-efficacy theory. *Cognitive Therapy and Research, 4,* 39–66.

Bandura, A., & Cervone, D. (1983). Self-evaluative and self-efficacy mechanisms governing the motivational effects of goal systems. *Journal of Personality and Social Psychology, 45,* 1017–1028.

Bandura, A., & Cervone, D. (1986). Differential engagement of self-reactive influences in cognitive motivation. *Organizational Behavior and Human Decision Processes, 38,* 92–113.

Bandura, A., Cioffi, D., Taylor, C. B., & Brouillard, M. E. (1988). Perceived self-efficacy in coping with cognitive stressors and opioid activation. *Journal of Personality and Social Psychology, 55,* 479–488.

Bandura, A., Reese, L., & Adams, N. E. (1982). Microanalysis of action and fear arousal as a function of differential levels of perceived self-efficacy. *Journal of Personality and Social Psychology, 43,* 5–21.

Bandura, A., & Schunk, D. H. (1981). Cultivating competence, self-efficacy, and intrinsic interest through proximal self-motivation. *Journal of Personality and Social Psychology, 41,* 586–598.

Bandura, A., Taylor, C. B., Williams, S. L., Mefford, I. N., & Barchas, J. D. (1985). Catecholamine secretion as a function of perceived coping self-efficacy. *Journal of Consulting and Clinical Psychology, 53,* 406-414.

Bandura, A., & Wood, R. E. (1989). Effect of perceived controllability and performance standards on self-regulation of complex decision making. *Journal of Personality and Social Psychology, 56,* 805-814.

Bassett, G. A. (1979). A study of the effects of task goal and schedule choice on work performance. *Organizational Behavior and Human Performance, 24,* 202-227.

Basso, M. R., Schefft, B. K., & Hoffman, R. G. (1994). Mood-moderating effects of affect intensity of cognition: Sometimes euphoria is not beneficial and dysphoria is not detrimental. *Journal of Personality and Social Psychology, 66,* 363-368.

Batson, C. D., Coke, J. S., Chard, F., Smith, D., & Taliaferro, A. (1979). Generality of the "glow of goodwill": Effects of mood on helping and information acquisition. *Social Psychology Quarterly, 42,* 176-179.

Baucom, D. H., & Aiken, P. A. (1981). Effect of depressed mood on eating among obese and nonobese dieting and nondieting persons. *Journal of Personality and Social Psychology, 41,* 577-585.

Baumeister, R. F. (1986). *Identity: Cultural change and the struggle for self.* New York: Oxford University Press.

Baumeister, R. F. (1987). How the self became a problem: A psychological review of historical research. *Journal of Personality and Social Psychology, 52,* 163-176.

Baumeister, R. F. (1991). *Escaping the self: Alcoholism, spirituality, masochism, and other flights from the burden of selfhood.* New York: Basic Books.

Baumeister, R. F., & Leary, M. R. (1995). The need to belong: Desire for interpersonal attachments as a fundamental human motivation. *Psychological Bulletin, 117,* 497-529.

Baumeister, R. F., Smart, L., & Boden, J. M. (1996). Relation of threatened egotism to violence and aggression: The dark side of self-esteem. *Psychological Review, 103,* 5-33.

Beach, F. A. (1955). The descent of instinct. *Psychological Review, 62,* 401-410.

Beatty, J. (1982). Task-evoked pupillary response, processing load, and the structure of processing resources. *Psychological Bulletin, 91,* 276-292.

Beatty, J. (1986). The pupillary system. In M. G. H. Coles, E. Ponchin, & S. W. Proges (Eds.), *Psychophysiology: Systems, processes, and applications* (Chpt. 3, pp. 43-50). New York: The Guilford Press.

Beatty, W. W. (1982). Dietary variety stimulates appetite in females but not in males. *Bulletin of the Psychonomic Society, 19,* 212-214.

Beck, A. T. (1967). *Depression: Clinical, experimental, and theoretical aspects.* New York: Hoeber.

Beck, A. T. (1976). *Cognitive therapy and the emotional disorders.* New York: International Universities Press.

Beck, A. T. (1984). Cognition and therapy. *Archives of General Psychiatry, 41,* 1112-1114.

Beck, A. T., & Beamesderfer, A. (1974). Assessment of depression: The depression inventory. *Modern Problems of Pharacopsychiatry, 7,* 1-10.

Beck, R. C. (1979). Roles of taste and learning in water regulation. *Behavior and Brain Sciences, 1,* 102-103.

Beck, S. P., Ward-Hull, C. I., & McLear, P. M. (1976). Variable related to women's somatic preferences of the male and female body. *Journal of Personality and Social Psychology, 34,* 1200-1210.

Becker, L. J. (1978). Joint effect of feedback and goal setting on performance: A field study of residential energy conservation. *Journal of Applied Psychology, 63,* 428-433.

Bell, A. P., Weinberg, M. S., & Hammersmith, S. K. (1981). *Sexual preference: Its development in men and women*. Bloomington, IN: Indiana University Press.

Bellak, L. (1993). *The T.A.T., C.A.T., and S.A.T. in clinical use*. Needham Heights, MA: Allyn and Bacon.

Bem, D. J. (1967). Self-perception: An alternative interpretation of cognitive dissonance phenomena. *Psychological Review, 74*, 183–200.

Bem, D. J. (1972). Self-perception theory. In L. Berkowitz (Ed.), *Advances in experimental social psychology* (Vol. 6, pp. 1–62). New York: Academic Press.

Bem, D. J., & McConnell, H. K. (1970). Testing the self-perception explanation of dissonance phenomena: On the salience of premanipulation attitudes. *Journal of Personality and Social Psychology, 14*, 23–31.

Benjamin, Jr., L. T., & Jones, M. R. (1978). From motivational theory to social cognitive development: Twenty-five years of the Nebraska Symposium. *Nebraska symposium on motivation* (Vol. 26, pp. ix–xix). Lincoln: University of Nebraska Press.

Benware, C., & Deci, E. L. (1984). The quality of learning with an active versus passive motivational set. *American Educational Research Journal, 21*, 755–765.

Berenbaum, S. A., & Snyder, E. (1995). Early hormonal influences on childhood sex-typed activity and playmate preferences: Implications for the development of sexual orientation. *Developmental Psychology, 31*, 31–42.

Bergler, E. (1957). *The psychology of gambling*. London: International Universities Press.

Bergmann, G., & Spence, K. W. (1941). Operationism and theory construction. *Psychological Review, 48*, 1–14.

Berkowitz, L. (1962). *Aggression: A social psychological analysis*. New York: McGraw-Hill.

Berlyne, D. E. (1966). Curiosity and exploration. *Science, 153*, 25–33.

Berlyne, D. E. (1967). Arousal and reinforcement. In D. Levine (Ed.), *Nebraska symposium on motivation* (Vol. 15, pp. 1–110). Lincoln: University of Nebraska Press.

Berlyne, D. E. (1975). Behaviourism? Cognitive theory? Humanistic psychology—To Hull with them all. *Canadian Psychological Review, 16*, 69–80.

Bernard, L. L. (1924). *Instinct: A study of social psychology*. New York: Holt.

Berry, D. S., & McArthur, L. Z. (1985). Some components and consequences of a babyface. *Journal of Personality and Social Psychology, 48*, 312–323.

Berry, D. S., & McArthur, L. Z. (1986). Perceiving character in faces: The impact of age-related craniofacial changes on social perception. *Psychological Bulletin, 100*, 3–18.

Berry, S. L., Beatty, W. W., & Klesges, R. C. (1985). Sensory and social influences on ice cream consumption by males and females in a laboratory setting. *Appetite, 6*, 41–45.

Berscheid, E. (1982). Attraction and emotion in interpersonal relations. In M. S. Clark & S. T. Fiske (Eds.), *Affect and cognition*. Hillsdale, NJ: Lawrence Erlbaum.

Betz, N. E., & Hackett, G. (1986). Applications of self-efficacy theory to understanding career choice behavior. *Journal of Social and Clinical Psychology, 4*, 279–289.

Bexton, W. H., Heron, W., & Scott, T. H. (1954). Effects of decreased variation in the sensory environment. *Canadian Journal of Psychology, 8*, 70–76.

Bindra, D. (1979). *Motivation, the brain, and psychological theory*. Unpublished manuscript, Psychology Department, McGill University, Montreal.

Biner, P. M., Angle, S. T., Park, J. H., Mellinger, A. E., & Barber, B. C. (1995). Need state and the illusion of control. *Personality and Social Psychology Bulletin, 21*, 899–907.

Birch, D., Atkinson, J. W., & Bongort, K. (1974). Cognitive control of action. In B. Weiner (Ed.), *Cognitive view of human motivation*. New York: Academic Press.

Birch, H. G. (1956). Sources of odor in maternal behavior in animals. *American Journal of Orthopsychiatry, 26*, 279–284.

Birch, L. L., Zimmerman, S. I., & Hind, H. (1980). The influence of social affective context on the formation of children's food preferences. *Child Development, 51*, 856-861.

Birney, R. C., Burdick, H., & Teevan, R. C. (1969). *Fear of failure*. New York: Van Nostrand.

Blai, B., Jr. (1964). An occupational study of job satisfaction and need satisfaction. *Journal of Experimental Education, 32*, 383-388.

Blank, P. D., Reis, H. T., & Jackson, L. (1984). The effects of verbal reinforcements on intrinsic motivation for sex-linked tasks. *Sex Roles, 10*, 369-387.

Blankenship, V. (1987). A computer-based measure of resultant achievement motivation. *Journal of Personality and Social Psychology, 53*, 361-372.

Blascovich, J., Brennan, K., Tomaka, J., Kelsey, R. M., Hughes, P., Coad, M. L., & Adlin, R. (1992). Affect intensity and cardiac arousal. *Journal of Personality and Social Psychology, 63*, 164-174.

Blasi, A. (1976). Concept of development in personality theory. In J. Loevinger (Ed.), *Ego development* (pp. 29-53). San Francisco: Jossey-Bass.

Blass, E. M., & Hall, W. G. (1976). Drinking termination: Interactions among hydrational, orogastric, and behavioral controls in rats. *Psychological Review, 83*, 356-374.

Block, J. (1982). Assimilation, accommodation, and the dynamics of personality development. *Child Development, 53*, 281-295.

Block, J., & Kremen, A. M. (1996). IQ and ego-resiliency: Conceptual and empirical connections and separateness. *Journal of Personality and Social Psychology, 70*, 349-361.

Boggiano, A. K., Barrett, M., Silvern, L., & Gallo, S. (1991). Predicting emotional concomitants of learned helplessness: The role of motivational orientation. *Sex Roles, 25*, 577-592.

Boggiano, A. K., Flink, C., Shields, A., Seelbach, A., & Barrett, M. (1993). Use of techniques promoting students' self-determination: Effects on students' analytic problem-solving skills. *Motivation and Emotion, 17*, 319-336.

Boggiano, A. K., & Main, D. S. (1986). Enhancing children's interest in activities used as rewards: The bonus effect. *Journal of Personality and Social Psychology, 51*, 1116-1126.

Boggiano, A. K., & Ruble, D. N. (1979). Competence and the overjustification effect: A developmental study. *Journal of Personality and Social Psychology, 37*, 1462-1468.

Bolles, R. C. (1975). *A theory of motivation* (2e). New York: Harper & Row.

Bolm-Avdorff, J., Schwammle, J., Ehlenz, K., & Kaffarnik, H. (1989). Plasma level of catecholamines and lipids when speaking before an audience. *Work and Stress, 3*, 249-253.

Boyatzis, R. E. (1972). *A two factor theory of affiliation motivation*. Unpublished doctoral dissertation, Harvard University.

Boyatzis, R. E. (1973). Affiliation motivation. In D. C. McClelland & R. S. Steele (Eds.), *Human motivation: A book of readings*. Morristown, NJ: General Learning Press.

Brehm, J. W. (1956). Postdecision changes in the desirability of alternatives. *Journal of Abnormal and Social Psychology, 52*, 384-389.

Brehm, J. W. (1966). *A theory of psychological reactance*. New York: Academic Press.

Brehm, S. S., & Brehm, J. W. (1981). *Psychological reactance: A theory of freedom and control*. New York: Academic Press.

Brenner, C. (1957). *An elementary textbook of psychoanalysis*. Garden City, NY: Doubleday.

Brewer, M. B. (1979). Ingroup bias in the minimal intergroup situation: A cognitive-motivational analysis. *Psychological Bulletin, 86*, 307-324.

Brewin, C. R. (1985). Depression and causal attribution: What is their relation? *Psychological Bulletin, 98*, 297-309.

Brigham, T. A., Maier, S. M., & Goodner, V. (1995). Increased designating driving with a program of prompts and incentives. *Journal of Applied Behavior Analysis, 28*, 83-84.

Brill, A. A. (1938). Introduction. In *The basic writings of Sigmund Freud* (pp. 3-32). New York: The Modern Library.

Broadbent, D. E., Cooper, P. F., FitzGerald, P., & Parkes, K. R. (1982). The cognitive failures questionnaire (CFQ). *British Journal of Clinical Psychology, 21*, 1-16.

Brobeck, J. R. (1960). Food and temperature. *Recent Progress in Hormone Research, 16*, 439.

Brophy, J. (1981). Teacher praise: A functional analysis. *Review of Educational Research, 51*, 5-32.

Brothers, K. J. (1994). Office paper recycling: A function of container proximity. *Journal of Applied Behavior Analysis, 27*, 153-160.

Brown, A. S. (1991). A review of the tip-of-the-tongue experience. *Psychological Bulletin, 109*, 204-223.

Brown, I., Jr., & Inouye, D. K. (1978). Learned helplessness through modeling: The role of perceived similarity in competence. *Journal of Personality and Social Psychology, 36*, 900-908.

Brown, L. T., Ruder, V. G., Ruder, J. H., & Young, S. D. (1974). Stimulation seeking and the change seeker index. *Journal of Consulting and Clinical Psychology, 42*, 311.

Brownell, K. D. (1982). The addictive disorders. In C. M. Franks, B. T. Wilson, P. C. Kendall, & K. D. Brownell (Eds.), *Annual review of behavior therapy: Theory and practice* (Vol. 8). New York: Guilford Press.

Bruner, J. S. (1962). *On knowing: Essays for the left-hand*. Cambridge: Harvard University Press.

Buck, R. (1984). *The communication of emotion*. New York: Guilford Press.

Buck, R. (1985). Prime theory: An integrated view of motivation and emotion. *Psychological Review, 92*, 389-413.

Buck, R. (1988). *Human motivation and emotion*. New York: John Wiley & Sons.

Bugental, J. F. T. (1967). *Challenges and humanistic psychology*. New York: McGraw-Hill.

Bugental, J. F. T. (1970). The humanistic ethic: The individual in psychotherapy as a societal change agent. *Journal of Humanistic Psychology, 10*, 11-25.

Burger, J. M. (1984). Desire for control, locus of control, and proneness to depression. *Journal of Personality, 52*, 71-89.

Burger, J. M. (1985). Desire for control and achievement-related behaviors. *Journal of Personality and Social Psychology, 48*, 1520-1533.

Burger, J. M. (1986). Desire for control and illusion of control: The effects of familiarity and sequence of outcomes. *Journal of Research in Personality, 20*, 66-76.

Burger, J. M. (1990). Desire for control and interpersonal interaction style. *Journal of Research in Personality, 24*, 32-44.

Burger, J. M. (1992). *Desire for control: Personality, social, and clinical perspectives*. New York: Plenum.

Burger, J. M., & Arkin, R. M. (1980). Prediction, control, and learned helplessness. *Journal of Personality and Social Psychology, 38*, 482-491.

Burger, J. M., & Cooper, H. M. (1979). The desirability of control. *Motivation and Emotion, 3*, 381-393.

Burger, J. M., Oakman, J. A., & Bullard, N. G. (1983). Desire for control and the perception of crowding. *Personality and Social Psychology Bulletin, 9*, 475-479.

Burger, J. M., & Schnerring, D. A. (1982). The effects of desire for control and extrinsic rewards on the illusion of control and gambling. *Motivation and Emotion, 6*, 329-335.

Bursik, K. (1991). Adaptation to divorce and ego development in adult women. *Journal of Personality and Social Psychology, 60*, 300-306.

Buss, A. H., & Plomin, R. (1984). *Temperament: Early developing personality traits*. Hillsdale, NJ: Lawrence Erlbaum.

Buss, D. M., & Schmitt, D. P. (1993). Sexual strategies theory: An evolutionary perspective on human mating. *Psychology Review, 100,* 204-232.

Byrne, B. M. (1984). The general/academic self-concept nomological network: A review of construct validation research. *Review of Educational Research, 54,* 427-456.

Bryne, D. (1961). Anxiety and the experimental arousal of affiliation need. *Journal of Abnormal and Social Psychology, 63,* 660-662.

Cabanac, M., & Duclaux, P. (1970). Obesity: Absence of satiety aversion to sucrose? *Science, 168,* 496-497.

Cacioppo, J. T., Petty, R. E., Losch, M. E., & Kim, H. S. (1986). Electromyographic activity over facial muscle regions can differentiate the valence and intensity of affective reactions. *Journal of Personality and Social Psychology, 50,* 260-268.

Cameron, J., & Pierce, W. D. (1994). Reinforcement, reward, and intrinsic motivation: A meta-analysis. *Review of Educational Research, 64,* 363-423.

Campion, M. A., & Lord, R. G. (1982). A control systems conceptualization of the goal-setting and changing process. *Organizational Behavior and Human Performance, 30,* 265-287.

Camras, L. (1977). Facial expressions used by children in a conflict situation. *Child Development, 48,* 1431-1435.

Cannon, W. B. (1927). The James-Lange theory of emotion: A critical examination and an alternative theory. *American Journal of Psychology, 39,* 106-124.

Cannon, W. B. (1932). *The wisdom of the body*. New York: W. W. Norton.

Cantor, N., Markus, H., Niedenthal, P., & Nurius, P. (1986). On motivation and the self-concept. In R. M. Sorrentino & E. T. Higgins (Eds.), *Handbook of motivation and cognition* (Vol. 1, pp. 96-121). New York: Guilford Press.

Carlsmith, J. M., Ellsworth, P. C., & Aronson, E. (1976). *Methods of research in social psychology*. New York: Random House.

Carlson, N. C. (1988). *Discovering psychology*. Boston: Allyn & Bacon.

Carnelley, K. B., Pietromonaco, P. R., & Jaffe, K. (1994). Depression, working models of others, and relationship functioning. *Journal of Personality and Social Psychology, 66,* 127-140.

Carnevale, P. J. D., & Isen, A. M. (1986). The influence of positive affect and visual access on the discovery of integrative solutions in bilateral negotiation. *Organizational Behavior and Human Decision Processes, 37,* 1-13.

Carver, C. S., & Blaney, P. H. (1977). Avoidance behavior and perceived control. *Motivation and Emotion, 1,* 61-73.

Carver, C. S., & Scheier, M. F. (1981). *Attention and self-regulation: A control theory approach to human behavior*. New York: Springer-Verlag.

Carver, C. S., & Scheier, M. F. (1982). Control theory: A useful conceptual framework for personality: Social, clinical, and health psychology. *Psychological Bulletin, 92,* 111-135.

Carver, C. S., & Scheier, M. F. (1990). Origins and functions of positive and negative affect: A control-process view. *Psychological Review, 97,* 19-35.

Chen, M., & Isen, A. M. (1992). *The influence of positive affect and success on persistence on a failed task*. Unpublished manuscript, Cornell University.

Cialdini, R. B., Petty, R. E., & Cacioppo, J. T. (1981). Attitudes and attitude change. *Annual Review of Psychology, 32,* 357-404.

Cioffi, D. (1991). Beyond attentional strategies: A cognitive-perceptual model of somatic interpretation. *Psychological Bulletin, 109,* 25-41.

Clark, L. A., & Watson, D. (1994). Distinguishing functional from dysfunctional affective responses. In P. Ekman & R. J. Davidson (Eds.), *The nature of emotion: Fundamental questions* (pp. 131-136). New York: Oxford University Press.

Clark, L. A., Watson, D., & Leeka, J. (1989). Diurnal variation in the positive affects. *Motivation and Emotion, 13,* 205-234.

Clark, M. S. (1984). Record keeping in two types of relationships. *Journal of Personality and Social Psychology, 47,* 549-557.

Clark, M. S., & Mills, J. (1979). Interpersonal attraction in exchange and communal relationships. *Journal of Personality and Social Psychology, 37,* 12-24.

Clark, M. S., Mills, J., & Powell, M. C. (1986). Keeping track of needs in communal and exchange relationships. *Journal of Personality and Social Psychology, 51,* 333-338.

Clark, M. S., Ouellette, R., Powell, M. C., & Milberg, S. (1987). Recipient's mood, relationship type, and helping. *Journal of Personality and Social Psychology, 53,* 94-103.

Clarke, R. A. (1973). Measures of achievement and affiliation motivation. *Review of Educational Research, 43,* 41-51.

Clement, R., & Jonah, B. A. (1984). Field dependence, sensation seeking and driving behavior. *Personality and Individual Differences, 5,* 87-93.

Clifford, M. M. (1984). Thoughts on a theory of constructive failure. *Educational Psychologist, 19,* 108-120.

Clifford, M. M. (1988). Failure tolerance and academic risk-taking in ten- to twelve-year old students. *British Journal of Educational Psychology, 58,* 15-27.

Clifford, M. M. (1990). Students need challenge, not easy success. *Educational Leadership, 48,* 22-26.

Clore, G. L. (1994). Why emotions require cognition. In P. Ekman & R. J. Davidson (Eds.), *The nature of emotion: Fundamental questions* (pp. 181-191). New York: Oxford University Press.

Clore, G. L., Ortony, A., & Foss, M. (1987). The psychological foundations of the affective lexicon. *Journal of Personality and Social Psychology, 53,* 751-766.

Cofer, C. N. (1972). *Motivation and emotion.* Glenview, IL: Scott, Foresman.

Cofer, C. N., & Appley, M. H. (1964). *Motivation: Theory and research.* New York: John Wiley.

Cohen, S., Lichtenstein, E., Prochaska, J. O., Rossi, J. S., Gritz, E. R., Carr, C. R., Orleans, C. T., Schoenbach, V. J., Biener, L., Abrams, D., DiClemente, C., Curry, S., Marlatt, G. A., Cummings, K. M., Emont, S. L., Giovino, G., & Ossip-Klein, D. (1989). Debunking myths about self-quitting: Evidence from 10 prospective studies of persons who attempt to quit smoking by themselves. *American Psychologist, 44,* 1355-1365.

Coles, M. G. H., Ponchin, E., & Porges, S. W., (Eds.) (1986). *Psychophysiology: Systems, processes, and applications.* New York: Guilford Press.

Condry, J. (1977). Enemies of exploration: Self-initiated versus other-initiated learning. *Journal of Personality and Social Psychology, 35,* 459-477.

Condry, J. (1987). Enhancing motivation: A social development perspective. *Advances in motivation and achievement: Enhancing motivation, 5,* 23-49.

Condry, J., & Chambers, J. (1978). Intrinsic motivation and the process of learning. In M. R. Lepper & D. Greene (Eds.). *The hidden costs of reward: New perspectives on the psychology of human motivation.* Hillsdale, NJ: Lawrence Erlbaum.

Condry, J., & Stokker, L. G. (1992). Overview of special issue on intrinsic motivation. *Motivation and Emotion, 16,* 157-164.

Connell, J. P. (1990). Context, self, and action: A motivational analysis of self-system processes across the life-span. In D. Cicchetti (Ed.), *The self in transition: From infancy to childhood* (pp. 61–97). Chicago: University of Chicago Press.

Connell, J. P., & Wellborn, J. G. (1991). Competence, autonomy, and relatedness: A motivational analysis of self-system processes. In M. R. Gunnar & L. A. Sroufe (Eds.), *Self processes in development: Minnesota symposium on child psychology* (Vol. 23, pp. 167–216). Chicago: University of Chicago Press.

Connolly, K., & Smith, P. K. (1972). Reactions of pre-school children to a strange observer. In N. G. Blurton-Jones (Ed.), *Ethological studies of child behavior*. Cambridge: Cambridge University Press.

Conti, R., Amabile, T. M., & Pollak, S. (1995). The positive impact of creative activity: Effects of creative task engagement and motivational focus on college students' learning. *Personality and Social Psychology Bulletin, 21*, 664–675.

Cooper, J., & Croyle, R. T. (1984). Attitudes and attitude change. *Annual Review of Psychology, 35*, 395–426.

Cooper, J., & Fazio, R. H. (1984). A new look at dissonance theory. In L. Berkowitz (Ed.), *Advances in experimental social psychology* (Vol. 17, pp. 229–266). New York: Academic Press.

Cooper, K. H. (1968). *Aerobics*. New York: Bantam Books.

Cooper, M. L., Frone, M. R., Russell, M., & Mudar, P. (1995). Drinking to regulate positive and negative emotions: A motivational model of alcohol use. *Journal of Personality and Social Psychology, 69*, 990–1005.

Cooper, W. H. (1983). An achievement motivation nomological network. *Journal of Personality and Social Psychology, 44*, 841–861.

Costa, P. T., Jr., & McCrae, R. R. (1980). Influence of extraversion and neuroticism on subjective well-being: Happy and unhappy people. *Journal of Personality and Social Psychology, 38*, 668–678.

Costa, P. T., Jr., & McCrae, R. R. (1988). From catalogue to classification: Murray's needs and the five-factor model. *Journal of Personality and Social Psychology, 55*, 258–265.

Costello, C. G. (1978). A critical review of Seligman's laboratory experiments on learned helplessness and depression in humans. *Journal of Abnormal Psychology, 87*, 21–31.

Cotton, J. L. (1981). A review of research on Schachter's theory of emotion and the misattribution of arousal. *European Journal of Social Psychology, 11*, 365–397.

Covington, M. W., & Omelich, C. L. (1984). Task-oriented versus competitive learning structures: Motivational and performance consequences. *Journal of Educational Psychology, 76*, 1038–1050.

Cox, R. (1987). The rich harvest of Abraham Maslow. In A. Maslow's *Motivation and personality* (3e, pp. 245–271). New York: Harper & Row.

Coyne, J. C. (1976a). Towards an interactional description of depression. *Psychiatry, 39*, 28–40.

Coyne, J. C. (1976b). Depression and the response of others. *Journal of Abnormal Psychology, 85*, 186–193.

Coyne, J. C., & DeLongis, A. (1986). Going beyond social support: The role of social relationships in adaptation. *Journal of Consulting and Clinical Psychology, 54*, 454–460.

Crago, M., Yates, A., Beutler, L. E., & Arizmendi, T. G. (1985). Height-weight ratios among female athletes: Are collegiate athletics the precursors to an anorexic syndrome? *International Journal of Eating Disorders, 4*, 79–87.

Craig, R. L., & Siegel, P. S. (1980). Does negative affect beget positive affect? A test of the opponent-process theory. *Bulletin of the Psychonomic Society, 14*, 404–406.

Crandall, C. S. (1988). Social cognition of binge eating. *Journal of Personality and Social Psychology, 55,* 588-598.

Crary, W. G. (1966). Reactions to incongruent self-experiences. *Journal of Consulting Psychology, 30,* 246-252.

Cross, S. E., & Markus, H. R. (1991). Possible selves across the life span. *Human Development, 34,* 230-255.

Cross, S. E., & Markus, H. R. (1994). Self-schemas, possible selves, and competent performance. *Journal of Educational Psychology, 86,* 423-438.

Crowne, D. P., & Marlowe, D. (1964). *The approval motive.* New York: Wiley.

Croyle, R. T., & Cooper, J. (1983). Dissonance arousal: Physiological evidence. *Journal of Personality and Social Psychology, 45,* 782-791.

Csikszentmihalyi, M. (1975). *Beyond boredom and anxiety: The experience of flow in work and play.* San Francisco: Jossey-Bass.

Csikszentmihalyi, M. (1982). Toward a psychology of optimal experience. *Review of Personality and Social Psychology, 3,* 13-36.

Csikszentmihalyi, M. (1985). Reflections on enjoyment. *Perspectives in Biology and Medicine, 28,* 469-497.

Csikszentmihalyi, M. (1990). *Flow: The psychology of optimal experience.* New York: Harper & Row.

Csikszentmihalyi, M., & Csikszentmihalyi, I. (Eds.) (1988). *Optimal experiences: Psychological studies of flow in consciousness.* New York: Cambridge University Press.

Csikszentmihalyi, M., & LeFevre, J. (1989). Optimal experience in work and leisure. *Journal of Personality and Social Psychology, 56,* 815-822.

Csikszentmihalyi, M., & Nakamura, J. (1989). The dynamics of intrinsic motivation: A study of adolescents. In C. Ames & R. Ames (Eds.), *Research on motivation in education* (Vol. 3, pp. 45-71). San Diego: Academic Press.

Csikszentmihalyi, M., & Rathunde, K. (1993). The measurement of flow in everyday life: Toward a theory of emergent motivation. In J. E. Jacobs (Ed.), *Nebraska symposium on motivation: Developmental perspectives on motivation* (Vol. 40, pp. 57-97). Lincoln: University of Nebraska Press.

Csikszentmihalyi, M., Rathunde, K., & Whalen, S. (1993). *Talented teenagers: The roots of success and failure.* New York: Cambridge University Press.

Cunningham, M. R. (1986). Measuring the physical in physical attractiveness: Quasi-experiments on the sociobiology of female facial beauty. *Journal of Personality and Social Psychology, 50,* 925-935.

Cunningham, M. R., Barbee, A. P., & Pike, C. L. (1990). What do women want? Facialmetric assessment of multiple motives in the perception of male facial physical attractiveness. *Journal of Personality and Social Psychology, 59,* 61-72.

Cunningham, M. R., Roberts, A. R., Barbee, A. P., Druen, P. B., & Wu, C. (1995). "Their ideas of beauty are, on the whole, the same as ours": Consistency and variability in the cross-cultural perception of female physical attractiveness. *Journal of Personality and Social Psychology, 68,* 261-279.

D'Amato, M. R. (1974). Derived motives. *Annual Review of Psychology, 25,* 83-106.

Daniels, M. (1988). The myth of self-actualization. *Journal of Humanistic Psychology, 28,* 7-38.

Danner, F. W., & Lonky, E. (1981). A cognitive-developmental approach to the effects of rewards on intrinsic motivation. *Child Development, 52,* 1043-1052.

Darwin, C. A. (1859). *On the origin of species by means of natural selection.* London: John Murray; New York: Modern Library, 1936.

Darwin, C. A. (1872). *The expression of the emotions in man and animals*. London: John Murray.

Davidson, R. J. (1994). On emotion, mood, and related affective constructs. In P. Ekman & R. J. Davidson (Eds.), *The nature of emotion: Fundamental questions* (pp. 51-55). New York: Oxford University Press.

Davidson, R. J., Ekman, P., Saron, C., Senulis, J., & Friesen, W. V. (1990). Approach/withdrawal and cerebral asymmetry. *Journal of Personality and Social Psychology, 58*, 330-341.

Day, J. D., Borkowski, J. G., Punzo, D., & Howsepian, B. (1994). Enhancing possible selves in Mexican American students. *Motivation and Emotion, 18*, 79-103.

Deaux, K., Reid, A., Mizrahi, K., & Ethier, K. A. (1995). Parameters of social identity. *Journal of Personality and Social Psychology, 53*, 281-295.

deCharms, R. (1976). *Enhancing motivation: Change in the classroom*. New York: Irvington.

deCharms, R. (1984). Motivation enhancement in educational settings. In R. E. Ames & C. Ames (Eds.), *Research on motivation in education: Student motivation* (Vol. 1, pp. 275-310). New York: Academic Press.

deCharms, R., & Moeller, G. H. (1962). Values expressed in American children's readers: 1800-1950. *Journal of Abnormal and Social Psychology, 64*, 136-142.

Deci, E. L. (1971). Effects of externally mediated rewards on intrinsic motivation. *Journal of Personality and Social Psychology, 18*, 105-115.

Deci, E. L. (1972). Intrinsic motivation, extrinsic reinforcement, and inequity. *Journal of Personality and Social Psychology, 22*, 113-120.

Deci, E. L. (1975). *Intrinsic motivation*. New York: Plenum.

Deci, E. L. (1980). *The psychology of self-determination*. Lexington, MA: Lexington.

Deci, E. L. (1992a). On the nature and function of motivation theories. *Psychological Science, 3*, 167-171.

Deci, E. L. (1992b). The relation of interest to the motivation of behavior: A self-determination theory perspective. In K. A. Renninger, S. Hidi, & A. Krapp (Eds.), *The role of interest in learning and development* (pp. 43-70). Hillsdale, NJ: Erlbaum.

Deci, E. L., Betley, G., Kahle, J., Abrams, L., & Porac, J. (1981). When trying to win: Competition and intrinsic motivation. *Personality and Social Psychology Bulletin, 7*, 79-83.

Deci, E. L., & Casio, W. F. (April 1972). *Changes in intrinsic motivation as a function of negative feedback and threats*. Paper presented at the meeting of the Eastern Psychological Association, Boston, MA.

Deci, E. L., Connell, J. P., & Ryan, R. M. (1989). Self-determination in a work organization. *Journal of Applied Psychology, 74*, 580-590.

Deci, E. L., Driver, R. E., Hotchkiss, L., Robbins, R. J., & Wilson, I. M. (1993). The relation of mother's controlling vocalizations to children's intrinsic motivation. *Journal of Experimental Child Psychology, 55*, 151-162.

Deci, E. L., Eghrari, H., Patrick, B. C., & Leone, D. R. (1994). Facilitating internalization: The self-determination theory perspective. *Journal of Personality, 62*, 119-142.

Deci, E. L., Nezlek, J., & Sheinman, L. (1981). Characteristics of the rewarder and intrinsic motivation of the rewardee. *Journal of Personality and Social Psychology, 40*, 1-10.

Deci, E. L., & Olson, B. C. (1987). Motivation and competition: Their role in sports. In J. H. Goldstein (Ed.), *Sports, games, and play* (2e). Hillsdale, NJ: Erlbaum.

Deci, E. L., & Ryan, R. M. (1980). The empirical exploration of intrinsic motivational processes. In L. Berkowitz (Ed.), *Advances in experimental social psychology* (Vol. 13, pp. 39-80). New York: Academic Press.

Deci, E. L., & Ryan, R. M. (1985a). *Intrinsic motivation and self-determination in human behavior*. New York: Plenum.

Deci, E. L., & Ryan, R. M. (1985b). The General Causality Orientations Scale: Self-determination in personality. *Journal of Research in Personality, 19*, 109-134.

Deci, E. L., & Ryan, R. M. (1987). The support of autonomy and the control of behavior. *Journal of Personality and Social Psychology, 53*, 1024-1037.

Deci, E. L., & Ryan, R. M. (1991). A motivational approach to self: Integration in personality. In R. Dienstbier (Ed.), *Nebraska symposium on motivation: Perspectives on motivation* (Vol. 38, pp. 237-288). Lincoln: University of Nebraska Press.

Deci, E. L., Schwartz, A., Scheinman, L., & Ryan, R. M. (1981). An instrument to assess adult's orientations toward control versus autonomy in children: Reflections on intrinsic motivation and perceived competence. *Journal of Educational Psychology, 73*, 642-650.

Deci, E. L., Spiegel, N. H., Ryan, R. M., Koestner, R., & Kauffman, M. (1982). Effects of performance standards on teaching styles: Behavior of controlling teachers. *Journal of Educational Psychology, 74*, 852-859.

Delgado, J. M. R., & Anand, B. K. (1953). Increased food intake induced by electrical stimulation of the lateral hypothalamus. *American Journal of Physiology, 172*, 162-168.

DeLongis, A., Coyne, J. C., Dakof, G., Folkman, S., & Lazarus, R. S. (1982). Relations of daily hassles, uplifts, and major life events to health status. *Health Psychology, 1*, 119-136.

DeLongis, A., Folkman, S., & Lazarus, R. S. (1988). The impact of daily stress and mood: Psychological and social resources as mediators. *Journal of Personality and Social Psychology, 54*, 486-495.

Dember, W. N. (1965). The new look in motivation. *American Scientist, 53*, 409-427.

Dember, W. N. (1974). Motivation and the cognitive revolution. *American Psychologist, 29*, 161-168.

Dembroski, T. M., MacDougall, J. M., & Musante, L. (1984). Desirability of control versus locus of control: Relationship to paralinguistics in the Type A interview. *Health Psychology, 3*, 15-26.

Dempsey, E. W. (1951). Homeostasis. In S. S. Stevens (Ed.), *Handbook of experimental psychology* (pp. 209-235). New York: John Wiley.

DePaulo, B. (1992). Nonverbal behavior and self-presentation. *Psychological Bulletin, 111*, 203-243.

Depue, R. A., & Monroe, S. M. (1978). Learned helplessness in the perspective of the depressive disorders: Conceptual and definitional issues. *Journal of Abnormal Psychology, 87*, 3-20.

de Rivera, J. (1981). The structure of anger. In J. de Rivera (Ed.), *Conceptual encounter: A method for the exploration of human experience*. Washington, DC: University Press of America.

Derryberry, D., & Rothbart, M. K. (1988). Arousal, affect, and attention as components of temperament. *Journal of Personality and Social Psychology, 55*, 958-966.

Derryberry, D., & Tucker, D. M. (1991). The adaptive base of neural hierarchy: Elementary motivational controls on network function. In R. A. Dienstbier (Ed.), *Nebraska symposium on motivation* (Vol. 38, pp. 289-342). Lincoln: University of Nebraska Press.

Deutsch, J. A., & Gonzalez, M. F. (1980). Gastric nutrient content signals satiety. *Behavior Neural Biology, 30*, 113-116.

Deutsch, J. A., Young, W. G., & Kalogeris, T. J. (1978). The stomach signals satiety. *Science, 201*, 165-167.

DeVillis, R. F., DeVillis, B. M., & McCauley, C. (1978). Vicarious acquisition of learned helplessness. *Journal of Personality and Social Psychology, 36*, 894-899.

Dickerson, C., Thibodeau, R., Aronson, E., & Miller, D. (1992). Using cognitive dissonance theory to encourage water conservation. *Journal of Applied Social Psychology, 22*, 841-854.

Diener, C. I., & Dweck, C. S. (1978). An analysis of learned helplessness: Continuous changes in performance, strategy, and achievement cognitions following failure. *Journal of Personality and Social Psychology, 36,* 451-462.

Diener, C. I., & Dweck, C. S. (1980). An analysis of learned helplessness: II. The processing of success. *Journal of Personality and Social Psychology, 39,* 940-952.

Diener, E., & Emmons, R. A. (1984). The independence of positive and negative affect. *Journal of Personality and Social Psychology, 47,* 1105-1117.

Diener, E., & Iran-Nejad, A. (1986). The relationship in experience between various types of affect. *Journal of Personality and Social Psychology, 50,* 1031-1038.

Diener, E., Larsen, R. J., Levine, S., & Emmons, R. A. (1985). Frequency and intensity: The underlying dimensions of affect. *Journal of Personality and Social Psychology, 48,* 1253-1265.

Dienstbier, R. A. (1991). Introduction. In R. A. Dienstbier (Ed.), *Nebraska symposium on motivation* (Vol. 38, pp. ix-xiv). Lincoln: University of Nebraska Press.

Dimsdale, J. E., & Moss, J. (1980). *Journal of American Medical Association, 243,* 340-342.

Diserens, C. M. (1925). Psychological objectivism. *Psychological Review, 32,* 121-125.

Dollinger, S. J., & Thelen, M. H. (1978). Overjustification and children's intrinsic motivation: Comparative effects of four rewards. *Journal of Personality and Social Psychology, 36,* 1259-1269.

Donahue, E. M., Robins, R. W., Roberts, B. W., & John, O. P. (1993). The divided self: Concurrent and longitudinal effects of psychological adjustment and social roles on self-concept differentiation. *Journal of Personality and Social Psychology, 64,* 834-846.

Donahue, M. J. (1985). Intrinsic and extrinsic religiousness: Review and meta-analysis. *Journal of Personality and Social Psychology, 48,* 400-419.

Donovan, J. M., Hill, E., & Jankowiak, W. R. (1989). Gender, sexual orientation, and truth-or-consequences in studies of physical attractiveness. *Journal of Sex Research, 26,* 264-271.

Duffy, E. (1957). Psychological significance of the concept of "arousal" or "activation." *Psychological Review, 64,* 265-275.

Dunker, K. (1945). On problem-solving. *Psychological Monographs, 58,* Whole No. 5.

Dunlap, K. (1919). Are there any instincts? *Journal of Abnormal Psychology, 14,* 35-50.

Dunning, D., Leuenberger, A., & Sherman, D. A. (1995). A new look at motivated inference: Are self-serving theories of success a product of motivational forces? *Journal of Personality and Social Psychology, 69,* 58-68.

Durkheim, E. (1951). *Suicide.* New York: Free Press.

Dutton, D., & Aron, A. (1974). Some evidence for a heightened sexual attraction under conditions of high anxiety. *Journal of Personality and Social Psychology, 30,* 510-517.

Dweck, C. S. (1975). The role of expectancies and attributions in the alleviation of learned helplessness. *Journal of Personality and Social Psychology, 31,* 674-685.

Dweck, C. S. (1986). Motivational processes affecting learning. *American Psychologist, 41,* 1040-1048.

Dweck, C. S., & Repucci, N. D. (1973). Learned helplessness and reinforcement responsibility in children. *Journal of Personality and Social Psychology, 25,* 109-116.

Dworetzkey, J. P. (1988). *Psychology* (3e). St. Paul, MN: West.

Earley, P. C., Connolly, T., & Ekegren, G. (1989). Goals, strategy development and task performance: Some limits on the efficacy of goal setting. *Journal of Applied Psychology, 74,* 24-33.

Earley, P. C., & Perry, B. C. (1987). Work plan availability and performance: An assessment of task strategy priming on subsequent task completion. *Organizational Behavior and Human Decision Processes, 39,* 279-302.

Earley, P. C., Wojnaroski, P., & Prest, W. (1987). Task planning and energy expended: Exploration of how goals influence performance. *Journal of Applied Psychology, 72,* 107-113.

Eaves, L. J., Eysenck, H. J., & Martin, N. G. (1989). *Genes, culture, and personality: An empirical approach.* San Diego: Academic Press.

Eccles, J. S. (1984a). Sex differences in achievement patterns. In T. Sonderegger (Ed.), *Nebraska symposium on motivation: Psychology and gender* (Vol. 32, pp. 97-132). Lincoln: University of Nebraska Press.

Eccles, J. S. (1984b). Sex differences in mathematics participation. In M. Steinkamp & M. L. Maehr (Eds.), *Advances in motivation and achievement* (Vol. 2, pp. 93-137). Lincoln: University of Nebraska Press.

Eccles-Parsons, J. E., Adler, T. F., & Kaczala, C. M. (1982). Socialization of achievement attitudes and beliefs: Parental influences. *Child Development, 53,* 310-321.

Eckelman, J. D., & Dyck, D. G. (1979). Task- and setting-related cues in immunization against learned helplessness. *American Journal of Psychology, 92,* 653-667.

Eckenrode, J. (1984). Impact of chronic and acute stressors on daily reports of mood. *Journal of Personality and Social Psychology, 46,* 907-918.

Edwards, A. L. (1959). *Manual for the Edwards Personal Preference Schedule.* New York: The Psychology Corporation.

Edwards, R., Manstead, A. S. R., & MacDonald, C. J. (1984). The relationship between children's sociometric status and ability to recognize facial expressions of emotion. *European Journal of Social Psychology, 14,* 235-238.

Eibl-Eibesfeldt, I. (1971). *Love and hate.* London: Methuen.

Eibl-Eibesfeldt, I. (1972). Similarities and differences between cultures in expressive movements. In R. A. Hinde (Ed.), *Nonverbal communication.* Cambridge: Cambridge University Press.

Eibl-Eibesfeldt, I. (1989). *Human ethology.* New York: Aldine De Gruyter.

Eidelson, R. J. (1980). Interpersonal satisfaction and level of involvement: A curvilinear relationship. *Journal of Personality and Social Psychology, 39,* 460-470.

Eisen, S. V. (1979). Actor-observer differences in information inferences and causal attribution. *Journal of Personality and Social Psychology, 37,* 261-272.

Eisenstadt, D., & Leippe, M. R. (1994). The self-comparison process of self-discrepant feedback: Consequences of learning you are what you thought you were not. *Journal of Personality and Social Psychology, 67,* 611-626.

Ekman, P. (1972). Universal and cultural differences in facial expression of emotion. In J. R. Cole (Ed.), *Nebraska symposium on motivation* (Vol. 19, pp. 207-284). Lincoln: University of Nebraska Press.

Ekman, P. (1992). An argument for basic emotions. *Cognition and Emotion, 6,* 169-200.

Ekman, P. (1993). Facial expression and emotion. *American Psychologist, 48,* 384-392.

Ekman, P. (1994a). All emotions are basic. In P. Ekman & R. J. Davidson (Eds.), *The nature of emotion: Fundamental questions* (pp. 15-19). New York: Oxford University Press.

Ekman, P. (1994b). Strong evidence for universals in facial expressions: A reply to Russell's mistaken critique. *Psychological Bulletin, 115,* 268-287.

Ekman, P., & Davidson, R. J. (1993). Voluntary smiling changes regional brain activity. *Psychological Science, 4,* 342-345.

Ekman, P., & Davidson, R. J. (Eds.) (1994). *The nature of emotion: Fundamental questions* (pp. 20-24). New York: Oxford University Press.

Ekman, P., & Friesen, W. V. (1971). Constants across cultures in facial expressions of emotion. In J. K. Cole (Ed.), *Nebraska symposium on motivation* (pp. 207-283). Lincoln: University of Nebraska Press.

Ekman, P., & Friesen, W. V. (1975). *Unmasking the face*. Englewood Cliffs, NJ: Prentice-Hall.

Ekman, P., & Friesen, W. V. (1978). *Facial action coding system*. Palo Alto, CA: Consulting Psychologists Press.

Ekman, P., & Friesen, W. V. (1986). A new pan-cultural facial expression of emotion. *Motivation and Emotion, 10*, 159-168.

Ekman, P., Levenson, R. W., & Friesen, W. V. (1983). Autonomic nervous system activity distinguishes between emotions. *Science, 221*, 1208-1210.

Ekman, P., Sorenson, E. R., & Friesen, W. V. (1969). Pan-cultural elements in facial displays of emotion. *Science, 164*, 86-88.

Elkin, R., & Leippe, M. (1986). Physiological arousal, dissonance, and attitude change: Evidence for a dissonance-arousal link and a "don't remind me" effect. *Journal of Personality and Social Psychology, 51*, 55-65.

Ellenberger, H. F. (1966). The pathogenic secret and its therapeutics. *Journal of the History of the Behavioral Sciences, 2*, 29-42.

Elliot, A. J., & Devine, P. G. (1994). On the motivational nature of cognitive dissonance: Dissonance as psychological discomfort. *Journal of Personality and Social Psychology, 66*, 382-394.

Elliot, E., & Dweck, C. (1988). Goals: An approach to motivation and achievement. *Journal of Personality and Social Psychology, 54*, 5-12.

Ellsworth, P. C. (1994). William James and emotion: Is a century of fame worth a century of misunderstanding? *Psychological Review, 101*, 222-229.

Ellsworth, P. C., & Smith, C. A. (1988a). From appraisal to emotion: Differences among unpleasant feelings. *Motivation and Emotion, 12*, 271-302.

Ellsworth, P. C., & Smith, C. A. (1988b). Shades of joy: Patterns of appraisal differentiating pleasant emotions. *Cognition and Emotion, 2*, 301-331.

Elman, D., & Killebrew, T. J. (1978). Incentives and seat belts: Changing a resistant behavior through extrinsic motivation. *Journal of Applied Social Psychology, 8*, 73-83.

Emmons, R. A. (1996). Striving and feeling: Personal goals and subjective well-being. In P. M. Gollwitzer & J. A. Bargh (Eds.), *The psychology of action: Linking cognition and motivation to behavior* (pp. 313-337). New York: Guilford Press.

Emmons, R. A., & Diener, E. (1986). Influence of impulsivity and sociability on subjective well-being. *Journal of Personality and Social Psychology, 50*, 1211-1215.

Emmons, R. A., & McAdams, D. P. (1991). Personal strivings and motive dispositions: Exploring the links. *Personality and Social Psychology Bulletin, 17*, 648-654.

Engberg, L. A., Hansen, G., Welker, R. L., & Thomas, D. R. (1972). Acquisition of key-pecking via autoshaping as a function of prior experience: "Learned laziness"? *Science, 178*, 1002-1004.

Entwistle, D. R. (1972). To dispel fantasies about fantasy-based measures of achievement motivation. *Psychological Bulletin, 77*, 377-391.

Epley, S. W. (1974). Reduction of the behavioral effects of aversive stimulation by the presence of companions. *Psychological Bulletin, 81*, 271-283.

Epstein, A. N. (1973). Epilogue: Retrospect and prognosis. In A. N. Epstein, H. R. Kissileff, & E. Stellar (Eds.), *The neuropsychology of thirst: New findings and advances in concepts* (pp. 315-332). New York: Wiley.

Epstein, J. A., & Harackiewicz, J. H. (1992). Winning is not enough: The effects of competition and achievement orientation on intrinsic interest. *Personality and Social Psychology Bulletin, 18*, 128-138.

Erdelyi, M. H. (1985). *Psychoanalysis: Freud's cognitive psychology*. New York: W. H. Freeman.

Erdelyi, M. H. (1990). Repression, reconstruction, and defense: History and integration of the psychoanalytic and experimental frameworks. In J. L. Singer (Ed.), *Repression and dissociation* (pp. 1–31). Chicago: University of Chicago Press.

Erdelyi, M. H., & Goldberg, B. (1979). Let's not sweep repression under the rug: Toward a cognitive psychology of repression. In J. F. Kilstrom & F. J. Evans (Eds.), *Functional disorders of memory*. Hillsdale, NJ: Erlbaum.

Erez, M. (1977). Feedback: A necessary condition for the goal setting–performance relationship. *Journal of Applied Psychology, 62*, 624–627.

Erez, M., Earley, P. C., & Hulin, C. L. (1985). The impact of participation on goal acceptance and performance: A two-step model. *Academy of Management Journal, 28*, 50–66.

Erez, M., & Kanfer, F. H. (1983). The role of goal acceptance in goal setting and task performance. *Academy of Management Review, 8*, 454–463.

Erez, M., & Zidon, I. (1984). Effects of goal acceptance on the relationship to goal difficulty and performance. *Journal of Applied Psychology, 60*, 69–78.

Erikson, E. H. (1959). Identity and the life cycle. *Psychological Issues, 1*, 1–171.

Erikson, E. H. (1963). *Childhood and society* (2e). New York: Norton.

Erikson, E. H. (1964). *Insight and responsibility*. New York: Norton.

Erikson, E. H. (1968). *Identity, youth, and crisis*. New York: Norton.

Ethington, C. A. (1991). A test of a model of achievement behaviors. *American Educational Research Journal, 28*, 155–172.

Exline, R. V. (1962). Need affiliation and initial communication behavior in problem solving groups characterized by low interpersonal visibility. *Psychological Reports, 10*, 79–89.

Exner, J. E., Jr. (1986). *The Rorschach: A comprehensive system* (Vol. 1, 2e). New York: Wiley-Interscience.

Exner, J. E., Jr., & Exner, D. E. (1972). How clinicians use the Rorschach. *Journal of Personality Assessment, 36*, 403–408.

Eysenck, H. J. (1963). Experiments with drugs: Studies in the relation between personality, learning theory, and drug action. New York: Pergamon Press.

Eysenck, H. J. (1967). *The biological basis of personality*. Springfield, IL: Charles C. Thomas.

Eysenck, H. J. (1971). *Readings in extraversion-introversion: II. Fields of application*. London: Staples.

Eysenck, H. J. (1986). Can personality study ever be scientific? *Journal of Social Behavior and Personality, 1*, 3–19.

Eysenck, H. J. & Eysenck, S. B. G. (1968). *Manual of the Eysenck Personality Inventory*. London: University of London Press.

Eysenck, H. J., & Eysenck, S. B. G. (1969). *Personality structure and measurement*. New York: Routledge, Chapman, & Hall.

Eysenck, H. J., & Eysenck, S. B. G. (1985). *Personality and individual differences*. New York: Plenum.

Faust, I. M., Johnson, P. R., & Hirsch, J. (1977a). Adipose tissue regeneration following lipectomy. *Science, 197*, 391–393.

Faust, I. M., Johnson, P. R., & Hirsch, J. (1977b). Surgical removal of adipose tissue alters feeding behavior and the development of obesity in rats. *Science, 197*, 393–396.

Fazio, R. H. (1981). On the self-perception explanation of the over-justification effect. *Journal of Experimental Social Psychology, 17*, 417–426.

Fazio, R. H., & Cooper, J. (1983). Arousal in the dissonance process. In J. T. Cacioppo & R. E. Petty (Eds.), *Social psychophysiology: A sourcebook*. New York: Guilford.

Fazio, R. H., Zanna, M., & Cooper, J. (1977). Dissonance and self-perception: An integrative view of each theory's proper domain of application. *Journal of Experimental Social Psychology, 13*, 464–479.

Fazio, R. H., Zanna, M., & Cooper, J. (1979). On the relationship of data to theory: A reply to Ronis and Greenwald. *Journal of Experimental Social Psychology, 15*, 70-76.

Feather, N. T. (1961). The relationship of persistence at a task to expectation of success and achievement related motives. *Journal of Abnormal and Social Psychology, 63*, 552-561.

Feather, N. T. (1963). Persistence at a difficult task with alternative tasks of intermediate difficulty. *Journal of Abnormal and Social Psychology, 66*, 604-609.

Feather, N. T. (1966). Effects of prior success and failure on expectations of success and subsequent performance. *Journal of Personality and Social Psychology, 3*, 287-298.

Feather, N. T. (1992). Values, valences, expectations, and actions. *Journal of Social Issues, 48*, 109-124.

Feather, N. T. (1995). Values, valences, and choices: The influence of values on the perceived attractiveness of choice of alternatives. *Journal of Personality and Social Psychology, 68*, 1135-1151.

Feather, N. T., & Newton, J. W. (1982). Values, expectations, and the prediction of social action: An expectancy-value analysis. *Motivation and Emotion, 6*, 217-244.

Feather, N. T., & Saville, M. R. (1967). Effects of amount of prior success and failure on expectations of success and subsequent task performance. *Journal of Personality and Social Psychology, 5*, 226-232.

Fehr, B., & Russell, J. A. (1984). Concept of emotion viewed from a prototype perspective. *Journal of Experimental Psychology: General, 113*, 464-486.

Felson, R. B. (1984). The effect of self-appraisals of ability on academic performance. *Journal of Personality and Social Psychology, 47*, 944-952.

Fernandez-Dols, J.-M., & Ruiz-Belba, M.-A. (1995). Are smiles a sign of happiness? Gold medal winners at the Olympic games. *Journal of Personality and Social Psychology, 69*, 1113-1119.

Feshbach, S. (1984). The "personality" of personality theory and research. *Personality and Social Psychology Bulletin, 10*, 446-456.

Festinger, L. (1957). *A theory of cognitive dissonance*. Stanford: Stanford University Press.

Festinger, L., & Carlsmith, J. M. (1959). Cognitive consequences of forced compliance. *Journal of Abnormal and Social Psychology, 58*, 203-210.

Festinger, L., Riecken, H. W., & Schachter, S. (1956). *When prophecy fails*. Minneapolis: Minnesota University Press.

Festinger, L., Riecken, H. W., & Schachter, S. (1958). When prophecy fails. In E. E. Maccoby, T. M. Newcomb, & E. L. Hartley (Eds.), *Readings in social psychology* (pp. 156-163). New York: Holt, Rinehart, & Winston.

Fineman, S. (1977). The achievement motive construct and its measurement: Where are we now? *British Journal of Psychology, 68*, 1-22.

Fischer, (1990). How emotions develop and how they organize development. *Cognition and Emotion, 4*, 81-127.

Fisher, C. D. (1978). The effects of personal control, competence, and extrinsic reward systems on intrinsic motivation. *Organizational Behavior and Human Performance, 21*, 273-288.

Fisher, S., & Greenberg, R. P. (1977). *The scientific credibility of Freud's theories and therapy*. New York: Basic Books.

Fisher, W., Piazza, C., Cataldo, M., Harrell, R., Jefferson, G., & Comer, R. (1993). Functional communication training with and without extinction and punishment. *Journal of Applied Behavior Analysis, 26*, 23-36.

Flink, C., Boggiano, A. K., & Barrett, M. (1990). Controlling teaching strategies: Undermining children's self-determination and performance. *Journal of Personality and Social Psychology, 59*, 916-924.

Flink, C., Boggiano, A. K., Main, D. S., Barrett, M., & Katz, P. A. (1992). Children's achieve-ment-related behaviors: The role of extrinsic and intrinsic motivational orientations. In A. K. Boggiano & T. S. Pittman (Eds.), *Achievement and motivation: A social-developmental perspective* (pp. 189-214). New York: Cambridge University Press.

Foch, T. T., & McClearn, G. E. (1980). Genetics, body weight, and obesity. In A. E. Stunkard (Ed.), *Obesity* (pp. 48-71). Philadelphia: W. B. Saunders.

Foder, E. M., & Farrow, D. L. (1979). The power motive as an influence on the use of power. *Journal of Personality and Social Psychology, 37,* 2091-2097.

Fodor, E. M., & Smith, T. (1982). The power motive as an influence on group decision mak-ing. *Journal of Personality and Social Psychology, 42,* 178-185.

Folkman, S., & Lazarus, R. S. (1985). If it changes it must be a process: Study of emotion and coping during three stages of a college examination. *Journal of Personality and Social Psychology, 48,* 150-170.

Folkman, S., & Lazarus, R. S. (1990). Coping and emotion. In N. Stein, B. Leventhal, & T. Trabasso (Eds.), *Psychological and biological approaches to emotion* (pp. 313-332). Hillsdale, NJ: Lawrence Erlbaum.

Folkman, S., & Lazarus, R. S., Dunkel-Schetter, C., DeLongin, A., & Gruen, R. J. (1986). Dynamics of a stressful encounter: Cognitive appraisal, coping, and encounter outcomes. *Journal of Personality and Social Psychology, 50,* 992-1003.

Foote, N. N. (1951). Identification as the basis for a theory of motivation. *American Sociological Review, 16,* 14-21.

Ford, J. G. (1991a). Inherent potentialities of actualization: An initial exploration. *Journal of Humanistic Psychology, 31,* 65-88.

Ford, J. G. (1991b). Rogerian self-actualization: A clarification of meaning. *Journal of Humanistic Psychology, 31,* 101-111.

Ford, J. G. (1995). The temperament/actualization concept: A perspective on constitutional integrity and psychological health. *Journal of Humanistic Psychology, 35,* 57-77.

Forest, D., Clark, M. S., Mills, J., & Isen, A. M. (1979). Helping as a function of feeling state and nature of the helping behavior. *Motivation and Emotion, 3,* 161-169.

Forsterling, F. (1985). Attribution retraining: A review. *Psychological Bulletin, 98,* 495-512.

Fowles, D. C. (1983). Motivational effects of heart rate and electrodermal activity: Implications for research on personality and psychopathology. *Journal of Research in Personality, 17,* 48-71.

Fowles, D. C., Fisher, A. E., & Tranel, D. T. (1982). The heart beats to reward: The effect of monetary incentive on heart rate. *Psychophysiology, 19,* 506-513.

Frank, M. G., Ekman, P., & Friesen, W. V. (1993). Behavioral markers and recognizability of the smile of enjoyment. *Journal of Personality and Social Psychology, 64,* 83-93.

Frankl, V. (1960). Paradoxical intention: A logotherapeutic technique. *American Journal of Psychotherapy, 14,* 520-525.

Freud, A. (1946). *The ego and mechanisms of defense.* New York: International Universities Press.

Freud, S. (1900). *The interpretation of dreams* (translated by A. A. Brill, 1932). London: Allen & Irwin.

Freud, S. (1901). *Psychopathology of everyday life* (translated by A. A. Brill, 1914). New York: Macmillan.

Freud, S. (1905). *Wit and its relation to the unconscious* (translated by A. A. Brill, 1917). New York: Moffat, Yard.

Freud, S. (1915). Instincts and their vicissitudes (translated by J. Rivière, 1949). In *Collected papers of Sigmund Freud* (Vol. 4, pp. 60-83). London: Hogarth.

Freud, S. (1917). *A general introduction to psychoanalysis* (translated by J. Rivière). New York: Liverright.

Freud, S. (1920). *Beyond the pleasure principle* (translated, 1922). London: Hogarth.

Freud, S. (1923). *The ego and the id* (translated by J. Rivière, 1927). London: Hogarth.

Freud, S. (1926). *Inhibitions, symptoms, and anxiety*. Translated by A. Strachey & J. Strachey. In *The standard edition of the complete psychological works of Sigmund Freud*, edited by J. Strachey (Vol. 20). London: Hogarth Press, 1959.

Freud, S. (1927). Humour (translated by J. Rivière & J. Strachey). In *The standard edition of the complete psychological works of Sigmund Freud*, edited by J. Strachey (Vol. 21). London: Hogarth press, 1961.

Fridlund, A. J. & Izard, C. E. (1983). Electromyographic studies of facial expressions of emotions. In J. T. Cacioppo & R. E. Petty (Eds.), *Social psychophysiology*. New York: The Guildford Press.

Fried, C. B., & Aronson, E. (1995). Hypocrisy, misattribution, and dissonance reduction. *Personality and Social Psychology Bulletin, 21*, 925-933.

Friedman, M. I., & Stricker, E. M. (1976). The physiological psychology of hunger: A physiological perspective. *Psychological Review, 83*, 409-431.

Frijda, N. H. (1986). *The emotions*. London: Cambridge University Press.

Frijda, N. H. (1993). The place of appraisal in emotion. *Cognition and Emotion, 7*, 357-388.

Frijda, N. H. (1994). Universal antecedents exist, and are interesting. In P. Ekman & R. J. Davidson (Eds.), *The nature of emotion: Fundamental questions* (pp. 155-162). New York: Oxford University Press.

Fromm, E. (1941). *Escape from freedom*. New York: Rinehart.

Fromm, E. (1956). *The art of loving*. New York: Harper & Brothers.

Fromm, E. (1964). *The heart of man*. New York: Harper & Row.

Funder, D. C. (1987). Errors and mistakes: Evaluating the accuracy of social judgment. *Psychological Bulletin, 101*, 75-90.

Gaes, G. G., Kalle, R. J., & Tedeschi, J. T. (1978). Impression management in the forced compliance situation. *Journal of Experimental Social Psychology, 14*, 493-510.

Gagnon, J. H. (1974). Scripts and the coordination of sexual conduct. In J. K. Cole & R. Diensteiber (Eds.), *Nebraska symposium on motivation* (Vol. 21, pp. 27-59). Lincoln: University of Nebraska Press.

Gagnon, J. H. (1977). *Human sexualities*. Glenview, IL: Scott Foresman.

Gale, A. (1973). The psychophysiology of individual differences: Studies of extraversion and the EEG. In P. Kline (Ed.), *New approaches in psychological measurement*. London: Wiley.

Gale, A. (1983). Electroencephalogram studies of extraversion-introversion: A case study in the psychophysiology of individual differences. *Personality and Individual Differences, 4*, 371-380.

Gale, A., Coles, M. G. H., & Blaydon, J. (1969). Extraversion-introversion and the EEG. *British Journal of Psychology, 60*, 209-223.

Gale, A., & Edwards, J. A. (1986). Individual differences. In M. G. H. Coles, E. Donchin, & S. W. Proges (Eds.), *Psychophysiology: Systems, processes, and applications* (pp. 431-507). New York: Guilford Press.

Garbarino, J. (1975). The impact of anticipated reward upon cross-aged tutoring. *Journal of Personality and Social Psychology, 32*, 421-428.

Gardner, H. (1985). *The mind's new science: A history of the cognitive revolution*. New York: Basic Books.

Gecas, V., & Burke, P. J. (1995). Self and identity. In K. S. Cook, G. A. Fine, & J. S. House (Eds.), *Sociological perspectives on social psychology* (pp. 41-67). Boston, MA: Allyn & Bacon.

Geller, E. S., Altomari, M. G., & Russ, N. W. (1984). *Innovative approaches to drunk driving prevention*. Warren, MI: Societal Analysis Department, General Motors Research Laboratories.

Geller, E. S., Casali, J. G., & Johnson, R. P. (1980). Seat belt usage: A potential target for applied behavior analysis. *Journal of Applied Behavior Analysis, 13*, 669-675.

Geller, L. (1982). The failure of self-actualization theory: A critique of Carl Rogers and Abraham Maslow. *Journal of Humanistic Psychology, 22*, 56-73.

Gergen, K. J. (1971). *The concept of self*. New York: Holt.

Gibson, E. J. (1988). Exploratory behavior in the development of perceiving, acting and the acquiring of knowledge. *Annual Review of Psychology, 39*, 1-41.

Gill, D. L., Ruder, K., & Gross, J. B. (1982). Open-ended attributions in team competition. *Journal of Sport Psychology, 4*, 159-169.

Gilovich, T., Medvec, V. H., & Chen, S. (1995). Commission, omission, and dissonance reduction: Coping with regret in the "Monty Hall" problem. *Personality and Social Psychology Bulletin, 21*, 182-190.

Gjesme, T. (1981). Is there any future in achievement motivation? *Motivation and Emotion, 5*, 115-138.

Gloor, P., Oliver, A., & Quesney, L. F. (1981). The role of the amygdala in the expression of psychic phenomena in temporal lobe seizures. In Y. Ben-Ari (Ed.), *The amygdaloid complex*. New York: Elsevier.

Goebel, B. L., & Brown, D. R. (1981). Age differences in motivation related to Maslow's need hierarchy. *Developmental Psychology, 17*, 809-815.

Goethals, G. R., Cooper, J., & Naficy, A. (1979). Role of foreseen, foreseeable, and unforeseeable consequences in the arousal of cognitive dissonance. *Journal of Personality and Social Psychology, 37*, 1179-1185.

Goffman, E. (1959). *The presentation of self in everyday life*. Garden City, NY: Doubleday.

Goldberg, C. (1995). The daimenic development of the malevolent personality. *Journal of Humanistic Psychology, 35*, 7-36.

Goldsmith, H. H. (1994). Parsing the emotional domain from a developmental perspective. In P. Ekman & R. J. Davidson (Eds.), *The nature of emotion: Fundamental questions* (pp. 68-73). New York: Oxford University Press.

Goldstein, K. (1939). *The organism*. New York: American Book Company.

Gollwitzer, P. M., & Bargh, J. A. (Eds.) (1996). *The psychology of action: Linking cognition and motivation to behavior*. New York: Guilford Press.

Gonas, G. (1977). "Situation" versus "frame": The "interactionist" and the "structuralist" analysis of everyday life. *American Sociological Review, 42*, 854-867.

Goodenough, F. L. (1932). Expressions of emotions in a blind-deaf child. *Journal of Abnormal and Social Psychology, 27*, 328-333.

Goodenow, C. (1993). The psychological sense of school membership among adolescents: Scale development and educational correlates. *Psychology in the Schools, 30*, 79-90.

Goodman, R. A. (1968). On the operationality of Maslow's need hierarchy. *British Journal of Industrial Relations, 6*, 51-57.

Gottfried, A. (1985). Academic intrinsic motivation in elementary and junior high school students. *Journal of Educational Psychology, 77*, 631-645.

Gough, H. G. (1964). A cross-sectional study of achievement motivation. *Journal of Applied Psychology, 48*, 191-196.

Gould, D., Hodge, K., Peterson, K., & Giannini, J. (1989). An exploratory examination of strategies used by elite coaches to enhance self-efficacy in athletes. *Journal of Sport and Exercise Psychology, 11*, 128-140.

Gould, R., & Sigall, H. (1977). The effects of empathy and outcome on attribution: An examination of the divergent-perspectives hypothesis. *Journal of Experimental Social Psychology, 13*, 480–491.

Gray, J. A. (1994). Three fundamental emotion systems. In P. Ekman & R. J. Davidson (Eds.), *The nature of emotion: Fundamental questions* (pp. 243–247). New York: Oxford University Press.

Graziano, W. G., Feldesman, A. B., & Rahe, D. F. (1985). Extraversion, social cognition, and the salience of aversiveness in social encounters. *Journal of Personality and Social Psychology, 49*, 971–980.

Green, C. W., Reid, D. H., White, L. K., Halford, R. C., Brittain, D. P., & Gardner, S. M. (1988). Identifying reinforcers for persons with profound handicaps: Staff opinion versus systematic assessment of preferences. *Journal of Applied Behavior Analysis, 21*, 31–43.

Greenberg, J., & Pyszczynski, T. (1985). Compensatory self-inflation: A response to the threat to self-regard of public failure. *Journal of Personality and Social Psychology, 49*, 273–280.

Greenberg, J., Pyszcynski, T., & Solomon, S. (1982). The self-serving attributional bias: Beyond self-presentation. *Journal of Experimental Social Psychology, 18*, 56–67.

Greenberg, J., Solomon, S., Pyszczynski, T., Rosenblatt, A., Burling, J., Lyon, D., Simon, L., & Pinel, E. (1992). Why do people need self-esteem? Converging evidence that self-esteem serves an anxiety-buffering function. *Journal of Personality and Social Psychology, 63*, 913–922.

Greene, D., & Lepper, M. R. (1974). Effects of extrinsic rewards on children's subsequent intrinsic interest. *Child Development, 45*, 1141–1145.

Greening, T. (1995). Commentary. *Journal of Humanistic Psychology, 35*, 1–6.

Greeno, C. G., & Wing, R. R. (1994). Stress-induced eating. *Psychological Bulletin, 115*, 444–464.

Greenwald, A. G., & Ronis, D. L. (1978). Twenty years of cognitive dissonance: A case study in the evolution of a theory. *Psychological Review, 85*, 53–57.

Grilo, C. M., & Pogue-Geile, M. F. (1991). The nature of environmental influences on weight and obesity: A behavior genetics analysis. *Psychological Bulletin, 110*, 520–537.

Grolnick, W. S., Frodi, A., & Bridges, L. (1984). Maternal control styles and the mastery motivation of one-year-olds. *Infant Mental Health Journal, 5*, 72–82.

Grolnick, W. S., & Ryan, R. M. (1987). Autonomy in children's learning: An experimental and individual difference investigation. *Journal of Personality and Social Psychology, 52*, 890–898.

Gross, N., Mason, W. S., & McEachern, A. W. (1958). *Explorations in role analysis: Studies of the school superintendency role.* New York: Wiley.

Gruen, A. (1976). Autonomy and compliance: The fundamental antithesis. *Journal of Humanistic Psychology, 16*, 61–69.

Guisinger, S., & Blatt, S. J. (1994). Individuality and relatedness: Evolution of a fundamental dialectic. *American Psychologist, 49*, 104–111.

Hackett, G. (1985). The role of mathematics self-efficacy in the choice of math-related majors of college women and men: A path analysis. *Journal of Counseling Psychology, 32*, 47–56.

Hale, C. S. (1995). Psychological characteristics of the literary genius. *Journal of Humanistic Psychology, 35*, 113–134.

Hall, H. K., & Byrne, A. T. J. (1988). Goal setting in sport: Clarifying recent anomalies. *Journal of Sport and Exercise Psychology, 10*, 184–198.

Hall, R. V., Axelrod, S., Tyler, L., Grief, E., Jones, F. C., & Robertson, R. (1972). Modification of behavior problems in the home with a parent as observer and experimenter. *Journal of Applied Behavior Analysis, 5*, 53–64.

Hall, W. G. (1973). A remote stomach clamp to evaluate oral and gastric controls of drinking in the rat. *Physiology and Behavior, 173*, 897-901.

Hansford, B. C., & Hattie, J. A. (1982). The relationship between self and achievement/performance measures. *Review of Educational Research, 52*, 123-142.

Harackiewicz, J. (1979). The effects of reward contingency and performance feedback on intrinsic motivation. *Journal of Personality and Social Psychology, 37*, 1352-1363.

Harackiewicz, J. M., & Elliot, A. J. (1993). Achievement goals and intrinsic motivation. *Journal of Personality and Social Psychology, 65*, 904-915.

Harackiewicz, J. M., & Manderlink, G. (1984). A process analysis of the effects of performance-contingent rewards on intrinsic motivation. *Journal of Experimental Social Psychology, 20*, 531-551.

Harackiewicz, J. M., Sansone, C., & Manderlink, G. (1985). Competence, achievement orientation, and intrinsic motivation: A process analysis. *Journal of Personality and Social Psychology, 48*, 493-508.

Hardeman, M. (1979). A dialogue with Abraham Maslow. *Journal of Humanistic Psychology, 19*, 23-28.

Harlow, H. F. (1953). Motivation as a factor in the acquisition of new responses. In M. R. Jones (Ed.), *Nebraska symposium on motivation* (Vol. 1, pp. 24-49). Lincoln: University of Nebraska Press.

Harper, F. B. W. (1975). The validity of some alternative measurements of achievement motivation. *Educational and Psychological Measurement, 35*, 905-909.

Harris, R. N., & Snyder, C. R. (1986). The role of uncertain self-esteem in self-handicapping. *Journal of Personality and Social Psychology, 51*, 451-458.

Harter, S. (1974). Pleasure derived by children from cognitive challenge and mastery. *Child Development, 45*, 661-669.

Harter, S. (1978a). Effectance motivation reconsidered: Toward a developmental model. *Human Development, 21*, 34-64.

Harter, S. (1978b). Pleasure derived from optimal challenge and the effects of extrinsic rewards on children's difficulty level choices. *Child Development, 49*, 788-799.

Harter, S. (1981). A model of mastery motivation in children: Individual differences and developmental changes. In W. A. Collin (Ed.), *Aspects of the development of competence* (Vol. 14, pp. 215-255). Hillsdale, NJ: Erlbaum.

Harter, S. (1982). The Perceived Competence Scale for Children. *Child Development, 53*, 87-97.

Harter, S. (1988). The construction and conservation of the self: James and Cooley revisited. In D. K. Lapsle & F. C. Power (Eds.), *Self, ego, and identity: Integrative approaches* (pp. 43-70). New York: Springer-Verlag.

Harter, S. (1990). Causes, correlates and the functional role of global self-worth: A life-span perspective. In R. J. Sternberg & J. Kolligian, Jr. (Eds.), *Competence considered* (pp. 67-97). New Haven, CT: Yale University Press.

Harter, S. (1993). Visions of self: Beyond the me in the mirror. In J. E. Jacobs (Ed.), *Nebraska symposium on motivation: Developmental perspectives on motivation* (Vol. 40, pp. 99-144). Lincoln: University of Nebraska Press.

Harter, S., & Park, R. (1984). The pictorial perceived competence scale for young children. *Child Development, 55*, 1969-1982.

Hartmann, H. (1958). *Ego psychology and the problem of adaptation* (translated by D. Rapaport). New York: International Universities Press.

Harvey, J. H., & Weary, G. (1981). *Perspectives on attributional processes*. Dubuque, IA: Wm. C. Brown.

Hatfield, E., Cacioppo, J. T., & Rapson, R. L. (1993a). *Emotional contagion.* Cambridge: Cambridge University Press.

Hatfield, E., Cacioppo, J. T., & Rapson, R. L. (1993b). Emotional contagion. *Current Directions in Psychological Science, 2,* 96-99.

Heath, R. G. (1964). Pleasure response of human subjects to direct stimulation of the brain. In R. G. Heath (Ed.), *The role of pleasure in behavior* (pp. 219-243). New York: Harper & Row.

Heatherton, T. F., Herman, C. P., & Polivy, J. (1991). Effects of physical threat and ego threat on eating behavior. *Journal of Personality and Social Psychology, 60,* 138-143.

Heatherton, T. F., & Nichols, P. A. (1994). Personal accounts of successful versus failed attempts at life change. *Personality and Social Psychology Bulletin, 20,* 664-675.

Hebb, D. O. (1955). Drives and the C.N.S.: Conceptual nervous system. *Psychological Review, 62,* 245-254.

Heckhausen, H. (1967). *The anatomy of achievement motivation.* New York: Academic Press.

Heckhausen, H. (1977). Achievement motivation and its constructs: A cognitive model. *Motivation and Emotion, 1,* 283-329.

Heckhausen, H. (1980). *Motivation and Handeln.* New York: Springer-Verlag.

Heckhausen, H. (1982). The development of achievement motivation. In W. W. Harup (Ed.), *Review of child development research* (Vol. 6, pp. 600-668). Chicago: University of Chicago Press.

Heider, F. (1958). *The psychology of interpersonal relations.* New York: John Wiley.

Heise, D. R. (1979). *Understanding events: Affect and the construction of social action.* New York: Cambridge University Press.

Heise, D. R. (1985). Affect control theory: Respecification, estimation, and tests of the formal model. *Journal of Mathematical Sociology, 1,* 191-222.

Heise, D. R. (1989). Effects of emotion displays on social identification. *Social Psychology Quarterly, 52,* 10-21.

Helson, R., Stewart, A. J., & Ostrove, J. (1995). Identity in three cohorts of midlife women. *Journal of Personality and Social Psychology, 69,* 544-557.

Hendrick, S. S., & Hendrick, C. (1987). Love and sexual attitudes, self-disclosure, and sensation seeking. *Journal of Social and Personal Relationships, 4,* 281-297.

Herman, C. P., & Mack, D. (1975). Restrained and unrestrained eating. *Journal of Personality, 43,* 647-660.

Herman, C. P., Polivy, J., & Esses, J. M. (1987). The illusion of counter-regulation. *Appetite, 9,* 161-169.

Hermans, H. J. M. (1970). A questionnaire measure of achievement motivation. *Journal of Applied Psychology, 54,* 353-363.

Heron, W. (1957). The pathology of boredom. *Scientific American, 196,* 52-56.

Hess, E. H. (1975). *The tell-tale eye.* New York: Van Nostrand Reinhold.

Heyns, R. W., Veroff, J., & Atkinson, J. W. (1958). A scoring manual for the affiliation motive. In J. W. Atkinson (Ed.), *Motives in fantasy, action, and society.* Princeton, NJ: Van Nostrand.

Hidi, S. (1990). Interest and its contribution as a mental resource for learning. *Review of Educational Research, 60,* 549-571.

Higgins, E. T., Rhodewalt, F., & Zanna, M. P. (1979). Dissonance motivation: Its nature, persistence and reinstatement. *Journal of Experimental Social Psychology, 15,* 16-34.

Higgins, T., Lee, J., Kwon, J., & Trope, Y. (1975). When combining intrinsic motivation undermines interest: A test of activity engagement theory. *Journal of Personality and Social Psychology, 68,* 749-767.

Hilgard, E. R., & Hilgard, J. R. (1983). *Hypnosis in the relief of pain* (Rev. ed.). Los Altos, CA: Kaufman.

Hiroto, D. S. (1974). Locus of control and learned helplessness. *Journal of Experimental Psychology, 102*, 187-193.

Hiroto, D. S., & Seligman, M. E. P. (1975). Generality of learned helplessness in man. *Journal of Personality and Social Psychology, 31*, 311-327.

Hirt, M., & Genshaft, J. L. (1981). Immunization and reversibility of cognitive deficits due to learned helplessness. *Personality and Individual Differences, 2*, 191-196.

Hochschild, A. R. (1983). *The managed heart*. Berkeley: University of California Press.

Hodgson, R., & Rachman, S. (1974). Desynchrony in measures of fear. *Behaviour Research and Therapy, 12*, 319-326.

Hoebel, B. G., & Teitelbaum, G. (1966). Weight regulation in normal and hypothalamic hyperphagic rats. *Journal of Comparative and Physiological Psychology, 61*, 189-193.

Holahan, C. K., & Holahan, C. J. (1987). Self-efficacy, social support, and depression in aging: A longitudinal analysis. *Journal of Gerontology, 42*, 65-68.

Holmes, D. S. (1974). Investigation of repression: Differential recall of material experimentally or naturally associated with ego threat. *Psychological Bulletin, 81*, 632-653.

Holmes, D. S. (1990). The evidence for repression: An examination of sixty years of research. In J. L. Singer (Ed.), *Repression and dissociation* (pp. 85-102). Chicago: University of Chicago Press.

Holmes, T. H., & Rahe, R. H. (1967). The social readjustment rating scale. *Journal of Psychosomatic Research, 11*, 213-218.

Holstedge, G., Kuypers, H. G. J. M., & Dekker, J. J. (1977). The organization of the bulbar fibre connections to the trigeminal, facial, and hypoglossal motor nuclei: II. An autoradiographic tracing study in cat. *Brain, 100*, 265-286.

Holt, E. B. (1931). *Animal drive and the learning process*. New York: Holt.

Holt, R. R. (1980). Loevinger's measure of ego development: Reliability and national norms for male and female short forms. *Journal of Personality and Social Psychology, 39*, 909-920.

Holt, R. R. (1989). *Freud reappraised: A fresh look at psychoanalytic theory*. New York: Guilford Press.

Hom, Jr., H. L. (1994). Can you predict the overjustification effect? *Teaching of Psychology, 21*, 36-37.

Horowitz, M. J., Wilner, N., Kaltreidr, N., & Alvarez, W. (1980). Signs and symptoms of post-traumatic stress disorder. *Archives of General Psychology, 37*, 85-92.

Horvath, P., & Zuckerman, M. (1993). Sensation seeking, risk appraisal, and risky behavior. *Personality and Individual Differences, 14*, 41-52.

Horvath, T. (1979). Correlates of physical beauty in men and women. *Social Behavior and Personality, 7*, 145-151.

Horvath, T. (1981). Physical attractiveness: The influence of selected torso parameters. *Archives of Sexual Behavior, 10*, 21-24.

Huber, V. L. (1985). Effects of task difficulty, goal setting, and strategy on performance of a heuristic task. *Journal of Applied Psychology, 70*, 492-504.

Hudley, C., & Graham, S. (1993). An attributional intervention to reduce peer-directed aggression among African-American boys. *Child Development, 64*, 124-138.

Huebner, R. R., & Izard, C. E. (1988). Mothers' responses to infants' facial expressions of sadness, anger, and physical distress. *Motivation and Emotion, 12*, 185-196.

Hull, C. L. (1943). *Principles of behavior*. New York: Appleton-Century-Crofts.

Hull, C. L. (1952). *A behavior system: An introduction to behavior theory concerning the individual organism*. New Haven: Yale University Press.

Hunt, J. M. (1965). Intrinsic motivation and its role in psychological development. In D. Levine (Ed.), *Nebraska symposium on motivation* (Vol. 13, pp. 189-282). Lincoln: University of Nebraska Press.

Hupka, R. B. (1984). Jealousy: Compound emotion or label for a particular situation. *Motivation and Emotion, 8*, 141-155.

Hymbaugh, K., & Garrett, J. (1974). Sensation seeking among skydivers. *Perceptual and Motor Skills, 38*, 118.

Isen, A. M. (1970). Success, failure, attention, and reactions to others: The warm glow of success. *Journal of Personality and Social Psychology, 15*, 294-301.

Isen, A. M. (1984). Toward understanding the role of affect in cognition. In R. Wyer & T. Srull (Eds.), *Handbook of social cognition* (pp. 179-236). Hillsdale, NJ: Erlbaum.

Isen, A. M. (1987). Positive affect, cognitive processes, and social behavior. In L. Berkowitz (Ed.), *Advances in experimental social psychology* (Vol. 20, pp. 203-253). New York: Academic Press.

Isen, A. M., Clark, M. S., & Schwartz, M. F. (1976). Duration of the effects of good mood on helping: "Footprints in the sands of time." *Journal of Personality and Social Psychology, 34*, 385-393.

Isen, A. M., Daubman, K. A., & Nowicki, G. P. (1987). Positive affect facilitates creative problem-solving. *Journal of Personality and Social Psychology, 51*, 1122-1131.

Isen, A. M., & Geva, N. (1987). The influence of positive affect on acceptable level of risk: The person with a large canoe has a large worry. *Organizational Behavior and Human Decision Processes, 39*, 145-154.

Isen, A. M., Johnson, M. M. S., Mertz, E., & Robinson, G. F. (1985). The influence of positive affect on the unusualness of word associations. *Journal of Personality and Social Psychology, 48*, 1413-1426.

Isen, A. M., & Levin, P. F. (1972). The effect of feeling good on helping: Cookies and kindness. *Journal of Personality and Social Psychology, 21*, 384-388.

Isen, A. M., & Means, B. (1983). The influence of positive affect on decision-making strategy. *Social Cognition, 2*, 18-31.

Isen, A. M., Niedenthal, P., & Cantor, N. (1992). An influence of positive affect on social categorization. *Motivation and Emotion, 16*, 65-78.

Isen, A. M., & Nowicki, G. P. (1981). *Positive affect and creative problem solving*. Paper presented at the annual meeting of the Cognitive Science Society, Berkeley, CA.

Isen, A. M., & Patrick, R. (1983). The effect of positive feelings on risk-taking: When the chips are down. *Organizational Behavior and Human Performance, 31*, 194-202.

Isen, A. M., & Reeve, J. (1996). *The influence of positive affect on intrinsic motivation*. Unpublished manuscript, Cornell University.

Isen, A. M., Rosenzweig, A. S., & Young, M. J. (1991). The influence of positive affect on clinical problem solving. *Medical Decision Making, 11*, 221-227.

Isen, A. M., Shalker, T., Clark, M., & Karp, L. (1978). Affect, accessibility of material in memory, and behavior: A cognitive loop? *Journal of Personality and Social Psychology, 36*, 1-12.

Iso-Ahola, S. E. (1977). Immediate attributional effects of success and failure in the field: Testing some laboratory hypotheses. *European Journal of Social Psychology, 7*, 275-296.

Iversen, L., & Sabroe, S. (1989). Psychological well-being among unemployed and employed people after a company close down: A longitudinal study. *Journal of Social Issues, 44*, 141-152.

Iwata, B. A. (1987). Negative reinforcement in applied behavior analysis: An emerging technology. *Journal of Applied Behavior Analysis, 20*, 361-378.

Izard, C. E. (1971). *The face of emotion*. New York: Appleton-Century-Crofts.

Izard, C. E. (1972). *Patterns of emotion: A new analysis of anxiety and depression*. New York: Academic Press.

Izard, C. E. (1975). Patterns of emotion and emotion communication in hostility and aggression. In P. Pliner, L. Kammer, & T. Alloway (Eds.), *Nonverbal communication of aggression*. New York: Plenum.

Izard, C. E. (1979). Emotions as motivations: An evolutionary-developmental perspective. In R. A. Dienstbier (Ed.), *Nebraska symposium on motivation: Human emotion* (pp. 163–200). Lincoln: University of Nebraska Press.

Izard, C. E. (1982). Comments on emotion and cognition: Can there be a working relationship? In M. S. Clark & S. T. Fiske (Eds.), *Affect and cognition*. Hillsdale, NJ: Lawrence Erlbaum.

Izard, C. E. (1989). The structure and functions of emotions: Implications for cognition, motivation, and personality. In I. S. Cohen (Ed.), *The G. Stanley Hall lecture series* (Vol. 9, pp. 39–73). Washington, DC: APA.

Izard, C. E. (1990). Facial expressions and the regulation of emotions. *Journal of Personality and Social Psychology, 58*, 487–498.

Izard, C. E. (1991). *The psychology of emotions*. New York: Plenum.

Izard, C. E. (1992). Basic emotions, relations among the emotions, and emotion-cognition relations. *Psychological Review, 99*, 561–565.

Izard, C. E. (1993). Four systems for emotion activation: Cognitive and noncognitive development. *Psychological Review, 100*, 68–90.

Izard, C. E. (1994). Innate and universal facial expressions: Evidence from developmental and cross-cultural research. *Psychological Bulletin, 115*, 288–299.

Izard, C. E., Hembree, E. A., Dougherty, L. M., & Spizzirri, C. C. (1983). Changes in facial expressions of 2- to 19-month-old infants following acute pain. *Developmental Psychology, 19*, 418–426.

Izard, C. E., Huebner, R. R. Risser, D., McGinnes, G., & Dougherty, L. (1980). The young infant's ability to reproduce discrete emotion expressions. *Developmental Psychology, 16*, 132–140.

Izard, C. E., Malatesta, C. Z. (1987). Perspectives on emotional development: I. Differential emotions theory of early emotional development. In J. D. Osotsky (Ed.), *Handbook of infant development* (Ed. 2, pp. 494–554). New York: Wiley-Interscience.

Jackson, D. N. (1974). *Manual for the Personality Research Form*. Goshen, NY: Research Psychologists Press.

Jacobs, K. W., & Koeppel, J. C. (1974). Psychological correlates of the mobility decision. *Bulletin of the Psychodynamic Society, 3*, 330–332.

Jacobs, W. J., & Nadel, L. (1985). Stress-induced recovery of fears and phobias. *Psychological Review, 92*, 512–531.

James, W. (1884). What is an emotion? *Mind, 9*, 188–205.

James, W. (1894). The physical basis of emotion. *Psychological Review, 1*, 516–529.

James, W. (1890). *The principles of psychology* (2 Vols.). New York: Henry Holt.

Janis, I. L., & Field, P. B. (1959). The Janis and Field Personality Questionnaire. In C. I. Hovland & I. J. Janis (Eds.), *Personality and persuasibility*. New Haven: Yale University Press.

Jeffrey, D. B., & Knauss, M. R. (1981). The etiologies, treatments, and assessments of obesity. In S. N. Haynes & L. Gannon (Eds.), *Psychosomatic disorders: A psychophysiological approach to etiology and treatment* (pp. 269–319). New York: Praeger.

Jenkins, S. R. (1987). Need for achievement and women's careers over 14 years: Evidence for occupational structural effects. *Journal of Personality and Social Psychology, 53*, 922–932.

Jenkins, S. R. (1996). Self-definition in thought, action, and life path choices. *Personality and Social Psychology Bulletin, 22*, 99–111.

Jobe, J. B., Holgate, S. H., & Sorapansky, T. A. (1983). Risk-taking as motivation for volunteering for a hazardous experiment. *Journal of Personality, 51*, 95–107.

Johnson, D. W., & Johnson, R. T. (1985). Motivational processes in cooperative, competitive, and individualistic learning situations. In C. Ames & R. Ames (Eds.), *Research on motivation in education: The classroom milieu* (Vol. 2, pp. 249–286). Orlando, FL: Academic Press.

Johnson, R. W., Kelly, R. J., & LeBlanc, B. A. (1995). Motivational basis of dissonance: Aversive consequences or inconsistency. *Personality and Social Psychology Bulletin, 21*, 850–855.

Johnson-Laird, P. N., & Oatley, K. (1989). The language of emotions: An analysis of a semantic field. *Cognition and Emotion, 3*, 81–123.

Johnson-Laird, P. N., & Oatley, K. (1992). Basic emotions, rationality and folk theory. *Cognition and Emotion, 6*, 201–223.

Jones, E. E. (1985). Major developments in social psychology during the past five decades. In G. Lindzey & E. Aronson (Ed.), *Handbook of social psychology: Theory and method* (Vol. 1, pp. 47–107). New York: Random House.

Jones, E. E., & Davis, K. E. (1965). From acts to dispositions: The attribution process in person perception. In L. Berkowitz (Ed.), *Advances in experimental social psychology* (Vol. 2). *New York: Academic Press.*

Jones, E. E., & Nisbett, R. E. (1971). *The actor and the observer: Divergent perceptions of the causes of behavior*. Morristown, NJ: General Learning Press.

Jones, E. E., & Nisbett, R. E. (1972). The actor and the observer: Divergent perceptions of the causes of behavior. In E. E. Jones et al. (Eds.), *Attribution: Perceiving the causes of behavior*. Morristown, NJ: General Learning Press.

Jones, S. L., Nation, J. R., & Massad, P. (1977). Immunization against learned helplessness in man. *Journal of Abnormal Psychology, 86*, 75–83.

Josephs, R. A., Markus, H. R., & Tafarodi, R. W. (1992). Gender and self-esteem. *Journal of Personality and Social Psychology, 63*, 391–402.

Kagan, J. (1972). Motives and development. *Journal of Personality and Social Psychology, 22*, 51–66.

Kagan, J. (1989). Temperamental contributions to social behavior. *American Psychologist, 44*, 668–674.

Kagan, J., Reznick, J. S., Clarke, C., Snidman, N., & Garcia-Coll, C. (1984). Behavioral inhibition to the unfamiliar. *Child Development, 55*, 2212–2225.

Kagan, J., Reznick, J. S., & Snidman, N. (1988). Biological basis of childhood shyness. *Science, 240*, 167–171.

Kahneman, D. (1973). *Attention and effort*. Englewood Cliffs, NJ: Prentice-Hall.

Kapp, B. S., Pascoe, J. P., & Bixler, M. A. (1984). The amygdala: A neuroanatomical systems approach to its contributions to aversive conditioning. In N. Buttlers & L. R. Squire (Eds.), *Neuropsychology of memory* (pp. 473–488). New York: Guilford.

Karabenick, S. A., & Yousseff, Z. I. (1968). Performance as a function of achievement level and perceived difficulty. *Journal of Personality and Social Psychology, 10*, 414–419.

Kasser, T., & Ryan, R. M. (1993). A dark side of the American dream: Correlates of financial success as a central life aspiration. *Journal of Personality and Social Psychology, 65*, 410–422.

Kasser, T., & Ryan, R. M. (1996). Further examining the American dream: Differential correlates of intrinsic and extrinsic goals. *Personality and Social Psychology Bulletin, 22*, 280–287.

Katzell, R. A., & Thompson, D. E. (1990). Work motivation: Theory and practice. *American Psychologist, 45*, 144–153.

Kazdin, A. E. (1979). Imagery elaboration and self-efficacy in the covert modeling treatment of unassertive behavior. *Journal of Consulting and Clinical Psychology, 47*, 725-733.

Kazdin, A. E. (1980). *Behavior modification in applied settings* (rev. ed.). Homewood, IL: Dorsey Press.

Keating, C. F., Mazur, A., & Segall, M. H. (1981). A cross-cultural exploration of physiognomic traits of dominance and happiness. *Ethology and Sociobiology, 2*, 41-48.

Keesey, R. E. (1980). A set-point analysis of the regulation of body weight. In A. J. Stunkard (Ed.), *Obesity* (pp. 144-165). Philadelphia: Saunders.

Keesey, R. E., Boyle, P. C., Kemnitz, J. W., & Mitchell, J. S. (1976). The role of the lateral hypothalamus in determining the body weight set point. In D. Novin et al. (Eds.), *Hunger: Basic mechanisms and clinical implications*. New York: Raven Press.

Keesey, R. E., & Powley, T. L. (1975). Hypothalamic regulation of body weight. *American Scientist, 63*, 558-565.

Kelley, H. H. (1967). Attribution theory in social psychology. In D. Levine (Ed.), *Nebraska symposium on motivation* (Vol. 15, pp. 192-238). Lincoln: University of Nebraska Press.

Kelley, H. H. (1973). The process of causal attribution. *American Psychologist, 28*, 107-128.

Kellman, H. C., & Baron, R. M. (1968). Inconsistency as a psychological signal. In R. P. Abelson et al. (Eds.), *Theories of cognitive consistency: A sourcebook* (Chpt. 22, pp. 331-336). Chicago: Rand McNally.

Kelly, A. E., & Kahn, J. H. (1994). Effects of suppression of personal intrusive thought. *Journal of Personality and Social Psychology, 66*, 998-1006.

Kemper, T. D. (1987). How many emotions are there? Wedding the social and the autonomic components. *American Sociological Review, 93*, 263-289.

Kiesler, C. A., & Pallak, M. S. (1976). Arousal properties of dissonance manipulations. *Psychological Bulletin, 83*, 1014-1025.

Kihlstrom, J. F., & Cantor, N. (1984). Mental representations of the self. In L. Berkowitz (Ed.), *Advances in experimental and social psychology* (Vol. 17, pp. 2-47). New York: Academic Press.

Kimble, G. A. (1990). Mother nature's bag of tricks is small. *Psychological Science, 1*, 36-41.

Kirkpatrick, L. A., & Shaver, P. (1988). Fear and affiliation reconsidered from a stress and coping perspective: The importance of cognitive clarity and fear reduction. *Journal of Social and Clinical Psychology, 7*, 214-233.

Klein, C. S. (1967). Peremptory ideation: Structure and force in motivated ideas. In R. R. Holt (Ed.), Motives and thought: Psychoanalytic essays in honor of David Rapaport. *Psychological Issues, 5* (Monograph No. 18/19), 80-128.

Klein, D. C., & Seligman, M. E. P. (1976). Reversal of performance deficits in learned helplessness and depression. *Journal of Abnormal Psychology, 85*, 11-26.

Klein, H. J. (1991). Control theory and understanding motivated behavior: A different conclusion. *Motivation and Emotion, 15*, 29-44.

Klein, H. J., Whitener, E. M., & Ilgen, D. R. (1990). The role of goal specificity in the goal-setting process. *Motivation and Emotion, 14*, 179-193.

Kleinginna, Jr., P. R., & Kleinginna, A. M. (1981). Categorized list of motivation definitions, with a suggestion for a consensual definition. *Motivation and Emotion, 5*, 263-291.

Klesges, R. C., Coates, T. J., Brown, G., Sturgeon-Tillisch, J., Moldenhauer-Klesges, L. M., Holzer, B., Woolfrey, J., & Vollmer, J. (1983). Parental influences on children's eating behavior and relative weight. *Journal of Applied Behavioral Analysis, 16*, 371-378.

Klien, G. (1954). Need and regulation. In M. R. Jones (Ed.), *Nebraska symposium on motivation* (Vol. 2, pp. 224-274). Lincoln: University of Nebraska Press.

Klinnert, M. D., Campos, J. J., Sorce, J. F., Emde, R. N., & Suejda, M. (1983). Emotions as behavior regulators: Social referencing in infancy. In R. Plutchik & H. Kellerman (Eds.), *Emotion: Theory, research, and experience, emotions in early development* (Vol. 2, pp. 57-86). New York: Academic Press.

Klose, D. A. (1995). M. Scott Peck's analysis of human evil: A critical review. *Journal of Personality and Social Psychology, 35,* 37-66.

Knox, R. E., & Inkster, J. A. (1968). Postdecision dissonance at post time. *Journal of Personality and Social Psychology, 8,* 319-323.

Koch, S. (1951). The current status of motivational psychology. *Psychological Review, 58,* 147-153.

Koestner, R., Bernieri, F., & Zuckerman, M. (1992). Self-regulation and consistency between attitudes, traits, and behaviors. *Personality and Social Psychology Bulletin, 18,* 52-59.

Koestner, R., Ryan, R. M., Bernieri, F., & Holt, K. (1984). Setting limits on children's behavior: The differential effects of controlling versus informational styles on intrinsic motivation and creativity. *Journal of Personality, 52,* 233-248.

Koestner, R., Zuckerman, M., and Koestner, J. (1987). Praise, involvement, and intrinsic motivation. *Journal of Personality and Social Psychology, 53,* 383-390.

Kohn, A. (1993). *Punished by rewards: The trouble with gold stars, incentive plans, A's, praise, and other bribes.* Boston: Houghton Mifflin.

Kowaz, A. M., & Marcia, J. E. (1991). Development and validation of a measure of Eriksonian industry. *Journal of Personality and Social Psychology, 60,* 390-397.

Kramer, R. (1995). The birth of client-centered therapy: Carl Rogers, Otto Rank, and "The Beyond." *Journal of Humanistic Psychology, 35,* 54-110.

Krantz, P. J., & McClannahan, L. E. (1993). Teaching children with autism to initiate to peers: Effects of a script-fading procedure. *Journal of Applied Behavior Analysis, 26,* 121-132.

Kraut, R. E., & Johnston, R. E. (1979). Social and emotional messages of smiling: An ethological approach. *Journal of Personality and Social Psychology, 37,* 1539-1553.

Krettek, J. E., & Price, J. L. (1978). Amygdaloid projections to subcortical structures within the basal forebrain and brainstem in the rat and cat. *Journal of Comparative Neurology, 178,* 225-254.

Kroger, J. (1993). The role of historical context in the identity formation process of late adolescence. *Youth and Society, 24,* 363-376.

Kruglanski, A. W., Riter, A., Amitai, A., Margolin, B., Shabtai, L., & Zaksh, D. (1975). Can money enhance intrinsic motivation? A test of the content-consequence hypothesis. *Journal of Personality and Social Psychology, 31,* 744-750.

Kuhl, J. (1978). Standard setting and risk preference: An elaboration of the theory of achievement motivation and an empirical test. *Psychological Review, 85,* 239-248.

Kuhl, J., & Blankenship, V. (1979). The dynamic theory of achievement motivation. *Psychological Review, 86,* 141-151.

Kuhlman, D. M. (1975). Individual differences in casino gambling? In N. R. Eadington (Ed.), *Gambling and society.* Springfield, IL: Thomas.

Kuhn, T. S. (1962). *The structure of scientific revolutions.* Chicago: University of Chicago Press.

Kulik, J. A., Mahler, H. I. M., & Earnest, A. (1994). Social comparison and affiliation under threat: Going beyond the affiliative-choice paradigm. *Journal of Personality and Social Psychology, 66,* 301-309.

Kuo, Z. Y. (1921). Giving up instincts in psychology. *Journal of Philosophy, 17,* 645-664.

Labott, S. M., Martin, R. B., Eason, P. S., & Berkey, E. Y. (1991). Social reactions to the expression of emotion. *Cognition and Emotion, 5,* 397-417.

Lacey, J. I., Kagan, J., Lacey, B. C., & Moss, H. A. (1963). The visceral level: Situational determinants and behavioral correlates of autonomic responses. In P. Knapp (Ed.), *Expression of the emotions in man*. New York: International Universities Press.

Laird, J. D. (1974). Self-attribution of emotion: The effects of expressive behavior on the quality of emotional experience. *Journal of Personality and Social Psychology, 29*, 475–486.

Laird, J. D. (1984). Facial response and emotion. *Journal of Personality and Social Psychology, 47*, 909–917.

Laird, J. D., Wagener, J. J., Halal, M., & Szegda, M. (1982). Remembering what you feel: The effects of emotion on memory. *Journal of Personality and Social Psychology, 42*, 646–657.

Lane, J. D., & Wegner, D. M. (1995). The cognitive consequences of secrecy. *Journal of Personality and Social Psychology, 69*, 237–253.

Lang, P. J. (1994). The varieties of emotional experience: A mediation of James-Lange theory. *Psychological Review, 101*, 211–221.

Lange, C. (1885). The emotions (translated, 1922, by Istar A. Haupt for K. Dunlap, Ed.), *The emotions*. Baltimore: Williams & Wilkins.

Lange, R. D., & James, W. (1922). *The emotions*. Baltimore: Williams & Wilkins.

Langer, E. (1975). The illusion of control. *Journal of Personality and Social Psychology, 32*, 311–328.

Langer, E., & Rodin, J. (1976). The effects of choice and enhanced personal responsibility for the aged: A field experiment in an institutionalized setting. *Journal of Personality and Social Psychology, 34*, 191–198.

Lansing, J. B., & Heyns, R. W. (1959). Need affiliation and frequency of four types of communication. *Journal of Abnormal and Social Psychology, 58*, 365–372.

Lanzetta, J. T., Cartwright-Smith, J. E., Kleck, R. E. (1976). Effects of nonverbal dissimulation of emotional experience and autonomic arousal. *Journal of Personality and Social Psychology, 33*, 354–370.

LaPorte, R. E., & Nath, R. (1976). Role of performance goals in prose learning. *Journal of Educational Psychology, 68*, 260–264.

Larsen, R. J. (1988, June). *Individual differences in affect intensity*. Paper presented at the Motivation and Emotion conference at Nags Head, NC.

Larsen, R. J., & Diener, E. (1987). Affect intensity as an individual difference characteristic: A review. *Journal of Research in Personality, 21*, 1–39.

Larsen, R. J., Diener, E., & Cropanzano, R. S. (1987). Cognitive operations associated with individual differences in affect intensity. *Journal of Personality and Social Psychology, 53*, 767–774.

Larsen, R. J., Diener, E., & Emmons, R. A. (1986). Affect intensity and reactions to daily life events. *Journal of Personality and Social Psychology, 51*, 803–814.

Larsen, R. J., Kasimatis, M., & Frey, K. (1992). Facilitating the furrowed brow: An unobtrusive test of the facial feedback hypothesis applied to unpleasant affect. *Cognition and Emotion, 6*, 321–338.

Larsen, R. J., & Ketelaar, T. (1991). Personality and susceptibility to positive and negative emotional states. *Journal of Personality and Social Psychology, 61*, 132–140.

Latham, G. P., & Baldes, J. J. (1975). The "practical significance" of Locke's theory of goal setting. *Journal of Applied Psychology, 60*, 122–124.

Latham, G. P., Erez, M., & Locke, E. A. (1988). Resolving scientific disputes by the joint design of crucial experiments by the antagonists: Application to the Erez-Latham dispute regarding participation in goal setting. *Journal of Applied Psychology, 73*, 753–772.

Latham, G. P., & Locke, E. A. (1975). Increasing productivity with decreasing time limits: A field replication of Parkinson's law. *Journal of Applied Psychology, 60*, 524-526.

Latham, G. P., Mitchell, T. R., & Dossett, D. L. (1978). Importance of participative goal setting and anticipated rewards on goal difficulty and job performance. *Journal of Applied Psychology, 63*, 163-171.

Latham, G. P., & Saari, L. M. (1979). Importance of supportive relationships in goal setting. *Journal of Applied Psychology, 64*, 151-156.

Latham, G. P., & Yukl, G. A. (1975). Assigned versus participative goal setting with educated and uneducated woods workers. *Journal of Applied Psychology, 60*, 299-302.

Latham, G. P., & Yukl, G. A. (1976). Effects of assigned and participative goal setting on performance and job satisfaction. *Journal of Applied Psychology, 61*, 166-171.

Lau, R. R., & Russell, D. (1980). Attributions in the sports pages. *Journal of Personality and Social Psychology, 39*, 29-38.

Lavrakas, P. J. (1975). Female preferences for male physiques. *Journal of Research in Personality, 9*, 324-334.

Law, A., Logan, H., & Baron, R. S. (1994). Desire for control, felt control, and stress inoculation training during dental treatment. *Journal of Personality and Social Psychology, 67*, 926-936.

Lazarus, R. S. (1966). *Psychological stress and the coping process*. New York: McGraw-Hill.

Lazarus, R. S. (1968). Emotions and adaptation: Conceptual and empirical relations. In W. J. Arnold (Ed.), *Nebraska symposium on motivation* (Vol. 16, pp. 175-266). Lincoln: University of Nebraska.

Lazarus, R. S. (1982). Thoughts on the relations between emotion and cognition. *American Psychologist, 37*, 1019-1024.

Lazarus, R. S. (1983). The costs and benefits of denial. In S. Bresnitz (Ed.), *The denial of stress* (pp. 1-32). New York: International Universities Press.

Lazarus, R. S. (1984). On the primacy of cognition. *American Psychologist, 39*, 124-129.

Lazarus, R. S. (1991a). *Emotion and adaptation*. New York: Oxford University Press.

Lazarus, R. S. (1991b). Progress on a cognitive-motivational-relational theory of emotion. *American Psychologist, 46*, 819-834.

Lazarus, R. (1994). Universal antecedents of the emotions. In P. Ekman & R. J. Davidson (Eds.), *The nature of emotion: Fundamental questions* (pp. 163-171). New York: Oxford University Press.

Lazarus, R. S., & DeLongis, A. (1983). Psychological stress and coping in aging. *American Psychologist, 38*, 245-254.

Lazarus, R. S., & Folkman, S. (1984). *Stress, appraisal, and coping*. New York: Springer-Verlag.

Lazarus, R. S., & Smith, C. A. (1988). Knowledge and appraisal in the cognition-emotion relationship. *Cognition and Emotion, 2*, 281-300.

Leavitt, R. L., & Power, M. B. (1989). Emotional socialization in the postmodern era: Children and day care. *Social Psychology Quarterly, 52*, 35-43.

LeDoux, J. E. (1987). Emotion. In F. Plum (Ed.), *Handbook of psychology: I. The nervous system* (pp. 419-460). Bethesda, MD: American Physiological Society.

LeDoux, J. E. (1989). Cognitive-emotional interactions in the brain. *Cognition and Emotion, 3*, 267-289.

LeDoux, J. E. (1992a). Brain mechanisms of emotion and emotional learning. *Current Opinion in Neurobiology, 2*, 191-198.

LeDoux, J. E. (1992b). Emotion and the amygdala. In J. P. Aggleton (Ed.), *The amygdala: Neurobiological aspects of emotion, memory, and mental dysfunction* (pp. 339-351). New York: Wiley-Liss.

LeDoux, J. E., Iwata, J., Cicchetti, P., & Reis, D. J. (1988). Different projections of the central amygdaloid nucleus mediate autonomic and behavioral correlates of conditioned fear. *Journal of Neuroscience, 8*, 2517-2529.

Lefcourt, H. M., & Martin, R. A. (1986). *Humor and life stress: An antidote to adversity.* New York: Springer-Verlag.

Lehman, D. R., Ellard, D. R., & Wortman, C. B. (1986). Social support for the bereaved: Recipients' and providers' perspectives on what is helpful. *Journal of Consulting and Clinical Psychology, 54*, 438-446.

Lepper, M. R. (1981). Intrinsic and extrinsic motivation in children: Detrimental effects of superfluous social controls. In W. A. Collins (Ed.), *Aspects of the development of competence: The Minnesota symposium on child psychology* (Vol. 14, pp. 155-214). Hillsdale, NJ; Lawrence Erlbaum.

Lepper, M. R., & Greene, D. (1975). Turning play into work: Effects of adult surveillance and extrinsic rewards on children's intrinsic motivation. *Journal of Personality and Social Psychology, 31*, 479-486.

Lepper, M. R., & Greene, D. (Eds.) (1978). *The hidden costs of reward.* Hillsdale, NJ: Erlbaum.

Lepper, M. R., Greene, D., & Nisbett, R. E. (1973). Undermining children's intrinsic interest with extrinsic rewards: A test of the "overjustification" hypothesis. *Journal of Personality and Social Psychology, 28*, 129-137.

Levenson, H. M. (1981). Differentiating among internality, powerful others, and chance. In H. M. Lefcourt (Ed.), *Research with the locus of control construct: Vol. 1. Assessment methods* (pp. 15-63). New York: Academic Press.

Levenson, R. W. (1992). Autonomic nervous system differences among emotions. *Psychological Science, 3*, 23-27.

Levenson, R. W. (1994a). Human emotion: A functional view. In P. Ekman & R. J. Davidson (Eds.), *The nature of emotion: Fundamental questions* (pp. 123-126). New York: Oxford University Press.

Levenson, R. W. (1994b). The search for autonomic specificity. In P. Ekman & R. J. Davidson (Eds.), *The nature of emotion: Fundamental questions* (pp. 252-257). New York: Oxford University Press.

Levenson, R. W., Carstensen, L. L., Friesen, W. V., & Ekman, P. (1991). Emotion, physiology, and expression in old age. *Psychology and Aging, 6*, 28-35.

Levenson, R. W., Ekman, P., & Friesen, W. V. (1990). Voluntary facial action generates emotion-specific autonomic nervous system activity. *Psychophysiology, 27*, 363-384.

Lewin, K. (1935). *A dynamic theory of personality.* New York: McGraw-Hill.

Lindgren, H. C. (1976). Measuring need to achieve by NachNaff scale: a forced choice questionnaire. *Psychological Reports, 39*, 907-910.

Lindsley, D. B. (1957). Psychophysiology and motivation. In M. R. Jones (Ed.), *Nebraska symposium on motivation* (Vol. 5, pp. 44-105). Lincoln: University of Nebraska Press.

Linville, P. W. (1982). Affective consequences of complexity regarding the self and others. In M. S. Clark & S. T. Fiske (Eds.), *Affect and cognition* (pp. 79-109). Hillsdale, NJ: Erlbaum.

Litle, P., & Zuckerman, M. (1986). Sensation seeking and music preferences. *Personality and Individual Differences, 4*, 575-578.

Littig, L. W. (1963). Effects of motivation on probability preferences. *Journal of Personality, 31*, 417-427.

Lockard, J. S., Allen, D. J., Schielle, B. J., & Wiemer, M. J. (1978). Human postural signals: Stance, weight-shifts and social distance as intention movements to depart. *Animal Behavior, 26*, 219-224.

Locke, E. A. (1968). Toward a theory of task motivation and incentives. *Organizational Behavior and Human Performance, 3*, 157-189.

Locke, E. A., & Bryan, J. F. (1969). The directing function of goals in task performance. *Organizational Behavior and Human Performance, 4*, 35-42.

Locke, E. A., Chah, D. O., Harrison, S., & Lustgarten, N. (1989). Separating the effects of goal specificity from goal level. *Organizational Behavior and Human Decision Processes, 43*, 270-287.

Locke, E. A., & Latham, G. P. (1984). *Goal-setting: A motivational technique that works!* Englewood Cliffs, NJ: Prentice Hall.

Locke, E. A., & Latham, G. P. (1990). *A theory of goal setting and task performance.* Englewood Cliffs, NJ: Prentice Hall.

Locke, E. A., Shaw, K. N., Saari, L. M., & Latham, G. P. (1981). Goal setting and task performance: 1969-1980. *Psychological Bulletin, 90*, 125-152.

Loevinger, J. (1976). Stages of ego development. In J. Loevinger *Ego development* (pp. 13-28). San Francisco: Jossey-Bass.

Loevinger, J., Cohn, L., Bonneville, L., Redmore, C., Streich, D., & Sargent, M. (1985). Ego development in college. *Journal of Personality and Social Psychology, 48*, 947-962.

Loevinger, J., & Wessler, R. (1970). *Measuring ego development: Vol. 1. Construction and use of a sentence completion test.* San Francisco: Jossey-Bass.

Loewenstein, G. (1994). The psychology of curiosity: A review and reinterpretation. *Psychological Bulletin, 116*, 75-98.

Lorenz, K. (1965). *Evolution and modification of behavior: A critical examination of the concepts of the "learned" and the "innate" elements of behavior.* Chicago: The University of Chicago Press.

Losch, M., & Cacioppo, J. (1990). Cognitive dissonance may enhance sympathetic tonus, but attitudes are changed to reduce negative affect rather than arousal. *Journal of Personality and Social Psychology, 51*, 55-65.

Lowe, M. R. (1993). The effects of dieting on eating behavior: A three-factor model. *Psychological Bulletin, 114*, 100-121.

Lowe, M. R., & Fisher, E. B. (1983). Emotional reactivity, emotional eating, and obesity: A naturalistic review. *Journal of Behavioral Medicine, 6*, 135-149.

Lykken, D. T., & Tellegen, A. (1993). Is human mating adventitious or the result of lawful choice? A twin study of mate selection. *Journal of Personality and Social Psychology, 65*, 56-68.

MacDowell, K. A., & Mandler, G. (1989). Constructions of emotion: Discrepancy, arousal, and mood. *Motivation and Emotion, 13*, 105-124.

MacIver, D. J., Stipek, D. J., & Daniel, D. H. (1991). Explaining within-semester changes in student effort in junior high school and senior high school courses. *Journal of Educational Psychology, 83*, 201-211.

MacKinnon, N. J. (1994). *Symbolic interactionism as affect control.* Albany, NY: SUNY Press.

Maehr, M. L., & Kleiber, D. A. (1980). The graying of achievement motivation. *American Psychologist, 36*, 787-793.

Mahoney, E. R. (1983). *Human sexuality.* New York: McGraw-Hill.

Malmo, R. B. (1959). Activation: A neurological dimension. *Psychological Review, 66*, 367-386.

Manderlink, G., & Harackiewicz, J. M. (1984). Proximal versus distal goal setting and intrinsic motivation. *Journal of Personality and Social Psychology, 47*, 918-928.

Mandler, G. (1975). *Mind and emotion.* New York: John Wiley & Sons.

Mandler, G. (1982). The structure of value: Accounting for taste. In M. S. Clark & S. T. Fiske (Eds.), *Affect and cognition* (pp. 3-36). Hillsdale, NJ: Lawrence Erlbaum.

Mandler, G. (1984). *Mind and body: Psychology of emotion and stress.* New York: Norton.

Manstead, A. S. R. (1991). Emotion in social life. *Cognition and Emotion, 5*, 353-362.

Marcia, J. E. (1966). Development and validation of ego identity status. *Journal of Personality and Social Psychology, 3*, 551-558.

Marcia, J. E. (1980). Identity in adolescence. In J. Adelson (Ed.), *Handbook of adolescent psychology*. New York: Wiley.

Marcia, J. E., Waterman, A. S., Matteson, D. R., Archer, S. L., & Orlofsky, J. L. (1993). *Ego identity: A handbook for psychosocial research*. New York: Springer-Verlag.

Markus, H. (1977). Self-schemata and processing information about the self. *Journal of Personality and Social Psychology, 35*, 63-78.

Markus H. (1983). Self-knowledge: An expected view. *Journal of Personality, 51*, 543-565.

Markus, H., Cross, S., & Wurf, E. (1990). The role of self-esteem in competence. In R. J. Sternberg & J. Kolligian (Eds.), *Competence considered* (pp. 205-225). New Haven: Yale University Press.

Markus, H., & Nurius, P. (1986). Possible selves. *American Psychologist, 41*, 954-969.

Markus, H., & Sentisk, K. (1982). The self in social information processing. In J. Suls (Ed.), *Psychological perspectives on the self* (Vol. 1, pp. 41-70). Hillsdale, NJ: Erlbaum.

Markus, H., & Wurf, E. (1987). The dynamic self-concept: A social psychological perspective. *Annual Review of Psychology, 38*, 299-337.

Marlatt, G. P., & Parks, G. A. (1982). Self-management of addictive behaviors. In P. Karoly & F. H. Kanfer (Eds.), *Self-management and behavior change* (pp. 443-488). New York: Pergamon.

Marsh, H. W. (1990). Causal ordering of academic self-concept and academic achievement: A multivariate, longitudinal panel analysis. *Journal of Educational Psychology, 82*, 646-656.

Masling, J. (Ed.), (1983). *Empirical studies of psychoanalytic theories*. Hillsdale, NJ: Analytic Press.

Maslow, A. H. (1943). A theory of human motivation. *Psychological Review, 50*, 370-396.

Maslow, A. H. (1968). *Toward a psychology of being*. New York: Van Nostrand.

Maslow, A. H. (1971). *The farther reaches of human nature*. New York: Viking Press.

Maslow, A. H. (1987). *Motivation and personality* (3e). New York: Harper & Row.

Mason, A., & Blankenship, V. (1987). Power and affiliation motivation, stress, and abuse in intimate relationships. *Journal of Personality and Social Psychology, 52*, 203-210.

Masters, W. H., & Johnson, V. E. (1966). *Human sexual response*. Boston: Little, Brown.

Mathes, E. W. (1981). Maslow's hierarchy of needs as a guide for living. *Journal of Humanistic Psychology, 21*, 69-72.

Mathews, J. R., Hodson, G. D., Crist, W. B., & LaRoche, G. R. (1992). Teaching young children to use contact lenses. *Journal of Applied Behavior Analysis, 25*, 229-235.

Matsumoto, D. (1987). The role of facial response in the experience of emotion: More methodological problems and a meta-analysis. *Journal of Personality and Social Psychology, 52*, 769-774.

Mauro, R. (1988). Opponent processes in human emotions? An experimental investigation of hedonic contrast and affective interactions. *Motivation and Emotion, 12*, 333-351.

May, R. (Ed.), (1961). *Existential psychology*. New York: Random House.

May, R. (1982). The problem of evil: An open letter to Carl Rogers. *Journal of Humanistic Psychology, 22*, 10-21.

Mayer, D. J. (1952). The glucostatic theory of regulation of food intake and the problem of obesity. *Bulletin of the New England Medical Center, 14*, 43.

Mayer, D. J. (1953). Glucostatic mechanism of regulation of food intake. *New England Journal of Medicine, 249*, 13-16.

McAdams, D. P. (1980). A thematic coding system for the intimacy motive. *Journal of Research in Personality, 14*, 413-432.

McAdams, D. P. (1982a). Intimacy motivation. In A. J. Stewart (Ed.), *Motivation and society*. San Francisco: Jossey-Bass.

McAdams, D. P. (1982b). Experiences of intimacy and power: Relationships between social motives and autobiographical memory. *Journal of Personality and Social Psychology, 42*, 292-302.

McAdams, D. P., & Constantian, C. A. (1983). Intimacy and affiliation motives in daily living: An experience sampling analysis. *Journal of Personality and Social Psychology, 45*, 851-861.

McAdams, D. P., Healy, S., & Krause, S. (1984). Social motives and patterns of friendship. *Journal of Personality and Social Psychology, 47*, 828-838.

McAdams, D. P., Jackson, R. J., & Kirshnit, C. (1984). Looking, laughing, and smiling in dyads as a function of intimacy motivation and reciprocity. *Journal of Personality, 52*, 261-273.

McAdams, D. P., & Losoff, M. (1984). Friendship motivation in fourth and sixth graders:. A thematic analysis. *Journal of Social and Personal Relationships, 1*, 11-27.

McAdams, D. P., & Powers, J. (1981). Themes of intimacy in behavior and thought. *Journal of Personality and Social Psychology, 40*, 573-587.

McAdams, D. P., & Vaillant, G. E. (1982). Intimacy motivation and psychosocial adaptation: A longitudinal study. *Journal of Personality Assessment, 46*, 586-593.

McAuley, E., & Tammen, V. V. (1989). The effect of subjective and objective competitive outcomes on intrinsic motivation. *Journal of Sport and Exercise Psychology, 11*, 84-93.

McCaul, K. D., Holmes, D. S., & Solomon, S. (1982). Facial expression and emotion. *Journal of Personality and Social Psychology, 42*, 145-152.

McClelland, D. C. (1961). *The achieving society*. Princeton, NJ: Van Nostrand.

McClelland, D. C. (1965). Achievement and entrepreneurship: A longitudinal study. *Journal of Personality and Social Psychology, 1*, 389-392.

McClelland, D. C. (1975). *Power: The inner experience*. New York: Irvington.

McClelland, D. C. (1978). Managing motivation to expand human freedom. *American Psychologist, 33*, 201-210.

McClelland, D. C. (1980). Motive dispositions: The merits of operant and respondent measures. In L. Wheeler (Ed.), *Review of Personality and Social Psychology* (Vol. 1). Beverly Hills, CA: Sage.

McClelland, D. C. (1982). The need for power, sympathetic activation, and illness. *Motivation and Emotion, 6*, 31-41.

McClelland, D. C. (1985). *Human motivation*. San Francisco: Scott, Foresman.

McClelland, D. C. (1987). Characteristics of successful entrepreneurs. *The Journal of Creative Behavior, 21*, 219-233.

McClelland, D. C., Atkinson, J. W., Clark, R. A., & Lowell, E. L. (1953). *The achievement motive*. New York: Appleton-Century-Crofts.

McClelland, D. C., & Burnham, D. H. (March-April 1976). Power is the great motivator. *Harvard Business Review*, 100-110, 159-166.

McClelland, D. C., Coleman, C., Finn, K., & Winter, D. G. (1978). Motivation and maturity patterns in marital success. *Social Behavior and Personality, 6*, 163-171.

McClelland, D. C., Constantian, C., Pilon, D., & Stone, C. (1982). Effects of child-rearing practices on adult maturity. In D. C. McClelland (Ed.), *The development of social maturity*. New York: Irvington.

McClelland, D. C., Davis, W. B., Kalin, R., & Wanner, E. (1972). *The drinking man: Alcohol and human motivation*. New York: Free Press.

McClelland, D. C., & Pilon, D. A. (1983). Sources of adult motives in patterns of parent behavior in early childhood. *Journal of Personality and Social Psychology, 44*, 564-574.

McClelland, D. C., & Teague, G. (1975). Predicting risk preferences among power-related tasks. *Journal of Personality, 43*, 266-285.

McClelland, D. C., & Watson, R. I., Jr. (1973). Power motivation and risk-taking behavior. *Journal of Personality, 41*, 121-139.

McClelland, D. C., & Winter, D. G. (1969). *Motivating economic achievement*. New York: Free Press.

McCombs, B. L., & Pope, J. E. (1994). *Motivating hard to reach students*. Washington, DC: American Psychological Association.

McCoy, C. L., & Masters, J. C. (1985). The development of children's strategies for the social control of emotion. *Child Development, 56*, 1214-1222.

McDougall, W. (1908). *Introduction to social psychology*. London: Methuen.

McFarlin, D. B., & Blascovich, J. (1981). Effects of self-esteem and performance feedback on future affective preferences and cognitive expectations. *Journal of Personality and Social Psychology, 40*, 521-531.

McGinley, H., McGinley, P., & Nicholas, K. (1978). Smiling, body position and interpersonal attraction. *Bulletin of the Psychonomics Society, 12*, 21-24.

McGraw, K. O. (1978). The detrimental effects of reward on performance: A literature review and a prediction model. In M. R. Lepper & D. Greene (Eds.), *The hidden costs of reward* (pp. 33-60). New York: John Wiley.

McGraw, K. O., McCullers, J. C. (1979). Evidence of detrimental effects of extrinsic incentives on breaking a mental set. *Journal of Experimental Social Psychology, 15*, 285-294.

McHugh, P. R., & Moran, T. H. (1985). The stomach: A conception of its dynamic role in satiety. In J. M. Sprague & A. N. Epstein (Eds.), *Progress in psychobiology and physiological psychology* (Vol. 11, pp. 197-232). Orlando, FL: Academic Press.

McKeachie, W. J. (1976). Psychology in America's bicentennial year. *American Psychologist, 31*, 819-833.

McKeachie, W. J., Lin, Y., Milholland, J., & Issacson, R. (1966). Student affiliation motives, teacher warmth, and academic achievement. *Journal of Personality and Social Psychology, 4*, 457-461.

McNulty, S. E., & Swann, W. B., Jr. (1994). Identity negotiation in roommate relationships: The self as architect and consequence of social reality. *Journal of Personality and Social Psychology, 67*, 1012-1023.

Mednick, M. T., Mednick, S. A., & Mednick, E. V. (1964). Incubation of creative performance and specific associative priming. *Journal of Abnormal and Social Psychology, 69*, 84-88.

Medvec, V. H., Madey, S. F., & Gilovich, T. (1995). When less is more: Counterfactual thinking and satisfaction among Olympic medalists. *Journal of Personality and Social Psychology, 69*, 603-610.

Mehrabian, A. (1968). Male and female scales of the tendency to achieve. *Educational and Psychological Measurement, 28*, 493-502.

Mehrabian, A., & Bank, L. (1975). *Manual for the Mehrabian measure of achieving tendency*. Unpublished manuscript, University of California at Los Angeles.

Meilman, P. W. (1979). Cross-sectional age changes in ego identity status during adolescence. *Developmental Psychology, 15*, 230-231.

Mellstrom, M. Jr., Cicala, G. A., & Zuckerman, M. (1976). General versus specific trait anxiety measures in the prediction of fear of snakes, heights, and darkness. *Journal of Consulting and Clinical Psychology, 44*, 83-91.

Mento, A. J., Steel, R. P., & Karren, R. J. (1987). A meta-analytic study of the effects of goal setting on task performance: 1966-1984. *Organizational Behavior and Human Decision Processes, 39*, 52-83.

Meskin, B. B., & Singer, J. L. (1974). Daydreaming, reflective thought, and laterality of eye movements. *Journal of Personality and Social Psychology, 30,* 64-71.

Meyers, H. H., & Siegel, P. (1985). The motivation to breastfeed: A fit to the opponent-process theory? *Journal of Personality and Social Psychology, 49,* 188-193.

Mikulincer, M. (1988). The relationship of probability of success and performance following failure: Reactance and helplessness effects. *Motivation and Emotion, 12,* 139-152.

Mikulincer, M. (1994). *Human learned helplessness: A coping perspective.* New York: Plenum Press.

Milgrim, S. (1969). *Obedience to authority.* New York: Harper & Row.

Miller, D. L., & Kelley, M. L. (1994). The use of goal setting and contingency contracting for improving children's homework performance. *Journal of Applied Behavior Analysis, 27,* 73-84.

Miller, D. T., & Ross, M. (1975). Self-serving bias in the attribution of causality: Fact or fiction? *Psychological Bulletin, 82,* 213-215.

Miller, G. A., Galanter, E. H., & Pribrum, K. H. (1960). *Plans and the structure of behavior.* New York: Holt, Rinehart, & Winston.

Miller, I. W., & Norman, W. H. (1981). Effects of attributions for success on the alleviation of learned helplessness and depression. *Journal of Abnormal Psychology, 90,* 113-124.

Miller, N. E. (1948). Studies of fear as an acquirable drive: 1. Fear as motivation and fear-reduction as reinforcement in the learning on new responses. *Journal of Experimental Psychology, 38,* 89-101.

Miller, N. E. (1960). Motivational effects of brain stimulation and drugs. *Federation Proceedings, Federation of American Societies for Experimental Biology, 19,* 846-853.

Miller, N. E. (1978). Biofeedback and visceral learning. *Annual Review of Psychology, 29,* 373-392.

Mills, J., & Clark, M. S. (1982). Communal and exchange relationships. In L. Wheeler (Ed.), *Review of personality and social psychology* (Vol. 3, pp. 121-144). Beverly Hills, CA: Sage.

Mischel, W., Coates, B., & Raskoff, A. (1968). Effects of success and failure on self-gratification. *Journal of Personality and Social Psychology, 10,* 381-390.

Mitchell, M., & Jolley, J. (1988). *Research design explained.* New York: Holt, Rinehart & Winston.

Mitchell, T. R. (1974). Expectancy models of job satisfaction, occupational preference and effort: A theoretical, methodological, and empirical appraisal. *Psychological Bulletin, 81,* 1053-1077.

Mittelman, W. (1991). Maslow's study of self-actualization: A reinterpretation. *Journal of Humanistic Psychology, 31,* 114-135.

Moltz, H. (1965). Contemporary instinct theory and the fixed action pattern. *Psychological Review, 72,* 27-47.

Money, J. (1988). *Gay, straight, and in-between: The sexology of erotic orientation.* New York: Oxford University Press.

Money, J., Wiedeking, C., Walker, P. A., & Gain, D. (1976). Combined antiandrogenic and counseling program for treatment of 46 XY and 47 XYY sex offenders. In E. J. Sachar (Ed.), *Hormones, behavior, and psychopathology, 66,* 105-109.

Monson, T. C., & Snyder, M. (1977). Actors, observers, and the attribution process: Toward a reconceptualization. *Journal of Experimental Social Psychology, 13,* 89-111.

Mook, D. G. (1988). On the organization of satiety. *Appetite, 11,* 27-39.

Mook, D. G. (1996). *Motivation: The organization of action* (2e). New York: W. W. Norton.

Mook, D. G., & Kozub, F. J. (1968). Control of sodium chloride intake in the nondeprived rat. *Journal of Comparative and Physiological Psychology, 66,* 105-109.

Mook, D. G., & Wagner, S. (1989). Orosensory suppression of saccharin drinking in rat: The response, not the taste. *Appetite, 13*, 1–13.

Morgan, C. T., & Murray, H. A. (1935). A method for investigating fantasies. *Archives of Neurology and Psychiatry, 34*, 289–306.

Mossholder, K. W. (1980). Effects of externally mediated goal setting on intrinsic motivation: A laboratory experiment. *Journal of Applied Psychology, 65*, 202–210.

Murray, H. A. (1937). Facts which support the concept of need or drive. *Journal of Personality, 3*, 115–143.

Murray, H. A. (1938). *Explorations in personality*. New York: Oxford University Press.

Murray, H. A. (1943). *Thematic apperception test*. Cambridge: Harvard University Press.

Nasby, W., & Yando, R. (1982). Selective encoding and retrieval of affectively valent information. *Journal of Personality and Social Psychology, 43*, 1244–1255.

Neary, R. S., & Zuckerman, M. (1976). Sensation-seeking, trait and state anxiety, and the electrodermal orienting reflex. *Psychophysiology, 13*, 205–211.

Neemann, J., & Harter, S. (1986). *The self-perception profile for college students*. Manual. University of Denver.

Neher, A. (1991). Maslow's theory of motivation: A critique. *Journal of Humanistic Psychology, 31*, 89–112.

Neiss, R. (1988). Reconceptualizing arousal: Psychobiological states in motor performance. *Psychological Bulletin, 103*, 345–366.

Neisser, U. (1967). *Cognitive psychology*. Englewood Cliffs, NJ: Prentice-Hall.

Newcomb, M. D., & McGee, L. (1991). Influence of sensation seeking on general deviance and specific problem behaviors from adolescence to young adulthood. *Journal of Personality and Social Psychology, 61*, 614–628.

Newell, A., Shaw, J. C., & Simon, H. A. (1958). Elements of a theory of human problem solving. *Psychological Review, 65*, 151–166.

Newman, E. B., Perkins, F. T., & Wheeler, R. H. (1930). Cannon's theory of emotion: A critique. *Psychological Review, 37*, 305–326.

Newman, J., & Layton, B. D. (1984). Overjustification: A self-perception perspective. *Personality and Social Psychology Bulletin, 10*, 419–425.

Nezu, A. M., Nezu, C. M., & Blissett, S. E. (1988). Sense of humor as a moderator of the relation between stressful events and psychological distress: A prospective analysis. *Journal of Personality and Social Psychology, 54*, 520–525.

Nicholls, J. G. (1978). The development of the concepts of effort and ability, perceptions of academic achievement, and the understanding that difficult tasks require more ability. *Child Development, 49*, 800–814.

Nicholls, J. G. (1979). Development of perception of own attainment and causal attributions for success and failure in reading. *Journal of Educational Psychology, 71*, 94–99.

Niedenthal, P. M., Tangney, J. P., & Gavanski, I. (1994). "If only I weren't" versus "If only I hadn't": Distinguishing shame and guilt in counterfactual thinking. *Journal of Personality and Social Psychology, 67*, 585–595.

Nisbett, R. E., & Ross, L. (1980). *Human inference: Strategies and shortcomings of social judgment*. Englewood Cliffs, NJ: Prentice-Hall.

Nisbett, R. E., & Wilson, T. D. (1977). Telling more than we can know: Verbal reports on mental processes. *Psychological Review, 84*, 231–259.

Noller, P. (1984). *Nonverbal communication and marital interaction*. Oxford: Pergamon.

Nurius, P. (1991). Possible selves and social support: Social cognitive resources for coping and striving. In J. A. Howard & P. L. Callero (Eds.), *The self-society interface: Cognition, emotion, and action* (pp. 239–258). New York: Cambridge University Press.

Oatley, K., & Duncan, E. (1994). The experience of emotions in everyday life. *Cognition and Emotion, 8*, 369-381.

O'Hara, M. (1989). When I use the term humanistic psychology . . . *Journal of Humanistic Psychology, 29*, 263-273.

Oldham, G. R. (1975). The impact of supervisory characteristics on goal acceptance. *Academy of Management Journal, 18*, 461-475.

Olds, J. (1956). A preliminary mapping of electrical reinforcing effects in the rat brain. *Journal of Comparative and Physiological Psychology, 49*, 281-285.

Olds, J. (1969). The central nervous system and the reinforcement of behavior. *American Psychologist, 24*, 114-132.

Olds, J., & Milner, P. (1954). Positive reinforcement produced by electrical stimulation of septal area and other regions in the rat brain. *Journal of Comparative and Physiological Psychology, 47*, 419-427.

Olds, M. E., & Fobes, J. L. (1981). The central basis of motivation: Intracranial self-stimulation studies. *Annual Review of Psychology, 32*, 523-574.

Olson, B. C. (1985). *The effects of informational and controlling feedback on intrinsic motivation in competition*. Unpublished doctoral dissertation, Texas Christian University, Fort Worth, TX.

O'Malley, M. N., & Becker, L. A. (1984). Removing the egocentric bias: The relevance of distress cues to evaluation of fairness. *Personality and Social Psychology Bulletin, 10*, 235-242.

Orbach, I., & Hadas, Z. (1982). The elimination of learned helplessness deficits as a function of induced self-esteem. *Journal of Research in Personality, 16*, 511-523.

Ortony, A., & Clore, G. L. (1989). Emotion, mood, and conscious awareness. *Cognition and Emotion, 3*, 125-137.

Ortony, A., Clore, G. L., & Collins, A. (1988). *The cognitive structure of emotions*. Cambridge: Cambridge University Press.

Ortony, A., & Turner, T. J. (1990). What's basic about basic emotions? *Psychological Review, 97*, 315-331.

Osgood, C. E., May, W. H., & Miron, M. S. (1975). *Cross-cultural universals of affective meaning*. Urbana: University of Illinois Press.

Osgood, C. E., Suci, G. C., & Tannenbaum, P. H. (1957). *The measurement of meaning*. Urbana: University of Illinois Press.

Oyserman, D., & Markus, H. (1990). Possible selves and delinquency. *Journal of Personality and Social Psychology, 59*, 112-125.

Ozer, E. M., & Bandura, A. (1990). Mechanisms governing empowerment effects: A self-efficacy analysis. *Journal of Personality and Social Psychology, 58*, 472-486.

Pace, G. M., Ivancis, M. T., Edwards, G. L., Iwata, B. A., & Page, T. J. (1985). Assessment of stimulus preference and reinforcer value with profoundly retarded individuals. *Journal of Applied Behavior Analysis, 18*, 249-255.

Panksepp, J. (1982). Toward a general psychobiological theory of emotions. *Behavioral and Brain Science, 5*, 407-467.

Panksepp, J. (1986). The anatomy of emotions. In R. Plutchik & H. Kellerman (Eds.), *Emotion: Theory, research, and experience: Biological foundations of emotions* (Vol. 5, pp. 91-124). New York: Academic Press.

Panksepp, J. (1994). The basics of basic emotion. In P. Ekman & R. J. Davidson (Eds.), *The nature of emotion: Fundamental questions* (pp. 20-24). New York: Oxford University Press.

Parkes, A. S., & Bruce, H. M. (1961). Olfactory stimuli in mammalian reproduction. *Science, 134*, 1049-1054.

Parkes, M. C., Benjamin, B., & Fitzgerald, R. G. (1969). Broken heart: A statistical study of increased mortality among widowers. *British Journal of Medicine, 1*, 740-743.

Parkinson, B. (1991). Emotional stylists: Strategies of expressive management among trainee hairdressers. *Social Psychology Quarterly, 5*, 419-434.

Parrott, W. G., & Smith, R. H. (1993). Distinguishing the experiences of envy and jealousy. *Journal of Personality and Social Psychology, 64*, 906-920.

Parsons, J. E., & Ruble, D. N. (1977). The development of achievement-related expectancies. *Child Development, 48*, 1975-1979.

Patrick, B. C., Skinner, E. A., & Connell, J. P. (1993). What motivates children's behavior and emotion? Joint effects of perceived control and autonomy in the academic domain. *Journal of Personality and Social Psychology, 65*, 781-791.

Paul, J. P. (1993). Childhood cross-gender behavior and adult homosexuality: The resurgence of biological models of sexuality. *Journal of Homosexuality, 24*, 41-54.

Pederson, N. C., Plomin, R., McClearn, G. E., & Friberg, L. (1988). Neuroticism, extraversion, and related traits in adult twins reared apart and reared together. *Journal of Personality and Social Psychology, 55*, 950-957.

Pennebaker, J. W. (1990). *Opening up*. New York: Morrow.

Perls, F. S. (1969). *Gestalt therapy verbatim*. Lafayette, CA: Real People Press.

Person, J. B., & Rao, P. A. (1985). Longitudinal study of cognitions, life events, and depression in psychiatric in-patients. *Journal of Abnormal Psychology, 94*, 51-63.

Peterson, C., & Barrett, L. C. (1987). Explanatory style and academic performance among university freshmen. *Journal of Personality and Social Psychology, 53*, 603-607.

Peterson, C., Maier, S. F., & Seligman, M. E. P. (1993). *Learned helplessness: A theory for the age of personal control*. New York: Oxford University Press.

Peterson, C., & Seligman, M. E. P. (1984). Causal explanations as a risk factor for depression: Theory and evidence. *Psychological Review, 91*, 347-374.

Peterson, C., Seligman, M. E. P., & Vaillant, G. E. (1988). Pessimistic explanatory style is a risk factor for physical illness: A thirty-five year longitudinal study. *Journal of Personality and Social Psychology, 55*, 23-27.

Peterson, C., Semmel, A., von Baeyer, C., Abramson, L. Y., Metalsky, G. I., & Seligman, M. E. P. (1982). The Attributional Style Questionnaire. *Cognitive Therapy and Research, 6*, 287-299.

Peterson, C., & Villanova, P. (1988). An expanded Attributional Style Questionnaire. *Journal of Abnormal Psychology, 97*, 87-89.

Pfaffmann, C. (1961). The sensory and motivating properties of the sense of taste. In M. R. Jones (Ed.), *Nebraska symposium on motivation* (Vol. 9, pp. 71-108). Lincoln: University of Nebraska Press.

Pfaffmann, C. (1982). Taste: A model of incentive motivation. In D. W. Pfaff (Ed.), *The physiological mechanisms of motivation* (pp. 61-97). New York: Springer-Verlag.

Phillips, D. (1984). The illusion of incompetence among academically competent children. *Child Development, 55*, 2000-2016.

Pierce, K. L., & Schreibman, L. (1994). Teaching daily living skills to children with autism in unsupervised settings through pictorial self-management. *Journal of Applied Behavior Analysis, 27*, 471-481.

Piliavin, J., Callero, P., Evans, D. (1982). Addiction to altruism: Opponent-process theory and habitual blood donation. *Journal of Personality and Social Psychology, 49*, 188-193.

Pittman, T. S., Boggiano, A. K., & Ruble, D. N. (1983). Intrinsic and extrinsic motivational orientations: Limiting conditions on the undermining and enhancing effects of reward on intrinsic motivation. In J. Levine & M. Wang (Eds.), *Teacher and student perceptions: Implications for learning* (pp. 319-340). Hillsdale, NJ: Erlbaum.

Pittman, T. S., Davey, M. E., Alafat, K. A., Wetherill, K. V., Kramer, N. A. (1980). Informational versus controlling verbal rewards. *Personality and Social Psychology Bulletin, 6*, 228–233.

Pittman, T. S., Emery, J., & Boggiano, A. K. (1982). Intrinsic and extrinsic motivational orientations: Reward induced changes in preference for complexity. *Journal of Personality and Social Psychology, 42*, 789–797.

Pittman, T. S., & Heller, J. F. (1988). Social motivation. *Annual Review of Psychology, 38*, 461–489.

Plutchik, R. (1970). Emotions, evolution, and adaptive processes. In M. B. Arnold (Ed.), *Feelings and emotions* (pp. 3–24). New York: Academic Press.

Plutchik, R. (1980). *Emotion: A psychoevolutionary analysis*. New York: Harper & Row.

Plutchik, R. (1985). On emotion: The chicken-and-egg problem revisited. *Motivation and Emotion, 9*, 197–200.

Polivy, J. (1976). Perception of calories and regulation of intake in restrained and unrestrained subjects. *Addictive Behaviors, 1*, 237–243.

Polivy, J., & Herman, C. P. (1976a). Clinical depression and weight change: A complex relation. *Journal of Abnormal Psychology, 85*, 338–340.

Polivy, J., & Herman, C. P. (1976b). Effect of alcohol on eating behavior: Influences of mood and perceived intoxication. *Journal of Abnormal Psychology, 85*, 601–606.

Polivy, J., & Herman, C. P. (1983). *Breaking the diet habit*. New York: Basic Books.

Polivy, J., & Herman, C. P. (1985). Dieting and binging. *American Psychologist, 40*, 193–201.

Pollak, L. H., & Thoits, P. A. (1989). Processes in emotional socialization. *Social Psychology Quarterly, 52*, 22–34.

Pope, L. T., & Smith, C. A. (1994). On the distinct meanings of smiles and frowns. *Cognition and Emotion, 8*, 65–72.

Powley, T. L., & Keesey, R. E. (1970). Relationship of body weight to the lateral hypothalamus feeding syndrome. *Journal of Comparative and Clinical Psychology, 70*, 25–36.

Premack, D. (1959). Toward empirical behavior laws: I. Positive reinforcement. *Psychological Review, 66*, 219–233.

Price, R. A. (1987). Genetics of human obesity. *Annals of Behavioral Medicine, 9*, 9–14.

Quattrone, C. A. (1982). Overattribution and unit information: When behavior engulfs the person. *Journal of Personality and Social Psychology, 42*, 593–607.

Quattrone, C. A. (1985). On the congruity between internal states and action. *Psychological Bulletin, 98*, 3–40.

Rachman, S. (1978). *Fear and courage*. San Francisco: Freeman.

Rachman, S., & Hodgson, R. I. (1974). Synchrony and desynchrony in fear and avoidance. *Behaviour Research and Therapy, 12*, 311–318.

Rajecki, D. W. (1990). *Attitudes*. Sunderland, MA: Sinauer.

Ramirez, E., Maldonado, A., & Markus, R. (1992). Attributions modulate immunization against learned helplessness in humans. *Journal of Personality and Social Psychology, 62*, 139–146.

Rapaport, D. (1960). On the psychoanalytic theory of motivation. *Nebraska symposium on motivation* (Vol. 8, pp. 173–247). Lincoln: University of Nebraska Press.

Raskin, D. C. (1973). Attention and arousal. In W. F. Prokasy & D. C. Raskin (Eds.), *Electrodermal activity in psychological research*. New York: Academic Press.

Ravlin, S. B. (1987). A computer model of affective reactions to goal-relevant events. Unpublished master's thesis, University of Illinois, Urbana-Champaign. (As cited in A. Ortony, G. L. Clore, & A. Collins, Eds., *The cognitive structure of emotions*. Cambridge: Cambridge University Press.)

Raynor, J. O. (1969). Future orientation and motivation of immediate activity: An elaboration of the theory of achievement motivation. *Psychological Review, 76*, 606–610.

Raynor, J. O. (1970). Relationship between achievement-related motives, future orientation, and academic performance. *Journal of Personality and Social Psychology, 15*, 28-33.

Raynor, J. O. (1974). Future orientation in the study of achievement motivation. In J. W. Atkinson & J. O. Raynor (Eds.), *Motivation and achievement*. Washington, D. C.: V. H. Winston.

Raynor, J. O., & Entin, E. E. (1982). *Motivation, career striving, and aging*. New York: Hemisphere.

Redmore, C. (1983). Ego development in the college years: Two longitudinal studies. *Journal of Youth and Adolescence, 12*, 301-306.

Redmore, C., & Loevinger, J. (1979). Ego development in adolescence: Longitudinal studies. *Journal of Youth and Adolescence, 8*, 1-20.

Reeve, J. (1989). The interest-enjoyment distinction in intrinsic motivation. *Motivation and Emotion, 13*, 83-103.

Reeve, J. (1993). The face of interest. *Motivation and Emotion, 17*, 353-375.

Reeve, J., Olson, B. C., & Cole, S. G. (1987). Intrinsic motivation in competition: The intervening role of four individual differences following objective competence information. *Journal of Research in Personality, 21*, 148-170.

Reeve, J., & Deci, E. L. (1996). Elements of the competitive situation that affect intrinsic motivation. *Personality and Social Psychology Bulletin, 22*, 24-33.

Reeve, J., Olson, B. C., & Cole, S. G. (1985). Motivation and performance: Two consequences of winning and losing in competition. *Motivation and Emotion, 9*, 291-298.

Reifman, A. S., Larrick, R. P., & Fein, S. (1991). Temper and temperature on the diamond: The heat-aggression relationship in major league baseball. *Personality and Social Psychology Bulletin, 17*, 580-585.

Reis, I. L. (1986). A sociological journey into sexuality. *Journal of Marriage and the Family, 48*, 233-242.

Reisenzein, R., & Hofmann, T. (1990). An investigation of dimensions of cognitive appraisal in emotion using the repertory grid technique. *Motivation and Emotion, 14*, 1-26.

Renninger, K. A., Hidi, S., & Krapp, A. (Eds.) (1992). *The role of interest in learning and development*. Hillsdale, NJ: Lawrence Erlbaum.

Renninger, K. A., & Wozniak, R. H. (1985). Effect of interest on attentional shift, recognition, and recall in young children. *Developmental Psychology, 21*, 624-632.

Revelle, W., Amaral, P., & Turriff, S. (1976). Introversion/extraversion, time stress, and caffeine: Effect on verbal performance. *Science, 192*, 149-150.

Reynolds, P. C. (1982). Affect and instrumentality: An alternative view on Eibl-Eibesfeldt's human ethology. *Behavioral and Brain Science, 5*, 267-268.

Riess, M., & Taylor, J. (1984). Ego-involvement and attributions for success and failure in a field setting. *Personality and Social Psychology Bulletin, 10*, 536-543.

Rigby, C. S., Deci, E. L., Patrick, B. P., & Ryan, R. M. (1992). Beyond the intrinsic-extrinsic dichotomy: Self-determination in motivation and learning. *Motivation and Emotion, 16*, 165-185.

Rimé, B., Mesquita, B., Philippot, P., & Boca, S. (1991). Beyond the emotional event: Six studies on the social sharing of emotion. *Cognition and Emotion, 5*, 435-465.

Rinn, W. E. (1984). The neuropsychology of facial expression: A review of the neurological and psychological mechanisms for producing facial expressions. *Psychological Bulletin, 95*, 52-77.

Riordan, C. A., Thomas, J. S., & James, M. K. (1985). Attributions in a one-on-one sports competition: Evidence for self-serving biases and gender differences. *Journal of Sport Behavior, 8*, 42-53.

Riskind, J. H., & Gotay, C. C. (1982). Physical posture: Could it have regulatory or feedback effects on motivation? *Motivation and Emotion, 6,* 273-298.

Ritcher, C. P. (1957). On the phenomenon of sudden death in animals and man. *Psychosomatic Medicine, 19,* 191-198.

Ritvo, L. B. (1990). *Darwin's influence on Freud: A tale of two sciences.* New Haven, CT: Yale University Press.

Rizley, R. (1978). Depression and distortion in the attribution of causality. *Journal of Abnormal Psychology, 87,* 32-48.

Roberts, G. C. (Ed.) (1992). *Motivation in sport and exercise.* Champaign, IL: Human Kinetics Books.

Robertson, L. S., Kelley, A. B., O'Neil, B., Wixom, C. W., Eiswirth, R. S., & Haddon, W. (1974). A controlled study of the effect of television messages on safety belt use. *American Journal of Public Health, 64,* 1071-1080.

Robins, C. J. (1988). Attribution and depression: Why is the literature so inconsistent? *Journal of Personality and Social Psychology, 54,* 880-889.

Robinson, D. T., & Smith-Lovin, L. (1992). Selective interaction as a strategy for identity maintenance: An affect control model. *Social Psychology Quarterly, 55,* 12-28.

Robinson, D. T., Smith-Lovin, L., & Tsoudis, O. (1994). Heinous crime or unfortunate accident? The effects of remorse on responses to mock criminal confessions. *Social Forces, 73,* 175-190.

Rodin, J. (1981). Current status of the external-internal hypothesis for obesity. *American Psychologist, 36,* 361-372.

Rodin, J. (1982). Obesity: Why the losing battle? In B. B. Wolman (Ed.), *Psychological aspects of obesity: A handbook* (pp. 30-87). New York: Van Nostrand Reinhold.

Rodin, J., & Langer, E. J. (1977). Long-term effects of a control-relevant intervention with the institutionalized aged. *Journal of Personality and Social Psychology, 35,* 897-902.

Rofé, Y. (1984). Stress and affiliation: A utility theory. *Psychological Review, 91,* 251-268.

Rogers, C. R. (1951). *Client-centered therapy: Its current practice, implications, and theory.* Boston: Houghton Mifflin.

Rogers, C. R. (1959). A theory of therapy, personality, and interpersonal relationships, as developed in the client-centered framework. In S. Koch (Ed.), *Psychology: A study of a science* (Vol. 3, pp. 184-256). New York: McGraw-Hill.

Rogers, C. R. (1961). *On becoming a person.* Boston: Houghton Mifflin.

Rogers, C. R. (1963). Actualizing tendency in relation to "motives" and to "consciousness." *Nebraska symposium on motivation* (Vol. 11, pp. 1-24). Lincoln: University of Nebraska Press.

Rogers, C. R. (1966). *A therapist's view of personal goals* (A Pendle Hill pamphlet, #108). Wallingford, PA: Pendle Hill.

Rogers, C. R. (1969). *Freedom to learn: A view of what education might become.* Columbus, OH: Merrill.

Rogers, C. R. (1973). My philosophy of interpersonal relationships and how it grew. *Journal of Humanistic Psychology, 13,* 3-15.

Rogers, C. R. (1980). *A way of being.* Boston: Houghton Mifflin.

Rogers, C. R. (1982). Notes on Rollo May. *Journal of Humanistic Psychology, 22,* 8-9.

Rogers, C. R. (1995). What understanding and acceptance mean to me. *Journal of Humanistic Psychology, 35,* 7-22.

Rogers, J. L., & Rowe, D. C. (1993). Social contagion and adolescent sexual behavior: A developmental EMOSA model. *Psychological Review, 100,* 479-510.

Rokeach, M. (1973). *The nature of human values.* New York: Free Press.

Rolls, B. J. (1979). How variety and palatability can stimulate appetite. *Nutrition Bulletin, 5,* 78–86.

Rolls, B. J., Rowe, E. T., & Rolls, E. T. (1982). How sensory properties of food affect human feeding behavior. *Physiology and Behavior, 29,* 409–417.

Rolls, B. J., Wood, R. J., & Rolls, E. T. (1980). Thirst: The initiation, maintenance, and termination of drinking. In J. M. Sprague & A. N. Epstein (Eds.), *Progresses in psychobiology and physiological psychology* (Vol. 9, pp. 263–321). New York: Academic Press.

Ronis, D., & Greenwald, A. (1979). Dissonance theory revised again: Comment on the paper by Fazio, Zanna, and Cooper. *Journal of Experimental Social Psychology, 15,* 62–69.

Rose, S., Frieze, I. H. (1989). Young singles' scripts for a first date. *Gender and Society, 3,* 258–268.

Roseman, I. J. (1984). Cognitive determinants of emotion: A structural theory. In P. Shaver (Ed.), *Review of personality and social psychology: Emotions, relationships, and health* (Vol. 5, pp. 11–36). Beverly Hills, CA: Sage.

Roseman, I. J. (1991). Appraisal determinants of discrete emotions. *Cognition and Emotion, 5,* 161–200.

Rosen, B., & D'Andrade, R. C. (1959). The psychological origins of achievement motivation. *Sociometry, 22,* 185–218.

Rosenberg, E. L., & Ekman, P. (1994). Coherence between expressive and experiential systems in emotion. *Cognition and Emotion, 8,* 201–229.

Rosenfeld, P., Giacalone, R. A., & Tedeschi, J. T. (1984). Cognitive dissonance and impression management explanations for effort justification. *Personality and Social Psychology Bulletin, 10,* 394–401.

Rosenfield, D., Folger, R., & Aldeman, H. F. (1980). When rewards reflect competence: A qualification of the overjustification effect. *Journal of Personality and Social Psychology, 39,* 368–376.

Rosenhan, D. L., & Seligman, M. E. P. (1984). *Abnormal psychology.* New York: W. W. Norton.

Rosenholtz, S. J., & Rosenholtz, S. H. (1981). Classroom organization and the perception of ability. *Sociology of Education, 54,* 132–140.

Ross, L. (1977). The intuitive psychologist and his shortcomings: Distortions in the attribution process. In L. Berkowitz (Ed.), *Advances in experimental and social psychology* (Vol. 10, pp. 173–220). New York: Academic Press.

Ross, M. (1976). The self-perception of intrinsic motivation. In J. Harvey, W. J. Ickes, & R. F. Kidd (Eds.), *New direction in attribution research* (Vol. 1, pp. 121–141). Hillsdale, NJ: Erlbaum.

Ross, M., & Shulman, R. (1973). Increasing the salience of initial attitudes: Dissonance versus self-perception theory. *Journal of Personality and Social Psychology, 28,* 138–144.

Ross, R. (1975). Salience of reward and intrinsic motivation. *Journal of Personality and Social Psychology, 32,* 245–254.

Rothkopf, E. Z., & Billington, M. J. (1979). Goal-guided learning from text: Inferring a descriptive processing model from inspection times and eye movements. *Journal of Educational Psychology, 71,* 310–327.

Rotter, J. B. (1966). Generalized expectancies for internal and external control of reinforcement. *Psychological Monographs,* Whole No. 80.

Rowan, J. (1987). Nine humanistic heresies. *Journal of Humanistic Psychology, 27,* 141–157.

Rozin, P., & Fallon, A. E. (1987). A perspective on disgust. *Psychological Review, 94,* 23–41.

Rozin, P., Haidt, J., & McCauley, C. R. (1993). Disgust. In M. Lewis & J. Haviland (Eds.), *Handbook of emotions* (pp. 575–594). New York: Guilford Press.

Rozin, P., Lowery, L., & Ebert, R. (1994). Varieties of disgust faces and the structure of disgust. *Journal of Personality and Social Psychology, 66,* 870–881.

Rozin, P., & Schiller, D. (1980). The nature and acquisition of a preference for chili pepper by humans. *Motivation and Emotion, 4,* 77-101.

Ruble, D. N., Crosovsky, E. H., Frey, K. S., & Cohen, R. (1992). Developmental changes in competence assessment. In A. Boggiano & T. S. Pittman (Eds.), *Motivation and achievement: A social-developmental perspective* (pp. 138-166). New York: Cambridge University Press.

Ruble, D., Parsons, J., & Ross, J. (1976). Self-evaluative responses of children in an achievement setting. *Child Development, 47,* 990-997.

Rudd, J. R., & Geller, E. S. (1985). A university-based incentive program to increase safety belt use: Towards cost-effective institutionalization. *Journal of Applied Behavior Analysis, 18,* 215-226.

Ruderman, A. J. (1983). Obesity, anxiety and food consumption. *Addictive Behaviors, 8,* 235-242.

Ruderman, A. J., & Wilson, G. T. (1979). Weight, restraint, cognitions, and counter-regulation. *Behaviour Therapy and Research, 17,* 581-590.

Rummel, A., & Feinberg, R. (1988). Cognitive evaluation theory: A meta-analytic review of the literature. *Social Behavior and Personality, 16,* 147-164.

Russek, M. (1971). Hepatic receptors and the neurophysiological mechanisms controlling feeding behavior. In S. Ehrenpreis (Ed.), *Neuroscience research.* New York: Academic Press.

Russell, J. A. (1995). Facial expressions of emotion: What lies beyond minimal universality? *Psychological Bulletin, 118,* 379-391.

Russell, J. A., & Fehr, B. (1994). Fuzzy concepts in a fuzzy hierarchy: Varieties of anger. *Journal of Personality and Social Psychology, 67,* 186-205.

Rutledge, L. L., & Hupka, R. B. (1985). The facial feedback hypothesis: Methodological concerns and new supporting evidence. *Motivation and Emotion, 9,* 219-240.

Ryan, R. M. (1982). Control and information in the intrapersonal sphere: An extension of cognitive evaluation theory. *Journal of Personality and Social Psychology, 43,* 450-461.

Ryan, R. M. (1991). The nature of the self in autonomy and relatedness. In J. Strauss & G. R. Goethals (Eds.), *The self: Interdisciplinary approaches* (pp. 208-238). New York: Springer-Verlag.

Ryan, R. M. (1993). Agency and organization: Intrinsic motivation, autonomy, and the self in psychological development. In J. E. Jacobs (Ed.), *Nebraska symposium on motivation: Developmental perspectives on motivation* (Vol. 40, pp. 1-56). Lincoln: University of Nebraska Press.

Ryan, R. M., & Connell, J. P. (1989). Perceived locus of causality and internalization: Examining reasons for acting in two domains. *Journal of Personality and Social Psychology, 57,* 749-761.

Ryan, R. M., Connell, J. P., & Grolnick, W. S. (1992). When achievement is not intrinsically motivated: A theory of internalization and self-regulation in school. In A. K. Boggiano & T. S. Pittman (Eds.), *Achievement and motivation: A social-development perspective* (pp. 167-188). New York: Cambridge University Press.

Ryan, R. M., & Grolnick, W. S. (1986). Origins and pawns in the classroom: Self-report and projective assessments of individual differences in children's perceptions. *Journal of Personality and Social Psychology, 50,* 550-558.

Ryan, R. M., & Lynch, J. (1989). Emotional autonomy versus detachment: Revisiting the vicissitudes of adolescent and young adulthood. *Child Development, 60,* 340-356.

Ryan, R. M., & Powelson, C. L. (1991). Autonomy and relatedness as fundamental to motivation and education. *Journal of Experimental Education, 60,* 49-66.

Ryan, R. M., Rigby, S., & King, K. (1993). Two types of religious internalization and their relations to religious orientations and mental health. *Journal of Personality and Social Psychology, 65,* 586-596.

Ryff, C. D. (1989). Happiness is everything, or is it? Explorations on the meaning of psychological well-being. *Journal of Personality and Social Psychology, 57*, 1069–1081.

Ryff, C. D. (1995). Psychological well-being in adult life. *Current Directions in Psychological Science, 4*, 99–104.

Ryff, C. D., & Keyes, C. L. M. (1995). The structure of psychological well-being revisited. *Journal of Personality and Social Psychology, 69*, 719–727.

Saarni, C. (1979). Children's understanding of display rules for expressive behavior. *Developmental Psychology, 15*, 424–429.

Sabini, J., & Silver, M. (1987). Emotions, responsibility, and character. In F. Schoeman (Ed.), *Responsibility, character, and the emotions: New essays in moral psychology* (pp. 165–175). Cambridge: Cambridge University Press.

Sackeim, H. A. (1983). Self-deception, self-esteem, and depression: The adaptive value of lying to oneself. In J. Masling (Ed.), *Empirical studies of psychoanalytic theories* (Vol. 1, pp. 101–157). Hillsdale, NJ: Analytic Press.

Sackeim, H. A., Gur, R. C., & Saucy, M. C. (1978). Emotions are expressed more intensely on the left side of the face. *Science, 202*, 434–435.

Sacks, C. H., & Bugental, D. B. (1987). Attributions as moderators of affective and behavioral responses to social failure. *Journal of Personality and Social Psychology, 53*, 939–947.

Salomon, G. (1984). Television is "easy" and print is "tough": The differential investment of mental effort in learning as a function of perceptions and attributions. *Journal of Educational Psychology, 76*, 647–658.

Sandvik, E., Diener, E., & Larsen, R. J. (1987). The opponent-process theory and affective reactions. *Motivation and Emotion, 9*, 407–418.

Saudino, K. J., McGuire, S., Reiss, D., Hetherington, E. M., & Plomin, R. (1995). Parent ratings of EAS temperament in twins, full siblings, half siblings, and step siblings. *Journal of Personality and Social Psychology, 68*, 723–733.

Scanlan, T. K., Stein, G. L., & Ravizza, K. (1989). An in-depth study of former elite figure skaters: II. Sources of enjoyment. *Journal of Sport and Exercise Psychology, 11*, 65–83.

Schachter, S. (1959). *The psychology of affiliation*. Stanford, CA: Stanford University Press.

Schachter, S. (1964). The interaction of cognitive and physiological determinants of emotion. In L. Berkowitz (Ed.), *Advances in experimental social psychology* (Vol. 1, pp. 49–80). New York: Academic Press.

Schachter, S. (1968). Obesity and eating. *Science, 161*, 751–756.

Schachter, S. (1971a). *Emotion, obesity, and crime*. New York: Academic Press.

Schachter, S. (1971b). Some extraordinary facts about obese humans and rats. *American Psychologist, 26*, 129–144.

Schachter, S., Goldman, R., & Gordon, A. (1968). Effects of fear, food deprivation, and obesity on eating. *Journal of Personality and Social Psychology, 10*, 91–97.

Schachter, S., & Gross, L. (1968). Manipulated time and eating behavior. *Journal of Personality and Social Psychology, 10*, 98–106.

Schachter, S., & Rodin, J. (1974). *Obese humans and rats*. Hillsdale, NJ: Erlbaum.

Schachter, S., & Singer, J. E. (1962). Cognitive, social, and physiological determinants of emotional states. *Psychological Review, 69*, 379–399.

Scheier, M. A., & Kraut, R. E. (1979). Increasing educational achievement via self-concept change. *Review of Educational Research, 49*, 131–150.

Scheier, M. F., & Carver, C. S. (1985). Optimism, coping, and health: Assessment and implications of generalized outcome expectations. *Health Psychology, 4*, 219–247.

Scheier, M. F., & Carver, C. S. (1988). A model of behavioral self-regulation: Translating intention into action. In L. Berkowitz (Ed.), *Advances in experimental social psychology* (Vol. 21, pp. 303–346). New York: Academic Press.

Scherer, K.R. (1984a). Emotion as a multicomponent process: A model and some cross-cultural data. In P. Shaver (Ed.), *Review of personality and social psychology* (Vol. 5, pp. 37-63). Beverly Hills, CA: Sage.

Scherer, K. R. (1984b). On the nature and function of emotion: A component process approach. In K. Scherer & P. Ekman (Eds.), *Approaches to emotion* (pp. 293-318). Hillsdale, NJ: Erlbaum.

Scherer, K. R. (1993). Studying the emotion-antecedent appraisal process: An expert systems approach. *Cognition and Emotion, 7*, 325-355.

Scherer, K. R. (1994a). An emotion's occurrence depends on the relevance of an event to the organism's goal/need hierarchy. In P. Ekman & R. J. Davidson (Eds.), *The nature of emotion: Fundamental questions* (pp. 227-231). New York: Oxford University Press.

Scherer, K. R. (1994b). Toward a concept of "modal emotions." In P. Ekman & R. J. Davidson (Eds.), *The nature of emotion: Fundamental questions* (pp. 25-31). New York: Oxford University Press.

Scherer, K. R., & Ekman, P. (1984). *Approaches to emotion*. Hillsdale, NJ: Lawrence Erlbaum.

Scherhorn, G., & Grunert, S. C. (1988). Using the causality orientations concept in consumer behavior research. *Journal of Consumer Psychology, 13*, 33-39.

Schiedel, D., & Marcia, J. (1985). Ego integrity, intimacy, sex role orientation and gender. *Developmental Psychology, 21*, 149-160.

Schiefele, U. (1991). Interest, learning, and motivation. *Educational Psychologist, 26*, 299-323.

Schierman, M. J., & Rowland, G. L. (1985). Sensation seeking and selection of entertainment. *Personality and Individual Differences, 6*, 599-603.

Schmale, A., & Iker, H. (1966). The psychological setting of uterine cervical cancer. *Annals of the New York Academy of Sciences, 125*, 807-813.

Schmitt, M. (1973). Influences of hepatic portal receptors on hypothalamic feeding and satiety centers. *American Journal of Physiology, 225*, 1089-1095.

Schooler, C., Zahn, T. P., Murphy, D. L., & Buchsbaum, M. S. (1978). Psychological correlates of monoamine oxidase in normals. *Journal of Nervous and Mental Disease, 166*, 177-186.

Schultz, D. P. (1987). *A history of modern psychology* (4e). San Diego, CA: Harcourt Brace Jovanovich.

Schunk, D. H. (1989a). Self-efficacy and achievement behaviors. *Educational Psychology Review, 1*, 173-208.

Schunk, D. H. (1989b). Self-efficacy and cognitive skill learning. In C. Ames & R. Ames (Eds.), *Research on motivation in education: Goals and cognition* (Vol. 3, pp. 13-44). San Diego: Academic Press.

Schunk, D. H. (1991). Self-efficacy and academic motivation. *Educational Psychologist, 26*, 207-231.

Schunk, D. H., & Cox, P. D. (1986). Strategy training and attributional feedback with learning disabled students. *Journal of Educational Psychology, 78*, 201-209.

Schunk, D. H., & Hanson, A. R. (1989). Self-modeling and children's cognitive skill learning. *Journal of Educational Psychology, 83*, 155-163.

Schwab, D. P., Olian-Gottlieb, J. D., & Heneman, H. G. III (1979). Between-subjects expectancy theory research: A statistical review of studies predicting effort and performance. *Psychological Bulletin, 86*, 139-147.

Schwartz, B. (1990). The creation and destruction of value. *American Psychologist, 45*, 7-15.

Schwartz, G. E. (1986). Emotion and psychophysiological organization: A systems approach. In M. G. H. Coles, E. Ponchin, & S. W. Proges (Eds.), *Psychophysiology: Systems, processes, and applications* (Chpt. 17, pp. 354-377). New York: Guilford Press.

Schwartz, G. E., Brown, S. L., & Ahern, G. L. (1980). Facial muscle patterning and subjective experience during affective imagery: Sex differences. *Psychophysiology, 17*, 75-82.

Schwartz, N., & Clore, G. L. (1983). Mood, misattribution, and judgments of well-being: Informative and directive functions of affective states. *Journal of Personality and Social Psychology, 45*, 513-523.

Sclafani, A. (1980). Dietary obesity. In A. J. Stunkard (Ed.), *Obesity* (pp. 166-181). Philadelphia: W. B. Saunders.

Sclafini, A., & Springer, D. (1976). Dietary obesity in adult rats: Similarities to hypothalamic and human obesity syndromes. *Physiology and Behavior, 17*, 461-471.

Seligman, M. E. P. (1975). *Helplessness: On depression, development, and death*. San Francisco: W. H. Freeman.

Seligman, M. E. P. (1990). *Learned optimism*. New York: Alfred A. Knopf.

Seligman, M. E. P., Abramson, L. Y., Semmel, A., & von Baeyer, C. (1979). Depressive attributional style. *Journal of Abnormal Psychology, 88*, 242-247.

Seligman, M. E. P., Castellon, C., Cacciola, J., Schulman, P., Luborsky, L., Ollove, M., & Downing, R. (1988). Explanatory style change during cognitive therapy for unipolar depression. *Journal of Abnormal Psychology, 97*, 13-18.

Seligman, M. E. P., & Maier, S. F. (1967). Failure to escape traumatic shock. *Journal of Experimental Psychology, 94*, 1-9.

Seligman, M. E. P., & Schulman, P. (1986). Explanatory style as a predictor of productivity and quitting among life insurance agents. *Journal of Personality and Social Psychology, 50*, 832-838.

Sepple, C. P., & Read, N. W. (1989). Gastrointestinal correlates of the development of hunger in man. *Appetite, 13*, 183-191.

Seyle, H. (1956). *The stress of life*. New York: McGraw-Hill.

Seyle, H. (1976). *Stress in health and disease*. Reading, MA: Butterworth.

Shaalvik, E. M., & Hagtvet, K. A. (1990). Academic achievement and self-concept. *Journal of Personality and Social Psychology, 58*, 292-307.

Shapira, Z. (1976). Expectancy determinants of intrinsically motivated behavior. *Journal of Personality and Social Psychology, 34*, 1235-1244.

Sharma, K. N., Anand, B. K., Due, S., & Singh, B. (1961). Role of stomach in regulation of activities of hypothalamic feeding centers. *American Journal of Physiology, 201*, 593-598.

Shaver, P., Schwartz, J., Kirson, D., & O'Connor, C. (1987). Emotion knowledge: Further exploration of a prototype approach. *Journal of Personality and Social Psychology, 52*, 1061-1086.

Sheffield, F. D., & Roby, T. B. (1950). Reward value of a non-nutritive sweet taste. *Journal of Comparative and Physiological Psychology, 43*, 471-481.

Shields, J. (1976). Heredity and environment. In H. J. Eysenck & G. D. Wilson (Eds.), *A textbook of human psychology*. Baltimore: University Park Press.

Shipley, T. E., Jr., & Veroff, J. (1952). A projective measure of need for affiliation. *Journal of Experimental Psychology, 43*, 349-356.

Shirey, L. L., & Reynolds, R. E. (1988). Effect of interest on attention and learning. *Journal of Educational Psychology, 80*, 159-166.

Sid, A. K. W., & Lindgren, H. C. (1981). Sex differences in achievement and affiliation motivation among undergraduates majoring in different academic fields. *Psychological Reports, 48*, 539-542.

Silverman, L. H. (1976). Psychoanalytic theory: The reports of my death are greatly exaggerated. *American Psychologist, 31*, 621-637.

Simon, L., Greenberg, J., & Brehm, J. (1995). Trivialization: The forgotten mode of dissonance reduction. *Journal of Personality and Social Psychology, 68*, 247-260.

Simon, W., & Gagnon, J. H. (1986). Sexual scripts: Permanence and change. *Archives of Sexual Behavior, 15*, 97-120.

Singh, D. (1993a). Adaptive significance of female physical attractiveness: Role of waist-to-hip ratio. *Journal of Personality and Social Psychology, 65*, 293-307.

Singh, D. (1993b). Body shape and women's attractiveness: The critical role of waist-to-hip ratio. *Human Nature, 4*, 297-321.

Singh D. (1995). Female judgment of male attractiveness and desirability for relationships: Role of waist-to-hip ratio and financial status. *Journal of Personality and Social Psychology, 69*, 1089-1101.

Skinner, B. F. (1938). *The behavior of organisms*. New York: Appleton-Century-Crofts.

Skinner, B. F. (1953). *Science and human behavior*. New York: MacMillan.

Skinner, B. F. (1986). What is wrong with daily life in the Western world? *American Psychologist, 41*, 568-574.

Skinner, E. A. (1996). A guide to constructs of control. *Journal of Personality and Social Psychology, 71*, 549-570.

Skinner, E. A., & Belmont, M. J. (1993). Motivation in the classroom: Reciprocal effects of teacher behavior and student engagement across the school year. *Journal of Educational Psychology, 85*, 571-581.

Sklar, L. S., & Anisman, H. (1979). Stress and coping factors influence tumor growth. *Science, 205*, 513-515.

Slade, L. A., & Rush, M. C. (1991). Achievement motivation and the dynamics of task difficulty choices. *Journal of Personality and Social Psychology, 60*, 165-172.

Smith, III, A. C., & Kleinman, S. (1989). Managing emotions in medical school: Students' contacts with the living and the dead. *Social Psychology Quarterly, 52*, 56-69.

Smith, C. A., & Ellsworth, P. C. (1985). Patterns of cognitive appraisal in emotion. *Journal of Personality and Social Psychology, 48*, 813-838.

Smith, C. A., & Ellsworth, P. C. (1987). Patterns of appraisal and emotion related to taking an exam. *Journal of Personality and Social Psychology, 52*, 475-488.

Smith, C. A., Haynes, K. N., Lazarus, R. S., & Pope, L. K. (1993). In search of the "hot" cognitions: Attributions, appraisals, and their relation to emotion. *Journal of Personality and Social Psychology, 65*, 916-929.

Smith, C. P. (Ed.) (1992). *Motivation and personality: Handbook of thematic content analysis*. New York: Cambridge University Press.

Smith, E. A., & Lazarus, R. S. (1993). Appraisal components, core relational themes, and the emotions. *Cognition and Emotion, 7*, 233-269.

Smith, E. R., & Miller, F. D. (1978). Limits on perception of cognitive processes: A reply to Nisbett and Wilson. *Psychological Review, 85*, 355-362.

Smith, R. A., Wallston, B. S., Wallston, K. A., Forsberg, P. R., & King, J. E. (1984). Measuring desire for control of health care processes. *Journal of Personality and Social Psychology, 47*, 415-426.

Smith, R. G., Iwata, B. A., & Shore, B. A. (1995). Effects of subject- versus experimenter-selected reinforcers on the behavior of individuals with profound developmental disabilities. *Journal of Applied Behavior Analysis, 28*, 61-71.

Smith-Lovin, L. (1990). Emotion as confirmation and disconfirmation of identity: An affect control model. In T. D. Kemper (Ed.), *Research agendas in the sociology of emotions*. New York: SUNY Press.

Smith-Lovin, L. (1991). An effect control view of cognition and emotion. In J. A. Howard &

P. L. Callero (Eds.), *The self-society dynamic: Cognition, emotion, and action* (pp. 143–169). New York: Cambridge University Press.

Smith-Lovin, L., & Heise, D. R. (Eds.) (1988). *Analyzing social interaction: Advances in affect control theory*. New York: Gordon & Breach.

Snyder, M., & Ebbesen, E. B. (1972). Dissonance awareness: A test of dissonance theory versus self-perception theory. *Journal of Experimental Social Psychology, 8*, 502–517.

Sobal, J., & Stunkard, A. J. (1989). Socioeconomic status and obesity: A review of the literature. *Psychological Bulletin, 105*, 260–275.

Solomon, R. L. (1977a). An opponent-process theory of motivation. IV. The affective dynamics of addition. In J. D. Maser & M. E. P. Seligman (Eds.), *Psychopathology: Experimental models*. San Francisco: Freeman.

Solomon, R. L. (1977b). An opponent-process theory of motivation. V. Affective dynamics of eating. In L. M. Barker, M. R. Best, & M. Domjan (Eds.), *Learning mechanisms in food selection*. Waco, TX: Baylor University Press.

Solomon, R. L. (1980). The opponent-process theory of motivation: The costs of pleasure and the benefits of pain. *American Psychologist, 35*, 691–712.

Solomon, R. L. (1982). The opponent processes in acquired motivation. In D. W. Pfaff (Ed.), *The physiological mechanisms of motivation* (pp. 321–336). New York: Springer-Verlag.

Solomon, R. L., & Corbit, J. D. (1973). An opponent-process theory of motivation: II. Cigarette addiction. *Journal of Abnormal Psychology, 81*, 158–171.

Solomon, R. L., & Corbit, J. D. (1974). An opponent-process theory of motivation: I. Temporal dynamics of affect. *Psychological Review, 81*, 119–145.

Solomon, S., Greenberg, J., & Pyszczynski, T. (1991). A terror management theory of social behavior: The psychological functions of self-esteem and cultural worldviews. In M. P. Zanna (Ed.), *Advances in experimental social psychology* (Vol. 24, pp. 93–159). San Diego, CA: Academic Press.

Sorrentino, R. M., & Higgins, E. T. (1986). Motivation and cognition. In R. M. Sorrentino & E. T. Higgins (Eds.), *Handbook of motivation and cognition: Foundations of social behavior* (pp. 3–19). New York: Guilford.

Spangler, W. D., & House, R. J. (1991). Presidential effectiveness and the leadership motive profile. *Journal of Personality and Social Psychology, 60*, 439–455.

Spencer, J. A., & Fremouw, W. J. (1979). Binge eating as a function of restrained and weight classification. *Journal of Abnormal Psychology, 88*, 262–267.

Spielberger, C. D., & Starr, L. M. (1994). Curiosity and exploratory behavior. In H. F. O'Neil, Jr., & Drillings, M. (Eds.), *Motivation: Theory and research* (pp. 221–243). Hillsdale, NJ: Lawrence Erlbaum.

Spink, K. S. (1978). Win-lose causal attributions of high school basketball players. *Canadian Journal of Applied Sports Sciences, 3*, 195–201.

Spitzer, L., & Rodin, J. (1981). Human eating behavior: A critical review of studies in normal weight and overweight individuals. *Appetite, 2*, 293–329.

Sprecher, S., Sullivan, Q., & Hatfield, E. (1994). Mate selection preferences: Gender differences examined in a national sample. *Journal of Personality and Social Psychology, 66*, 1074–1080.

Squire, S. (1983). *The slender balance*. New York: Pinnacle.

Stafford-Clark, D. (1966). *What Freud really said*. New York: Schocken Books.

Stagner, R. (1977). Homeostasis, discrepancy, dissonance: A theory of motives and motivation. *Motivation and Emotion, 1*, 103–138.

Steele, C. M. (1988). The psychology of self-affirmation: Sustaining the integrity of the self. In L. Berkowitz (Ed.), *Advances in experimental social psychology* (Vol. 20, pp. 261–302). New York: Academic Press.

Steele, C. M., & Josephs, R. A. (1990). Alcohol myopia: Its prized and dangerous effects. *American Psychologist, 45*, 921-933.

Steele, C. M., Liu, T. J. (1983). Dissonance processes as self-affirmation. *Journal of Personality and Social Psychology, 45*, 5-19.

Steele, R. S. (1977). Power motivation, activation, and inspirational speeches. *Journal of Personality, 45*, 53-64.

Stein, G. L., Kimiecik, J. C., Daniels, J., & Jackson, S. A. (1995). Psychological antecedents of flow in recreational sport. *Personality and Social Psychology Bulletin, 21*, 125-135.

Stein, M. (1989). Gratitude and attitude: A note on emotional welfare. *Social Psychology Quarterly, 52*, 242-248.

Stein, N. L., & Trabasso, T. (1992). The organisation of emotional experience: Creating links among emotion, thinking, language and intentional action. *Cognition and Emotion, 6*, 225-244.

Stellar, J. R., & Stellar, E. (1985). *The neurobiology of motivation and reward*. New York: Springer-Verlag.

Stepper, S., & Strack, F. (1993). Proprioceptive determinants of emotional and nonemotional feelings. *Journal of Personality and Social Psychology, 64*, 211-220.

Stern, J. A., Walrath, L. C., & Goldstein, R. (1984). The endogenous eyeblink. *Psychophysiology, 21*, 22-33.

Stern, J. S., & Lowney, P. (1986). Obesity: The role of physical activity. In K. D. Brownell & J. P. Foreyt (Eds.), *Handbook of eating disorders: Physiology, psychology, and treatment of obesity, anorexia, and bulimia* (pp. 145-158). New York: Basic Book.

Stevenson, J. A. F. (1969). Neural control of food and water intake. In W. Haymaker et al. (Eds.), *The hypothalamus*. Springfield, IL: Thomas.

Stewart, A. J. (1992). Self-definition and social definition: Personal styles reflected in narrative style. In C. P. Smith (Ed.), *Motivation and personality: Handbook of thematic content analysis*. New York: Cambridge University Press.

Stewart, A. J., & Rubin, Z. (1976). Power motivation in the dating couple. *Journal of Personality and Social Psychology, 34*, 305-309.

Stewart, A. J., & Winter, D. G. (1974). Self-definition and social definition in women. *Journal of Personality, 42*, 238-259.

Stipek, D. J. (1983). A developmental analysis of pride and shame. *Human Development, 26*, 42-56.

Stipek, D. J. (1984). Young children's performance expectations: Logical analysis or wishful thinking? In J. G. Nicholls (Ed.), *The development of achievement motivation* (pp. 33-56). Greenwich, CT: JAI.

Stokols, D. (1972). On the distinction between density and crowding: Some implications for future research. *Psychological Review, 79*, 275-277.

Storm, C., & Storm, T. (1987). A taxonomic study of the vocabulary of emotions. *Journal of Personality and Social Psychology, 53*, 805-816.

Strack, F., Martin, L. L., & Stepper, S. (1988). Inhibiting and facilitating conditions of the human smile: Unobtrusive test of the facial feedback hypothesis. *Journal of Personality and Social Psychology, 54*, 768-777.

Strang, H. R., Lawrence, E. C., & Fowler, P. C. (1978). Effects of assigned goal level and knowledge of results on arithmetic computation: A laboratory study. *Journal of Applied Psychology, 63*, 446-450.

Straub, R. R., & Roberts, D. M. (1983). Effects of nonverbal oriented social awareness training program on social interaction ability of learning disabled children. *Journal of Nonverbal Behavior, 7*, 195-201.

Straub, W. F., & Williams, J. M. (Eds.) (1984). *Cognitive sport psychology*. Lansing, NY: Sport Science Associates.

Strube, M. J., Boland, S. M., Manfredo, P. A., & Al-Falaij, A. (1987). Type A behavior pattern and the self-evaluation of abilities: Empirical tests of the self-appraisal model. *Journal of Personality and Social Psychology, 52*, 956–974.

Stunkard, A. J. (1988). Some perspectives on human obesity: Its causes. *Bulletin of New York Academy of Medicine, 64*, 902–923.

Sullivan, H. S. (1953). *The interpersonal theory of psychiatry*. New York: Norton.

Sutherland, S. (1993). Impoverished minds. *Nature, 364*, 767.

Swann, W. B., Jr. (1983). Self-verification: Bringing social reality into harmony with self. In J. Suls & A. Greenwald (Eds.), *Psychological perspectives on the self* (Vol. 2, pp. 33–66). Hillsdale, NJ: Lawrence Erlbaum.

Swann, W. B., Jr. (1985). The self as architect of social reality. In B. Schlenker (Ed.), *The self and social life* (pp. 100–125). New York: McGraw-Hill.

Swann, W. B., Jr. (1987). Identity negotiation: Where two roads meet. *Journal of Personality and Social Psychology, 53*, 1038–1051.

Swann, W. B., Jr. (1990). To be adored or to be known: The interplay of self-enhancement and self-verification. In R. M. Sorrentino & E. T. Higgins (Eds.), *Handbook of motivation and cognition: Foundations of social behavior* (Vol. 2, pp. 408–448). New York: Guilford Press.

Swann, W. B., Jr. (1992a). Why people self-verify. *Journal of Personality and Social Psychology, 62*, 392–401.

Swann, W. B., Jr. (1992b). Seeking "truth," finding despair: Some unhappy consequences of a negative self-concept. *Current Directions in Psychological Science, 1*, 15–18.

Swann, W. B., Jr., & Hill, C. A. (1982). When our identities are mistaken: Reaffirming self-conceptions through social interactions. *Journal of Personality and Social Psychology, 43*, 59–66.

Swann, W. B., Jr., Hixon, J. G., & De La Ronde, C. (1992). Embracing the bitter "truth": Negative self-concepts and marital commitment. *Psychological Science, 3*, 118–121.

Swann, W. B., Jr., Hixon, J. G., Stein-Seroussi, A., & Gilbert, D. T. (1990). The fleeting gleam of praise: Behavioral reactions to self-relevant feedback. *Journal of Personality and Social Psychology, 59*, 17–26.

Swann, W. B., Jr., Pelham, B. W., & Krull, D. S. (1989). Agreeable fancy or disagreeable truth: Reconciling self-enhancement and self-verification. *Journal of Personality and Social Psychology, 57*, 782–791.

Swann, W. B., Jr., & Pittman, T. S. (1977). Initiating play activity in children: The moderating influence of verbal cues on intrinsic motivation. *Child Development, 48*, 1125–1132.

Swann, W. B., Jr., & Predmore, S. C. (1985). Intimates as agents of social support: Sources of consolation or despair? *Journal of Personality and Social Psychology, 49*, 1609–1617.

Swann, W. B., Jr., Wenzlaff, R. M., & Tafarodi, R. W. (1992). Depression and the search for negative evaluations: More evidence of the role of self-verification strivings. *Journal of Abnormal Psychology, 101*, 314–317.

Sweeney, P. D., Anderson, K., & Bailey, S. (1986). Attributional style in depression: A meta-analytic review. *Journal of Personality and Social Psychology, 50*, 974–991.

Taylor, C. B., Bandura, A., Ewart, C. K., Miller, N. H., & DeBusk, B. F. (1985). Raising spouse's and patient's perception of his cardiac capabilities after clinically uncomplicated acute myocardial infarction. *American Journal of Cardiology*.

Taylor, S. E., & Brown, J. D. (1988). Illusion and well-being: A social psychological perspective on mental health. *Psychological Bulletin, 103*, 193–210.

Taylor, S. E., & Brown, J. D. (1994). Positive illusions and well-being revisited: Separating fact from fiction. *Psychological Bulletin, 116*, 21-27.

Taylor, S. E., & Fiske, S. T. (1978). Salience, attention, and attribution: Top of the head phenomena. In L. Berkowitz (Ed.), *Advances in experimental social psychology* (Vol. 11). New York: Academic Press.

Teasdale, J. D., & Fogarty, S. J. (1979). Differential effects of induced mood on retrieval of pleasant and unpleasant events from episodic memory. *Journal of Abnormal Psychology, 88*, 248-257.

Tedeschi, J. T., Schlenkier, B. R., & Bonoma, T. V. (1971). Cognitive dissonance: Private ratiocination or public spectacle? *American Psychologist, 26*, 685-695.

Teichman, Y. (1973). Emotional arousal and affiliation. *Journal of Experimental Social Psychology, 9*, 591-605.

Tennen, H., & Affleck, G. (1987). The costs and benefits of optimistic explanations and dispositional optimism. *Journal of Personality, 55*, 377-393.

Tennen, H., & Eller, S. J. (1977). Attributional components of learned helplessness and facilitation. *Journal of Personality and Social Psychology, 35*, 265-271.

Terasaki, M., & Imada, S. (1988). Sensation seeking and food preferences, *Personality and Individual Differences, 9*, 87-93.

Terborg, J. R. (1976). The motivational components of goal setting. *Journal of Applied Psychology, 61*, 613-621.

Terhune, K. W. (1968). Studies of motives, cooperation, and conflict within laboratory microcosms. In G. H. Snyder (Ed.), *Studies in international conflict* (Vol. 4, pp. 29-58). Buffalo, NY: University of Buffalo.

Tesser, A. (1987). Toward a self-evaluation maintenance model of social behavior. In L. Berkowitz (Ed.), *Advances in experimental social psychology* (Vol. 20). New York: Academic Press.

Thibaut, T. W., & Kelley, H. H. (1959). *The social psychology of groups.* New York: Wiley.

Thibodeau, R., & Aronson, E. (1992). Taking a closer look: Reasserting the role of the self-concept in dissonance theory. *Personality and Social Psychology Bulletin, 18*, 591-602.

Thoits, P. A. (1984). Coping, social support, and psychological outcomes. In P. Shaver (Ed.), *Review of personality and social psychology* (Vol. 5, pp. 219-238). Beverly Hills, CA: Sage.

Thorndike, E. L. (1898). Animal intelligence: An experimental study of the associative process in animals. *Psychological Monographs, 2*, No. 8.

Thorton, J. W., & Jacobs, P. D. (1971). Learned helplessness in human subjects. *Journal of Experimental Psychology, 87*, 369-372.

Thorton, J. W., & Powell, G. D. (1974). Immunization to and alleviation of learned helplessness in man. *American Journal of Psychology, 87*, 351-367.

Tiggenmann, M., & Winefield, A. H. (1987). Predictability and timing of self-report in learned helplessness experiments. *Personality and Social Psychology Bulletin, 13*, 253-264.

Timberlake, W. (1980). A molar equilibrium theory of learned performance. In G. H. Bower (Ed.), *The psychology of learning and motivation* (Vol. 14, pp. 1-58). San Diego, CA: Academic Press.

Timberlake, W., & Allison, J. (1974). Response deprivation: An empirical approach to instrumental performance. *Psychological Review, 81*, 146-164.

Timberlake, W., & Farmer-Dougan, V. A. (1991). Reinforcement in applied settings: Figuring out ahead of time what will work. *Psychological Bulletin, 110*, 379-391.

Toates, F. M. (1979). Homeostasis and drinking. *Behavior and Brain Science, 2*, 95-139.

Tolman, E. C. (1923). The nature of instinct. *Psychological Bulletin, 20*, 200-218.

Tolman, E. C. (1925). Purpose and cognition: The determinants of animal learning. *Psychological Review, 32*, 285-297.

Tolman, E. C. (1932). *Purposive behavior in animals and man.* New York: Century.

Tolman, E. C. (1938). The determinants of behavior at a choice point. *Psychological Review, 45*, 1-44.

Tolman, E. C. (1959). Principles of purposive behavior. In S. Koch (Ed.), *Psychology: A study of a science* (Vol. 2, pp. 92-157). New York: McGraw-Hill.

Tolman, E. C., Ritchie, B. F., & Kalish, D. (1946a). Studies in spatial learning: 1. Orientation and the short cut. *Journal of Experimental Psychology, 36*, 13-24.

Tolman, E. C., Ritchie, B. F., & Kalish, D. (1946b). Studies in spatial learning: 2. Place learning versus response learning. *Journal of Experimental Psychology, 36*, 221-229.

Tomaka, J., Blascovich, J., Kelsey, R. M., & Leitten, C. L. (1993). Subjective, physiological, and behavioral effects of threat and challenge appraisals. *Journal of Personality and Social Psychology, 65*, 248-260.

Tomkins, S. S. (1962). *Affect, imagery, and consciousness: The positive affects* (Vol. 1). New York: Springer.

Tomkins, S. S. (1963). *Affect, imagery, and consciousness: The negative affects* (Vol. 2). New York: Springer.

Tomkins, S. S. (1970). Affect as the primary motivational system. In M. B. Arnold (Ed.), *Feelings and emotions* (pp. 101-110). New York: Academic Press.

Tomkins, S. S. (1984). Affect theory. In K. R. Scherer & P. Ekman (Eds.), *Approaches to emotion* (pp. 163-196). Hillsdale, NJ: Lawrence Erlbaum.

Tooby, J., & Cosmides, L. (1990). The past explains the present: Emotional adaptations and the structure of ancestral environment. *Ethology and Sociobiology, 11*, 375-424.

Tourangeau, R., & Ellsworth, P. C. (1979). The role of facial response in the experience of emotion. *Journal of Personality and Social Psychology, 37*, 1519-1531.

Tranel, D. T., Fisher, A. E., & Fowles, D. C. (1982). Magnitude of incentive on heart rates. *Psychophysiology, 19*, 514-519.

Trice, A. D., & Ogdon, E. P. (1986). Informed consent: I. The institutional nonliability clause as a liability in recruiting research subjects. *Journal of Social Behavior and Personality, 1*, 391-396.

Trope, Y. (1975). Seeking information about one's own ability as a determinant of choice among tasks. *Journal of Personality and Social Psychology, 32*, 1004-1013.

Trope, Y. (1983). Self-assessment in achievement behavior. In J. Suls & A. G. Greenwald (Eds.), *Psychological perspectives on the self* (Vol. 2, pp. 93-121). Hillsdale, NJ: Lawrence Erlbaum.

Trope, Y., & Brickman, P. (1975). Difficulty and diagnosticity as determinants of choice among tasks. *Journal of Personality and Social Psychology, 31*, 918-925.

Trudewind, C. (1982). The development of achievement motivation and individual differences: Ecological determinants. In W. Hartrup (Ed.), *Review of Child Development Research* (Vol. 6, pp. 669-703). Chicago: University of Chicago Press.

Tubbs, M. E. (1986). Goal-setting: A meta-analytic examination of the empirical evidence. *Journal of Applied Psychology, 71*, 474-483.

Turner, J. H. (1987). Toward a sociological theory of motivation. *American Sociological Review, 52*, 15-27.

Vaillant, G. E. (1977). *Adaptation to life.* Boston: Little, Brown, & Company.

Valenstein, E. S. (1973). *Brain control.* New York: Wiley.

Vallerand, R. J., & Bissonnette, R. (1992). Intrinsic, extrinsic, and amotivational styles as predictors of behavior: A prospective study. *Journal of Personality, 60*, 599-620.

Vallerand, R. J., Deci, E. L., & Ryan, R. M. (1985). Intrinsic motivation in sport. In K. B. Pandolf (Ed.), *Exercise and sport sciences reviews* (Vol. 15, pp. 389-425). New York: Macmillan.

Vallerand, R. J., Gauvin, L. I., & Halliwell, W. R. (1986). Negative effects of competition on children's intrinsic motivation. *Journal of Social Psychology, 126*, 649-656.

Vallerand, R. J., Pelletier, L. G., Blais, M. R., Briere, N. M., Senecal, C., & Vallieres, E. F. (1992). The Academic Motivation Scale: A measure of intrinsic, extrinsic, and amotivation in education. *Educational and Psychological Measurement, 52*, 1003-1017.

Vallerand, R. J., & Reid, G. (1984). On the causal effects of perceived competence on intrinsic motivation: A test of cognitive evaluation theory. *Journal of Sport Psychology, 6*, 94-102.

Van Der Plight, J., & Eiser, J. R. (1983). Actors' and observers' attributions, self-serving bias, and positivity bias. *European Journal of Social Psychology, 13*, 95-104.

van Hooff, J. A. R. A. M. (1962). Facial expressions in higher primates. *Symposium of the Zoological Society of London, 8*, 97-125.

van Hooff, J. A. R. A. M. (1972). A comparative approach to the phylogeny of laughter and smiling. In R. A. Hinde (Ed.), *Non-verbal communication*. Cambridge: Cambridge University Press.

Veitch, R., & Griffitt, W. (1976). Good news-bad news: Affective and interpersonal effects. *Journal of Applied Social Psychology, 6*, 69-75.

Veroff, J. (1957). Development and validation of a projective measure of power motivation. *Journal of Abnormal and Social Psychology, 54*, 1-8.

Veroff, J., Depner, C., Kulka, R., & Douvan, E. (1980). Comparison of American motives: 1957 versus 1976. *Journal of Personality and Social Psychology, 39*, 1249-1262.

Viken, R. J., Rose, R. J., Kaprio, J., & Kosken, V. U. O. (1994). A developmental genetic analysis of adult personality: Extraversion and neuroticism from 18 to 59 years of age. *Journal of Personality and Social Psychology, 66*, 722-730.

Visintainer, M., Volpicelli, J. R., & Seligman, M. E. P. (1982). Tumor rejection in rats after inescapable or escapable shock. *Science, 216*, 437-439.

Volmer, F. (1986). Why do men have higher expectancy than women? *Sex Roles, 14*, 351-362.

Vroom, V. H. (1964). *Work and motivation*. New York: Wiley.

Wahba, M. A., & Bridwell, L. G. (1976). Maslow reconsidered: A review of research on the need hierarchy theory. *Organizational Behavior and Human Performance, 15*, 212-240.

Waterman, A. S. (1982). Identity development from adolescence to adulthood: An extention of theory and a review of research. *Developmental Psychology, 18*, 341-358.

Waterman, A. S. (1988). Identity status theory and Erikson's theory: Communalities and differences. *Developmental Review, 8*, 185-208.

Watson, D., & Clark, L. A. (1994). The vicissitudes of mood: A schematic model. In P. Ekman & R. J. Davidson (Eds.), *The nature of emotion: Fundamental questions* (pp. 400-405). New York: Oxford University Press.

Watson, D., Clark, L. A., McIntyre, C. W., & Hamaker, S. (1992). Affect, personality, and social activity. *Journal of Personality and Social Psychology, 63*, 1011-1025.

Watson, D., Clark, L. A., & Tellegen, A. (1988). Development and validation of brief measures of positive and negative affect: The PANAS scales. *Journal of Personality and Social Psychology, 54*, 1063-1070.

Watson, D., & Tellegen, A. (1985). Toward a consensual structure of mood. *Psychological Bulletin, 98*, 219-235.

Watson, J. B. (1919). *Psychology from the standpoint of a behaviorist*. Philadelphia: Lippincott.

Watson, J. B. (1924). *Behaviorism*. New York: W. W. Norton.

Wegner, D. M. (1989). *White bears and other unwanted thoughts.* New York: The Guilford Press.

Wegner, D. M. (1992). You can't always think what you want: Problems in the suppression of unwanted thoughts. In M. P. Zanna (Ed.), *Advances in experimental social psychology* (Vol. 25, pp. 193–225). San Diego: Academic Press.

Wegner, D. M. (1994). Ironic processes of mental control. *Psychological Review, 101*, 34–52.

Wegner, D. M., & Erber, R. (1993). Hyperaccessibility of suppressed thoughts. *Journal of Personality and Social Psychology, 63*, 903–912.

Wegner, D. M., Schneider, D. J., Carter, S. III, & White, T. (1987). Paradoxical effects of thought suppression. *Journal of Personality and Social Psychology, 53*, 5–13.

Weil, J. L. (1974). *A neurophysiological model of emotional and intentional behavior.* Springfield, IL: Charles C. Thomas.

Weinberg, R., Bruya, L., & Jackson, A. (1985). The effects of goal proximity and goal specificity on endurance performance. *Journal of Sport Psychology, 7*, 296–305.

Weinberg, R. S., Bruya, L., Longino, J., & Jackson, A. (1988). Effect of goal proximity and specificity on endurance performance of primary-grade children. *Journal of Sport and Exercise Psychology, 10*, 81–91.

Weinberg, R., Gould, D., & Jackson, A. (1979). Expectations and performance: An empirical test of Bandura's self-efficacy theory. *Journal of Sport Psychology, 1*, 320–331.

Weiner, B. (1972). *Theories of motivation: From mechanism to cognition.* Chicago: Rand McNally.

Weiner, B. (1974). An attributional interpretation of expectancy-value theory. In B. Weiner (Ed.), *Cognitive views of human motivation* (pp. 51–69). New York: Academic Press.

Weiner, B. (1979). A theory of motivation for some classroom experiences. *Journal of Educational Psychology, 71*, 3–25.

Weiner, B. (1980). *Human motivation.* New York: Holt, Rinehart, & Winston.

Weiner, B. (1982). The emotional consequences of causal attributions. In M. S. Clark & S. T. Fiske (Eds.), *Affect and cognition.* Hillsdale, NJ: Lawrence Erlbaum.

Weiner, B. (1985). An attributional theory of achievement motivation and emotion. *Psychological Review, 92*, 548–573.

Weiner, B. (1986). *An attributional theory of motivation and emotion.* New York: Springer-Verlag.

Weiner, B. (1990). History of motivational research in education. *Journal of Educational Psychology, 82*, 616–622.

Weiner, B., Frieze, I., Kukla, A., Reed, L., Rest, S., & Rosenbaum, R. M. (1971). Perceiving the causes of success and failure. In E. E. Jones et al. (Eds.), *Attribution: Perceiving the causes of behavior.* Morristown, NJ: General Learning Press.

Weiner, B., & Graham, S. (1989). Understanding the motivational role of affect: Life-span research from an attributional perspective. *Cognition and Emotion, 3*, 401–409.

Weiner, B., Russell, D., & Learman, D. (1978). Affective consequences of causal ascriptions. In J. Harvey, W. J. Ickes, & R. F. Kidd (Eds.), *New directions in attribution research* (Vol. 2, pp. 59–88). Hillsdale, NJ: Erlbaum.

Weiner, B., Russell, D., & Learman, D. (1979). The cognition-emotion process in achievement-related context. *Journal of Personality and Social Psychology, 37*, 1211–1220.

Weingarten, H. P. (1985). Stimulus control of eating: Implications for a two-factor theory of hunger. *Appetite, 6*, 387–401.

Weiss, J. M. (1972). Psychological factors in stress and disease. *Scientific American, 226*, 104–113.

Weiss, J. M., Glazer, H. I., Pohorecky, L. A. (1976). Coping behavior and neurochemical changes in rats: An alternative explanation for the original "learned helplessness" experiments. In G. Serban & A. King (Eds.), *Animal models in human psychobiology*. New York: Plenum.

Weiss, J. M., Stone, E. A., & Harrell, N. (1970). Coping behavior and brain norepinephrine level in rats. *Journal of Comparative and Physiological Psychology, 72*, 153-160.

Wertheimer, M. (1978). Humanistic psychology and the humane but tough-minded psychologist. *American Psychologist, 33*, 739-745.

Wheeler, L., Reis, H. T., & Nezlek, J. (1983). Loneliness, social interaction, and sex roles. *Journal of Personality and Social Psychology, 45*, 943-953.

Whitbourne, S. K., Zuschlag, M. K., Elliot, L. B., & Waterman, A. S. (1992). Psychosocial development in adulthood: A 22-year sequential study. *Journal of Personality and Social Psychology, 63*, 260-271.

White, G. L. (1981). A model of romantic jealousy. *Motivation and Emotion, 5*, 295-310.

White, H. R., Labourvie, E. N., & Bates, M. E. (1985). The relationship between sensation seeking and delinquency: A longitudinal analysis. *Journal of Research in Crime and Delinquency, 22*, 197-211.

White, R. W. (1959). Motivation reconsidered: The concept of competence. *Psychological Review, 66*, 297-333.

White, R. W. (1960). Competence and the psychosexual stages of development. In M. R. Jones (Ed.), *Nebraska symposium on motivation* (Vol. 8, pp. 97-141) Lincoln: University of Nebraska Press.

Wicker, A. W. (1969). Attitudes versus action: The relationship of verbal and overt behavioral responses to attitude objects. *Journal of Social Issues, 25*, 41-78.

Wickland, R. A., & Brehm, J. W. (1976). *Perspectives on cognitive dissonance*. Hillsdale, NJ: Erlbaum.

Wilder, D. A., & Thompson, J. E. (1980). Intergroup contact with independent manipulations of in-group and out-group interaction. *Journal of Personality and Social Psychology, 38*, 589-603.

Williams, D. G. (1990). Effects of psychoticism, extraversion, and neuroticism in current mood: A statistical review of six studies. *Personality and Individual Differences, 11*, 615-630.

Williams, G. C., Grow, V. M., Freedman, Z. R., Ryan, R. M., & Deci, E. L. (1996). Motivational predictors of weight loss and weight-loss maintenance. *Journal of Personality and Social Psychology, 70*, 115-126.

Williams, G. C., Wiener, M. W., Markakis, K. M., Reeve, J., & Deci, E. L. (1994). Medical students' motivation for internal medicine. *Journal of General Internal Medicine, 9*, 327-333.

Williams, J. G., & Solano, C. H. (1983). The social reality of feeling lonely: Friendship and reciprocation. *Personality and Social Psychology Bulletin, 9*, 237-242.

Wilson, G. (1978). Introversion/Extraversion. In H. London & J. E. Exner, Jr. (Eds.), *Dimensions of personality* (pp. 217-261). New York: John Wiley.

Wilson, T. D., & Linville, P. W. (1982). Improving the academic performance of college freshman: Attribution therapy revisited. *Journal of Personality and Social Psychology, 42*, 367-376.

Wilson, T. D., & Linville, P. W. (1985). Improving the performance of college freshman with attributional techniques. *Journal of Personality and Social Psychology, 49*, 287-293.

Winchie, D. B., & Carment, D. W. (1988). Intention to migrate: A psychological analysis. *Journal of Applied Psychology, 18*, 727-736.

Winefield, A. H. (1982). Methodological differences in demonstrating learned helplessness in humans. *Journal of General Psychology, 107*, 255-266.

Winefield, A. H., Barnett, A., & Tiggemann, M. (1985). Learned helplessness deficits: Uncontrollable outcomes or perceived failure? *Motivation and Emotion, 9*, 185-195.

Winer, D. L., Bonner, T. O., Jr., Blaney, P. H., & Murray, E. L. (1981). Depression and social attraction. *Motivation and Emotion, 5*, 153–166.

Winter, D. G. (1973). *The power motive*. New York: Free Press.

Winter, D. G. (1987). Leader appeal, leader performance, and the motive profiles of leaders and followers: A study of American presidents and elections. *Journal of Personality and Social Psychology, 52*, 196–202.

Winter, D. G. (1988). The power motive in women—and men. *Journal of Personality and Social Psychology, 54*, 510–519.

Winter, D. G. (1993). Power, affiliation, and war: Three tests of a motivational model. *Journal of Personality and Social Psychology, 65*, 532–545.

Winter, D. G., & Stewart, A. J. (1978). Power motivation. In H. London & J. Exner (Eds.), *Dimensions of personality*. New York: Wiley.

Winterbottom, M. (1958). The relation of need for achievement to learning experience in independence and mastery. In J. Atkinson (Ed.), *Motives in fantasy, action, and society* (pp. 453–478). Princeton, NJ: Van Nostrand.

Wirtshafter, D., & Davis, J. D. (1977). Body weight: Reduction by long-term glycerol treatment. *Science, 198*, 1271–1274.

Wise, R. A., & Bozarth, M. A. (1984). Brain reward circuitry: Four circuit elements wired in apparent series. *Brain Research Bulletin, 12*, 203–208.

Woike, B. A. (1994). The use of differentiation and integration processes: Empirical studies of "separate" and "connected" ways of thinking. *Journal of Personality and Social Psychology, 67*, 142–150.

Wolfe, R. N., & Kasmer, J. A. (1988). Type versus trait: Extraversion, impulsivity, sociability, and preferences for cooperative and competitive activities. *Journal of Personality and Social Psychology, 54*, 864–871.

Wolff, P. H. (1969). The natural history of crying and other vocalizations in early infancy. In B. M. Foss (Ed.), *Determinants of infant behavior* (pp. 81–109). London: Methuen.

Wong, M. M., & Csikszentmihalyi, M. (1991). Affiliation motivation and daily experience: Some issues on gender differences. *Journal of Personality and Social Psychology, 60*, 154–164.

Wood, R. E., & Bandura, A. (1989). Impact of conceptions of ability on self-regulatory mechanisms and complex decision making. *Journal of Personality and Social Psychology, 56*, 407–415.

Wood, R. E., Bandura, A., & Bailey, T. (1990). Mechanisms governing organizational performance in complex decision-making environments. *Organizational Behavior and Human Decision Processes, 46*, 181–201.

Wood, R. E., Mento, A. J., & Locke, E. A. (1987). Task complexity as a moderator of goal effects: A meta-analysis. *Journal of Applied Psychology, 72*, 416–425.

Woods, D. J., Beecher, G. P., & Ris, M. D. (1978). The effects of stressful arousal on conjugate lateral eye movement. *Motivation and Emotion, 2*, 345–353.

Woods, D. J., & Steigman, K. B. (1978). Conjugate lateral eye movement and interpersonal arousal: Effects of interviewer sex and topic intimacy. *Personality and Social Psychology Bulletin, 4*, 151–154.

Woods, S. C. (1991). The eating paradox: How we tolerate food. *Psychological Review, 98*, 488–505.

Woods, S. C., Decke, E., & Vaselli, J. R. (1974). Metabolic hormones and regulation of body weight. *Psychological Review, 81*, 26–43.

Woodworth, R. S. (1918). *Dynamic psychology*. New York: Columbia University Press.

Woody, E. Z., Costanzo, P. R., Leifer, H., & Conger, J. (1981). The effects of taste and caloric perceptions on the eating behavior of restrained and unrestrained subjects. *Cognitive Research and Therapy, 5*, 381-390.

Wortman, C. B., & Brehm, J. W. (1975). Responses to uncontrollable outcomes: An integration of reactance theory and the learned helplessness model. In L. Berkowitz (Ed.), *Advances in experimental social psychology* (Vol. 8, pp. 277-336). New York: Academic Press.

Wortruba, T. R., & Price, K. F. (1975). Relationships among four measures of achievement motivation. *Educational and Psychological Measurement, 35*, 911-914.

Younger, J. C., Walker, L., & Arrowood, A. J. (1977). Postdecision dissonance at the fair. *Personality and Social Psychology Bulletin, 3*, 284-287.

Zajonc, R. B. (1980). Feeling and thinking: Preferences need no inferences. *American Psychologist, 35*, 151-175.

Zajonc, R. B. (1981). A one-factor mind about mind and emotion. *American Psychologist, 36*, 102-103.

Zajonc, R. B. (1984). On the primacy of affect. *American Psychologist, 39*, 117-123.

Zanna, M. P., & Cooper, J. (1976). Dissonance and the attribution process. In J. H. Harvey, W. J. Ickes, & R. F. Kidd (Eds.), *New directions in attribution research* (Vol. 1, pp. 199-217). Hillsdale, NJ: Lawrence Erlbaum.

Zimmerman, B. J., & Ringle, J. (1981). Effect of model persistence and statements of confidence on children's self-efficacy and problem-solving. *Journal of Educational Psychology, 73*, 485-493.

Zoeller, C. J., Mahoney, G., Weiner, B. (1983). Effects of attribution training on the assembly task performance of mentally retarded adults. *American Journal of Mental Deficiency, 88*, 109-112.

Zubek, J. P. (Ed.), (1969). *Sensory deprivation*. New York: Appleton-Century-Crofts.

Zuckerman, M(arvin). (1978). Sensation seeking. In H. London & J. E. Exner (Eds.), *Dimensions of personality* (pp. 487-559). New York: John Wiley.

Zuckerman, M. (1979). *Sensation-seeking: Beyond the optimal level of arousal*. Hillsdale, NJ: Erlbaum.

Zuckerman, M. (1984). Sensation seeking: A comparative approach to a human trait. *Behavior and Brain Science, 7*, 413-471.

Zuckerman, M. (1987a). Biological connection between sensation seeking and drug abuse. In J. Engle, L. Oreland, D. H. Ingvar, B. Pernow, S. Rossner, & L. A. Pellborn (Eds.), *Brain reward systems and abuse* (pp. 165-176). New York: Raven Press.

Zuckerman, M. (1987b). Is sensation seeking a predisposing trait for alcoholism? In E. Gottheil, K. A. Druley, S. Pashkey, & S. P. Weinstein (Eds.), *Stress and addiction* (pp. 283-301). New York: Bruner/Mazel.

Zuckerman, M. (1994). *Behavioral expressions and biosocial bases of sensation seeking*. New York: Cambridge University Press.

Zuckerman, M. (1995). Good and bad humors: Biochemical bases of personality and its disorders. *Psychological Science, 6*, 325-332.

Zuckerman, M., Ball, S., & Black, J. (1990). Influences of sensation seeking, gender, risk appraisal, and situational motivation on smoking. *Addictive Behaviors, 15*, 209-220.

Zuckerman, M., Bone, R. N., Neary, R., Mangelsdorff, D., & Brustman, B. (1972). What is the sensation seeker? Personality trait and experience correlates of the Sensation Seeking Scale. *Journal of Clinical Counseling Psychology, 39*, 308-321.

Zuckerman, M., Buchsbaum, M. S., & Murphy, D. L. (1980). Sensation seeking and its biological correlates. *Psychological Bulletin, 88*, 187-214.

Zuckerman, M., & Neeb, M. (1980). Demographic influences in sensation seeking and expressions of sensation seeking in religion, smoking, and driving habits. *Personality and Individual Differences, 1*, 197–206.

Zuckerman, M., Tushup, R., & Finner, S. (1976). Sexual attitudes and experience: Attitude and personality correlates and changes produced by a course in sexuality. *Journal of Consulting and Clinical Psychology, 44*, 7–19.

Zuckerman, M(iron). (1979). Attribution of success and failure revisited, or: The motivational bias is alive and well in attribution theory. *Journal of Personality, 47*, 245–287.

Zuckerman, M., Gioioso, C., & Tellini, S. (1988). Control orientation, self-monitoring, and preference for image versus quality approach to advertising. *Journal of Research in Personality, 22*, 89–100.

Zuckerman, M., Klorman, R., Larrance, D. T., & Spiegel, N. H. (1981). Facial, autonomic, and subjective components of emotion: The facial feedback hypothesis versus the externalizer-internalizer distinction. *Journal of Personality and Social Psychology, 41*, 929–944.

Zuckerman, M., Porac, J., Lathin, D., Smith, R., & Deci, E. L. (1978). On the importance of self-determination for intrinsically motivated behavior. *Personality and Social Psychology Bulletin, 4*, 443–446.

Zullow, H. M., Oettingen, G., Peterson, C., & Seligman, M. E. P. (1988). Pessimistic explanatory style in the historical record: CAVing LBJ, presidential candidates, and East versus West Berlin. *American Psychologist, 43*, 673–682.

Name Index

SUBJECT INDEX